To Floyd & Connie
Best wishes
[signature]
7-12-12

A WESLEYAN THEOLOGY OF HOLY LIVING FOR THE TWENTY-FIRST CENTURY:
The Pursuit of Perfection Across Twenty Centuries

Volume One

Vic Reasoner

Fundamental Wesleyan Publishers

2120 Culverson Ave
Evansville, IN 47714-4811

ISBN 978-0-9761003-2-4

Library of Congress Control Number:
2011940557

Dedicated to
Beverly Nora Brush Reasoner,
my wife since December 23, 1976.
Although she knows I am not perfect, she loves me anyway.
οὐχ ὅτι ἤδη τετελείωμαι

CONTENTS

II. HISTORICAL THEOLOGY

— Volume 2 —

III. PRACTICAL THEOLOGY

In the 1970s a small group of men met together for fellowship and to share their common understanding that the indwelling of the Holy Spirit was the common and necessary ingredient of the New Testament Christian. This indwelling was also evidenced by the direct witness of the Holy Spirit. We also held that saving faith was the gift of God and not the working of man himself. Every person had his personal testimony of how God's Holy Spirit had let them to embrace this truth. We were everywhere spoken against, many were warned, and some were coerced to distance themselves from this tiny fellowship.

The opposition was strong and the numbers were few, which forced us to ponder disbanding. To that possible action an age-old question arose, "To whom shall we go?" Under severe duress we pressed on, although not as forcefully as we had contemplated in our minds.

Onto this scene came Vic Reasoner, who had, in pursuance of his masters, written defending the Fundamental Wesleyan Society position that the Baptism of the Holy Spirit produces the birth. The backlash that started with our original position continued in spite of the courageous and definitive proclamation written by Dr. Reasoner in his flagship work, *The Hole in the Holiness Movement.*

What we had envisioned as a catalyst to revival and a fresh awakening was met with nearly unilateral opposition within the conservative holiness movement. Today Dr. Reasoner boldly pushes this forward in systematic form in *The Arminian Magazine* and with this somewhat revised format of a vital truth.

Neither Vic nor myself have any illusions about the costliness of "truth as it is in Jesus." Twenty years have not softened the opposition, but we press on persuaded that this is Kingdom work and we commit this work both to the reader who seeks to "know truth as it is in Jesus" and to the Great Judge of the Ages, before whom we all will one day stand.

Reader, read with the enlightenment of the Holy Spirit and a keen desire to better comprehend the truth. Then this book will aid you in your quest for eternal life.

Rev. C. Marion Brown, chairman
Fundamental Wesleyan Society

I first met Dr. Reasoner in 2007 after he accepted a teaching position at Southern Methodist College in Orangeburg, SC. Being familiar with his many published writings and the fact that he is considered an academic leader in the area of Wesleyan Theology, I was surprised at his unassuming nature and his ability to easily converse with those of us who are "non-academics." Over the past three years I have come to know "Dr. Vic" as we have both labored in The Southern Methodist Church (he has asked that I drop the Dr., but he has earned that title and I just can't bring myself to let it go). The more exposure I have had to his teaching and writing, the more I admire not only his intelligence, his deep understanding of Scripture, and his ability to communicate, but also his integrity and commitment to "rightly divide the Word of Truth."

In this latest project, *A Wesleyan Theology of Holy Living*, Vic Reasoner has outdone even himself. This rather large and exhaustive work is written in such a way that those without an extensive background in Wesleyan Theology can easily understand as he leads the reader through a thorough Biblical exegesis of holiness. He then turns his attention to the detailed historical development of his subject over the two thousand years of church history. From early Gnosticism and Monasticism to John Wesley's concept of Christian perfection on to the American holiness movement up to the modern Charismatic and Third Wave movements, every major move is detailed and supported with almost 3300 footnotes. And yes, for all the "academics" that read this work, the almost 3300 footnotes offer a wealth of information to keep the most diligent researcher content for many, many hours. The final chapter, Living the Holy Life Today, examines attitudes and teachings concerning holiness and sanctification as the church enters the twenty-first century. And with the conclusion we find a simple, yet profound, definition of what Christian Perfection truly is.

As a fairly recent student of the life and teachings of John Wesley, this book meets so many practical and academic needs. In this one book you have thorough Biblical exegesis, extensive historical data, and simple practical application on this sometimes confusing and often misunderstood doctrine of holiness and sanctification. This is not a book to read quickly and not one you will read once and recall all the important information it contains. This book will become your primary reference on all subjects pertaining to holiness and sanctification, and I suspect you will find yourself going back to it again and again. I highly recommend this latest work of Dr. Vic Reasoner for every pastor and lay person who is seeking to understand the true meaning and application of God's command to "be holy, for I am holy!"

Rev. James O. Jones, Jr.
Director of Light of Life Ministry (Nashville, TN)
Director of Christian Education for the Southern Methodist Church
Director of Continuing Education of Southern Methodist College (Orangeburg, SC)

Before reading a volume of this size and scope, one should always ask why him/herself, "Why should I read this? Will reading this book be worthy of the investment of the hours required to read and comprehend it, when there are other pursuits call for my attention?"

Please allow me to try to answer that question with regard to the book before you – at least to my own satisfaction, and, hopefully, to your satisfaction.

First, you should read this volume because of the character of the person who has written it. Dr. Vic Reasoner is a husband and father and doting grandfather. He's a writer, Christian leader, pastor, college professor and administrator. Furthermore, he is a truth loving student of the Word of God.

Above all else he may be, through years of Christian living and service, Dr. Reasoner has proved himself to be a man of God. Having been his denominational superintendent for about a dozen of the twenty years I have been his friend, I fear neither to say I know him well, nor that he is a man of great Christian character. Vic writes about what he has experienced in his daily life, as well as what he has studied. He *knows* his subject not only intellectually, but having *"learned obedience by the things which he* [*has*] *suffered."* That allusion is strong, I know, but it is accurate and I do not believe the Lord is insulted in this case.

A second reason you should read this book is because of the wealth of historical and contemporary resource material in its pages. In this volume, Dr. Reasoner has brought together a compendium of theological thought from a large number of writers of influence within the Wesleyan-Arminian holiness movement since the days of the Wesleys. He has added thousands of pages of reading, a wealth of research and 20 years of maturity to his earlier study on the same subject. With well over 3,000 reference notes, the present work reads nearly like a *Who's Who In Holiness Theology*, making it a valuable reference work for seekers after the blessing and searchers for the truth. I know of no other contemporaneous volume with similar characteristics.

A third reason you should read this work is because it also addresses a number of other very vitally important issues which we in the Wesleyan-Arminian holiness movement face today. I name four which seem to me to be paramount among our needs as a people.

1. We need to reaffirm, and, in some cases, to reestablish our commitment to the revelation, inspiration, inerrancy, authority and sufficiency of the Bible as the Word of God.
2. We need to understand our roots in order to fully comprehend the revealed nature of our doctrinal statements and beliefs. We need to understand that Wesleyan doctrine did not begin with the Wesleys, but arose directly from the teachings of the Apostles and Prophets. Through

the Wesleys, the doctrines of our movement were given an English voice for their time and ours as well.

3. We need a revival of deep hermeneutical, exegetical and theological thought, both in the pulpit, and in the pew. If the understanding in the pew about the Biblical truths of sanctification and holiness is any indication, we need purposefully to deepen our movement's comprehension of the Scripture in general and doctrine in particular.
4. We need to let our voice be heard clearly above the confusing cacophony of voices clamoring for the hearts of our people. So *many* times, we simply lose our doctrine by default. We allow other doctrinal preachers and writers to influence our people with poor doctrinal positions. If we are content to allow that to continue to happen, we can expect nothing better than continued confusion and harmful syncretism. This is an unacceptable risk which *must* be addressed by our movement if we really believe what we say.

Though perhaps not intentionally aimed at *all* of these goals, this volume addresses them all in one way or another, as it leads us toward the glories of holiness of heart and life.

Finally, you should read this work as an act of worshiping God with your whole mind. Dr. Reasoner may not agree with your particular view on some issues. But whatever else this book will do for you, it will cause you to think more deeply about God's Word and your theology. And *that*, friend, is an act of worship to the Almighty God. May God make it so for all of us.

So, work your way through what's written here. Read the attending Scriptures. Pay attention to the reasoning. And let God speak to you through these pages.

Dr. William H. Sillings
General Superintendent
International Fellowship of Bible Churches

A Wesleyan Theology of Holy Living for the Twenty First Century is a valuable contribution to the theology, history, experience and practice of holiness. The arguments, insights and conclusions reached in this book is, first of all, scholarly. Dr. Reasoner has demonstrated his depth and insight as a scholar by meticulously examining the theological, historical, practical relevance of the message of holiness.

Second, the book is valuable because the author brings into it his many years of pastoral experience. As a pastor he has taken into account the many struggles of Christians in the quest to become holy. Thus the book not only has a scholarly appeal, but it is a must read by pastors and church members as well. The third reason why I believe this book is relevant is because of my many years of personal acquaintance with Dr. Vic Reasoner as my pastor and friend. I have seen him lived out the life of holiness as a believer in Jesus. He is not merely a scholar or professor of religion, but a student in the school of holiness with Jesus, earnestly pursuing the life of holiness and seeking to be like Christ.

You may not agree with all that the author has written concerning the teaching of holiness, but you can not dispute the fact that holiness is demanded of all Christians irrespective of theological and denominational affiliation.

Finally, this book demonstrates from the history of the church and the holiness movement across the century that holiness can be experienced and practiced, and lived out in our world by the earnest and sincere seeker.

This book will no doubt be beneficial to the many Christians in Africa who are yearning to understand and live out the holiness message daily. It is my prayer that God will use this book to stir up holiness and revival within His church.

William Udotong, Ph D,
Provost, West Africa Theological Seminary,
Lagos, Nigeria

PREFACE

People approach a topic differently. Some people want the "bottom line" and often that is sufficient for them. If you are that type of person, I would encourage you to read the last chapter first. However, it will not be as well documented as the previous chapters because it is the conclusion drawn from the previous chapters. If, after reading my conclusion, you want to know what influenced me, you may want to go back and read the first four chapters of biblical exegesis.

Other minds, like mine, demand to know the historical development of a subject. Chapters 5-8 attempt to provide that historical foundation. Although tradition is not as important as Scripture, because I am covering two thousand years of Church history, these chapters are necessarily longer. Some people may have little need to consult these chapters at all.

A secondary purpose for this work is to provide readers access to primary sources with which they may not be aware or which are inaccessible to them. This also makes for a longer text, but serves to provide readers with something more than my opinion. I do not desire to make things as complicated and technical as possible, but I do want to make a comprehensive statement and hopefully a meaningful contribution to the body of Christ.

My Spiritual Pilgrimage

I was raised in an environment where the doctrine of holiness was preached strongly.[1] But no one else besides us heard the preaching. I remember as a small boy looking out the car window on Sunday as we passed other churches and wondered why none of them preached what we believed. I was told that was because they did not preach the Bible.

One day, however, I noticed a Bible church had opened up on the road we traveled to our holiness church, but that church did not preach holiness either. I wondered, if it is really in the Bible, like I hear it preached, why does no one else preach it?

Some years later when I was studying for the ministry, I filled the pulpit

---

[1]C. E. Cowen and Dale M. Yocum were two of my pastors. Yocum refers to me in *Conformed to Christ*, 134-136.

in a small Missouri town. I had determined to preach entire sanctification from Romans 8 for the evening service. That afternoon as I worked on the sermon, verse 9 contradicted what I thought was a perfectly good sermon. For me, it became a crisis of whether I would preach my notions or stick with the text. Ultimately I scrapped my whole outline and started over.

In 1977, I took my first pastorate, although I had been preaching nearly every week for the preceding year and a half. I had been taught in college to base everything I preached on the Bible, but at twenty-one years of age I tended to repeat what I had heard preached. Yet sometimes I felt the Spirit check me; insisting I ensure that my preaching was biblically based. I became aware that some of our favorite proof texts did not necessarily bear the weight placed upon them. My chosen text did not always make the point I wanted to make. I came to a crisis where I had to decide whether I would *preach the Word or what I had heard*. Did the Bible really teach the doctrine of holiness? I turned to the books I had accumulated and found that many of them did not base their teaching on solid Bible exposition. I went through a short period of agnosticism when I really was not convinced the doctrine I had been taught was biblically based. As early as 1978 I was wrestling with many of the issues with which this book deals.

Some years later, Douglas Crossman told me that at one point in his ministry Martyn Lloyd-Jones was open to the doctrine of holiness. During that period he read a standard holiness classic, *Perfect Love* by J. A. Wood and longed for an experience like the one described in that book. But he said the Spirit convicted him that the teaching of that book was not based on Scripture. Lloyd-Jones knew that if preaching is anything, it must be based upon the Word of God. When he did not find an adequate Scriptural foundation for the doctrine in Wood's book, he turned against it and fought it the rest of his ministry.

The Fundamental Wesleyan Society had been formed in 1979 and by 1981 they asked me to become their editor. But the denominational board to which I was accountable passed a resolution advising me not to accept the position — although they claimed to be Wesleyan-Arminian in doctrine. In 1992 the Fundamental Wesleyan Society asked me a second time to serve as their editor. By this time I was in the process of transferring my credentials to the International Fellowship of Bible Churches and was free to accept the invitation.

In 1993 I did a random sampling of 5 percent of the ministers within the Inter-Church Holiness Convention, a broad umbrella of conservative holiness groups, for my doctoral dissertation. I asked these preachers to list the three main holiness texts that they used to preach the doctrine and then compiled a list of texts based upon frequency of their use. I found that neither of the top two biblical passages would support the doctrine as they believed.

In my own search for truth I turned to John Wesley's *A Plain Account of Christian Perfection*. Although it was written in 1765, I found that he based his presentation so squarely upon Scripture that I could not deny that what he taught was true. If anything, he understated the case. Wesley's defense of Christian perfection was based upon Scriptural promises, commands, prayers, and examples. His presentation was marked by reasonableness and careful exegesis. It had to be, since he was reviving a teaching which was not popular in his day. Edmund Gibson, the bishop of London once asked Wesley what he meant by perfection. After he explained himself, the bishop replied, "Mr. Wesley, if this be all you mean, publish it to all the world."[2]

Yet as the teaching gained wider acceptance, preachers became more careless in how they presented it. While exponents of holiness claim the Bible is the sole authority for faith and practice, I have heard whole messages which were nothing more than the minister sharing his personal experience. I am not interested in seeking any experience which the Bible does not command me to pursue.

Thus, it is my conviction is that I should be a Bible preacher. I am more comfortable saying that I am a Bible preacher than to say I am a holiness preacher. However, I preach holy living because I find it in the Bible.

When I preach on the subject of holiness I assume my congregation does not understand it. I have often been told by my generation and the younger generation that they have never understood it. I am convinced that many who preach the doctrine of holiness do not have an adequate understanding of it either. I am not interested in using hollow cliches and generalizations which do not adequately convey biblical concepts.

Pat answers and shibboleths[3] may gain acceptance into the "holiness club," but some holiness organizations are not all that holy. The wife of a holiness evangelist wrote, "In traveling the length and breadth of this land . . . I am repeatedly appalled and grieved to find every type of sexual sin and perversion surfacing again and again among our clergy and lay leaders, but creating very little ripple to mar our pious complacency."[4] Another holiness denomination reportedly has lost a pastor a week over a four-year period due to clergy misconduct.

In other words we failed to convince the rest of the church concerning our doctrine of holiness for two reasons: we have failed to present it biblically and we have often failed to live it. More than anything else, I want to succeed at those two priorities: to live holy and preach the Word clearly. I want my mind to be clear and my heart to be full.

---

[2]Wesley, *Works*, 11:374.

[3]A *shibboleth* is a way of saying things which is primarily used to distinguish one group of people from another. See Judges 12:6.

[4]Lawrence, "I Protest!"12.

In 1987 I wrote a Master's thesis[5] on aspects of this doctrine and there were some requests for me to publish my research. In 1991 *The Hole in the Holiness Movement* was published. While I received some congratulations for a clever title, others misinterpreted the title as an attack on the doctrine of holiness. That was never my intention! In 1994 my doctoral dissertation was an expansion of the same subject.[6] I was privileged in 1995 to make a presentation of my material to the Wesleyan Theological Society, which was published the following year in their journal.[7] However, James 3:1 warns that the teacher will be judged more strictly. If I only please one person, I want to hear God say "well done." And if I do not live what I preach, everything I have written is wood, hay, and stubble to be burned. May God help us to serve this present age by clearly articulating the doctrine *and* by consistently living a holy life.

---

[5]Reasoner, "Spirit and Sanctification: Changing Emphasis within American Wesleyanism."

[6]Reasoner, "Spirit and Sanctification: Changes within American Wesleyanism."

[7]Reasoner, "American Holiness Movement's Paradigm Shift Concerning Pentecost," 132-146. This title was mistakenly confused on the journal cover as "concerning *holiness*." Perhaps this typo reflects the tendency to conflate the two terms.

I. BIBLICAL THEOLOGY

CHAPTER 1
THE HOLINESS OF GOD

"'Sanctification' cannot stand alone in theology. It cannot be lifted up out of the complex of theological doctrines to be separated from them. The interlocking relationships of all Christian doctrines are integral to the life and meaning of every other one."[8]

A systematic study of the doctrine of holiness must begin then with God. In Leviticus 11:44-45 God declares that he is holy. The angels worship him crying, "Holy, holy, holy" (Isa 6:3; Rev 4:8). This is the only attribute of God which is repeated three times in succession. "Holy" is used more often as a prefix to God's name than any other attribute.[9]

The most important concept to be contemplated is our concept of God.[10] Isaiah 57:15 describes his intrinsic holiness in the phrase "whose name is holy." Isaiah also describes his transcendent holiness. He is "the high and lofty One" who dwells in the high and holy place. He is greater than his creation and is separate from the creation and our sin. This same verse describes his immanent holiness in the promise "I dwell . . . with him who has a contrite and humble spirit." He provides his holiness to the humble through faith in Jesus Christ.[11]

Thomas Watson wrote that God is holy *intrinsically*, *efficiently*, and *transcendentally*. God is holy *intrinsically*, meaning that he is holy in his name. God is holy *primarily*, meaning that he is the origin and pattern of holiness. God is holy *efficiently*, meaning that he is the cause of all that is holy in others. He is holy *transcendently*. No angel in heaven can take the just dimensions of God's holiness.[12]

The first petition in the model prayer which Jesus gave is that God's name be kept holy (Matt 6:9). His name is holy because his nature is holy. Holiness is so essential to God's character that "I am the Lord" and "I am holy" are used

---

[8]Wynkoop, *Theology of Love*, 305.

[9]Charnock, *Existence and Attributes of God*, 2:110.

[10]Tozer, *Knowledge of the Holy*, 6-13.

[11]Moritz, "*Be Ye Holy*," 9, 17.

[12]Thomas Watson, *Body of Divinity*, 83.

interchangeably in Leviticus 11:44-45 and throughout the rest of Leviticus.[13] In Psalm 89:35 God swears by his own name or nature — his holiness. In Psalm 111:9 his name is holy and awesome. Isaiah calls God "the holy one" twenty-eight times. In Ezekiel 36:20-23 God was concerned to vindicate the holiness of his great name. When Amos speaks of him swearing "by his holiness" (4:2), it is the same as saying "the Sovereign Lord has sworn by himself" (6:8). Thus, to say God is holy is just another way of saying he is God.

It is on this basis that some theologians argue that holiness is not simply an attribute of God, but his essence. For example, "Holiness is not so much one of His attributes as the entirety of the divine character. It is the 'godness' of God."[14] Ora Lovell wrote that the holiness of God was intrinsic to God's character. It is the union of all existing excellences. Holiness is the title which defined the essential perfection of God as opposed to everything not in harmony with it.[15] David Peterson regarded holiness as a synonym for deity.[16]

However, this distinction hinges upon how the word "attribute" is defined. If an attribute is defined as an essential characteristic of a person or thing, it seems a matter of semantics to distinguish between attribute and essence.

Twice the Bible declares that God is love (1 John 4:8, 16). Holiness is his essence and love is the expression of that holiness. Jerry Bridges wrote, "The holiness of God also includes His perfect conformity to His own divine character. That is, all of His thoughts and actions are consistent with His holy character."[17]

However, for Kenneth Grider love is not an attribute but an action. Grider argued, "If love is an attribute of God, then when God loves us, He is only doing what is His nature to do and not what is His free decision to do in spite of what His nature is like — which is holy."[18] Samuel Powell also concluded that we should not think of God's love as an attribute. "Instead, we must think of God's being as love."[19]

Richard Rice said, "From a Christian perspective, *love* is the first and last

---

[13]Lev 19:2-4, 10, 12, 14, 16, 18, 25, 28, 30-31, 34, 36-37; 20:3, 7-8, 23-24, 26; 21:8, 15, 23; 22:2-3, 8-9, 16, 30-33.

[14]Baab, *Theology of Old Testament*, 34.

[15]Lovell, "The Holiness of God,"50-53.

[16]Peterson, *Possessed by God*, 17.

[17]Bridges, *Pursuit of Holiness*, 23.

[18]Grider, *Wesleyan-Holiness Theology*, 116.

[19]Powell, *Discovering our Christian Faith*, 332.

word in the biblical portrait of God."[20] While openness theology tends to emphasize love as the primary characteristic of God, we cannot exalt his love above other attributes since his love and his holiness interpenetrate each other.[21] Tozer warned that equating love with God is a major mistake which has produced much unsound religious philosophy. If God and love are identical, we destroy the concept of personality in God and deny all his attributes save one and that one we substitute for God. The God we have left is not the God of Scripture.[22]

Furthermore, the Bible specifically attributes truth to all three members of the Trinity (John 3:33; 14:6; 1 John 5:6). Is truth any less fundamental to the nature of God than holiness? Some determinists have emphasized God's sovereignty, describing God as free to be and do whatever he chooses. But God cannot be or do anything inconsistent with his own nature. His freedom has bounds. He cannot contradict himself. God can do anything consistent with his nature. He cannot sin (2 Tim 2:13) nor lie (Heb 6:17-18; Titus 1:2).

Donald Bloesch warned that in our delineation of the attributes of God, we must guard against singling out any of them as giving an exhaustive definition of God.[23] Theologians have typically emphasized a fundamental attribute of God which uniquely describes his essence more fundamentally than other attributes. For Thomas Aquinas, Exodus 3:14-15 taught that "being itself" is the most proper name for God. For Duns Scotus, God's fundamental attribute was infinity. For some Reformed theologians it was aseity. Cornelius Jansenius held that it was veracity. For Saint-Cyran it was omnipotence. According to the Socinians it was the will. According to G. W. F. Hegel it was reason. For Albrecht Ritschl it was

---

[20]Rice, "Biblical Support for a New Perspective," 18.

[21]Schubert Ogden described God as unbounded love. In suggesting that love is an image of the divine nature, Charles Hartshorne came close to redefining love as God [Stone, "Process and Sanctification," 76]. Karl Barth is emphatic that God is the free event of love. T. F. Torrance writes that in Bultmann's theology we are "flung back upon ourselves," so that the word "God" becomes merely "a cipher for our *relations* with God" [Torrence, *Theological Science*, 327, 329–330]. A student of Bultmann, Herbert Braun wrote that God was a "cipher for love" By that he seemed to mean that God did not exist apart from loving human relationships [Braun, *Gesammelte Studien*, 243–309].

Carl F. H. Henry explained that in process theology the nature of divine love is necessarily *eros*, not *agape* since God needs the universe ["The Stunted God of Process Theology," 364. See also Henry, *God, Revelation, and Authority*, 6:70-75; 30]. This discussion is continued under the section on process sanctification, p. 759.

[22]Tozer, *Knowledge of the Holy*, 104.

[23]Bloesch, *God the Almighty*, 42; see also Dunning, *Grace, Faith, and Holiness*, 192-198; Seamands, *Holiness of Heart and Life*, 71-72.

love. For Herman Lotze and Isaac Dorner it is absolute personality. Friedrich Schliermacher overemphasized immanence and Karl Barth overemphasized transcendence. Martin Buber and Emil Brunner emphasized person and Jürgen Moltmann emphasized futurity.

In his discussion, John Frame admits his temptation is to make lordship the fundamental attribute. But he warns against making any favorite attribute central. These theologians may all be right in what they say, but wrong in what they deny. For example, Ritschl is right to say that love is God's essence, but wrong to deny his holiness. "Often, when a theologian makes God's love central, he intends to cast doubt on the reality or intensity of God's wrath and judgment." That was the case with Ritschl and with some modern evangelicals, including open theists of today.[24]

However, Wesley's emphasis was on a holy love. Wesley wrote,

> When God is termed holy, it denotes that excellence which is altogether peculiar to himself; and the glory flowing from all his attributes conjoined, shining forth from all his works, and darkening all things beside itself, whereby he is, and eternally remains, in an incomprehensible manner, separate and at a distance, not only from all that is impure, but likewise from all that is created. . . . Hence it is, that holy and holiness mean the same as God and Godhead. . . . And as God swears by his name, so he does also by his holiness, that is, by himself.[25]

Wesley called God's love "his darling, his reigning attribute, the attribute that sheds an amiable glory on all his other perfections."[26]

God also reveals his character through his חסד, his covenant love. חסד (*chesed* or *hesed*) means steadfast love, mercy, grace, faithfulness, goodness, loving kindness, reliability and consistency. It is covenant love. Thomas Torrance called *hesed* the great sacramental word of the Old Testament.[27] It occurs 246 times in the Old Testament. It has no cognate in any other Semitic language.[28]

According to Wilbur Dayton, the pagan Greeks had no noun to describe this kind of unmixed love because they knew no such love. The Greek noun

---

[24]Frame, *Doctrine of God*, 38; 392-393.

[25]Wesley, *Notes*, 667.

[26]Wesley, *Notes*, 637.

[27]Torrance, "Doctrine of Grace in the Old Testament,"55-65.

[28]Baer and Gordon, חסד, *NIDOTTE*, 2:211-218.

agape was coined to translate the Old Testament *hesed* into the Septuagint Greek and then became very much a key word in the new Testament.[29]

"All demonstrations of the divine covenant of grace are the issues of divine holiness."[30] "God is holy and that is why he chooses to enter into the covenant; man, on the contrary, can become holy only by entering into the covenant."[31] Therefore, Oswalt concluded, "If the giving of the covenant demonstrated that God's holiness is gracious, and if the content of the covenant demonstrated that it is ethical, then the outworking of the covenant demonstrated that holiness is faithful and kind."[32]

The Hebrew word for "holy," קדש (*kodesh* or *qadash*) appears 842 times in the Old Testament. Al Truesdale wrote that this word "refers positively to what is uniquely God's, to the essential difference between God and man. He is Yahweh, and His glory He does not share with any other. Holiness distinguished him from everything else."[33] This word "holy" carries the concepts of separation, glory, and purity.

Holiness conveys the concept of <u>separation</u>. The concept of separation means something is unapproachable because of danger, because of excellence, or set aside for moral excellence and worship. Stated negatively holiness means that God is separate from sin. Habakkuk declared, "Your eyes are too pure to look on evil; you cannot tolerate wrong (1:13). "Who can stand in the presence of the Lord, this holy God?" (1 Sam 6:20). "For I am God, and not man — the Holy One among you" (Hosea 11:9). Thus, holiness has been described as "a general term for the moral excellence of God, and His freedom from all moral limitations in His moral perfection . . . a declaration expressive of the moral sensitiveness of God, shrinking from all evil and sin."[34]

James wrote that God cannot be tempted by evil (1:13). God is transcendent. He is above us. He is unlike us. He is distinct from us. While all religions recognize their god to be holy, not all these gods manifested ethical virtue. Oswalt pointed out that by definition, the word "holy" was used in reference to all gods. However, the plagues of Egypt started the process of separating the one true God from all other pagan gods since the plagues were

---

[29]Dayton, *Contemporary Wesleyan Theology*, 1:533.

[30]Oehler, *Theology of Old Testament*, 1:157.

[31]Jacob, *Theology of Old Testament*, 90.

[32]Oswalt, *Called to Be Holy*, 34-35.

[33]Truesdale, *A Contemporary Wesleyan Theology*, 1:117.

[34]Finlayson, *The Holiness of God*, 4.

attacks upon Egyptian deities.[35]

Stephen Neill pointed out that it is possible for an earnest Hindu to seek contact with the "holy" and yet not to be convinced that such an experience need be in any way related to a demand for ethical righteousness or that such an experience has any direct effect on his moral conduct in the future.[36] In fact the word *kodesh* could refer to the prostitutes in pagan temples who were dedicated to the service of their gods. While זנה (*zonah*) described ordinary prostitutes, קדשה (*kedeshah* - which is related to *kodesh*) referred to dedicated, consecrated, or sanctified prostitutes.[37] According to Dennis Kinlaw, Tamar the prostitute was the first person to be called holy in the Scriptures.[38] In India, some ascetics flee from the world of the flesh while other holy men practice total sensuality as the way of holiness. Both ways are accepted because of the dualistic philosophy which is held.

Yet the true God is morally holy, separate from sin. Theologians have attempted to express this separateness by explaining that God is "wholly other" and unapproachable.[39] "God is unapproachable because of his complete

---

[35]Oswalt, *Called to Be Holy*, 19.

[36]Neill, *Christian Holiness*, 19.

[37]The feminine form occurs in Gen 38:21-22; Deut 23:17; Hos 4:14. The masculine form occurs in Deut 23:17; 1 Kings 14:24; 15:12; 22:46; 2 Kings 23:7; Job 36:14 and refers to sodomites who are morally unclean and yet were ritually holy.

[38]Kinlaw, *Lectures in Old Testament Theology*, 62-63.

[39]While Rudolf Otto was the first to use the phrase "wholly other," John W. Harvey, the English translator, in his preface to the second edition thirty-two years after *The Idea of the Holy* was first published in German, wrote that for Otto God was not "*wholly* 'wholly other'" [Otto, *The Idea of the Holy*, xviii]. This aspect of God's transcendence cannot be so exaggerated that we fail to recognize that this "high and lofty One" also dwells with him who is contrite and lowly in spirit (Isa 57:15).

Apophatic (negative) theology asserts that God can only be defined by what he is not, because there are no adequate positive models to express God's attributes. While God is incomparable, he reveals himself in Scripture in relationship to his people. Donald Metz cautioned that Otto's concept is more in harmony with Oriental mysticism than with the personal God of biblical revelation [Metz, *Studies in Biblical Holiness*, 37]. Harold B. Kuhn objected that Otto's premise, that "holiness" originally was a morally neutral category connoting some vague numinous or mysterious quality which elicited a sense of awe, was a radical reinterpretation of the history of Israel's religion [Kuhn, *God: His Names and Nature*, 6-17].

Dennis Kinlaw said that Otto was over-influenced by post-Enlightenment history of religion. For Otto the moral and the holy were distinct and unrelated. For him, the religion of Israel was simply another religion. Otto was looking for what all religions had in common and he concluded it was "the holy." However, "the holy" had 'otherness' and perfection when compared with all created things."[40] A. W. Tozer wrote, "We cannot grasp the true meaning of the divine holiness by thinking of someone or something very pure and then raising the concept to the highest degree we are capable of."[41] According to Emil Brunner, the conflict between Yahweh and Baal was a conflict between the God who is "wholly other" and the gods of nature. Thus, divine holiness is inseparably connected with the absolute intolerance of recognition of other gods.[42]

Yahweh is God alone. Beside him there is none other. "To whom will you compare me? Or who is my equal? says the Holy One" (Isa 40:25). According to Allan Coppedge this aspect of separation is revealed in his transcendence as creator and his sovereignty as king.[43] And the Church of God is the *ekklesia*, the called-out ones.

Wrapped up in this word is also the concept of brilliance, radiance, or glory.[44] James I. Packer wrote, "Holiness is the outshining of all that God is."[45]

---

no element of either the rational or the ethical/moral. Yet humans can be religious without being moral or ethical. Yahweh alone, the Holy One of Israel, is the source of all holiness. Contact with him always quickens moral consciousness [Kinlaw, *Let's Start with Jesus*, 90-92]. See also Maquarrie, *In Search of Humanity*. According to Colin Crowder, Otto was a child of his age, following the theology of Schleiermacher [Crowder, "Rudolf Otto's *The Idea of the Holy* Revisited," 22-47]. On Schleiermacher, see p. 405 of this book.

[40]Eichrodt, *Theology of the Old Testament*, 1:273.

[41]Tozer, *The Knowledge of the Holy*, 111.

[42]Brunner, *The Christian Doctrine of God*, 159-160.

[43]Coppedge, *Portraits of God*, 57.

[44]Koehler and Baumgartner, *Lexicon In Veteris Testament Lubros*, 825-827. Fuerst, *A Hebrew and Chaldee Lexicon to the Old Testament*, 1221.

The Hebrew word for "glory" is כבוד (*kabod*) as in "Ichabod" which means the glory is departed (1 Sam 4:21). It can also mean "heavy" as in "eternal weight of glory" (2 Cor 4:17). When related to God it means "honor." Greathouse wrote that when God revealed his presence, "*kabod* refers to a perceptible manifestation of the Reality to which humanity would otherwise have no access" [Greathouse, *Wholeness in Christ*, 18].

The word *shekinah* does not occur in the Bible. It first occurs in the Jewish Targums and was borrowed by Christians to express the visible majesty of God's presence. The word was derived from שכן (*shakan* - to dwell). To say that God dwelt in any place was to say that his glory was there. The *shekinah* was the visible presence of the glory of God. This *shekinah* glory became incarnate in Jesus Christ.

[45]Packer, "God Is,"136.

Alfred Edersheim held that the primary meaning for the Hebrew word "holy" was "splendid, beautiful, pure, uncontaminated.[46] Thus, true holiness produces an inward beauty which is reflected in character.

The English word "holy" does not occur in Genesis, but when Jacob realized that God was present where he was, he declared the place was awesome (Gen 28:17). The concept of glory corresponds to the presence of God. According to Exodus 15:11 God is glorious in his holiness.

J. Agar Beet said, "The idea of holiness was not revealed definitely to man until the time of Moses."[47] The first specific reference to holiness occurs when Moses encountered the burning bush and found himself on holy ground. The ground was holy because God was there. Moses was warned not to come closer. He removed his sandals as an act of worship and he hid his face (Exod 3:2-6). Then as he set forth to return to Egypt, God almost killed him because his son was uncircumcised (Exod 4:24). Circumcision was required because human nature was unclean. All that we procreate is a reproduction of our sinfulness.

Thus, the holiness of God required separation. Ultimately God separated his people from Egypt (Exod 11:7; Psalm 105:37-45). Separation is *from* sin and *unto* God Under the new covenant God requires circumcision of the heart (Rom 2:29; 4:9-12; Col 2:11-13).[48] In his sermon "The True Circumcision," Adam Clarke defined the circumcised as those who have entered into covenant with God and not simply nominal Christians.[49]

At Sinai Israel was separated to serve as a kingdom of priests and be a holy nation (Exod 19:5-6). God intended for Israel to lead the nations in his

---

[46]Edersheim, *Bible History: Old Testament*, 2:110.

[47]Beet, *Holiness As Understood by Writers of the Bible*, 13.

[48]Yet even under the old covenant it was described as circumcision of the heart, which delivered them from being stiff necked (Deut 10:16). According to Clarke, this was evidence that God's intention was spiritual. Circumcision was not a cutting of the flesh, but a purification of the soul [*Commentary*, 1:767].

[49]Clarke, Sermon #61, *Works*, 8:335. Yet circumcision comes after birth. Col 2:11 describes spiritual circumcision as a putting off of the body of the flesh. Is this to be interpreted as a cleansing from the sinful nature in entire sanctification? The next verse, however, implies that circumcision has been replaced with baptism. Baptism is an initiatory rite and does not symbolize Christian maturity. Rom 2:28-29; Phil 3:3; Col 2:11 all connect the circumcision of the heart with identification as Christians and not with the deeper cleansing of entire sanctification. Just as Abraham was circumcised after he was justified, so we are baptized after we are justified. Abraham was not saved because he was circumcised nor are we saved because we are baptized. But for us, baptism is a means of grace. It is an outward sign of identification with Christ and it is also an outward sign of an inward grace — the seal or baptism of the Spirit.

worship. Abraham Heschel wrote, "The idea of the holiness of an entire people, Israel as a holy people, is without parallel in human history."[50]

Israel sanctified herself ceremonially by washing her clothes (Exod 19:10), by avoiding the mountain which was set apart temporarily as God's throne (vv 17; 23), and by abstaining from sex for three days (v 15; see also Lev 15:18; 1 Sam 21:5). While the surrounding nations incorporated sex in their worship, believing that they communed with the gods and participated in creation, Israel was taught that salvation did not come through man's power.

Jon Huntzinger wrote of the world of holiness in which Israel lived. The Sabbath and special festivals were set apart as holy times. Space was also viewed as holy. Specific areas were designated as more or less holy; as places where people could experience God's presence and participate in his purpose. The holy of holies in the tabernacle, and later in the temple, was the center of God's creation.[51] Here the divine and the human could meet without the divine destroying the human or the human polluting the divine.

God met with the children of Israel at the door of the Tabernacle and the place was sanctified by his glory (Exod 29:43; Lev 10:3). The pillar of fire by night and the pillar of cloud by day represented the protection of God's glory. This glory was manifested as a consuming fire on top of Mount Sinai (Exod 24:17). Moses asked to see God as he is (Exod 33:18-20). He was not allowed to see God in his holiness because he could not stand the trauma. Thus, we cannot know God unless he accommodates himself to our human frailty and manifests himself in some form of incarnation.[52] Yet Moses saw his glory, the manifestation of his activity in the world, and that revelation made his face radiant (Exod 33:22; 34:30; see Psalm 34:5 NIV). Under the new covenant every person can now behold this glory and as a result experience transformation (2 Cor 3:18). If the three basic meanings of קדש (*kodesh* or *qadash*) are separation, glory, and purity, it would seem that this transformation was the result of separation from sin and being purified by the Holy Spirit.

At the dedication of Solomon's temple this glory so filled the house that the priests could not stand to minister (1 Kings 8:10-11). Jehoshaphat appointed men to sing to the Lord and praise him for the splendor of his holiness (2 Chron 20:21). We are called to ascribe to the Lord the glory due his name and that is done as we worship the Lord in the splendor of his holiness (Psalm 29:2; see also 96:6-9; 110:3; 1 Chron 16:29; 2 Chron 20:21). He is resplendent with light (Psalm 76:4).

---

[50]Heschel, *God in Search of Man: A Philosophy of Judaism*, 245.

[51]Huntzinger, "Goodness and Worship,"36. Notice Heb 9:1 in the *English Standard Version* speaks of "the place of holiness."

[52]Greathouse, *Wholeness in Christ*, 18.

When Isaiah had his revelation of God, in which he saw the glory of God filling the whole earth, he was made painfully aware of his own uncleanness (6:5).[53] Everyone in scripture who even saw a holy angel was so overcome with the brilliance that they expected to die. Ezekiel described the glory of the Lord as a cloud filling the temple. "The cloud filled the temple, and the court was full of the radiance of the glory of the Lord" (10:4). When Christ returns, the splendor or brightness of Christ will defeat Satan (2 Thess 2:8).

According to 1 John 1:5 God is light and in him there is no darkness at all. Here "light" refers to holiness and purity. God's power is incredible, his glory awesome, and his majesty unrivaled. Wesley said, "Holiness is covered glory, and glory is uncovered holiness."[54]

Holiness also means that God is pure. There is no mixture of the pure and impure. It also means he is 100% perfect. He is transparent and perfectly good. "For to say that God is holy is nothing other than to say that God is perfect in goodness."[55] Yet it is universally agreed that while the word "holy" connotes among other meanings absolute goodness, that it is a mistranslation to reduce the term to merely "good."[56] W. B. Pope wrote that holiness is the standard of goodness and that it is the holy nature of God "that declares what is morally good."[57]

In Deuteronomy 32:4 his work is *perfect.* The Septuagint uses the word ὅσιος (*hosios*) conveying the idea of holiness as devoutness or piety, undefiled by sin, free from wickedness, observing every moral obligation, pure, pious.[58]

Pope wrote that "absolute perfection which belongs to God in His eternal essence is . . . Holiness: His nature is the sum and the standard of all goodness;

---

[53]Kornfeld wrote that this emphasis on holiness is not cultic, but ethical [Kornfeld, קדשׁ, *TDOT*, 12:536]. Dunning warned that if we derive our definition of holiness from a dictionary we will miss the biblical perspective. While dictionary definitions invariably interpret sanctification language from its original ceremonial source, the Wesleyan understanding of sanctification emphasizes an ethical transformation [Dunning, *Grace, Faith, and Holiness*, 482].

[54]Wesley, *Notes*, 667.

[55]Oden, *The Living God*, 99.

[56]Otto, *The Idea of the Holy*, 6.

[57]Pope, *Compendium*, 1:333.

[58]Thayer, *Greek English Lexicon of the New Testament*, 456; Seebass, "Holy,"*NIDNTT*, 2:236.God is also said to be *hosios* in Acts 2:27; 13:35; Rev 15:4; 16:5.

and it is eternally opposed to all that is not good in the creature."[59] He is absolute perfection, above the weaknesses and imperfections of mankind, and free from every moral evil.[60] According to 1 Samuel 2:2, "There is none holy like the Lord." He alone is holy (Rev 15:4). "Holiness in human beings (or things) is present only when in relation to God. That is, no finite person or object has any inherent holiness. The holiness of things or persons is derived and dependent. This derived holiness is present only as the person or thing is in right relationship to God."[61] We share in *his* holiness (Heb 12:10). Charles Wesley wrote,

Holy as thee, O Lord, is none!
Thy holiness is all thy own;
A drop of that unbounded sea
Is ours, a drop derived from thee.

And when thy purity we share,
Thy only glory we declare;
And humbled into nothing, own
Holy and pure is God alone.[62]

God's wrath is his resistance to everything unholy. The Old Testament used more than twenty words in reference to the wrath of God for a total of more than 580 references to God's wrath. Old Testament references to divine wrath outnumber references to human anger almost five to one.[63] Rudolf Otto wrote that the Old Testament writers saw the wrath of God as a natural and indispensable expression of God's holiness.[64] Gustav Stählin wrote that the Old Testament proclaims God's love and mercy just as impressively as his wrath and the New Testament preaches his wrath as well as his mercy.[65]

This wrath of God is not an uncontrollable outburst of passion from a

---

[59]Pope, *Compendium*, 1:331.

[60]The word *qahash* occurs in several dialects of Akkadian with the basic meaning of clean, pure, consecrated [McComiskey, קדש, *TWOT*, 2:787].

[61]Dunning, *A Layman's Guide to Sanctification*, 23-24.

[62]Wesley, *BE Works*, 7:380.

[63]Jacob, *Theology of the Old Testament*, 114.

[64]Otto, *The Idea of the Holy*, 18.

[65]Stählin, ὀργή, *TDNT*, 5:422.

pagan god, but the reverse side of a holy love.[66] Sam Powell explained

> Judgment is not contrary to God's love and creative power. It is, on the contrary, a manifestation of that love and power. Accordingly, we must guard against the easy assumption that wrath and punishment come from God's holiness and that redemption comes from God's love. This could be true only if holiness and love were distinct realities. However, they are not two realities but are an indivisible unity in the one God.[67]

Jesus teaches us in Matthew 6:9 and Luke 11:2 to conceive of God as father and as holy. "Father" implies love (Psalm 103:13). Yet God's love makes him vulnerable to wrath. Passive indifference, not anger, is the antithesis of love. "When love is pure, the anger from abused love is righteous. . . . To confess God without acknowledging His wrath is to suggest He is ethically indifferent toward sin."[68] Wrath is God's righteous reaction toward sinners who refuse his grace and mercy. "It is a dreadful thing to fall into the hands of the living God" (Heb 10:31). Karl Barth called Heb 10:26-31 "perhaps the most emphatic in the whole Bible on the theme of God's holiness."[69]

"Wrath is the reaction of God, the necessary reaction of God's holiness against sin."[70] He is repulsed by our sin and his anger burns hot when we deliberately break his holy law. "The law is holy, and the commandment holy, and just, and good" (Rom 7:12).

Yet he does not abandon us. Love is the link between his holiness and our sinfulness. H. Orton Wiley wrote, "God is not holy because He loves, but loves because He is holy."[71] Holiness without love is legalism. Love without holiness is antinomianism. Emil Brunner said, "Holiness erects barriers; love breaks through them."[72] And yet while God's holiness is informed by his love, the nature

---

[66]Morris, *Apostolic Preaching of the Cross*, 184. According to Dunning, God's wrath is the dark side of his love [Dunning, *Grace, Faith, and Holiness*, 191].

[67]Powell, *Discovering our Christian Faith*, 149-150.

[68]Murphree, *Divine Paradoxes*, 126-128.

[69]Barth, *Church Dogmatics*, 2/1:362.

[70]Bloesch, *God the Almighty*, 142-143.

[71]Wiley, *Christian Theology*, 1:383.

[72]Brunner, *Christian Doctrine of God*, 188.

of God cannot be reduced to a lawless love that violates his holiness.[73] God's love does not violate his own law, but his love provided a sacrifice before the foundation of the world (1 Peter 1:19-20). Neither holiness nor love alone would have been enough to have provided salvation. "For love without holiness would not be just in ignoring the offensiveness of sin, and holiness without love would not be able to effect the reconciliation."[74]

I. Howard Marshall explained that God is both holy and loving. While holiness and love are inseparable facets of the same character, we have no word that expresses both qualities simultaneously. God cannot be simply reduced to one or the other. "God's love wants to see justice done, and his justice requires that people be loved."[75]

Love makes a transcendent God immanent. And love is the highest expression of his holiness. Martin Luther said that God is "an abyss of eternal love."[76] Wynkoop wrote that love takes the harshness out of holiness and the incredibility out of perfection.[77] Wesley preached, "But we must love God before we can be holy at all; this being the root of all holiness."[78] Outler expanded on this theme,

> To love God is not merely a friendly feeling toward the ground of being, nor a mood of prayer and piety toward "The Man Upstairs." It is, rather, an awareness of our radical dependence upon God's grace and our gladness that this is the truth about our lives. It means a sense of Holy Presence and of security and warmth in that Presence. It means our recognition of God's upholding love and our gratitude for his love. It means serenity in the face of death because of our confidence that God's love cannot be conquered or cancelled by death. And, most of all, it means having no other gods of our own, since the *First* Commandment is also the *last*![79]

---

[73]Bloesch, *God the Almighty*, 141. "Agape transcends *nomos*, but it does not cancel *nomos*" [p. 151]. *Nomos* is the Greek word for "law."

[74]Oden, *The Living God*, 124.

[75]Marshall, *Aspects of the Atonement*, 39.

[76]Quoted by Philip S. Watson, *Let God Be God!* 133.

[77]Wynkoop, *Theology of Love*, 13.

[78]Wesley, "The Witness of the Spirit, I," Sermon #10, 1.8.

[79]Outler, *Theology in the Wesleyan Spirit*, 84-85.

Love unites the persons within the Trinity. God's love also desires fellowship with us, but his holiness cannot accept our sin, so his holy love provides a means through which he can share his holiness with us. God makes us like himself so that he can enjoy fellowship with us. To be holy we must imitate his love. While God is holy (*qodesh*), he acts in covenant love (*hesed*). God's holiness and covenant love are expressed in his righteousness and justice. After Moses saw the glory of God, the Lord declared, "The Lord, the Lord, the compassionate and gracious God, slow to anger, abounding in love (*hesed*) and faithfulness, maintaining love to thousands, and forgiving wickedness, rebellion and sin. Yet he does not leave the guilty unpunished; he punished the children and their children for the sin of the fathers to the third and fourth generation" (Exod 34:6-7).

It is a mistake to portray God as either all anger or all mercy. His anger is holy; his love is holy. Yet he is good all the time. Because he loves us, he gets angry with us. Parents understand this. We would give our lives for our children, but sometimes are so angry with them we threaten to kill them! God will not let us get by with our sin, because he cares. While his holy anger toward us is justified, his holy love provides a way out. His anger is understandable. His love is beyond comprehension.

Yet it is his love, not his wrath, which is generally considered to be an attribute of God. According to Micah 7:18 he does not retain his anger forever, but his love is steadfast (see also Psalm 103:8-11; Isaiah 54:7-8; Hosea 14:4). His pure love toward us is the highest expression of his holiness. "Whenever holiness is spoken of in Scripture, love is nearby; wherever God's love is manifested, it does not cease to be holy."[80]

Jealousy is also the result of his holiness. This is not a petty emotion which desires to possess its lover at all costs. This is a passionate concern for the covenant relationship. Hebrews 12:29 reminds us that God is a consuming fire. These words were originally stated in Deuteronomy 4:24, where Moses added that God is a jealous God. Dunning explained that this does not mean God envies the accomplishments of someone else. Instead, it means that God maintains his position and will not share his glory with anyone else. "His holiness gives God the right to claim undivided or unshared love and worship."[81] When the sons of Aaron were careless with the holy fire and in its place offered strange fire, God consumed them with his fire explaining, "I will show myself holy" (Lev 10:3).

So the meaning of "holiness" is brilliance or glory, purity, and separation. John Huntzinger summarized holiness in the Old Testament as separation,

---

[80]Oden, *The Living God*, 124.

[81]Dunning, *Grace, Faith, and Holiness*, 188.

wholeness, and otherness.[82] When we come in contact with his holiness there is mystery. It is supernatural. It is awe-inspiring. It is fearful. It is frightening, yet attractive; it is overwhelming, yet fascinating. Rudolf Otto called it the *mysterium tremendum*, the awful mystery. He said that when the human comes in contact with the divine it produces a sense of awe, majesty, vitality,[83] otherness, fascination.[84] The revelation of God's holiness is a traumatic experience.[85] All five of these elements are present in the revelation of God at Mount Sinai in Exodus 19.[86] There the mountain was concealed by smoke and was roped off lest the people draw near and be killed.

Although Eliphaz did not understand the purposes of God in the life of Job, Eliphaz reported a dreadful encounter which left him asking, "Can mortal man be in the right before God. Can a man be pure before his Maker?" (Job 4:12-17). Although Isaiah was already a prophet, when he saw the holiness of God he cried out, "Woe is me" (Isa 6:5). Peter fell at the feet of Jesus and said, "Depart from me, for I am a sinful man, O Lord" (Luke 5:8).

God's holiness produces a sense of unworthiness and uncleanness. His holiness makes us uncomfortable. Man in his sinful condition hates nothing more than an encounter with the holy. He loves darkness rather than light. Yet we were originally created in the image and likeness of God.

The world crucified Jesus, the holy One of God[87] because he made them

---

[82]Huntzinger, "Goodness and Worship,"32.

[83]Otto used such synonyms as urgency, energy, and consuming fire.

[84]By this term Otto meant mystery, mysticism, or numinous. See the discussion of the *numinous* in Lewis, *Problem of Pain*, 17-23 where Lewis describes an awareness of the supernatural which leads to a consciousness of moral law. This sense of "ought" leads to a recognition of that supernatural power as the authority behind the moral law. The highest level of revelation is that Jesus Christ is the son of, and at one with, this supreme being. If Christ is who he claimed to be, everything else claimed by Christianity becomes credible.

[85]Otto, *The Idea of the Holy*, 12-40. John G. Gammie however argued that Otto's classification of five aspects of holiness was inadequate. "Nowhere does Otto sufficiently probe the notion that the holy calls for purity, cleanness, and that frequently purity is to be attained by means of separation" [Gammie, *Holiness in Israel*, 6-8]. See also Kaiser, *New Interpreter's Bible*, 1:1132. Coppedge lists the six components of holiness as: separation, brilliance, righteousness, love, power, and goodness [Coppedge, *Portraits of God*, 51].

[86]Gammie, *Holiness in Israel*, 6-7.

[87]Jesus is called "the holy One of God" in Mark 1:24; Luke 4:34; John 6:69; Acts 2:27; 3:14; 13:35; 1 John 2:20; Rev 3:7.

too uncomfortable. The absolute holiness of Jesus Christ is implied since he was said to be of the same nature as God (Phil 2:6). Christ is the image of God (Col 1:15). He is one with the Father. Nine times he is specifically described as "holy" in the New Testament. Even before his birth he was declared to be "the holy one" (Luke 1:35). Even the demons recognized Jesus as "the Holy One of God" (Mark 1:24; Luke 4:34). The disciples also confessed that Christ was the Holy One of God (John 6:69; Acts 3:14). Matthew 17:2 records that Jesus was transfigured before his disciples. His face shone like the sun and his clothes became as white as the light. Mark added that his clothes became dazzling white, "Whiter than anyone in the world could bleach them" (9:3). Wesley explained that at this moment of transformation, he no longer bore the form of a servant. "The indwelling Deity darted out its rays through the veil of the flesh."[88]

Christ described himself as "holy and true" (Rev 3:7). He had no sin (2 Cor 5:21; Heb 4:15; 7:26; 1 John 3:5). He was without spot or blemish (1 Peter 1:19). He committed no sin (1 Peter 2:22). Thus, he is our righteousness, holiness, and redemption (1 Cor 1:30). Diane Leclerc wrote that Jesus represents for us the actualization of God's call to holiness. "Jesus Christ showed his disciples a life of full obedience to God and of the fullest expression of love to others."[89]

The Holy Spirit is termed the *Holy* Spirit and the Spirit of *holiness* not only because he is holy in himself, but because it is his office and work to sanctify and make us holy.[90] Wesley explained that the infinite and eternal Spirit of God was not only equal with the Father and the Son, not only perfectly holy in himself, but the immediate cause of all holiness in us. Then Wesley explained how the Spirit works to make us holy, "enlightening our understandings, rectifying our wills and affections, renewing our natures, uniting our persons to Christ, assuring us of the adoption of sons, leading us in our actions, purifying and sanctifying our souls and bodies, to a full and eternal enjoyment of God."[91]

The holiness of God is also manifested through his Word. A literal translation of the Hebrew text of Psalm 138:2 reads, "For you have exalted above all your name your word." In the culture of the Old Testament people already understood that the "name" of God was exalted above all things. On the other hand, to say that God exalted his Word above his very name would be an amazing

---

[88]Wesley, *Notes*, 58.

[89]Leclerc, *Discovering Christian Holiness*, 145.

[90]John Tilly, "On Grieving the Holy Spirit," included in the Jackson edition of Wesley's *Works*, 7:486, but not by Wesley; see also Wiley, *Christian Theology*, 1:377. The New Testament calls the Spirit of God "holy" eighty-three times, as compared with just three times in the Old Testament.

[91]Letter to a Roman Catholic, 18 July 1749, ¶ 8. *Works*, Jackson, ed, 10:82.

revelation. Thus, through the full revelation of Scripture God has surpassed all earlier revelations of himself.

A man's words are an extension of his character. Out of the overflow of the heart the mouth speaks (Matt 12:34). Our words justify or condemn us (v 37). Thus, the Scriptures are holy because they come from a holy God. The Scriptures are true because they come from the God of truth. All Scripture is God-breathed (2 Tim 3:15-16). It is the Scriptures which equip, prepare, and perfect us for the work of the ministry and unto all good works (2 Tim 3:17; Eph 4:12). The Scripture is perfect and its goal is to prepare or equip us completely and perfectly.

Preaching before the Sheffield Conference of the Methodist Church in 1811, John Stephens referred both to personal perfection and professional competency.

> The Bible should be the chief book of the man of God. This he should study, if possible, in its original languages, with the help of the best biblical critics and commentators, by the beams of the morning sun, and the rays of the midnight lamp, with earnest prayers to God, and under the irradiating influence of the Spirit by whom it was inspired. If he thus aim at perfection he shall not be disappointed.[92]

Yet the Word of God also came through men. According to1 Peter 1:11 the prophets of old had the Spirit of Christ within them. 2 Peter 1:21 says they did not write under their own impulse, but were impelled by the Holy Spirit.

Therefore the words of the Lord are flawless (Psalm 12:6). Here the word "flawless" טהור (*tahor*) is used of the product of pure gold without alloy. The process of refining gold is used of God's word in Psalm 18:30; 119:140; Proverbs 30:5. Here the word "flawless" is צרף (*sarap*) meaning to burn or purge. What God says is completely reliable since it has been refined. According to Psalm 19:7 the law of the Lord is "perfect," "what is complete, entirely in accord with truth and fact."[93] This adjective תמים (*tamim*) is also used fifty-six times of animals without blemish. In six passages *tamim* is used to describe walking *uprightly*.[94] These passages suggest fellowship with God. To walk before God means to live consciously in his presence. And those who are walking straight are free from crookedness.

In 2 Samuel 22:31 and Psalm 18:30 the way of God is perfect and the

---

[92]Stephens, "Truth, Importance, and Design of Revelation," 253-254.

[93]BDB, *Lexicon*, 1071.

[94]Gen 6:9; 17:1; Psalm 15:1-2; 84:11; 101:2; Prov 28:18.

word of God is flawless. Here the word *tamim* is used of God's attributes and the word *sarap* is used of God's revelation.[95] Because of the nature of Hebrew parallelism, the two descriptive words are being used as synonyms. Two verses later, in both passages, David declared that God made his way perfect (*tamim*). Theologically, the perfection of God's attributes and revelation are absolutely perfect, while the perfect of David was an imputed perfection.

Elihu claimed his words were not false, because he was perfect in knowledge (Job 36:4). Elihu's words were not perfect, but the words of God are perfect. Not the smallest letter nor the smallest part of a letter will pass from the law until all is accomplished (Matt 5:18).

The Word is active in our sanctification (Psalm 19:7-9). It is written on our hearts (Jer 31:31-34). Jesus not only declared that the word of God is truth, but that we are sanctified or made holy by that truth (John 17:17). "You are already clean because of the word I have spoken to you" (John 15:3). "How can a young man keep his way pure? By living according to your word" (Psalm 119:9). Thus, the Trinity is absolutely holy and the Word of God, which is an extension of his character, is also holy and true.

According to Gustaf Aulén, a proper understanding of God's holiness serves as a sentinel to monitor our understanding of him in three ways. First, it guards against philosophical abstraction and superficial speculation about God which reduces our faith to merely a system of ethics. It proclaims that God is unfathomable and it frustrates all rationalistic efforts to define God. God cannot be reduced to a manageable size.

Second it guards against the notion that the Christian faith is simply a projection of the human mind which we employ for our personal fulfillment. Were God merely a figment of our imagination, we would have never conceived of such a holy being. Thus, we need to recover our sense of awe and reverence for God.

Third, a proper understanding of God resists all forms of mysticism which blur the distinction between the human and the divine.[96] Brunner wrote, "The borderline which separates the nature of God from all other forms of existence . . . is not only a frontier line, it is a *closed* frontier."[97]

Samuel Powell said it was important to distinguish the awe caused by experiencing God from the terror caused by God's judgment. "Only the wicked feel this terror; however, the sense of awe is felt by everyone who experiences the

---

[95]Benson said the word of the Lord is free from deceit as gold refined by fire [*Notes*, 2:708]. *Sarap* is used in Deut 32:4 to describe the works of God. Thus, his works and his words are pure and free from any mixture of error.

[96]Aulén, *Faith of the Christian Church*,104-106.

[97]Brunner, *Christian Doctrine of God*, 159.

holy presence of God."[98] We need to recover a wholesome fear of God. According to the book of Proverbs, the fear of God is the beginning of knowledge (1:7), produces hatred of evil (8:13), produces strong confidence (14:26), is the fountain of life (14:27), and leads a man to avoid evil (16:6).

[98]Powell, *Discovering our Christian Faith*, 92.

CHAPTER 2
THE SINFULNESS OF MAN

Humanity was created holy, with an inclination or tendency toward God and toward good. That holiness was more than innocence, it was an enlightened understanding of God and a will wholly inclined toward spiritual things.[99]

We were originally created in the image and likeness of God. The problem in the Garden of Eden was not that the fruit was poisonous; the problem was that Adam and Eve made a choice to disobey God. Eating the forbidden fruit was an act of disobedience. They were promised they would experience good and evil. They experienced the loss of good and the consequences of evil. They would know evil by participating in evil and the knowledge they gained was knowledge about their sinfulness.

When God said, "Let there be" — whatever he commanded happened, whether it was light or sky or dry land or vegetation or sun and moon or life. There was not a chance that it would not happen. But God also made us in his image and gave us the freedom to choose. When he gave the first negative command, not to eat of this tree, he suspended his sovereignty and allowed the possibility that we might not obey his command.

Willful sin is rebellion against God's sovereignty. Sin is autonomy; the setting up of ourselves as gods. Sin is the breech of fellowship which God intended to maintain with man. It results in man, and not God, being at the center. Richard Howard wrote that original sin is "self-sovereignty." Howard concluded that for a man to live according to the flesh is to live according to himself.[100]

According to Gary Anderson the predominate Old Testament metaphor for sin is the picture of sin as a weight or burden. But Jesus never talked about sin as an enormous weight. Instead, he depicted sin predominately as debt. Thus, he taught us to pray "forgive our debts." This carries the idea of God deciding not to collect.[101]

Using relational language, Wynkoop described sin as "self-separation

---

[99]Wiley, *Christian Theology*, 2:44-45.

[100]Howard, *Newness of Life*, 35-44; 29; 33.

[101]Wilson, "The Evolution of Sin,"30-33. The interview of Gary Anderson was based on his book *Sin: A History*.

from God" in moral unlikeness and spiritual alienation.[102] We have turned every one to his own way (Isa 53:6). Luther described this condition as *in se curvatos* (the heart turned in upon itself).[103]

Genesis 3 is the classic Old Testament passage on sin, yet most modern scholars reject the idea of a historic Fall. For the first seventeen hundred years of Church history the opening chapters of Genesis were regarded as historical. With the advent of Enlightenment philosophy, Baruch Spinoza was one of the first to reject the biblical account. Jean-Jacques Rousseau is considered to be the first to formulate a secular version of the Fall. Georg Hegel introduced an evolutionary model, teaching it was both necessary and good for Adam to eat the forbidden fruit. By the twentieth century liberal theologians had abandoned Genesis for Darwin.

Kierkegaard held that Genesis 3 was not literal, but was an existential cross section of the primal act of sinning. Tillich held that Genesis 3 was a symbol for the human predicament and should not be taken literally. Barth declared that Genesis 3 was not history, but saga. Emil Brunner, Reinhold Niebuhr, and Donald Bloesch held Genesis 3 was myth. Even Clark Pinnock, Millard Erickson, and Bernard Ramm, who are regarded as evangelical theologians, do not think Genesis 3 is necessarily literal history.

But the origin of sin in the human race must be a space and time historical event, argued David L. Smith. A meta-historical Fall would be unjust.[104] Liberals want us to believe that Adam is theologically significant, even though he did not exist historically. But theological significance must be grounded in historical reality. The man through which sin entered the world must be the father of our race, not an just an abstract concept. Romans 5:12-21 teaches that what one man got us into, the other man got us out of. If Christ is historical, Adam cannot be mythical. Furthermore, Jesus regarded the creation narrative as literal history (Matt 19:4-6; Mark 13:19). Paul does as well in Romans 5, 1 Corinthians 15:45, and 1 Timothy 2:13-14.

It is legitimate to describe the effects of sin in relational language, provided the historic Fall is not denied or explained exclusively in terms of

---

[102]Wynkoop, *Theology of Love*, 51. Wynkoop said sin must be interpreted in keeping with the "existential" terminology of Scripture and the terms are all very personal [p. 150]. "God seeks our love and gives His love without measure. Sin is simply the absence of this relationship because man has repudiated it" [p. 154]. "Sin is love, but love gone astray. . . . Sin is love locked into a false center, the self" [pp. 157-158]. It is perverted love [pp. 155; 252].

[103]*Luther's Works*, 10:241; 25:245, 291, 313, 345, 351, 513; 33:175.

[104]Smith, *With Willful Intent*, 107-119; 146; 339-343.

existential philosophy.[105] However, a mythical view of the Fall tends to lead to a psychological view of sin. For Friedrich Schleiermacher sin is misspent energy which interferes with God-consciousness. For Tillich sin is existential estrangement from the "Ground of his being." For process theologians, sin is perverted or misdirected love.

Søren Kierkegaard also explained original sin psychologically. When faced with the freedom of choice, Adam and Eve felt anxiety. They chose to leap from freedom into sin and this resulted in more anxiety. While the presence of God had originally kept anxiety at bay, after his relationship with mankind was estranged, despair and dread amount to the original sin which resulted. But what was it that broke the relationship? Perhaps anxiety and dread are the condition that elicits temptation.

But is sin defiance or weakness? The emphasis is not so much on rebellion or guilt as it is on the fractured self. According to Kierkegaard, we each become sinners when we also leap into sin. This is our original sin. And salvation, for Adam or any one of us, is a wholeness which results from a leap of faith back toward God.[106] Kierkegaard declared that man is not born as a sinner in the sense that he is presupposed as being a sinner before he is born.[107] Thus, there is no sinful nature passed on from Adam. We are either saved or lost based upon which way we choose to jump. More recently Brad Mercer explained

---

[105]Donald Metz warned that a relational idea of original sin is more in harmony with evolutionary naturalism than it is in traditional Wesleyan theology. Metz then argued that Wesley regarded both original righteousness and original sin as more than relational. He argued that such righteousness and sin were substantive states. And yet some of his citations from Wesley seem to also convey a relational dimension. While Colin Williams reinterpreted Wesleyan thought in liberal terms which rejected the historic Fall, it does not necessarily follow that all relational explanations of sin amounts to liberalism [Metz, *Some Crucial Issues*, 145-149]. The reference to Colin Williams is from his *John Wesley's Theology Today*, 55-56. Williams reinterpreted the whole Adam story as a myth which did not happen historically, but is still true existentially. It has become a popular option among "evangelical" intellectuals to deny that Adam and Eve were actual historical people. However, this denial brings into question passages such as Rom 5:12-19; 1 Cor 15:20-23; 42-49; Acts 17:26. See Ostling, "Search for the Historical Adam," 23-27.

[106]Leclerc, "Holiness: Sin's Anticipated Cure,"114-126; *Discovering Christian Holiness*, 167-169. My concern is that Leclerc attempted to promote Wesleyan theology to the postmodern mind by showing how compatible it is with the existentialism of Kierkegaard. Kiergaard's leap of faith is not based on propositional truth. The subjectivity of existentialism must be balanced by the objectivity of propositional truth as Dunning seems to concede [Dunning, *Grace, Faith, and Holiness*, 128-129].

[107]Bretall, *Kierkegaard Anthology*, 218.

original sin as inadequate self worth and identity. Holiness, then, is finding our worth and identity through our relationship with Christ. Such descriptions are more psychological than theological.[108]

Dennis Kinlaw explained that Adam and Eve together chose a relationship of personal distrust, distance, suspicion, and disobedience. Because they turned their faces away from God, the result was a chasm and God's face could no longer be seen. This amounted to a deliberate reorientation away from God and toward our own way. The result was a self-centered inversion; a kingdom within the self where the "I" could reign unchallenged.[109]

Not only is our relationship with God broken; Talley wrote that the fall continues to impact human relationships. The effects of the fall on gender are evident in every area of life. In Genesis 1-3 man and woman are presented as equal under God, co-laborers together in performing the tasks of their Creator. They come together to have children. They rule over the earth as overseers of God's creation. Yet their failures are distinct because their created purpose is distinct. The woman abdicates her helping role by disregarding the Word of the Creator and disregarding the leadership of her husband. The man abdicates his role by disregarding the Word of the Creator and shifting blame to his helper.

Their punishment, therefore, was different. Gordon Wenham explained, "The sentences on the man and woman take the form of a disruption of their appointed roles."[110] The resulting issue for the woman becomes one of safety. It is difficult for the man to lead because the woman and the ground now "fight back." Therefore he copes by abdicating his leadership and focusing on whatever he perceives to be his competency.[111]

Sam Powell wrote that sin is the revival of chaos. "In creation God overcomes the power of chaos and thus fashions a world for our existence. But chaos is not utterly destroyed; it is only kept at bay. . . . Sin is the power of chaos manifesting itself in human being, resisting and distorting the creative power of God's coming into the world." Yet sin is more than relational, it is an independent reality which is a distortion of God's creation. He observed that John wrote of the *world* both as God's creation and as the system of sin. Paul's favorite term for the corporate nature of sin is *flesh*.[112]

Biblically, the essence of sin is unbelief, pride (self-centeredness),

---

[108]Online: Mercer, "Sin and Holiness." See the section on "Relational Sanctification," p. 750.

[109]Kinlaw, *Let's Start with Jesus*, 111-125; 137.

[110]Wenham, *Genesis 1-15*, 81.

[111]Talley, "Gender and Sanctification," 6-16.

[112]Powell, *Discovering our Christian Faith,* 111; 128-131.

disobedience, and sensuality (self-gratification). Wesley identified five elements which constitute the root of sin: atheism, idolatry, pride, self-will, and love of the world.[113] Mark Mueller wrote that the universal antecedent of all sin was the historic fall of Adam.

- Atheism is the universal cause of all sin
- Self-idolatry is the universal nature of all sin
- Self-pride is the universal attitude of all sin
- Self-will is the universal assertion of all sin
- Love of the world is the universal desire of all sin.[114]

This lust for forbidden knowledge is deceptive. We are like goldfish who demand to live outside the bowl as an expression of our freedom. This knowledge of good and evil provides a knowledge we never had previously. It is like being told not to put your hand in the fire. We never knew how good it felt not to be burnt and we never knew how badly it felt to be burned!

Adam and Eve did gain knowledge. They learned that they would have been better off had they obeyed God and not eaten what he had forbidden. But by the time they learned that lesson, it was too late. They chose the wrong tree. This acquired knowledge of evil did not lift them to a higher level. Instead, they opened the door to sin and Satan — not only for themselves, but for us all. Adam was the head of the human race. He was the authorized agent. All of us are implicated by his original sin. Mankind fell and we did not fall upward.[115]

As a result of the Fall, the moral image of God in man was lost. Our affections are alienated, our intellect is darkened, our will is perverted. We are sinful from the moment of conception (Psalm 51:5). The wicked are estranged from the womb; they go astray from birth (Psalm 58:3). The heart is deceitful above all things (Jer 17:9). Jesus said we are evil (Matt 7:11). There is not even one who is righteous (Rom 3:10-18). We are dead in transgressions and sins, gratifying the cravings of our sinful nature (Eph 2:1-3). Our old self is corrupt through deceitful desires (Eph 4:22). It is at war with God (Rom 8:7). We quarrel and fight, covet and murder because we have passions warring within

---

[113]Wesley, "Original Sin," Sermon #44, 2.4-9; 3.1; see also Chiles, *Theological Transitions*, 119; Lindström, *Wesley and Sanctification*, 27; Collins, *Theology of John Wesley*, 69-70.

[114]Mueller, "A Biblical Examination," 21. Diane Leclerc argues that the primary definition of original sin is idolatry [Leclerc, *Singleness of Heart*].

[115]In contrast, Mormon theologian Sterling W. Sill taught, "Adam fell, but he fell in the right direction. He fell toward the goal. . . . Adam fell but he fell upward" [Sill, *Deseret News*, 7].

(James 4:1-2). Sinful desire is the corruption that is in the world (2 Peter 1:4). All have sinned (Rom 3:23) because all are sinners. Sinful actions proceed from a sinful heart (Mark 7:21-22). The sinner is:

- energized by Satan (Eph 2:1-2)
- blinded by Satan (2 Cor 4:3-4)
- controlled by Satan (1 John 5:19)

The sinful nature controls us. Our sin condemns us. We have not only inherited depravity, but we acquire depravity by wrong choices. We stand guilty before God because of our sins. The wages of sin is death (Rom 6:23). The sinner is dead in sin (Eph 2:1). The sinner faces the second death, eternal separation from God (Rev 2:11; 20:14; 21:8).

According to Sam Powell, the twofold consequence of living in the world of sin is *alienation*, which manifests itself as spiritual death and judgment, which implies separation. Another result of sin is *corruption*, manifested as wrong desire, loss of true freedom, distortion of thought and ethical conduct, and in wickedness.[116] Cornelius Plantinga observed, "Sin is more than the sum of what sinners do. Sin acquires the powerful and elusive form of a spirit."[117]

Man has been tempted ever since the Fall to express his freedom through disobedience. This is the essence of sin. The basic meaning of *sin* in the Old Testament means missing or transgressing an implied absolute standard of God. The Hebrew language has at least ten words for sin, which is more terms than it has for "goodness." The basic New Testament meaning is to miss the mark (ἁμαρτία - *harmartia*). Used over two hundred times in the New Testament, *harmartia* can refer to sin in the abstract or to sinful acts.[118] The New Testament contains twenty-eight synonyms for sin, derived from eight different roots. They carry these variations in meaning and emphasis: wrongdoing, unrighteousness, injustice, overstepping, transgression, disobedience, failure to hear, carelessness, trespass, a false step, oversight, error, mistake (unintentional), lawlessness, iniquity, godlessness, falling short, an error, ignorance, a defect, loss, a fault, a crime, evil, wicked, unbelief. Several of these words, *asebeia, anomia,* and *adikia* refer to an inward orientation toward sin. Kinlaw observed that in Romans 1:18-32 Paul uses *asebeia* first and then speaks of *adikia*. The point is that *asebeia* describes a relationship with God that is not proper and *adikia* describes all other relationships which are not right. Thus *asebeia* is cause and *adikia* is

---

[116]Powell, *Discovering our Christian Faith*, 139-143.

[117]Plantinga, *Not the Way It's Supposed to Be*, 75.

[118]Trench, *Synonyms of the New Testament*, 241.

result.[119]

Other phrases in the New Testament, such as "filthiness" (2 Cor 7:1), "the body of sin" (Rom 6:6), "the sin which does so easily beset us" (Heb 12:1), and "filthiness and all that remains of wickedness" (James 1:21, *NASB*) also denote inward depravity.

There may be sin without guilt when the person is not conscious that an action is sinful. The biblical concept of sin is blurred, however, when it is assumed that all of man's deeds are sinful because he is human. All guilt presupposes sin, but all sin does not necessarily presuppose guilt.

Thus, all sin is not treated equally. Numbers 35 distinguishes between an accidental killing and an intentional murder. The word "murder" is not attributed to the man who kills accidently. Passages such as Matthew 12:31; Luke 12:47-48; John 9:41 imply a gradation view of sin. Arminius rejected the Stoics teaching which make all sin equal.[120] Calvin also acknowledged a gradation of sin.[121]

Kenneth Kinghorn asserted there is no precise biblical definition of sin; that the Bible is more concerned with the remedy for sin than with a definition of sin. Sin is both willful transgression and falling short. It is both objective and subjective; both ethical and legal. Kinghorn concluded that sin is essentially a wrong relationship with God.[122] Because there are degrees and types of sin, there are various definitions of sin found in Scripture.

- *Sin* is not believing in Christ (John 16:9).
- *Sin* is suppression of the truth (Rom 1:18).
- *Sin* is defiance against God's law (Rom 8:7).
- *Sin* is whatever does not come from faith (Rom 14:23).
- *Sin* is lawlessness (1 John 3:4).
- *Sin* is refusal to do good (James 4:17).

Unintentional Sin?

A careful study of the terms used to describe sin will bear out these distinctions:

- sin as a condition and as an act

---

[119]Kinlaw, *Let's Start with Jesus*, 122.

[120]Arminius, *Works*, 2:160.

[121]Calvin, *Institutes*, 4.12.4.

[122]Kinghorn, "Biblical Concepts of Sin," 21; 23-26.

- sins of commission and sins of omission
- unintentional and deliberate sin

Leviticus 4:27-28 also refers to inadvertent errors, which are still called "sin." Restitution to man and a sacrifice offering to God were required for these unintentional sins. Leviticus 4-5 uses the word שגגה (*segaga*) which means sin of error, inadvertence. This word is set over against sins of intention.[123]

Numbers 15:22-31 makes a distinction between unintentional and defiant sin. Flagrant sin resulted in a member removed from the covenant community, but this was not the case with a sin of ignorance or unintentional sins. George Allen Turner wrote that the Old Testament treats sin in three broad categories: deliberate acts of rebellion, sins of ignorance, and a chronic disposition to sinfulness.[124] Psalm 19:12-13 makes a distinction between errors and hidden faults and willful or presumptuous sins. If I am kept from willful sins, I am blameless [*tam*][125]and declared innocent of great transgression.[126]

Hebrews 10:26 speaks of sinning deliberately, which implies that Christians may also sin inadvertently. There is no atonement for those who draw back (v 38) into total apostasy.[127] Paul called himself the foremost sinner, yet two verses earlier, in 1 Timothy 1:13, said he had acted in ignorance.

W. T. Purkiser argued that the category "sins of ignorance," which is found sparingly in Leviticus and Numbers, refer to unconscious transgressions of the ceremonial law with its many requirements. However, even in the Old Testament the prevailing use is that which regards sin as rebellion against God.[128] Yet Wesley said of New Testament believers, "The best of men still need Christ, in his priestly office, to atone for their omissions, their shortcomings (as some not improperly speak), their mistakes in judgment and practice, and their defects of various kinds. For these are all deviations from the perfect law, and consequently

---

[123]BDB, *Lexicon*, 993. A form of this word is used seven times in Lev 4-5.

[124]Turner, *Vision Which Transforms*, 26; see also Purkiser, *Exploring Our Christian Faith*, 291-295.

[125]The Hebrew word *tam*, also discussed at ftnt #700, is a derivative of תמם (*tamam*), which means to be complete.

[126]Clarke defined "great transgression" as habitual sinning, apostasy, and besetting sin [*Commentary*, 3:283]. Benson said that innocence from great transgression meant to be kept pure from the guilt of presumptuous sin, which are, indeed, very great transgressions [*Notes*, 2:714-715].

[127]Dale Moody connected Heb 10:26 with Numb 15:30 [Moody, *Apostasy*, 53].

[128]Purkiser, *Exploring Our Christian Faith*, 292.

need an atonement."[129] Thus, while we walk in obedience our fellowship with God remains unbroken and the blood of Christ continually cleanses us from unconscious sin (1 John 1:7). Wesley replied to Miss J. C. March,

> There cannot be a more proper phrase than that you used, and I will understand your meaning; yet it is sure you are a transgressor still – namely, of the perfect, Adamic law. But though it be true all sin is a transgression of this law, yet it is by no means true on the other hand (though we have so often taken it for granted) that all transgressions of this law are sin: no, not at all — only all voluntary transgressions of it; none else are sins against the gospel law.[130]

J. T. Crane defended Wesley's distinction between sins of ignorance and presumption. "There are cases where ignorance is itself a grievous sin." Yet they do not result in peace with God being forfeited. "So far as the ultimate salvation of the soul is concerned, the difference between Wesley and Calvinism is that what Wesley concludes in regard to the believer's involuntary infractions of the perfect law Calvinism affirms in regard to all manner of deliberate sin."[131]

In his *A Right Conception of Sin*, Richard S. Taylor does admit that unintentional sins are called "sin" in the Bible, but he says that under the dispensation of grace the definition of sin is different from the dispensation of the law. "It makes all the difference in the world to remember that in the problem of defining sin we are *not under law but under grace*. . . . Grace . . . takes into full consideration the circumstances and emotions and motives involved. If it was an unintentional, unforeseen, and inescapable commission or omission, grace pronounces the man innocent; that is, grace says he is *not* a sinner." Taylor continued, "True, such things as misinterpretation of God's will and mistakes of ignorance need to be guarded against and need the atoning blood of Christ, but only because they are results of the fall and not because they are in themselves acts of sin.[132]

---

[129]Wesley, *Works*, 11:396. In contrast, Finney taught that sanctified Christians were dependent upon the atonement only for their past sins [Finney, *Lectures to Professing Christians*, 393]. Mudge is also in error to reject this teaching of Wesley [Mudge, *Growth in Holiness*, 187].

[130]Wesley, *Letter*, May 31, 1771.

[131]Crane, "Christian Perfection and the Higher Life," 710-711.

[132]Taylor, *Right Conception*, 61-63. Diane Leclerc, however, acknowledges that these omissions are sin [Leclerc, *Discovering Christian Holiness*, 162]. In the sense that we could always care for more of the poor, visit more of the sick and

John Hartley concluded in the light of the teaching of the Old Testament that Taylor's statement should be tempered.[133] Ironically, Taylor is the same author who in an earlier chapter berated Calvinists for actually implying that "God's method of redeeming the race is by changing the nature of sin rather than by removing it and delivering from it."[134] It is more consistent to hold that sins of ignorance are not imputed against us.

Calvinists such as Louis Berkhof accuse Wesleyans of holding that we are not obligated to fulfill the original moral law. Berkhof said that Perfectionists lower the standard of the law and externalize the idea of sin in order to maintain their theory.[135] However, in 1851 an earlier Wesleyan voice, Thomas Summers, declared "the holiness of which we speak is both legal and evangelical." He explained that while we are not under the ceremonial law, we are under moral law.[136] Berkhof's accusation applies more to Oberlin theology. Finney taught that there must be some relaxation of the moral law if man whole-heartedly does the best that he can.[137]

Richard S. Taylor said he was baffled that Wesley would not call human imperfection "sin," yet acknowledged it needed atonement. Taylor's solution is that sin can only be willful and that unintentional mistakes do not need atonement.[138] However, what Wesley actually said was that all deviations from the perfect law are not properly sins according to the definition given in Romans 13:10. Thus, through the unconditional benefits of the atonement, sins of ignorance are not imputed. Clarke admonished us to often pray for cleansing from sins of ignorance.[139]

---

imprisoned, and do more acts of mercy — everyone sins through omission. But these sins of omission are not imputed to us if we are walking as 1 John 1:7 describes.

[133]Hartley, "Old Testament Studies in the Wesleyan Mode," 76.

[134]Taylor, *Right Conception of Sin*, 24.

[135]Berkhof, *Systematic Theology*, 538; 540.

[136]Summers, *Treatise on Sanctification*, 52.

[137]Erickson said, in describing the governmental theory of the atonement, as taught by Grotius, "It is possible for God to relax the law so that he need not exact a specific punishment or penalty for each violation" [*Christian Theology*, 807].

[138]Taylor, "The Question of 'Sins of Ignorance,'" 71-77; Wesley, *Works*, 11:396. Tennant argued, "Unconscious sin is a contradiction in terms" [Tennant, *The Concept of Sin*, 101]. See the discussion by Sangster, *Path to Perfection*, 71-76; Steele, *Leviticus*, 41.

[139]Clarke, *Commentary*, 1:520. Mudge denied the category of sins of ignorance [Mudge, *Growth in Holiness*, 38-56]. While Granbery said his book was helpful,

Therefore, Wesleyans have not necessarily redefined sin, but instead teach that it is not imputed unless willful. W. B. Pope explained that the Methodist doctrine did not lower the law, but instead taught that Christian perfection is an obedience which is counted as perfection.[140]

Delbert Rose wrote, "The margin between what a perfect Adam attained under the *Edenic law* and what a perfect-hearted Christian realizes under the *Evangelical law* is covered by the atoning merits of Christ. God does not impute to believers as sin those 'shortcomings' which arise out of a defective body and mind, yet they need the atoning merits of Christ in the light of God's perfect law, His perfect righteousness."[141]

John Wesley declared, "*All* deviation from perfect holiness *is sin*."[142] But he also spoke of sin, properly so called and sin, improperly so called.[143] Here he distinguishes between willful sins and unintentional sins. He defined sin, properly so called, as a "voluntary transgression of a known law of God."[144]

> Nothing is sin, strictly speaking, but a voluntary transgression of a known law of God. Therefore, every voluntary breach of the law of love is sin; and nothing else, if we speak properly. To strain the matter farther is only to make way for Calvinism. There may be ten thousand wandering thoughts and forgetful intervals without any breach of love, though not without transgressing the Adamic law. But Calvinism would fain confound these together. Let love fill your heart, and it is enough.[145]

Granbery went on to say his treatise would have been more satisfactory if he had not been so absorbed in his contention that all sin is voluntary and guilty [Granbery, "Dr. Mudge on Growth in Holiness,"198; 201; 207].

Steele rightly exposes his view as inadequate in *Defense of Christian Perfection*, 41, 100-101, pointing to Lev 4:13; Heb 5:2; 9:7. Lewis R. Dunn protested, "I totally disagree with Dr. Mudge, and so do all our leading theologians, when he says; 'Unavoidable infirmities and ignorances *need no expiation*'"[Dunn, *Manual of Holiness*, 72-73].

[140]Pope, *Higher Catechism*, 273.

[141]Rose, "Wesleyan Understanding of Sin," 27-28. Rose cited Rom 4:15; 5:13.

[142]Wesley, *Notes*, 641.

[143]Wesley, *Works*, 11:396.

[144]Wesley, *Works*, 10:394.

[145]Wesley, *Letter* to Elizabeth Bennis, 16 June, 1772.

Other systems tend to make little distinction between these issues, preferring to emphasize that we all sin daily because we are human or finite. This discounts the possibility of deliverance from willful sin. Yet Sam Powell argued that Wesley did not intend for this definition to be a complete or adequate definition. Sin in multidimensional and therefore no brief definition of sin can be adequate. "There is much to sin besides voluntarily transgressing the command of God. It is therefore a mistake to think that the Wesleyan view of sin is principally about voluntary transgressions of God's law."[146]

However, Calvinists such as Charles Hodge believed that Wesley had a deficient view of sin.[147] Calvinists basically hold a legal definition of sin as any transgression of the law of God. While Wesley recognized the reality of involuntary transgressions, he felt they were covered under the unconditional benefits of the atonement. So long as the human will was not in rebellion, man did not incur any guilt or punishment. The Old Testament law did make a distinction between voluntary and involuntary transgressions. According to W. E. Vine, παράπτωμα (*paraptoma*) is a stronger term than *hamartema* because it describes the breach of a known law.[148] Thus, both the Old and New Testaments appear to make the distinction Wesley also made.

Colin Williams wrote that Wesley resorted to two definitions of sin: one of conscious separation from God and the other of absolute conformity to the perfect will of God. "Thus when he spoke of the time or moment when the believer becomes perfect, he was speaking in terms of the first definition, but in light of the second he still spoke of the necessity for the perfect to confess their sins and grow in grace."[149]

Wesley wrote that those cleansed from all sin are the most deeply conscious of their need of Christ both as Prophet, Priest, and King. "'But are they not sinners?' Explain the term one way, and I say, Yes; another, and I say, No. 'Are they cleansed from all sin?' I believe they are; meaning all sinful tempers. 'But have they then need of Christ?' I believe they have." Wesley then argued that this position was no contradiction, that it was consistent with right reason, and the whole oracles of God.[150]

---

[146]Powell, *Discovering our Christian Faith*, 116.

[147]Hodge, *Systematic Theology*, 3:254-255; 258. This was also the opinion of Flew, *The Idea of Perfection*, 332-336.

[148]Vine, *Expository Dictionary*, 4:155.

[149]Williams, *John Wesley's Theology Today*, 170.

[150]Wesley, *Letter* to Samuel Furly, 15 September 1762. When Wesley referred to "sinful tempers" or "unholy tempers" he meant a disposition toward pride, self-will, and the love of the world. To be cleansed from this disposition means the believer no

While Wesley's view has received much criticism,[151] the scriptures do distinguish between being blameless and faultless. The difference between blameless and faultless is that faults are not imputed as sin when the motive was pure before God. Even R. J. Rushdoony, a proponent of Calvinism, conceded, "In this life, we can be perfect in the sense of being blameless in our faithfulness to God's purpose, but to be blameless does not mean being faultless."[152]

Yet this view can also lead to the danger of presumption. In his Addendum to the 2002 edition of *A Right Conception of Sin,* Richard S. Taylor contrasts the shallow view of sin held by some Wesleyans with the deeper view held by Wesley himself:

> We have subtly shifted from unintentional transgressions of the law in Old Testament terms to violation of a Christian spirit. This is more serious and introduces a new dimension. . . . To brush aside these failures as being sinless simply because they do not fully qualify as sins under Wesley's definition is to foster hardheartedness . . . Impatient words, rash judgments, apparent injustices, and attitudes which at least seem petulant and selfish cannot simply be swept under the carpet and forgotten, as if they carried no moral significance, simply because they are not 'voluntary transgressions of a known law.' This is an abuse of Wesley's definition. Wesley himself would not tolerate it. In evaluating the profession of a group of Methodists in London, he found among some of them many telltale evidences of remaining

---

longer senses this contrary principle within but instead experiences freedom. Wesley spoke of the wholly sanctified as purified from pride, self-will, and anger, based on the example of Christ [Wesley, "Christian Perfection," Sermon #40, 2.26]. On the other hand, Mudge expressed doubt whether there be any soul who enjoys every right temper. By this he meant that an error in judgment almost always led to an error in disposition. Thus, Mudge distinguished between sin and depravity. He declared that we may be saved from all sin in this life, but not from all depravity [Granbery, "Dr. Mudge on Growth in Holiness, 199-201].

[151]For example, see Flew who argued that our worst sins are often those of which we are unconscious and if Wesley's view of sin is adopted our sanctification is limited to our own insight and knowledge of ourselves [Flew, *The Idea of Perfection*, 333; 412]. However, there can be further revelations of ourselves and deeper cleansings. Leo Cox wrote, "Wesley would agree with Flew that sometimes the worst sins of the believer are unconscious although Flew thought Wesley had no such concept" [Cox, *John Wesley's Concept of Sin*, 91].

[152]Rushdoony, *Institutes of Biblical Law*, 629. See the discussion on blameless and faultless on p. 162.

double mindedness. He says: 'Some are wanting in gentleness. They resist evil, instead of turning the other cheek. They do not receive reproach with gentleness; no, nor even reproof. Nay, they are not able to bear contradiction without the appearance, at least, of resentment. If they are reproved or contradicted, though mildly, they do not take it well; they behave with more distance and reserve than they did before. If they are reproved or contradicted harshly, they answer it with harshness, with a loud voice, or with an angry tone, or in a sharp and surly manner.' . . . [Also] he faults them for a lack of meekness and quietness of spirit. He concludes with the verdict: 'You have not what I call perfection.' . . . In other words, your profession of holiness is defective. You are carnal; and carnality is sin, no matter how much you hide behind Wesley's definition of sin 'properly so-called.' For while a sinful disposition may not be expressed in a deliberate act of wrongdoing in the sense of stealing or lying, it is nevertheless positive unChristlikeness which needs repentance and forgiveness.[153]

Wesley explained,

(1). Every one may mistake as long as he lives. (2.) A mistake in opinion may occasion a mistake in practice. (3.) Every such mistake is a transgression of the perfect law. Therefore, (4.) Every such mistake, were it not for the blood of atonement, would expose to eternal damnation. (5.) It follows, that the most perfect have continual need of the merits of Christ, even for their actual transgressions, and may say for themselves, as well as for their brethren, "Forgive us our trespasses."
This easily accounts for what might otherwise seem to be utterly unaccountable; namely, that those who are not offended when we speak of the highest degree of love, yet will not hear of living without sin. The reason is, they know all men are liable to mistake, and that in practice as well as in judgment. But they do not know, or do not observe, that this is not sin, if love is the sole principle of action.[154]

The Lost Image

---

[153]Taylor, *Right Conception* (2002), 115-116.

[154]Wesley, *Works*, 11:395.

The "image of God" has been interpreted as substantive, referring to something inherent within humanity, such as reason, the intellect, or innate holiness. It has also been understood as something relational, referring to how humanity relates to each other and to God. And it has been explained as functional, describing how humanity exercises stewardship or dominion over creation.

Wesley understood the image of God to consist of three components: the natural image, the political image, and the moral image. The natural image consists of reason, will, and freedom. The political image is the responsibility of mankind as steward and caretaker of creation.[155] The moral image is righteousness and holiness.[156]

The natural image and the political image of God was marred — not completely lost, but greatly damaged. If our destiny is defined by the image of God in which we were created, sin is the rejection of our identity. Mankind is a magnificent ruin due to the results of sin. Blaise Pascal said that man is "the glory and refuse of the universe."[157] Yet according to Genesis 9:6 and James 3:9 that image of God in man still exists in some sense.[158]

Irenaeus distinguished between the image of God and our likeness or similitude to God. According to him, the image of God was an endowment in humans of the capacity for relationship with God. Our likeness to God is the proper functioning of this capacity, as expressed in a righteousness relationship with God.

Yet the terms "image" and "likeness" occur together only in Genesis 1:26. However, in v 27, which deals with the actual work of creation, only "image is used." In Genesis 5:1 the Hebrew word for "likeness" is not translated in the Septuagint by the usual Greek word *homoiosis*, but by *eikon*, which means "image."

Wesley did not contrast image and likeness. Instead he used the language

---

155Recently Veli-Matti Kärkkäinen described a modern "green" or ecological doctrine of the Spirit. He described Jürgen Moltmann's call for a new state in the relationship between theology and science or the relationship between Spirit and nature [*Pneumatology*, 159-164]. See also Howard Snyder, "Holiness and the Five Calls of God," 130-132.

156Wesley, "The New Birth," Sermon #45, 1,1; 'The General Deliverance," Sermon #60, 1.1-5; "The End of Christ's Coming," Sermon #62, 1.3-7; "The Image of God," Sermon #141.

157Pascal, *Penśees*, frag. 131, 34.

1581 Cor 11:7 also refers to the image of God in males as a present reality. Paul is not here denying that women are also created in God's image. Instead he is delineating role distinctions.

of natural image and moral image. While Martin Luther understood "image" and "likeness" as Hebrew parallelism, Roman Catholic theology tends to understand that our likeness was lost in the Fall but the "image" was not affected. This likeness or reflection of God was not part of man's essential personality, but consisted of supernaturally added gifts (*donum superadditum*). The recovery of the likeness, then, is perfection which has been bestowed in addition to the *donum naturale*, which was not lost in the Fall. Only the *donum superaddita* was lost as a result of the Fall.

In the teaching of the Eastern church, "image" is a gift while "likeness" is the goal. Adam and Eve bore the image of God, but were to grow into the divine likeness. According to Orthodox teaching this likeness is the doctrine of theosis.[159] While humanity lost the likeness of God, we did not lose the image of God.

In her relational theology, Wynkoop also distinguished between "image" and "likeness." However, she rejected both the Protestant and Catholic interpretations. Instead she argued for a third position, that the image of God was not something *in* man, but that it is man's relationship before God.[160] It seems like reductionism for her to explain the image of God as love. Yet Dunning makes this same claim,[161] as does Leclerc.[162] Theodore Runyon expressed the same concept that the image is not something that humanity has, but it is an ongoing relation in which humanity receives and gives. "And what is received is *love*."[163]

Wynkoop defined "image" as resemblance or family tie. She taught that all essential to human personality was never lost, that the image of God continues after the Fall.[164] However, she defined "likeness" as an approximation of Christ which was lost and needs to be recovered.[165] She declared that the Scripture

---

[159]Payton, "Keeping the End in View,"66-68. *Theosis* will be discussed on pp. 330-331.

[160]Wynkoop, *Theology of Love*, 105.

[161]Dunning, *Grace, Faith, and Holiness*, 465.

[162]Leclerc, *Discovering Christian Holiness*, 144; 158.

[163]Runyon, "Holiness as the Renewal," 80.

[164]Wynkoop, *Theology of Love*, 146-147.

[165]Wynkoop, *Theology of Love*, 105-145. She declared that the image of God is marred in every part but not destroyed, because to destroy the "image" would rob men of humanhood [Wynkoop, *Foundations*, 98]. I find it interesting that Wynkoop felt it necessary twice to declare that her theology was not Pelagian [*Theology of Love*, 171; 177]. Richard S. Taylor said Wynkoop's *A Theology of Love* was "essentially Pelagian" and that there is no original sin in it ["Why the Holiness Movement Died," 50; 53].

makes a distinction between "God's image in man" and "man made in God's image."[166] She felt that "God's image in man" refers to the "likeness" which we lost, but "man made in God's image" can never be lost.

Yet if the "image of God" was not lost are we totally depraved? Ray Dunning concluded that the image was both lost and retained at one and the same time.[167] How then can the image be restored if not lost? Dunning asked, "Is it then possible to sustain a position that speaks of fallen man as standing in a relation to God that is a perpetual relation, not lost through the original sin, or if lost, restored by an act of sovereign grace?" His conclusion is that prevenient grace "is simply another way of talking about that aspect of the *imago Dei* as a relationship within which man perpetually stands."[168] Dunning did not distinguish between "image" and "likeness," but specified that the "image of God" consists in man's relation before God or the image of God is reflected in man because of his position before God. Thus, original sin involves the loss of or the perversion of that relationship in which man stood in a state of integrity.[169] The image of God in the sanctified life, according to Dunning, is a set of relationships that include a relation to God, to other persons, and to one's possessions.[170]

Dunning wrote that the image was totally lost as a consequence of the Fall, but a reflection of it is restored by the activity of prevenient grace. This

---

Dunning said that relational theology can appear to be Pelagian if it is not understood [*Grace, Faith, and Holiness*, 15]. *Pelagianism* will be discussed on pp. 61-62.

[166]Wynkoop, *Foundations*, 99-100.

[167]Dunning, *Reflecting the Divine Image*, 52.

[168]Dunning, *Grace, Faith, and Holiness*, 157-158. Metz objected that such an emphasis denies any inherent human nature. Thus, man is not sinful by nature for he has not nature as such. Instead of a state of sinfulness, man exists in a broken relationship. Metz rejected the philosophic teaching that man is essentially good but existentially estranged [*Some Crucial Issues*, 151-156]. Perhaps, however, we can affirm that man is both essentially and relationally sinful without adopting philosophical concepts which undermine biblical teaching on the nature of our sinfulness.

[169]Dunning, "Holiness, Technology and Personhood,"177; 180. See Dunning, *Grace, Faith, and Holiness*, 488-498. In *Reflecting the Divine Image* Dunning also said the image of God involves a fourfold relationship: with God, with other, with the earth and with self [p. 45]. Leclerc wrote that many who have followed Dunning, including herself, see the last two categories in a more positive light: an appropriate love for ourselves and our stewardship of the earth [*Discovering Christian Holiness*, 300]. I am not sure we can have a relationship with the earth. Perhaps "responsibility" is a better term.

[170]Dunning, "Holiness: Experience or Relationship?" 45.

restored aspect is what constitutes personhood. Since personhood involves choice, if the image of God was completely destroyed, mankind would be incapable of sin. "In fact it is this graciously restored aspect of the *imago* that constitutes personhood."[171]

Has the moral image of God in man been lost or have the effects of the Fall been reversed through prevenient grace? Has preliminary grace so restored humanity that we are all under a perpetual state of grace? Preliminary grace can be so construed to mean that depravity was never transferred to the race or that all are saved because of this irrevocable gift. Thus, original sin can be identified as the sin of Adam, but it did not result in total depravity for humanity. I do not question that prevenient grace is an unconditional benefit of the atonement. I do question whether it is to be understood as a permanent condition which results in a universal salvation.

It was said of Nathan Bangs that "he was a strong believer of prevenient grace but not at the expense of total depravity. He argued that because of grace, humankind does have the ability to respond to God."[172] However, according to John Miley there is no intrinsic sinfulness in the inherited corruption of nature.[173] Albert Knudson also wrote,

> Original sin in its traditional form is a fiction, and so are all themes that seek to explain its origin by a catastrophic act either in time or out of it. There is no such thing as inherited guilt or inherited moral depravity. . . . It is in the will . . . and its free activity, not in anything extra volitional, that we must seek the origin of sin.[174]

Some modern descriptions of prevenient grace seem to be describing a "spark of goodness" within every person or human personality. Theodore Runyon sees prevenient grace as "God's presence in every human life."[175] Bradford McCall defined prevenient grace as "the omnipresent, omni-relational God acting in each moment to empower creatures to respond freely and then luring them to

---

[171]Dunning, *Reflecting the Divine Image*, 51. William Arnett wrote that the natural image is summed up in the word *personality* ["The Wesleyan Arminian Teaching on Sin," 58]. Jon Tal Murphree contends that being social is one of the ways we are created in God's image [*Love Motive*, 13].

[172]Online: "Biography of Nathan Bangs."

[173]Miley, *Systematic Theology*, 1:526; see Metz, *Some Crucial Issues*, 143.

[174]Knudson, *Systematic Theology*, 2; 76.

[175]Runyan, *New Creation*, 34.

choose responses that increase overall complexity."[176]

Thomas Lessmann believed that prevenient grace is a freeing perspective. "It places in a hopeful light even the human being who has turned away from and against God, and who is hardened in his or her sins."[177] John Cobb declared, "The Holy Spirit *is* God's gracious presence in all people."[178] He went on to connect the Holy Spirit with grace, so that he could have made the same statement about prevenient grace — that grace was God's gracious presence in all people. But is this prevenient grace to be understood an almost universal and permanent state? If everyone is under some degree of preliminary grace and if this grace is salvific, this leads to the logical conclusion of universalism. Kenneth Collins rightly insists that a distinction must be made between this preliminary grace and justification.[179]

Randy Maddox wrote that Eastern theologians did not hold that the Fall deprived us of all grace.[180] The Eastern Orthodox Church believe humans are born with the curse of Adam, which is to be mortal and die. They do not believe humans are born in sin.[181] Thus, original sin is not passed on; it is the mortality which we inherit from Adam.

If the Fall did not result in total depravity, if the image of God is not lost, and all are under grace — then are all saved? Does preliminary grace constitute salvation? Maddox defines prevenient grace as "a crucial degree of regeneration prior to the New Birth."[182] Maddox also defines the faith of a servant as justifying faith.[183] He also wrote about the universal restoring presence of the Spirit.[184] Maddox distinguished between original sin and inbeing sin. We are spiritually diseased, but not spiritually dead.

For the Western church, sin is viewed as a legal problem. For the Eastern

---

[176]McCall, "Emergence Theory and Theology,"192.

[177]Lessmann, *John Wesleys*, 131.

[178]Cobb, *Grace and Responsibility*, 42.

[179]Collins,"The State of Wesley Studies," 23-24.

[180]Maddox, *Responsible Grace*, 66.

[181]Harakas, *Toward Transfigured Life*, 81-84. See the discussion by Collins, *Theology of John Wesley*, 72-73.

[182]Maddox, *Responsible Grace*, 159.

[183]This is also the position of Felleman, "'Servant of God,'"72-86. See the concerns expressed by Collins, "Recent Trends in Wesley Studies," 67-74; "The State of Wesley Studies" 19.

[184]Maddox, *Responsible Grace*, 123.

church, sin is a disease. While the Western church held that we inherit the guilt of original sin, the Eastern church denies this. Maddox explained the present corruption of human nature relationally, that we were born into a world already separated from the empowering Divine Presence.[185] Yet prevenient grace is the beginning of restoration and thus, humanity is beginning to be restored.[186] The effects of original sin are annulled by prevenient grace.[187]

Therefore, the question must be asked, Is prevenient grace a permanent condition or a temporary window of opportunity? Concerning prevenient grace, Wesley taught

> salvation begins with what is usually termed (and very properly) "preventing grace;" including the first wish to please God, the first dawn of light concerning his will, and the first slight, transient conviction of having sinned against him. All these imply some tendency toward life, some degree of salvation, the beginning of deliverance from a blind, unfeeling heart, quite insensible of God and the things of God.[188]

Wesley said that "preventing grace" included

> all the 'drawings' of 'the Father,' the desires after God, which, if we yield to them, increase more and more; all that 'light' wherewith the Son of God 'enlighteneth everyone that cometh into the world,' *showing* every man 'to do justly, to love mercy, and to walk humbly with his God' all the *convictions* which his Spirit from time to time works in every child of man. Although it is true the generality of men stifle them as soon as possible, and after a while forget, or at least deny, that ever they had them

---

[185]Maddox, *Responsible Grace*, 74-82.

[186]Maddox, *Responsible Grace*, 83-90.

[187]Wesley taught that original guilt was cancelled as an unconditional benefit of the atonement [*Letter* to John Mason, 21 Nov. 1776; "God's Love to Fallen Man," Sermon #59, 2.14]. Yet Maddox here blurs the distinction between original guilt and original sin. In his discussion on "original sin or inbeing sin?" he conflates original sin with original guilt and infers that since Wesley rejected original guilt that he was in agreement with the Eastern theologians who also rejected original sin [Maddox, *Responsible Grace*, 74-75]. See the analysis by Collins, *Theology of John Wesley*, 73. In his doctrine of original sin, Wesley followed Augustine and not Eastern theology.

[188]Wesley, "On Working Out Our Own Salvation," Sermon #85, 2.1.

at all.[189]

Wesley preached,

> For allowing that all the souls of men are dead in sin by *nature*, this excuses none, seeing there is no man that is in a state of mere nature; there is no man, unless he has quenched the Spirit, that is wholly void of the grace of God. No man living is entirely destitute of what is vulgarly called "natural conscience." But this is not natural; it is more properly termed "preventing grace."[190]

In his dialogue with Richard Hill, Fletcher wrote, "We believe that no child of Adam is a "natural man" in the Calvinian sense of the word, (that is, absolutely destitute of all saving grace,) except he who has actually sinned away his day of grace."[191] Yet both Fletcher and Wesley also held to original sin *and* total depravity.

Original Sin and Total Depravity

A consistent theology of sin and holiness, according to Richard S. Taylor, depends on the fundamental distinction between original holiness and original sin.[192] Lindström explained what "original sin" meant for Wesley,

> The Fall, he believed, had deprived man of his original perfection and occasioned total corruption of human nature. Consequently, Adam's descendants are spiritually dead at birth and utterly devoid of the righteousness and holiness in which he himself was created. Sometimes original sin is described as an inclination to evil, or a condition in which all the faculties of man, understanding and will and affections, have been perverted. But he can use stronger language, defining it as total corruption of the whole of human nature.[193]

---

[189]Wesley, "The Scripture Way of Salvation," Sermon #43, 1.2.

[190]Wesley, "On Working Out Our Own Salvation," Sermon #85, 3.4.

[191]Fletcher, *Works*,1:409.

[192]Taylor, *Theological Formulation*, 38.

[193]Lindström, *Wesley and Sanctification*, 27.

The classic New Testament passage on sin is Romans 1:18-3:20. In Romans 1:29-31 Paul begins with four vices with which we are "filled to the brim" — unrighteousness, as well as two synonyms for evil which are separated by greed. Then Paul lists five vices of which we are full: we are full of envy, murder, strife, deceit, and a tendency to put the worst construction upon everything. Finally Paul lists twelve vices: whisperers, back-talkers, God-haters, those who insult, arrogant, boastful, inventors of evil, disobedient to parents, senseless, faithless, loveless, and merciless.

In Romans 2 Paul shifts from the rebellious sinner to the religious sinner and argues that those with greater privilege are liable to greater punishment. In Romans 3:9-20, Paul closes his argument by indicting the whole human race as sinners. In a corporate sense, we all sinned with Adam and continue to fall short.

Adam's sin was conveyed to the whole human race. Thus there is a corporate dimension of sin. Theologians use several phrases to explain the permanent condition which resulted from Adam's first sin: original sin, the Adamic nature; the sin nature; the carnal nature; total depravity. According to Grider, "Original sin refers to a state of sin in us due to that original act of sin on Adam's part."[194] Sam Powell wrote that original sin is more than the first sin. "*Original* means *universal*."[195]

The Articles of Religion of the Methodist Episcopal Church state, "Original sin standeth not in the following of Adam (as the *Pelagians* do vainly talk) but it is the corruption of the nature of every man, that naturally is engendered of the offspring of Adam, whereby man is very far gone from original righteousness, and of his own nature inclined to evil, and that continually."[196]

Isaiah 53:5 promised that Christ would become the substitute for our transgressions[197] and our iniquities.[198] David prayed for cleansing from secret faults and from presumptuous sins (Psalm 19:12-13). Both the words of our mouth and the meditations of our heart need to be accepted by God (Psalm 19:14). Thus we need clean hands and a pure heart (Psalm 24:4). Wesley preached the two-fold nature of sin; that our sins are both guilt and disease.

---

[194]Grider, *Wesleyan-Holiness Theology*, 277.

[195]Powell, *Discovering our Christian Faith*, 134.

[196]Schaff, *Creeds of Christendom*, 3:492-493. Article 7 of the Articles of Religion of the Methodist Episcopal Church. Adapted by John Wesley from Article 9 of the Anglican Articles of Religion and sent to America. Adopted by the Christmas Conference of 1784.

[197]פשע - *pesha*; refers to outward sins, deliberate transgression, rebellion

[198]עון - *avon*; refers to inborn crookedness or perversion.

> Indeed we are already bound hand and foot by the chains of our own sins. These, considered in regard to ourselves, are chains of iron and fetters of brass. They are wounds wherewith the world, the flesh, and the devil, have gashed and mangled us all over. They are diseases that drink up our blood and spirits, that bring us down to the chambers of the grave. But considered . . . with regard to God, they are debts, immense and numberless.[199]

Dunning concluded, "Humanity is wrong, all wrong, before God, and therefore everything that is done is wrong. It is in this way that actual sin is always an expression of original sin."[200]

Wesley's evangelical sermons were based on three main assumptions:

- natural man is totally corrupt
- this corruption is the result of original sin
- man can be justified only through God's grace in Christ[201]

Olin Curtis said that the sinner has three things the matter with him: "First, he is *guilty*; second he is morally *powerless*; and third, his inherent and inherited *disposition is wrong*."[202] The point is we are in such a condition that we cannot save ourselves. We must have outside help. Anyone who understands the biblical doctrine of man's sinful condition will not waste his time trying to save himself through good works. Yes, sinners can do wonderful acts of kindness and charity, but those works are not good enough to save them. Wesley explained, "All works done before justification are not good, in the Christian sense, forasmuch as they spring not of faith in Jesus Christ."[203]

On the other hand, seemingly good people can surprise us by hideous acts of cruelty. The term total depravity does no imply that every person is as bad as he can possibly be. Instead we are describing the extent of sin's influence.[204] The corruption of sin extends to the whole of man's nature. It affects the entire being of man: the affections are alienated, the intellect is darkened, the will is

---

[199]Wesley, "Sermon on the Mount VI," Sermon #26, 3.13.

[200]Dunning, *Grace, Faith, and Holiness*, 301.

[201]Lindström, *Wesley and Sanctification*, 21.

[202]Curtis, *Christian Faith*, 382.

[203]Wesley, "Justification by Faith," Sermon #5, 3.5.

[204]Whedon distinguished between *extensive* and *intensive* depravity [*Statements*, 331]. We can also distinguish between *inherited* and *acquired* depravity.

perverted.[205] Francis Schaeffer wrote, "Since the Fall, there is no truly healthy person in his body, and there is no completely balanced person psychologically. The results of the Fall spoils us as a unit and in all our parts."[206]

We are deprived of all that is good (Rom 7:18). There was a total loss of innocence, original righteousness and holiness. We are inclined to evil continually (Gen 6:5).

The original sin on Adam's part was imputed to us and we have inherited his sinful tendencies. Thus, original sin is inherited sin. According to Romans 7:18, in our natural condition we are deprived of all that is good. There was a total loss of original righteousness.[207] Because we are liable for Adam's sin, we are deprived of the Spirit of God who makes us holy. Thus, we experience a lost relationship. Because of our identification with Adam we inherit a propensity or inclination to sin like him, which is an inherited condition. And by our continued choice to sin, that inherited tendency from Adam becomes even more depraved. This is an acquired condition.

In the science fiction trilogy written by C. S. Lewis, a character explained "our world is very bent."[208] Yet while all earthlings were "bent," some were also "broken." Here Lewis seems to distinguish between inherited and acquired depravity.

Dissenting from both the Pelagian and the Calvinistic views, R. S. Foster stated the Arminian view that the actions of Adam as the head of the human race affected his posterity. Yet he represents himself regarding his actions morally. His sin caused two results: he became guilty and divine favor was withdrawn from him. This resulted in a loss of balance in which he became extremely averse to good and inclined to evil. There was no recovering power remaining in him. He was totally overthrown. Since like begets like, children born to him inevitably inherited his evil tendencies and disabilities. Potentially we died in him. As we all died potentially in the first Adam, we were all made alive potentially in the second Adam. The existence of the race is a provision of redemption. We partake of Adam's fall, inherit his degenerate and corrupt nature, his tendency to evil. Yet this inherited depravity is not itself ground of guilt, but becomes ground of guilt when it is voluntarily perpetuated by the refusal to have it overcome or removed.[209]

---

[205]Wiley, *Christian Theology*, 2:128-129.

[206]Schaeffer, *Works*, 3:321.

[207]Wakefield, *Christian Theology*, 1:299.

[208]Lewis, *Out of the Silent Planet*, 121. "We are all a bent race" [p. 82].

[209]Foster, *Studies in Theology*, 6:236-238. Foster said that Calvinism is more damaging to the character of God, while Pelagianism is more dangerous to the morality

Sin is transferred to us legally because Adam was our legal representative or federal head. In one sermon Wesley referred to the wide influence of "parent sins . . . from which all the rest derive their being."[210] Wesley explained, "Sin is entailed upon me, not by immediate generation, but by my first parent. In Adam all died; by the disobedience of one, all men were made sinners; all men without exception, who were in his loins when he ate the forbidden fruit."[211]

Richard S. Taylor is wrong in defining Wesley as a"geneticist." The sinful nature is not transmitted from Adam to his posterity by natural generation.[212] Nor is his hypothesis credible that the sin nature is transmitted through DNA chromosomes.[213] Neither Calvinists nor Wesleyans hold to a genetic theory of original sin. "This misuse of language is especially detrimental to the Wesleyan-Holiness movement, which places great emphasis on how God deals with the problem of original sin through the work of entire sanctification. Obviously, a confused perception of original sin will result in a confused perception of entire sanctification."[214]

James Mudge argued that if a total cleansing occurred within parents, that their children would be born without sin. "The only sufficient and satisfactory reason that we have been able to find, why no child is begotten or born without some degree of depravity, is that there are no parents wholly free from it."[215] But the sinful nature is passed on through our connection to Adam. Yet Mudge denied the statement of Wesley that sin is entailed upon us through our first parents. Mudge wrote, "Adam can reach us in no other way than through our father and mother."[216] But this is not exactly the case either. Adam implicated us legally through his original act of sin and the condition of our immediate parents has no bearing on this fact.

Richard Treffry explained that parents propagate their species but not

---

of men [p. 134]. Calvinism holds that the guilt of Adam was transmitted to his descendants, while Pelagianism regards mankind as in a state of spiritual health but in need of moral discipline.

[210]Wesley, "Sermon on the Mount, XI," 1.3.

[211]Wesley, *Works*, 11:400.

[212]Taylor, "Geneticism,"231-232.

[213]Taylor, *Theological Formulation*, 97-98. David L. Smith advocates a similar error in *With Willful Intent*, 369.

[214]Burnett, *In the Shadow of Aldersgate*, 76-77.

[215]Mudge, *Growth in Holiness*, 69-70.

[216]Mudge, *Growth in Holiness*, 68.

their endowments.[217] Thus, Pope said that we must cease to belong to the lineage of Adam before our unsinning state becomes sinless. "The entirely sanctified believer may be, as touching his relation to Christ and in Christ, without spot and blameless; at the same time that in relation to Adam and in him he is only a sinful man among sinful men."[218]

Concerning the transmission of original sin, Wesley replied to a correspondent who had asserted that "there are but three opinions" that "I care not if there were none. The fact I know, both by Scripture and by experience. I know it is transmitted; but *how* it is transmitted I neither know nor desire to know."[219]

> And if you ask me, how, in what determinate manner, sin is propagated; how it is transmitted from father to son: I answer plainly, I cannot tell; no more than I can tell how man is propagated, how a body is transmitted from father to son. I know both the one and the other fact; but I can account for neither.[220]

Wesley was trying to interpret scripture, such as Romans 5:12, where he noted, "These words assign the reason why death came upon *all men*; infants themselves not excepted, *in that all sinned.*"[221] The later Methodists were arguing against the implications of Calvinism on the basis of philosophy.

However, Pope attempted to explain what Wesley sidestepped by distinguishing between our being susceptible to punishment, which was passed on to all men through Adam, and our being held responsible and therefore guilty for Adam's sin.[222]

---

[217]Treffry, *Treatise on Christian Perfection*, 61-62.

[218]Pope, *Compendium*, 3:47; 59. Lowrey objected to these statements by Pope as a concession that the sanctified man is still a sinner [*Possibilities of Grace*, 24; 144]

[219]Wesley, *Letter* to Dr. John Robertson, 24 Sept, 1753.

[220]Wesley, *Works*, 9:335.

[221]Wesley, *Notes*, 375; Reasoner, *Romans* 195-202

[222]Moss, *Pope*, 81; see also Pope, *Compendium*, 2:48-51. Wesley also held that there were two kinds of guilt: personal and corporate [Cox, *John Wesley's Concept of Perfection*, 31; 49; Lindström, *Wesley and Sanctification*, 34-37]. Wesley declared, "God does not look upon infants as innocent, but as involved in the guilt of Adam's sin" [*Works*, 9:316]. Yet on the previous page Wesley had declared, "But with regard to parents and their posterity, God assures us, children 'shall not die for the iniquity of their fathers.' No, not eternally. I believe none ever did, or ever will, die eternally, merely for the sin of our first father" [*Works*, 9:315].

Pope said that depravity is twofold, "the absence of original righteousness and the bias to all evil."[223] Because we are charged with Adam's sin we are deprived of the Spirit of God who makes us holy and thus our relationship with God is lost. Because of our identification with Adam we inherit a propensity or inclination to sin and thus the condition of sinfulness is transferred.

In the fifth century, Pelagius, a British monk, opposed the doctrines of original sin and prevenient grace. He argued that Adam had set a bad example, but that his descendants did not inherit Adam's corruption. Every person has the same choice that Adam and Eve had in the garden. Thus, Pelagius taught that it is possible to live without sinning. He held that if an act is necessary, it is not a sin; if it is voluntary, it can be avoided.[224]

Pelagius was opposed by Augustine. The Pelagian teaching was championed by John Taylor[225] and a hundred years later by Charles Finney. Pelagius essentially held that we were only damaged in the Fall. We remain capable of resisting sin by our own natural power.

Wesley held that we were guilty *corporately* through Adam but that this guilt was not imputed through prevenient grace and cancelled through the unconditional benefits of the atonement. Later Methodist theologians, such as Miley, Foster, Raymond, and Tillett, rejected the doctrine of original guilt based on logic. It was upheld by Summers and Daniel Curry [Sheldon, "Changes in Theology Among American Methodists,"38-39].

While Miley argued that Wesley had edited the Ninth Article of the Anglican Church to omit references to original guilt, this is not positive proof that Wesley had changed his mind. However, Miley concluded, "Dr. Pope may speak for himself and for his own Church if so it be, but he may not speak for the Methodist Episcopal Church. We have the same article, but only in part, and with the omission of every phrase and word which expresses this doctrine." Miley also referenced an article by Albert Bledsoe which analyzed the doctrinal significance of Wesley's change to Article 9. Bledsoe maintained that Wesley did not touch the quest of our native depravity except with regard to the separate Calvinistic doctrine of original guilt [Miley, "Pope's Christian Theology," 401-406; see also Miley, *Systematic Theology*, 1:525; Bledsoe, "Review of Pope," 253–301].

[223]Pope, *Compendium*, 2:59.

[224]Augustine, *Treatise Concerning Man's Perfection*, 2.1, *NPNF,* First Series, 5:160. Notice, however, that this summary comes from the opponent of Pelagius and Augustine is describing the teachings of Celestius, a disciple of Pelagius. Since none of the writings of Pelagius have survived, Wesley expressed some ambiguity about the man. However, Wesley condemned the theological position we have labeled as "Pelagian" [Campbell, *John Wesley and Christian Antiquity*, 6].

[225]Wesley's 272-page treatise, "The Doctrine of Original Sin," was a reply to John Taylor.

In the 1804 General Conference of the Methodist Episcopal Church, a motion was made that the word "preventing" be changed to "assisting" in the Articles of Religion. Thomas Coke sprang to his feet and exclaimed, "Where am I? In a Methodist conference? I thought so; but have we turned Pelagians? Do we think we can get along in our natural depravity with a little assistance, without preventing grace?" Coke explained that the word "preventing" did not mean "hindering." After further remarks on the necessity of grace before salvation, he declared, "Brethren, Do not change that word. I would go to the stake — yes — to the stake as soon as any word in the Bible."[226]

Classic liberal theology teaches that the will is fallen, but not the intellect. The autonomous mind is untainted and unfallen. The human mind is the starting point of modern philosophy, based on Descartes, "I think, therefore I am." Thus, we start with a clean, blank pad.

Semi-Pelagianism holds that we are fallen, but retain free will and the ability to seek God apart from any special grace. Thus, the free will to choose grace to overcome sin is preserved, but the free will to overcome sin itself is not.

In contrast, James Arminius taught that while we did not lose our will, we lost the power to will any good thing.[227]

> But in his *lapsed and sinful state*, man is not capable, of and by himself, either to think, to will, or to do that which is really good; but it is necessary for him to be regenerated and renewed in his intellect, affections or will, and in all his powers, by God in Christ through the Holy Spirit, that he may be qualified rightly to understand, esteem, consider, will, and perform whatever is truly good. When he is made a partaker of this regeneration or renovation, I consider that, since he is delivered from sin, he is capable of thinking, willing and doing that which is good, but yet *not without the continued aids of Divine Grace.*[228]
> In this state, the Free will of man towards the True Good is not only wounded, maimed, inform, bent and weakened; but it is also imprisoned, destroyed, and lost.[229]

These statements on free will, along with Wesley's declaration, "Such is

---

226Cowan, "The Arminian Alternative," 225.

227Arminius, *Works*, 3:178.

228Arminius, *Works*,1:659-660.

229Arminius, *Works*, 2:192.

the freedom of his will — free only to evil,"[230] affirm both a libertarian view of freedom and total depravity. *Libertarian freedom* means that God did not cause sin. When Calvinists refer to free will they believe the will is free only in the sense that this is compatible with determinism. Thus, while both Calvinists and Arminians hold to total depravity, according to Arminianism man sins because it is his nature and according to Calvinism man sins because he could not do otherwise.

Dale Dunlap concluded that Methodist theology does not view the fall as ontological, but as relational, and recognizes that freedom is part of human nature under grace.[231] But early Methodist held that the fall not only broke our relationship with God, but that the resulting original sin or total depravity affected man's being in every area. While later Methodists such as Daniel D. Whedon could write *The Freedom of the Will as a Basis of Human Responsibility and a Divine Government* (1864),[232] the earlier position was that the will was also

---

[230]Wesley, "The Spirit of Bondage and of Adoption," Sermon #9, 2.7-8.

[231]Dunlap, "Methodist Theology,"42; 111. "Ontological" is a philosophical term which refers to a state of being. I am arguing that sin is a state of being which has relational results.

[232]Daniel Steele felt that Whedon and Miley had undermined the doctrine of original sin by their stress on the philosophical doctrine of responsible freedom and guilt [Steele, *Gospel of the Comforter*, 288; Chiles, *Theological Transitions*, 199]. In the broader sense, Whedon's book *The Freedom of the Will* was a philosophical argument against the Calvinistic "necessitarian" view that free will is compatible with a divine sovereignty that is deterministic. In that debate I would agree with Whedon's "freedomist" or libertarian position. And Whedon does acknowledge prevenient grace. "In the case of the volitional decision to repent, God's prevenient grace does exert an enabling influence on the will. . . . Furthermore, the grace of God frees the Will from being completely bound by sin since the Fall, but it does not determine or cause which way the Will volitionally decides" [Whedon, *Freedom of the Will*, 74]. Whedon argued that fallen man is unable to keep the Law, yet he held that hereditary depravity is not totally responsible for our actions [pp. 281-284]. Yet too much emphasis is put on free will and natural ability. Cox concluded that Whedon was the ablest writer to deal with Calvinism in the nineteenth century and his argument on the basis of free will became representative of the trend in Methodism. Yet Cox argued that Wesley never argued for natural ability. Wesley's emphasis was on free grace [Cox, *Perfection*, 41]. According to Langford, "Whedon was instrumental in reshaping Wesleyan theology in North America by placing more emphasis upon human capability and giving less weight to the grounding of this ability in prevenient grace" [*Wesleyan Theology*, 91; see Langford's extended discussion in *Practical Divinity*, 101-106].

Whedon's article, "Doctrines of Methodism," originally published in *Bibliotheca Sacra*, 241- 273, starts out by defending the freedom of the will, but does not mention prevenient grace. This article also appears in Whedon, *Essays, Reviews,*

corrupted by the Fall and that man could will to do right only under the influence of prevenient grace. Wesley declared, "Since the fall, no child of man has a natural power to choose anything that is truly good."[233] Sam Powell wrote that the corruption of sin results in the loss of freedom. While we still exercise choice, because we are slaves to our passions, we are not free to respond faithfully to God.[234]

Arminius taught that Adam committed the actual sin. The result of this original sin was that the human race was deprived of its original righteousness. Some Catholic and liberal Arminian theologians have emphasized the privation of good rather than the depravity of nature.[235] For them perfection is the recovery of our potential. On the other hand, some Calvinistic theologians have so emphasized man's depravity that we remain sinners even after the reception of the Spirit. Properly understood, Wesleyan-Arminianism teaches that original sin is "a depravation arising from deprivation."[236] The sin principle is the condition resulting from a breach in relationship; a depravity based on a depravation. Yet depravity is also corruption, a corruption extends to the whole of man's nature. Arminius wrote,

> The whole of this sin, however, is not peculiar to our first parents, but is common to the entire race and to all their posterity, who, at the time when this sin was committed, were in their loins, and who have since descended from them by the natural mode of propagation, according to the primitive benediction: For in Adam "all have sinned." (Rom 5:12) Wherefore, whatever punishment was brought down upon our first parents, has likewise pervaded and yet pursues all their posterity: So that all men "are by nature the children of wrath," (Eph 2:3), obnoxious [liable] to condemnation, and to temporal as well as to eternal death; they are also devoid of that original

---

and Discourses, 109-146.

[233]Wesley, *Works*, 10:350.

[234]Powell, *Discovering our Christian Faith*, 140-141.

[235]Reed, "Thomas Merton," 92. However, Leclerc affirms total deprivity *and* total depravity [*Discovering Christian Holiness*, 158-159].

[236]Wiley used these words to describe the position of Arminius [*Christian Theology*, 2:123-124]. They were first used by Richard Watson [*Theological Institutes*, 2:79]. This concept is also affirmed by Ralston, Raymond, Wakefield, Sheldon, and Gamertsfelder, Summers, Pope, and Luther Lee [Hynson, "Original Sin as Privation," 72-76].

> righteousness and holiness (Rom 5:12, 18-19)[237] This was the reason why all men who were to be propagated from them in a natural way, became obnoxious to death temporal and death eternal, and devoid of this gift of the Holy Spirit or original righteousness: This punishment usually receives the appellation of "a privation of the image of God," and "original sin."
>
> But we permit this question to be made a subject of discussion: Must some contrary quality, beside the absence of original righteousness, be constituted as another part of original sin?; though we think it much more probable, that this *absence of original righteousness* only is *original sin itself*, as being that which alone is sufficient to commit and produce any actual sins whatsoever.[238]

Arminius also wrote that human depravity is the depravation of the image of God, specifically the forfeiture of the Holy Spirit and the loss of original righteousness. "On account of this transgression, man fell under the displeasure and the wrath of God, rendered himself subject to a double death, and deserving to be deprived of the primeval righteousness and holiness in which a great part of the image of God consisted."[239]

While Carl Bangs represented Arminius as holding "that the effect of the *depravity* language could be gained in terms of a *simple privation*,"[240] Arminius also wrote, "In this state, the Free will of man towards the True Good is not only wounded, maimed, inform, bent and weakened; but it is also imprisoned, destroyed, and lost."[241] Leon Hynson observed that the definition of sanctification, given by Arminius, "leads to the conclusion that deprivation results

---

[237] Arminius, *Works*, 2:156-157. Wesley preached, "Thus 'by one man sin entered into the world, and death by sin. And so death passed upon all men,' as being contained in him who was the common father and representative of us all. Thus 'through the offense of one' all are dead, dead to God, dead in sin, dwelling in a corruptible, mortal body, shortly to be dissolved, and under the sentence of death eternal ["Justification by Faith," Sermon #5, 1.6.].

[238] Arminius, *Works*, 2:375.

[239] Arminius, *Works*, 2:151.

[240] Bangs, *Arminius*, 338-340.

[241] Arminius, *Works*, 2:192. See Picirilli, *Grace, Faith, Free Will*, 149-153; 157.

in depravity."[242] Thus, Wesley could declare, "No man that ever lived, not John Calvin himself, ever asserted either original sin, or justification by faith, in more strong, more clear and express terms, than Arminius has done."[243]

Although Arminius and Wesley were separated in history by two hundred years, Stephen Gunter compared their teachings. He concluded they both sounded similar notes in their anthropological notions about humanity as originally created. And they both agreed about the state of human affairs as a result of disobedience. Both taught prevenient grace which led to justification. Both emphasized the work of God through Christ rather than divine decrees. "Given their respective concepts of prevenient and ongoing/continued grace, it would not then be accurate to say that either Arminius or Wesley taught a human-centered voluntarism that initiates even the slightest move apart from grace in the direction of salvation. That the human will is free to respond to God's overtures and offer of salvation is the result of being *set free* by the Holy Spirit."[244]

In "Salvation by Faith," Wesley preached that "only corrupt fruit grows on a corrupt tree. And his heart is altogether corrupt and abominable, being 'come short of the glory of God', the glorious righteousness at first impressed on his soul, after the image of his great Creator."[245] In "The Righteousness of Faith" he declared that it was foolish for any man to seek life by keeping the law.

> Is it not then the very foolishness of folly for fallen man to seek life by this righteousness? For man, who was 'shapen in wickedness', and 'in sin did his mother conceive him'; man, who is by nature all 'earthly, sensual, devilish'; altogether 'corrupt and abominable'; in whom, till he find grace, 'dwelleth no good thing'; nay, who cannot of himself think one good thought? Who is indeed all sin, a mere lump of ungodliness, and who commits sin in every breath he draws; whose actual transgressions, in word and deed, are more in number than the hairs of his head! What stupidity, what senselessness must it be for such an unclean, guilty, helpless worm as this to dream of seeking

[242]Hynson, "Original Sin as Privation," 69. The reference Hynson made was to the definition by Arminius that sanctification was "a gracious act of God by which He purifies man who is a sinner, and yet a believer, from the darkness of ignorance, from indwelling sin and from its lusts or desires, and imbues him with the Spirit of knowledge, righteousness and holiness" [Arminius, *Works*, 2:408].

[243]Wesley, "The question 'What is an Arminian?' Answered. By a lover of Free Grace," *Works*, 10:359.

[244]Gunter, "John Wesley," 78-82.

[245]Wesley, Sermon #1, §2.

> acceptance by 'his own righteousness', of living by 'the righteousness which is of the law![246]

In "The Way to the Kingdom" Wesley described the inbred corruption of the sinner.

> Know that thou art corrupted in every power, in every faculty of thy soul, that thou are totally corrupted in every one of these, all the foundations being out of course. The eyes of thine understanding are darkened, so that they cannot discern God or the things of God. The clouds of ignorance and error rest upon thee, and cover thee with the shadow of death. Thou knowest nothing yet as thou oughtest to know, neither God, nor the world, nor thyself. Thy will is not longer the will of God, but is utterly perverse and distorted, averse from all good, from all which God loves, and prone to all evil, to every abomination which God hateth. Thy affections are alienated from God, and scattered abroad over all the earth. All thy passions, both thy desire and aversions, thy joys and sorrows, thy hopes and fears, are out of frame, are either undue in their degree, or placed on undue objects. So that there is no soundness in thy soul, but "from the crown of the head to the sole of the foot" (to use the strong expression of the prophet) there are only "wounds, and bruises, and putrefying sores."[247]

In "The Spirit of Bondage and Adoption" Wesley taught that when the sinner is shaken out of his sleep, he sees himself naked, stripped of all the fig-leaves which he had sewed together.

> His heart is bare, and he sees it is all sin, "deceitful above all things, desperately wicked"; that it is altogether corrupt and abominable, more than it is possible for tongue to express; that there dwelleth there no good thing, but unrighteousness and ungodliness only; every motion thereof, every temper and thought, being only evil continually.[248]

---

[246]Wesley, Sermon #6, 2.5.

[247]Wesley, Sermon #7, 2.1. See Wiley's summary statement that the affections are alienated, the intellect is darkened, the will is perverted [*Christian Theology*, 2:128-129].

[248]Wesley, Sermon #9, 2.3.

Wesley preached that anyone who denied original sin was but a heathen still. He claimed this as the first grand distinguishing point between heathenism and Christianity.

> This, therefore, is the first, grand, distinguishing point between heathenism and Christianity. The one acknowledges that many men are infected with many vices, and even born with a proneness to them; but supposes withal that in some the natural good much overbalances the evil. The other declares that all men are "conceived in sin", and "shapen in wickedness"; that hence there is in every man a "carnal mind which is enmity against God, which is not, cannot be, subject to his law", and which sin infects the whole soul that "there dwelleth in him, in his flesh", in his natural state, "no good thing;" but "all the imagination of the thoughts of his heart is evil," "*only* evil", and that "continually." [249]

In Wesley's 272-page treatise, "The Doctrine of Original Sin," which was a reply to John Taylor, Wesley declared without this doctrine "the Christian system falls at once."[250] Here Wesley taught that the Fall completely reversed the conditions of human life. Primitive perfection was replaced by total corruption. Man suffered spiritual, temporal, and eternal death.[251] Thorsen called this "the most systematic treatise Wesley produced."[252]

Yet Albert Knudson (1873-1953), who represented Methodist theology for the first third of the twentieth century, denied original sin and explained that the universality of sin was because natural, human impulses, and environmental factors get a head start before moral sense can be developed. According to Chiles the resulting transition was from sinful man to moral man.[253]

Some liberal Arminians also teach that God does not even know in advance the outcome of man's future free choices — otherwise our choices would not be free. They exalt human nature and human potential believing people will do right because of an inner imperative. They emphasize the role of Christ as our

---

[249]Wesley, "Original Sin," Sermon #44, 3.1.

[250]Wesley, *Works*, 9:194.

[251]Wesley, *Works*, 9:291; 245.

[252]Thorsen, *Wesleyan Quadrilateral*, 104.

[253]Knudson, *Principles of Christian Ethics*, 90-95; Chiles, *Theological Transitions*, 35; 140-142. See the discussion about personalism, which he advocated, p. 761.

example, not our redeemer. These views have combined the teachings of Pelagius, a British monk in the fifth century, Faustus Socinus in the sixteenth century, Charles Finney in the nineteenth century, and Gordon Olson in the twentieth century. Yet the role of Jesus merely as our great example and pattern would only serve to awaken unfulfilled aspirations within us.[254]

However Finney wrote, "To talk of a sinful nature, or sinful constitution, in the sense of physical sinfulness, is to ascribe sinfulness to the Creator, who is the author of nature. It is to overlook the essential nature of sin, and to make sin a physical virus, instead of a voluntary and responsible choice."[255] J. W. Jepson stated, "Finney did not think much of this doctrine of original sin. In fact, he was quite opposed to it. For one thing, he did not believe that the Bible really teaches that we are born with a sinful nature or a natural disposition toward sin per se."[256]

More recently Gordon Olson taught that man is born morally neutral and is capable of choosing whether to sin. Both sin and holiness are free voluntary acts of will or states of mind. Thus, Olson, combines the teachings of Pelagius, Socinus, and Finney, denying the doctrine of original sin.[257] Yet this teaching does not square with the description of the unregenerate given in Romans 7:14-25.

In comparing early Methodism with later liberal Methodist theology, Robert Chiles wrote, "Human goodness was Wesley's goal, not his starting point."[258] Thus, freedom is not autonomy but deliverance from the slavery of sin into which all humans are born.

Yet John Miley, a transitional Methodist theologian, objected that most of the Arminian treatment of original sin is unsatisfactory. Miley rejected the federal headship of Adam. In so doing, he broke with every Methodist theologian prior to him. According to Watson it is the legal consequence of Adam's disobedience which is imputed to his descendants.[259] Miley was critical of Watson's position,[260] but his own position failed to satisfy "many of his

---

[254]So argued Benjamin Gregory, *Perfect in Christ Jesus*, 16-17.

[255]Finney, *Systematic Theology*, 172.

[256]Jepson, *Don't Blame It all On Adam*,109; see also A. M. Hills, *Holiness and Power*, 33.

[257]Beisner, "The False God," 20-23; 41-44. Olson was a leader in Youth with a Mission (YWAM).

[258]Chiles, *Theological Transition*, 143.

[259]Watson, *Theological Institutes*, 2:54.

[260]Miley, *Systematic Theology*, 2:507-509; 522-524.

contemporaries and most of his successors."[261]

The transition, as Chiles documented, was from an earlier emphasis on free grace to an emphasis on free will which tended to deny depravity. "The realities which Wesley attributed to prevenient grace were gradually incorporated into man's created nature, depreciating his estrangement and helplessness apart from God. . . . Steadily the areas of achievement assigned to man's freedom were increased." By the time of Albert Knudson free will was part of man's nature.[262]

While Miley claimed that the doctrine of original sin concedes the Calvinistic doctrine of election and reprobation, this does not necessarily follow.[263] Adam Clarke argued for a universal atonement based on the federal headship of Christ. If humanity is of one race and if Christ took on himself the nature of man and in human nature made expiation for the sins of nature, then redemption is general and the benefits of his death must necessarily apply to every human being who has descended from Adam. All who share the human nature have a right to apply to God, by virtue of that redemption, for remission of sins.[264]

Yet according to Miley, "If God is a moral ruler over responsible subjects, they must be morally free." Thus Miley argued that such subjects were in not in need of prevenient grace, but could choose the good by virtue of their native ability.[265]

The holiness movement tended to follow the influence of Miley and Finney, emphasizing man's free agency. In his *Fundamental Christian Theology*, Hills quoted from Finney who argued for man's natural ability rejecting the gracious ability taught by Methodism. Hills abridged twelve pages from Finney to prove that "gracious ability"was inconsistent with moral accountability. Hills concluded, "We think Finney's reasoning on this point unanswerable."[266]

On the other hand, Calvinism affirms both original sin and original guilt. Augustine had mistranslated Romans 5:12 to teach that all sinned with Adam. The phrase ἐφ ' ᾧ (*eph' ho*) should be translated "because," but Augustine, who relied on the Latin translation *in quo* instead of the Greek, translated it "in him." While the interpretation question is whether all sinned *like* Adam or *with* Adam, the bottom line is that "all sinned." Romans 5:19 declares that through Adam's

---

[261]Chiles, *Theological Transition*, 130.

[262]Chiles, *Theological Transition*, 186; 178.

[263]Knudson, *Systematic Theology*, 1:521; 2:505-524.

[264]Clarke, "A Fragment in Favour of General Redemption," in *Works*, 8:439-440.

[265]Miley, *Systematic Theology*, 2:274; 280.

[266]Hills, *Fundamental Christian Theology*, 230-234.

disobedience many were constituted sinners. As Cox pointed out, Wesley believed in at least two kinds of sin and two kinds of guilt: personal and racial or corporate.[267] While this concept was upheld by Watson and Pope, it was rejected by Whedon, Foster, and Miley.[268]

Augustine held that the primary effect of original sin is guilt, but that guilt may be negated through infant baptism. The Wesleyan doctrine is that the human race is implicated by Adam's sin, but personal sin is not imputed until an age of accountability is attained. The basis for this doctrine is a logical deduction from the fact that God warned Adam that they would die in the day that they ate of the fruit of the forbidden tree. While they did die spiritually, meaning they were separated from God, the preservation of the race was an unconditional benefit of a future atonement. While we were implicated by Adam's sin, so that in some sense we sinned with Adam according to Romans 5:12, the guilt of Adam's sin was not imputed to the race.[269] Thus, no person goes to hell solely for Adam's sin. Therefore, the justice of God requires that children not be damned until they personally and intelligently choose to sin. Thus, all children are saved whether or not they have been baptized.[270]

In 1928 the General Assembly of the Church of the Nazarene replaced the paragraph titled "Inherited Depravity" with a new paragraph entitled "Free Agency" in their Articles of Faith.[271] To his credit, Wiley's *Christian Theology*

---

[267]Cox, *Perfection*, 31; 49. Thus, Wesley would have rejected original guilt at a personal level and taught that corporately it was not imputed to the human race due to the unconditional merits of Christ's atonement.

[268]Cox, *Perfection*, 31; see also Cox, *Sin*, 111-113.

[269]Dale Yocum taught that as the head of a race, Jesus Christ also acted on behalf of all men. He chose life for the entire race until each man chooses responsibly for himself. Thus, all are covered by the benefits of Christ's atonement until they are awakened to the point of personal responsibility [Yocum, *Conformed to Christ*, 51-52].

[270]The purpose of infant baptism is that it is a sign and seal of the covenant made by the child's parents. Under the Old Testament, circumcision was that sign and seal, but according to Col 2:12 baptism has replaced circumcision in the New Testament. Infant baptism symbolizes, but does not constitute spiritual regeneration. Rather it means that the child is under prevenient or preliminary grace. While Wesley taught that baptism cleanses from original sin, Wesley was not entirely consistent on this matter, but I am not convinced that his mature conclusion was that infant baptism actually imparts saving grace [see Reasoner, *Romans*, 168-169; 210-211; Cho, "John Wesley's View on Baptism," 60-73; Staples, *Outward Sign*, 167-172; 177-195].

[271]Quanstrom, *Century of Holiness Theology*, 72.

did not follow the emphasis of Miley and Hills on free moral agency.[272] He carefully argued for prevenient grace. But this theology was not published until 1940, long after holiness theology had solidified.

More recently Kevin Lowery has proposed to salvage Wesley's agenda. Yet part of Lowery's proposal was a new paradigm which does not see human beings as utterly depraved. Therefore, prevenient grace is not necessary to restore the natural faculties, such as conscience, because these faculties were never lost.[273]

But Kenneth Collins explained a "weak doctrine of original sin could only result in an equally weak doctrine of the new birth. For if the extensiveness of the problem was relinquished or soft-pedaled, the radical nature of the solution would be lost as well."[274] It is this condition of total depravity that makes the new birth necessary. Since we were born in sin, we must be born again. Holiness must be restored and perfected.

If man is basically good, he needs only the right environment, heredity, and circumstances. If man is not connected with Adam, but is neutral or born with a blank slate, he only needs to be encouraged toward the light. But if man is basically sinful, he cannot save himself and needs God's help. Total depravity means total inability except for prevenient grace. We are helpless but not hopeless. Without God's grace we cannot be saved; without our grace-enabled, but uncoerced, participation, God's grace will not save.[275]

Richard Watson agreed with John Calvin's evaluation concerning the natural state of man "that man is so totally overwhelmed, as with a deluge, that no part is free from sin, and therefore whatever proceeds from him is accounted sin." Watson wrote, "The true Arminian, as fully as the Calvinist, admits the doctrine of the total depravity of human nature in consequence of the fall of our first parents; and is indeed enabled to carry it through his system with greater consistency that the Calvinist himself."[276]

---

[272]Quanstrom, *Century of Holiness Theology*, 77-78.

[273]Lowery, *Salvaging Wesley's Agenda*, 56.

[274]Collins, *Wesley on Salvation*, 22.

[275]Maddox, *Responsible Grace*, 19.

[276]Watson, *Theological Institutes*, 2:48. Yet Calvin's doctrine of common grace is not the same as Wesley's doctrine of prevenient grace, since common grace is nonsaving grace to the nonelect. In fact, Frame argues that it would be better to speak of God's common goodness or love, rather than his common grace to the nonelect. According to Frame, God restrains sin, restrains his wrath, and gives temporal blessings to the nonelect. Thus the unregenerate can do good, know truth, and experience some of the blessings of the Holy Spirit through this common goodness of God [Frame,

Concerning early Arminian teaching, A. W. Harrison wrote, "The Arminian of that period accepted the doctrine of the total depravity of human nature as fully as the Calvinist did."[277] Samuel Wakefield declared, "True Arminianism, therefore, as fully as Calvinism, admits the total depravity of human nature in consequence of the fall of our first parents; and to represent this doctrine as being exclusively Calvinistic, which has often been done, is an entire delusion."[278] A Calvinistic journal even conceded that eighteenth-century Wesleyans properly affirmed,

> Man's ruin by the fall; his native depravity and alienation from God; his absolute need of a Saviour, and utter inability to save himself; the necessity of regeneration by the Holy Spirit; justification, not by works, but by faith alone in blood and righteousness of Jesus; the free offer of salvation to every human being, without money and without price; the necessity of holiness, not to merit heaven, but to become meet for it — these articles constituted the very burden of their preaching.[279]

Thus, Scripture teaches that mankind is sinful. We are unholy in our actions, in our speech, and in our thoughts because we are sinful by nature. And the more God-conscious we become, the more sin-conscious we are. There is no spiritual good in the sinner's relationship to God. And the sinner is completely unable to correct his corrupt nature. But while we are disabled by the fall we are enabled by preliminary grace.

While the Calvinistic and Arminian systems can be compared as similar or contrasted as dissimilar, it must be realized that there is not total uniformity of thought within each system. However, in broad terms the real difference is not over the doctrine of original sin but over the consequences of that teaching. By denying the reality of prevenient grace Calvinists come to different conclusions from Wesleyan-Arminians over original guilt and the nature of human freedom of choice. Calvinists tend to emphasize the intensive nature and permanent condition of depravity to the point of denying the possibility of Christian perfection. Thus

Doctrine of God, 429-437].

[277]Harrison, *Arminianism*, 234. Harald Lindström said that Wesley was "at one with the Reformed outlook" insisting "on the total corruption of natural man, grounding the tenet on the doctrine of original sin" [*Wesley and Sanctification,* 20].

[278]Wakefield, *Christian Theology*, 1:291.

[279]Anonymous, "Annals of the American Pulpit," 507. The classic Calvinist theologian Charles Hodge also recognized that Wesley held that man since the fall is in a state of absolute depravity [*Systematic Theology*, 2:329].

while both systems affirm total depravity, Calvinists tend to give the doctrine of depravity priority over the sovereignty of sanctifying grace.

Diane Leclerc wrote,

> Void of an understanding of prevenient grace, we find no way of explaining how the steps of faith are possible except as an act of the human will. It is we who must move ourselves toward reconciliation and faith. While we can find a Christ who suffered for us, we really do not find the mechanism by which we have faith to begin with, or to explain how faith overcomes estrangement. If it is the presence of God that effectively vanquishes the power of sin, is it we who must find our way into that presence, or is there a movement toward us, even in our estrangement, that does not override our will? It is here that the power of the concept [and certainly the reality of prevenient grace solves the problem of deciding between predestination and our hidden Pelagianism.[280]

Neo-orthodox theologians such as Niebuhr and Barth "have made the sinfulness of man so inherent in his nature as to be irremediable."[281] But we must not overemphasize depravity to the exclusion of the power of the blood of Christ to completely sanctify. Wesley believed that prevenient grace had been unconditionally bestowed upon the human race. This grace spared the race from extinction in Adam who deserved to die immediately for his crime. It clears all men from any and all guilt of Adam's actual sin which might have been transmitted to his offspring. It renders all men salvable by sustaining in man a capacity for God, for righteousness and true holiness. It enables man's natural powers to function so as to produce a tolerable state of affairs in human society. It assists man in his response to the overtures of saving grace that he might be redeemed.[282]

On the other hand, liberal Arminianism does not help the cause of truth by asserting the perfectability of the human nature based on a denial of the scriptural doctrine of original sin. Merne A. Harris and Richard S. Taylor noted that liberalism was essentially Pelagian in its denial of original sin.[283]

---

[280]Leclerc, *Discovering Christian Holiness*, 168.

[281]Reinhold Niebuhr chided Wesleyans for their preoccupation with perfection in *The Nature and Destiny of Man*.

[282]Rose, "Wesleyan Understanding of Sin," 22.

[283]Harris and Taylor, "The Dual Nature of Sin," 101.

The Real Danger of Apostasy

What is apostasy? The Greek word ἀποστασία (*apostasia*) occurs only twice, to describe Jews forsaking Moses (Acts 21:21) and to describe a rebellion or falling away at the end of the millennium (2 Thes 2:3). It certainly does not describe the departure of the church or correspond to the "rapture" of 1 Thess 4:17.[284]

A related word, ἀποστάσιον (*apostasion*), is used three times for "divorce." And so we have the concept of departure, but always in a negative connotation.

But our study of apostasy must also consider synonymous words such as ἀφίστημι (*aphistemi*), which literally means to stand apart from. It is sometimes used in narrative passages to describe departure from a location, to leave a person, or to take something away. Doctrinally, it is used in Luke 8:13 to describe those who believe for awhile, but fall away. In 1 Timothy 4:1 it describes those who will abandon the faith. It is used in a positive sense in 2 Timothy 2:19, "Everyone who confesses the name of the Lord must *turn away* from wickedness." But Hebrews 3:12 warns against turning away from or forsaking the living God.

Πίπτω (*pipto*) is a third word used for apostasy. Normally it is used to describe a literal fall, but in 1 Corinthians 10:12 it describes falling from grace. In 2 Peter 3:17-18 there is a warning against falling from our secure position. Here the compound verb is *ekpipto*. Joseph Benson preached that growth in grace is the only security against falling from it.[285] According to 2 Peter 1:10, those who keep on confirming their salvation shall never πταίω (*ptaio*) stumble, trip, sin, fail, or fall.

A fourth word, ἀφίημι (*aphiemi*), can be used in a positive sense to describe the release of forgiveness. It can also refer to the release of permission. But in Revelation 2:4 it describes the Ephesians who have left or abandoned their first love. And now their light will be removed.

In 1 Timothy 5:12 Paul describes widows who have broken their pledge. But the Greek text is stronger than the NIV translation. They ἀθετέω (*atheteo*) or set aside, cast off, or rejected their previous faith. In 2 Timothy 4:10 Demas abandon or forsook Paul (ἐγκαταλείπω - *egkataleipo*). Clarke explained that Demas preferred Judaism to Christianity.[286] While this is a case of apostasy, the text does not reveal any formal renunciation of Christ, only a love for this present world. That same love for the world causes many to forsake (same Greek word)

---

[284]House, "Apostasia in 2 Thessalonians 2:3."

[285]Benson, *Sermons*, 7:230-232. Sermon #251.

[286]Clarke, *Commentary*, 6:638.

the assembly of believers. Perhaps apostasy is more prevalent that we acknowledge.

Romans 14:15 warns that a brother's faith can be destroyed. This destruction comes in stages. He is first distressed or grieved. Ultimately he is destroyed. This word, ἀπόλλυμι (*apollumi*), means damnation.

Three times in Romans 1:24-28 God gave up the reprobate. In all three instances the verb παραδίδωμι (*paradidomi*) is used. It describes a give up or giving over through the withdrawal of the influence and restraint of the Holy Spirit. The word used to describe the reprobate is ἀδόκιμος (*adokimos*) which denotes the negation of approval. The depraved mind has been rejected by God because it has first rejected God. Paul used the same word, *adokimos*, in 1 Corinthians 9:27 to say that he himself could become disqualified or a castaway if he did not mortify the deeds of the flesh. Thus the elect could become the reprobate.

The New Testament also contains metaphors for apostasy.

- In 1 Timothy 1:18-19 we are warned that some did not maintain their hold on faith and their faith was *shipwrecked*.
- Romans 11:17 describes Israel as a branch which was broken off because of unbelief (v 20). Jude 12 describes apostates who are twice dead. They were originally dead in trespasses and sins, but they had been made alive. Now they are once more dead. Jude describes them as trees without fruit. Revelation 3:2 also describes those who are ready to die.
- This is the sin which leads to spiritual death (1 John 5:16).[287]
- This is a removal of the candlestick (Rev 2:5).
- This is a name taken from the book of life (Rev 3:5). Robert Thomas conceded, "The promise to the overcomer is an empty one unless the

---

[287]George Findlay observed that the nature and tendency of all sin is unto death, as cause and effect. John is not making a distinction between venial and mortal sins. The expression "sin unto death" comes from Numb 18:22 where sacrilege was denoted as a capital offence. "There may come, and sometimes does come, in the present life a crisis at which the soul's doom is practically fixed and after which it proves 'impossible to renew' the sinner 'again unto repentance' (Heb 6:6). *When* that point is reached, *when* the sin has been committed which closes the heart against the visitings of compunction and plunges the guilty man beyond saving help, or what shape the decisive sin may take, God alone can judge" [*Studies in John's Epistles*, 421-426].

Daniel Steele adds, "This sin is not limited to a single act, such as a crime worthy of punishment by death, or a manifestly Divine visitation, or a sin punished by the church with excommunication. It is rather a course of wilful sin in defiance of the known law of God persisted in so obstinately against the influences of the Holy Spirit, that repentance becomes a moral impossibility, just as a man may starve himself so long as to lose the power to appropriate, digest and assimilate food" [*Half-Hours with St. John's Epistles*, 144].

possibility exists that such blotting out could occur. What incentive is furnished by being promised deliverance from something that could not happen?"[288]

We still have to consider the five warning passages of Hebrews. In Hebrews 2:1-4 the warning is against drifting away, slipping away, or losing sight (παραρέω - *pararheo*). They neglected their salvation. Here Wesley comments that the Greek verb signifies "as water out of a leaky vessel."[289]

The second warning is in Hebrews 3:7-4:13. The verb ἀφίστημι (*aphistemi*) has already been noted, but in the context this turning away is the result of hardening the heart. This hardening comes as a result of disobedience and the result is falling short. Dale Moody says that ἀπιστία (*apistia*) is a synonym for apostasy. It is used in Hebrews 3:12 and 19 and means unbelief. A second synonym is ἀπείθεια (*apeitheia* - disobedience; 4:6, 11). Thus, hardness of heart is the result of falling away, unbelief, and disobedience. He also says that ὑστερέω (*hustereo*), falling short (4:1), is a synonym of *aphistemi*, falling away (3:12).[290]

The third warning is Hebrews 5:11-6:12. The danger is that those who have not reached maturity may fall away. Here the verb is a compound form of πίπτω (*pipto*) - παραπίπτω (*parapipto*) and the meaning is not to fall away, but to deliberately turn away. According to Grant Osborne, to repudiate the Son, as described in Hebrews 6:4-6 is to commit the unpardonable sin.

The fourth warning in Hebrews 10:19-39 is to those who deliberately keep on sinning or persist in wilful sin. Osborne declared that Heb 10:26 was the closest thing to a definition of apostasy in Hebrews.[291] They cast away or thrown off (ἀποβάλλω- *apoballo*) their confidence (v 35) and draw back (ὑποστολή - *hupostole* - noun form of *hupostello* used in v 38) unto destruction (v 39).

The final warning, Hebrews 12:14-29, is against falling behind or lacking (ὑστερέω - *hustereo*) the grace of God which results in a bitter root which grows up to cause trouble and defile.

Thus, the NT uses at least twelve synonyms and five metaphors to define apostasy. The passages which describe *how* apostasy occurs normally use

---

[288]Thomas, *Revelation 1-7*, 261.

[289]Wesley, *Notes*, 566; see also Clarke, *Commentary*, 6:694-695. *Paparheo* occurs only here in the NT. It is debated whether this word depicts a drifting ship or a leaking vessel. Regardless of whether the metaphor is a ship drifting off course or a vessel which runs dry, the result is still the same — a gradual backsliding which ultimately results in the loss of salvation.

[290]Moody, *Apostasy*, 29-30.

[291]Osborne, "Classical Arminian View," 120.

gradual language.

Having surveyed the warnings in the New Testament against apostasy, we must now draw some theological conclusions.

- Calvinism denies the possibility of apostasy for the elect.[292] Theologically, Calvinism may interpret these warnings as hypothetical, but that violates the graphic language of Hebrews 6:4-5. Those who depart from the faith actually never were elect. But this violates the very concept of apostasy. One cannot abandon what he never possessed.

- Some who are Arminian also embrace unconditional eternal security. They want to reject the predestination of Calvinism, but embrace the perseverance of the believer. They, too, must dismiss the possibility of apostasy.

In his defense of Arminius, Roger Olson reported the strongest statement that Arminius made about perseverance was, "I should not readily dare to say that true and saving faith finally and totally fall away."[293] But these are the opening words in a section which evaluates William Perkins' belief that true and saving faith cannot fail either totally or finally. According to Carl Bangs, Perkins had raised a new issue with Arminius and he approaches it cautiously. But Arminius proceeded to dismantle that proposition for the next sixteen pages and then concluded, "In the beginning of faith in Christ and conversion to God the believer becomes a living member of Christ; and, if persevering in the faith of Christ, and keeping a conscience void of offense, remains a living member. But if it happens that this member grows slothful, is not careful over itself, gives place to sin, by little and little it becomes half-dead; and so at length, proceeding still further, dies altogether, and ceases to be a member." Ultimately Arminius held that it is impossible for believers, as long as they remain believers, to decline from salvation, but that a believer who ceases to trust God is no longer a believer.[294]

- According to Scot McKnight, blasphemy against the Spirit and apostasy are related. Apostasy, whether defined in the Calvinistic or Arminian sense, is committed by those who have had some relationship to God through Christ. Thus, apostasy is acceptance followed by repudiation of Jesus Christ. Blasphemy against the Spirit is not preceded by acceptance. It describes overt repudiation before any kind of commitment is made.

---

[292]Feinburg, "God Ordains All Things," 35.

[293]Olson, *Arminian Theology*, 187.

[294]Arminius, *Works*, 3:470.

While we may distinguish these two sins in this manner, it also needs to be observed that the two sins amount to largely the same stance. For both involve an overt repudiation of God's work in Christ. Both the "unpardonable sin" and final apostasy are irreversible.[295]

Dispensationalists believe that the blasphemy against the Holy Spirit, which is warned against in Matthew 12:22-32, could only be committed while Jesus was living on earth.[296] The reason for this is directly related to their understanding of the sin itself. Chafer explains, Matt 12:22-32

> It should be noted that this sin against the Holy Spirit consisted in asserting that Christ's works, which were wrought by the Holy Spirit, were accomplished on the contrary by Satan. Such a setting could not be found now since Christ is not in the world as He was then, nor is He undertaking in the same way to do works by the Holy Spirit. It is therefore impossible for this particular sin to be committed today.[297]

Thus, the sin was limited to the time or *dispensation* that Christ was on earth. According to Chafer the warnings against apostasy apply to Israel, since the believer is eternally secure.[298] However, while believers cannot lose their salvation, Chafer predicts apostasy for the church in the last days. And apostasy was a real danger for Jewish believers in the first century. But it is not a real possibility in between. Charles Stanley explains that Hebrews 6:4-6 deals with a "unique situation."[299]

- Reformed or Classical Arminianism does accept the possibility of a narrowly-defined apostasy — a once-for-all, irremediable event; a

---

[295]McKnight, "Apostasy," 68.

[296]Chafer, *Systematic Theology*, 7:48; Enns, *Moody Handbook of Theology*, 265–66; Franklin, "The Blasphemy Against the Holy Spirit," 232–33; Gaebelein, *Matthew*, 250; Gromacki, *Holy Spirit*, 133; Pentecost, *Words and Works of Jesus Christ*, 207; Ryrie, *Holy Spirit*, 54.

While Wesley defines this sin as "neither more nor less than the ascribing those miracles to the power of the devil, which Christ wrought by the power of the Holy Ghost" [*Notes*, 44], he does not restrict this sin to the first century.

[297]Chafer, *Systematic Theology,* 7:48.

[298]Chafer, *Salvation*, 99.

[299]Stanley, *Eternal Security*, 146.

complete shipwreck of saving faith. In contrast, Robert Shank defines apostasy as "any departure from God and saving grace, whether deliberate or casual."[300]

Matthew Pinson asserts that sin does not cause a loss of salvation in a believer.[301] A. B. Brown said that apostasy is committed by willful unbelief, not by sin.[302] But unbelief *is* sin! This is antinomian. It is dangerous to teach that we can sin and not lose our salvation. How else would we lose it? According to Stephen Ashby, a believer who dies in a state of unconfessed sin would not lose his salvation.[303]

Thus, this position holds that apostasy is a real possibility, but it is a decisive renunciation of Christ which is more of a theoretical possibility. And they also hold that such apostasy is an irrevocable condition. While many of the passages do not describe *how* apostasy occurs, at least four of the five warnings in Hebrews seem to be describing a gradual process.

- Historically, Wesleyan-Arminianism defined apostasy differently. The early Methodists took sin and holy living seriously. However, this is mis-characterized by Ashby as having to get saved all over again each time we commit sin. Ashby declares that we all sin and the implication is that we must do something much worse in order to lose our salvation. According to Ashby we must cease believing.[304] But the real question is whether an unrepentant believer can maintain faith while living in a state of continued disobedience and sin.

Adam Clarke said, "Apostasy begins in the closet: no man ever backslid from the life and power of Christianity who continued constant and fervent,

---

[300]Shank, *Life in the Son*, 312.

[301]Ashby, "Reformed Arminian View," 15.

[302]Brown, *Modified Arminian Theology*, 336.

[303]Ashby, "Reformed Arminian View," 182. Forlines, Pinson, Brown, and Ashby call themselves Reformed Arminians. However, the position of Arminius and the Remonstrants is that sin *does* affect justification. Arminius declared that if David had died after his adultery with Bathsheba and murder of Uriah, he would have been condemned to death eternal [Arminius, *Works*, 2:725]. "True believers are capable by their own fault of falling into flagrant crimes and atrocious wickedness, to persevere and die in them, and therefore finally to fall away and perish" [Five Points of the Remonstrants," Article 5, Proposition 4; Watson, *Dictionary*, 898].

[304]Ashby, "Reformed Arminian View,"186-187.

especially in private prayer."[305]

In his treatise *Serious Thoughts on the Perseverance of the Saints*, Wesley is persuaded that a true believer can make shipwreck of his faith and perish everlastingly. He bases this on Hebrews 6:4,6; 10:26-29; 2 Peter 2:20-21 and other New Testament texts.[306] In *What Is an Arminian?* Wesley believed that final perseverance was contingent upon the continuing cooperation of the believer's will with the justifying and sanctifying grace of God.

Whedon declared "as the doctrine of apostasy constitutes a real warning against backsliding and sin, so the doctrine of Christian perfection is a living incitement to progressive holiness."[307]

There can be individual apostasy, apostasy within the church, or national apostasy. 2 Thessalonians 2:7-12 also describe the final apostasy of Revelation 20:7-10.

Richard Watson notes that the early church distinguished several types of apostasy.

1. Relapse from Christianity into Judaism
2. Judaism and Christianity blended together into legalism
3. Relapse into paganism

Watson also noted the difference between an apostate and a heretic, that the heretic only abandons part of his faith, while the apostate abandons it all.[308]

There can be degrees of apostasy. Apostasy is the final step in backsliding. Not all apostasy is final. Adam Clarke taught that where there is life there is hope."[309] Steve Harper declared, "Even when we fall *from* grace, we do not fall *beyond* grace."[310] Even in Romans 11 the national apostasy of Israel was *not* final; all Israel will be saved. The Remonstrants taught that one can be renewed should he fall away. "Yet though true believers sometimes fall into grievous sins, and such as destroy the conscience, we do not believe that they immediately fall away from all hope of repentance; but we acknowledge this to be an event not impossible to occur, that God, according to the multitude of His

---

[305]Clarke, *Commentary,* 1:391.

[306]Wesley, *Works*, 10:284-98.

[307]Whedon, *Essays*, 144.

[308]Watson, *Dictionary*, 72.

[309]Clarke, *Christian Theology*, p. 366-367.

[310]Harper, "Wesleyan Arminian View," 241.

mercies may again call them by His grace to repentance."[311]

Southern Methodist theologian, Thomas Summers defended the thesis that saints may and do fall from grace — some partly but not totally or finally, some totally but not finally, and others both totally and finally.[312]

Grant Osborne, writing as a Classical Arminian, concludes that we can backslide by allowing sin to crowd Christ out of our life. This kind of apostate can be brought back to Christ. But we can actually repudiate Christ and this type of apostate will never want to come back nor will God ever convict that person again.[313]

Apostasy is the culmination of backsliding and that backsliding is the result of sin. Apostasy is not merely a hypothetical possibility, nor can it be committed by the nominal Christian who never was regenerate. It cannot be relegated to another dispensation, to Israel or to the Church. The warning in Heb 3:12 and 4:1 is to individuals - "none of you."

The corporate body is composed of individual members, who according to dispensationalism cannot lose their salvation.

Apostasy is not necessarily a decisive renunciation of Christ or attributing his works to the power of Satan. I doubt that one in a thousand cases of apostasy is that dramatic or decisive. The more dramatic and decisive mode is more properly associate with committing the unpardonable sin. However, Wilson Hogue, a Free Methodist bishop, taught the blasphemy against the Holy Spirit was not some isolated and independent act. He described it as a culminating transgression, "the final link in a long chain of malignant and rebellious acts. . . . This state is usually reached through a protracted series of resistances against the drawing and impulses of the Spirit."[314]

It seems, then, that both *final* apostasy and the blasphemy of the Spirit occur gradually and the only real difference is that only true believers may become apostate, while non-believers may blasphemy the Spirit. Thus, apostasy may occur incrementally or decisively.[315]

---

[311]Article 5, Proposition 5 in Watson, *Dictionary*, 898.

[312]Summers, *Systematic Theology*, 2:177.

[313]Osborne, "Classical Arminian View," 87. Harper also articulates two ways in which apostasy may occur ["Wesleyan Arminian View," 244].

[314]Hogue, *Holy Spirit*, 385-391.

[315]In my own ministry I have witnessed several gradual cases of apostasy in which members simply wanted their own agenda more than they wanted to obey God. Some of them still even profess to be right with God, but their lives argue otherwise. I have known only one dramatic and decisive renunciation of Christianity and that instance was the result of several years of subjection to higher criticism in seminary.

According to the warning passages in Hebrews, apostasy results when believers drift away, disobey, harden their hearts, and fall short. They deliberately persist in wilful sin. The root of bitterness springs up because they fail to appropriate the grace of God.

We are either moving forward or sliding backward. Anyone who is sliding backward is in danger of apostasy. The only question is how far back to they have to slide? And is apostasy always irreversible? Wesley preached

> If it be asked, "Do any real apostates find mercy from God? Do any that have 'made shipwreck of faith and a good conscience,' recover what they have lost? Do you know, have you seen, any instance of persons who found redemption in the blood of Jesus, and afterwards fell away, and yet were restored, — renewed again unto repentance?'" Yea, verily and not one or an hundred only, but, I am persuaded several thousands. . . . Indeed, it is so far from being an uncommon thing for a believer to fall and be restored, that it is rather uncommon to find any believers who are not conscious of having been backsliders from God, in a higher or lower degree, and perhaps more than once, before they were established in faith.[316]

But Wesley also interpreted Hebrews 6, as "absolute, total apostasy." He felt that Hebrews 6:4-6 and 10:26-27 describes such a case."[317] Yet he continues in the same sermon to declare, "A believer may fall, and not fall away. He may fall and rise again. And if he should fall, even into sin, yet this case, dreadful as it is, is not desperate." But Wesley went on to warn that a believer may "sink lower and lower till he wholly fall away."[318] But elsewhere he has described the warning on Hebrews 6 as a formal renunciation of Jesus of Nazareth as an impostor, a deceiver, and deserving of the cross.[319]

However, not all Arminians agree that Hebrews 6 is necessarily warning of final apostasy. Robert Shank devotes an entire chapter to the question, "Is apostasy without remedy?" Shank argues that even the warning in Hebrews 6 is regarding not merely a past defection, but a present deliberate hostility toward

---

[316]Wesley, "Call to Backsliders," Sermon #86, 2.2.

[317]Wesley, "Sermon on the Mount, IV," Sermon #24, 1.9; "Call to Backsliders," Sermon #86, 2.3.i. See also his *Notes* on Heb 6:6. Ironically, he seems to conflate his interpretation of Hebrews 6 with the blasphemy of the Holy Ghost in "Call to Backsliders," 2.5.i.

[318]Wesley, "Sermon on the Mount, IV," 1.9.

[319]Wesley, "Call to Backsliders," 2.4.

Christ.[320]

This is the position of Boyce Blackwelder who explained that the temporal force of the two present participles in Hebrews 6:6, *while crucifying* and *while putting to open shame*, "implies that if person guilty of such sin will cease it, and repent, they can be reclaimed."[321]

While this is not Wesley's interpretation, he reports that some who backsliders have been restored to their first love. And his general conclusion is that we should not give up on those who have no hope of restoration.[322] He even claimed that he knew of several thousand real apostates who were restored.[323] Thus, apostasy was not always final.

W. J. Parks, an old Southern Methodist pastor, taught that we avoid apostasy by keeping God's word, by watching and praying, by putting on the whole armor of God, by striving, by giving all diligence, by maintaining faithfulness until death, by keeping the word of God's patience, by fighting the good fight of faith, by pressing toward the mark for the prize, by keeping the faith, by not drawing back to perdition, by now casting away our confidence, by not being let away with the error of the wicked but separating from them, and by resisting the devil.[324]

Parks warned that the first step toward final apostasy begins in the heart when we regard iniquity. The second step is a loss of life and zeal which were formerly in the soul. This is accompanied by an abatement in attending the means of grace. The third step is to relish what was once loathed and abhorred. The fourth step is the utter abandonment of the Church and moral obligation. The last step is their utter abandonment to the service of the devil and the desires of their own evil heart.[325]

In his comments on Hebrews 3:12, Clarke observed five degrees of apostasy

- Consenting to sin, being deceived by its solicitations.
- Hardness of heart, through giving way to sin.
- Unbelief in consequence of this hardness which lead to calling the truth of the Gospel into question.

---

[320]Shank, *Life in the Son*, 318;

[321]Blackwelder, *Light from the Greek New Testament*, 103-104.

[322]Wesley, "Call to Backsliders," § 5; 2.1.v; 2.4-6.

[323]Wesley, "Call to Backsliders," 2.2.

[324]Parks, *Short Essay on Apostasy*, 94-97.

[325]Parks, *Short Essay on Apostasy*, 111-123.

- Speaking evil of the Gospel and the provision God has made for our salvation, as a result of this unbelief.
- Apostasy itself or falling off from the living God.

Clarke concluded, "He who begins to give the least way to sin is in danger of final apostasy; the best remedy against this is to get the evil heart *removed*."[326]

[326]Clarke, *Commentary*, 6:706.

CHAPTER 3
THE CALL TO HOLINESS

According to Carl F. H. Henry, the Bible has three major emphases in its exposition of holiness: the holiness of the living transcendent God, the holiness of God in Christ Jesus the incarnate Son and Servant, and the holiness of the believing community.[327]

We have seen how absolutely pure; how absolutely perfect God is. He is awesome and glorious. He is unimpeachable. He is separate from and above all that is sinful. The holiness of God should lead us to worship (1 Chron 16:29; 2 Chron 20:21; Psalm 29:2; 96:9), gratitude (1 Chron 16:35; Psalm 30:4; 97:12), and even rejoicing (1 Chron 16:10).

If Christ is of the same nature as the Father, he is also absolutely holy. Nine times he is specifically described as "holy" in the New Testament. Christ described himself as "holy and true" (Rev 3:7). He had no sin (2 Cor 5:21; Heb 4:15; 7:26; 1 John 3:5). He was without spot or blemish (1 Peter 1:19). He committed no sin (1 Peter 2:22). Thus, he is our righteousness, holiness, and redemption (1 Cor 1:30).

We have also seen that we are sinners by nature and by choice. We are very far gone from our original righteousness. Confronted with the holiness of God, Isaiah confessed his own sinfulness (Isa 6:5). Yet in spite of our sinful state, the shocking command of Scripture is "be holy." How holy can God make a sinner?

Holiness in the Old Testament

There are six Hebrew terms used to express the idea of perfection.

- כלה (*kala*) means to bring a process to completion and can denote the accomplishment of a design
- כלל (*kalal*) is used to denote perfection in beauty or wholeness
- חרם (*haram*) is the ban; something devoted or separated to God for destruction
- שלם (*shalom*) means to be complete or sound, describing prosperity and

[327]*God, Revelation and Authority*, 6:336.

well-being, which tends to perfection

- תמם (*tamam*) describes that which is ethically sound, wholly God's, and integrity.
- ישר (*yashar*) means to be upright or straight

A seventh way to express perfection is the Hebrew construction in which the infinitive absolute is used either before or after a finite verb to give intensity by the repetition. Isaiah 26:3 is an example. *Shalom* is doubled to emphasize completeness and this construction is translated "perfect peace."

The Hebrew word for holy is קדש (*kodesh* or *qadash*). Walter Kornfeld concluded separation was the primary meaning of קדש.[328]

The same passage in Leviticus that declares the holiness of God, commands us to be holy (Lev 19:2). According to Leviticus 19 we are to reverence our parents (v 3), practice righteous judgment (vv 15, 35-36), love our neighbor (v 18), respect the elderly (v 32), and love the stranger (vv 33-34).

The law, as stated in Leviticus 19-20 also forbid idolatry and witchcraft, stealing, fraud, and lying. We are not to discriminate against the handicapped, spread slander, hate, bear a grudge, or curse our parents. We are not to engage in sexual misconduct such as prostitution, adultery, homosexuality, bestiality or other forms of perversion.[329]

Obedience to the positive commands and separation from the forbidden actions are a reflection of God's holiness in our conduct. Nathan Bangs devoted two letters to the proposition that keeping the commandments is the external evidence of entire sanctification.[330] R. J. Rushdoony wrote,

> Every Biblical law is concerned with holiness. All law creates a line of division, a separation between the law-abiding and the law-breaking peoples. Without law, there can be no separation.

---

[328]Kornfeld, *TDOT*, 12:523. It is probable that the word is derived from the root *qad* which means "to cut." This is the conclusion of BDB, *Lexicon*, 871, Girdlestone, *Synonyms*, 175, Procksch, ἅγιος, *TDNT*, 1:89, Klein, *Etymological Dictionary*, 284], Erickson, *Christian Theology*, 1:284], and Sproul who suggested a more accurate translation would be "a cut above" [*Holiness of God*, 54].

[329]Yet William Blake declared, "For every thing that lives is holy" in *Marriage of Heaven and Hell*, 148-160. Allen Ginsberg carried this philosophy to its logical conclusion, declaring in his poem "Howl" (1955) that "everything is holy." The revolutionary sexuality advocated by the Marquis de Sade who taught that evil was natural inspiration was advanced by Jean-Paul Sartre who taught that man purifies himself by committing evil systematically. According to Sartre the will to evil is spirituality [*Saint Genet*]. Albert Camus wrote, "I rebel, therefore we exist" [*The Rebel*].

[330]Bangs, *Necessity, Nature, and Fruits*, 145-160.

> The modern antipathy to and open hatred of law is also a hatred of holiness. It is an attempt to destroy the line of separation between good and evil by abolition of law. But because God is holy, law is written into the structure of all being; law cannot be abolished: it can only be enforced, if not by man, then surely by God.[331]

Keeping the Sabbath was considered a mark of Israel as a holy nation. God's people were to sanctify the seventh day as a way of honoring the Holy One who sanctified them (Exod 31:13-17).[332] Wesley equated the rest which remains for the people of God (Heb 4:9), as descriptive of Christian perfection.[333]

The words which are translated "perfect" or "perfection" originally denoted something other and less than ideal perfection.[334] Under the old covenant holiness was imputed. This means that God accepted their obedience to his law as an expression of their faith and that on the basis of that obedient faith he sanctified them or set them apart as belonging to him. God was reinforcing the distinction between the holy and the unholy.

Only five times, when the reference is to God does "perfect" mean absolute perfection.[335] When the Old Testament describes holiness related to anything other than God, it is describing a state of consecration effected by Levitical ritual. In fact, whatever came in contact with that which was ritually sanctified also became holy (Exod 30:29; Lev 6:27; Ezek 46:20). This does not imply that the person or object became ethically or morally pure, but that they were set apart for holy use. "The holiness of the creature always goes back to an act of the divine will, to divine election and institution."[336] Whenever the term holiness is used to describe a person or object, it never refers to a natural quality. Instead the subject is regarded as holy because of its relationship with God. "These holy objects stand in a special relation to God as his property. They have no human owner who can do with them as he pleases. None can touch them except at the bidding of God."[337]

---

[331]Rushdoony, *Institutes*, 88.

[332]Peterson, *Possessed by God*, 22.

[333]Wesley, *Works*, 11:382; see also Wood, *Pentecostal Grace*, 47-49.

[334]Campbell, "Perfection." *IDB*, 3:730.

[335]Deut 32:4; 2 Sam 22:31; Job 37:16; Psalm 18:30; 19:7.

[336]Oehler, *Theology of the Old Testament*,1:155.

[337]Beet, *Holiness as Understood*, 18. Beet also contended that Christian holiness is the true explanation of the Mosaic ritual [Section 8, 47-48].

Yet Sinclair Ferguson explained this was not a cold formality. "God separates men and things for his own possession and purpose. More fully, 'to sanctify' means that God repossesses persons and things that have been devoted to other uses, and have been possessed for purposes other than his glory, and takes them into his own possession in order that they may reflect his own glory."[338] Thus, according to this definition, the opposite of *holy* is common and that which is *holy* is set apart, dedicated or devoted unto the Lord.

The words "holy," "holiness," and "sanctification" are used about a thousand times in the Bible. Of all the occurrences of the word קדש (*kodesh* or *qadash*) in the Old Testament, 18% or 152 occurrences are in Leviticus — more than any other Old Testament book. The word "Leviticus" is the Latin form for the priests of Levites which God set apart for holy service.

Leviticus 11-12 defines the clean and the unclean. Leviticus 13-14 deals with leprosy, which typified sin. Again, chapter 15 dealt with sexual uncleanness. Chapter 16 deals with the atonement for sin.

The largest section of holiness code in Leviticus (chapters 17-27) is given over largely to ceremonial and external regulations. However, even in this context Leviticus 19 describes holiness in behavioral or ethical terms.[339] Ceremonial holiness did not imply that the person or object became ethically or morally pure. It meant that they were set apart for holy use. While the most common use of the word "holy" in the Old Testament describes what Beet called "objective holiness" in which God sanctified objects or creatures for himself, he also described "subjective holiness" in which intelligent beings surrendered themselves and their possessions to God.[340]

According to Sam Powell, created things are holy when they are devoted to God's service.[341] The tabernacle, anointing oil, incense, showbread, the priest's clothing, holy days or seasons were all sanctified in this objective sense. They were hallowed or sacred. Kings were anointed for leadership. Priests served in a holy function. Prophets spoke the Word of God. However, they were holy in function, not as a person. While the law refers to holy places, holy things, and

---

[338]Ferguson, *Holy Spirit*, 140.

[339]However, William Dyrness argued that the idea of holiness was associated with moral purity very early. Dyrness pointed to the incident of Nadab and Abihu [*Themes in Old Testament Theology*, 52]. Not only were they punished for ceremonial violations but perhaps for being intoxicated (Lev 10:1-11).

[340]Beet, *Holiness As Understood*, 29. Wynkoop used similar language in *Theology of Love*, 264.

[341]Powell, *Discovering our Christian Faith*, 91.

holy days, none of these places, things, or days are inherently holy.[342] Dennis Kinlaw explained, "Nothing in the Old Testament is holy in itself except Him."[343]

Angels, Moses, the tent of meeting, the ark of the covenant, the temple, the holy of holies, and the high priest were all mediators which allowed interaction with God while protecting and preserving divine transcendence and holiness. As a result of this function, these mediators were also holy in a functional sense.[344]

Daniel Steele declared that "entire sanctification except in a ceremonial sense was not enjoyed by the Old Testament saints."[345] Charles Carter noted that about three-fourths of all the references to the Spirit in the Old Testament describe Him as an external influence. Carter wrote, "Men upon whom God placed His Spirit for the accomplishment of certain redemptive acts were not always men of right hearts or approved ethical conduct. Such, however, cannot be said of New Testament believers indwelt by the Spirit of God."[346]

Holiness to the first-century Jew meant boundaries. Their land was holy and their temple was holy. Fidelity to the Law meant the observance of the Sabbath and circumcision. Yet the Old Testament prophets looked forward to a personal holiness under the new covenant which went beyond ceremonial holiness. This ethical concept of holiness becomes more prominent in the prophetic section of the Old Testament. Jeremiah 31:31-34 describes the new covenant. "I will put my law in their minds; write it on their hearts." This moves beyond the ceremonial and refers to an internal transformation. Ezekiel said God's Spirit would enable us to keep God's commandments. The reference to a new heart is a reference to regeneration (36:25-29). According to Joel, this gift of the Spirit is not merely corporate, but individual (2:28-29).

Beet pointed out that the Septuagint translators could have used ἱερός (*hieros*) for the Hebrew קדש, but instead they used ἅγιος (*hagios*), which contains an ethical element. Because *hieros* was tainted by association with the gods of heathendom, in the substantive sense of "sanctuary" it was only used once, in Ezekiel 28:18 to describe the sanctuary of Tyre.[347] According to Kinlaw,

---

[342]Sproul lists twenty-two holy things in *Holiness of God*, 55-56.

[343]Kinlaw, *Lectures in Old Testament Theology*, 220.

[344]Waters, "Holiness in New Testament Perspective,"47.

[345]Steele, *Gospel of the Comforter*, 38.

[346]Carter, *Person and Work*, 60. See also the discussion by Oswalt, *Called to Be Holy*, 86-87; the summary of Waters, "Holiness in New Testament Perspective,"56.

[347]Beet, *Holiness as Understood*, 30-32; see also Beet, *Manual of Theology*, 253. Carl Henry makes the same point in *God, Revelation and Authority*, 6:338. *Hieros* connotes consecration [Thayer, *Greek English Lexicon*, 229; Seebass, *NIDNTT*, 2:232].

the Septuagint translators had a least five Greek words which could have been used to translate the Hebrew word for "holy." However, the word they chose was relatively unknown and did not have the baggage of the other Greek words. While the other choices conveyed religious, sacred, separate, numinous, or sublime concepts, they did not adequately convey the idea of "wholly other."[348]

But Turner explained, "While the terms associated with 'holiness' stress the contrast between Jehovah and man, which can be bridged by an act of cleansing, those associated with 'perfection' point to man's kinship with God and the possibility of fellowship."[349]

Regarding the Old Testament emphasis on perfection, Turner concluded:

> 1. The exhortation to moral integrity, wholeness, soundness, sincerity, or perfection is very prominent in the Old Testament, especially in the prophetic literature.
> 2. Of the some two hundred and thirty occurrences of synonyms of perfection about seventy-two refer to man's character.
> 3. A "perfect" man is one characterized by moral integrity, sincerity, and loyalty to Jehovah.
> 4. Such perfection is commanded and expected of all the people of God.
> 5. This concept of perfection emphasizes the possibility of man's becoming like Jehovah in character.
> 6. Such a divine-human fellowship is based on the ideas of holiness, such as separation unto God and cleansing from all defilement whether ceremonial or moral.[350]

According to Perkins, the Old Testament taught that no man can live the perfect life except in immediate and continual communion with God. The ideal life was epitomized by the life of Enoch. However, stress on the ceremonial law came to be laid in the Priestly Code of Leviticus, as well as in the writings of Jubilees. From this emphasis the Pharisaic concept of holiness arose. But there was also a growing emphasis on th ethical ideal. "Man could still only reach the goal by an inward communion with God, which would necessarily express itself towards Him by the outward sign of adoring love and toward one's fellows by the fulfilment of the moral law."[351]

---

[348]Kinlaw, *Lectures in Old Testament Theology*, 230-234.

[349]Turner, *More Excellent Way*, 31.

[350]Turner, *More Excellent Way*, 38.

[351]Perkins, *Evangelical Perfection*, 46-47.

The Hebrew word שלום (*shalam*) is used of a perfect heart in fourteen passages.[352] It describes the condition of wholeness or completeness, an undivided heart and spiritual health.[353] According to Dunning *shalom* best describes the wholeness of the Edenic, pre-Fall state. To experience a restoration of the image of God means that man is in tune with God and in proper relationship to himself, man is in harmony with each other and with nature.[354] 2 Kings 20:3 and Isaiah 38:3 refer to a perfect heart. The term *shalem*, the adjective form of *shalom* is also used, to carry the meaning of wholeness.

Holiness Through the Atonement of Christ

In both the Old and New Testaments the goal is the restoration of the divine image. The motive remains the same: being holy as God is holy. The law of God is the pattern in both covenants. But now the goal, the motive, and the pattern are all brought into sharper focus in the person of Jesus Christ. Christ has become our righteousness, holiness, and redemption (1 Cor 1:30). Beet wrote, "We notice in passing that the holiness both of God and of man is set forth in the old covenant only in symbolic outline. For a complete conception of it we must wait till in the face of Jesus Christ we see the full glory of God."[355]

The perfect revelation of God is in Christ (Col 2:9). Thus he is our perfect prophet. According to Hebrews 5:8-9, Christ learned perfect obedience. His priesthood is perfect (Heb 7:11-28). He is the ideal king (Rev 19:16).

The grace of God has been made available to us through the atonement of Christ. Wesley wrote, "Indeed, nothing in the Christian system is of greater consequence that the doctrine of Atonement. It is properly the distinguishing point between Deism and Christianity. . . . Here, then, we divide. Give up the Atonement, and the Deists are agreed with us."[356]

P. T. Forsyth emphasized the holiness of God in the atonement.

> By the atonement, therefore, is meant that action of Christ's death which has a prime regard to God's holiness, has it for its first charge, and finds man's reconciliation impossible except as

---

[352]Deut 25:15; 1 Kings 8:16; 11:4; 15:3, 14; 2 Kings 20:3; 1 Chron 12:38; 28:9; 29:19, 2Chron 15:17; 16:9; 25:2; Isa 26:3; 38:3.

[353]Girdlestone, *Synonyms*, 95-96.

[354]Dunning, *Grace, Faith, and Holiness*, 486-498.

[355]Beet, *Holiness As Understood*, 22; see also p. 26 and Section 6, "The Holiness of Jesus Christ,"36-39.

[356]Wesley, *Letter* to Mary Bishop, 7 Feb, 1778.

> that holiness is divinely satisfied once for all on the cross. Such an atonement is the key to the incarnation.[357]

Love prompted the atonement, but holiness is the basis on which it was necessary. Richard S. Taylor said, "The biblical doctrine of holiness is inextricably bound up with the biblical doctrine of atonement. . . . Any theory of atonement falls short that fails to see it as *extensive* (to all men) and *intensive* (for all sin) as the effects of the Fall."[358]

The atonement is universal in scope. It is substitutionary in its nature. The purpose of substitution is propitiation and the purpose of propitiation was to satisfy the justice and holiness of God. Thus Wiley could say, "Propitiation, therefore, becomes the dominant idea of the atonement."[359] Wesley said the law is "an incorruptible picture of the high and holy One that inhabiteth eternity. . . . It is the face of God unveiled; God manifested to his creatures as they are able to bear it . . . that they may see God and live. It is the heart of God disclosed to man."[360] Mudge added, "The moral law is a transcript of the divine mind; and, hence, God could as easily change his own immutable nature as lower the standard of obedience. If he could lower the standard of obedience he could have release man from all obligation to keep the law and so have saved the trouble of the atonement."[361]

Christ also came to conquer Satan, sin, and death. Because we were bound by evil, Christ partook "of flesh and blood that through death he might destroy him who had the power of death" (Heb 2:13-14). Not only did Christ defeat Satan, he destroyed sin itself. "The reason the Son of God appeared was to destroy the works of the devil" (1 John 3:8). According to 1 John 3:4, Christ came to destroy the principle of lawlessness (ἀνομία - *anomia*), which was the devil's chief work in man. Christ's victory for us in the atonement becomes Christ's victory in us through the indwelling Spirit. This victory begins in conversion (Rom 6:1-11; 1 John 4:4; 5:4, 18). Greathouse explained the victory of sanctification "has the character of a spiritual warfare in which our victory over sin is assured as we permit Christ to live moment by moment in us." Sanctification is the repetition of Christ's victory in us. It is not simply an

---

[357]Forsyth, *Cruciality of the Cross*, viii.

[358]Taylor, *Theological Formulation*,107.

[359]Wiley, *Christian Theology*, 2:283.

[360]Wesley, "The Original, Nature, Properties, and Use of the Law," Sermon #34, 2.3.

[361]Mudge, *Growth in Holiness*, 41-42; see also Hunt, *Letters on Sanctification*, 246.

imputed righteousness based on our identification with Christ but a renewal of the image of God through our relationship to Christ and the work of the Spirit to establish the character of holiness in us. Thus Christ gives us victory over the dominion of sin in conversion, over sin itself in sanctification, and over the racial consequences of sin in glorification.[362]

John Deschner described the three aspects of Christ's victory: the victory in the atonement, in our sanctification, and in the last day. Deschner explained that Wesley did not interpret the victory of the atonement as confirming the elect, lest the believer relax too soon. "Christ's ultimate victory is certain, while our salvation is not. Wesley wants the power of Christ's certain victory offered to all men in such a way that its results may become visible in their sanctification."[363]

Christ gave himself to redeem us from all iniquity and to purify unto himself a people who belong to him (Titus 2:14). According to Ephesians 5:25-27 Christ also gave himself in his atoning work that he might sanctify and cleanse the Church that it should be holy, without spot or wrinkle. Nathaniel Burwash wrote,

> The ideal of the holy people is to be found in Christ Himself. He is the Elect Servant and the Head of the church. Hence "unity with Christ," the "mind of Christ," and "growing up into Christ" are the terms in which this ideal is set before us, and its perfection is expressed by St John in these words: "As He is so are we in this world."[364]

The atonement demonstrates the love of God. Although God foreknew who would believe, he provided a universal atonement demonstrating the extravagance of his love. While his anger is righteous, his justice is tempered by love. Thus, it is a holy love which provides a substitute. And yet this sacrificial lamb of God was not merely sent to turn away the just wrath of God, he came to take away the sin of the world (John 1:29). According to Romans 5:12-21 the last Adam reversed the judgment on the first Adam's sin. If Christ reversed the curse on Adam and yet does not address the problem of sin unattended, how can it be said that many are made righteous?

Building upon the two-fold nature of sin, Wesley referenced the atonement.

> Here is a remedy provided for all our guilt: he "bore all our sins in his body on the tree". And "if any man have sinned, we have

---

[362]Greathouse, "Sanctification and the Christus Victor Motif," 49-55.

[363]Deschner, *Wesley's Christology*, 125.

[364]Burwash, *Manual of Christian Theology*, 2:315.

an advocate with the Father, Jesus Christ the righteous." And here is a remedy for all our disease, all the corruption of our nature. For "God hath also", through the intercession of his Son, "give us his Holy Spirit", to "renew" us both "in knowledge", in his natural image . . . and also in his moral image, namely, "righteousness and true holiness."[365]

We are cleansed by his blood (1 John 1:7-9). John sees a great multitude that no one could count. They have come out of great tribulation; they have washed their robes and made them white in the blood of the Lamb (Rev 7:14). Therefore, every aspiration to holiness within the human heart can only be met through faith in the work of Christ and not through man's efforts to sanctify himself.

Thus, there is more enabling grace available today. We can be made righteous and morally pure. While it has always been God's will that we be holy, now we have the intercession of Christ and his cleaning blood, as well as the gift of the Spirit. Therefore, Hebrews 12:14 tells us to "make every effort" to be holy. Literally we are told to pursue[366] holiness like an animal pursuing its prey. This command is in the present tense; the pursuit after holiness is to be our lifelong priority.

Holiness in the New Testament

The New Testament utilizes words that convey the idea of preparedness:

- ἄρτιος (*artios*) comes from *arios*, a limb or joint, and is used in 2 Timothy 3:17 in the sense of being fitted or complete. A compound word, ἐξαρτίζω (*exartizo*) is also used in 2 Timothy 3:17. The prefix is used to intensify the verb and the meaning is to prepare perfectly or completely.
- καταρτίζω (*katartizo*) is used of mending nets in Matthew 4:21 and Mark 1:19. In Galatians 6:1 it describes restoration.

- The word ὅλος (*holos*) is used in various forms to convey the idea of wholeness of completeness.

- The word πληρόω (*pleroo*) is used in various forms to convey the idea of fullness or fulfillment.

---

[365]Wesley, "On the Fall of Man," Sermon #57, 2.8.

[366]διώκετε - *diokete*; second person plural present active indicative.

- The word τέλος (*telos*) is used in various forms and means to be finished, to reach the end, to be complete or perfect, to be mature.

The idea of holiness as devoutness or piety, undefiled by sin, free from wickedness, observing every moral obligation, pure, pious is expressed in the Greek word ὅσιος (*hosios*).[367]

A second word ἱερος (*hieros*) refers to that which is sacred or consecrated. Normally in the New Testament it describes the priest or the temple.

The major Greek word for holiness is ἅγιος (*hagios*). Thomas Summers wrote that *hagios* had three meanings. The natural meaning was to be clean or free from filth. The ceremonial meaning was purification or consecration to service. The moral meaning was holy.[368]

In the New Testament holiness (*hagiasmos*) refers not primarily to a ritual act, but to an ethical standard and a moral perfection which adheres to God's commandments. The emphasis "becomes increasingly ethical, having advanced from the outward to the inward, from the negative to the positive, from the merely ceremonial act to the moral and spiritual motive."[369]

While the New Testament maintained the Hebrew emphasis on separateness, holiness became synonymous for purity of heart. *Hagiasmos* is a noun expressing action and it is properly translated "sanctifying," rather than "sanctification" as a state or condition.[370] "The sacred no longer belongs to things, places or rites, but to the manifestations of life produced by the Spirit."[371]

> In the NT God is seldom described as holy (John 17:11; 1 Peter 1:15; Rev 4:8; 6:10). Christ is only once called holy in the same sense as God (Rev 3:7). The concept of holiness in the NT is determined rather by the Holy Spirit. Following from this, the proper sphere of the holy in the NT is not the cult but the prophetic. The sacred no longer belongs to things, places, or

---

[367]Thayer, *Lexicon*, 456; Seebass, *NIDNTT*, 2:236. God is also said to be *hosios* in Acts 2:27; 13:35; Rev 15:4; 16:5.

[368]Summers, *Treatise on Sanctification*, 12-18.

[369]Coats, "Holiness," *Encyclopedia of Religion and Ethics*, 6:743-744.

[370]Procksch, ἅγιος,"*TDNT*,1:100-113.

[371]Seebass, "Holy" in *NIDNTT*, 2:228. In Matt 23:17 Jesus refers to the ceremonial cleansing of inanimate objects by the Jews.

rites, but to manifestations of life produced by the Spirit.[372]

Kenneth Waters summarized the New Testament perspective on holiness as purity of heart and mind. He defined the *heart* as the emotional self and the *mind* as the rational self. *Purity* means the absence of base impulses or emotions, such as lust, greed, anger, hate, envy, and jealousy, that drive people toward egotism, arrogance, dishonesty, excessive indulgence in bodily pleasure, depravity, and violence. *Purity* also means the presence of love, generosity, kindness, self-control, humility, and mercy that motivate people toward justice, service, self-sacrifice, heroism, and peace-making.[373]

Gaddis called Jesus the leader of the first perfection movement in Christian history.[374] In Matthew 15:1-20; Mark 7:1-23 Jesus implied that Old Testament prescriptions about defilement and purification were about to be transcended by challenging the traditional ways of thinking about cleansing. He taught that the gift of the Holy Spirit would be the means by which the disciples would be sustained in a new and distinct relationship with the Father.[375] In describing this gift of the Holy Spirit, Nathan Bangs described the work of the Spirit effecting repentance, faith, regeneration, and sanctification.[376]

According to E. Stanley Jones, Matthew 5:1-47 gives twenty-seven marks of the perfect life.[377] God's purpose was for a holy people who were the heirs of his kingdom. Jesus taught the present reality of his kingdom in this world. What Jesus meant by perfection is contained in his teaching on the kingdom. The kingdom is perfection because Christ is at its center. His proclamation of this kingdom carries with it the doctrine of Christian perfection which may be lived out in this present world. This kingly rule of God within the human heart implies the communion of the individual soul with God. But this rule also implies a realm or a society where a life of love is lived in community. This kingdom was present in Jesus himself and he established it when he entered this world. Yet this ideal of the kingdom included the cross. We enter this kingdom through the new birth and the kingdom is actualized through the supernatural life in the Spirit. Yet growth in this kingdom also requires suffering and death. The kingdom grows on earth as those within the kingdom grow in Christlikeness. Yet the cross was also

---

372Naudé, קדש in *NIDOTTE*, 3:887.

373Waters, "Holiness in New Testament Perspective,"*Holiness Manifesto*, 38.

374Gaddis, *Christian Perfection*, 19.

375Peterson, *Possessed by God*, 27-28; 153.

376Bangs, *Necessity, Nature, and Fruits*, 85-87.

377Jones, *Christ of the Mount*, 36; 194.

the final victory of love. There is a victory to be won in this world and it is freedom from sin.[378]

God calls for our imitation of himself. The call "Be holy because I am holy" is as impossible as the command to "be perfect" (Matt 5:48). Wesley observed, "There is scarce any expression in Holy Writ which has given more offence than this. The word 'perfect' is what many cannot bear. The very sound of it is an abomination to them."[379] While most people object that perfection is only an attribute of deity, if it is only a prerogative of deity this call is just as inapplicable to us in the future as now. Yet in his overview regarding the New Testament emphasis on perfection, Turner wrote

> On the whole the New Testament ideal of perfection, while more implicit than explicit, envisions the complete redemption of man from sin. It emerges from the following beliefs: (1) sin is not only an act but a principle: (2) this remains in believers; (3) believers have the alternative of either (a) maintaining the "status quo," or (b) going on to perfection — purification and maturity in love and grace; (4) God is holy and heaven is a holy place, hence sin must be dealt with either in the next life, at death, or in this life: (5) it is during this life that God promises to "save his people from their sins" and to perfect them in love.[380]

Christian perfection in this life was described by Burwash, "Intellect is quickened, taste is refined, judgment is made clear, imagination is purified, memory is strengthened, affections are given a nobler action, appetites are moderated to their true ends, and even the body itself attains a higher perfection and a more perfect beauty."[381]

Such language implies that Christian perfection is a balance of human personality. If original sin affected the total personality so that affections are alienated, the intellect is darkened, the will is perverted, then Christian perfection involves the restoration of human personality to loving God with our whole being.

---

[378]This paragraph is my summary of Flew's chapter on the teaching of Jesus in *The Idea of Perfection*, 3-40. In his exposition of the Sermon on the Mount, Wesley made three applications of the phrase" thy kingdom come." He referred first to the reign of Christ in the individual believer, then in the establishment of the kingdom on earth, and finally to the eternal state [Wesley, "Sermon on the Mount, VI," Sermon #26, 3.8].

[379]Wesley, "Christian Perfection," Sermon #40, § 1.

[380]Turner, *More Excellent Way*,113.

[381]Burwash, *Manual of Christian Theology*, 2:325.

Leclerc argues that a theology of holiness should be affectional as well as cognitive and behavioral.[382]

Wynkoop wrote, "sanctification is God's method of *healing a soul.*"[383] Here she borrowed Wesley's language at the close of his sermon "Original Sin" where he declared that the religion of Jesus Christ is the healing of the soul. Wesley was influenced by the Eastern tradition which stressed therapeutic salvation, not merely a legal justification. He exhorted his hearers,

> Know your disease! Know your cure! Ye were born in sin; therefore "ye must be born again", "born of God". By nature ye are wholly corrupted; by grace ye shall be wholly renewed. "In Adam ye all died;" in the second Adam, "in Christ, ye all are made alive." You "that were dead in sins hath he quickened". He hath already given you a principle of life, even "faith in him who loved *you*, and gave himself for *you*"! Now "go on" "from faith to faith", until your whole sickness be healed.[384]

Charles Wesley also preached, "The one work we have to do is to return from the gates of death to perfect soundness; to have our diseases cured, our wounds healed, and our uncleanness done away."[385] Leclerc wrote that sanctification is the grace "which heals the *dis-ease* of sin and empowers us for sacrificial living."[386]

In Romans 8:1-4 the will of the Father is that the righteousness of the law might be fulfilled in us. This is accomplished through life in Christ Jesus and the law of the Spirit. As we walk in the Spirit we are enabled to keep God's law. Through the new life in Christ Jesus, which is regeneration, we are filled full of righteousness. There is no condemnation from the penalty of sin because we are

---

[382]Leclerc, *Discovering Christian Holiness*, 274. By "affectional," Leclerc refers to inclinations or Wesley's term "tempers." She argues that love involves such emotions as affection, delight, and desire. We are not to be Stoic nor to suppress the emotional aspect of personality [p. 275].

[383]Wynkoop, *Foundations*, 117. The English word "holy" is from "halig." "Hal" means well or whole, according to Tozer, *Knowledge of the Holy*, 113. Apparently "hale" is derived from "hal."

[384]Wesley, Sermon #44, 3.3,5. However, healing may be instantaneous or gradual. This metaphor emphasizes the result over the method.

[385]*Sermons of Charles Wesley*, Sermon #21, 1.5, 364; also published in the *BE Works of John Wesley*, "The One Thing Needful," Sermon #146, 1.5.

[386]Leclerc, *Discovering Christian Holiness*, 151.

justified. There is no condemnation from the power of sin because are set free. Commenting on Wesley's sermon "The Scripture Way of Salvation," Sugden explained that

> regeneration is the impartation of the new *life* through the indwelling of the Holy Spirit; sanctification is the gift of holiness or spiritual *health*, holiness and health being a derivation of the same. Of course there can be no life without some measure of health; but we can distinguish between life and health; and whilst there are no degrees in life — a man is either alive or dead — there are degrees of health, and it is capable of improvement.[387]

As the Father is holy, so he has predestined that his children should resemble him. *Because* he is holy, he has appropriated the grace to make us like him. Holiness is conformity to the character of God. Thus, we are pessimistic about man's plight, but optimistic about God's grace. The command to be holy is repeated in 1 Peter 1:16. A. W. Tozer said,

> God is holy with an absolute holiness that knows no degrees, and this He cannot impart to His creatures. But there is a relative and contingent holiness which He shares with angels and seraphim in heaven and with redeemed men on earth as their preparation for heaven. This holiness God can and does impart to His children. He shares it with them by imputation and by impartation, and because he has made it available to them through the blood of the Lamb, He requires it of them. To Israel first and later to His Church God spoke, saying "Be ye holy; for I am holy." He did not say, "Be ye as holy as I am holy," for that would be to demand of us absolute holiness, something that belongs to God alone. . . . No honest man can say 'I am holy,' but neither is any honest man willing to ignore the solemn words of the inspired writer, "Follow peace with all men, and holiness, without which no man shall see the Lord."[388]

While 1 Peter 1 gives seven components to our holiness, most approaches to holiness tend to emphasize one or two and neglect the rest. The biblical text refers to the originating cause, the procuring cause, the efficient cause, the instrumental cause, the realization of need, the requirement of faith, and the

---

[387]Sugden, *Works of John Wesley*, 2:446.

[388]Tozer, *Knowledge of the Holy*, 113-114.

response of obedience. The first four components emphasize God's overture of grace, while the last three focus on our response enabled by grace.

In 1 Peter 1:15-16 the command to be holy is repeated. Each member of the Trinity is involved in our holiness. George Peck argued that entire sanctification is attainable in this present life based on the provisions of the Gospel.[389] The plan of God, motivated by his holy love, is the *originating cause* of our holiness. According to 1 Peter 1:2, God in his foreknowledge saw our sinful plight and before the foundation of the world chose Christ to be the lamb of God (vv 19-20) who would take away the sin of the world. Peter further declares the perfection of Christ, the sacrificial lamb. Thus, the sprinkling of the precious blood of Christ (v 2) and the resurrection of Jesus Christ (v 3) are the *procuring causes* of our holiness.

The Holy Spirit is the *efficient cause* of our holiness. Peter also declares that we who are God's elect are made holy through the sanctification of the Spirit (1 Peter 1:2). Enabled by preliminary grace, those who respond in obedient faith to the Gospel call are chosen by God. Selection is not based on God's foreknowledge. All persevering believers in Jesus Christ constitute "the elect." There is no direct connection between the elect in 1 Peter 1:1 and God's foreknowledge in v 2. 1 Peter 1:2 does not teach that God chose us according to his foreknowledge. The verb "to choose" (ἐκλέγω - *eklego*) is never used once by Peter. The *New International Version* has it right in v 1; the letter is addressed to God's elect. But then the NIV mistranslates v 2. "Chosen" is not in the text.[390]

Nor is foreknowledge connected to predestination. In fact Peter does not use the word for predestination. However, the concept is implied in 1 Peter 2:9 and 2 Thessalonians 2:13. According to Peter, the Church[391] is a chosen race and

---

[389]Peck, *Christian Perfection*, 371-372. Peck argued on the basis of the work of Christ, the outpouring of the Holy Spirit, and the instrument of God's Word. Asbury Lowrey spoke of four agents of entire sanctification: the atonement, the truth, faith and the Holy Spirit [*Possibilities of Grace*, 342].

[390]There are four possibilities for the subject of the prepositional phrases of v 2. It could be referring to Peter the apostle, to the elect, to the strangers, or to the grace and peace in v 4. There is just as much precedent to connect the adjective "strangers" with the three prepositions in v 2 (both words are adjectives used as nouns - masculine dative plural). It could just as well be asserted that they were strangers according to the foreknowledge of God. Edwin Blum writes that Peter is here announcing some basic themes of his letter that will be later expanded and developed [Blum, *Expositor's Bible Commentary*, 12:219]. These themes are not necessarily connected to the doctrine of election.

[391]The Greek word for "church" is ἐκκλησία (*ekklasia*), from ἐκκαλέω (*ekkaleo* - to call out). The Greek word for "elect" is ἐκλεκτός (*eklektos*) is from ἐκλέγω (*eklego* - to pick out). Thus calling and choosing are not the same. "Called"

a holy nation and it is comprised of those who respond to God's call out of darkness and into light.

God foreknew that we would sin and would need a Savior. So Christ was chosen before Creation (v 20). He was the Lamb that was slain from the creation of the world (Rev 13:8). The only other place the noun *foreknowledge* (πρόγνωσις - *prognosis*) is used is Acts 2:23 and it also refers to the crucifixion of Christ.

God calls all men everywhere to repent, but that call is not irresistible. "Many are called, but few are chosen" (Matt 20:16; 22:14). Those who respond to God's grace are the elect. In 2 Peter 1:10 the same writer tells us to make our calling and election sure.

God predestined the plan of salvation, not the selection of those individuals who would be saved. God has not predestined who will be saved, but he has predestined that those who are born again will be holy (Rom 8:29). Thus, through election God chose Israel for fellowship and therefore Israel is holy because it is devoted to God's service. God's election calls for a response and that response is consecration. This consecration results in righteousness through keeping God's law. Obedience is the condition of the covenant.[392]

The Church is the New Israel of God (Gal 6:16) and according to Peter we are a chosen or elect race, a holy nation (1 Peter 2:9). Peter states that God chose us who are being saved through the sanctifying work of the Spirit (1 Peter 1:2, 9). The verb "choose" does not restrict who is chosen, rather it defines what they are chosen to become. The Church is the called-out ones. We are called out of the world system and called to be holy. We are called to be saints (Rom 1:7). "For he chose us in him before the creation of the world to be holy and blameless in his sight" (Eph 1:4). We are predestined to be conformed to the image of the Son (Rom 8:29).[393]

It is the call to holiness in 1 Peter 1:15-16 which is *according to* God's foreknowledge of our fall. This is accomplished *through* the work of the Spirit. Those who respond to initial grace are given more grace and the purpose of this grace is *unto* obedience.[394] Thus, through faith we are enabled to obey. While the

---

implies a summons or invitation which has been obeyed and does not imply coercion. *Effectual calling* is not a biblical term. Those who respond to God's call are the elect.

[392]This is developed by Powell, *Discovering our Christian Faith*, 91-106.

[393]Steele, *Half-Hours with St. Paul*, "St. Paul's 'Election' is Unto Sanctification," chapter 19, 105-110. See also John Knight, *In His Likeness*, 28.

[394]According to the three clauses in v 2, the call to holiness is in accordance with God's foreknowledge, by means of the Spirit (this phrase is in the instrumental case), and the cleansing of the blood of Christ is for the purpose of our obedience of the law of God.

blood belongs to him; the obedience belongs to us. Both the divine and human activity are here blended.

The Word is the *instrumental cause* of our holiness. The command to be holy stands written (v 16). This Word stands forever and it is the word which was preached to us. We were born again through this living and enduring word of God (v 23).[395] That same Word sanctifies us (John 17:17).

The circumstance of adversity tests our faith and purifies it (vv 6-7). Adversity may also help us *realize our need* for more grace. Thus, trials and suffering serve to test the genuineness of our holiness. According to James 1:4, perseverance will produce a complete perfection - if perseverance is allowed to do its perfecting work.[396]

Persevering faith is the *requirement* for more holiness (vv 5-9). Grace is actualized through faith. Wesley said, "I believe this perfection is always wrought in the soul by a simple act of faith."[397] He preached,

> Exactly as we are justified by faith, so are we sanctified by faith. Faith is the condition, and the only condition of sanctification, exactly as it is of justification. It is the condition: none is sanctified but he that believes; without faith no man is sanctified. And it is the only condition: this alone is sufficient for sanctification.[398]

Through faith we are kept by the power of God until our final salvation is realized (v 5). While we await the return of Jesus Christ we continually receive the perfection of our faith, the salvation of our soul (vv 8-9). When Christ returns he will not bring provision for the removal of sin since he already put away sin at his first appearing.[399] Romans 6:6, 2 Corinthians 7:1, and 1

---

[395]The change of prepositions in 1 Peter 1:23, from εκ (*ek*) to δια (*dia*) indicates that the Word itself is not the seed, but rather the means by which the new life is mediated. We are saved *through means of* the Word. According to Romans 10:17 faith comes by hearing the Word. Yet the Word alone does not save us. Rather it tells us how to be saved. We have been born again by incorruptible seed. This σπορά (*spora*) is synonymous with the σπέρμα (*sperma*) in 1 John 3:9 and is a reference to the nature of God implanted by the Holy Spirit.

[396]McKnight explained that perfection for James is not just eschatological or an inner orientation toward God, but "concretely behavioral" [*James*, 81].

[397]Wesley, *Works*, 11:446.

[398]Wesley, "Scripture Way of Salvation," Sermon # 43, 3.3.

[399]Pope, *Compendium*, 3:51.

Thessalonians 5:23 all indicate that entire sanctification is possible before death and that this condition may be preserved until the coming of Christ. According to 1 Peter 1:13 the revelation of Jesus Christ will bring grace, but the Scriptures never claim we must wait until that moment to be perfected in love.[400]

Finally we are made holy as we *respond in obedience* (v 2). There must be an initial surrender to enter the kingdom and a continued surrender to advance in the kingdom.[401] This phrase "unto obedience" not only refers to initial obedience, but to continued obedience. In v 14 Peter tells the chosen that as obedient children they are to be holy. They were already sanctified, but now there is a deeper call to holy living. The way for God's children to become like Christ and to be holy as their Father is holy is through continued obedience.

This pursuit after holiness begins with God drawing us by his prevenient grace. Prevenient grace is preliminary grace; the grace which precedes salvation.[402] "Holiness has its genesis in prevenient grace." Put in other language, sanctification begins with prevenient grace.[403]

The Awakened State

It is important that we understand the awakened state. This awareness that we are a sinner and have fallen far from God's original intention for us is often referred to as being "awakened." Paul cried out, "Wake up, O sleeper, rise from the dead, and Christ will shine on you" (Eph 5:14).

In our natural condition, we are said to be both spiritually asleep and

---

[400]Warfield taught that entire sanctification is obtained *at* the second advent [*Studies in Perfectionism*, appendix to abridged edition, 462-464], but Paul's prayer is that they would be kept blameless in this life, culminating - not beginning - when Christ returns.

[401]Wynkoop declared that surrender is not a biblical word and ought never to be used in relation to salvation [*A Theology of Love*,178]. She is reflecting a philosophy of personalism which sees salvation as a voluntary relationship. However, Rom 6:13-19 commands us to yield five times. Paul will use the same word again in Rom 12:1. This yielding to the will of God does not result in the loss of human personality or passive quietism, but it does involve the surrender of our will. Perkins observed that while Buddhism and Stoicism taught some form of self-surrender, Jesus taught surrender to our Father in heaven, not to the Universal Reason or the Eternal Void [Perkins, *Evangelical Perfection*, 82].

[402]Lindström, *Wesley and Sanctification*, 44-50.

[403]Greathouse, *Wholeness in Christ*, 129; *Historical Development*, 211. See also Lindström, *Wesley and Sanctification*, 113. Leclerc, *Discovering Christian Holiness*, 151.

spiritually dead. The natural man neither fears nor loves God. He is not troubled by his sin. But perhaps in a moment, perhaps by degrees, the eyes of his understanding are opened and he sees the danger he is in. He is now awakened to his need and is under the conviction of the law. He has a desire to please God. He fears God, but does not yet have a relationship with God. He is a servant, but not yet a son. This dawning of preliminary grace is stifled as soon as possible by most people, but God visits every soul, though most forget or deny the experience.[404]

Thus, Collins argues that prevenient grace is irresistible grace. "Irresistibility in this context pertains not to the call or overtures made to these faculties (that can be resisted) but to the reestablishment of these faculties that constitute responsible personhood and accountability."[405]

Wesley taught that the difference between a servant and a son was a point of no small importance.[406] He said many devout and earnest people never pass beyond this stage. He wrote in his *Journal* that this is the state most who are called Christians are content to live and die in.[407] Wesley used several phrases to differentiate between the awakened state and the new birth. He called the convicted sinner "the almost Christian." He described this as "the legal state" or "the faith of a servant."[408]

While all sons and daughters of God also serve him,[409] not all who fear God and work righteousness (Acts 10:35) have received the gift of the Holy Spirit which brings new life (Acts 11:18) and adoption into the family of God. While Romans 6:16-22 contrasts servants of sin with servants of righteousness, Romans 8:14-17 describes servants of righteousness who have also received the Spirit of adoption.

John expressed wonder at the present status of believers that "now we are the children of God" (1 John 3:1-2). Paul follows this same pattern in Romans.

---

[404]Wesley, "The Scripture Way of Salvation," Sermon #43, 1.1-2. See also "On Working Out Our Own Salvation," 3.4 where Wesley drew on John 1:9 as his principal text.

[405]Collins, *Theology of John Wesley*, 80-81. Here Collins disagrees with Maddox who emphasizes only a co-operant grace while ignoring free grace.

[406]Wesley, "On the Discoveries of Faith," Sermon #117, ¶ 13.

[407]Wesley, *Journal*, 24 May, 1738, ¶ 10.

[408]See Wesley, "The Spirit of Bondage and Adoption," Sermon # 9; Lindström, *Wesley and Sanctification*, 109-110; Mitton, *Clue to Wesley's Sermons*.

[409]John MacArthur claims that the proper translation of *doulos* is "slave." We are bought with a price. We belong to Christ. We are his own possession [MacArthur, *Slave*].

"We did not receive again the spirit of slavery, but the Spirit of sonship. And if we are now sons we are also heirs who will share in His glory" (Rom 8:14-17). The difference in the relationship of the Spirit to believers in the Old Testament and the New Testament is illustrated by Paul with the image of a master to a servant and a father to a son.[410]

Those who kept the law before Christ were servants of God, but with the coming of Christ we may now receive the "full rights of sons" (Gal 4:5). Paul concludes, "So you are no longer a servant, but a son" (Gal 4:7). While the privileges of believers are greater because of the new covenant, yet it is possible for our relationship with God to be that of a servant instead of a son. In his analysis of the theology of John Fletcher, Daniel Steele said that someone who held to a false doctrine might be a servant of God who had never personally entered the dispensation of Christ or the Holy Spirit.

> Now and then an honest Deist, a devout Unitarian, with the head warped by early implanted error, but a sincere heart, may be found amid the full blaze of Gospel truth, still serving God in the same dispensation with uncircumcised Abram in Mesopotamia.[411]

The teaching of Galatians 4:21-31 illustrates the difference between servant and son. Abraham's two wives, Hagar and Sarah, represent two covenants. John Fletcher felt that Galatians 3 clearly distinguishes between Jewish and Christian faith, although many nominal Christians live below their privileges.[412] Here Paul uses Isaac and Ishmael as an allegory. There are four major points made:

1. Ishmael had an ordinary birth; Isaac had a supernatural birth. Abraham fathered Ishmael in an attempt to help God. Fourteen years later Abraham and Sarah were too old to reproduce and Isaac's birth was a miracle. The new birth is always a miracle; it not based upon our works. The true seed of Abraham are those who by faith in Jesus Christ have been born again (3:26-29).

2. Ishmael's identity is associated with servanthood. Five times in this section he is described as the son of a slave woman. Isaac is associated with freedom. Four times he is the son of the free woman. In order to understand the significance, we have to go back to the previous section 3:26-4:20. Here Paul teaches that when

---

[410]McClintock and Strong, *Cyclopedia*, 9:947.

[411]Steele, *Love Enthroned*, 99.

[412]Fletcher, *Works*,1:573-574.

we are baptized into Christ, we are no longer servants but sons.

3. The major difference between a servant and a son is that one is in the family; the other is not. How do we know we are in the family? According to 4:6 we have the Spirit's witness. If you do not have this witness, you are still a servant.[413]

Notice that both the servant and the son experience training and discipline, but the difference is that only the son has the promise of a future. Isaac alone is the heir to the promises made to Abraham. While sons and daughters still obey the Father, the servant has no relationship with the Father. According to David Seamands,

> The servant is accepted and appreciated on the basis of *what he does*, the child on the basis of *who he is*. The servant starts the day *anxious and worried*, wondering if his work will really please his master. The child *rests in the secure love* of his family. The servant is accepted because of his *workmanship*, the son or daughter because of a *relationship*. The servant is accepted because of his *productivity and performance*. The child belongs because of his *position as a person*. At the end of the day, the servant has peace of mind only if he is sure he has *proven his worth by his work. The next morning his anxiety begins again*. The child can be *secure all day, and know that tomorrow won't change his status*. When a servant *fails, his whole position is at stake*; he might lose his job. When a child fails, he will be grieved because he has hurt his parents, and he will be corrected and disciplined. But *he is not afraid of being thrown out. His basic confidence is in belonging and being loved, and his performance does not change the stability of his position*.[414]

4. Ishmael persecuted Isaac. The religious who have never been born again will always fight this emphasis. That is why Paul persecuted the church before his conversion. This is not a popular teaching, but it will bring revival. The new

---

[413]Kenneth Collins has observed that while all servants lack assurance and are under the spirit of bondage, not all who lack assurance are necessarily servants nor under the spirit of bondage. There are exceptional cases which are usually the result of bodily infirmaries or ignorance of the gospel promises [Collins, *Scripture Way of Salvation*, 136-144]. One exceptional case was Wesley's own brief bout with depression, recorded in his *Journal*, 4 January 1739.

[414]Seamands, *Healing Grace*, 23.

birth has always been a predominate theme in true revival.

John Wesley came to Georgia in order to convert the Indians, but on his return trip home he became concerned that he did not have assurance that he was saved by faith. He described his faith as the faith of a servant, though not of a son.[415] His experience at 28 Aldersgate Street was not entire sanctification, as some have tried to make it, nor simply the time of his assurance that he was born again. It was his new birth experience.[416] Mark Olson concluded,

> Therefore, all views that see Aldersgate at the time when JW experienced perfection are mistaken. Equally so are the views that merely identify it with JW receiving assurance or as just another step in the faith journey process. JW interpreted it differently: this was the time when he became born again, a child of God.[417]

Wesley later explained that the early Methodists at first did not understand the difference between a servant and a son. They felt that all those who did not have assurance of forgiveness were children of the devil. But they came to understand a transition stage in which we fear God, but do not have the adoption of sons.[418] He said this point was "of no small importance." He exhorted the one who feared God and kept his commandments to keep seeking God until he passed from the faith of a servant to the faith of a son, was born of God, and had

---

[415]Wesley, *Journal*, 29 January 1738.

[416]Wesley frequently referred to events in his journal in terms of *anno meae conversionis,* dating them from 24 May 1738 [Cell, *Rediscovery of John Wesley*, 185]. In the memorial sermon preached by Joseph Benson about four months after Wesley's death, Benson spoke of Wesley's Aldersgate experience as his conversion or salvation [Benson, *Sermons*, "The Life and Labours of the Late Rev. John Wesley," Sermon #9, 199-203; reprinted in Brush and Reasoner, *Wesley Workbook*, 12-15].

In John Telford, *Life of John Wesley*, 380, the chronology of Wesley's life cites his Aldersgate experience as his conversion. See also Collins, "Twentieth-Century Interpretations of John Wesley's Aldersgate Experience,"18-31. For alternate views, see Maddox, *Aldersgate Reconsidered.* See the 1910 interpretation by the French Catholic J. Augustin Leger who argued that Wesley was born once and that his conversion was a gradual process which began around 1724-1725 [*L'Angleterre religieuse*]. This point is debated in *Methodist History*: Maddox, "Celebrating Wesley" 63-75; Collins, "Other Thoughts on Aldersgate," 10-25; Maddox, "Continuing the Conversation," 235-241; Collins, "Reply to Randy Maddox," 51-54.

[417]Olson, "Aldersgate II,"171.

[418]Wesley,"On Faith," Sermon #106, 1.11.

the witness of the Spirit.[419] In another sermon he referred to the sinner as "the natural man," the servant as "the awakened man," and the child of God as the "evangelical man."[420]

And now He takes me to His heart—a son;
He asks me not to fill a servant's place.
The far off country wanderings all are done;
Wide open are His arms of grace.[421]

In Wesley's *Notes* on 1 John 4:18, he wrote, A natural man neither fears nor loves God. One that is awakened, fears without love. A babe in Christ loves and fears. A father is Christ loves without fear.[422]

Twas grace that taught my heart to fear
And grace my fears relieved.[423]

What is the awakened sinner to do? He is called upon by Scripture to repent. Repentance is the first step in human response. Our response is enabled by prevenient grace. Repentance is the gift of God. It is impossible to exercise saving faith until we have genuinely repented. Faith is also the gift of God (Eph 2:8; Phil 1:29). Yet we are commanded to believe. Wesley wrote, "When we urge any to believe, we mean, 'Accept that faith which God is now ready to give.' Indeed, believing is the act of man, but it is the gift of God. For no one ever did believe unless God gave him the power."[424] Clarke taught

> Without the *grace* or *power* to believe no man ever did or can believe; but with that *power* the *act* of *faith* is a man's own. God never believes *for* any man, no more than he *repents* for him; the penitent, through this grace enabling him, believes for himself. . . . God gives the power, man uses the power thus given, and brings glory to God: without the power no man can

---

[419]Wesley, "On the Discoveries of Faith," Sermon #117, ¶ 13-14.

[420]Wesley, "The Spirit of Bondage and of Adoption," Sermon #9.

[421]C. Bishop, "Such Love," Kansas City: Lillenas Publishing, © 1929.

[422]Wesley, *Notes*, 638.

[423]John Newton, "Amazing Grace."

[424]Wesley, *Letter* to Theophilus Lessey, 7 January 1787.

believe; with it, any man may.[425]

Romans 7 describes the awakened state. Here the awakened sinner finds the pleasure of sin is gone. Although he purposes to improve his life, he discovered he is bound by sin. Sin is the problem. It causes a breakdown between us and God. It causes a breakdown in human relationships. It causes an interpersonal breakdown. The struggle in Romans 7 is between conscience and will. It is the struggle between what we ought to do and what we want to do. Unless our desires are transformed by grace, they will win out over our conscience. We may approve of right, but eventually we find ourselves doing wrong.

Romans 6 asserts that justification and initial sanctification are bound together and we cannot have the one without having the other. Sin is not to reign. We have been set free from sin. It is both an inconsistency to teach that one can become born again without any change and an inconsistency to teach that a believer can switch back and forth between the old lifestyle and the new.

In Romans 7 Paul flashes back to his pre-Christian experience. Although Paul shifts to the present tense in vv 14-25 this should be understood as the historical present, in which a past event is viewed with the vividness of a present occurrence.[426]

Romans 7 makes no mention of enabling grace. It depicts a man who sins compulsively; who is under the bondage of sin. He confesses, "I do evil" (v 19), "I am a slave of sin" (v 25), "I am sold under" (v 14). The personal pronoun "I" is used 32 times and the emphatic form ἐγώ *(ego)* is used eight times in this chapter. This is climaxed in v 25 where the double pronoun is used for emphasis, "I myself" (αὐτὸς ἐγὼ - *autos ego*).

The Greek word σάρξ (*sarx*) or σαρκικός (*sarkikos*) is used four times in Romans 7. It is often translated "flesh," "carnal," or "sinful nature." In this context it clearly is used to describe those who have not been born again. Paul explains in the following chapter that "the mind of the sinful man" or "the minding of the flesh" is death). Obviously he means that a person in this condition is spiritually dead. Paul goes on to say that those controlled by this sinful nature cannot please God. That is our natural condition — not I, but sin.

Romans 7 then is the classic psychological description of an awakened sinner struggling without the Holy Spirit. The struggle in Romans 7 is between conscience and will. It is the struggle between what we ought to do and what we

---

[425]Clarke, *Commentary*, 5:439.

[426]Dana and Mantey, *Grammar*, 185; Blackwelder, *Light from the Greek New Testament*, 67. In *Toward Understanding Romans* Blackwelder claimed the use of the historical present was common in Koine Greek and that the use of γάρ (*gar* - translated "for" in the KJV and not translated in the NIV) "connotes an explanation and continuation of the thought of the previous section" [54-55].

want to do. Unless our desires are transformed by grace, they will win out over our conscience. We may approve of right, but eventually we find ourselves doing wrong.

> My reason this, my passion that persuades;
> I see the right, and I approve it, too;
> Condemn the wrong and yet the wrong pursue.[427]

Wesley describes this inner struggle:

> Now he truly desires to break loose from sin, and begins to struggle with it. But though he strive with all his might he cannot conquer; sin is mightier than he. He would fain escape; but he is so fast in prison that he cannot get forth. He resolves against sin, but yet sins on. . . . Such is the freedom of his will - free only to evil. . . . Thus he toils without end, repenting and sinning, and repenting and sinning again, till at length the poor sinful, helpless wretch is even at his wit's end, and can barely groan, "O wretched man that I am, who shall deliver me from the body of this death?"[428]

Is there any deliverance from sin? "Who will rescue me from this body of death?" (v 24) In some theological systems the consciousness of sin and the concern over it is considered sufficient evidence that a person is born again. But the harder you try to live holy, the more impossible it will become. "I have the desire to do what is good, but I cannot carry it out" (v 18).

Romans 7 is a watershed chapter and how it is interpreted will largely determine your theology of holiness. Alexander Whyte, often called "the last of the Puritans," once told his Edinburgh congregation, "You'll never get out of the seventh of Romans while I'm your minister."[429] Yet according to E. Stanley Jones, "The eighth chapter is normal Christianity." He said that many stop at the seventh chapter as if this constituted the Christian life. They must go on or go under.[430]

According to Romans 8:9, if anyone does not have the Spirit of Christ,

---

[427]The Roman poet, Ovid, A. D. 8, *Metamorphoses*, 7.19, quoted by Clarke, *Commentary*, 6:88.

[428]Wesley, "The Spirit of Bondage and of Adoption," Sermon #9, 2.7-8.

[429]Packer, *Quest for Godliness*, 197-198; see also Packer, *Keep in Step*, 129.

[430]Jones, *Christ of Every Road*, 93; 216.

he does not belong to Christ.[431] We receive the Holy Spirit when we get saved and if we are saved we walk in the Spirit. The description in chapter 7 then is of someone who is *not* saved.

It was this very interpretation that began the controversy for James Arminius. His *A Dissertation on the True and Genuine Sense of the Seventh Chapter of the Epistle to the Romans* (1612) demonstrated that for the first four hundred years of the Church, Romans 7 was generally regarded as pre-Christian experience. This same interpretation was uniformly held by John Wesley and all of early Methodism.

Wesley warned that we should never fancy ourselves "a believer in Christ, till Christ is revealed in you, and till His Spirit witnesses with your spirit that you are a child of God."[432] We are enabled to live holy because we have made righteous, the dominion of sin has been broken, and we have received the Holy Spirit. This is the biblical standard of the new birth, which Wesley described as a "vast, inward change."[433]

Initial Sanctification

In the Gospels and Acts, different people were given different instructions for salvation. David Kendall observed that the way Jesus dealt with people was tailor-made to each individual.[434] Although God deals with each person individually, there is a basic order of salvation. "The Holy Ghost cannot make us holy without our co-operation; and we cannot take a step in the matter apart from his gracious influence."[435] Wesley described the process of salvation saying:

> Salvation begins with what is usually termed (and very properly) "preventing grace"; including the first wish to please God, the first dawn of light concerning his will, and the first slight, transient conviction of having sinned against him. All these imply some tendency toward life, some degree of salvation, the beginning of a deliverance from a blind, unfeeling heart, quite

---

[431]There has been an attempt to distinguish between "having" the Spirit and the indwelling of the Spirit [see Taylor, *God, Man, and Salvation*, 488; Wood, *Pentecostal Grace*, 85]. Yet the Corinthians were said both to have the Spirit (1 Cor 6:19) and be indwelt by the Spirit (1 Cor 3:16). However, at best they were immature Christians.

[432]Wesley, "The Nature of Enthusiasm," Sermon #37, ¶ 35.

[433]Wesley, *BE Works*, 11:107.

[434]Kendall, "Jesus and a Gospel of Holiness,"68.

[435]Summers, *Treatise on Sanctification*, 109.

> insensible of God and the things of God. Salvation is carried on by "convincing grace'; usually in Scripture termed "repentance", which brings a larger measure of self-knowledge, and a farther deliverance from the heart of stone. Afterwards we experience the proper Christian salvation whereby "through grace" we "are saved by faith", consisting of those two grand branches, justification and sanctification. By justification we are saved from the guilt of sin, and restored to the favor of God: by sanctification we are saved from the power and root of sin, and restored to the image of God. All experience, as well as Scripture, show this salvation to be *both instantaneous and gradual.* It begins the moment we are justified, in the holy, humble, gentle, patient love of God and man. It gradually increases from that moment, as a "grain of mustard seed, which at first is the least of all seeds, but" gradually "puts forth large branches", and becomes a great tree; till in another instant the heart is cleansed from all sin, and filled with pure love to God and man. But even that love increases more and more, till we "grow up in all things into him that is our head", "till we attain the measure of the stature of the fullness of Christ".[436]

Initial sanctification begins at the new birth. Wesley believed the new birth to be an entire change of our inmost nature from the image of the devil (in which we were born) to the image of God, a change from the love of the creature to the love of the Creator.[437] James Bartlet wrote,

> Thus sanctification begins subjectively as faith (see Acts 26:18), or trustful self abandonment to God's revealed will, and ends as love. Attitudes pass into character, the soul becoming assimilated to its object, the God to whom it is consecrated. This means that Justification, which involves regeneration, is implicit Sanctification; and actual Sanctification means the subjective attitude of the justified becomes explicit in moral life.[438]

---

[436]Wesley, "On Working Out Our Own Salvation," Sermon #85, 2.1. Italics added.

[437]Wesley, *Journal*, 13 Sept, 1739.

[438]Bartlet, "Sanctification" 4:394. Claude Thompson referred to Bartlet of Oxford as a non-Wesley who gave a Wesleyan interpretation of holiness ["Witness of American Methodism," 200-203].

Wesley preached, "When we are born again, then our sanctification, our inward and outward holiness, begins. And thenceforward we are gradually to 'grow up in him who is our head.'"[439] This phrase "inward and outward holiness" implies not only an inward cleansing but an outward righteousness.

R. S. Foster wrote of the new birth as "holiness begun."[440] Asbury Lowrey declared that "real regeneration is incompatible with sinning." Lowrey said the new birth "implies power over sin, but not entire deliverance from its taint and remains."[441] Cox said that Wesley did not lower the first experience in order to make room for a second grace. "Even though justification and regeneration are gates to holiness, it is also true that a real holy life has begun. Righteousness is infused into the believer."[442]

Where the Bible speaks of "sanctification," it is initial sanctification unless qualified by an adjective such as "entire" or "wholly."[443] Those who are born again are holy because they have received the Holy Spirit. They are delivered from sinful habits. They walk in the Spirit and have assurance that they have been adopted into the family of God. They manifest the fruit of the Spirit in their lives and are used by God to lead sinners to Christ.

The Bible gives various definitions of sin and we must pay attention to the context. The Old Testament does provide atonement for sins of ignorance. If that

---

[439]Wesley, "The New Birth," Sermon #45, 4.3. According to Sangster, Wesley taught that justification was the first stage of sanctification [*Pure in Heart*, 186]. See also Cox, *Perfection*, 97.

[440]Foster, *Christian Purity*, 106. According to Thomas Langford, Foster's *Christian Purity* was one of the more representative statements on holiness within Methodism [*Practical Divinity*, 94]. Yet this second edition was a complete rewrite of the 1851 first edition. The National Holiness Association condemned this second edition as "one of the most unsatisfactory discussions of the subject of Christian Purity, from a professedly Methodistic stand point, that we have yet met with." It was suggested in the *Advocate of Christian Holiness* that Foster needed to revise it again. In particular the editor objected to Foster's emphasis on the progressive element of sanctification and he did not appreciate the concerns Foster expressed over Palmer's emphasis on "appropriating faith" [McDonald, "Book Notices," 178-179].

[441]Lowrey, *Possibilities of Grace*, 186-187.

[442]Cox, *Perfection*, 82.

[443]Wesley, *BE Works*, 10:195; *Works*, 11:388; Steele, *Love Enthroned*, 9; Wilcox, *Profiles in Wesleyan Theology*, 2:236. Incredibly, Laurence Wood has it exactly backwards, "It was normal for Wesley and his preachers to mean full sanctification when they simply used the term sanctification. If they were denoting initial sanctification, they usually spoke of justifying faith" [Wood, *Meaning of Pentecost*, 288].

is the operative definition, then we all do fall short. In Romans 3:23 Paul makes a distinction between the fact that all sinned in Adam and all continue to fall short. He moves to a different vantage point in Romans 5:15-20 where he describes Adam's sin as a trespass. Here we are dealing with deliberate sin. The word translated "transgress" or "offense" (παράπτωμα -*paraptoma*) is used six times in these six verses. And the word "disobedience"(παρακοή -*parakoe*) also occurs in v 19. It means a refusal to hear. And so the context defines sin as a deliberate refusal to obey.

Romans 6:1 contains the connecting word "then" (οὖν-*oun*), a particle expressing consequence. The subject has not changed. Now that Paul has introduced the subject of grace, he declares four times (Rom 6:7, 14, 18, 22) that Christians have victory over sin. They do not deliberately refuse to obey God's law. They may accidently step over a line they do not see, but they do not willfully disobey what they know to be God's righteous requirements. This victory over sin is normal Christianity. Wesley preached that those who are justified, who are born again in the lowest sense, do not continue in sin. In making his case he quoted much of Romans 6.[444] In this chapter Paul gives four reasons why believers have victory over sin:

- We died to sin - vv 1-2
- We have been buried - vv 3-4
- We have been crucified - vv 5-7
- We have been resurrected - vv 8-10

We have victory over sin because we died to the old life in repentance and we receive a new life through faith. This new life is life in the Spirit, but Paul will not explain that until Romans 8. This victory over sin is commonly explained as nothing more than freedom from the penalty of sin. It is popular to teach a positional theology which says that by faith I am "in Christ" and when God looks at me he can only see Jesus.[445] But that does not do justice to the truth that Christ is also in me. Too many in the world have lost confidence in the church because they have not seen Christ in us. The believer is not only delivered from the penalty of sin, but from the power of sin.

---

[444]Wesley, "Christian Perfection," Sermon #40, 2.3. Laurence Wood tried to separate Rom 6:1-11 from vv 12-23 and make the second half of the chapter the perfection of the believer's sanctification [Wood, *Pentecostal Grace*, 41-42]. Yet Wesley cited from the chapter indiscriminately to make the point that victory over sin occurs at justification.

[445]"In Christ we are sinlessly perfect, while in ourselves we remain unclean" [Carnell, *Philosophy of the Christian Religion*, 77].

Wesley declared that "none can be holy except he be born again."[446] In addition to the four reasons stated in Romans 6, there are five additional reasons why a truly saved person is holy:

- *We are made just by faith*
- *We are given a new nature*
- *We receive the Holy Spirit*
- *We have been sanctified*
- *We are called "holy ones"*

1. We are made just by faith. God no longer charges us with our past sins. He also credits us who believe with righteousness. Our faith is credited as righteousness (Rom 4:5).

For just as through the disobedience of the one man the many were made sinners. Adam's sin imputed to us. So also through the obedience of the one man the many will be made righteous. The righteousness of Christ imparted to us (Rom 5:19).[447]

The popular teaching today is that we are legally declared to be just and holy, but we do not live righteous lives. Instead the obedience of Christ is reckoned to us while we continue to live in disobedience. The Scriptural teaching is not that the *obedience* of Christ is credited to us, but that our *faith* is credited to us as righteousness and that we are both declared justified and made righteousness.[448] There is no text in the New Testament which categorically states that Christ's righteousness is imputed to believers.[449]

---

[446]Wesley, "The New Birth," Sermon #45, 3.2.

[447]The verb καθίστημι (*kathistemi*) is used twice in this verse. It means to set down, to set in order, appoint, make, constitute, cause someone to become something. While we are made to share legally in Adam's sin, it means more than to be put in the category of sinners. We actually became sinners. Likewise, we were not only declared righteous; we were made righteous. David Peterson concluded that justification was not only the declaration of a legal state, but it must also be viewed within a covenantal and relational context [Peterson, *Possessed by God*, 45]. See Wright, *Justification*, which is a response to the Calvinism of John Piper in *Future of Justification*.

[448]See Watson, *Theological Institutes*, 2:216; 224; 241; Raymond, *Systematic Theology*, 2:338-342; Ralston, *Elements of Divinity*, 385.

[449]Bird, *Saving Righteousness of God*, 2. Bird surveyed the new perspective on Paul, which includes this dialog on justification. Robert Gundry has also concluded that the biblical texts used to support imputed righteousness do not espouse imputation ["The Nonimputation of Christ's Righteousness,"17-45]. See also Gathercole, "What

Wesley objected to a distortion of the doctrine of imputation which results in God being deceived in those whom he justifies, "that he think them to be what in fact they are not, that he accounts them to be otherwise than they are. . . . He can no more in this manner confound me with Christ than with David or Abraham."[450]

To justify means to make just. The adjective δίκαιος (*dikaios*) can be translated "just" or "righteous." It has been argued by those who advocate the new perspective on Paul that δικαιοσύνη (*dikaiosune*) is based on the Hebrew background of צדק (*sadeq*), which denotes righteousness in terms of personal and social relationships.[451] In Romans δίκαιος (*dikaios*) is translated "just" four times and "righteous" three times in the KJV. Justification is imputed and righteousness is imparted.

Fletcher explained that we are made righteous, not by a speculative imputation of the works of Christ, but by being made partakers of the divine nature, begotten of God, and clothed with righteousness and true holiness.[452]

2. We are given a new nature. Regeneration is the work of the Holy Spirit in the believer. In the new birth the bondage of sin is broken. John Miley said that "there is conceded to the regenerate a power of repression or subjugation over the remnants of depravity."[453] Romans 6 teaches that sin no longer has dominion. Sin remains, but does not reign.[454] We have been set free from sin. David Peterson wrote that freedom from sin, in an absolute sense, is possible only for those who share in Christ's bodily resurrection. "Nevertheless, his resurrection life casts its shadow into the present, and gives us the promise of defeating sin and living for God here and now . . . Those who belong to the crucified and resurrected Lord Jesus need no longer live as the helpless slaves of sin."[455] While we can only

---

Did Paul Really Mean?" 22-28.

[450]Wesley, "Justification by Faith," Sermon #5, 2.4.

[451]Dunn, *Romans 1-8*, 40-43. Dunn asked if the verb to justify (δικαιοῦν - *dikaioun*) means "to *make* righteous" or "to *count* righteous." As Michael Bird frames the question, is righteousness transformative or forensic? [*Saving Righteousness of God*, 12-18].

[452]Fletcher, *Works*, 1:308.

[453]Miley, *Systematic Theology*, 2:364.

[454]Wesley, "On Sin in Believers," Sermon #13, 4.3. Wesley first learned this theology from Christian David, a Moravian.

[455]Peterson, *Possessed by God*, 99-100; see also Wesley, "Christian Perfection," Sermon #40, 2.3, where he connects the victory of Rom 6 with being born again "in the

anticipate our own final resurrection, we can participate in the resurrection life and power of Jesus Christ now through faith.

According to Colossians 3:9 the believer has put off the old man with its practices and has put on the new man. And Ephesians 4:24 teaches that the new man is created to be like God in true righteousness and holiness.[456] Initial sanctification is closely related to regeneration.

> When a person truly believed, he was justified, regenerated, and initially sanctified. Justification is the forgiveness of his sins and his acceptance with God. . . . At the same instant he is born again, renewed, changed from death to life. . . . At that same moment there is a deliverance from sinning, a breaking of the power of sin, and a beginning of holiness or perfection. This last can be properly classified as initial sanctification.[457]

"No one who is born of God will continue to sin, because God's seed remains in him; he cannot go on sinning, because he has been born of God" (1 John 3:9). According to Nathan Bangs the adopted child of God cannot sin because the body of sin was destroyed by the baptism of the Holy Ghost. Thus he is entirely separated from sin. "Not that he has not power to sin, for he still possesses all the natural moral power he ever did." He might turn away from the holy commandment as easily as Eve and Adam did, but he cannot sin so long as the seed remains in him as a living, active principle and so long as his heavenly Father purges him that he might bring forth more fruit.[458]

Thus, grace is not only exhibited in the forgiveness of sin, but grace is power over sin. Wesley preached,

> Through this faith they are saved from the power of sin as well as from the guilt of it. . . . He that is by faith born of God sinneth not, (1) by any habitual sin, for all habitual sin is sin reigning; but sin cannot reign in any that believeth. Nor, (2), by any wilful sin; for his will, while he abideth in the faith, is utterly set against all sin, and abhorreth it as deadly poison. Nor, (3), by

---

lowest sense."

[456]Here the Greek word ὅσιος (*hosios*) conveys the idea of holiness as devoutness or piety, undefiled by sin, free from wickedness, observing every moral obligation, pure, pious. See also ftnt #367.

[457]Cox, *Perfection*, 86.

[458]Bangs, *Necessity, Nature, and Fruits*, 109-110.

> any sinful desire; for he continually desireth the holy and perfect will of God; and any unholy desire he by the grace of God stifleth in the birth. Nor, (4), doth he sin by infirmities, whether in act, word, or thought; for his infirmities have no concurrence of his will; and without this they are not properly sins.[459]

Wesley preached

> An immediate and constant fruit of this faith whereby we are born of God, a fruit which can in no wise be separated from it, no, not for an hour, is power over sin: power over outward sin of every kind; over every evil word and work; for wheresoever the blood of Christ is thus applied it "purgeth the conscience from dead works". And over inward sin; for it "purifieth the heart" from every unholy desire and temper.[460]

He declared that a person "has power both over outward and inward sin, even from the moment he is justified."[461] "By a Christian I mean one who so believes in Christ as that sin hath no more dominion over him."[462] Charles Wesley wrote, "He breaks the power of cancelled sin, he sets the prisoner free."[463] John Wesley rejected the concept that the new birth delivers from habitual, but not occasional, sin.[464] He ridiculed this doctrine in a letter to William Dodd,

> I tell my neighbor here, "William, you are a child of the devil; for you commit sin: you was drunk yesterday." "No, sir," says the man, "I do not live or continue in sin . . . I am not drunk continually, but only now and then, once in a fortnight or a month." Shall I tell him he is in the way to heaven or to hell? I

---

[459]Wesley, "Salvation by Faith," Sermon #1, 2.5-6. Originally Wesley defined justification to mean both forgiveness of sins and complete freedom from original sin. When this sermon was first preached in 1738 Wesley defined justification as "a deliverance from the whole body of sin." In 1771 he edited that phrase to read that justification is deliverance from "the power of sin" [Wesley, *BE Works*, 1:124].

[460]Wesley, "The Marks of the New Birth," Sermon #18, 1.4.

[461]Wesley, "On Sin in Believers," Sermon #13, 2.4.

[462]Wesley, *Letter* to Samuel Wesley, Jr, 30 October 1738.

[463]"O for a thousand tongues to sing," (1739) Hymn #1 in *A Collection of Hymns for the use of the People called Methodists* (1780).

[464]Wesley, "Marks of the New Birth," Sermon #18, 1.5.

> think he is in the high road to destruction, and that if I tell him otherwise his blood will be upon my head.[465]

He also taught that the newly justified and regenerated soul is initially sanctified and made "so far perfect as not to commit sin."[466] Therefore, it is a distortion for Laurence Wood to claim that phrases such as "salvation from sin," "conquerors over sin," "righteousness and true holiness,""created anew in Christ Jesus,"and "the love of God shed abroad in our hearts by the Holy Spirit were common ways of describing entire sanctification for Wesley and early Methodists.[467] In contrast, Wesley wrote

> "He that is born of God keepeth himself, and that wicked one toucheth him not? God has "purified his heart by faith," so that his wickedness is departed from him. "Old things are passed away, and all things" in him "are become new." So that his heart is no longer desperately wicked, but renewed "in righteousness and true holiness." Only let it be remembered, that the heart, even of a believer, is not wholly purified when he is justified. Sin is then overcome, but it is not rooted out; it is conquered, but not destroyed."[468]

3. We receive the Holy Spirit. Nathaniel Burwash wrote, "But this regeneration is effected by the indwelling of God's Holy Spirit, the promised Comforter, whose office it is to reveal to us the things of God."[469] More recently Dunn wrote, "The

---

[465]Wesley, *Letter*, 12 March 1756.

[466]Wesley, "Christian Perfection," Sermon #40, 2.20-21; see also 2.2-3, "Those who are born again in the lowest sense, do not 'continue in sin.'"

[467]Wood, *Meaning of Pentecost*, 163-165; 209-210.

[468]Wesley, "The Deceitfulness of the Human Heart," Sermon #128, 2:5. Richard Ballard wrote, "Wood, however, has restricted the meaning of such expressions for the sake of his theology. Notice that Wesley is not as restricted in his use of these expressions as Wood suggests. For example, Wesley uses the terms 'purified' and '[sin] is conquered' to describe one who has been justified, but not entirely sanctified. Only by adding the word 'wholly' does Wesley clarify his use of the expression 'purified.'" Ballard also noted that Wood seldom tries to exegete passages. When he does, his approach is subject driven rather than context driven. Wood has allowed his theology to dictate his methodology, which amounts to the text disappearing and the reader creating the meaning. "Thus Wood has forced *his* interpretation into the writings of early Methodism: [Ballard, "Acts," 77-79].

[469]Burwash, *Romans*, 157.

high point in conversion-initiation is the gift of the Spirit, and the beginning of the Christian life is to be reckoned from the experience of Spirit-baptism."[470] Regeneration is accomplished through the baptism with the Holy Spirit. Robert Tuttle explained

> The new birth is the side of conversion that denotes a turning to righteousness — what God does in us by the Holy Spirit. It is the beginning of an imparted righteousness or that which is realized in us through the power of the Holy Spirit — a real change. In most instances Wesley would have associated the outset of this transformation into the likeness of Jesus Christ with the "baptism of the Holy Spirit."[471]

The baptism with the Spirit is never mentioned in the Old Testament. The promise of John the Baptist that Christ will baptize you with the Holy Spirit is recorded in Matt 3:11; Mark 1:8; Luke 3:16; John 1:33. The second different reference is the promise of Jesus that the disciples would be baptized with the Holy Spirit (Acts 1:5; 11:16).

In the book of Acts the terms "baptized" (1:5), "come upon" (1:8), "filled" (2:4) and "receiving the gift of the Holy Spirit" (2:38) all refer to the same event; that event is regeneration.[472]

---

[470]Dunn, *Baptism in the Holy Spirit*, 4.

[471]Tuttle, *Sanctity without Starch*, 104.

[472]Actually the term "filled with the Spirit" is used only by Luke, with the exception of Eph 5:18. Pentecostal scholar Howard Ervin agreed that the terms "baptism in the Holy Spirit" and "filled with the Holy Spirit" are used interchangeable "as related aspects of the same experience." Ervin is also correct that "came upon," "filled with," "received," "fell upon," and "poured out" all amount to the same experience [Ervin, *Spirit-Baptism,* 25-26; 44]. However, Ervin understands this experience as subsequent to regeneration. "It is a consensus of the classical Pentecostal view that the baptism of the Holy Spirit (Acts 2:4) is *subsequent* to conversion and the new birth" [Ervin, *Conversion-Initiation*, vii]. Laurence Wood examined the writings of John Calvin, Rudolf Bultmann, F. X. Durrwell, Karl Barth, Alan Richardson, Ernst Kasemann, Oscar Cullmann, Joachim Jeremias, Markus Barth, and William Barclay. He researched the widely recognized New Testament commentaries, as well. He failed to find a significant writer who distinguished among these various phrases "receiving the Spirit, the baptism with the Spirit, the Spirit "falling upon," and "filled with the Spirit." Wood then proceeded to argue that there was a difference between having the Spirit and a Pentecostal fullness [Wood, *Truly Ourselves*, 198-199; 236]. Robert Lyon demonstrated that "baptizing, coming upon, filling, pouring out, receiving — are equivalent expressions" and all believers receive the Holy Spirit in his fullness at

John Larsson explained that the scriptural foundation on which the doctrine of the baptism of the Spirit rests is different from those on which the teaching of entire sanctification is built.

> This is an important point. From the angle of scriptural support, the ‘ experiences ’are not just two sides of the same coin. The scriptural backing for Wesley’s original concept is built up from a series of Scripture texts dealing with cleansing from sin, putting on the new man, and concepts of holiness and perfection. Though the positive element is also there, for example, as in the text ‘perfect love casteth out fear’ (1 John 4:18)—and the positive element in the form of the indwelling Holy Spirit has received increasing attention in the holiness movement—the basic idea, however modified, remains that of cleansing.

Regarding Spirit baptism as a second experience, Larsson concluded,

> Against this must be set the many other instances of conversion mentioned or implied in Acts in which the matter of subsequent Spirit baptism does not appear to arise, and the fact that nowhere in the Scriptures does it expressly say or even hint that the reception of the Spirit is a second experience. On the contrary, the reception of the Spirit is often expressly linked with conversion itself, as in Romans 8:9: ‘If a man does not possess the Spirit of Christ, he is no Christian.’[473]

All believers have the Holy Spirit (Rom 8:9) and there is no command in the New Testament for Christians to receive the baptism with the Holy Spirit. Baptism is a once-for-all experience. Therefore, the phrase “*baptism of the Holy Spirit*” is stressing the initial or first experience with the Holy Spirit. The phrase “*gift of the Holy Spirit*” emphasizes that this is something that God gives to us, not something that we earn through observing some spiritual formula. The “*filling of the Holy Spirit*” stresses the result of our encounter with the Holy Spirit, but does not describe a single experience in a Christian’s life. If you are baptized, even by immersion, in a short time, you will be dry and you will only have a memory of your experience. However, if you fill something, it is likely to remain in that condition much longer. The results of the filling will continue for a long time. Thus, the filling of the Holy Spirit is primarily stressing the result

---

conversion [Lyon, “Baptism and Spirit-Baptism,”18; 24].

[473]Larsson, *Spiritual Breakthrough*, 64; 66.

of the encounter with the Holy Spirit that we have when we are baptized by the Holy Spirit.

Murphree reminds us that the phrase "filled with the Spirit" is a metaphor which uses a spatial analogy. But we are talking about something that is not spatial. The Holy Spirit is not material and we are not receptacles. Thus, we actually mean that we are united with and controlled by the Spirit. Every Christian is filled with the Spirit *to the extent* that he or she is emptied of self and surrendered to Christ. No Christian is filled with the Spirit, in the sense of being full, until that person is fully surrendered. A person cannot be occupied with the presence of Christ so long as he or she is preoccupied with self.[474]

It is like the difference between a wedding and marriage. Though we use the two words somewhat interchangeably, the wedding is like the baptism. It is a once-for-all event and only lasts for a few hours. However, marriage is like the filling. When one gets married, that marriage lasts for the rest of our life. The command in Ephesians 5:18 is a present tense command to keep filled with the Spirit.[475] No one is filled permanently. It is a mistake to conceive of a container which is filled at a point in time and neither gains nor loses any of the contents.[476] The Christian life is like a conduit which has a continual infilling and a continual outflowing. This flow of the Spirit may be restricted or blocked by anything which is inconsistent with divine love. Turner wrote, "The more nearly one approximates Christian perfection, the more constantly he is filled with the Holy Spirit."[477]

---

[474]Murphree, *Love Motive*, 62; 65.

[475]Mudge was in error by stating that Ephesians 5:18 "appears like an exhortation from them to get something more than the initiatory imparting" [Mudge, *Perfect Life*, 270]. However, Pope also distinguished between having the Spirit and being filled with the Spirit. While he explained that fullness was a comparative term and that God gives himself entire to every one of us so far as we are capable of receiving him, Pope seemed to emphasize a greater infilling which empowers the believer against besetting sin [Pope, *Sermons*, "Be Filled with the Spirit," 237; 235; 240]. J. Baines Atkinson believed that every Christian is baptized with the Spirit at conversion but that not everyone is filled with the Spirit [Atkinson, *Beauty of Holiness*,151]; see also Hunt, *Letters on Sanctification*, 52.

[476]According to Wesley, Heb 2:1 describes water leaking out of a barrel [Wesley, *Notes*, 566]. The verb is used only here in the New Testament and it seems to convey the image of a drifting ship, not a leaking barrel. The leaking barrel metaphor has been connected to Eph 5:18, but the Hebrews passage does not reference the infilling of the Holy Spirit.

[477]Turner, *Vision Which Transforms*, 154. Henry Holloman wrote that there is no command in Scripture for Christians to be indwelt, baptized, or sealed by the Spirit, but believers may be filled with the Spirit repeatedly. Yet later he wrote that the normal

It is through this baptism with the Spirit that we are added to the body of Christ (1 Cor 12:13; Gal 3:27). Water baptism is an outward sign of the inward work of Spirit baptism (Acts 10:47). When Paul states in Ephesians 4:5 that there is one baptism, it is best to understand that water baptism and Spirit baptism are two parts of the one baptism.[478]

4. We have been sanctified. According to 1 Corinthians 6:9-11, those in the Corinthian congregation who were justified were also washed and sanctified to the extent that they were set apart from the outward expression of sin. This same deliverance from sin is taught in 1 Thessalonians 4:3.

William Cooke taught that the believer is initially sanctified in the sense that he is separated from the practice of wilful and overt acts of transgression. He has been separated from the love of sin through repentance. And he has been separated from the guilt of sin through justification. He is also dedicated to God as a living sacrifice (Rom 12:1).[479]

5. We are called "holy ones." All believers are called holy, sanctified, or saints in the New Testament.[480] "Saint" or "holy one" is the primary New Testament term for a Christian and is used as such over sixty times. The New Testament, however, uses the term "saints" or "holy ones"(ἅγιοι- *hagioi*) to refer to believers not yet entirely sanctified (for example, see 1 Cor 1:2 and Eph 4:12). Five of Paul's letters are addressed to the saints or "holy ones"(ἅγιοι- *hagioi*) at a particular church.[481] They have already been separated to God as his possession (1 Cor 6:18-19), separated from the common or ordinary, and separated from all that is sinful (1 Peter 1:14-16; 2 Peter 1:4; 1 John 3:9).

Yet while they are initially sanctified, Paul urges them on to entire

---

Christian life is to be filled with the Spirit. "Every Christian is Spirit-filled or Spirit controlled to some extent, but for some Christians the Spirit's control of their lives is not sufficient for them to be characterized as 'Spirit-filled.' Even Christians characterized as 'Spirit-filled' can become more Spirit-filled" [Holloman, *Forgotten Blessing*, 85; 234]. It seems Holloman labors here to defend an artificial distinction.

478John P. Brooks recognized that 1 Cor 12:13 described incorporation into the body of Christ, but because he interpreted Acts 2:1-4 as *another* Spirit baptism by which believers are sanctified, he was forced to the conclusion that the "one baptism" of Eph 4:5 could not be Spirit baptism because there are two Spirit baptisms. Therefore, Eph 4:5 must be referring to water baptism [Brooks, *Divine Church*, 79; 174-175].

479Cooke, *Entire Sanctification*, 10-11.

480Wynkoop, *Theology of Love*,322; Peterson, *Possessed by God*, 41.

4811 Cor 1:2; 2 Cor 1:1; Eph 1:1; Phil 1:1, Col 1:2

sanctification. But he acknowledges that they are already holy. "Clearly, the term 'saint' is used in Scripture to refer to the believer and 'sinner' is used in reference to the unbeliever." The New Testament never clearly identifies the believer as a sinner. "Though believers can still sin, the New Testament uses the term 'sinners' only of unbelievers."[482] In thirty-eight New Testament passages where the Christian is described, they are never referred to as sinners.[483]

Mudge objected that the holiness movement had appropriated the word "holy" to describe a special class in the Church, when nothing can be plainer than that it belongs to the whole. This resulted in "the great majority of Christ's true Church, who have been genuinely born again and are happy in the love of God" branded as unholy and classified with sinners.[484]

J. C. Granbery wrote,

> Dr. Mudge strongly and justly protests against the restriction of such words as holy, sanctified, saints, to a special class in the Church, when nothing can be plainer than that they belong to all Christ's disciples. This he proves beyond dispute. We may add that all believers are described in God's word as dead unto sin, alive unto God, crucified with Christ, risen with Christ, partakers of the divine nature, sealed by the Holy Spirit unto the day of redemption. Whoever are not holy, and do not follow after holiness, are not Christ's. They who do not preach holiness do not preach the gospel. Moreover, everyone who received Christ by faith is a child of God, an heir of God, a joint heir with Christ; he is begotten again unto a living hope, which hope we have as an anchor of the soul, both sure and steadfast. Any preaching is false which discredits the title of a true disciple, however feeble and immature.[485]

It is amazing that Wilcox could state that the title "Holy Spirit" never

---

[482]Anderson and Saucy, *Common Made Holy*, 42.

[483]The only exception might be 1 Tim 1:15-16 where Paul describes himself twice as a sinner. But the question is whether that is his present state or his previous identity. V 13 seems to settle the question, that Paul was recalling his previous state.

[484]Mudge, *Growth in Holiness*, 75; see also 100; 114. One of the best contributions Mudge made to the discussion of holiness was to connect it with regeneration. See chapter 3, "Regeneration and Holiness" in *Growth in Holiness*.

[485]Granbery, "Dr. Mudge,"203-204.

appears in regeneration texts.[486] Acts 2:38, Ephesians 1:13, Titus 3:5, and 1 Peter 1:22-23 all refer to regeneration. But according to Wilcox, believers do not have the Holy Spirit and are not holy. Therefore he finds significance in the fact that when they receive the *Holy* Spirit, they are entirely sanctified.

While all true Christians are holy, according to 2 Corinthians 7:1 that holiness may be perfected. The English Standard Version says, "bringing holiness to completion." Fletcher explained, "For the same Spirit of faith, which *initially* purifies our hearts when we cordially believe the pardoning love of God, *completely* cleanses them when we fully believe his sanctifying love."[487]

Growth in holiness

In John 15:1-17 Jesus taught that those who have trusted in him must remain, abide, rest, and be steadfast in him; to rely and depend upon God. *Abiding* implies a present tense obedience of faith (v 10). Those who abide in him bear fruit. This fruit of the Spirit is described in Galatians 5:22-23. Summers observed that Galatians 5:22-24 referred to "fruit" not "fruits" to indicate their essential identity, their inseparable connection and harmonious combination.[488] "The fruit of the Spirit are the virtues of Christ."[489] W. H. Poole also observed that the fruit of the Spirit is love:

- Joy is love in action; it is love running over
- Peace is love resting
- Patience is love suffering
- Kindness is love showing consideration
- Goodness is love at work helping others
- Faithfulness is love believing
- Gentleness is love learning self discipline
- Self-control is love submitting[490]

Thus love binds together all other virtues (Col 3:14). Benjamin Gregory

---

[486]Wilcox, *Power from on High*, 11.

[487]Fletcher, *Works*, 2:645.

[488]Summers, *Treatise on Sanctification*, 49.

[489]Friedrich Schleiermacher, quoted by Dunning in *Grace, Faith, and Holiness*, 427.

[490]Poole, *Ripe Grapes*. See also the discussion by Sangster, *Pure in Heart*, 100-180.

called love "the belt of perfectness."[491] Wesley said, "The love of God contains the whole of Christian perfection, and connects all the parts of it together."[492]

- Love must be holy.
- Faith must be obedient.
- Grace must be empowering.

Those who do not bear the fruit of the Spirit will be cut off. Every Christian is already clean or initially sanctified, but every branch abiding in Christ through saving faith will also be purged so that he will become more fruitful.[493] "Thus, as a possibility and an obligation, Christian perfection signifies the full cluster and maturity of the specifically Christian graces which give the Christian character its completeness for life and service within the conditions of its earthly environment."[494] As we endure trials and persevere in faith, the full effect is that we are perfect and complete, adorned with every Christian grace (James 1:4). Wesley said that joy was the highest degree of patience or perseverance and contains all the rest.[495]

According to John 15:3 the disciples whom Jesus addressed were already sanctified ceremonially by their obedience to the Mosaic law.[496] But the emphasis of v 3 is that they were sanctified by their association with Jesus (see John 13:3-11). They were set apart from the world by following Christ. They were then cleansed through the Word (John 15:3), but not yet by the Spirit. And they were instructed to remain in that condition by their obedience to the commands of Christ (John 15:10). They had renounced the world, submitted to the demands of discipleship, and had preached Christ.

All this had been a great help toward future fruit-bearing.[497] Yet not all of them were clean. But between John 13:10 and John 15:3 the disciples were purged of Judas. In v 3 καθαρός (*katharos*) is the adjective form of the verb just used in v 2. As a verb καθαίρω (*kathairo*) means to cleanse or purge; to prune

---

[491]Gregory, *Perfect in Christ Jesus*, 71.

[492]Wesley, *Notes*, 522.

[493]According to Asbury Lowrey, this purging which results in more fruit is entire sanctification [*Possibilities of Grace,* 251].

[494]Platt, "Perfection," 9:728.

[495]Wesley, *Notes*, 597.

[496]Wesley said the apostles were clean before Christ died by Jewish faith, for the Holy Ghost was not then given [*Works*, 8:287].

[497]Mantey, *John*, 297.

or trim clean. Its noun form is also used in 13:10. But while the disciples were set apart, pruned, and potentially clean, as in 13:10 and 17:19, through God's revelation in Christ, they needed the washing of regeneration and the purging of entire sanctification.[498] They would not bear fruit until Pentecost.

Poole observed that when we are regenerated we experience love, joy, and peace instantly. But the other manifestations require "time and cultivation for their proper development."[499] Thus their love would be completed or fulfilled (v 11). Apart from continued faith we can do nothing. But continued faith results in progressive sanctification which produces *much* fruit. "'Much fruit' is the result of this progressive sanctification and growth in grace."[500] The progression is from no fruit to bearing fruit; from fruitfulness to more fruit (v 2); and from more fruit to much fruit (v 5). We bear much fruit by dying (John 12:24) and by abiding (John 15:5).

But this growth in grace is retarded by the remains of sin. While sin no longer reigns in the heart of the born again, it does remain. John Hunt wrote, "Our carnal nature will strive within us, though it does not reign; and it will weaken, interrupt, and perplex us in loving and serving God, though it cannot hinder us."[501]

George Smith explained that a new nature was implanted in the soul when we were born again. This life is maintained in the heart by the indwelling Spirit. But there is one consideration connected with this subject too frequently overlooked — progress in this spiritual life. Yet it is the privilege of ordinary believers to make considerable progress in piety after the attainment of a sense of pardon.

We are commanded to grow in grace (2 Peter 3:18). The apostolic descriptions of spiritual life as little children, young men, and fathers (1 John 2:12-13), as well as the exhortations of Ephesians 4:13-15 and Hebrews 5:12-14, all show that when born again, we ought to go on increasing in grace, knowledge, and holy action, until we attain the measure of the stature of the fulness of Christ.

Smith explained the results of that change when we were born again were perhaps so glorious, that for a season we were not conscious of any indwelling

---

[498]B. F. Westcott wrote that the spiritual work represented by this cleansing was potentially completed, but it remained that it should be realized by them [Westcott, *John*, 217]. Donald Bloesch wrote that they were on their way to regeneration. They were cleaned proleptically by virtue of the word addressed to them, but they were not yet regenerated [Bloesch, *Holy Spirit*, 306-307]; see also Peterson, *Possessed by God*, 153.

[499]Poole, *Ripe Grapes*, 81

[500]Turner, *John*, 298.

[501]Hunt, *Letters on Sanctification*, 210.

enemy to our peace. "At length, however, roots of bitterness sprang up and trouble us. We became sensible of the existence of pride, anger, unbelief, envy, worldly-mindedness, or other similar evils." While we have power over these corruptions to restrain their action and by looking to Jesus by faith we do not commit sin, yet the existence of these remains of corrupt nature is painful and dangerous. They are sources of pain, as they are felt to be contrary to the will of God by a mind that pants to do his will. They are dangerous because many under their influence have fallen into the snare of the devil. Few have fully escaped being drawn into condemnation under their influence and have consequently had to apply again for pardoning mercy through faith in Jesus Christ. "From these evils, we teach that it is the privilege of all believers to be delivered."[502]

Romans 8:12-13 infers a sinful nature remaining *after* regeneration. We are warned not to live according to the flesh, or according to the sinful nature. To do so leads to spiritual death. Yet apparently the sinful nature still remains.

Tillett argued that Galatians 5:17 is addressed to the unregenerate man.[503] However, the context is speaking to Christians. So long as they live in the Spirit, they will not gratify the desires of the sinful nature. This passage implies that the sinful nature does *remain* after regeneration, but the Christian does not walk according to it.

While some teach that entire purity is not only the privilege, but the actual experience of every child of God, that the carnal mind is utterly destroyed at the moment Christ is received by faith, J. C. Granbery asked where we should find these men and women who are thoroughly free from egotism, vanity, love of the world, undue self-seeking, impatience, irritability, discontent, censoriousness, and every other wrong spirit. He concluded,

> That the carnal mind lingers in the great body of believers, not cherished nor dominant, but hated, resisted, overcome; that it causes them great grief and trouble, but undergoes gradual weakening and extinction, is Methodist doctrine; and, if we except the being and perfection of God, meets as nearly as any other article of faith the celebrated test of catholicity, "what has

[502]Smith, *Elements of Divinity*, 298-303.

[503]Tillett, *Personal Salvation*, 367-368. Miley conceded that there is no *explicit* scriptural proof of depravity remaining after regeneration [Miley, *Systematic Theology*, 2:361], but I think he overlooked this passage in Galatians 5. Greathouse concluded that Miley made a strong case that Gal 5:17 reflects a degenerate state, but felt that his case against 1 Cor 3:1-3 was not as strong [Greathouse, *Historical Development*, 283]. My own evaluation would be just the opposite.

been taught always, everywhere, and by all Christians."[504]

In his comments on James 1:21 concerning the prevalence of evil which the believer is admonished to get rid of, Theodor Zahn translated this phrase "residue — remainder" and explained, "The writer means the old, hereditary faults which still cling even to those born of God."[505] Wesley argued that sin remains in believers from Galatians 5:17, from the experience of innumerable believers, from the prayers of the whole Christian tradition, and from reason. If the premise of complete freedom from sin after justification is true, then anyone who feels a sinful desire cannot be a believer. This produces hopelessness, not faith.[506]

Wesley depicted the believer who was partially, but not entirely sanctified.

> He was humble, but not entirely; his humility was mixed with pride: He was meek; but his meekness was frequently interrupted by anger, or some uneasy and turbulent passion. His love of God was frequently damped by the love of some creature; the love of his neighbor by evil surmising, or some thought, if not temper, contrary to love. His will was not wholly melted down into the will of God; but although in general he could say, "I come 'not to do my own will but the will of him that sent me'", yet now and then nature rebelled, and he could not clearly say, "Lord, not as I will, but as thou wilt."[507]

John Miley wrote, "The doctrine of an incompleteness of the work of regeneration underlies that of entire sanctification, particularly in its Wesleyan form. Without such incompleteness there could be no place for the definite second-blessing view."[508] The new birth provides deliverance from the bondage of outward sin. However, we do not have to adopt an all or nothing approach. The

---

[504]Granbery, *Entire Sanctification*, 32-34. Granbery was citing Vincent of Lérins, see ftnt #1151.

[505]Zahn, *Introduction to the New Testament*, 1:96. This language will become significant when we encounter later Methodists who rejected Wesley's "residue theory."

[506]Oden, *Scriptural Christianity*, 336-337.

[507]Wesley, "On Patience," Sermon #83, § 10. For those who argue that Wesley changed his mind after writing "On Sin in Believers" in 1763, this sermon was written in 1784.

[508]Miley, *Systematic Theology*, 2:357.

new birth does do all it was intended to do, but the commencement of spiritual life does not imply its maturity. R. S. Foster explained,

> The difficulty is to make plain what that sin is, from which Christian men are not free, which remains in, or is found still cleaving to, believers; how to discriminate between the some sin that is removed in regeneration and the some sin that remains. And it is just around this point that revolves the whole question of entire sanctification, both as to what it is and its possibility. It has to do what that sin that remains. It removes that remainder of sin. Regeneration took some sin away; entire sanctification takes away what was left.[509]

Elijah Hedding explained that the justified soul does not voluntarily commit known sin, yet he finds in himself the remains of inbred corruption or original sin such as pride, anger, envy, a feeling of hatred or rejoicing at a calamity which has fallen upon an enemy. While he has a new heart which hates all these evil, resists and overcomes them as soon as the mind perceives them, he wishes these evils were not in his heart. Yet he has in himself no power to destroy them. Though he does not feel guilty for this depravity as he would feel if he had voluntarily broken the law of God, yet he is often grieved over this sinfulness of his nature.[510]

Miley cautioned, "That remnant must not be exaggerated in the interest of the doctrine of sanctification, or to the detriment of the truth of regeneration."[511] I no longer walk after the flesh, but that fleshly nature still remains and according to Galatians 5:16-18 I will struggle with it. Sangster wrote that while we do not willingly sin against him in anything, "sinful tempers remain, and though they are resisted, and resisted successfully, they remain."[512] However there is a contrast between the spiritual condition described in Romans 7 and the condition depicted in Galatians 5.

1. In Romans 7 the struggle was between the conscience and the will. In

---

[509]Foster, *Christian Purity*,117.

[510]Quoted by George Peck, *Christian Perfection*, 61-62. Hedding was a bishop in the Methodist Episcopal Church from 1824-1852.

[511]Miley, *Systematic Theology*, 2:366.

[512]Sangster, *Path to Perfection*, 27.

Galatians 5 the struggle is between the Spirit and the sinful nature.[513]

2. In Romans 7 sin is in control. In Galatians 5 the Spirit is in control. "So that we do not do what you want" is ambiguous. Do you want to do what is right or what is wrong? Wesley comments, "Being thus strengthened by the spirit, ye may not fulfil the desire of the flesh, as otherwise ye would do."[514] The Spirit is restraining him from pleasing the sinful nature. Gordon Fee wrote that the phrase "you cannot do the things that you would" in Galatians 5:17 does not contain the slightest hint of inability. Instead, it expresses God's enabling power over against the flesh."[515] This is confirmed by v 18, that there is no condemnation of the law.

Ambrosiaster, the name given to the anonymous author of the first complete Latin commentary on Paul's epistles, connected Galatians 5:17 with Romans 7:14-25. However, in Galatians 5:17,

---

[513]Pope described the awakened condition as a struggle between the flesh and the law. In the regenerate the struggle is between the flesh and the Spirit [Pope, *Higher Catechism*, 248].

[514]Wesley, *Notes*, 485; see also "The First-fruits of the Spirit," Sermon #8, 1.2. Summers wrote, "The struggle in Gal 5:17 is very different from that in Romans 7" [Summers, *Romans*, 88]. See also Peck, *Christian Perfection*, 290. More recently Ronald Fung concluded that Gal 5:17 "refers to a different situation from that envisaged in Rom 7:14ff" ["The Impotence of the Law," 37]. Martyn Lloyd-Jones went so far as to say that Romans 7 says the exact opposite as Galatians 5. One passage describes failure; the other victory [*Law*, 230-232].

In his 1941 commentary on Romans, Anders Nygren claimed that Gal 5:17 was substantially the same as Romans 7. In his review of Nygren, Leslie Mitton wrote that by omitting from the quotation the words which immediately precede Gal 5:17, Nygren "has seriously distorted Paul's meaning. Whereas, v 17, quoted in isolation, sounds a powerful ally to [the position that Romans 7 describes Paul's mature Christian experience], when it is linked with v 16, it can more easily be claimed as support for [the position that Romans 7 describes Paul's pre-conversion experience]… . Romans 7 portrays the mastery of the flesh in unaided man, and Gal 5:17 the persisting strength of the flesh in the Christian. But neither declares the mastery of the flesh to be a permanent evil from which there is no deliverance. It is an evil, and an enduring one, but it is one for which an enduring remedy has been supplied. Gal 5:14 offers that remedy. The Christian will still be aware of the continuing strength of the flesh, and of the need for unceasing watchfulness, but he need not any longer 'fulfil its promptings.' The strong man has been bound by a stronger" [Mitton, "Romans vii. Reconsidered,"102]. Gordon Fee wrote that the differences between Gal 5:17 and Rom 7:18-20 are far greater than their similarity [Fee, *God's Empowering Presence*, 435-436].

[515]Fee, *God's Empowering Presence*, 435; see also Steele, *Steele's Answers*, 93.

> The divine law clamps down on this [the desires of the flesh] and drives out the law of sin by advising people to follow the strength of their nature and not be captivated by wicked things. The law of sin, on the other hand, works insidiously and afflicts people with temptations, so that they reject the commandments of the divine law. Therefore when a person submits ot the law of God, the law of sin counterattacks by trying to persuade him not to do what the divine law commands. But the law of God works against this by calling him back and telling him not to do what the law of sin suggests, which the person concerned does not find absurd because he knows that it is in his nature to do what the law of God commands, and in the end he is glad when he does it. But if he does what the law of sin suggests, he is ashamed and horrified afterwards. Therefore the commands of the law of the Spirit are to be kept and those of the flesh are to be avoided. Even his conscience accuses him if he agrees to the law of sin, because it knows how terrible what it suggests is.

Ambrosiaster concluded at v 18, "It is clear that anyone who is led by the Holy Spirit will not go astray."[516]

In a 1659 sermon, Robert Gell explained that the flesh desires what is contrary to the Spirit. This is evidence of man's fall. Even among those who have the Spirit, there are motions contrary to the Spirit, a proneness and strong inclination to do the lusts of the flesh, yet there is no necessity of doing them because the Spirit desires what is contrary to the flesh. Parenthetically, Paul explains that the flesh and the Spirit are contrary to the other. However, this does not mean that those with the Spirit cannot do the spiritual things which they would do because v 16 promises that if we walk in the Spirit we will not fulfill the desires of the flesh.

Therefore, the promise of v 17 is that we may not do the things of the flesh which we otherwise would do. Gell argued that if a commander exhorted his men to be valiant and take a fort, promising them great reward if they take it and threatening them with death if the fort is not taken, but added that the fort is impregnable, impossible to win. Truly a man would think such a commander little more than a fool.[517]

---

[516]Ambrosiaster, *Galatians-Philemon*, 29-30.

[517]Gell, *Essay*, 774-784. Sermon #19, "Contrary Principles, Mutual Impediments." In this book Gell evaluates the King James Version which had been printed in 1611. Wesley mentioned Gell in his *Journal* 17 April 1777, "surely he was a man mighty in the Scriptures and well acquainted with the work of God in the soul."

3. There is no mention of the Holy Spirit in Romans 7. The struggle against sin was an attempt to earn salvation through works. This legalism produced deep condemnation. In Galatians 5 the person is led by the Spirit and is not under the condemnation of the law.

4. In Romans 7 the individual is awakened to his sin. In Galatians 5 the individual is not committing acts of sin (see vv 19-21).

The person described in Galatians 5 is born again, but needs to go on unto perfection (Heb 6:1). He both loves God and fears God, but perfect love casts out fear (1 John 4:18). Fear produces a restraint. The ground of boldness is conformity to Christ.[518]

While this believer does not live under condemnation, he will be convicted over inward sin, such as pride, self-will, love of the world, lust, anger, peevishness, unbelief — as well as sins of omission. He knows he is of God because he has the witness of the Spirit; yet he sees sin cleaving to even his best actions and holiest duties. Every babe in Christ is holy; yet not altogether so. While we do not yield to sin, we feel it. While we do not give way to sin, we have it. Burwash explained that in the life of the regenerate, "The flesh no longer rules, but the Spirit."

> But the flesh still strives, rebels, and is not subject to the law of God. But its power is broken, and it is now controlled by the new will directed by conscience and animated by the love of God. And as the work of grace is perfected the perfect control becomes easy, the will grows strong in spirit. The passions still exist, and still must be governed, but now that the centre of life, the interest and energy of our being, is transferred from them, they lose the abnormal strength which they once possessed, and fall back to the position for which God made them, the servants of the Spirit. But they must ever be governed as servants, otherwise they may again seek to be masters.[519]

The Scriptures do not speak of the regenerate as "carnal." They are not in the flesh (*sarx*), but in the Spirit (Rom 8:9). Those who are carnal (*sarx*) cannot please God (Rom 8:8), but the regenerate please God because they have their mind set on what the Spirit desires (Rom 8:5). Therefore, the regenerate are not

---

[518]Gregory, *Perfect in Christ Jesus*, 64.

[519]Burwash, *Manual of Christian Theology*, 2:323. Notice the implications of this statement concerning the question of eradication.

carnal.[520] Clarke called the epithet "carnal" the "characteristic designation of an unregenerate man."[521]

To be "in the flesh" is to be unregenerate. This word σάρξ (*sarx*) occurs 150 times in the New Testament. The majority of the occurrences refer to the physical body, but Paul also uses it to refer to the carnal or sinful nature.[522] Notice in 2 Corinthians 10:2-3 Paul distinguishes between walking according to the flesh and walking in the flesh. Although we live in a human body, we do not live according to the sinful nature.

Sarx is a noun, but used adjectivally to refer to persons, behavior, or dispositions. It is a tendency, not a substance. Therefore, it is improper to speak of "carnality," a term which never appears in Scripture.[523] W. B. Pope wrote,

---

[520]Arminius, *Works*, 2:513.

[521]Clarke, *Commentary*, 6:86.

[522]In classical Greek *sarx* is used only in the physical sense. In the New Testament, however, *sarx* can refer to humanity, the human body, the incarnation of Christ, the unregenerate nature in man, or the remaining sinful nature in the regenerate. Paul's use of the word psychologically is based upon it usage in the Septuagint, the Greek translation of the Old Testament. For example, Psalm 63:1 says, "My *soul* thirsts for you, my body longs for you." In this Hebrew parallelism, the Psalmist is referring to himself in two alternate forms. In the Septuagint, the translators used ψυχή *(psuche)* for *soul* and σάρξ (*sarx*) for *body*. Yet *sarx* is used metaphorically for humanity.

Therefore, in the New Testament when Paul uses the term metaphorically the distinction made by Trench [*Synonyms*, 272-274] and picked up by Vine [*Expository Dictionary*, 1:170] regarding the variation in meaning between the two suffixes in classical Greek does not hold because Paul uses these term in a psychological and not a physical sense. However, both words, *sarkikos* and *sarkinos*, are used to describe the same group of people, regardless of this issue. The interpretive question relates to what kind of people is Paul describing.

Concerning σαρκικός, James Strong wrote, "Wicked or unconverted men are represented as under the dominion of a 'carnal mind, which is enmity against God'"[*Cyclopedia*, 2:127]. F. F. Bruce wrote, "Though 'my flesh' is still present with me, I am no longer 'in the flesh.' To be 'in the flesh' is to be unregenerate, to be still 'in Adam,' in a state in which one 'cannot please God' (Rom. 8:8). Believers were formerly 'in the flesh,' (7:5), but now they 'are not in the flesh, but in the Spirit,' if indeed the Spirit of God dwells within them — and if He does not, they do not yet belong to Christ (8:9)" [Bruce, *Romans*, 44].

[523]Dunning, *Grace, Faith, and Holiness*, 483; 16. Wynkoop said that sin is not a substance but rebellion. The concept that sin is a substance which can be removed it based on the dualism in Platonic philosophy which understood sin as inherent in the physical body [Wynkoop, *Theology of Love*, 49]. Purkiser also said that sin "is best defined not as a thing, an entity or quality having ontic status [being], but as the moral condition of a personal being [*God, Man, and Salvation*, 87].

"Fallen human nature is Flesh or σάρξ: the whole being of man, body and soul, soul and spirit, separated from God, and subjected to the creature."[524]

But does 1 Corinthians 3:1-4 teach there are "carnal" Christians?[525] How carnal can we be and yet still be spiritual?

First, there is no necessity in declaring that all in a particular local church are in the same spiritual condition. John describes antichrists as going out from the church. "They were not [really] of us; for if they had been of us, they would no doubt have continued with us" (1 John 2:19). Obviously all professing Christians are not in the same state or degree of grace. To refer to a church collectively as Christians does not mean all in that church are saved. Miley warned that "there is a mistaken use of certain instances of defective Christian life, particularly in the churches of Corinth, Galatia, and Asia, which leads to a false view of regeneration. The mistake arises in the treatment of such instances just as though they represented a true and normal regenerate life, whereas the Scriptures treat them as instances of very serious degeneration.[526]

Paul addressed some were initially sanctified and yet they were called to be even more holy (1:2). Paul addressed some who were not spiritual (3:1) while he recognized that God's Spirit lived in others (3:16). There was also immorality within the church (5:1) and some who called themselves "brothers" were not only immoral, but greedy, idolaters, slanders, drunkards, or swindlers (5:11). Yet *some* who used to be immoral, idolaters, thieves, greedy, drunkards, slanderers, or swindlers had been washed, sanctified, and justified (6:9-11). We create serious theological error when we assume that everyone who attended the Christian church in Corinth were in the same spiritual relationship. Paul concluded his second letter to the church at Corinth with an appeal for them to test themselves to see whether they were even in the faith (2 Cor 13:5). The

---

[524]Pope, *Compendium*, 2:65.

[525]Whedon explained that if they were wholly carnal they would not even be babes, but would be unregenerate [*Commentary*, 4:27]. Yet Paul says they are acting "carnally." According to Gordon Fee, Paul is not suggesting classes of Christians or grades of spirituality. He is trying to get the Corinthians to stop acting like people of the present age [Fee, *NICNT*, 122]. Thus, the question concerning their spiritual status remains.

There is a textual variant in 1 Corinthians 3:1. Σάρκινος is the preferred reading over σαρκικός. Both are adjectival forms of *sarx*. The basis for the preference is that the -νος ending is used less frequently and is therefore more likely to be the original word. However, most authorities agree that there is probably no difference in meaning. The fact that there is also the same textual variant in Romans 7:14, with the -νος ending there altered to the -κος ending suggests that the terms are synonymous.

[526]Miley, *Systematic Theology*, 2:367. The reference to Asian church is to situations discussed in Revelation 2-3.

possibility existed that some were not true Christians. He had also just expressed concern that there might be quarreling, jealousy, outbursts of anger, factions, slander, gossip, arrogance, and disorder within the church. He was even concerned that some may not have repented of the impurity, sexual sin, and debauchery in which they have indulged (2 Cor 12:20-21).

Second, the key words *brethren*, *babes in Christ*, and *carnal* must be properly understood. *Brethren* does not always mean Christian in the true sense. Sometimes it is used of mankind in general or of those in a community relationship which are united by common interests or members of the same congregation, but does not mean all such are regenerated.[527]

Babes in Christ does not necessarily mean all in the church were actually born again, but babes in the sense of just beginning to understand the teachings of Christianity, or as Adam Clarke states, "Just beginning to acquire some notion of the Christian religion."[528] These babes in Christ were not the same as the *newborn* babes of 1 Peter 2:2.[529] Paul uses strong language in 1 Corinthians 3:3, "For you are *yet* carnal." They always were and still are carnal, which in a strict sense means they are still unregenerate.

Then Paul cites the inconsistences of their lives. Religious, yes, but sinful in their actions. Paul points to the inconsistencies of every strife and division. Since you have all this among you, are you not yet carnal (unregenerate) and live like or act the same as unregenerate man? In 2 Corinthians 12:20-21 Paul reveals their sexual sin and debauchery, anger, slander, gossip, envying, strife. Paul, in Galatians 5:19-21 tell us they which do such things will not inherit the kingdom of God.

Paul states in the second letter to the Corinthians that he was afraid when he came to them he would be embarrassed and find *many* which had sinned and not repented of the uncleanness, fornication, and lasciviousness which they had committed. He feared there would be quarreling, jealousy, outbursts of anger,

---

[527]Vine, *Dictionary*, #4-8, 1:154-155, Arndt and Gingrich, *Lexicon*, 16, ¶ 3 "fellow countryman," ¶ 4 "neighbor." In such passages as Acts 2:29; 3:17; 9:17; 22:1; 28:17, and Rom 9:3 the term "brethren" (ἀδελφος - *adelphos*) is used of non-Christians.

[528]Clarke, *Commentary* 6:202; see also Coke, *Commentary*, 6:189. Clarke concluded that these "brethren" had no more religion that the people of the world.

[529]Peter used ἀρτιγέννητος (*artigennetos*) which means newborn. Paul used νήπιος (*nepios*) which means immature or babyish. It cannot be inferred from this word that the subject is born again. Wynkoop said Paul never used this word for *son* or *child*. Rather he was emphasizing "babyishness." She said this term always had a unpleasant connotation; a spoiled baby or arrested development. Yet she recommended sanctification as the cure [Wynkoop, *Theology of Love*, 205-206; 287]. Thus, it seems for Wynkoop the subject in 1 Cor 3:1, while born again, was not spiritually healthy.

factions, slander, gossip, arrogance and disorder (2 Cor 12:20-13:5). These were in the visible church, but not considered saved. In fact, Paul states real Christians should not fellowship with these "carnal Christians" (1 Cor 5:11-13).

Some seem to think the only one in the Corinthian church who was unsaved was the one who was living immorally with his mother or maybe stepmother, but from the verses quoted above it seems there were many in an unconverted state. Yet there were no doubt saved, regenerate, upright Christians in that church as well, but Paul feared *many* who had sinned would not have repented when he arrived (2 Cor 12:20).

Wesley did apply the term "carnal," as found in 1 Corinthians 3:1-3 to Christians. In "The First-fruits of the Spirit" he describes those who walk after the Spirit. They are filled with the Holy Ghost and demonstrate the fruits of the Spirit, yet inward sin still remains in them. He calls them "carnal."[530] Yet he taught that while they feel sin they do not yield to it; while they have sin they do not give way to it.[531]

The interpretation of Adam Clarke is more accurate. The Bible never calls Christians "carnal" in an unqualified sense. However, John Wesley has been misunderstood, as though he contradicts Clarke's position that Christians are not carnal. In his sermon "On Sin in Believers," Wesley said they were unquestionably believers who were still *in a measure* carnal.[532] Later in the same sermon Wesley said they "were still (in part) carnal and that they were "in some degree, carnal."[533] In his *Journal* he wrote that they had some degree of faith, but they were in a sense carnal.[534]

Wesley distinguished between being *controlled* by the carnal mind and having the carnal mind *remaining*. While Wesley and Clarke differed in their evaluation of the spiritual condition of those at Corinth, Wesley never used the term "carnal" in an unqualified sense to describe Christians. Elsewhere in his comments about he "carnal" Christians at Corinth, Wesley said they were "in a great measure carnal."[535] In at least three other references Wesley qualified his description: "still in a measure carnal," "still (in part) carnal," "which is in some

---

[530]Wesley, "First-fruits,"1.6; 2.5.

[531]Wesley, "On Sin in Believers,"4.13.

[532]Wesley, "On Sin in Believers,"3.2.

[533]Wesley, "On Sin in Believers," 4.1.

[534]Wesley, *Journal*, 4 June 1738.

[535]Wesley, *Notes*, 412.

measure 'carnal.'"[536] Fletcher made a similar qualification.[537]

Yet it is clear that those described in 1 Corinthians 5:11-13 were altogether carnal! Wesley and Adam Clarke did not interpret 1 Corinthians 3:1-3 alike. This fact was noted by Dennis Kinlaw, who also noted that Wilbur F. Tillett had concluded that unless the professors of religion at Corinth repented they could not inherit the kingdom of God.[538]

However, Tillett rejected the doctrine of sin in believers. He said the epistle of 1 Corinthians is addressed collectively to saints, even though the church contained unregenerate men in it. Here the church is collectively reproved as if it were collectively responsible for offenses of which only a portion of its membership was guilty. The guilty are not called "babes in Christ." The whole emphasis is that they are "babes" and are not "in Christ." Here "babes" is used as a term of reproach. They were "carnal" and must not be confused with John's "little children."

Even if it could be shown that these Christians are recognized as truly regenerate believers, and yet carnal, it would not prove that all babes in Christ are also carnal. It could only prove that some may be carnal. Tillett argued that the incestuous person in chapter 5 was not regenerate. Paul accused them in chapter 6 of doing wrong and defrauding their brethren. Paul then warned, "Know ye not that unrighteous shall not inherit the kingdom of God?"[539]

But Wesley's unguarded and unqualified use of the word "carnal"in one statement cannot be equated with the later development of the "carnal Christian" doctrine by dispensationalists and other antinomians. The expression "carnal Christian" is a misnomer. Over a hundred names are given for Christians, but "carnal" is never mentioned. Therefore, because of these problems, this passage cannot be used to demonstrate the need for entire sanctification. Nor can Romans 7. However, Galatians 5 does make the case adequately.

Third, according to 1 Corinthians 2:14-15 there are two spiritual classes: the natural man and the spiritual man. The men Paul addressed in 1 Corinthians 3:1 were not spiritual. James R. Graham expressed a consistent Wesleyan understanding

Some say that there are three classes of men: the natural man, the

---

[536]Wesley, "On Sin in Believers," 3.2; 4.1; "The Repentance of Believers," 1.10.

[537]Fletcher, *Works*, 2:541-542.

[538]Kinlaw, "Sin in Believers,"121. Kinlaw cited Tillett, *Personal Salvation*, 367.

[539]Tillett, *Personal Salvation*, 360-367

> carnal man, and the spiritual man. The natural man, is, of course, the unsaved child of the world. The carnal man is a saved man who, however, still walked in the flesh. The spiritual man is the higher quality of saved man, who walks in the Spirit and in the course of obedience. Much of this is directly contrary to the teaching of the eighth chapter of Romans … the teaching, then of the three classes: natural man, carnal man, and spiritual man is deeply pernicious and is deluding many who are continuing in sin into thinking they are saved. . . . It is the worst kind of antinomianism and is part of the base alloy of fundamentalist instruction that is abroad today. . . . The Scripture knows of two places — heaven and hell; two beings — God and Satan; two ways — the narrow way that leadeth to life and the broad that leadest to destruction; two principles of walk — the Spirit principle and the flesh principle.[540]

The command to seek holiness (Heb 12:14) is still applicable to those who are growing in holiness. As we walk in light, the blood cleanses (1 John 1:7). We are to attend to the means of grace: prayer and fasting, daily Bible reading and reading of devotional literature, spiritual conversation, public worship and the sacraments, be accountable to a small group, and giving financially. We will grow spiritually as we learn spiritual discipline. "In its broadest sense discipleship is the metaphor most descriptive of the doctrine of 'progressive sanctification.'"[541] But while all this will weaken sin, it will not drive it out. God alone can cleanse us. Sangster wrote that saints do not usually set out to attain perfection. They set out for God. "They gaze on God in love and longing, and the Holy Spirit makes them holy as they gaze."[542]

According to Beet, Revelation 22:11 should be translated, "He that is holy, let him be sanctified still further."[543] We need to go on unto perfection (Heb 6:1) and that perfection is a loving of God with our total being and our neighbor as ourselves — so filled with the love of God that it displaces everything contrary to that love. The sinner neither fears nor loves God. The awakened sinner fears, but does not yet love God. The born again believer both loves God and fears God,

---

[540]Graham, "Are There Carnal Christians?"158-164. See also Smith, *Bible Holiness*, Chapter 10, "Where There Carnal Christians in the Corinthian Church?" 73-79.

[541]Wilkins, *Following the Master*, 343.

[542]Sangster, *Pure in Heart*, 200-201.

[543]Beet, *Holiness as Understood*, 62.

but perfect love casts out fear (1 John 4:18).

Christian perfection

Holiness and perfection are related terms. Frederic Platt observed that "many Christians who urge the possibility of holiness plead the impossibility of perfection." Yet perfection is distinguished from holiness and from sanctification as a question of degree, or as the specific from the generic.[544]

Wesley may have not distinguished them adequately when he wrote that Christian perfection is "only another term for holiness. They are two names for the same thing. Thus everyone that is perfect is holy, and everyone that is holy is, in the Scripture sense, perfect."[545] All true Christians are holy, but according to 2 Corinthians 7:1 that holiness may be perfected. Entire sanctification is the perfection of the regenerate state.[546] The New Testament speaks of perfection as the goal in thirty-three places.[547] "Christian perfection implies a conformity to the will of Christ, in all that relates to inward and outward holiness, to the temper of our minds, and the conduct of our lives."[548]

W. B. Pope explained that 2 Corinthians 7:1 reveals the will of God. Five rhetorical questions in 6:14-18 express our total severance from the world:

- What do righteousness and wickedness have in common?
- What fellowship can light have with darkness?
- What harmony is there between Christ and Belial?
- What does a believer have in common with an unbeliever?
- What agreement is there between the temple of God and idols?

If we are part of the temple of God, we must be his entirely. That is the holiness which we are exhorted to perfect; a holiness which gives to God literally and perfectly all that is ours because it is already his and acknowledged to be his in the temple. The word "holiness" expresses both consecration to God in his

---

[544]Platt, "Perfection," *Encyclopedia of Religion and Ethics*, 9:728.

[545]Wesley, "Christian Perfection," Sermon #40, 1.9. David Peterson wrote that perfection is not synonymous with cleansing from sin or sanctification, although the concepts are related. The terminology of perfection refers to fulfilment or consummation [Peterson, *Possessed by God*, 36].

[546]Yet the term perfection does not always connote Christian perfection. For example, Matt 19:21; 1 Cor 13:10; Heb 2:10.

[547]Jones, *Christ of the Mount*, 38.

[548]Treffry, *Treatise on Christian Perfection*, 13.

temple and separation from the world without. Thus, we are a chosen people (1 Peter 2:9).

This passage reveals the promise of God. Nothing is demanded of us for which the covenant of grace does not make provision. The promise in 2 Corinthians 6:18 is that God will be our father, making us his sons and daughters, if we will separate ourselves from the world and consecrate ourselves to him. And the very relationship in which we stand with the God of the temple itself involves a gracious promise. The Spirit of holiness separates from the world those he brings into the temple and sanctifies all that he brings into the temple. The temple makes provision for positional holiness and the paternal relationship makes that holiness attractive and affectionate. Thus, our relationship is an incentive to perfect holiness.

This passage also provides encouragement to our own personal endeavor. While we would have expected Paul to exhort us to seek more grace through the sanctifying Spirit, the apparent contradiction in exhorting us to sanctify ourselves is resolved in the word "promise." What we do in the power of God is the work of God within us, who fulfills his own promises through our instrumentality. What the power of God accomplishes through our energies exerted in faith is counted by his as our own act. Thus, if we cleanse ourselves God by the Holy Ghost will cleanse us. But he will not cleanse us without our constant and most earnest cooperation. There can be no corporate holiness which is not the result of the communion of many individual saints.[549]

Whatever we have to do or to renounce, whatever the cost may be, however often we have failed, even though most of life seems to have gone in fruitless striving, still we must make perfection our motto. The personal cleansing from all defilement of flesh and spirit is accomplished by the Spirit blessing our own endeavors. Yet the perfecting of holiness is spoken of as always going on; a perfecting that knows no limit. It is a constant, continuous, fulfillment of the claims of holiness. "Having been delivered from all defilement of flesh and spirit, you shall be made every whit whole in the sight of God; and, in that blessed consciousness, every day perfect your holiness as in His holy presence, until the end comes and hour holiness shall be no longer in the course of perfecting but perfected for ever." Therefore, let us come out from the world this day and separate ourselves more fully than ever we have been separated from its defilements. Let us enter the house of God where we shall find him ready to receive us as a father and into the temple which is still the same house, where we

[549]While 1 Peter 2:9 describes the corporate holiness of the Church as a holy nation, the Church is holy because of its individual members (2 Tim 2:20-22). If "the great house" refers to the Church, then its purity or holiness comes from those who individually offer themselves as purified vessels.

shall find him a sanctifying Spirit.[550]

We are to be carried on unto perfection (Heb 6:1).[551] The gradual or *progressive* work of *sanctification* is the work of the Spirit beginning with prevenient grace and continuing until final glorification. Wesley declared, "There is no 'perfection of degrees', as it is termed; none which does not admit of a continual increase. So that how much soever any man hath attained, or in how high a degree soever he is perfect, he hath still need to 'grow in grace', and daily to advance in the knowledge and love of God his Saviour."[552] In fact, R. S. Foster believed that there would be continued progress in holiness even after death. It will expand through time and beyond time, throughout eternity.[553] This concept is reflected in the song "In the New Jerusalem"(1911), where Charles B. Widmeyer wrote that we "will grow in perfect love in the new Jerusalem." Thus we can experience an infinite increase in perfection after we have been perfected.

McCain observed that the higher life of Christianity, as referenced in Hebrews 6:1, results in an acquaintance with the teachings of righteous living (Heb 5:13) and the ability to distinguish good from evil (Heb 5:14). "The more we learn about righteousness, the more we are able to discern between right and wrong." However, this level of maturity requires time and is beyond the initial entry point of Christianity.[554]

When Christ baptizes us with his Spirit we are born again. His Spirit bears witness with our spirit and enables us to rise above conscious acts of sin. We are sanctified and holy so long as we walk in obedience and live by faith.

The entire salvation process is the work of the Holy Spirit, from prevenient grace to awakening, conviction to the gift of faith, to regeneration, assurance, initial, progressive, entire, and final sanctification. Holiness is to be experienced through receiving and experience the daily presence of the Holy Spirit. Holiness to be expressed through daily growth in and working out of what

---

[550]The previous four paragraphs are a summary from W. B. Pope, "Perfecting Holiness" in *Inward Witness*, 212-228.

[551]The verb, φερώμεθα (*pherometha*) is first person plural present passive subjunctive. The passive voice indicates that the action is done by the agency of God. B. F. Westcott explained, "The thought is not primarily of personal effort, but of personal surrender to an active influence. The power is working: we have only to yield ourselves to it. At the same time the influence and the surrender are continuous and not concentrated in one momentary crisis" [Westcott, *Hebrews*, 143].

[552]Wesley, "Christian Perfection," Sermon #40, 1.9.

[553]Foster, *Christian Purity*, 70-71. Wesley also suggested this in *Farther Thoughts Upon Christian Perfection*, Q 29, *Works*, 11:426.

[554]McCain, *Lord Lift Me Up!* 43-47.

God works in through the presence of the Spirit. Holiness to be expected through the holiness of glorification.

Just as the Spirit distributes the gifts as he chooses, so he can work in each life as he chooses. The mistake of the early holiness movement was to reduce the scope of sanctification to a second crisis experience. Turner said the emphasis on a second work of grace "is the feature of Wesley's doctrine of sanctification which has the least *explicit* scriptural warrant." Yet Turner felt there was some justification based on the twofold nature of sin and the fact that commands to be holy, perfect, or Christlike were addressed to believers.[555]

Can sanctification be entire? Sinclair Ferguson, representing the Calvinistic perspective, quoted Anselm, "You have not yet considered how great the weight of sin is."[556] But we cannot put limits upon the sovereign grace of God. In surveying the New Testament conception, Platt concluded, "No limit is set to Christian privilege."[557] Sangster declared that "no man has a right to put a limit to what the grace of God can do."[558] If God be sovereign, there is no limit to the grace he can extend to mankind. Outler explained, "For Wesley, the doctrine of perfection was yet another way of celebrating the *sovereignty* of grace!"[559] Even J. I. Packer commended Wesley "and his refusal to set limits to the transforming power of God's Spirit in us here and now."[560]

However, we are usually cleansed to the level of consciousness. Whenever any lack of conformity to the whole will of God is recognized, there will be an immediate consecration in order to bring a new harmony. This often comes in a second crisis, but further crises may also be experienced. John Barker wrote, "Entire Sanctification is a fullness of love and grace up to the capacity of the moment."[561] Charles W. Rishell explained that

> there is not a fixed, definite standard, no one line which all must cross alike in order to the experience of perfect love. Since perfect love is consistent with many mistakes and imperfections, and since these are not identical in any two individuals, there is no absolute standard. The ideal of one may be far higher than

---

[555]Turner, *Vision Which Transforms*, 257-258.

[556]Ferguson, *Christian Spirituality*, 125.

[557]Platt, "Perfection," *Encyclopedia of Religion and Ethics*, 9:728.

[558]Sangster, "The Church's One Privation,"493-507.

[559]Outler, *John Wesley*, 253.

[560]Packer, *Keeping in Step*, 137.

[561]Barker, *This Is the Will of God*, 88.

> that of another. The "second blessing" will lift him far higher morally and spiritually than it will the other. And this is exactly what we observe in fact. So far as it appears to the consciousness of both, however, they have passed through almost identical experiences. A religious "experience" is revealed only in consciousness. Both are conscious of hating sin and loving righteousness. Both are conscious of having entirely consecrated themselves to God. Both are conscious of having been set free from the bondage of sin. Both are conscious of a blessedness and purity never before experienced. Both will have perfect confidence toward God as long as they remain in this state. But as soon as the nature of the remaining imperfection is revealed to the mind of one thus saved there is room for a new consecration and a still higher salvation. It is entirely possible that a third crisis might come, and a third blessing of a nature similar to the second be received. But it is more likely that the state of enlightenment in a person who has reached this stage of experience will lead to a gradual discovery of the defects, and separation from them, without a repetition of the sharp and painful struggle which preceded the blessing of perfect love.[562]

Wynkoop wrote that Wesley was aware of the problems posed by the unconscious life and declared that "the most perfect have continual need of the merits of Christ."[563] Yet W. E. Sangster declared that the unconscious cannot sin. The Holy Spirit does influence the unconscious and no one can say to what depths this holy influence may extend, but the Spirit does not violate our personality. We can be cleansed to the level of all conscious sin.[564]

E. Stanley Jones taught that the work of the Spirit in entire sanctification was largely, if not entirely, in the subconscious.[565] In conversion the Holy Spirit entered the conscious mind, but in entire sanctification the Spirit entered the subconscious. Previously the subconscious was suppressed, but not redeemed. In entire sanctification the subconscious is also redeemed. The drives — self, sex,

---

[562]Rishell, "The Doctrine of Sanctification," 528.

[563]Wynkoop, *Foundations*, 107-108.

[564]Sangster, *Path to Perfection*, 118-123; see also Mudge, *Growth in Holiness*, 97; see also Steele, *Defense of Christian Perfection*, 60; Marston, "Christian Holiness,"306-308.

[565]Brown, *Meaning of Sanctification*, ii. Jones wrote his testimony at the request of Brown and it is located in the flyleaf of Brown's book; see also Jones, *Christ of the Mount*, 272-273.

and the herd mentality, were all cleansed but not eradicated. No longer do they pull against the conscious mind, but in entire sanctification both are under the control of the Spirit. Jones taught that if we would surrender the conscious mind to the Holy Spirit — all that we know and do not know, that the Spirit would cleanse at the depths beyond our control.[566]

Yet Kenneth Grider argued that while we are cleansed from original sin, the subconscious mind is not cleansed. He argued, "If the subconscious were cleansed in entire sanctification, we would be cleansed of far more than the Adamic sin we come into the world with." He contended that if the subconscious mind was cleansed all our dreams while we are asleep would be just as spiritual as our conscious thoughts.[567] Sudgen argued that our strongest instincts can be so suppressed that we are not conscious of them. We can be so overwhelmed by a sense of God's love that we are not conscious of any sin. Sugden then used the well-known phrase, "the expulsive power of a higher affection."[568] Richard Treffry explained, "Neither the pleasures of sin, nor the seductions of the world, nor the lures of the flesh, will then be able to hold any ascendancy over the heart, or alienate the affections from the sole object that has engrossed them; for when love has the supreme authority in the mind, every other passion is made its willing captive, and becomes sub-servient to its sway."[569]

Leroy Frolines argued σύμμορφος (*summorphos*), the Greek word for "conformed" in Romans 8:29, denotes an inward and thorough, not merely superficial likeness. In Romans 12:2 and 2 Corinthians 3:18 Paul used a related word μεταμορφόω (*metamorphoo*), which refers to a deep, basic change in the inner nature of the Christian. "It is a change of our personality on the subconscious level that manifests itself in conscious actions."[570]

The Holy Spirit within us will lead us on to Christian perfection. We can love God with all our heart, and soul, and mind, and strength and love our

---

[566]Jones, *Song of Ascents*, 53-56. Yet Sangster questioned the popular language of Jones earlier in *Victorious Living* which seemed to imply that natural desires and instincts are eradicated [Sangster, *Path to Perfection*, 114-115].

[567]Grider, *Entire Sanctification*, 126-127. Dunning also rejected this teaching of Jones ["Christian Perfection,"158]. Sangster is more optimistic that the Holy Spirit does influence the unconscious mind. See his chapter "The Holy Spirit and the Unconscious," in *Path to Perfection*, 118-123.

[568]Sugden, *Works*, 2:150. Umphrey Lee used the phrase "the expulsive power of a new affection" to distill the central claim of Wesley's concept of Christian perfection [*John Wesley and Modern Religion*, 185]. See also p. 623 of this book.

[569]Treffry, *Treatise on Christian Perfection*, 16.

[570]Frolines, *Quest for Truth*, 224-225.

neighbor as ourselves. This occurs as we trust Christ moment-by-moment and are moment-by-moment cleansed by his blood and filled with his Spirit. Yet there will be moments when we realize an attitude, a word, or a deed was not Christlike. These may be revelations of deeper needs and become crisis points when we repent as believers and surrender anew to his Lordship. Kenneth Kinghorn explained,

> Growth in the Lord involves both moments of crises and periods of process. By crises I mean those special times when we consciously make deeper commitments to Christ, as the Holy Spirit reveals personal needs and deeper possibilities. By process I mean the daily growth in grace that we undergo as we walk in faithful obedience to Christ.[571]

As we trust Christ moment-by-moment we are cleansed by his blood and filled with his Spirit. The Holy Spirit develops Christian character and maturity within those who are consistently led by the Spirit. Those who walk closest are the most conscious of their imperfections. Yet they can be cleansed at least from all conscious sin. The fruit of the Spirit can be increased in quality and quantity. In his eloquent way, Fletcher described Christian perfection as

> a spiritual constellation, made up of these gracious stars, perfect repentance, perfect faith, perfect humility, perfect meekness, perfect self denial, perfect resignation, perfect hope, perfect charity for our *visible* enemies, as well as for our *earthly* relations; and, above all, perfect love for our *invisible* God, though the explicit knowledge of our Mediator Jesus Christ. And as this last star is always accompanied by all the others, as Jupiter is by his satellites, we frequently use, as St. John, the phrase"perfect love," instead of the word *perfection*; understanding by it the pure love of God shed abroad in the hearts of established believers by the Holy Ghost, which is abundantly given them under the fulness of the Christian dispensation.[572]

John Hunt wrote of the maturity of knowledge, of righteousness, of peace, of joy, of hope, of meekness, of patience, of love, and of confidence.[573] Yet Miley

---

[571]Kinghorn, "Question and Answer," 9.

[572]Fletcher, *Works*, 2:492-493.

[573]Hunt *Letters on Sanctification*, 51-114.

wrote, "The Christian graces of the same person must differ in perfection or strength, whatever the grade of his attainment in holiness. One may excel in one grace; another in another; but none in all."[574]

We can have a greater delight in God's law and a greater consistency in keeping it. We may enjoy a greater sense of God's favor and blessing. We can develop a greater sensitivity and compassion for our neighbor. Yet this does not necessarily all happen instantaneously. Thomas Summers described sanctification as a progressive work which begins, but does not end with regeneration.

> In the new birth all the principles of a holy nature are implanted in the soul; but they must take root downward and bring forth fruit upward; and this cannot be done to perfection until every root of bitterness is extracted by sanctifying grace. And after this is accomplished, there is still room for development. When we no longer need the renewing of the Holy Ghost, in the work of regeneration — when we no longer need it in those cleansing operations which result in our entire sanctification — it is necessary that our inward man should be renewed day by day, by an application of that grace which keeps us clean — which strengthens all the holy principles and affections of our souls, and which can enlarge our capacity for divine communications until mortality is swallowed up on life.[575]

E. R. Hendrix explained that one may love the Lord with all the mind and heart, and yet "his power of moral discernment and his intellectual development be capable of increase as long as he lives. His very power of love will increase with his enlarging knowledge of God. His is a growing capacity both to know and to love."[576]

David Seamands explained, "You and I may be filled with the Holy Spirit today, but tomorrow our vessel should be bigger than it was today. And if it is, unless it is replenished it will no longer be full."[577]

Yet the holiness movement has insisted that entire sanctification must happen instantaneously and in so doing have emphasized the nature of the experience instead of the nature of the holy life. According to the holiness movement the sinful nature is a unit and thus it is impossible for it to be gradually

---

[574]Miley, *Systematic Theology*, 2:377.

[575]Summers, *Treatise on Sanctification*, 40-41.

[576]Hendrix, *The Perfecting of the Saints*, 16.

[577]Seamands, "Unclogging the Wells,"12-13.

cleansed away by degrees.[578] Therefore, they taught that the sinful nature was cleansed by the baptism with the Holy Spirit and that maturity was progressively realized *after* entire sanctification.[579]

Mark Mueller concluded, "As the concepts of Spirit-baptism and unitary sin developed and gained popular support throughout the nineteenth century, the meaning of maturity shifted. With its emphasis on instantaneous Spirit-baptism and the cleansing of original sin as a unitary evil, the Holiness Movement could no longer speak of entire sanctification using the vocabulary of maturity with its strong connotations of growth and its affinity to progressive purification."[580] Yet Miner Raymond wrote that the remains of original sin are generally removed by a gradual process, but perhaps sometimes instantaneously.[581] According to Maddox, Wesley recognized the need for continual awakenings to remaining sin within the Christian life.[582]

More recently Colin Urquhart described this gradual process, "God does not immediately convict us of every sin; many of the desires of the heart have yet to be refined, purified and changed. He deals with each of us step by step, purging us of one area of disobedience after another. Matters that at one time seemed minor and trivial concern us because we realise they grieve the Lord; they offend His holiness and righteousness."[583]

In the late nineteenth century the McClintock and Strong *Cyclopedia* explained that Wesleyans "differ to some degree among themselves as to the instantaneous or progressive character of this experience [of entire sanctification], and also as to its date with reference to conversion, but they all agree in looking for it during life and health, on precisely the same terms of consecration, faith, and

---

[578]For example, Thomas K. Doty opposed "depravity in layers" [*Lessons in Holiness*, 30]. "The nature of sin is such that where one of its attributes appears every other attribute is present . . . So if there is one carnal manifestation in the soul, all the rest are there, though they may lie dormant for the time being. . . . Carnality is indivisible" [Baldwin, *Lessons for Seekers of Holiness*, 11]; see also Baldwin, *The Carnal Mind*, chapter 12, "Carnality a Unit," 90-93.

[579]John Miley held to a progressive sanctification until completeness is attained, but he did not see maturity as its consequence. Miley was aware that he differed with Wesley "in respect to the element of time in the attainment of perfection or maturity" [*Systematic Theology*, 2:369; 375].

[580]Mueller, "A Biblical Examination," 35. J. A. Wood affirmed the unitary nature of sin [*Perfect Love*, 77]. James Mudge denied it [*Growth in Holiness*, 228-229].

[581]Raymond, *Systematic Theology*, 2:350.

[582]Maddox, *Responsible Grace*, 161.

[583]Urquhart, *Holy Fire*, 50.

co-operation as required by regeneration."[584]

However, early Methodism spoke of entire sanctification in terms of maturity because they understood it was the culmination of the process of inner cleansing.[585] Although Wesley talked about an instantaneous experience of entire sanctification, his major emphasis was the continuous process of going on to perfection. In his sermon "The Repentance of Believers," Wesley declared, "But if there be no such second change, if there be no instantaneous deliverance after justification, if there be none but a gradual work of God then we must be content, as well as we can, to remain full of sin till death."[586] He also wrote in a letter, "Gradual sanctification may increase from the time you was justified; but full deliverance from sin, I believe is always instantaneous — at least, I never yet knew an exception."[587] Wesley made a similar observation in his sermon "On Patience," but conceded "the Scriptures are silent upon the subject; because the point is not determined — at least, not in express terms — in any part of the oracles of God."[588]

Yet Wesley recognizes that "from the time of our being 'born again,' the gradual work of sanctification takes place."[589] He said that "generally speaking, it is a long time, even many years, before sin is destroyed." But he argued that God might cut short his usual work in a moment. Therefore, he concluded that he could speak of sanctification as both gradual and instantaneous "without any manner of contradiction."[590] The instantaneous aspect is a logical implication of the reality that entire sanctification is a gift of God's grace. Thus Wesley

---

[584]McClintock and Strong, *Cyclopedia*, 10:936.

[585]For example, Pope explained that there is a "gradual and sure depression of the sinful principle down to its zero or limit of nonentity" [Pope, *Compendium*, 3:38]. Miner Raymond described entire sanctification as "a point that is in Scripture designated as a point of maturity" [Raymond, *Systematic Theology*, 2:374]. Stephen Merrill stated that maturity, and not purity, was perfection [*Doctrinal Aspects*, 234-235]. David Cubie wrote that for Wesley and Fletcher "original or indwelling sin is not a single-nondivisible entity which is wholly present in one moment and then removed in a single, radical faith-grace event. Instead, it is removed gradually, the Comforter 'expelling according to the degree of our faith'" ["Perfection in Wesley and Fletcher,"25]. See also Sangster, *Pure in Heart*, 227-228.

[586]Wesley, Sermon #14, 1.20.

[587]Wesley, *Letter* to Sarah Rutter, 5 December1789.

[588]Wesley, Sermon #83, 2.11-12.

[589]Wesley, "The Scripture Way of Salvation," Sermon #43, 1.8.

[590]Wesley, *Works*, 11:423.

preached we should expect it every moment.[591] If it is ever received at all, it is received by a simple act of faith.[592]

Wesley taught that Christian perfection is not absolute, but a dynamic that can constantly be improved and can always be forfeited. Wesley was impressed with the phrase from Fénelon — *moi progressus ad infinitum* — "my progress is without end."[593] Wesley wrote, "You do well strongly to insist that those who do already enjoy [Christian perfection] cannot possibly stand still. Unless they continue to watch and pray and aspire after higher degrees of holiness, I cannot conceive not only how they can go forward but how they can keep what they have already received."[594] Jabez Bunting preached

> And if the divine fire, thus kindles in the heart of the pardoned believer, be not chilled by relapses into sin or omissions of duty — if his faith continue to work by love, and to overcome the world — if he persists to follow Christ in the path of self-denial and mortification, constantly exercising himself unto godliness, waiting on God in the use of all instituted means of grace, and wrestling for larger measures of the Spirit and its fruits, according to his faith it shall be done unto him. Every enemy shall be vanquished, every thought shall be brought into captivity to grace; and he shall comprehend, with all saints, what is the height and depth of the love of Christ and be filled with the fullness of God. The good seed shall produce not only the blade, but the ear; yea and after that the full corn in the ear. And still shall the believer grow up into Christ his living Head in all things, by doing and suffering His will; till, when the fruit is fully ripe, angels shall put in the sickle and gather the harvest.[595]

---

[591]Wesley, *Works*, 11:393; Wesley, "On Patience," Sermon #83, § 13.

[592]Bangs, *Necessity, Nature, and Fruits*,163.

[593]Tuttle, "John Wesley,"1164; Tuttle, *Mysticism in the Wesleyan Tradition*, 156.

[594]Wesley, *Letter* to Mrs. Pawson, 16 Nov 1789. See also *Letter* to Francis Wolfe, 22 Nov 1772, "strongly exhort the believers everywhere to 'go on to perfection'; otherwise they cannot keep what they have." Nathan Bangs wrote, "We must be either gaining or losing; either going forward or backward" [*Necessity, Nature, and Fruits*, 185].

[595]Bunting, "The Sanctifier and the Sanctified," Sermon #34, *Bunting's Sermons*, 2:117-126. Richard S. Taylor is concerned that Bunting does not emphasize this entire sanctification as received at a distinct point in time [Taylor, *Leading*

Wesley learned that the only way to keep Methodists alive is to keep them moving.[596] He preached, "You cannot stand still; you must either rise or fall — rise higher or fall lower. Therefore the voice of God to the children of Israel, to the children of God, is 'Go forward.'"[597] Turner said, "No feature of doctrine gave Wesley more difficulty than this one. His answer was that it was both a process and a crisis. Most of the time he dwells on the gradual work, probably as a carry-over from the tradition in which he grew up and partly to counteract the position of those extremists who said sanctification was complete at regeneration." Turner thought that toward the end of his life Wesley placed greater stress on the instantaneous aspect, but concluded that Wesley taught sanctification is gradual but is often consummated in a moment.[598] White observed that after 1771 Wesley spoke increasingly about instantaneous sanctification in his letters, yet he conceded the Scripture never settles the issue. The later letters do not repudiate his earlier statements about the gradual process. Therefore, White concluded that Wesley did not change his mind but felt the Methodists were in danger of upsetting the balance between the gradual and instantaneous by forgetting the instantaneous, so he continually emphasized that side of the balance in his letters.[599]

Based on the teachings of B. T. Roberts, Leslie Marston taught that entire sanctification was a crisis experience and that Christian perfection was a life process. Entire sanctification is an event which is part of the continuing process of Christian perfection. Roberts believed that the biblical command to be perfect applied to every phase and stage of Christian life.[600] This seems to be the definition by which Paul Bassett operated.[601] Yet properly understood, entire sanctification is not a static, once-for-all state of grace. And contrary to Roberts, Wesley applied the term Christian perfection only to mature Christians. According to Thomas Ralston, "perfected holiness, entire sanctification, and perfect love, are synonymous terms, all implying the same as Christian

---

Wesleyan Thinkers, 57].

596Tuttle, "John Wesley,"1164. Whedon declared "as the doctrine of apostasy constitutes a real warning against backsliding and sin, so the doctrine of Christian perfection is a living incitement to progressive holiness"[Whedon, *Essays*, 144].

597Wesley, "On Faith," Sermon #106, 2.5.

598Turner, *Vision Which Transforms*, 259; 255.

599White, *Beauty of Holiness*, 286.

600Marston, "The Crisis-Process Issue," 3-15.

601Bassett, *Historical Development*, 19-20.

perfection."[602] George Peck said that entire sanctification and Christian perfection were identical.[603] According to Turner, "be ye therefore perfect" was a paraphrase of "Be ye therefore holy."[604] Oscar Cullman said that τελειόω (*teleioo* - "to make perfect") is "almost a synonym for *hagiadzo* (to sanctify)."[605]

The emphasis on crisis is based on a misinterpretation of the Greek aorist tense and the use of logic. The Greek aorist tense is used to overemphasize crisis. In *Mile-Stone Papers* Daniel Steele wrote a famous chapter, "The Tense Readings of the Greek New Testament."[606] Steele argued that when the work of purification is described in the New Testament, both in the new birth and in entire sanctification, the aorist tense is almost always used. While that is true, the problem is that the aorist tense does not always denote instantaneous action. It represents past action, but not specifically continuous nor necessarily punctiliar action. It can be used to describe a process that took a period of time to complete, but that process is described from a "bird's eye view." For example, in John 2:20 the aorist tense is used to describe the construction of Herod's temple. It took forty-six years to complete, but the aorist tense is used simply to view the project as a unit or as a whole, not to discuss the process or the length of time involved. Therefore, the aorist tense cannot be used in and of itself to prove that entire sanctification is a crisis. While that interpretation is possible, it becomes probable only when the context supports it.[607]

Randy Maddox argued that Steele's understanding of the aorist tense was inadequate. The aorist tense does not necessarily imply crisis fulfillment; only the

---

[602]Ralston, *Elements of Divinity*, 461.

[603]Peck, *Christian Perfection*, 65.

[604]Turner, *Vision Which Transforms*,155.

[605]Cullmann, *Christology of the New Testament*, 100.

[606]Steele, *Mile-Stone Papers*, 44-72.

[607]Blackwelder, *Light from the Greek New Testament*, 61. See Lyon, "The Baptism of the Spirit — Continued,"70-74. See also Robert Shank's discussion of the aorist tense. The aorist presents the mere fact of an action without reference to the progress of the action. Aorists may represent actions requiring extended periods of time [Shank, *Life in the Son*, 77-78]. Prescott Johnson conceded that neither Wesley, Watson, nor Pope appealed to the Greek tense in support of their position regarding sanctification [Johnson, "Crisis and Con-Sequence,"175].

A stronger argument for a crisis might be argued from the perfect tense, which indicates completed action with abiding results. It is found in Heb 12:23; 1 John 2:5; 4:12, 17, 18. It is also found in Heb 10:14 and yet the same verse goes on to describe sanctification as an ongoing process!

context can determine that.[608] Samuel Powell wrote that generations of holiness scholars had appealed to the aorist tense to support their understanding that sanctification was an instantaneous event. "Today, it seems odd that anyone could ever have placed so much doctrinal weight on what turned out to be an utterly mistaken understanding of the Greek language. Yet a review of Holiness literature in the 1960s and 1970s shows that this understanding died a hard but inevitable death as a new generation of scholars arose with better linguistic tools and fewer aberrant presuppositions."[609]

While there are passages which describe sanctification in terms of the end result, there are also passages which describe sanctification by using the present tense. It is purging (John 15:2), "be filled" (Eph 5:18), "bearing fruit and growing in the full knowledge of God" (Col 1:10), and "the blood cleanses us from all sin" (1 John 1:7).[610]

The emphasize on crisis is also based on logic. In Galatians 5:24, "Those who belong to Christ Jesus have crucified their sinful nature with its passions and desires." Wesley's comment here is that all true believers have nailed their fleshly nature to a cross, where it continually grows weaker and weaker.[611] Pope described the crucifixion referenced in Romans 6:6 and Galatians 5:24 as a "gradual mortal process."[612] While Jesus was crucified at nine o'clock in the morning, he did not die until three o'clock that afternoon.

In his sermon "Crucifixion with Christ," Pope stated that Galatians 2:19-20 describes a sinner appropriating the sacrifice of the Great Substitute and is set

---

[608]Maddox, "Use of the Aorist,"106-118.

[609]Powell, "The Theological Significance,"134. See also Charles N. Dillmann, "It seems to me to be time for us either to come to grips with the masters of Greek grammar and correct them, or stop making assertions about grammar — and in particular about the aorist tense — which are out of tine with the masters" ["Book Reviews," 102].

[610]Steele explained the present tense verb in 1 John 1:7 as describing a collective cleansing in which one person after another in the human family is instantaneously cleansed, not a progressive cleansing of one individual [Steele, *Half-Hours with John*,12]. While John consistently writes in the first person plural, which Steele terms the "editorial 'we,'" he means any one [p. 17]. Thus, by Steele's own explanation, John is not speaking collectively.

[611]Wesley, *Notes*, 485. According to Donald Campbell this crucifixion refers to the fact that by means of the baptism of the Holy Spirit Christians were identified with Christ in his death and resurrection [Campbell, "Galatians,"609]. This is the experience of all believers (Rom 6:1-6; Col 2:11; 3:9), yet regeneration is the beginning, and not the end, of the process.

[612]Pope, *Compendium*, 3:37.

free from condemnation through personal union with the Redeemer's death. In Galatians 5:24 the flesh or the old man remaining in the pardoned believer is delivered unto death in the same mystical fellowship. The first act of their regenerate life was to deliberately renounce the old Adam which regeneration did not kill. Every Christian must have his own Calvary. He must crucify there and keep crucified until crucifixion ends in death all that belongs to his flesh with its affections and lusts. Crucifixion is not death, but it is unto death. It is the business of the Christian man to use every sacred effort to hasten that death. Though we have crucified our flesh, and keep it bound to the cross, it is not the rigor of our ascetic severity that destroys our sin. It is the breath of the Holy Ghost which withers the fruits of evil in our nature. Though it is said most explicitly that we crucify the flesh, it is not said that we put it to death and destroy the "body of sin." That is the sole work of the Divine Spirit. We must not doubt that he will finish the work he has begun in us, which is the case described in Galatians 6:14. Here the crucifixion is perfect and entire. Pope advocated this theme must be preached as a balance between the inward power of the Spirit and the personal disciplines of mortification and self denial.[613]

Wesley wrote that inward sanctification begins in the moment a man is justified. "From that time a believer gradually dies to sin, and grows in grace."[614] Wesley added,

> A man may be dying for some time; yet he does not properly speaking, die, till the instant the soul is separated from the body; and in that instant he lives the life of eternity. In like manner, he may be dying to sin for some time; yet he is not dead to sin, till sin is separated from his soul, and in that instant he lives the full life of love.[615]

In answer to the question, "Is the change gradual or instantaneous?" Wesley answered:

> It is both one and the other. From the moment we are justified, there may be a gradual sanctification, a growing in grace, a daily advance in the knowledge and love of God. And if sin cease before death, there must, in the nature of the thing, be an instantaneous change; there must be a last moment wherein it

---

[613]Pope, *Sermons*, 292-313.

[614]Wesley, *Works*, 11:387.

[615]Wesley, *Works*, 11:402.

does exist, and a first moment wherein it does not.[616]

Therefore, Wesley sees logically there must be a moment when the work is complete. If we can be sanctified wholly in this life, as the Bible teaches, then this crisis moment is a logical necessity. But he also taught that some could not perceive the instant when they were perfected in love or when sin ceased to be.[617] Pope wrote, "There is a consummation of the Christian experience which may be said to introduce perfection, when the Spirit cries, 'It is finished,' in the believer. The moment when sin expires, known only to God, is the Divine victory over sin in the soul: this is the office of the Spirit alone."[618] George Peck declared, "We make no question as to the gradual growth of a Christian, either before or after his entire sanctification, but acknowledge and maintain the fact in relation to both periods. But the question we raise is, whether the body of sin in the Christian must necessarily *live*, and, if it is not 'rampant and furious,' at least be asleep, 'calm and still,' as long as he lives." Peck pointed out that the process of mortification, with reference to the human body, is not slow and long, continuing for years.[619]

For early Methodism sanctification was both a process and a crisis. The important issue was living the holy life, not a certain experience. The end is Christian maturity and complete holiness, the means to the end cannot be substituted for that end. For Wesley Christian perfection was the goal, not the beginning of Christian life.[620] In *A Plain Account of Christian Perfection* he said some believers have had an instantaneous change, but that others could not perceive the instant when they were perfected in love.[621] He declared that the scriptures were silent concerning whether entire sanctification was gradual or instantaneous.[622] He wrote in the preface to the journal of Elizabeth Harper, which he published in 1769, "concerning the circumstances we need not dispute, whether it be wrought gradually or instantaneously. Only let the change be wrought. Only let our souls be renewed in the whole Image of God."[623] Thomas

---

616Wesley, *Works*, 8:329.

617Wesley, "The Scripture Way of Salvation," Sermon #43, 3.18.

618Pope, *Compendium*, 3:43.

619Peck, *Christian Perfection*, 205-206.

620Cubie, "Perfection in Wesley and Fletcher," 22.

621Wesley, *Works*, 11:423; 442.

622Wesley, "On Patience," Sermon #83, ¶ 11.

623Wesley, *Works*, 14:263.

Ralston said,

> It matters but little whether this eminent state of holiness be gained by a bold, energetic, and determined exercise of faith and prayer, or by a more gradual process—whether it be instantaneous or gradual, or both the one and the other. The great matter is, with each and all of us, that we lose no time, but arise at once and "press toward the mark for the prize of the high calling of God in Christ Jesus."[624]

Elijah Hedding explained that the work of sanctification goes on gradually until it is finished and that event is instantaneous. However, "in some, the fact of its being finished in an instant is more apparent to the subject than it is in others."[625] R. S. Foster said in *Christian Purity* that regeneration and entire sanctification are not identical, but he did not hold that in all cases entire sanctification

> is so separate and marked as a distinct work that it must necessarily be known at precisely what moment it transpired. It may be reached by such gradual and imperceptible stages as to make it impossible to tell when the river widens to the sea—when the unfolding bud opens to the consummate flower—yet whenever reached, it is a line passed, which differentiates what follows from what preceded in kind and degree, as the mature differs from the immature.[626]

John Miley reacted to the "second-blessing view" by cautioning against a single mode. He observed that while the scriptures were full of the idea of entire sanctification, "they were quite empty of any such teaching respecting the mode of its attainment." He pleaded for tolerance noting that Wesley taught both a gradual and instantaneous work. He concluded, "Let those who hold rigidly the second-blessing view preach sanctification in their own way, but let them be

---

[624]Ralston, *Elements of Divinity*, 470. However, Richard S. Taylor reacted from a rigid holiness paradigm, "It really matters a lot!" [*Leading Wesleyan Thinkers*, 89]. However, Wesley had written Lady Maxwell, "Be this given in an instant or by degrees, hold it fast" [*Letter*, 5 July 1765].

[625]Quoted by Peck, *Christian Perfection*, 62-63.

[626]Foster, *Christian Purity*, 56-57. See the analysis of Langford, *Practical Divinity*, 95.

tolerant of such as preach it in a manner somewhat different."[627] Miner Raymond did not feel that an instantaneous work of grace was the only method by which entire sanctification was accomplished.[628] Thomas O. Summers wrote that indwelling sin in the heart of the regenerate is entirely destroyed "by gradual mortification, or by an instant and powerful exercise of faith."[629]

Some of the most holy men never testified to a definite crisis experience, including John Wesley, Richard Watson, and Francis Asbury. Wesley himself never testified directly to entire sanctification.[630] Wesley was once asked in 1777 at a love-feast in Macclesfield for his testimony to entire sanctification and he replied, "By the grace of God I am what I am."[631] When asked once regarding his own experience concerning sanctification Wesley responded by quoting a hymn by his brother based on Leviticus 6:13,

O thou who camest from above
The pure celestial fire t'impart,
Kindle a flame of sacred love
On the mean altar of my heart!

There let it for thy glory burn
With inextinguishable blaze,
And trembling to its source return
In humble love, and fervent praise.

Jesu, confirm my heart's desire
to work, and speak, and think for thee;
Still let me guard the holy fire,

---

[627]Miley, *Systematic Theology*, 2:370-371. John Tigert endorsed this view by Miley in "Purity and Peace," 317-318. According to Diane Leclerc, "John Miley represents the steps in Methodism's de-emphasis of entire sanctification" [*Discovering Christian Holiness*, 115].

[628]Raymond, *Systematic Theology*, 2:394. Yet Leslie Wilcox expressed concern over this concession and that Raymond used the word "maturity" to describe entire sanctification [*Profiles in Wesleyan Theology*, 2:264-265].

[629]Summers, *Treatise on Sanctification*, 117.

[630]See Tyerman, *Life and Times of John Wesley*, 1:462-463; 2:598; Wilcox, *Be Ye Holy*, 269-278. Wilcox gives a bibliography for four positions on this question. Additionally, see McPheeters, "Snowfields Christmas Eve 1744," 5. See also see Peters, *Christian Perfection*, 201-215; Maddox, *Responsible Grace*, 344, #218; Lindström, *Wesley and Sanctification*, 135-136.

[631]Strachan, *Recollections*; Wesley was quoting 1 Cor 15:10.

And still stir up thy gift in me;

Ready for all thy perfect will,
My acts of faith and love repeat,
Till death thy endless mercies seal,
And make the sacrifice complete.[632]

Chris Bounds pointed to a letter John Wesley wrote to Dr. Conyers Middleton on January 4, 1739. After describing the Christian life in ways that can only be understood as Christian perfection, Wesley stated, "So Christianity tells me; and so I find it, may every real Christian say. I am now assured that these things are so: I experience them in my own breast. What Christianity promised (considered as doctrine) is accomplished in my soul. And Christianity, considered as an inward principle, is the completion of all those promises. It is holiness and happiness, the image of God impressed on a created spirit, a fountain of peace and love springing up into everlasting life." This testimony appears to be further substantiated by Wesley's letter to Thomas Maxfield on November 2, 1762 in which he says, "But I dislike your supposing man may be perfect as an angel; that he can be absolutely perfect; that he can be infallible, or above being tempted; or that the moment he is pure in heart he cannot fall from it. I dislike the saying, "This was not known or taught among us till within two or three years." I grant you did not know it. You have over and over denied instantaneous sanctification; but I have known and taught it (and so has my brother, as our writings show) above these twenty years."

Still, these testimonies are not conclusive. If Wesley had experienced entire sanctification, why are there not more direct statements by Wesley regarding his experience? In response, we must keep in mind the culture in which Wesley lived. English Christians of his age were reluctant to talk about their personal spiritual lives and Wesley was especially careful not to widely publish his personal crisis experiences because of the fear of abuse or ridicule. Even Wesley's Aldersgate experience receives little attention in his published works. The only access we have to Wesley is his published thoughts which were intended for a general audience. We do not know what he may have shared in conversation with his intimate friends. He may have felt too much emphasis on his own experience might cause others to copy it. We also know that the influential mystics in Wesley's life cautioned their adherents to not talk about their personal

---

[632]Arthur, *Proceedings*, 46-47; Tillett, *Personal Salvation*, 414-415]. Samuel Bradburn reported that Wesley told him, that his experience might almost any time be found in the first two stanzas of this hymn [*Sketch of Mr. Wesley's Character* (1791). When asked to testify about his own state of sanctification in a class meeting, the aged Wesley would quote the last two stanzas [Mouzon, *Fundamentals of Methodism*, 68].

experiences because of the threat of pride. In 1780 Wesley wrote,

> I speak of myself very little to any one, were it only for fear of hurting *them.* I have found exceeding few that could bear it; so I am constrained to repress my natural openness. I find scarce any temptation from any *thing* in the world; my danger is from *persons.*[633]

However, the fact that Wesley must have had some measure of Christian perfection can be seen in the lack of personal challenges to him on the subject. Also, as we read his writings, he appears to know personally, experientially what he wrote about and it is difficult to read him without feeling that he in some measure experienced this holiness of heart and life which drove his life.[634]

Thomas Jackson noted that Watson, like Wesley "did not himself profess to have attained it; but during the subsequent part of his life he exhibited its fruits in fully maturity and beauty."[635] At the end of his three-volume biography of Wesley, Luke Tyerman concluded that while he was not faultless, his "physique, his genius, his wit, his penetration, his judgment, his memory, his beneficence, his religion, his diligence, his conversation, his courteousness, his manners, and his dress — made him as perfect as we ever expect man to be on this side of heaven."[636]

In Wesley's *Plain Account of Christian Perfection* the question is raised, "Can you show one such example now? Where is he that is thus perfect?" Wesley answered, "To some that make this inquiry one might answer, If I knew one here, I would not tell you; for you do not inquire out of love. You are like Herod; you only seek the young child to slay it. But more directly we answer: There are many reasons why there should be few, if any, indisputable examples. What inconveniences would this bring on the person himself, set as a mark for all to shoot at! And how unprofitable would it be to gainsayers! 'For if they hear not Moses and the Prophets,' Christ and his Apostles, 'neither would they be persuaded though one rose from the dead.'"[637]

But Phoebe Palmer insisted that the second blessing must be testified to

---

[633]Wesley, *Letter* to Sarah Crosby, 11 May 1780. See also Collins, *Real Christian*,154.

[634]Online: Bounds, "Wesley's Doctrine of Salvation."

[635]Jackson, *Memoirs*, 405; 424]. Concerning Asbury, see Salter, *America's Bishop*, 158; Peters, *Christian Perfection*, 217-219.

[636]Tyerman, *Life and Times of John Wesley*, 3:660.

[637]Wesley, *Works*, 11:391.

definitely and publically in order to retain this state of grace. People were often pressured into testifying to something they did not understand. On the other hand, Wesley advised, "Be particularly careful in speaking of yourself. You may not, indeed, deny the work of God; but speak of it when you are called thereto, in the most inoffensive manner possible. Avoid all magnificent, pompous words; indeed, you need give it no general name; neither perfection, sanctification, the second blessing, nor the having attained. Rather speak of the particulars which God has wrought for you. You may say, 'At such a time, I felt a change which I am not able to express; and since that time, I have not felt pride or self-will, or anger, or unbelief; not any thing but a fulness of love to God and to all mankind.'"[638] Notice, the emphasis was not on professing a certain experience, but the improvement in holy living.

How holy can we become? We can love God with all our heart, and soul, and strength, and mind and love our neighbor as ourselves (Luke 10:27). Adam Clarke explained that "a man may be said to be perfect who answers the end for which God made him; and as God requires every man to love him with all his heart, soul, mind, and strength, and his neighbor as himself; then he is a perfect man that does so; he answers the end for which God made him."[639] When Clarke refers to the end he is speaking of the Creator's purpose and is incorporating the meaning of the Greek word τέλος (*telos*), which means end, goal, completion, maturity, or the fulfilling of the law (Rom 2:27). Richard Hooker wrote, "We count those things perfect which want nothing requisite for the end whereunto they were instituted."[640] According to Richard Trench, "The τέλειος is one who has attained his moral *end*, that for which he was intended, namely, to be a man [or adult] in Christ."[641] Nathan Bangs declared, "Any is perfect which answers the end for which it is made."[642]

Ironically, R. J. Rushdoony labeled Wesley's concept of perfection as

---

[638]Wesley, *Works*, 11:434-435.

[639]Clarke, *Christian Theology*,183.

[640]Hooker, *Works*, 1:234. Quoted by Treffry, *Treatise on Christian Perfection*,10; Peck, *Christian Perfection*, 25. In context, Hooker was arguing for the sufficiency of Scripture in matters of church polity.

[641]Trench, *Synonyms*, 77.

[642]Bangs, *Necessity, Nature, and Fruits*, 41. While Plato had concluded that only God was perfect, Aristotle defined perfection as that which accomplishes the purpose for which it was created. This argument by Bangs reflects the philosophy of Aristotle. But for Wesley these virtues are not produced by internal motivation, they are produced in response to an external grace.

dualism.[643] Writing as a Calvinist, he never realized that he had articulated the Wesleyan doctrine of Christian perfection when he explained, "The law does not command us to do what man cannot do. . . . The Old Testament words translated as 'perfect' means upright, having integrity, blameless, and the New Testament words have the meaning of mature, complete. . . . Perfection means uprightness and maturity in terms of a goal or purpose, and end established by God. . . . . In this life, we can be perfect in the sense of being blameless in our faithfulness to God's purpose, but to be blameless does not mean being faultless. . . . God alone is holy; we are holy to the degree that we separate and dedicate ourselves to Him and to His Kingdom. . . . Our goal thus is to do the will of our Father, to serve Him with all our heart, mind, and being, to love God and our neighbor."[644]

1 John 2:12-14 does imply a maturity in the faith. We are all God's children and will always be dependant upon our heavenly Father. The aged John calls us children nine times in this short letter. However, in vv 12-14 he divides the children of God into three categories:

- children — τεκνιον - v 12; παιδιον - v 13 used of an infant just born and by John of the youngest believers in the family of God
- young men — νεανισκος - vv 13-14
- fathers — πατηρ - vv 13-14

John's emphasis is on spiritual development. *Little children* have the forgiveness of sins. It is on the basis that we have been forgiven that we can be adopted into the family of God. According to 1 John 2:13 those who have been born again know the Father. We know God as our Father by the Spirit witnessing with our spirit that we are the children of God. And yet Wesley adds a very insightful comment about new Christians. He says they have not yet overcome.[645]

Young men have a strong faith through which they have won some battles and overcome the evil one. The new believer is not defeated, but he or she has not yet learned spiritual warfare. How do we get strong enough to resist Satan? Our

---

643Rushdoony, *Law and Society*, 482-484.

644Rushdoony, *Institutes of Biblical Law*, 628-629. See also Rushdoony, *Law and Society*, 620. The last two sentences are taken from Rushdoony, "Holiness Versus Perfectionism," reprinted in Rushdoony, *Roots of Reconstruction*, 275-279. See also "Perfection versus Maturity," reprinted in *Roots of Reconstruction*, 1040-1042. Here Rushdoony insisted the biblical word *teleios* means fully grown or mature, not sinless. On the other hand the world of Eden was sinless, but it was not perfect in the sense of being fully developed.

645Wesley, *Notes*, 632.

strength comes from having the Word of God in us. Literally the Word of God remains in us. The Word lives in us and governs our conduct. According to 1 John 2:5 we must *obey* the Word. George Findlay wrote, "Obedience is the school of love's perfecting. For love's sake we obey rule, and by obeying learn to love better. Love reaches no height of perfectness in any family without commands to keep and tasks to do; where all is ease and indulgence, selfishness grows rank." Findlay connected this verse with James 2:22 which speaks of perfecting faith by works.[646] Notice also that Jesus himself was made perfect through suffering (Heb 2:10). While salvation from beginning to end is by faith, that faith is tested through suffering and confirmed by good works.

According to 1 John 2:7-11 the commandment has not changed. We are to love God with our whole heart and our neighbor as ourselves. At one point it was said of the children of Israel that they did not wholly follow God, except for Caleb and Joshua (Numb 32:11; see also 2 Kings 10:31; 2 Chron 25:2).

And yet verse 8 says there is a new emphasis. We are to love one another. Jesus said that he was giving us a new commandment, that we love one another (John 13:34). What does John mean that this matter of loving one another is both old and new? It is an old commandment, but we have new grace to keep it through the indwelling Spirit. Notice that the growing Christian is also fighting some battles and learning to win through faith.

According to 1 John 5:4 everyone born of God has overcome the world potentially. But we have to learn to stand in that victory. The victory that overcomes the world is our faith. And that victory does not come automatically; we have to exercise it and stand our ground. God must help us resist temptation and break sinful habits.

We will discover that while we are fighting and winning, we have a battle on three fronts: the world, the flesh, and the devil. According to 1 John 2:15-17 we do not love the world system. Anyone who loves the world system does not have the love of God.

And we have victory over the devil. According to 1 John 5:18 whoever is born of God does not continue to sin. Christ keeps us safe and the evil one cannot touch us.

But we also have an internal battle. We have a battle with our old self. This battle is described in Galatians 5:17. The sinful nature desires what is contrary to the Spirit and the Spirit what is contrary to the sinful nature. They are in conflict with each other. So long as we are led by the Spirit we do not give in to these sinful desires. Being strengthened by the Spirit we do not fulfil the desires of the flesh, as otherwise we would do.

Is it necessary for this struggle to continue as long as we live? Most theologians would answer "yes." Most theologians would not even concede that

---

[646]Findlay, *Studies in John's Epistles*, 158-159.

the new birth gives victory over sin. But according to the promise in 1 John 1:9, he not only will forgive; he can cleanse from all unrighteousness. *Fathers* have known God from the beginning point of the new birth and still know him. John indicates that we can reach a level of spiritual maturity. 1 John 2:13-14 both give the same description: "you have known him who is from the beginning." This indicates a deeper level of knowledge. Wesley explained, "Ye have known the eternal God, in a manner wherein no other, even true believers, know him."[647] They have a deep acquaintance with God; a full assurance of understanding and faith and hope.

According to Romans 5:5 when we are forgiven, at the stage of spiritual infancy, we receive God's love. But 1 John 2:5 promises that God's love can be perfected. The emphasis in on conformity to the law of God, not reluctantly but joyfully (1:4). Jean Baptiste Massillon said, "You cannot serve God with pleasure, only when you serve him without reservation. From the moment you make him entire master of your heart, hope, confidence, and joy will spring up in the depths of your soul."[648]

John will return to this subject of perfect love in chapter 4. There he refers to perfect love four times. In 4:12 the emphasis is on concern for others. Perfect love is to love our neighbor as ourselves. Hendrix observed that it is much easier to love God than it is to love our neighbor, for God is worthy of love and there is so much in man that is unlovely. Yet "no love is perfect toward God that is not perfect toward men."[649]

If his love is made complete in us or if we have grown to maturity, 1 John 4:17 promises that we will have confidence. Again the emphasis is on a full assurance or confidence. According to 1 John 4:18 this perfect love drives out fear. It displaces everything that is not consistent with the love of God. When that is happening, there is no longer a struggle with the fleshly desires. Notice that the emphasis on conformity, concern, and confidence covers the whole personality incorporating the volitional, the ethical, and the emotional.

George Findlay wrote that John's bold word must not be evaded nor softened. He enunciates a doctrine of perfect love, of full sanctification — a devotion to God that is complete as it covers man's whole nature and brings him to the realization os his proper end as a man, a love that reigns in the soul and suppresses every alien motive and desire.[650]

Wesley emphasized perfection as completeness, not faultlessness. Albert

---

[647]Wesley, *Notes*, 632.

[648]Quoted by J. A. Wood, *Perfect Love*, 130-131.

[649]Hendrix, *Perfecting of the Saints*, 18.

[650]Findlay, *Studies in John's Epistles*, 158-159.

Outler pointed out that the Latin word *perfectus* means unimprovable. The Latin understanding of perfection was static. But Wesley defined perfection with the understanding of the Greek word *teleios*, which meant completeness or fulfillment. The Greek understanding, which Wesley embraced, was a journey; a growth experience with new levels to be gained.[651] *Teleios* means wholeness, completeness, whole-heartedness, and total commitment without reservation.[652] *Teleios* implies a sense of continuing growth or progress toward completeness. Thus, continued growth is an aspect of perfection. It does not connote a static attainment, but rather an ongoing life of wholeness.[653] This perfection is said to be "complete" in the sense of our yieldedness toward God, our being filled with *agape* love, and that redemption has attained its goal. "The Greek word rendered *perfect* has *always a relative* significance, except when applied to God." Hebrews 9:11, in comparing the heavenly temple with its earthly counterpart, declared the heavenly temple to be *more* perfect. Thus the earthly temple was relatively perfect, but not absolutely.[654] Likewise, a Christian can only be relatively perfect.[655]

Richard C. Trench explained

> It will be seen that there is a certain ambiguity in our word 'perfect,' which, indeed, it shares with τέλειος itself; this, namely, that they are both employed now in a relative, now in an absolute sense; for only so could our Lord have said, "Be ye therefore *perfect* (τέλειοι), and your Heavenly Father is *perfect*" (τέλειος), Matt. 5:48; cf. 19:21. The Christian shall be 'perfect,' yet not in the sense in which some of the sects preach the doctrine of perfection, who, as soon as their words are looked into, are found either to mean nothing which they could not have expressed by a word less liable to misunderstanding; or to mean something which no man in this life shall attain, and which he who affirms he has attained is deceiving himself, or others, or both. The faithful man shall be 'perfect,' that is, aiming by the grace of God to be fully furnished and firmly established in the knowledge and practice of the things of God (James 3:2; Col 4:12; τέλειος καί πεπληροφορημένος); not

---

651Outler, *John Wesley,* 30-33; see also Wesley, *BE Works*, 1:74; 76.

652Guelich, *Sermon on the Mount*, 234-237.

653Delling, τέλειος, *TDNT*, 8:77.

654Gregory, *Perfect in Christ Jesus*, 33-34.

655Hunt, *Letters on Sanctification*, 163.

a babe in Christ to the end, 'not always employed in the elements, and infant propositions and practices of religion, but doing noble actions, well skilled in the deepest mysteries of faith and holiness.'[656]

Outler concluded that mainstream Methodism had thrown out the baby of true holiness with the "second blessing" bath water. The shift was from a notion of perfecting perfection over to a claim of perfected perfection.[657]

Wesley wrote, "Here are persons exceedingly holy and happy; rejoicing evermore, praying always, and in everything giving thanks; feeling the love of God and man every moment; feeling no price or other evil temper. If these are not perfect, that scriptural word has no meaning. Stop! you must not cavil at that word: you are not wiser than the Holy Ghost."[658]

But that holiness is a moment-by-moment condition which is maintained by a moment-by-moment obedient faith. This is to be our lifelong pursuit. We never cease seeking for more. "None feel their need of Christ"[659] like those who have experienced the greatest deliverance from sin. Holiness and perfection are related terms — we are unholy but the perfecting grace of God makes us holy. We should always be seeking more love, more grace, more holiness. Lindström explained,

> The distinction between the new birth and entire sanctification seems therefore to be nothing more than a difference in degree in a continuous development. But if so, how can they also be described as distinct stages in the Christian life? If we consider the definition of perfection as perfect love, it is clear that this love must be of the same kind as that granted to man at new birth. In this respect indeed Wesley could not indicate any difference. Entire sanctification is not a new kind of sanctity in relation to the earlier experience of the believer.

---

[656]Trench, *Synonyms*, 76. According to Trench, he drew from a discussion by Jeremy Taylor. Taylor also influenced the theology of John Wesley. The Greek phrase is lifted from Colossians 4:12, "perfect/complete/mature and fully assured." Trench (1807-1886) was an archbishop in the Church of England.

[657]Outler, *Theology in the Wesleyan Spirit*, 77-80.

[658]Wesley, *Letter* to Samuel Furly, 15 September 1762. According to Outler, Wesley connected the words "happy" and "holy" fifty-four times [*Theology in the Wesleyan Spirit*, 83-84]. Outler also observed there was much joy in Wesley [p. 86] and that Wesley died happy [p. 87].

[659]Wesley, *Works*, 11:395.

Lindström concluded that Christian perfection is not a new kind of holiness or a new kind of life. Instead it is a greater degree of love. "Entire sanctification involves a love incompatible with sin. It is a love unmixed with sin, a pure love."[660] Holiness is present in all Christians, but in varying degrees. Wesley explained, "The difference between one and the other properly lies in the degree of love."[661]

"In what sense, then, may *love* be said to be *perfect*? Simply in this, that it is now the *reigning* and *ruling* principle of the soul, and 'casteth out' every opposing principle."[662]

> Perfect love is the pure love of God so filling the heart as to exclude therefrom all unholy tempers, evil desires, wicked dispositions, and sinful tendencies. Love fills the heart, while all that is opposed to love and which is out of harmony with God is excluded. . . . It means sincerity, a single eye, pure motives, without the semblance of impurity, insincerity, or mixed motives. It is called "perfect love" simply because Divine love perfectly fills the soul. Everything of the nature of hatred, envy, pride, foolishness, covetousness, jealousy, and evil speakings is ruled out. Love cast out these things. . . . Just as a vessel filled allows no room for anything else in it, so the heart filled with pure love permits nothing to remain therein evil in nature or out of harmony with the God of love. Here is Christian Perfection, the only kind taught in God's Word . . . It is *perfection in love* — nothing more, nothing less. . . . Perfect love means that state of heart where the two great commandments laid down by our Lord are fully obeyed: "Thou shalt love the Lord thy God with all they heart," and "Thou shalt love thy neighbor as thyself." . . . Perfect love implies that love is the ruling passion of the believer, the spring of all his energies, and the controlling motive to duty. . . . Perfect love implies complete deliverance from all "fear which hath torment."[663]

---

[660]Lindström, *Wesley and Sanctification*, 141-142.

[661]Wesley, "On Patience," Sermon #83, § 10.

[662]Elmore Yocum (1806-1898), "Perfect Love," Sermon #7 in Thomson, *Sermons*, 135. Maddox observed the distinction between love present and love ruling. God's love is shed abroad in the lives of all Christians, but in the lives of the entirely sanctified there is no mixture of any contrary affections [*Responsible Grace*, 187; Maddox cites Wesley, "On Patience," § 10].

[663]Cary, *Holiness Sermons*, 76-81.

Benson wrote that to sanctify you wholly was to "carry on and complete the work of purification and renovation begun in your regeneration, redeeming you *from all iniquity*; cleansing you *from all filthiness of flesh and spirit*; stamping you with his whole image, and rendering you *a glorious church, not having spot or wrinkle, or any such thing*, but made holy toward God, dedicated to and employed in his service, and *without blame* in the whole of your conduct toward men."[664] Wesley himself explained

> By "perfection," I mean "perfect love," of the loving God with all our heart, so as to rejoice evermore, to pray without ceasing, and in everything to give thanks. I am convinced every believer may attain this; yet I do not say, he is in a state of damnation, or under the curse of God, till he does attain.[665]

Romans 6:6 teaches that the old life is crucified and also that the body of sin may be destroyed or abolished. This Greek word καταργέω (*katargeo*) means to put away, to render inoperative, inactive or powerless. It is also used in 1 Corinthians 13:11 where we are to put childish ways behind us. In *Putting Away Childish Things* David Seamands wrote that childish behavior patterns and attitudes keep us from maturity. Childish things don't simply fall away by themselves as dead leaves fall from a tree. We have to *katargeo* them.[666]

While Colossians 3:9 declares that we have put off the old man, Ephesians 4:22 commands us to put off the old man.[667] This refers to the process of mortification, which is addressed in Romans 8:13 and Colossians 3:5. Contrary to a passive approach to sanctification or to simply claim victory, mortification emphasizes human effort. We are called upon to abstain from fleshly lusts (1 Cor 6:18; 1 Peter 2:11). We are to make no provision for the flesh (Rom 13:14). Paul found it necessary to practice self denial (1 Cor 9:27). David Brown wrote, "If ye do not kill sin, it will kill you."[668] Yet self-inflicted pain may be an attempt at self atonement rather than faith in Christ. In occult teaching the endurance of pain or denial of appetites serves to increase spiritual powers. According to John Stott, biblical mortification is neither masochism nor

---

[664]Benson, *Notes*, 5:402.

[665]Wesley, *Works*, 12:227.

[666]Seamands, *Childish Things*, "Preface," also 10; 134.

[667]F. F. Bruce called this the tension between the indicative and the imperative; between the already and the not yet [*Colossians*, 357]. Pope made the same observation [*Compendium*, 1:425].

[668]Jamieson, Fausset, and Brown, *Commentary*, 3:240.

asceticism. Rather it is a clear recognition of evil which leads to a decisive and radical repudiation of it.[669] "We are forgiven because He died in our place. We are delivered because we have died with Him."[670]

Yet many who emphasize mortification most vigorously deny that the battle can ever be won. The paraphrase of J. B. Phillips at Romans 6:7 is misleading, "A dead man may safely be said to be immune to sin."[671] Freedom from the necessity of sin does not imply an immunity to sin. Douglas Crossman once said, "We can be dead to sin so long as we understand sin is not dead to us." Death is separation and to be dead to sin is separation from sin.

Entire sanctification is the condition of loving God with all our heart. It is not different from salvation, but it is more grace which enables us to become all that God wants us to be. Summers defined it as "the state of being entirely cleansed from sin, so as to love God with all our heart, and mind, and soul, and strength, and our neighbor as ourselves."[672] Pope wrote that entire sanctification "is the work of the Holy Spirit alone, applying the virtue of the atonement in the removal of the last trace of the indwelling or pollution of sin and consecrating the entire nature of the believer to God in perfected love."[673]

This love expels all sin, cleansing the heart from all unrighteousness. Benjamin Field defined Christian perfection as "a maturity of holy love, love which counteracts and expels all antagonistic influences, and molds the soul into the image of God; for 'God is love.'"[674]

Entire sanctification corresponds with the term *Christian perfection*, but neither term implies the end of growth or progress. *Perfection*, in its absolute sense, is an attribute of God alone. Yet Christ commands us to "be perfect" (Matt 5:48). A perfect Christian would not be as absolutely holy as God. He would not have the knowledge of angels. He would not have the innocence as Adam and Eve before the fall.[675] The highest perfection man can attain in this life does not exclude ignorance, error, and a thousand other infirmities.

---

[669]Stott, *Romans*, 228.

[670]Anderson and Miller, *Freedom From Fear*, 78.

[671]Phillips, *New Testament*. Assuming "dead" is used metaphorically, the revised edition of 1972 is an improvement: "for a dead man can safely be said to be free from the power of sin."

[672]Summers, *Way of Salvation*, 120.

[673]Pope, *Higher Catechism*, 256.

[674]Field, *Christian Theology*, 226.

[675]See Wesley's disclaimers in "On Perfection," Sermon #76.

> They are not perfect in knowledge. They are not free from ignorance, no, nor from mistake. We are no more to expect any living man to be infallible, than to be omniscient. They are not free from infirmities, such as weakness or slowness of understanding, irregular quickness or heaviness of imagination. Such in another kind are impropriety of language, ungracefulness of pronunciation; to which one might add a thousand nameless defects, either in conversation or behavior.[676]

Nor is this Christian perfection the same as *final sanctification,* attained in the resurrection when we are delivered from the very presence of sin. Paul makes this distinction in Philippians 3:12-15.[677] Final sanctification is also anticipated in 1 Corinthians 13:10.

While final sanctification is not a present possibility, entire sanctification is. In *A Plain Account of Christian Perfection* Wesley argued that God will save us from all sin because of his promises, his commands, scriptural examples, and scriptural prayers.[678]

Entire sanctification is promised. "And he will redeem Israel from all his iniquities" (Psalm 130:8). Wesley said this promise was expanded upon in Ezekiel 36:25, "I will sprinkle clean water on you, and you shall be clean from all your uncleanness, and from all your idols I will cleanse you." Wesley declared, "No promise can be more clear." Paul clearly is referring to this promise, "Since we have these promises, beloved, let us cleanse ourselves from every defilement of body and spirit, bringing holiness to completion in the fear of God" (2 Cor 7:1). In Deuteronomy 30:6 Moses promised, "And the Lord your God will circumcise your heart and the heart of your offspring, so that you will love the Lord your God with all your heart and with all your soul, that you may live."

"The reason the Son of God appeared was to destroy the works of the devil" (1 John 3:8). "Christ loved the church and gave himself up for her, that he might sanctify her, having cleansed her by the washing of water with the word, so that he might present the church to himself in splendor, without spot of wrinkle or any such thing, that she might be holy and without blemish" (Eph. 5:25-27). "By

---

[676]Wesley, *Works*, 11:374. Yet George Peck could write, "The complete sanctification of the intellect will correct all its *moral* aberrations. It will purify and regulate the thoughts, the conceptions, the imagination, the memory, and the judgment" [Peck, *Christian Perfection*, 37-38].

[677]Flew observed that because Warfield did not recognize Phil 3:12 as a reference to absolute perfection, he concluded that the whole course of the Christian life in this world must be marked by sin [Flew, *Idea of Perfection*, 52].

[678]Wesley, *Works*, 11:388-391.

sending his own Son in the likeness of sinful flesh and for sin, he condemned sin in the flesh, in order that the righteous requirement of the law might be fulfilled in us, who walk not according to the flesh but according to the Spirit" (Rom 8:3-4).[679] "He has given us his very great and previous promises, so that through them you may participate in the divine nature and escape the corruption in the world caused by evil desires" (2 Peter 1:4). According to Thomas Summers there is no question that 1 John 1:9 encompasses entire sanctification, as well as justification.[680] John McClintock declared, "If there be any text in the whole bible that declares the doctrine of Christian purity this does it."[681] Clarke declared that it is the birthright of every child of God to be cleansed from all sin.[682]

Entire sanctification is <u>commanded</u>. "Walk before me and be perfect" (Gen 17:1). "Serve Him with a perfect heart and a willing mind (1 Chron 28:9). "You therefore must be perfect, as your heavenly Father is perfect (Matt 5:48). The perfection or completeness commanded is explained in v 43 where Jesus said we are to love even our enemies. Thus the context prior to v 48 is dealing with perfect love and v 48 is a concluding statement which begins with the connecting

---

[679]The promises found in the Old Testament are translated in the future tense. The New Testament promises are in the subjunctive mood, expressing potential action which is contingent upon certain conditions. The verb in 2 Cor 7:1 is a hortatory subjunctive, which is an exhortation to action based upon the promises of God.

[680]Summers, *Treatise on Sanctification*, 47. Mudge denied that 1 John 1:7-9 describes anything beyond regeneration [*Growth in Holiness*, 107-109]. Granbery called this an unfortunate comment ["Dr. Mudge,"207].

Both *forgive* and *cleanse* in v 9 are aorist active subjunctives. The timing of these actions is relative to the main verb — *confess*. When we confess our sins, God is faithful to forgive us. When we receive a deeper revelation of our sinful nature and confess that, God is faithful to cleanse us from all iniquity.

Howard Marshall explained that most commentators regard the two terms, forgive and cleanse, as synonymous, but he said it is possible that purification signifies the removal not only of the guilt of sin but also of the power of sin. Marshall suggested that John may be thinking of the destruction of sinful desires which defile us in God's sight [Marshall, *Epistles of John*, 114]. Alford held that cleansing is distinguished from forgiveness as sanctification is distinct from justification and that the sanctification referenced is to sanctify wholly and entirely [cited by Steele, *Half-Hours with John*, 16].

The present tense cleaning, described in v 7, is the continuation of that initial sanctification and includes cleansing from the actual practice of sin and as we seek for a deeper cleansing, cleansing from the sinful nature. Wesley understood the cleansing of v 7 to include cleansing from both original and actual sin, which resulted in taking away all the guilt and all the power [*Notes*, 631].

[681]Crooks, *Life of John McClintock*, 161.

[682]Clarke, *Commentary*, 6:905.

word "therefore."

"You shall love the Lord your God with all your heart and with all your soul and with all your mind" (Matt 22:37; Mark 12:30). Paul commanded the Corinthian believers to "be perfect" (2 Cor 13:11). "You shall be holy, for I am holy" (1 Peter 1:16).[683]

A second class of texts could be categorized as exhortations: "I urge you to present your bodies a living sacrifice, holy, acceptable to God" (Rom 12:1). Under the old covenant worship involved offering sacrifices to God. There were burnt offerings, grain or meat offerings, peace offerings, guilt or sin offerings. Normally animals were put to death. This symbolized substitution as human guilt was transferred to the animal sacrifice. By the time of the temple in Jerusalem, so much blood was spilled into the drainage system that the brook Kidron, into which it dumped, ran red.

Then Christ came and became our sacrifice, doing away with animal sacrifices. The worship of the church in Rome with its breaking of the bread and sharing of the communion cup must have appeared strange to the Jews, because there were no animal sacrifices and to the Romans because there was no sacrifices offered to Caesar. But although God took the blood our of sacrifice, he did not take the sacrifice out of worship. Now he calls on us to present ourselves as *living* sacrifices. This is a paradox since the very word *sacrifice* implies to kill or slay.[684] But God wants us to live for him as a freed servant (see Exod 21:2-11), not necessarily to die for him.

There are no unsurrendered Christians. In Romans 6:13 believers were told that they are to stop presenting themselves, handing themselves over or giving in to sin. This present tense command indicates an action which was occurring but now must stop. Instead they are to present themselves for surrender to God. In Romans 6 the verb *present* occurs five times.[685] When it is used again in Romans 12:1 it is not a recapitulation, but a deeper surrender based upon the awareness of a deeper need. Wynkoop said that the entire man is involved in sanctification and that sanctification is not subject to the descriptive terms *initial*

---

[683]These verbs are all future indicatives and express a command — "you will be" or "you will." Thus they are classified as imperative future. This compares to לא (not) with the imperfect form of the Hebrew verb used in the ten commandments. "You will not ever . . . ." Some Old Testament scholars hold that the ten commandments do not merely contain negative commands, but actually give promise of future conformity to them [Ferguson, *Holy Spirit*, 141].

[684]θυσία (*thusia*) is from the root θύω (*thuo*) which means "to kill in sacrifice or slay." It occurs for the first and only time in Romans at 12:1.

[685]παρίστημι (*paristemi*) or παριστάνω (*paristano*) occurs twice in v 13, v 16, twice in v 19.

or *entire*. "These qualifications are human ways to distinguish man's spiritual progress and are legitimate expressions only when so understood."[686]

Awakened sinners come to Christ repenting for what they have done, but eventually the Christian must come to realize the problem is not simply what they have done, but who they are. In one sense, "This continuing, yielding consecration is not qualitatively different from the initial consecration, but rather it is growing and developing under conditions of temptation and contextual hearing of the word. It is a continuing unfolding of what was implied in the initial act of consecration."[687] But if original sin is "self-sovereignty,"[688] then it is at this point where the "delusion of self-sovereignty"[689] is shattered. Jesse Peck explained,

> In conversion, the consecration to God is sincere, but not discriminating. The further study of the heart, the aid of genuine experience, and the searching power of God's Holy Spirit will — in nearly, if not quite all cases — reveal defects in the consecration, will bring to our notice strongly marked mental reservations in favor of our own way. We see that in many things we choose our own way in distinction from God's way and detect ourselves in practically carrying out our own wills in preference to God's will. We see it, feel it, repent of it, mourn and grieve over it, seek and obtain forgiveness for it, and yet find it returning with more or less power, evincing what is unquestionably true — that the source of the difficulty is within us, that a more complete and final separation of conscious self from fallen worldly and selfish elements is indispensable to required success in the Christian life.[690]

The initial yielding of a sinner involves repentance for evil; the advanced yielding of a believer involves a consecration of what is good. Sinners surrender to Christ because they are guilty, afraid, and miserable. Now God calls those who have been justified to dedicate their lives a second time because of God's mercy (see Rom 11:31-32). When we were sinners condemned to die, God had

---

686Wynkoop, *Theology of Love*, 352.

687Oden, *Life in the Spirit*, 229; see also Doty, *Lessons in Holiness*, 54; Daniel Steele, *Love Enthroned*, 21.

688Howard, *Newness of Life*, 35-44.

689Dunning, *Grace, Faith, and Holiness*, 288.

690Peck, *Central Idea of Christianity*, 29-30.

mercy on us and provided a way of escape. In his mercy he offered his own Son as our substitute. In view of God's mercy in justifying us, we ought to give the rest of our lives to him — realizing that without his mercy we would have no life anyway. And so the motive of this second dedication is not fear, but love.

According to Wesley, Jane Green "never was in darkness or heaviness one hour during the second conviction. Only she felt in a manner not to be expressed her own foolishness, emptiness and nothingness."[691] Nathan Bangs described the Christian who did not lose the consciousness of pardon, even amidst the conflicts which arose from the inward feeling of inbred sin. Despite "fightings without and fears within" he held fast his confidence in God, his faith in Christ, and retained an evidence of his acceptance "in the Beloved."[692] Thus, the believer repents at a deeper level of consciousness.[693]

Paul also calls for a deeper surrender because it is reasonable to do so. The word *reasonable* or *spiritual* in the Greek word λογικός (*logikos*) which literally means *logical*. Christian worship does not bypass the mind. Worship which seeks to manipulate the emotions while bypassing the mind, and especially the will, is not Christian. God first renews our minds and then makes his appeal to that renewed mind.

There is a progressive realization of God's purpose. These Christian brothers and sisters are already alive through regeneration, holy through initial sanctification, and accepted by God through adoption. Their transformation[694] has been initiated, but not completed. Since you have found God's will for you to be good and since you have accepted his plan for your life and he has accepted you, now enter into his perfect will.[695]

---

[691]Wesley, *Letter* to Mr. Jones, 22 August 1759. See also *Journal* for 28 Nov 1761 and 15 Nov 1763 for other examples of evangelical repentance.

[692]Bangs, *Necessity, Nature, and Fruits*, 57.

[693]See John Wesley's sermon, "The Repentance of Believers." Even the Puritan Thomas Hooker spoke of a "second repentance" [Hambrick-Stowe, *Practice of Piety*, 81].

[694]Here Paul uses the term μεταμορφόω (*metamorphoo*), the basis of our word "metamorphosis." It is also used in 2 Cor 3:18 where the emphasis is on progressive sanctification. The other two uses of this word refer to the transfiguration of Christ (Matt 17:2; Mark 9:2). This transfiguration was a manifestation of the holiness of Christ through the revelation of his glory.

[695]*Good*, *well-pleasing*, and *perfect* are not adjectives which modify "will." Rather they are adjectival nouns or substantival adjectives in apposition to or equivalent to "will." The article, though not repeated, applies to each statement — the good, the acceptable, the perfect. Martin Luther caught something of this progressive nature in his comment that the good will of God was to do good, the acceptable will of God was

We are to present our bodies to God. Our bodies are to be temples of the Holy Spirit. So by specifying that we should present our bodies, Paul is singling out a part for the whole person as in Romans 6:13.[696] God wants the whole person. If we understand our essence as a soul which possesses a body, this will lead to a depreciation of our physical nature in our quest for spiritual perfection.[697] Because of the Incarnation and Resurrection of Christ, our physical nature is redeemed and sanctified. Thus, the physical realm is not necessarily sinful. The human body is not a prison nor are physical appetites always to be mortified — even if they must be surrendered and consecrated. Thus, we are called to yield our whole self and experience God's perfect will.

> I am no longer my own, O Lord, but Thine. Put me to what thou wilt: rank me with whom thou wilt; put me to doing, put me to suffering. Let me be employed for Thee or laid aside for Thee. Exalted for Thee or brought low for Thee. Let Me be full; let me be empty. Let me have all things; let me have nothing. I freely and heartily yield all things to thy pleasure and disposal.[698]

When I consecrate myself to God, the indwelling Spirit of God will sanctify me wholly. In the rest of Romans 12 Paul lists ten changes which result:

---

that we should be chaste and keep ourselves pure, and the perfect will of God was that we should desire to please God alone [*Romans*, 152]. See also Gregory, *Perfect in Christ Jesus*, 47; Wynkoop, *Theology of Love*, 288-289.

[696]Wesley, *Notes*, 396; see also Pope, *Prayers of St Paul*, 134 which ties Rom 12:1; 1 Thes 5:23; Heb 4:12 as the three passages where our nature is divided. Pope agreed that the body presented by the spirit is representative of a whole life dedicated to God. Although a tripartite or trichotomy view of body, soul, and spirit is a popular position, according to Joel Green this position is rarely found in biblical studies or in theological literature [Green and Palmer, *In Search of the Soul*, 14; see also Green, *Body, Soul, and Human Life*, Moreland and Rae, *Body and Soul*, Ladd, "Greek Versus the Hebrew View of Man,"13-40].

In his *Notes*, Wesley argued that man cannot possibly consist of three parts [p. 532]. David Cubie argues that Paul in 1 Thess 5:23-24 is teaching that it is "indeed the whole person who is the object of sanctification" ["'Entire' Sanctification, 154].

[697]See Powell, *Discovering our Christian Faith*, 68, who claims the soul-body dualism is based on the philosophy of Plato and Descartes, not the Bible.

[698]John Wesley, *Order of Worship* (1780); *Directions for Renewing our Covenant*, 14. Based on Richard Alleine's *Vindication of Godliness*, which Wesley included in his *Christian Library*, Vol. 30 (1753). See Wesley, *Journal*, 6-11 Aug 1755; 30 Sept 1764.

- Humility. According to v 3 we will not think of ourselves more highly than we ought. Psychology says our problem is low self-esteem. The Bible has very little to say about it. Instead it warns that we esteem ourselves too highly. Verse 10 says to honor one another above ourselves. According to v 16 we are not to be proud or conceited, but willing to associate with people under us. While the word for "high" is neuter in gender, referring to high things, the word for "low" could be either masculine or neuter. Therefore, Paul could be referring to people of low status or to menial tasks. In both cases we should demonstrate humility.

- Generosity. Whatever gifts we have been given are to be dedicated for the good of the whole body (v 5). Verses 6-8 list seven gifts. This is not a complete list, but every believer has some gift. We are to use what we have been given to minister to others and not advance our own agenda. "Be devoted to one another in brotherly love" (v 10). "Share with God's people who are in need. Practice hospitality" (v 13).

- Purity. Our love is sincere and pure. It is not pretended or hypocritical (v 9). It is to will one thing.

- Fervency. We are not lacking in zeal (v 11). The same word σπουδή (*spoude*) is used in v 8, where leaders are to be diligent, eager, and earnest. We need such a dedication to the work of the Lord. A second word ζέω (*zeo*) means fervent or zeal. Literally this word means "seething" or "burning." Our passion should be for Christ and his kingdom.

- Positivity. According to v 12 we are joyful in the hope of the gospel.

- Consistency. According to v 12 we are patient and endure affliction, and we are faithful in prayer.

- Sympathy. We rejoice in the success of other and weep with those who mourn (v 15). It takes more grace to rejoice when other are doing well than to sympathize when they are doing poorly.

- Unity. We get along with others (v 16). As far as it depends on us, we try to get along with everyone (v 18).

- Integrity. Holiness is integrity (v 17). It will make us careful to do what is right in all circumstances. We are glued to whatever is good and we hate what is evil (v 9).

- Victory. Finally v 21 says we can be overcomers. We are not overwhelmed by evil, but we overcome evil with good. We bless and do not curse those who persecute us (v 14). We do not repay evil for evil (v 17), we do not take revenge (vv 19-20).

Other exhortations include, "Let us cleanse ourselves from all filthiness of the flesh and spirit, perfecting holiness in the fear of God" (2 Cor 7:1). "But let patience have its perfect work, that you may be perfect and complete, lacking nothing (James 1:4).

The New Testament gives examples of entire sanctification.[699] Paul included himself with all those of whom he exhorted in Philippians 3:15, "Let those of us who are perfect think this way." Three verses earlier Paul declared that he was not already perfected in the sense that he had not already been resurrected from the dead. Here he does testify to Christian perfection, even if not

---

[699]Even Old Testament Enoch pleased God (Heb 11:5). Noah was a just man and perfect in his generation (Gen 6:9). Asa's heart was perfect (1 Kings 15:14). Job was also perfect and upright (Job 1:1). Here the synonyms *blameless* (*tam*) and *upright* (*yashar*) are used to describe personal integrity, faithful adherence to God's statutes, and honest compassion in relating to others. These two words are also utilized in Psalm 37:37 [Hartley, *Job*, 67].

Notice that God said prior to the trial that Job was blameless or perfect (1:1, 8; 2:3; 12:4). The Hebrew word תמם (*tamam*) carries the idea of completeness. When used to describe a sacrificial animal it meant "spotless, without blemish." When used of a person it meant personal integrity.

The feminine noun תמה (*tummah* - from *tamam*) occurs in Job 2:3, 9; 27:5; 31:6 and is best translated "innocence." It is a judicial term meaning that Job maintains he is not guilty as charged. The Hiphil stem (causitive mode) conveys the sense of entering into a state and remaining in it.

Job's integrity and innocence was not absolute perfection; it was balance and completeness. It is not to be as perfect as archangels who are superior to angels. It is not to be as perfect as angels, with their superior knowledge. It is not to be as perfect as Adam and Eve in their innocence. Noah, Job, Hezekiah, David's soldiers, and the entire congregation at the time of Solomon's dedication were also said to be perfect. While these are not examples of *Christian* perfection, Fletcher would explain that they were perfect in their dispensation. On "gentile perfection," see Fletcher, *Works*, 2:524-525. George Rawlinson said, "We must suppose Job to have reach as near perfection as was possible for men at the time" [*Job*, 2].

to final perfection.[700]

Paul wrote to the Thessalonians, "You are witnesses, and so is God, of how holy, righteous and blameless we were among you who believed" (1 Thess 2:10). All three of these adverbs describe Christian perfection.

John included himself with all those of whom he said, "By this is love perfected with us, so that we may have confidence for the day of judgment, because as he is so also are we in this world" (1 John 4:17). Thus we reflect the likeness of Christ now, as a student reflects the character of his teacher (Luke 6:40).

In 1 Corinthians 13 Paul describes mature Christianity. Paul used, *agape*, the word for commitment or covenantal love. The Greek language used four different words for *love*: *eros*, *philos*, *storgos*, and *agape*. All of these types of love are legitimate. However, *agape* is a completely different dimension of love, according to Wynkoop. She described it as a principle by which one orders life. It is a personal orientation to God and to all other persons and things in life. It is a deliberate policy by which all relationship are kept in balance by our deliberate orientation to God and ourselves. *Agape* love is God's dimension of love which he wants to restore to all men. It is holiness and it results in fellowship. When our life is aimed at God and centered in God, that dedication brings holiness, wholeness, and fellowship with God. This Christian *agape* love is not a substitute for the other loves, but it is a quality of the entire person as it is centered in Christ. Thus, it becomes our goal to bring Christian character into *eros, storgos*, and *philos*.

Based on the use of *agape* in 1 John 2:15, Wynkoop also said the essence of sin was to be thus devoted to anything other than God. "Sin is love locked into a false center, the self." "Everyone is centering his love somewhere. He is biased. The gospel call is a radical thing and presumes to create a radical revolution in personality." Therefore, entire sanctification is the reorientation of our misdirected love "in which the antagonistic and feuding sectional gods tearing the human heart apart by contrary loves are cleansed by the presence of the Holy Spirit. This happens as Christ is made the absolute Lord of all the heart, mind, soul, and strength."[701]

The word ἀγάπη (*agape*) occurs nine times in 1 Corinthians 13. When we are born again this *agape* love is poured out into our hearts (Rom 5:5). Yet according to 1 John 4:17-18 this love can grow to a state of completeness or perfect love.

---

[700]In Phil 3:12 the verb is τελειόω and in v 15 the adjective is τέλειος, both from the root word τέλος.

[701]Wynkoop, *Theology of Love*, 31-37; 158; 178.

Perfect love is patient and kind with people. It does not envy[702] or boast. It is not puffed up with pride. The perfect Christian is not rude or out of line. Nor is he self-seeking. Such a person is not provoked to anger.[703] It should not be inferred that the entirely sanctified are incapable of righteous anger, but that they get angry over the things that anger God and not over personal insults. The only other time this word παροξύνω (*paroxuno*) occurs is in Acts 17:16 where Paul was stirred up over the idolatry he witnessed in Athens. Wesley himself testified, "Anger, for instance, is natural to me; yea, irregular, unreasonable anger. I am naturally inclined to this, as I experience every day. Yet I can help it, by the grace of God; and do so, as long as I watch and pray."[704]

Perfect love keeps no record of wrongs. It does not delight in evil but rejoices in truth. It seeks to protect like a roof covers. It chooses to believe the best and is not suspicious. Even when it learns the worst to be true, it remains optimistic and hopeful. It refuses to take failure as final. Wesley wrote, "The longer I live, the larger allowances I make for human infirmities. I exact more from myself and less from others."[705]

Finally, this grace enables us to persevere regardless of the circumstances. In v 4 the word μακροθυμέω (*makrothumeo*) means patience with people; in v 7 ὑπομένω (*hupomeno*) means patience with circumstances. Such a love never fails so long as it is maintained.

Therefore when perfection comes, it brings to an end (καταργέω - *katargeo*) that which is imperfect, immature, and childish. Thus, Wesley concluded,

> There is nothing higher in religion; there is, in effect, nothing else; if you look for anything but more love, you are looking wide of the mark, you are getting out of the royal way. And when

---

[702]The verb ζηλόω (*zeloo*) is from the root ζέω (*zeo*). It occurs thirty-five times in all its related formed. Only by context can it be determined whether the meaning is good or bad. Thus, it means *jealous* nineteen times and *zealous* sixteen times.

[703]"Anger I no more shall feel, Always even, always still"[Wesley, *BE Works*, 7:508, Hymn #345]; "Be anger to my soul unknown; hate, envy, jealousy, be gone!" [Wesley, *BE Works*, 7:502. Hymn #341].

[704]Wesley, *Works*, 9:273. Yet Wesley also wrote, "A man strikes me. Here is a temptation to anger. But my heart overflows with love. And I feel no anger at all; of which I can be as sure, as that love and anger are not the same" [*Works*, 11:419]. Cox declared, "It can be wished that Wesley had made himself more clear at this point" [*Perfection*, 159].

[705]Wesley, *Letter* to Samuel Furly, 25 January 1762.

> you are asking others, "Have you received this or that blessing?" if you mean anything but more love, you mean wrong; you are leading them out of the way, and putting them upon a false scent. Settle it then in your heart, that from the moment God has saved you from all sin, you are to aim at nothing more, but more of that love described in the thirteenth of the Corinthians. You can go no higher than this, till you are carried into Abraham's bosom.[706]

Everything that is substituted for perfection can be duplicated by some other means. "It may be fanatical philanthropy, or moralism, such as an undue concern about dress and adornment and austerity of life. It eagerly seeks persecution because of one's 'standards.' Or it may be an obsession with emotional displays and experience such as shouting, tongues, visions, and ecstatic trances which substitutes for the less spectacular quiet walk of love in daily life." Nothing, however, that Christian perfection is can be counterfeited.[707] Sangster said the testimony of the saints is that they have seen the burning heart of God. Their own love has leaped out in flaming response, and they have loved the Lord their God with all their heart and soul and strength and mind — and their neighbor as themselves. As their egotism is broken, their love widens to embrace the world.[708] Yet Richard Treffry wrote that love

> may not always burn with an equally perceptible intensity; there may be seasons when the soul is in heaviness through manifold temptations, when the enemy may come in like a flood, when the body loaded with pains and infirmities may weigh down the mind; but the extent of a Christian's love to God must not be estimated by any ecstasy of feeling, or flights of rapture, for these are often accidental circumstances attendant on this live, rather than properties essential to its existence.

Instead, this love should be understood "as a predominant and powerfully operative principle of heavenly origin and tendency, drawing the soul into the closest union with its God, making it jealous of His honor, attentive to His ordinance, observant of His precepts, and emulous to behold His glory."[709]

---

[706]Wesley, *Works*, 11:430.

[707]Wynkoop, *Theology of Love*, 281

[708]Sangster, *Pure in Heart*, 239.

[709]Treffry, *Treatise on Christian Perfection*, 17.

The New Testament contains prayers for entire sanctification.[710] Wesley declared that if there were no such thing as entire sanctification, such prayers "would be mere mockery of God." Wesley also explained that if we pray, as Jesus taught us to pray, "Deliver us from evil" (Matt 6:13), "when we are delivered from all evil, there can be no sin remaining."[711] Thus Wesley would understand 1 John 1:8 to refer to any person *before* the blood of Christ has cleansed him.[712] 1 John 1:8 cannot be interpreted so as to contradict 1 John 1:7 and 9 or 1 John 3:9. Findlay wrote, "The man of 'sinless perfection,' who imagines he has nothing left to confess, nothing that needs forgiveness, verily 'deceives himself'; rarely does he deceive his neighbor on this point, — never his God."[713] Yet Findlay affirmed Christian perfection as taught in 1 John 1:9.

The disciples would be kept from evil as they were kept in or by the power of God's name.[714] This meant that God's character, as revealed in the person of his Son, would keep them from being overwhelmed by the world and its values, so that they might be devoted or sanctified to the Father and his values.[715] In his high priestly prayer, Jesus prayed,

> Sanctify them in the truth; your word is truth.[716] As you sent me

---

[710]Many of these prayers utilize the optative mood, which expresses a wish or prayer.

[711]Wesley, *Works*, 11:390.

[712]Wesley, *Notes*, 631. Lowrey explained, "Salvation from all sin implies the prior existence of sin, but not it continuance in a fully saved state" [*Possibilities of Grace*, 74]. Westcott held that "to have sin" should be distinguished from "to sin,"thus distinguishing the sinful principle from the sinful act [cited by Steele, "Sanctification,"4:2686].

[713]Findlay, *Studies in John's Epistles*, 123.

[714]According to Harald Riesenfeld, τηρέω (*tareo*) meant to protect, preserve, and guard [*TDNT*, 8:142]. The aorist active imperative denotes continuous action. The time of action is lost in the imperative mood. Aorist imperative has to do with action which has not yet started.

[715]Peterson, *Possessed by God*, 29-30.

[716]"Consecrate them by the anointing of thy Spirit to their office; and perfect them in holiness, by means of thy word" [Wesley, *Notes*, 263]. Thus the disciples were to be consecrated to the work to which Christ had called them. Therefore, this verse is not necessarily proof that the disciples were initially or entirely sanctified at that point in time. Nor does the sanctification of the Savior refer to the categories of initial or entire sanctification. However, all this is potentially included when the prayer is expanded to include all who will believe.

> into the world, I have sent them into the world. For them I sanctify myself, that they too may be truly sanctified. I do not ask for these only, but also for those who will believe in me through their word, that they may all be one, just as you, Father, are in me, and I in you, that they also may be in us, so that the world may believe that you have sent me. The glory that you have given me I have given to them, that they may be one even as we are one, I in them and you in me, that they may become perfected in one (John 17:17-23).

What did Christ mean by saying that his disciples were "kept by the name" the Father had given to him? (John 17:11-12) Leon Morris says, "This probably means keep them from evil, but the object is not expressed, and the end of the verse makes it possible that what is meant is keeping them from disunity. But the wider meaning is more likely."[717]

Such statements collectively imply no more than that up to the event of Pentecost the disciples were in a unique relationship to Christ in a way that can never be repeated again. Therefore, we cannot pattern our salvation after theirs, because they were a unique group of men who played a unique role in God's plan of salvation. They were the first of Christ's disciples; the forerunners, the exception, not the rule.

In Luke 24:13-32 the disciples had given up on Christ. "We had hoped" (v 21) in the imperfect tense indicates past action. They were no longer hoping. Does this mean they became apostate? No, in answer to the prayer of Christ they were kept. They had not as yet experienced the new birth by the Spirit. That still lay in the future for them as it did for all future believers. But despite their doubts, the Holy Father would "keep them,"just as Jesus had kept all but Judas, until they received the promised gift of the Holy Spirit on the day of Pentecost.

As our great high priest, Jesus was first prepared for his mission through suffering (Heb 5:9) and then devoted himself as a victim to be sacrificed, consecrating himself to the Father's will and separating himself from everything which would hinder him. He dedicated himself to become a sacrifice for sin (John 17:19).[718] He had no sin of which he needed purging, but he set himself apart for the work of redemption, consecrating himself entirely to do his Father's will. The result of this atoning sacrifice is that the sanctification, both initial and entire, now provided produces in us deliverance through the Word, unity within the body of Christ, access into the presence of God, a reflection of the nature of God, and

---

[717]Morris, *John*, 643.

[718]Peterson, *Possessed by God*, 29 and 33-34 where he discussed the self-sanctification of the Savior.

credibility within the world. Ironically the Holy Spirit is not mentioned in John 17, but his sanctifying work may be implied from chapters 14-16.[719]

Hendrix observed that Paul prayed for the entire sanctification of believers in all his epistles except one.[720] W. B. Pope observed that all of Paul's prayers are more or less devoted to the grand concept of the perfect Christian life. "The word Perfection is the seal with which they are all alike stamped, and that ideal which is found in them is to be personally realized."[721] The next five prayers[722] to be considered are prayers of Paul which are each part of a letter addressed to the saints [ἅγιοι- *hagioi*] or literally to the holy ones. They are initially sanctified, but not entirely.

In Romans 15 the example of Christ is held up in vv 3-4; 7-8. We are told not to please ourselves, but rather that each of us should please his neighbor (vv 1-2). The mature Christian should thus exemplify a spirit of consideration and a spirit of cooperation. The prayer of Paul in Romans 15:5-6 is for the grace of unity between Jewish and Gentile believers within the Roman church. Paul prayed that they might receive patience and encouragement. The example of Christ teaches his people to endure the contempt of the world and to bear with each other. The basis of this patience endurance is hope. Christian maturity should produce hope (see vv 4-5; 12-13). Again in v 13 Paul prays. In this benediction he refers to God as the source and object of our hope. Clarke paraphrased Paul's prayer, "That ye may be excited to take more enlarged views of the salvation which God has provided for you, and have all your *expectations* fulfilled *by the power of the Holy Ghost*, enabling you to *hope and believe*; and then sealing the fulfilment of the promises upon your hearts."[723]

Paul prays that we might be filled with *all* joy and peace. This implies the displacement of anything inconsistent with the fruit of the Spirit. According to Pope, this prayer "takes up the fundamental doctrine of Christian salvation by

---

[719]Peterson, *Possessed by God*, 31.

[720]Hendrix, *Perfecting of the Saints*, 20. While Hendrix does not name the one epistle, apparently it is 1 Corinthians and apparently Hendrix is not considering the pastoral epistles.

[721]Pope, *Prayers of St. Paul*, 29-30.

[722]By my count this brings us to the letter of 1 Thessalonians, which is not specifically addressed to "saints." Most of Paul's letter contain prayers for Christian perfection. However, there are no such prayers in the pastoral letters. The significance may be that Timothy and Titus were already mature believers. I reject the assertion by higher critics that the pastoral epistles were not written by Paul since each of them names Paul as its author.

[723]Clarke, *Commentary*, 6:157.

faith, and prays for the abounding experience of the blessings of that salvation. . . . Here we have set before us as the object of prayer the abundance of peace and joy and hope as the result of the abounding power in us of the Holy Ghost." This prayer speaks not of our hope in eternity, but rather of an eternal hope.[724]

In 2 Corinthians 13:9 Paul declared, "Our prayer is for your perfection." This is a prayer for restoration and wholeness. This includes a restoration of order in the Corinthian church, as well as the recovery of moral purity. But the prayers of Paul always rise above their immediate occasion. Although this prayer scarcely mentions the individual believer, every application of Scriptural truth must find its way to the individual and only through the individual will it reach the community.[725]

Originally this word *perfection* was used for setting dislocated bones. Even after we are born again, there are areas of our personality that are out of alignment and need to be relocated. These idiosyncracies should not be excused. Verse 11 tells us to aim for perfection.[726]

Sangster declared that the emphasis of the New Testament is not on perfection but on growth. The major concern is that man shall grow rapidly to holiness.[727] And yet Ephesians 4:11-16 declares that a major purpose in pastoral ministry is to produce growth *and* spiritual maturity.

In Ephesians 1:15-23 Paul prays that God would give the saints in Ephesus the Spirit of wisdom and revelation so that they may know him better.[728] The Spirit inspired the revelation of the mind of God through Scripture, but he is also in every believer revealing Christ as a personal Savior. Pope asserted that the same Spirit who presided over the inspiration of Scripture presides over this personal revelation. Nothing less than this will satisfy the language of the prayer nor should satisfy the aspiration of the Christian.

---

[724]Pope, *Prayers of St. Paul*, 183; 196.

[725]Pope, *Prayers of St. Paul*, 176; 182.

[726]In v 9 the noun κατάρτισις comes from the same root word as καταρτίζω, the verb in v 11. The meaning is to mend, restore, or perfect. This concept of perfection is implied in Ephesians 4:12-13 which also uses *perfecting (*καταρτίζω), *perfect* (τέλειος), and *full stature* (πλήρωμα ἡλικία - *pleroma helikia*) (v 13).

[727]Sangster, *Pure in Heart*, 39.

[728]It is impossible from the Greek to determine whether v 17 is a reference to the Holy Spirit or the human spirit, but as A. T. Robertson said, "It is open to question if it is possible to obtain this wisdom and revelation apart from the Holy Spirit" [*Word Pictures*, 4:520]. Ralph Earle argued that the human spirit may possess wisdom, but not revelation. *Apokalypto* is always used for a divine disclosure. The most important revelation is the knowledge of God and that knowledge is beyond mere human understanding [*Word Meanings*, 4:246]. Through revelation we see the glory of God.

Here Pope acknowledged the best and purest mystical teaching which described the way of perfection as moving through three stages:

- purification from sin
- illumination by grace
- perfect union with God

These three steps are not only successive but also simultaneous. Every fresh revelation of the Lord is a deeper experience of union, while it makes sin and self more loathsome and thus purifies the soul from both.[729]

The believer has already received the seal of the Spirit (v 13), an internal assurance of acceptance which no mere rational ascent could bring. Yet there is more to behold: the hope of his calling, the riches of our glorious inheritance, and the might of the divine power made available to us.[730]

We are called to experience the treasury of blessings for the people of God in time and in eternity. Our glorious inheritance does not mean the glory of heaven, but "the present manifestation of the glory of grace in believers who are gradually 'perfected into one' through their union with the Redeemer." This resurrection power has already raised the dead sinner to life and will raise our bodies from physical death in the future. In the present, we sit in heavenly places with the resurrected Christ and he exercises his authority through us.[731]

Paul resumes this prayer in Ephesians 3:14-21, praying that we might become mighty through the Spirit (v 16). Not only does Paul pray for a supernatural empowerment, in v 17 Paul prays that Christ may dwell in our hearts through faith. While the Spirit of Christ indwells all believers, here Paul uses a compound word κατά + οἰκεω, meaning to settle down or to make a home in your hearts. The Spirit makes himself at home in the sense that we become rooted and grounded in love. When we are justified by faith, the love of God is poured out into our hearts (Rom 5:5). Now Paul prays that we might become established in love. In this deeper relationship, we are enabled to realize the magnitude of God's love — how wide, how long, how high, and how deep. As our spiritual capacity increases, we can receive a fuller measure of the Holy Spirit.[732] Miner

---

[729]Pope, *Prayers of St. Paul*, 235.

[730]In vv 19-20 Paul uses four synonyms for *power*: incomparably great δύναμις (*dunamis*); ἐνέργεια (*energeia* - "energy"); κράτος (*kratos*); ἰσχύς (*ischus*).

[731]Pope, *Prayers of St. Paul*, 223-238.

[732]Wynkoop protested, "We cannot divide the Holy Spirit up so that we receive a part of Him at one time and more of Him at another time. The Holy Spirit is a person and comes as a Person and he relates himself to persons. When one is saved, the Holy Spirit comes to him" [*Theology of Love*, 199]. Wykoop was rejecting the old holiness

Raymond observed,

> The blessing prayed for is a knowledge of the fullness of redemption, the length of which may be its extend in duration, from the eternal purpose of God in Christ Jesus throughout all ages, world without end; its breadth may be the extent of its provisions, being a salvation provided for the whole human family; its depths the peril from which it saves — the depths of depravity and perdition; its height the eternal glory to which it elevates. To know the love of Christ, to apprehend the vastness, fullness, and completeness of redemption, is of no avail, if the knowledge be merely an intellectual apprehension; the prayer evidently reaches to the designed results of such knowledge in the affections and volitions of him who has it.[733]

Clarke commented,

> In reference to human beings, the love of God, in its BREADTH, is a girdle that encompasses the globe; its LENGTH reaches from the *eternal* purpose of the mission of Christ to the *eternity* of blessedness which is to be spent in his ineffable glories; its DEPTH reaches to the *lowest fallen* sons of Adam, and to the *deepest* depravity of the human heart; and its HEIGHT to the infinite dignities of the throne of Christ. [According to Rev 3:21] Thus we see that the *Father*, the *Son*, and all true believers in him are to be seated on the *same throne*! This is the *height* of the love of God and the *height* to which that love raises the souls that believe in Christ Jesus![734]

"Christ's four-dimensional love embraces all mankind in all times and conditions and provides a basis for the Church's evangelization of all men."[735]

"The third and chief blessing . . . is the presence of the Holy Trinity

---

paradigm which taught the Spirit was *with* us in regeneration, but *within* us in sanctification. We cannot distinguish between receiving and being baptized in the Spirit. However, according to Wynkoop's emphasis, our relationship with the Spirit can grows deeper.

[733]Raymond, *Systematic Theology*, 2:386.

[734]Clarke, *Commentary*, 6:448.

[735]Carter, *Wesleyan Bible Commentary*, 5:404.

abiding in its fullness in the soul of man."[736] While all true Christians have the Spirit, Daniel Steele explained, "The vessel is too weak and too small to contain all that God desires to pour into it. It must be enlarged and strengthened."[737] Godet wrote, "Man is a vessel destined to receive God, a vessel which must be enlarged in proportion as it is filled and filled in proportion as it is enlarged."[738] Joseph Benson remembered John Fletcher's visits at Trevecca. Benson said he saw Fletcher so filled with the love of God that he cried out "O my God, withhold Thy hand, or the vessel will burst." However, Fletcher later told Benson he was afraid he had grieved the Spirit of God, that he ought to have prayed that the Lord would have enlarged the vessel.[739]

While Raymond conceded that the expression "filled with all the fullness of God" is considered by some as figurative, he concluded that the idea is that of completeness, fullness, all the subject can contain. The only limitation is the capacity of the person.[740] Pope wrote,

> Here it is needful to observe that reference is made to an abiding influence of the Spirit on the inner man of the Christian, who has already received that Spirit under two aspects, as the Spirit of the son in adoptions, and as the Earnest of an always future inheritance. The Holy Ghost is once for all given in both these latter senses: it is the believer's privilege, as a believer, to have the abiding access to God, and hope of future salvation. But the continuous and ever-increasing strength of the Holy Ghost is granted by degrees, and the measure of these degrees makes the difference between one Christian and another. As there is a growth into the fulness of God, and a gradual establishment into permanence of the indwelling of Christ, so there is a progression in the inward operation of the Spirit. That progression is very clearly marked in our Epistle. In the first chapter all believers are sealed by the Spirit as the earnest of God's possession and their inheritance; in this prayer the ever-increasing might of the Spirit is presented as a promise; and towards the close we are all

---

736Raymond, *Systematic Theology*, 2:387-389.

737Steele, *Half-Hours with St. Paul*,18; see also Steele, *Love Enthroned*, 86-97.

738Quoted by Oden, *Life in the Spirit*, 226.

739Benson, *Life of John Fletcher*, 139.

740Raymond, *Systematic Theology*, 2:390.

exhorted to "be filled with the Spirit."[741]

To be filled with God is to be emptied of self. John Wesley commented this describes "a perfection far beyond a bare freedom from sin."[742] While we can never contain the fullness of God, we can be filled unto the full measure of blessing and maturity God has for us. This does not indicate a static state of fullness, but rather a progressive filling.[743] Raymond concluded that the state of grace described here is a state of grace to be sought after and prayed for by regenerated persons. It is the highest state which we conceive as attainable in this life and it is Christian perfection.[744]

In Philippians 1:4-6, Paul prays that the Spirit will carry his ongoing work in us unto completion or perfection (ἐπί - *epi* + τελέω - *teleo*). According to verses 9-11 this would produce

- a love growing in knowledge of the truth and discernment which is able to react properly in every crisis
- an ability to discern the more excellent way. Love functions as an internal monitor "instructing us always what to believe and what to reject, what to do and what to shun, what to leave behind us as unworthy and what to make the mark of our supreme pursuit."[745]
- a purity of character that reflects sincerity (simplicity of motive) and is not offensive
- a fullness of the fruit of righteousness, which Wesley defined as "all inward and outward holiness."[746] All Christians have an imputed righteousness that comes through faith in Christ (Phil 3:9), but here Paul describes a condition of being full of this righteousness. "Here also the apostle is far from speaking of justification only."[747]

In Philippians 3:10-11 Paul himself longs to know Christ better. While Christ suffered and died, then was resurrected, the order for the Christian is

---

[741]Pope, *Prayers of St. Paul*, 245.

[742]Wesley, *Notes*, 495.

[743]Carter, *Wesleyan Bible Commentary*, 5:404. See Rom 15:29 where Paul used πλήρωμα (*pleroma*) to describe the full measure of the blessing of Christ.

[744]Raymond, *Systematic Theology*, 2:390-391.

[745]Pope, *Prayers of St. Paul*, 264.

[746]Wesley, *Notes*, 506.

[747]Wesley, *Notes*, 512.

reversed. First he is raised from spiritual death. Thus, we first know God in the power of Christ's resurrection.

Then we come to know Christ through the fellowship of his sufferings. The only suffering which becomes a means of grace is suffering which causes us to look away from ourselves and focus upon his passion. Although Christ suffered alone, I need not ever suffer alone. I was not present historically when Christ suffered on the cross, but my suffering can connect with his. Yet suffering does not sanctify. Richard S. Taylor explained, "Suffering is intended, not to be the purifying agent, but to drive the soul to Him who is. Suffering . . . serves one great purpose: it shows us our helplessness, our littleness, our insecurity, our need of God."[748]

The third level of intimacy with God is through death. This seems like a paradox, but it is a deeper death to self-centeredness. It is the death of what remains of the old life. Thus, entire sanctification is death. It is a more perfect conformity to the nature of Christ.[749] The only change that counts is becoming like him.[750]

In Colossians 1:9-14, Paul continued to pray that they would have a growing knowledge of God's will which would result in a practical conformity with that will in three areas:

- more fruit — the holiness of the regenerate life is the fruit of a tree of life within as well as his own habits and acts. But the fruitfulness of the Christian life knows no limits. Thus, as our knowledge of God's will grows the fruits of obedience will also grow.
- a greater power in our lives producing more strength, endurance, patience, and joy
- thankfulness — gratitude for the benefits of redemption

John Frame, writing from a Calvinistic perspective, explained that although we are not sinlessly perfect in this life, the Lord is working to perfect in us the image of Christ (Jer. 32:39-40; Eph. 5:25-27). "So we pray that God will

---

[748]Taylor, *Disciplined Life*, 53-54.

[749]The word translated "conformable" or "becoming like him" is συμμορφίζω (*summorphizo*). Paul took the word *morphe*, which mean "form," and added the prefix "with." Just as Paul distinguished between Christian perfection and bodily perfection in verses 12 and 15, so he distinguished between a conformity to the image of Christ in v 10 and the future change of our physical bodies in v 21.

[750]The previous two paragraphs were drawn from my article, "Knowing Christ," 8-9. This article was written for the *Holiness Digest* and was not a reprint from the *Evangelical Advocate* as incorrectly cited.

enable us to please him, for we know that this is his will, and that only he can make that happen (Col. 1:10-12)."[751] Yet we evidently are not to be passive in this process. Paul said he labored, struggling with all the energy he could muster, counseling and teaching so that every person might be presented perfect (*teleios*) in Christ (1:28-29). Clarke argued that Paul must mean something.

> Call it by what name we please, it must imply the pardon of all transgression, and the removal of the whole body of sin and death; for this must take place before we can be like him, and see him as he is, in the effulgence of his own glory. This fitness, then, to appear before God, and thorough preparation for eternal glory, is what I plead for, pray for, and heartily recommend to all true believers, under the name of *Christian perfection.*[752]

The verb πληροφορέω (*plerophoreo*) is made up of two words: *full* and *to carry*. It means to be fully assured.[753] It is used as a noun in Colossians 2:2 where Paul expressed his desire that they might know the freedom of mind and confidence that comes from a full understanding of the mystery of God in Christ. The full assurance of understanding includes a systematic grasp of all the truths and treasures of the faith; "the fullest and clearest understanding and knowledge of the Gospel."[754] It is the realization that all truth is united in the person of Christ (v 3). It was their safeguard against the deceitfulness of empty philosophy (2:8), as well as the emerging gnosticism and later forms of scepticism.[755]

Adam Clarke defined the full assurance of understanding as "the most indubitable certainty of the truth of Christianity, of their own salvation, and of the general design of God to admit the Gentiles into his Church."[756] Richard Watson wrote that it was "a perfect knowledge and entire persuasion of the truth of the doctrine of Christ."[757] Joseph Benson connected this full assurance of understanding with John 8:32, writing that it would

---

[751]Frame, *Doctrine of God*, 76.

[752]Clarke, *Christian Theology*, 184.

[753]A second and more commonly used word for assurance is παῤῥησία (*parrhesia*) and refers to confidence or boldness. See its usage in 1 John 2:28; 3:21; 4:17; 5:14.

[754]Wesley, *Notes*, 519; Benson, *Notes*, 5:369.

[755]Pope, *Prayers of St. Paul*, 214-218.

[756]Clarke, *Commentary*, 6:521.

[757]Watson, *Biblical and Theological Dictionary*, 101.

> scatter their doubts, bring satisfaction, peace, and serenity to their minds; and also that it would free them from the slavery of sin and Satan, the love of the world, and the lusts of the flesh, and all the consequences thereof; and even from the yoke of the ceremonial law, under which they at present groaned, from the spirit of bondage, and the tormenting fear of death.[758]

Beet explained,

> This knowledge is possible only to those whom Christian love knits together in a union which fills their hearts with encouragement; and only to those who are themselves in Christ and thus know and possess, in measure, whatever is in Him. . . . Such union will open the channels of the inner life, and will enrich them with an assured comprehension of the great realities known only to those who know Christ.[759]

Thus, this full assurance of understanding is an abiding and continual affirming by the Spirit of truth which produces a life of confidence. The result is that we are no longer infants, tossed back and forth by the waves, and blown here and there by every wind of teaching (Eph 4:14). Church leaders are to hold the deep truths of the faith with a pure consciousness (1 Tim 3:9). We can know we are of the truth (1 John 3:19). It is an anointing from Christ which confirms truth and discerns error (1 John 2:20, 27; 4:6). It is an understanding which reveals the truth about Christ (1 John 5:20).

In Colossians 4:12 a colleague of Paul also prays earnestly for two things — that we may stand perfect or complete (τέλειος - *teleios*) and fully assured, having a greater sense of God's presence and acceptance.

In the first letter written to the church at Thessalonica we read that they are in God the Father and in the Lord Jesus Christ (1:1). If any man be in Christ, he is a new creation (2 Cor 5:17). According to v 4 they are brethren, elect by God. In 4:8 we also discover that they have the Holy Spirit. God is giving them the Spirit.[760] And he came in much assurance (1:5). According to Sutcliffe this included the full assurance of faith and hope.[761] He also gave them joy (1:6).

---

[758]Benson, *Notes*, 4:582.

[759]Beet, *Ephesians,* 171-172. See also Foster, *Christian Purity*, 236-237 for a good description of the full assurance of understanding and faith.

[760]present tense

[761]Sutcliffe, *Commentary*, 2:808.

According to 1:3 their faith produced good works; their love prompted labor, and their hope inspired endurance. According to 1:7 they were a model or pattern. Verse 8 records their witness was like a trumpet blast that covered all of Macedonia. They had turned from idols to serve the living and true God and the news of their conversion had covered their whole region.

In chapter 3, Timothy had returned to Paul bringing a good report (3:6) about their faith and love. In 4:9 Paul acknowledged that he had no need to instruct them about brotherly love.

Therefore, it might come as a surprise that Paul states in 3:10 "night and day we pray most earnestly." Nebuchadnezzar's furnace was heated up "excessively" (Dan 3:22), but here Paul adds a prefix, he is praying super-excessively,[762] that what is lacking in their faith might be perfected. The verb *perfect* (καταρτίζω - *katartizo*) means to put in right order or restore to its former condition. It is a medical term.

They needed an increase in love (3:12). Pope said that the first blessing invoked in Paul's supplication is love, "that gift of God and grace in man which always has the preeminence. It is the ruling emotion of the regenerate soul," but here Paul prays for the enlargement of their souls. The word "increase" signifies the growth of the soul in the sphere of love and the word "abound" signifies the outward manifestation of that love. Thus, Paul has utilized two words which defy restriction. "The soul in which the Divine love is shed abroad in its fulness can give no place to evil desires; this is a light which leaves no part dark, — a law, royal in its authority, that allows nothing rebellious to remain."[763]

According to 1:3 their labor was prompted by their love. They had love, but they needed more love. God's love can flow from us only when he continually flows into us. God wants to increase our intake and our outflow. Sometimes, however, it seems the demand is greater than the supply. But God can enlarge our capacity to love each other and to love everyone. Paul seems to indicate in the last part of v 12 that he has that kind of love for them. And he is praying that they will also have that kind of love. They also needed more stability (3:13). It is God's plan to so cleanse the Church that they are holy and blameless (Eph 5:27). Paul testified in 1 Thessalonians 2:10 that he had lived holy, righteous, and blameless among them. Now he is praying that they may be established blameless in holiness (3:13) and again in 5:23 he prays that their spirit, soul, and body be kept blameless.[764] According to Daniel Steele this blamelessness

---

[762]ὑπερεκπερισσοῦ - *huperekperissou*

[763]Pope, *Prayers of St. Paul*, 109-113.

[764]In Phil 2:15 and 1 Thess 3:13 ἄμεμπτος (*amemptos*) "blameless"is used as an adjective. In Eph 1:4; 5:27; Col 1:22; Jude 24; Rev 14:5 a related adjective ἄμωμος (*amomos*) is used. In 1 Thess 2:10; 5:23 it is used as an adverb (ἀμέμπτως -

portrays what perfect Christians should be.[765] To be holy is to be morally blameless. In this life we will never know freedom from ignorance, mistake, temptation, or a thousand infirmities, but we can be blameless. Our motives can be pure.

> There is a state possible to Christians, corresponding to the ideal of their calling, in which they can be described as "unblamable in holiness," and into which they may be brought by the grace of God in this life. Therein they stand hallowed through and through, every part of their being abiding by grace in a condition fit to bear the scrutiny of their Lord's presence without rebuke. Such is the teaching of 1 Thess. 3.13 and 5.23. The fidelity of God to his purpose in calling men to be Christians is pledged to this achievement (1 Thess. 5.24), though there is no definite time, as measured from the initial hallowing of the Spirit in conversion, at which it must needs be accomplished. God, who begins the good work in the soul, also continues to work at its perfecting right up to the day of Jesus Christ (Phil. 1.6); and yet, ere that day dawns, Christians may become already "pure in purpose [Matt. 5.8] and void of offense," and so remain "until the day of Christ" (Phil. 1.10). It is this state of realized sanctification of conduct, or "walk," so as to "please God," that Saint Paul has constantly in view in exhorting his converts to holy living (for example, 1 Thess. 4.1). This is what he means, at times, by his use of ἁγιασμός [*hagiasmos* - sanctification].[766]

Part of what it means to be blameless is stated in Philippians 2:14, "Do everything without complaining or arguing so that you may become blameless and

---

amemptos).

The Hebrew word תמם (*tamim*) occurs in various forms over 200 times in the Old Testament. It describes the concept of integrity, that which is complete, blameless, just, honest, perfect. It refers to animals for sacrifice which were "without blemish" or "without spot." It is also used of man's moral character 23 times. The Septuagint usually translates *tamim* with the Greek word *teleios* (perfect) or *amomos* (blameless). Richard Treffry cited Augustine Calmet's definition as entire, complete, without blemish or defect, irreprehensible — perfect [Treffry, *Treatise on Christian Perfection*, 11].

[765]Steele, *Half-Hours with St. Paul*, 103.

[766]Bartlet, "Sanctification,"4:393.

pure." According to Colossians 3:13-14, if any man have a complaint, and the word "complaint" is a related word to "blame,"[767] we are to bear with each other, forgive each other [not cast blame] and above all put on love, which binds them all together in perfect unity.

God can deliver from a complaining spirit. In Ephesians 5:27 Paul says he can cleanse us from it — that is the negative side. 1 Thessalonians 3:12-13 is the positive answer — he strengthens, establishes, reinforces, and braces in holiness. This results in an increase and overflow of love.

Notice the Thessalonians already had some holiness, but it needed reinforcement. God can provide extra bracing that will stabilize us. Notice this stabilization is not provided by death nor by the return of Christ. Paul's prayer was that they would be found blameless and holy *when* the Lord Jesus appeared. This appearing of Christ will then confirm us in a permanent state of holiness which implies the end of probation.

They needed a completion of sanctification. They were already initially sanctified. In 1 Thessalonians 4:3 Paul teaches that their sanctification was God's will. Paul says it is God's will that they should keep on abstaining[768] from these sexual sins. Thus, they were already partially sanctified and separate from sexual impurity. So were the Corinthians. Paul wrote that some of them were involved in sexual sins, "but you were washed, you were sanctified, you were justified" (1 Cor 6:11). This is initial sanctification which comes along with justification. God calls all believers to live such a holy life (1 Thess 4:7).

But in 1 Thessalonians 5:23 this is more than a wish, although in the optative mood. Stephen Gibson surveyed 120 commentaries on this passage. The majority of the commentators surveyed either ignored the primary theme of sanctification in 1 Thessalonians or interpreted this passage in light of their theology. Gibson concluded, "The necessity they feel to juggle terms, dodge the point, and ignore the obvious comes from a sort of pessimism. Their emphasis of human depravity and inability actually translates into a divine inability. They simply cannot believe that God will make possible what He requires of a believer."[769]

It is the desire of the Spirit that our sanctification or holiness be entire.[770]

---

[767]μομφή (*momphe*) occurs only in Col 3:13. It is related to μεμψίμοιρος (*mempsimoiros*) [Grundmann, *TDNT*, 4:571-574].

[768]present imperative

[769]Gibson, *Sincerity of God*, 84; see also p. 7.

[770]This is the only place in the New Testament where ὁλοτελής (*holoteles*) occurs. It is comprised of ὅλος (*holos*), meaning all, whole, or entirely and τέλος (*telos*) which means to perfect. It speaks strongly of a completeness to sanctification.

The second word ὁλόκληρος (*holokleros*) means entire, complete, sound in

Paul prays that they would completely attain the goal. This prayer was expressed for those who had experienced the grace of God. Paul said in 3:10 that he prayed earnestly night and day that God would supply what was lacking in their faith. He prays for sanctifying grace that reaches the whole life and the whole person. All believers are cleansed as they walk in light, so that their mistakes and shortcomings are not imputed against them, but this is a deeper cleansing which leaves nothing out, penetrating body, soul, spirit and cleansing through and through, entirely and completely.[771] George Peck explained, "To Christian

---

every part. Wesley took it as a synonym with *teleios*, both meaning "whole" or "complete" [Wesley, *BE Works*, 3:179; see also Trench, *Synonyms*, 74-77].

Regarding the first word, however, Wilber Tillett argued that "wholly" is an adjective, not an adverb and therefore it does not modify "sanctify." Thus, he concluded, "It means that wholeness or entireness or completeness that is reached only at the end (*telos*) of a process; it means "entire and final perfection," and, as used here, it indicates that perfection admits of degrees" [Tillett, *Personal Salvation*, 267]. But if "wholly" does not modify the verb, sanctify," the prayer for the subject cannot be understood without incorporating the verb. You cannot separate the subject and verb. Simply because this adjective technically modifies the noun, the prayer for the noun cannot be understood apart from the action of the verb. Therefore, Paul prays that something will happen to us which will make us complete. Since the verb is "sanctify" the focus of the prayer is that we are sanctified completely. In Greek syntax an adjective can be used as an adverb. "Frequently an adjective is used in its pure adjectival relation where English idiom would require an adverb" [Dana and Mantey, *Manual Grammar*, 119]. Charles Wanamaker calls this adjective a "predicate adjective" and translates it as though it were an adverb [*Thessalonians*, 206]. The process of sanctification may occur in stages or degrees, but Paul's concept is that it can reach a point of completeness. Hermann Cremer wrote that *telos* never refers merely to an end with regard to time or space in and for itself. It always includes the idea of an inner completion or qualitative end [*Biblico-Theological Lexicon*, 541].

[771]Laurence Wood objected that James Mudge rejected Christian perfection and instead argued for a growth in holiness *toward*, but not *to* perfection [Wood, *Meaning of Pentecost*, 318]. Here Wood reflects the criticism of Daniel Steele [*Defense of Christian Perfection*, 11]. Steele observed that Mudge did not say "Christian perfection," but referred to absolute perfection. Steele concluded that the Wesleyan emphasis would be "growth in holiness unto Christian perfection through entire sanctification attainable by faith." Mudge explained that we are to pursue absolute purity and holiness, but that it will not be attained until the resurrection [*Growth in Holiness*, 196-197; 221]. Since Wesley did not advocate absolute perfection, Steele concluded much of Mudge's book "is directed against a man of straw" [p. 52]. Yet entire sanctification is complete in its scope and is imputed as we walk in the light.

Timothy Smith wrote that Mudge was much less revolutionary than Boland had been. "He did not deny the traditional doctrine that believers were sanctified after they were justified. He did, however, acknowledge his divergence from Wesley's view

perfection, then, we must necessarily attach the idea of *holiness*, or *sanctification to the fullest extent of which we are capable in our present state*: — what St. Paul means by being sanctified *wholly*, (1 Thess. 5:23,) and by standing *complete in all the will of God*. Col. 4:12."[772]

It cannot be assumed that Paul is praying for the wholeness of the Thessalonian church since he referred in his prayer to the components of human personality. While the Savior prayed for the unity of his spiritual body in John 17, here Paul prays for the individuals comprising that body that this entire sanctification pervade their whole being. What will this entire sanctification do? Verses12-22 imply at least nine graces:

- It will give us a respect for spiritual authority and for preaching (v 20)
- It will help us live in peace with one another (v 13b)
- It will give us a sensitivity to spiritual needs. The lazy need to be admonished, the fearful need to be encouraged, the weak need to be propped up — it will take patience to deal with them all (v 14).
- It will deliver us from a vindictive, get-even spirit (v 15) and make us kind.
- It will make us joyful and deliver us from blaming and grumbling (v 16)
- It will make our prayer life more consistent (v 17)
- It will make us more thankful; thankful in all circumstances (v 18). Actually vv 16-18 describes unbroken praise to God, unbroken communion with God, and unbroken awareness of God. Wesley said this is Christian perfection.[773]
- It will make us more obedient to the Spirit and more discerning of the Spirit (vv 19, 21)
- It will help us live more consistent and avoid every evil and questionable practice (v 22)

Then Paul prayed that this condition be maintained in them until the return of Christ. Pope observed that the same power which sanctifies as an act preserves that sanctification as a state. This state of holiness is without defect. The whole person becomes entirely the Lord's as his property and as his servant. "Faith in the power of God working by love, keeps the spirit and soul faithful to

---

of an instantaneous experience and denounced as well the sectarian and divisive tendencies of the second-blessing movement" [*Called Unto Holiness*, 45]. However, to categorize Wesley's view of entire sanctification as instantaneous does not do justice to Wesley's thought.

[772]Peck, *Christian Perfection*, 27.

[773]Wesley, *Notes*, 531.

God as the supreme object of worship and source of happiness." All is done with the aim, conscious or latent, to glorify God. "Life has no higher perfection than this; and he who is preserved in this state is wholly sanctified." God does not impute blame to those in this state of entire consecration.[774]

According to v 24, the one who calls you is faithful and he will do it, not simply impute it. "The fidelity of God is pledged to the accomplishment of this." Yet "the Faithful Caller demands faith in the called."[775]

John Wesley said no man can live higher than this, but no man need to live short of this. "Farther than this we cannot go; and we need not stop short of it."[776] "Now to him who is able to do immeasurably more than all we ask or imagine, according to his power that is at work within us" (Eph 3:20). The process has already begun. The Holy Spirit is already at work. And so with Charles Wesley we sing,

Finish then thy new creation,
Pure and spotless let us be;
Let us see thy great salvation
Perfectly restored in Thee;
Changed from glory into glory,
Till in heaven we take our place,
Till we cast our crowns before thee,
Lost in wonder, love, and praise.[777]

In 2 Thessalonians 1:11-12 Paul prayed that the church, who were called out of sin and called unto holiness, be deemed worthy of this calling and thus be glorified by the grace that counts them and makes them worthy.

Pope said the two phrases employed describe the whole of religion. "By his power he may fulfill every good purpose of yours" refers to the perfect realization of all that the regenerate heart can desire. "By his power he may fulfill every act prompted by your faith" refers to the perfect discharge of every obligation that law can impose. In other words these two phrases express Paul's prayer for inward an inward perfection of goodness and an outward perfection of faithfulness and consistency. Finally Paul carries us forward in his prayer to the day when this worthiness shall be acknowledged to be complete "on the day he comes to be glorified in his holy people" (v 10). "What they shall be He will have

---

[774]Pope, *Prayers of St. Paul*, 131-133.

[775]Pope, *Prayers of St. Paul*, 134-135.

[776]Wesley, *Notes*, 531.

[777]Charles Wesley, *Collection of Hymns*, 547.

made them" is the meaning of the last phrase in Paul's prayer. "When we use this prayer, we ask that we may be among the number of those whose imputed and whose imparted worthiness shall both and alike reflect honor on the name of Jesus!"[778]

In the next chapter Paul again prays. He prays in 2:16-17 that the Thessalonian Christians be consoled and established. Through the love and grace of God they have already experienced everlasting comfort and good hope. According to Pope "everlasting consolation" implies nothing less than the healing of the great wound of sin and the removal of its consequences. "Good hope" describes that part of the everlasting gift which has reference to the future. Paul prayed that the Lord himself, in unity with the Father, console their inner man by the word that invigorates and keeps their outer life steadfast in every good work and in every good doctrine.

While they had already received eternal encouragement, Paul is concerned that they not become quickly unsettled or alarmed (2 Thess 2:2). Therefore he prays that their hearts will be kept strong in this same consolation[779] and their life established in obedience. According to Pope the term "comfort" stands for both encouragement in word and invigoration for act. The precise burden of the prayer is that God may bless in them the formation of a character which produces a consistent life of holiness. According to Pope, when the word *every* is added, nothing is lacking in this prayer to qualify it as another of Paul's prayers for a complete Christian perfection. The consistency of a full obedience, implied by *every* good word and deed, depends on the establishment of a firm faith in the Christian doctrine, according to v 15. The life that a Christian should desire is a life of entire goodness based upon perfect truth. In 3:3 Paul declares that the Lord is faithful and will establish us.[780]

In the third chapter of 2 Thessalonians Paul has been requesting prayer for himself when he breaks out in prayer for them at v 5. Paul prays for their direction into the love of God and into the patience of Christ. "In the strength of the love of God, always poured abundantly upon and around, and into the soul, there is no duty past performance, and no difficulty that may not be overcome. No higher prayer can be offered to God than this, that by the sweet influence of His Spirit we may be drawn from every lower affection, released from every base impediment, and have our entire being and all that is in it thrown open to the

[778]Pope, *Prayers of St. Paul*, 136-144

[779]In v 16 παράκλησις (*paraklesis*) is a noun which may be translated *comfort* or *consolation*; in v 17 the verb form of the same word is used (παρακαλέω - *parakaleo*) is aorist active optative. The related word *parakletos* is used elsewhere to describe both Christ and the Holy Spirit as *comforter* or *advocate.*

[780]Pope, *Prayers of St. Paul*, 145-153.

unhindered operation of the love of God." Then Paul literally prays for the stedfastness of patience that is Christ's. This will result in the steadfast obedience described in v 4. The specific meaning of this prayer is that it may please the Lord to remove every hindrance to our perfect union and harmony with our Lord in his example of endurance unto death. In Paul's mind "all that the Christian needs for the struggle and victory of life is the abundant effusion of the love of God into the heart as an active principle and the perfect defense of the heart by the patience of Christ as a passive grace."[781]

At v 16 Paul returns to conclude his prayer. He prays that the Savior himself administer the blessings of his peace. That peace abides on the entire assembly through the abiding presence of the Lord. He can give us peace at all times and in all circumstances. The result is that we may expect a permanent, uninterrupted assurance of his acceptance. This peace of Christ incorporates all that is included in perfect spiritual prosperity. Yet this bold petition also demands that the rage of Satan and the wrath of men should not only praise God, but be turned to the deeper joy of his servant. The previous verses teach the Thessalonians to expect that the unrest and disorder of evil men should result in a far more exceeding peace for the devout. The voice of the Lord may not always hush the storm around or within the soul, but always and by all means he will give his peace in that inner man which ought never to be penetrated by anxiety.[782]

In Hebrews 13:20-21, the writer prays "May God equip you with everything good for doing his will." Here the verb "equip" is καταρτίζω (*katartizo*) one of the New Testament words for perfection. This perfection "signifies the entire deliverance of the soul from everything that would hinder the complete performance of the will of God." Pope connected this perfection with the united heart in Psalm 86:11. Then the God of holiness is petitioned to do his own good pleasure within us so that we are able to manifest his good pleasure externally. He works internally, conforming us to his own image and thus we are enabled to do every good work.[783]

Finally, Peter prays "And the God of all peace, who called you to his eternal glory in Christ, after you have suffered a little while, will himself restore you and make you strong, firm and steadfast. To him be the power for ever and ever. Amen" (1 Peter 5:10-11).

Here the emphasis is not upon suffering, but upon grace. Suffering demonstrates our need for growth in grace. Although Peter's emphasis in this first letter is that Christians will suffer (see 1:6) and that trials should not take us by

---

[781]Pope, *Prayers of St. Paul*, 154-158.

[782]Concepts and phrases in this paragraph originate from Pope, *Prayers of St. Paul*, 159-166.

[783]Pope, *Prayers of St. Paul*, 279-280.

surprise (4:12), persecution and stress, trials and afflictions do not sanctify — they reveal to what degree we are sanctified. Alfred Cookman wrote in the last days of his life, "I used to maintain that the blood was sufficient, but I am coming to know that tribulation brings us to the blood that cleanseth."[784]

Wesley believed that most who are justified gradually die to sin and grow in grace, until at or near the point of death God perfects them in love. God usually gives a considerable time for men to receive light, to grow in grace, to do and suffer his will, before they are either justified or sanctified; but he does not invariably adhere to this; sometimes he 'cuts short his work:' He does the work of many years in a few weeks; perhaps in a week, a day, an hour. He justifies or sanctifies both those who have done or suffered nothing, and who have not had time for a gradual growth either in light or grace.[785]

While this statement is open to misunderstanding, the bottom line is that often we need to go through some things before we become aware of a deeper need. There are four synonyms, all future tense verbs, in 1 Peter 5:10 which are a promise of what God's grace can do in you between now and the end. He can *restore* you (καταρτίζω - *katartizo*). He can supply what is lacking in your faith (1 Thess 3:10 - same word *katartizo*).[786]

He can *establish* you (στηρίζω - *sterizo*). Peter says the grace of God will confirm and support us. The word is used in v 9 where it tells us to stand firm in the faith. We have an invisible means of support. God has the grace to help us stand firm; make you hard, firm, solid. In Acts 14:22 Paul and Barnabas strengthened the disciples and encouraged them to remain true. They preached that we must go through many hardships to enter the kingdom of God. The kingdom is both now and later. We enter the kingdom now through the new birth; we enter heaven later by remaining true. We need this establishing grace so that we will persevere. Paul ends Romans with this same word; "Now to him who is able to establish you by my gospel" (Rom 16:25).

He can *strengthen* you (σθενόω - *sthenoo*). Although this is the only

---

[784]Ridgaway, *Life of Alfred Cookman*, 443.

[785]Wesley, *Works*, 11:423. Yet because this sanctifying grace is by faith and not by works it can happen in a moment and ought to be expected every moment. "Believe . . . that he is not only able, but willing to do it *now*! Not when you come to die; not at any distant time; not tomorrow, but *today*. He will then enable you to believe, *it is done*, according to his word" [Wesley, "On Patience," Sermon #83, § 13].

[786]In his sermon "The God Of All Grace,"Clarke taught that the word perfection signifies to put things dislocated into their places. The Church was here compared to a building which was established on the foundation of Christ, strengthened and supported, and settled — when temptations come to unsettle us [Sermon #55, *Works*, 8:237-239].

place this verb is found in the New Testament, it is found in noun form in the Septuagint, the Greek translation of the Old Testament, where Eliphaz speaks of the strength of a lion (Job 4:10). Satan roars *like* a lion (1 Peter 5:8), but he is not a real lion. Jesus is the lion of the tribe of Judah and he gives us his strength. Grace will keep us from collapsing.

He will *settle* you (θεμελιόω - *themelioo*). He will establish us on a firm foundation. Grace will prevent you from being swept away. S*terizo* denotes solid support *around* us; *themelioo* describes a secure foundation *under* us.[787]

Wesley ended a sermon on hypocrisy with this benediction,

> May the God of all grace, who is long-suffering, of tender mercy, and repenteth him of the evil, fix these things in your hearts, and water the seed he hath sown with the dew of heaven! May he correct whatsoever he seeth amiss in us! May he supply whatsoever is wanting [lacking]! May he perfect that which is according to his will and so establish, strengthen, settle us, that this place may again be a faithful city to her Lord, yea the praise of the whole earth."[788]

Every true Christian hungers for these dynamics. Some theologies offer little encouragement, but Pope declared that "no desire of holiness can be vain."[789] Even though Calvinism teaches there is no deliverance from sin in this life, there is still among godly Calvinists a God-given desire to rise above it. "I often pray, Lord, make me as holy as a pardoned sinner can be made,"confessed Robert Murray M'Cheyne. [790]

The Wesleyan emphasis is the most optimistic, teaching that these hungers are God-given. I am intrigued by the titles of Asbury Lowrey, an old Methodist writer, who wrote *Positive Theology* (1853) and *Possibilities of Grace* (1884).[791] God can save completely or to the uttermost (Heb 7:25). This phrase,

---

[787]In the Septuagint, *sterizo* is used to describe the support of Moses by Aaron and Hur. They put a stone under the hands of Moses and then supported his hands, one on the one side and one on the other (Exod 17:12).

[788]Wesley, "Hypocrisy in Oxford," Sermon #150, 2.16.

[789]Pope, *Compendium*, 3:56.

[790]Bonar, *Memoirs of McCheyne*, 209.

[791]According to Quanstrom, however, no other holiness writer approached Lowrey's claims for the results of an instantaneous eradication which resulted from the grace of entire sanctification. "The language he used to describe the entirely sanctified believer was language that those outside the Holiness tradition had reserved for

εἰς τὸ παντελὲς (*eis to panteles*) means salvation is to the farthest extent, to the greatest degree, to the most distant point.[792] Full salvation is not only freedom from the guilt, the bondage, and the power of sin, but cleansing from the pollution and nature of sin and ultimately deliverance from the very presence of sin. But how much of this complete salvation may be experienced in this life? "Now to him who is able to do immeasurably more than all we ask or imagine, according to his power that is at work with us" (Eph 3:20).

This sanctifying work of the Spirit occurs in all true believers, whether or not they embrace Wesleyan theology. While it is not necessary to adhere to a particular theological system to experience perfecting grace, it is the duty of the Church to counsel, teach, and provide spiritual guidance for believers. The Wesleyan synthesis is the most adequate framework in which to diagnose spiritual needs, discern spiritual unbalance, and direct spiritual formation.

---

glorification" [Quanstrom, *Century of Holiness Theology*, 46]. Lowrey's book, *Possibilities of Grace*, was dropped from the Nazarene ministerial course of study in 1960. Quanstrom explained that according to the Nazarene theologians of the second half of the twentieth century, Lowrey's description of the entirely sanctified state was not longer accepted by them as accurate [p. 127].

[792]The *New American Standard Bible* translated this phrase "forever." Does it express duration or completeness? While it could have a temporal sense, the *New International Version* translated it "completely." It might be translated "utterly," "perfectly," "altogether," or "entirely." The phrase is found in only one other reference, Luke 13:11. It is used to describe a woman who was bent over and unable to straighten completely up. Just as the healing touch of Jesus helped her reach her full height physically, so God enables us spiritually to reach our full potential which is to love God with all our heart. See Robertson, *Word Pictures*, 5:386; Wiley, *Hebrews*, 254-255; Brown, *Meaning of Sanctification*, 192-194.

CHAPTER 4
THE MINISTRY OF THE HOLY SPIRIT

Each member of the Trinity has a role in our sanctification. The Father is the ultimate source of our sanctification. His will for us is that we be sanctified and as our heavenly Father he disciplines us that we might share in his holiness (Heb 12:10).

The Son provided our sanctification through his atonement and through our union with him we are conformed into his image. Hebrews 10:10 combines the will of the Father and the provision of Christ's atonement. "And by that will we have been sanctified through the sacrifice of the body of Jesus Christ once for all."

The Holy Spirit is the direct agent of our sanctification. "God chose you to be saved through the sanctifying work of the Spirit" (2 Thess 2:13). He is the divine enabler who helps us keep the commands of Christ and realize the will of God.

In his study on the use of the word "holiness," Beet observed that the concept of holiness advanced little beyond the development attained in the Old Testament until the book of Acts. There is a greater frequency of holiness as an attribute of the Spirit prior to Acts, but it is in the Acts of the Apostles that church members are call saints or holy persons. This is a complete contrast to 2 Chronicles 23:6 where only the priests are holy.[793]

The Ministry of the Spirit before Pentecost

Pentecost was the Greek name for the Jewish Feast of Weeks, which came on the day after the seventh weekly Sabbath after Passover. It marked the completion of the barley harvest and thus it was also the feast of harvest. Later it also commemorated the giving of the Law at Sinai. Then on Pentecost, in Acts 2, the new covenant was inaugurated with the outpouring of the Holy Spirit.

Daniel Steele contrasted the work of the Spirit prior to Pentecost giving seven observations:

---

[793]Beet, *Holiness as Understood*, 35; 40.

> 1. The conviction for sin does not seem to have been so pungent. Men were driven back from their apostasies by repentance, more through the scourge of divine judgments, wars, locusts, plagues, captivities, than by an inner sense of the exceeding turpitude of sin.
> 2. The Old Testament conversion was a moral change wrought by the will of the penitent, influenced by the Spirit of God, rather than a new creation or a new birth. The very surprise of Nicodemus indicates that the idea of regeneration as a radical spiritual transformation was unfamiliar to the Jewish mind. . . .
> 3. There was no assurance of acceptance with God certified to the penitent soul, no witness of the Spirit, in fact no pardon, but rather the pretermission of sins, as Paul teaches in Romans 3:25. . . .
> 4. Old Testament piety was characterized by bondage, the New by freedom. . . .
> 5. It naturally follows that there was no permanent state of reconciliation, because there was no permanent basis for it in an atonement made once for all and all-sufficient during all time. . . .
> 6. There was no conscious indwelling of the Spirit in Old Testament saints because there was no new or spiritual man in which he could abide. . . . The notion of divine sonship as conferred upon Israel as a nation, and then upon the anointed king, is found in the Old Testament. But the sonship of individuals is a glorious gospel promise, the distinctive prerogative of believers in Christ. . . .
> 7. Of course entire sanctification except in a ceremonial sense was not enjoyed by the Old Testament saints.[794]

Jesus expressed the difference between the work of the Spirit before and after Pentecost by saying "He lives with you and will be in you" (John14:17).[795] Milton S. Agnew outlined the administrative work of the Holy Spirit before Pentecost.

1. He was the divine creative agent
2. He was the divine author of the Scriptures

---

[794]Steele, *Gospel of the Comforter*, 36-38.

[795]Shaw, *Spirit in Redemption*, 41-57.

3. He was active in the redemptive life and ministry of Jesus.[796]

The Old Testament references to the Holy Spirit may be divided into three categories. *First*, there are references to the Spirit's general activity in the world such as his creative work depicted in Genesis 1:2.

Second are references which speak of God acting through specific people. Frequently the Holy Spirit came upon a leader and gave him supernatural power. George Lyons observed that the experience of the Spirit was "an intermittent and temporary endowment of a few specially favored individuals given to them to deal with a specific crisis."[797] The Spirit came upon chosen people enduing them with special spiritual, intellectual, and physical gifts. Such men as Balaam, Saul, Samson, and Cyrus had a special anointing of the Spirit, but their lives did not necessarily demonstrate ethical holiness.

Richard S. Taylor wrote that the baptism of the Spirit is unique to our dispensation. He allowed that there was an emotional or ecstatic fullness in the Old Testament, but it did not necessarily produce ethical results.[798] This observation was based on Daniel Steele's categories of ecstatic fullness, a temporary emotional fullness of the Spirit which leaves no permanent moral effect, charismatic fullness in which the person might not be a real Christian but exhibits some extraordinary gift of the Spirit, and ethical fullness which results in entire sanctification.[799] Charles W. Carter believed that only a few special individuals in the Old Testament were indwelt by the Spirit. He noted:

> Approximately seventy-five, or about three-fourths, of the total references to the Spirit in the Old Testament describe Him as influencing men externally, and in some cases at least, using them instrumentally. On the other hand only approximately one-fourth of the references to the Spirit in the Old Testament represent Him as in some manner inhabiting man internally, though not necessarily permanently.[800]

The Old Testament refers to the Spirit as "holy" three times; twice in

---

[796]Agnew, "Pneumatology,"1:421-425.

[797]Lyons, "Spirit in the Gospels," 34. Dunning made a very similar statement in *Grace, Faith, and Holiness*, 401-402.

[798]Taylor, *God, Man, and Salvation*, 496-497.

[799]Steele, *Defense of Christian Perfection*, 108-111. See also Rose, "Distinguishing the Things That Differ," 8-12.

[800]Carter, *Person and Ministry*, 83; 60.

Isaiah 63 and once in Psalm 51:11. W. T. Purkiser explained:

> It is not to be claimed that these passages teach a regenerating or sanctifying work of the Holy Spirit in Old Testament times that was exactly equivalent to what we find in the New Testament. The age of the Spirit was yet to come. John comments concerning Jesus' promise of the Spirit that the Spirit had not been given, because Jesus was not yet glorified (John 7:39).[801]

Israel's holiness was corporate. However, some Old Testament characters seemed to have a relationship with God that was not the common experience. Richard S. Taylor thinks the experience of Isaiah was a "leap ahead of his dispensation."[802] In one of his sermons, Wesley insisted "David was unquestionably born of God."[803] But in another sermon, when he commented on Matthew 11:11, he realized the Christian dispensation was higher than the Jewish standard. He reasoned that if we enter the kingdom of God by the new birth as John 3:5 teaches, and if John the Baptist was not in the kingdom because it did not come until Pentecost, then neither John the Baptist, Abraham, David, nor any Jew was born again.[804] Wesley declared, "The faith through which we are saved . . . is not barely that which the apostles themselves had while Christ was yet upon the earth."[805] Wesley concluded, "The Apostles themselves had not the proper Christian faith till after the Day of Pentecost."[806] The death, burial, and

[801]Purkiser, *God, Man, and Salvation*, 169. Purkiser made a similar statement in *Exploring Our Christian Faith*, 168.

[802]Taylor, "New Covenant,"364. However, in *Theological Formation*, 118-121, Taylor seems to discount an emphasis on dispensational differences, although admitting that Wesley and Fletcher did make such a distinction [pp. 121-124].

[803]Wesley, "The Great Privilege of those that are Born of God," Sermon #19, 2.4.

[804]Wesley, "Christian Perfection," Sermon #40, 2.10-11. Fletcher spoke of Pentecost as the time when God "set up his kingdom" in the hearts of believers [*Works*, 1:590].

[805]Wesley, "Salvation by Faith," Sermon #1, 1.3.

[806]Wesley, *BE Works*, 10:192; Minutes of 16 June 1747. Yet the disciples before Pentecost were justified under the old covenant [see Wesley's *Notes* on John 14:24; 15:3; 17:17]. Bloesch wrote, "The disciples were justified like the Old Testament patriarchs and prophets were justified — by the promise of the blood, not by actual immersion or participation in the blood. . . . They were on the way to regeneration but not yet totally cleansed" [Bloesch, *Holy Spirit*, 307]. Yet Laurence

resurrection of Jesus Christ could not be proclaimed nor believed until they had become facts. Elmer Long explained that

> Gospel faith is to believe with the heart that God raised Jesus from the dead. This the disciples did not have (Rom 10:9)! It is also very clear to anyone who reads the epistles that all who have this faith are indwelt by the Holy Spirit! This the disciples did not have for the Bible says that he that believeth on the Son hath the witness in himself (1 John 5:10). Anyone who reads the Gospels as well as other parts of the Scriptures will see that the terms "baptism with the Spirit," "being endued," "coming upon," "receiving," and being "filled with the Spirit" are all terms meaning the same experience. Now the Bible clearly teaches that all Christians have this if they are true believers (Rom 8:9; Gal 4:6; Eph 1:13). Pentecost was the beginning of the new covenant which was promised. The disciples were not in that covenant until the Spirit came at Pentecost. While they were with Christ on earth, they had faith enough to leave their nets and follow Him, yet they did not believe in Christ's atonement. Before His resurrection they had no witness of the Spirit (John 14:20). "And they all forsook him and fled" (Mark 14:50). This is not New Testament regeneration![807]

Henry Holloman explained that although some select individuals in Old Testament times were indwelt by God's Spirit, that indwelling was temporary. God's relationship to his people under the old covenant was primarily through his manifested presence among them as a corporate nation. "Only under the New Covenant does the Spirit permanently indwell each believer. . . . The Christ-in-you relationship began at Pentecost for all believing Jews and Gentiles."[808]

Robert Tuttle concluded, "In effect, there were no Christians prior to Pentecost. Oh, there were people in right relationship with God, but there were no Christians, as such, since to be a Christian is not only to be a descendant of Abraham; but, once again, to be baptized by the Holy Spirit into the body of Jesus

---

Wood thinks that Wesley may have gone too far in minimizing the possibilities of grace prior to Pentecost [*Pentecostal Grace*, 55]. I think that under the old covenant we have imputed righteousness, but under the new covenant we have both imputed *and* imparted righteousness. This was the theology of John Fletcher who taught that pre-Pentecost believers were justified, but not regenerated [*Works*, 3:151].

[807]Long, "Pentecost," 1.

[808]Holloman, *Forgotten Blessing*, 27; 40.

Christ, *his Church*, and empowered to bear fruit."[809]

David's prayer that God would not take the Holy Spirit from him (Psalm 51:11) does not prove that he was born again or entirely sanctified. According to 1 Samuel 16:13 when David was anointed as king the Spirit came upon him. This was the normal operation of the Holy Spirit in the Old Testament. There was a special anointing of the Spirit for leaders. As the "anointed one" David was a type of the coming King, the Messiah. It is significant that 1 Samuel 16:14 records the Spirit had departed from Saul. If David was anointed because Saul was rejected (16:1), then for David to lose the anointing would mean that he, too, was rejected as king. Richard Watson observed that David's prayer for a clean heart and a right spirit was not proof of his regeneration, but it was evidence that he needed to be born again.[810]

Regeneration is the restoration of life to the spirit of man. Thomas Ralston explained that

> here all the important doctrines of the gospel meet; and any radical error in the theories of men may generally be detected. For it may well be said, that whoever is sound in his entire view of the doctrine of regeneration, cannot be seriously erroneous in any essential doctrine of salvation; but, on the other hand, a radical error as this doctrine will not only extend its influence to almost every leading doctrine of Christianity, but it will endanger the salvation of the soul.[811]

Wesley declared,

> No man is able to work it in himself. It is a work of omnipotence. It requires no less power thus to quicken a dead soul than to raise a body that lies in the grave. It is a new creation; and none can create a soul anew but he who at first created the heavens and the earth.[812]

While the term "justification" refers to our legal standing, regeneration is "that work of the Holy Spirit by which we experience a change of heart." Richard Watson continued, "The change in regeneration consists in the recovery

---

[809]Tuttle, *Sanctity without Starch*, 111.

[810]Watson, *Theological Institutes*, 2:254.

[811]Ralston, *Elements of Divinity*, 417.

[812]Wesley, *An Earnest Appeal to Men of Reason and Religion*, ¶ 9, *Works*, 8:5.

of the moral image of God upon the heart."[813] Watson declared,

> It is a mighty change in man, wrought by the Holy Spirit, by which the dominion which sin has over man in his natural state, and which he deplores and struggles against in his penitent state, is broken and abolished.[814]

According to Luther Lee,

> Regeneration is a renewal of our fallen nature, by the power of the Holy Spirit, received through faith in Jesus Christ, whereby the regenerate are delivered from the power of sin which reigns over all the unregenerate, so that they love God, and through grace serve Him with the affections of the heart.[815]

Ray Dunning explained the role of the Spirit in Christian experience:

> The Holy Spirit is the life-giving agent in the new birth by which the process of being transformed into the image of God is begun; and the Spirit continues to function as the Agent of growth and transformation with this same goal until it is finally achieved in its fullness at the consummation.[816]

The moral image of God which was lost in the first Adam was to be regained in the last Adam, Jesus Christ, and implanted in the believer through the new birth. If this definition is accepted, then it leads to the conclusion that regeneration was not a common privilege under the old covenant. It awaited the atoning work of Christ and the outpouring of the Spirit.

Josephus called the return of his people from exile a "regeneration," but the Jews "did not describe themselves or others as regenerate." According to the *Theological Dictionary of the New Testament*, "the thought of regeneration was adopted as an expression of their hope, though not, of course of their experience.

---

[813]Watson, *Biblical and Theological Dictionary*, 815.

[814]Watson, *Theological Institutes*, 2:267. Clarke taught, "Justification comes through what Christ has done FOR man. Sanctification comes through what Christ's Spirit does IN man" ["The Corruption That Is In the World Through Lust," Sermon #30, *Works*, 6:381].

[815]Lee, *Elements of Theology*, 194.

[816]Dunning, "A Wesleyan Perspective,"193.

. . . After the resurrection of Jesus it was a present reality."[817] Edersheim explained that in Jewish liturgy when proselytes were baptized they were considered "born anew." "But this new birth was not 'a birth from above' in the sense of moral or spiritual renovation, but only as implying a new relationship to God, to Israel, and to his own past, present, and future."[818]

Nowhere in the Old Testament are individual believers called "sons of God." Daniel Steele wrote, "That individual sonship to God was a strange doctrine to the Jews, who were diligent students of their Scriptures, is seen in their indignant surprise that Jesus should dare call God His Father."[819] Israel collectively is called the son of God (Exod 4:22-3) and every reference in the Old Testament to "sons of God is a reference to God's people collectively or to the angelic host. "The description of God as Father refers in the OT only to His relationship with the people of Israel or to the king of Israel. It never refers to any other individual or to mankind in general."[820]

In the days of Christ the distance between God and man was widening in popular thought, rather than growing narrower. No one ever addressed God directly as "My Father," because it would have been considered disrespectful. The Old Testament does not contain a clear reference to God as the Father of an individual believer.[821] Jeremias asserted that in the literature of early Palestinian Judaism "there is no evidence of 'my Father' being used as a personal address to God."[822] Yet in the Gospels Jesus called God "Father" 170 times. Jewish slaves were never allowed to address their master as "father."[823] Yet Jesus always addressed God as "Father" except in Matthew 27:46. When Jesus authorized his disciples to address God as "Father," he completely reversed the trend of his day. Yet under the new covenant the sons of God have received the Holy Spirit who leads us to cry, Abba, Father" (Rom 8:14-16; Gal 4:6-7). Leon Morris explained,

> Not many people in the Old Testament are said to have actually known the Lord. In those days it was rather an aspiration, something that people might greatly long for, but which they felt

---

[817]Buchsel, ἀναγεννάω, *TDNT*, 1:674-675.

[818]Edersheim, *Life and Times of Jesus*, 2:746.

[819]Steele, *Mile-Stone Papers*, 13.

[820]Hofius, "Father,"1:617.

[821]Payne, "אבא,"1:6.

[822]Jeremias, *Prayers of Jesus*, 57.

[823]Sutcliffe, *Commentary*, 2:458; Watson, *Sermons*, 2:342.

> they were not likely to attain. The new covenant would see a radical alteration of this situation. It would bring all God's people into a personal knowledge of him.[824]

Two individuals in the Old Testament were called "friends" of God. Abraham was called the friend of God in 2 Chronicles 20:7, Isaiah 41:8, and James 2:23. Apparently Abraham was more than God's slave in the sense that God did not hide his purpose from Abraham (Gen 18:17; John 8:56).

Moses spoke face to face with God, as a man speaks with his friend (Exod 33:11; Numb 12:8). God spoke directly to Moses and not through any kind of medium.[825] However, we must remember that Moses spoke to God on behalf of the people of Israel and that no one else in his day enjoyed this special relationship (Exod 20:19).

In 2 Corinthians 3:13 Paul tells us that Moses veiled his face to hide the fact that the glory of his encounter with God was fading away. Paul uses this historic event to illustrate a doctrinal truth; the new covenant is more glorious than the old. The glory of the old covenant was external, but the glory of the new covenant is intimate and internal.[826] Paul said that we do not need to cover our faces because we have the abiding presence of the Spirit. The glory of God shines on our face because the Spirit of God lives in our heart. According to Paul the old covenant brought bondage and death, while the new covenant brings life and liberty.[827] The chapter ends with the explanation that we are being transformed into his likeness and this results in an ever-increasing glory (2 Cor 3:18).

In John 15:15 Jesus said to His disciples, "I no longer call you servants, because a servant does not know his master's business. Instead, I have called you friends, for everything that I learned from my Father I have made known to you." This new relationship is based on confidence. Cole explained, "The mark of a friend (as opposed to the servant) is that he knows the purpose and meaning of the commands given to him."[828]

The *third* category of references to the Holy Spirit in the Old Testament relates to the prophecies of a new age of the Spirit.[829] The Old Testament prophets predicted the outpouring of the Spirit, although they did not witness that

---

[824]Morris, *Atonement*, 29.

[825]Keil and Delitzsch, *Commentary*, 2:234.

[826]Hughes, *Second Corinthians*, 103.

[827]Steele, *Half-Hours with Paul*, 176-179.

[828]Cole, *Exodus*, 224.

[829]Greathouse, *Fullness of the Spirit*, 41-46.

outpouring.[830] In the New Testament the metaphor changes from "outpouring" to "baptism." Prior to John the Baptist "baptism" was never used in this context.

As the leader of his people, Moses had a special relationship with God. God communicated with his prophets through dreams and visions, but God spoke face to face with Moses (Numb 12:6-7). When the Holy Spirit came on seventy elders of Israel, Joshua felt that only Moses was to have such an anointing. But Moses exclaimed, "Are you jealous for my sake? I wish all the Lord's people were prophets and that the Lord would put his Spirit on them!" (Numb 11:29).

While the gift of the Spirit was not a common privilege in those days, Joel looked forward to a day in which the Spirit would be poured out upon all flesh—even slaves and women! He said, "I will pour out my Spirit on all people. Your sons and daughters will prophesy, your old men will dream dreams, your young men will see visions. Even on my servants, both men and women, I will pour out my Spirit in those days" (Joel 2:28-29).

This promise is quoted in one way or another in nine New Testament contexts. In the most important connection, Peter made it clear that Pentecost was the beginning of the fulfillment when he said, "This is it" (Acts 2:16).

The early church was living at the end of the old age and the beginning of the new age. Peter called this period of time "the last days." Two events marked the beginning of "the last days:" the old system was destroyed by the Jerusalem holocaust and the new covenant was inaugurated by the Jerusalem Pentecost (Acts 2:17-21). In symbolic language the prophet said it would seem that everything was breaking loose at once when God intervened.[831]

While Joel may have limited this giving of the Spirit to Israel, yet Paul made it clear that both Jew and Gentile were part of the new Israel (Rom 10:12-13) and quoted from the Joel passage. We are living in the new age and there is no longer any distinction between bond and free (Gal 3:28).

The only passage in the Old Testament which refers specifically to the "new covenant" is Jeremiah 31:31-34.[832] The Jews needed a new covenant because they had broken the old one. Since the context, again, is a covenant made with Israel, some dispensationalists have concluded that there must be two new covenants—one to Israel and another to the Church. It is better to conclude that the new covenant was enlarged to include Gentiles (Rom 11:17-20). In Hebrews 8 the promise of Jeremiah 31:31-34 is quoted as a present reality, not the future promise of a Jewish millennium. According to Paul the days of segregation are

---

[830]For example, see Isa 32:15; 44:3; Ezek 39:25-29; Joel 2:28-29.

[831]Stuart, *Hosea-Jonah*, 31:261.

[832]Thompson, *Jeremiah*, 579.

over (Gal 3:28-29; Eph 2:12-13, 3:6).[833]

Jeremiah prophesied that God would put his law in "their minds and write it on their hearts." According to Charles L. Feinberg this implies the new birth. "The new covenant will include a revolutionary change in will, heart, and conscience. It will be an internal rather than an external covenant."[834] Paul expressed this thought to the Corinthians, saying "You show that you are a letter from Christ, the result of our ministry, written not with ink but with the Spirit of the living God, not on tablets of stone but on tablets of human hearts" (2 Cor 3:3).

John Wesley said that Jeremiah's purpose was to express the difference between the law and the gospel. He continued to explain:

> The first shows duty, the latter brings the grace of regeneration, by which the heart is changed, and enabled for duty. All under the time of the law that came to salvation, were saved by this new covenant; but this was not evidently exhibited; neither was the regenerating grace of God so common under the time of the law, as it hath been under the gospel.[835]

Under the new covenant, Jeremiah said the people of God would no longer rely on intermediaries such as Moses, priests, prophets, and teachers. This does not mean the gift of teaching is not necessary, but it does mean that every believer can know God personally. Keil explained,

> The knowledge of Jahveh, of which the prophet speaks, is not the theoretic knowledge which is imparted and acquired by means of religious instruction; it is rather knowledge of divine grace based upon the inward experience of the heart, which knowledge the Holy Spirit works in the heart assuring the sinner that he has indeed been adopted as a son of God through the forgiveness of sins.[836]

"Probably the most significant contribution which Jeremiah made to religious thought was inherent in his insistence that the new covenant involved a one-to-one relationship of the spirit."[837] Along with regeneration and a personal

---

[833]Fuller, *Gospel and Law*, 165-166.

[834]Feinburg, *Jeremiah*, 6:576.

[835]Wesley, *Notes*, 3:2209.

[836]Keil and Delitzsch, *Jeremiah*, 20:40.

[837]Harrison, *Jeremiah and Lamentations*, 19:140.

relationship with God is the promise of forgiveness: "For I will forgive their wickedness and remember their sins no more" (Jer 31:34).

What was an external commandment under the old covenant becomes an internal principle of life. The demands of the law to be holy cannot be fulfilled by sinful man. He forgives our transgressions of the law, but he does not eliminate the standard for holiness. Rather, he enables the believer to keep his commandments.

Ezekiel prophesied that we would be enabled through the power of the Holy Spirit. Of the thirty major passages on which John Wesley based his doctrine of Christian perfection, Ezekiel 36:25-29 was the only Old Testament passage.[838] This is in contrast to later holiness preachers who seemed to realize no difference between experience under the old covenant and the new covenant. Stephen Gibson conceded that the conservative holiness movement handled the Old Testament deplorably in many cases.

> We use it as a book of illustrations and say that the people who lived then could not be saved as we are, because Jesus had not died yet. Yet we teach that the disciples were saved before Pentecost, so that event can be an example of a second work of grace, which means they must have been saved before Jesus died.[839]

Richard S. Taylor is helpful in categorizing holiness texts. In class A texts the holiness meaning is primary and must carry the weight of our doctrinal preaching. In class B texts the holiness meaning is implicit, but not explicit. These texts are only inferences. Class C texts are texts which more or less illustrate holiness truth. He recognized many familiar Old Testament texts can only be used to illustrate New Testament privileges.[840]

Through Ezekiel God promised to put his Spirit in us and this would enable us to keep God's commandments. Again the prophet promised a new heart and a new spirit which refers to regeneration.[841] The major difference between this description of the new covenant and other such passages is Ezekiel's emphasis on the Holy Spirit. Wesley commented that the Spirit promised was "the Holy Spirit

---

[838]Sangster, *Path to Perfection*, 37.

[839]Gibson, *Held by Conviction*, 75.

[840]Taylor, *Preaching Holiness Today*, 94-96; 144-145.

[841]However, Richard S. Taylor used the metaphor of removing the heart of stone to imply eradication ["Why the Holiness Movement Died," 135].

of God, which is given to, and dwelleth in all true believers."[842]

God also promised through Ezekiel to cleanse the believer from all impurities. Edwin Yamauchi pointed out that in denouncing moral uncleanness, the prophets used ritual uncleanness as a metaphor for the wickedness which only God could cleanse.[843] According to Wesley this sprinkling spoken of by Ezekiel symbolized both the cleansing of a guilty conscience and the purification of the soul from all corrupt inclinations and dispositions.[844] Adam Clarke said every true Christian was filled with the nature and Spirit of Christ. However it is the birthright of every Christian believer to be cleansed from all unrighteousness—"the complete destruction of all sin in his soul."[845] Wesley made use of this scripture four times in *A Plain Account of Christian Perfection.* However, he realized the regenerating and sanctifying work of the Holy Spirit was not a present reality in Ezekiel's day, but a future hope realized in the new covenant.

Jesus made it clear that the Holy Spirit would not be given until he was glorified (John 7:39). "Here we see a clear reference to Pentecost as the time when those who would follow Christ are born of water and the Spirit."[846] Jesus said that unless he went away the Comforter would not come, but that after he left he would send the Spirit (John 16:7). Of course, as God, the Holy Spirit was omnipresent and we do find him at work in the world as early as Genesis 1:2. But to do the work promised by the Old Testament prophets, Jesus had to first return to heaven and then send the Spirit.

The writer of Hebrews used four different words to tell us that the Old Testament sacrifices were pointing ahead to something better—a time of reformation (9:10). They were an illustration or parable (9:9), copies (9:23), an antitype (9:24), and a shadow (10:1). According to Hebrews 9:16, the new covenant did not take effect until after Christ died.

The writer of Hebrews used the word *better* thirteen times in comparing the spiritual life of the Jewish believer with the privileges of the new covenant. Through the atonement of Jesus Christ we have the forgiveness of sins and a place among those who have been sanctified.

According to Hebrews 10:11-12 the Old Testament ritual restored the Jew and made him eligible to participate in the worship ceremonies, but it did not deal with the inward sense of guilt. Each new sin required a new sacrifice and the

---

[842]Wesley, *Notes*, 3:2385.

[843]Yamauchi, טמא.1:349.

[844]Wesley, *Notes*, 3:2385.

[845]Clarke, *Commentary*, 4:521.

[846]Bloesch, *Holy Spirit*, 305.

sacrifices could "never take away sins." These rituals "were not able to clear the conscience of the worshipper" (9:9), but only produced ceremonial purity (9:13-14). Daniel Steele explained that there was no permanent state of reconciliation, because there was no permanent atonement made once for all.[847]

Paul stated in Romans 3:25 that God passed over the sins committed before the atonement of Christ. According to John Murray, "passing over" occurs only here in the New Testament and is not equivalent to justification. "This by-passing is not to be equated with remission. Suspension is not equivalent to forgiveness."[848] This understanding was the background for Paul's sermon in Athens. "In times past," he said, "God overlooked such ignorance" (Acts 17:30).[849]

The writer of Hebrews also stresses that perfection was not possible under the Levitical priesthood (7:11). He explained that the law made nothing perfect (7:19; 10:1). However, the same writer exhorts the believer to go on unto perfection (6:1) in light of the fact that it is possible for spiritual infants to grow up to full mature (5:13-14).[850] The author also writes of just men who have been perfected (12:23). H. Orton Wiley wrote that this last clause "may apply to either the present or the future state of man, and in a true sense does apply to both."[851]

Hebrews 6 encourages us not to go back but to go on and be diligent to the very end. We are told in v 12 not to be slothful or dull but to pursue the promises of God. But we will not move forward without hope. Our hope is based upon God's Word. It is an anchor for the soul. It provides consolation. It is our security. It leads us into the presence of God (see Psalm 91:1). Therefore, we enter the into the most holy place. Perfection did not come through the Levitical priesthood (7:11), but Christ is able to save us to the uttermost (7:25). Through the blood of Christ we can enter into a deeper, more intimate relationship with God.

During the process of sanctification, described by a present participle in Hebrews 10:14, the believer reaches a point of relative perfection.[852] Through the

---

[847]Steele, *Gospel of the Comforter*, 37.

[848]Murray, *Romans*, 119.

[849]While Taylor cited this reference as proof that ignorance is an excuse before God [*Theological Formulation*, 59], the real point is that God did not impute sin where there was complete ignorance.

[850]The adjective τέλειος (*teleios*) in Heb 5:14 is related to the noun τελειότης (*teleiotes*) in Heb 6:1.

[851]Wiley, *Hebrews*, 404.

[852]Sangster objected to the term "relative perfection," asking whether the best that once can do in any circumstance should be equated with perfection [*Path to*

sacrifice of Christ sanctification is possible (10:10) and through that same atonement those who are being sanctified may be perfected (10:14). There is a sense in which our sanctification is an ongoing process. Those who have become holy are called to become holy. However, this does not mean that sanctification is an endless process because the same verse also says that the provision for our perfection was completed forever by one offering. Thus, Christ has done everything that was needful in order to provide for our sanctification. Therefore, while Hebrews 11 lists many great men and women of faith under the old covenant, none of them realized this "better thing," which included perfection (v 40), until Christ finished his work. Now, however, he is the author and perfector of our faith (Heb 12:2). The result, however, is not "once sanctified, always sanctified" but the continuous cleansing of the blood which keeps us holy. This Christian perfection is described as being saved to the uttermost and it is based, not only on the finished work of Christ in atonement, but upon his continual work of intercession (Heb 7:25).

It is important to understand that while God has not changed in either his holy nature or his requirements for holy living, something has changed between the Old Testament and the New Testament. That change is the ministry of the Holy Spirit. Chrysostom compared the old and new covenants, distinguishing between ceremonial separation and moral purification:

> What then is the distinction between the first and the second? The first is the honor of a name, in the second the thing goes with it. Of the first the Prophet says, "I have said, Ye are gods, and all of you are children of the Most High" (Psalm 82:6); but of the latter, that they "were born of God." How, and in what way? By the washing of regeneration, and renewing of the Holy Ghost. For they, even after they had received the title of sons, retained the spirit of slavery, (for while they remained slaves they were honored with this appellation,) but we being made free, received the honor, not in name, but in deed. And this Paul has declared

---

Perfection, 179; 185]. That is not my concept of relative perfection. Rather, I am making a distinction between absolute perfection of which only God is capable and *Christian* perfection. Murphree came at this question differently, but arrived at the same conclusion. He contended that "perfection" was an absolute term. Therefore, there could be no comparative or superlative degrees of perfection. But he explained that perfection is only absolute in the area to which the perfection refers. Thus, he concluded that perfection refers to a controlling motive rather than actions [Murphree, *Love Motive*, 55-56]. Majorie Hewitt Suchocki wrote that this perfection could be called a "processive condition, adapted to the situation of the believer, and always luring the believer on toward yet fuller realization of love" [Suchocki, "Coming Home," 59-60].

> and said, "For ye have not received the spirit of bondage again to fear, but ye have received the Spirit of adoption, whereby we cry, Abba, Father." (Rom 8:15) For having been born again, and, as one may say, thoroughly remade, we so are called "sons." And if one consider the character of the holiness, what the first was and what the second, he will find there also great difference. They, when they did not worship idols, nor commit fornication or adultery, were called by this name; but we become holy, not by refraining from these vices merely, but by acquiring things greater. And this gift we obtain first by means of the coming upon us of the Holy Ghost; and next, by a rule of life far more comprehensive than that of the Jews. To prove that these words are not mere boasting hear what He saith to them, "Ye shall not use divination, nor make purification of your children, for ye are a holy people. So that holiness with them consisted in being free from the customs of idolatry; but it is not so with us. "That she may be holy," saith Paul, "in body and spirit." (1 Cor 7:34) "Follow peace, and holiness, without which no man shall see the Lord" (Heb 12:14): and, "Perfecting holiness in the fear of God." (2 Cor 7:1).[853]

The Acts of the Holy Spirit

When we turn to the book of Acts we find the Holy Spirit is given six times (2:4, 4:31, 8:17, 9:17, 10:44, and 19:6). These references have often been appealed to as proof of a second crisis experience by the Keswick and Holiness movements, as well as some within the Pentecostal movement. However, there are some problems with such a model. The book of Acts is not primarily a doctrinal book, but instead it records the history of the early church. It marks the transition between the Old and New Testaments.

Sinclair Ferguson wrote that the experience of the disciples is not a paradigm for the church, "for the obvious reason that they, uniquely, span the period of transition from old to new covenant faith. Their experience is epoch-crossing, and consequently atypical and non-paradigmatic in nature."[854]

> The first disciples' experience in this context was obviously in some elements unique. They alone belonged to the time before and after Christ. Like other believers of the Old Testament era,

---

[853]Chrysostom, *NPNF*, First Series, 14:48; Homily 14:2.

[854]Ferguson, *Holy Spirit*, 80.

> they were regenerated before the death, resurrection, ascension and Pentecost events (and in some sense, united to Christ). But like believers in all ages thereafter, they also received the Spirit of the *ascended* Christ, an event which (in their case necessarily) was chronologically separated from their regeneration. Their entrance into all that union with Christ means to New Testament believers was therefore progressive. By contrast, for Christians after the initial period of overlap between the Old and New epochs of redemption, the experiences of faith, regeneration *and* baptism with the Spirit take place simultaneously — a threefold perspective on the one event in which no perspective is simply reducible to either of the other two.[855]

Yet Laurence Wood misrepresented the Wesleyan view by responding,

> A Wesleyan view does not hold to a rigid notion of time in a purely sequential way. It may be that the experience of some believes on the continuum of salvation history are pre-Abrahamic; others are pre-Mosaic; some are pre-Pentecostal; some are Pentecostal Christians. The quality of one's Christian life is measured in terms of where one is participating in the timeline of salvation history. . . . The several instances in Acts where there is a distinction in time between believer's repentance and initial faith in Christ and a subsequent reception of the Pentecostal Spirit implies that this pattern is typical in the life of believers.[856]

While John Fletcher and Daniel Steele observed that it is possible experientially to be living like Old Testament servants, the question is whether believers under the old covenant could be living experientially under the new covenant *before* that grace was made available. The disciples were not fully Christian before Pentecost. Therefore, the transition from the old to the new is not a paradigm for Christian growth. Wood erroneously uses a unique situation to

---

[855]Ferguson, *Christian Spirituality*, 51-52.

[856]Wood, *Christian Spirituality*, 86-87. This leads to more erroneous conclusions on p. 100, where Wood argues for a distinction between receiving the Son and the sending of the Spirit. But the Trinity cannot be divided, a fact which Wood tried to reconcile with his theology on p. 101. Wood then attempts to illustrate what he had failed to demonstrate through a reference to topography and Israel's exodus-conquest pattern [pp. 102-109].

become a typical pattern.[857]

The subsequent "Pentecosts" in the book of Acts at Samaria, Caesarea, and Ephesus were all connected with and an extension of the inaugural event in Jerusalem. Ferguson wrote that Pentecost was a unique historical event which is not repeated any more than the death or resurrection of Christ is a repeatable event. However "implications of the baptism with the Spirit which took place on that occasion overflow the banks of that day and flow on, down through the centuries." According to 1 Corinthians 12:13 "all believers are baptized with the Spirit and drink the water of the Spirit. Elements of the Pentecost event are thus reduplicated in believers in every age."[858] Yet the message of the holiness movement was that the baptism with the Holy Spirit was entire sanctification and Pentecost *can* be repeated. This was carried to its logical conclusion by the pentecostal movement which tried to emphasize the once-for-all non-repeatable aspects.

In *The Path to Perfection,* Sangster listed the basic texts which John Wesley used to preach the doctrine of Christian perfection. We have already noted that only one is from the Old Testament (Ezekiel 36), and of the twenty-four remaining texts not one is from the book of Acts.[859] Peter Böhler had searched the Scriptures with Wesley and they had concluded that there were scarcely any instances other than instantaneous conversion in the book of Acts.[860] Thus, Wesley interpreted experience in the book of Acts as initial and not entire sanctification.

However, Charles Ewing Brown, trying to advocate that the baptism of the Holy Spirit was a second work of grace, wrote that these accounts in the book

---

[857]This point is made by Gerhard Forde, "it seems questionable to draw dogmatic conclusion from what was considered even in Acts to be highly irregular" [*Christian Spirituality*, 121-122].

[858]Ferguson, *Holy Spirit*, 86-88.

[859]Sangster, *Path to Perfection*, 37-52: Matt 5:8; Matt 5:48; Matt 6:10; John 8:34-36; John 17:20-23; Rom 2:29; Rom 12:1-2; 2 Cor 3:17; 2 Cor 7:1; Gal 2:20; Eph 3:14-19; Eph 5:27;
Phil 3:15; 1 Thess 5:23; Titus 2:11-14; Heb 6:1; Heb 7:25; Heb 10:14; James 1:4; 1 John 1:5-7; 1 John 1:8-9; 1 John 2:6; 1 John 3:3; 8-10; 1 John 5:13. Sangster promised thirty passages but only gave twenty-six. *The Wesley Study Bible* gives "The Thirty Texts of Wesley," [Harper, 1951-1952]. It is the same as the list above, but adds Matt 22:37 and Heb 12:14 and omits 2 Cor 3:17 and 1 John 2:6. Thus, it does not give 30 texts either.

[860]Wesley, *Journal*, 22 April 1738. The one specific exception Wesley mentioned was the conversion of Paul which took three days. Scarcely any other conversion was as slow.

of Acts "concerning the baptism of the Holy Spirit have been a source of confusion and bewilderment to the technical theologians from time out of mind." Brown then presented two of their alternatives as unsatisfactory: the "clever little theory" of the cessationists who taught that miracles were confined to the apostolic age or the liberal interpretation that the baptism of the Spirit recorded in Acts represents hysterical excitement of ignorant men in a superstitious age. Rejecting both of these alternatives, Brown then declared,

> Even the early Methodist theologians were so far misled by the technical theologians that they failed to put proper emphasis on the baptism of the Holy Spirit. They tended to interpret sanctification as a crisis experience, it is true, but found most of their proof texts in other parts of the New Testament.[861]

Yet Brown cannot legitimately conclude that the early Methodist theologians did not interpret Acts as he did for either of these reasons. In fact the early Methodists were accused of being "enthusiasts" because they did believe in the personal ministry of the Holy Spirit, especially his direct assurance of salvation.[862]

Daniel Steele was probably the first holiness writer to cite Acts 15:8-9 as evidence that the Pentecostal baptism accomplishes the heart cleansing of entire sanctification.[863] While this was Steele's emphasis in *Love Enthroned* (1875), he did not take this view later in life. Even in *Love Enthroned* Steele allowed that Acts 10:44 and perhaps 9:17 were exceptional cases in which the baptism of the Holy Ghost was blended with regeneration.[864] In *A Defense of Christian Perfection* (1896), Steele conceded that the phrase "baptism or fullness of the Spirit" "may mean something less than entire sanctification. . . . The phrase 'fullness of the Spirit' is not a certain proof text of entire sanctification."[865]

Asbury Lowrey (1816-1898) was a Methodist who advocated the holiness message. Yet he had a wholistic understanding of the baptism of the Holy Spirit, defining it at a generic name for all the offices of the Spirit such as Comforter,

---

[861]Brown, *Meaning of Sanctification*, 114-115.

[862]The Methodist emphasis was neither charismatic nor cessationist. See the discussion in Reasoner, *Romans*, 35-37.

[863]Greathouse, *Historical Development*, 313. See also Steele, "Personal Pentecosts," 49-51, where he taught the disciples moved from justification to sanctification at Pentecost.

[864]Steele, *Love Enthroned*, 71.

[865]Steele, *Defense of Christian Perfection*, 109; 111.

unction, seal, and earnest. He felt the whole subject of baptism had been confused by controversy over the mode of water baptism. Lowrey did not make a direct equation of Spirit baptism and entire sanctification, but declared "the baptism of the Holy Spirit is the gist of Christianity, the key-note of the new dispensation, the motive power that moves all its machinery. There is nothing to differentiate Christianity from Judaism but the substitution of the Holy Ghost for the cumbrous externalism of the Levitical code."[866]

On the back dust jacket of the Schmul Publishers reprint of Whedon's *Commentary*, Leslie Wilcox endorsed Whedon for affirming pentecostal sanctification. While Whedon used this phrase in his comments on Acts 2:4, Whedon distinguished between a higher and lower sanctification. For Whedon, supernatural works do not necessarily imply a regenerate character. The higher sanctification, however, implies some conformity to the heavenly image. Whedon continued to explain that before Pentecost the disciples were holy in the sense of the lower, Mosaic dispensation. However, it was by this outpouring that they were raised to the highest level of sanctification in the new dispensation of the Spirit. Thus, Whedon seems to imply that the disciples were both regenerate *and* entirely sanctified at Pentecost. This interpretation does not square with that of the conservative holiness movement, of which Wilcox was a spokesman.[867]

The key to understanding the Biblical emphasis on the Spirit is found in Acts 2:38. The Bible nowhere gives us any encouragement to seek a duplication of pentecostal phenomenon. Peter does tell us what God's plan is for us. First, we are convicted by the gracious work of the Holy Spirit (v 37), and in response, we confess our sins. Then we are to confess our faith in the Lord Jesus Christ through water baptism. We receive the forgiveness of sins and the gift of the Holy Spirit. This promise of the Spirit is for all whom the Lord calls (Acts 2:39) and the many that the Lord our God will call amounts to "those who receive his word" (v 41).

There are two commands in Acts 2:38. The first is for you all (plural) to repent. There are two promises, the forgiveness of your (plural) sins and you all (plural) will receive the Holy Spirit. The second command is for each one of you (singular) who repents to be baptized.

James Dunn wrote, "It should be noted that no possibility of delay is envisaged here." All are commanded to repent and all who repent will be forgiven. Those who do truly repent and believe do receive the Spirit and those who have received the Spirit are to be baptized. The command to be baptized is on this basis, every one of you (singular) who have received the Spirit, be baptized.

While faith is not mentioned explicitly in this passage, according to Dunn,

---

[866]Lowrey, *Possibilities of Grace*, 344-346.

[867]Whedon, *Commentary*, 3:28.

Luke uses three different words to describe man's act of faith. In faith we turn from [ἀπό - *apo*] sin and toward [ἐπί - *epi*] God. In faith we commit ourselves to [εἰς - *eis*] Christ.[868] As a public testimony that we do believe, we identify with the Church through water baptism. Dunn summarizes the teaching of the New Testament thus:

Faith demands baptism as its expression;
Baptism demands faith for its validity.
The gift of the Spirit presupposes faith as its condition;
Faith is shown to be genuine only by the gift of the Spirit.[869]

Some holiness commentators have argued that since God only gives the Holy Spirit to believers, the gift of the Spirit is a second blessing. George Lyons noted that the passage in John 14:17 does not imply that the world cannot become believers or that the Spirit is received by believers in an experience subsequent to the new birth. He explained that "those who turn from unbelief to faith in Jesus receive the Holy Spirit, which is eternal life."[870] However the normal salvation order as given in Acts 2:38 demonstrates that all receive the Spirit when they truly believe. This was the view of early Methodism and is reflected in the comments of Joseph Benson:

> Observe, reader, all that receive the remission of sins, and are adopted into God's family, receive the gift of the Holy Ghost, as a Spirit of adoption and regeneration; to assure them of their sonship, and renew them after God's image.[871]

Luther Lee, a founder of the Wesleyan Methodist Connection in 1843, wrote that the subjects of Acts 2:38 were not yet regenerated or pardoned, but they were baptized in water *before* they were regenerate.[872]

One extreme view of Acts 2:38 teaches baptismal regeneration. While the

---

[868]Dunn, *Baptism in the Holy Spirit*, 91. The preposition *apo* is found in v 40; *epi* and *eis* are both in v 38. To be baptized *into* the name of Jesus means we are to embrace everything the name of Jesus represents: that he is both Lord and Christ (Acts 2:36). Jesus himself commanded us to be baptized in the name of the Trinity (Matt 28:19).

[869]Dunn, *Baptism in the Holy Spirit*, 228.

[870]Lyons, "The Spirit in the Gospels,"72.

[871]Benson, *Notes*, 4:693.

[872]Lee, *Elements of Theology*, 550-551.

command is to "be baptized *for* the remission of sins," the preposition εἰς (*eis* - for) can mean "because of," or "on the basis of" forgiveness of sins.[873] It is like saying, "I took an aspirin *for* a headache" or "I was jailed *for* a crime." The opposite extreme, which some within the holiness movement have taken, teaches that Spirit baptism replaces water baptism. However, F. F. Bruce declared that "the idea of an unbaptized Christian is simply not entertained in the New Testament."[874] It is not water baptism which produces regeneration, but the gift of the Holy Spirit. Howard Marshall explained, "The Spirit accomplishes the inner cleansing of which baptism is the outward symbol."[875]

John Wesley taught that "every man, in order to believe unto salvation, must receive the Holy Ghost."[876] However, W. B. Godbey claimed that the Holy Spirit gives the gifts of conviction, repentance, regeneration, justification, and adoption to the sinner and then when you are truly converted you may receive the gift of the Holy Spirit which, according to Godbey, is to be sanctified wholly.[877] Leslie Wilcox also believed that regeneration is a work of the Spirit, but we do not receive the Spirit until entire sanctification.[878] Russell R. Byrum taught that "every Christian has the Holy Spirit in him, but this is not saying every believer has the baptism with the Spirit."[879] Richard S. Taylor tried to distinguish between the birth of the Spirit and the baptism of the Spirit.[880] Holiness writers often try to make a distinction between receiving the Spirit and the baptism of the Spirit, but it is difficult to see that the baptism of the Spirit is subsequent to receiving the Spirit. Bruce believes that "in general, it seems to be assumed throughout the New Testament that those who believe and are baptized have also the Spirit of God."[881]

Biblical writers refer to the giving of the Holy Spirit at Pentecost as

---

[873]Dana and Mantey, *Manual Grammar*, 103-104; Turner, *Syntax*, 3:266; Wallace, *Greek Grammar*, 369-371.

[874]Bruce, *Acts*, 70; 363.

[875]Marshall, *Acts*, 81.

[876]Wesley, *Works*, 8:49.

[877]Godbey, *Commentary*, 5:65.

[878]Wilcox, *Be Ye Holy*, 352-359. "We cannot say that one receives the Holy Ghost at the time of conversion" [p. 356].

[879]Byrum, *Christian Theology*, 389.

[880]Taylor, *Theological Foundation*, 135-166. Jimmy Swaggart said the difference between the two is vast [*Speaking in Tongues*, 5].

[881]Bruce, *Acts*, 169.

receiving, being filled, being baptized, and being endued with power. The Spirit was sent, given, poured out, and fell. These terms are synonymous and cannot be used to make artificial distinctions. Luke uses seven different phrases a total of twenty-three times to describe the coming of the Spirit and they are merely different aspects of the same operation.[882] Writing a consensus of Christian belief from the first five centuries of the Church, Thomas Oden concluded that "though indwelling is not precisely the same as baptism, sealing, and filling of the Spirit, none of these is detachable from the new birth through the Spirit and baptism of the Spirit. . . . The New Testament understands baptism of and by the Spirit as the privilege of all who have faith, all Christians, all who belong to the body of Christ."[883] Fletcher also wrote,

> For in the language of the Scriptures the *giving* — the *pouring out*— the shedding forth — and the *baptism of the Holy Ghost*, are phrases of the same import. And *to receive the Holy Ghost* — to be *sealed with the Spirit of promise* — to *be baptized with the Holy Ghost* — and to have *the Holy Ghost falling upon one* — and to *be endued with* (Pentecostal) *power from on high*, are expressions, which convey the same meaning.[884]

The death and resurrection of Jesus Christ would be ineffective without the gift of the Holy Spirit. R. C. Moberly said, "Calvary without Pentecost would not be an atonement to us."[885] Pentecost was regarded by the Jews as the feast which celebrated the giving of the Mosaic law. It was no accident that the new covenant was inaugurated on the same day. Just as Luke's gospel ends with the ascent of Christ, so Luke's church history begins with the descent of the Spirit.

Yet Kenneth Grider expressed a common concern of holiness writers that if Pentecost was not entire sanctification, then the history of the early church was

---

[882]Dunn, *Baptism in the Holy Spirit*, 70-72. When such terms as effusion, baptism, or outpouring are used by writers of the eighteenth century in a collective sense, they describe a "revival of religion" [Murray, *Revival*, 20]. Yet such a revival of religion can only occur after it has been established. Murray contends that Pentecost is an unrepeatable event, but that *revival* consists in receiving more of what Christians already possess [Murray, *Pentecost-Today?*, 31].

[883]Oden, *Life in the Spirit*, 3:178; 182. Oden described baptism of the Spirit as the means "by which the new person becomes dead to the old way and alive to the new" [Oden, *Transforming Power*, 195].

[884]Fletcher, "Essay on the New Birth,"45.

[885]Moberly, *Atonement and Personality*, 152.

written without any reference to this important doctrine.[886] But the purpose of Luke was to record the history of the early church. He gives particular emphasis to the spread of the gospel among the Gentiles. Apparently it was not his purpose to teach doctrine so much as to recount the gracious work of God in planting the church among diverse peoples. Certainly when Paul writes to these churches their perfection is one of his major themes. We are not encouraged to seek the experience of the apostles, but to follow the teachings of the apostles. While Jack Deere asserted that "the book of Acts is the *best* source that we have to demonstrate what normal church life is supposed to look like,"[887] in contrast John Stott wrote that the

> revelation of the purpose of God in Scripture should be sought primarily in its *didactic* rather than its *descriptive* parts. More precisely, we should look for it in the teaching of Jesus and in the sermons and writings of the apostles, rather than in the purely narrative portions of Acts. . . . I am *not* saying that the descriptive passages of the Bible are valueless, for "all Scripture is inspired by God and profitable" (2 Tim 3:16). What I *am* saying is that what is descriptive is valuable only in so far as it is interpreted by what is didactic.[888]

Gordon Fee, who is Pentecostal, wrote, "Our assumption, along with may others, is that *unless Scripture explicitly tells us we must do something, what is merely narrated or described can never function in a normative way.*"[889]

Contrary to the usual evangelical interpretation, that Luke's history must be interpreted by Paul's theology, Roger Stronstad argued that Luke was just as

---

[886]Grider, *Entire Sanctification*, 44.

[887]Deere, *Surprised by the Power*, 114.

[888]Stott, *Baptism and Fullness*, 15. The first edition was entitled *The Baptism and Fullness of the Holy Spirit* (1964). This booklet received a less than adequate review by Turner in "An Evaluation," 45-51.

Stott said that he practically rewrote the first edition because he felt he had been less than generous in his evaluation of the charismatic movement [McCloughry, "Basic Stott," 30]. Yet Stott objected to the charismatic stereotype of Christian experience that everybody has to go through the same two hoops. While the Pentecostal still concentrates on the three supernatural gifts of healing, prophecy, and tongues, Stott feels that the gift of teaching is the most needed gift today.

[889]Fee and Stuart, *How to Read the Bible*, 97. In the second edition (1993) Fee added, "unless it can be demonstrated on other grounds that the author intended it to function in this way."

good a theologian as he was a historian. Stronstad believed that Luke did not relate the Spirit to salvation. Instead, the Spirit was a new source of power subsequent to salvation.[890] In fact Robert Menzies claimed, "Luke does not view the gift of the Spirit as a necessary element in conversion."[891] Thus, it is claimed that Luke and Paul are not in full agreement.[892] However, if we understand that the same Spirit inspired both Luke and Paul, this interpretation creates more problems that it solves.

John Wesley was taught by Christian David that the disciples before Pentecost were in an intermediate state. They were servants of God, but they did not yet have "new hearts" nor "the gift of the Holy Ghost."[893]Pentecost cannot be an adequate model for entire sanctification for the following six reasons:

- Pentecost was a unique and unrepeatable event in salvation history
- The physical phenomenon of wind, tongues of fire, and speaking in other languages are not necessary to attest to the indwelling of the Spirit
- Until the Holy Spirit was given at Pentecost neither regeneration nor entire sanctification was possible
- Pentecost is not a model because there is no seven-day waiting period
- The concept of heart purity or cleansing is not prominent in the Acts passages concerning the gift of the Holy Spirit
- Jesus taught that we enter the kingdom of God through the new birth

1. Pentecost was a unique and unrepeatable event in salvation history.[894] It marked the beginning of a new era of divine grace. Luke calls it the "beginning" in Acts 11:15. James Mudge, in stating the historic position of the Methodist Church, said Pentecost was practically "a change from one religion to another." He continued:

> It was the inauguration of a new dispensation, that is, a new phase in the process of salvation. Before this the disciples had been Jews, rather than Christians; they had been thoroughly Jewish in their views, their practices, their expectations. They were far from being Christians, in the complete sense in which we use the word now of those who are born anew in the full

---

[890]Stronstad, *Charismatic Theology*, 12.

[891]Menzies, *Development of Early Christian Pneumatology*, 275.

[892]William and Robert Menzies, *Spirit and Power*, 50-58. See also Hummel, *Fire in the Fireplace*, 185.

[893]Wesley, *Journal*, 8 August 1738.

[894]This was the conclusion of Lyon, "Baptism and Spirit-Baptism," 21.

blaze of the dispensation of the Holy Ghost.[895]

Pentecost marked the giving of the Holy Spirit, the beginning of the new covenant, and the coming of the kingdom of God. Thomas Coke recognized the significance of Pentecost:

> He had indeed already in some degree formed the body of his new visible church, while he was here on earth, conversing with and instructing his disciples; but by this last act, the descent of the Holy Ghost, he infused a soul into that his mystical body; he endowed it with a vigorous principle of life and action, a heart that might always correspond and sympathize with him, its head. See 1 Cor. xii. 12, 13.[896]

Acts 2

Joseph Sutcliffe wrote these reflections on Acts 2,

> From this great display of glory we may learn that conversion is always a work of argument; their judgment was gained by truth. Conversion is also a work of conviction; they were pricked in the heart. Conversion is likewise a work of enquiry; men and brethren, what must we do to exonerate our conscience from so great a guilt? Lastly, conversion is a work of comfort; ye shall receive remission of sins, and the gift of the Holy Ghost. But the gift of the Holy Spirit, absolutely essential to regeneration, is twofold in its operations. First, ordinary, to warm and cheer the heart of every believer. So we have remarked on Luke 24. Next, it is extraordinary, in the gift of tongues, and the power of working miracles. The latter is confined solely to as many as the Lord shall call to that high office and ministry.[897]

W. B. Pope taught that the tongue of fire which sat upon each of the one hundred and twenty symbolized God's acceptance and seal. The Holy Ghost came "in the fulness and glory of his sealing office, to imprint upon their foreheads by a symbol, upon their consciences by his secret influence, the assurance that their sins were blotted out, that their renunciation of the world was accepted, that their

---

[895]*Growth in Holiness*, 248-249.

[896]Coke, *Commentary*, 5:949-950.

[897]Sutcliffe, *Commentary*, 2:392-393.

self-abandonment to the Lord was well-pleasing to Him, and that He made them His own from that day for ever." The symbol left as suddenly as it came. Outward and visible signs ceased, but the reality remains, "they were all filled with the Holy Ghost." While the sign departed, the inward witness remains. The penitent believer in Christ can know that he is released from condemnation. The prodigal led back to the father becomes a child of God and has the "Spirit of adoption." The worshiper laying himself upon the altar is silently sealed by the Spirit of consecration. We do not need to sigh after the symbolic token. Every one of us may "be filled with the Holy Ghost" as the witness in himself.[898]

2. The physical phenomena of wind, tongues of fire, and speaking in other languages are not necessary to attest to the indwelling of the Spirit. W. T. Purkiser called these "inaugural signs."[899] It was natural that when the holiness movement made this their model for entire sanctification that the emphasis would shift from the ethical to the emotional. The new age of the Holy Spirit was ushered in with special signs, but Pentecost has never been exactly duplicated. What justification do Pentecostals have for emphasizing only one of the three signs as the sign of the Holy Spirit? If the giving of the Holy Spirit is always accompanied by languages, why is there no record of languages in three of the six instances in Acts?

3. Until the Holy Spirit was given at Pentecost neither regeneration nor entire sanctification was possible. Holiness writers often argue that the new birth was available before Pentecost, but that entire sanctification was not possible until after Pentecost. Yet both are the work of the Holy Spirit. To interpret Pentecost as entire sanctification empties the new birth and results in practical antinomianism.[900]

Holiness writers have labored to show a connection between Pentecost and Christian perfection and then have labored to avoid the pentecostal emphasis on signs and wonders. They typically point out that in the upper room discourse

---

[898]Pope, *Sermons*, "The Tongues of Fire," 274-275. While Acts 2:3-4 was the text, Pope never associated the day of Pentecost with Christian perfection in this sermon. Pope declared that Methodism "preached the testimony of the Holy Ghost in the heart of the believer as the common prerogative; and further, the attainableness in this life of a state of entire sanctification and acceptableness in the sight of God" [Moss, *Pope*, 89].

[899]Purkiser, *Biblical Foundation*, 119-121.

[900]This was the conclusion of Kenneth Collins, stated in personal correspondence with the author 25 May 2010.

(John 13-17), Jesus said the disciples were clean,[901] they belonged to him, he had chosen them, they were his, they were not of the world, they were heirs, and their names were written in heaven (Luke 10:20). The phrases just cited apply to all Old Testament saints. However, the faith of the disciples was not primarily in Jesus Christ, for he told them to trust in him, just as they believed in the Father (John 14:1, 11). The new birth was made possible through the death of Christ and his shed blood.[902]

That their names were written in heaven (Luke 10:20) does not necessarily mean the disciples had been born again prior to Pentecost. Even under the old covenant the name of Moses was written in God's book (Exod 32:32) and according to Malachi 3:16 all who feared the Lord were written in heaven. According to Revelation 13:8; 17:8 the names of believers were written in the book of life from the foundation of the world, based on the foreknowledge of God that they would believe.[903] Thus, the reference in Luke 10:20 does not require us to conclude that the disciples were even then born again, having believed on the death and resurrection of Christ which had not yet happened. According to Mark 4:40 the disciples had no faith.

Thus, Wesley concluded that "the faith through which we are saved . . . is not barely that which the apostles themselves had while Christ was yet upon the earth."[904] Although the disciples had left all to follow him, A. J. Smith pointed out their motive in forsaking all was to gain a position of status in the coming kingdom.[905] In the upper room, they argued over who was the greatest (Luke 22:24).

Although they had the power to work miracles and had authority over demons, after they returned from their preaching mission Jesus termed them "a faithless generation" (Luke 9:41). Jesus explained they could not cast out a

---

[901]R. A. Torrey argued from John 13:10; 15:3 that the disciples were regenerate before Pentecost [*Holy Spirit*, 112-115]. The defense of this position by Richard S. Taylor is especially weak [*Theological Formation*, 3:119-121].

Bloesch argued that they were clean by virtue of being covered by the blood of Christ, but they were not actually clean. Even though Jesus washed their feet, that act symbolized their future cleansing through the blood. "They did not yet have regeneration because they were not yet baptized into the death of Christ (Mk 10:35-45). . . . They were cleaned proleptically by virtue of the word addressed to them. They were on the way to regeneration but not yet totally cleansed" [*Holy Spirit*, 306-307].

[902]Smith, *Bible Holiness*, 33-34.

[903]See Reasoner, *Revelation*, 198-204.

[904]Wesley, "Salvation by Faith," Sermon #1, 1.3.

[905]Smith, *Bible Holiness*, 70.

demon because of their unbelief (Luke 9:40; Mark 6:6). When the disciples prayed for their faith to be increased, Jesus told them plainly that they had none of this faith at all (Luke 17:5-6).[906] Nor did they manifest the fruits of the Spirit described in Galatians 5:22-23. Instead they were selfish and intolerant.[907] Nor did they yet have the peace which results from justification by faith (Rom 5:5). "My peace I give you" (John 14:27) speaks of the future Comforter whom the Father would send (John 14:26).[908]

In other references they are rebuked for little faith.[909] They really did not have saving faith. They really did not know who Jesus was nor grasp his teaching because their hearts were hardened (Matt 15:16; Mark 6:52; Luke 18:34).

In John 14:7 Jesus said, "If you had known me, [but you do not] you would have known my Father also." Here a second-class conditional statement is made — a statement contrary to fact.[910] The disciples did not yet have a saving knowledge of Jesus Christ. According to John 14:17 their knowledge of the Holy Spirit was based only on his external work in the world. He did not yet indwell them. Only through him could they truly know Christ.

Nor did they love him, according to John 14:28. Again, this states a second-class conditional statement which is contrary to fact.[911] *Agape* love comes from God. Everyone who has this *agape* love has been born of God and knows God. Whoever does not have *agape* love does not know God (1 John 4:7-8; 3:14; see also John 5:42). It is impossible to have *agape* love until we are regenerate. Love must be produced in us before it can be perfected in us. According to Romans 5:1-5 the *agape* love of God is poured out into our hearts by the Holy Spirit who is given to us at the same time we are justified.[912] Therefore it is

---

[906]Wesley, "Salvation by Faith," Sermon #1, 1.3.

[907]Smith, *Bible Holiness*, 128; 26.

[908]Wesley, *Notes*, 256; Clarke, *Commentary*, 5:624 both say that Jesus used the present for the future tense.

[909]Matt 6:30; 14:31; 16:8; 17:16-17; Mark 6:52; 7:18; 8:17-18, 21, 32-33; 9:19; 16:13-14; Luke 24:25; John 16:31.

[910]Robertson, *Word Pictures*, 5:250. See also Vine's explanation of the two words for "know" in John 14:7 [*Expository Dictionary*, 2:298-299]. According to the definition of γινώσκω (*ginosko*), the disciples did not have an active relationship with Christ, therefore they did not οἶδα (*oida*) or perceive the identity of the Father.

[911]Robertson, *Word Pictures*, 5:256.

[912]δικαιωθέντες (*dikaiothentes* - aorist passive participle - having been justified) and δοθέντος (*dothentos* - aorist passive participle - having been justified) both occur at the moment of saving faith.

significant that twice when Jesus asked Peter, "Do you truly love (*agapao*) me?" that both times Peter replied he was fond of (*phileo*) the Lord (John 21:15-16).

Peter was not yet born again. B. F. Westcott explained, "Love (*agape*) in its truest form includes Faith. St. Peter in his answer affirms his personal attachment to the Lord, appealing to the Lord's own knowledge. . . . He lays claim only to the feeling of natural love, of which he could be sure. He does not venture to say that he has attained to that higher love which was to be the spring of the Christian life."[913]

While Peter once declared that Jesus was the Christ, a few verses later Christ rebuked him as "Satan" (Matt 16:16-23). Peter confessed in Luke 5:8 that he was a sinful man. Furthermore, the disciples did not exemplify the Christian life when they all forsook him and fled (Mark 14:50) nor when Peter cut off the ear of Malchus (John 18:10). According to Luke 22:32 Peter was not converted. Jesus is not describing a restoration. He is describing the change of heart which occurs in the new birth. The usual word for conversion (ἐπιστρέφω - *epistrepho*) is used. Luke used the same word in Acts 3:19 to describe the result of repentance and in Acts 26:18 to describe the turn from darkness to light. Thus, the burden of proof rests upon those who want to define it differently in Luke 22:32. Thomas Coke wrote,

> Three long years had the apostles been in the school of Christ, and had tried even his patience with their gross stupidity, and incapacity to apprehend his spiritual doctrine. Though they had made some progress in the way of truth by leaving their little all to follow him: though they daily heard his precepts, and saw his practice, that living comment upon his doctrine—yet nothing could rectify their false notions, nothing could wean them from their vain desires of secular grandeur and magnificence. When our Lord informed them of the necessity of sufferings, the benefits of poverty, the blessedness of persecution, it was all a riddle to them. *They understood none of these things; these sayings were hid from them, neither knew they the things that were spoken,* Luke, xviii. 34. Even after the resurrection of Christ the cloud was still upon their minds, and they were yet hankering after an immediate possession of worldly grandeur and dominion. *Lord,* say they, *wilt thou at this time restore again the kingdom to Israel?* Acts, I. 6. Christ no longer opposed their carnal prejudices, but referred them to the Holy Ghost for full

---

[913]Westcott, *John*, 302-303. William Hendriksen argued conclusively that *agapeo* and *phileo* are not used as synonyms in this passage [*John*, 2:494-500]. See also Lenski, *John*, 1418-1421; McKay, "Style and Significance," 319-333.

> information and conviction. According to the promise of Christ, the Holy Ghost came. Immediately, all darkness, error, and mistake fled before him. They understood, they believed, they taught, they practised, they were ready to lay down their lives for those truths, which before they could not receive, they could not bear, nor endure. The cross of Christ was no longer an offence to them, but their boast and their glory; and they rejoiced, that they themselves were *counted worthy* to partake of it, and to *suffer shame for his name.* Such and so effectual were the fruits of the Spirit, enlightening the minds of the apostles as a Spirit of *truth. . . .* Is this the illiterate fisherman? Is this the carnal disciple who presumed to rebuke his Lord, when he first mentioned the cross to him? Is this the fugitive apostate, the abjuring Peter? But *with God all things are possible.* Peter had now received the Holy Ghost, *the Spirit of Power,* whose property it is to strengthen us with might in the inward man, to create a new heart, and renew a right spirit within us.[914]

It is true that Jesus said of his disciples before Pentecost they are not of the world (John 17:14). They had believed in God and were given to Christ. Christ in turn would ascend to his throne and give them his Spirit which would make them New Testament believers or Christians. Since Pentecost all who truly belong to Christ have received his Spirit. They were hated by the world because they were different. They were servants of God and friends of Christ, but they were not Christians until they received the Holy Spirit (Rom 8:9).

To the opposer who contended, "But I got sanctified when I was converted," C. B. Jernigan argued from John 17:6-16, "Surely, then, they are saved men. The world hates them because they are not of the world, even as Jesus is not of the world; and yet, in this state, they are not sanctified, for Jesus in the

---

[914]Coke, *Commentary*, 5:951-953. Laurence Wood cited part of this section in Coke's *Commentary* as proof that he taught the baptism of the Holy Spirit as the means of full sanctification. However, Coke is describing their conversion. In his introduction to the book of Acts, Coke said one of Luke's purposes was to describe the effusion of the Holy Ghost by which the Christian religion was established [*Commentary*, 5:933]. Coke did not connect the baptism with the Holy Ghost with Christian perfection in this section. In fact, he never used the term Christian perfection or entire sanctification in any of his comments on Acts 2. Ironically, Wood said that Coke excerpted this material from an unpublished manuscript by John Fletcher [*Meaning of Pentecost*, 262]. Yet an careful reading of this unpublished Fletcher manuscript, reprinted in *The Asbury Theological Journal* (Spring 1998), reveals that Fletcher was quoting from John Heylyn [pp. 55-56].

next verse cries, 'Sanctify them.'"[915] Yet Donald Bloesch explained,

> It is important to understand that the disciples were not believers until Pentecost. They were under the law but not yet under grace. They had been converted to the "way" of the cross, yet not to the gospel of the cross. They had accepted Jesus as messiah in the Jewish sense, but they did not embrace him as the Savior of the world. The Holy Spirit was *with* them, not yet *in* them (Jn 14:17). They were in the sphere of the kingdom, but not yet sealed in the body of Christ. Jesus declared, "I tell you this now, before it takes place, that when it does take place you may believe that I am he" (Jn 13:19; cf. 14:29). Even at the time of the ascension the disciples still regarded Jesus only as Messiah of Israel rather than God in human flesh, as is evident in their words: "Lord, will you at this time restore the kingdom to Israel?" (Acts 1:6). The disciples before Pentecost were seekers rather than believers. They had an incipient faith but not the faith that is "the power unto salvation." They were faithful as servants, but not as sons (cf. Heb 3:5-6). They received the gift of the Spirit when their hearts were purified by faith (Acts 15:8-9 JB).[916]

The fact that Jesus prayed for their sanctification in John 17:20-23 does not prove that they were ready to receive *entire* sanctification. Wynkoop observed that Jesus did not here equate sanctification with the coming of the Holy Spirit. In fact the Holy Spirit is not mentioned in this prayer. The Pentecostal experience is not said to be an answer to the prayer of Jesus. In fact the coming of the Spirit at Pentecost is never directly identified with sanctification.[917]

The promise of living water in John 4:13-14 contains five future tense verbs. Mudge realized that it was not possible to compare the condition of the disciples before Pentecost and the condition of Christian believers now.

---

[915]Jernigan, *Entire Sanctification*, 4.

[916]Bloesch, *Holy Spirit*, 297-298. George Turner claimed the Spirit was *with* the disciples from conversion, but not *in* them until after Pentecost. He implies that the disciples were converted prior to Pentecost. However, he conceded that the Holy Spirit comes to believers at conversion in baptism (1 Cor 12:13) and in his sealing (Eph 1:14; 2 Cor 1:22) ["Doctrine of Sanctification," 98]. Yet the disciples were neither baptized nor sealed by the Spirit prior to Pentecost.

[917]Wynkoop, *Theology of Love*, 321.

It is asked, sometimes with much indignation, "What! were the apostles, when with Jesus, not converted?" But the answer would have to depend on the meaning attached to the word "converted." It is a very ambiguous term, meaning many things. It does not mean precisely the same thing when used of a little child as when used of an adult, or when used of one who turns from another form of faith to be a Christian as when used of one who simply changes his conduct, not his views. In a certain sense the apostles were doubtless converted; but the word, if applied to them, could not signify exactly the same thing as when applied to sinners who give their hearts to God in an ordinary church revival today. The case of the disciples before Pentecost, of Cornelius before Peter preached to him, of the twelve at Ephesus before Paul catechized them is paralleled in heathen lands now much more nearly than in Christian countries.[918]

James Dunn said we might as well make the civilization of the Roman Empire the standard for civilization today as to make the experience of the disciples the standard for spiritual experience today. "The new age has come, and in comparison the old age reeks of condemnation and death (2 Cor 3:6-8)."[919] The one thing that Jesus does not say about the disciples is that they have the Holy Spirit. If the gift of the Holy Spirit is the beginning of Christian experience, the disciples before Pentecost do not make a good example. It will not do to point out that Abraham was used as a model for justification in Romans 4.[920] The issue is the nature of regeneration, not justification.

A few holiness commentators have realized the dilemma of their position and have pointed to John 20:22 as the disciples' regeneration.[921] There are three major interpretations of John 20:22, according to Robert Lyon.[922]

1. The view that in John 20:22 there are two separate bestowals of the Spirit. Those who hold this interpretation do not necessarily agree concerning the purpose, meaning, and impact.

Relying on this interpretation, some Pentecostals very early taught that the disciples were already born again and were entirely sanctified in John 20:22.

---

[918]Mudge, *Growth in Holiness*, 249-250.

[919]Dunn, *Baptism in the Holy Spirit*, 53.

[920]Grider, *Entire Sanctification*, 54.

[921]Godbey, *Commentary*, 7:513-514; Grider, *Entire Sanctification*, 25.

[922]Lyon, "John 20:22,"73-86.

They concluded that their baptism in Acts 2 was a third crisis experience.[923] Howard M. Ervin, professor at Oral Roberts University, argued that if the disciples were born again before Pentecost it implies Jesus' disciples entered the new covenant while their Lord was still subject to the provisions of Sinai's legal covenant. He goes on to conclude, however, that they were born again after the resurrection and before Pentecost. He rightly argues that the new covenant could not be available until Jesus provided it, but how could it be available until the Holy Spirit was given?[924]

Dunn argued that the baptism of Jesus in the Spirit at the Jordan River initiated the new covenant and Jesus entered the new covenant as our representative. It was at this time he also initiated his public ministry.[925] Therefore, Dunn argued that our Spirit baptism is an initiation into the new covenant and therefore is not a subsequent work of grace.

Ervin argued that the work of the Spirit in the life of Jesus began with his conception and Incarnation and therefore this anointing at the beginning of his public ministry supported the Pentecostal paradigm. He also argued that the absence of water baptism at Pentecost argues against the conversion-initiation paradigm.[926]

Actually both arguments are based on an analogy from the life of Christ which breaks down when we understand that the work of the Spirit in the life of Christ does not constitute a work of salvation. As the sinless Lamb of God, Christ was not in need of salvation, but instead came to provide it for us. Therefore, we cannot establish the order of salvation from the life of Christ. Instead the order of salvation is stated in Acts 2:38. Walter Kaiser argued, "It is difficult to set forth 'any sort of *second blessing* account' of Jesus' baptism. To do so runs the risk of diminishing the full deity and known mission of our Lord. And if that caution is of any value, then how can what happened to our Lord be 'paradigmatic for us' in the sense of our being equipped with power and authority for our mission?"[927]

Dunn recognized that it was especially important for the Pentecostal to show that the disciples were regenerate before Pentecost and that they had received the Spirit before Pentecost. While Dunn is willing to grant this interpretation, he pointed out that the Pentecostal thesis must argue for more than

---

[923]Godbey, *Spiritualism*, 29. Godbey claimed the disciples were in a backslidden condition and reclaimed at John 20:22 [pp. 30-31].

[924]Ervin, *Spirit-Baptism*, 7; 14-21.

[925]Dunn, *Baptism in the Holy Spirit*, 32

[926]Ervin, *Conversion-Initiation*, 5-11; 15-19.

[927]Kaiser, "Baptism in the Holy Spirit,"178.

this, "namely, that the experience of the apostles is, or can be a pattern which may be repeated in the lives of later Christians. It is with this further step that he definitely misses the way. For the chronological sequence of events in the lives of the apostles is unique and unrepeatable." The transition period in the life of the apostles was "unique and unrepeatable." Thus, Dunn concluded that the normal pattern is not found in John 20:22 or Acts 2:4, but in Acts 2:38.[928] Therefore, Pentecostalism is mistaken in separating Spirit-baptism from the event of conversion-initiation, and has made the gift of the Spirit an experience which follows after conversion. "The gift of the Spirit may not be separated in any way from conversion, whether to be set before conversion as its presupposition, or after conversion as a merely empowering, confirmatory or charismatic gift. The gift of the Spirit (that is, Spirit-baptism) is a distinct element within conversion-initiation, indeed, in the NT, the most significant element and focal point of conversion-initiation."[929]

Laurence Wood, however, thought the conversion of the three thousand on the day of Pentecost "was an extraordinary occurrence and not the usual pattern because believers normally are justified believers first and later receive the baptism with the Holy Spirit."[930] Such a statement reflects a general denial that a mighty effusion of the Spirit is necessary to bring a penitent from the state of spiritual death to a resurrection of spiritual life in the new birth. To those who were cut in their hearts, as a result of Peter's sermon, the Apostle clearly promised the receiving of the gift of the Holy Ghost after they meet the condition of repentance (Acts 2:37-38).

Later in his book, Wood asserts that Fletcher believed this conversion of the three thousand on the day of Pentecost was an extraordinary event when the Jewish believers "simultaneously received forgiveness of sins through faith in Christ and received that fullness of sanctification through faith in the Spirit."[931] However, a review of the closing paragraphs of Fletcher's *Essay on Truth* does

---

[928]Dunn, *Baptism in the Holy Spirit*, 173-182. Dunn describes properly the disciples entrance into the new covenant as a staggered entrance, yet the three decisive milestones he suggests do not necessarily reflect that process.

[929]Dunn, *Baptism in the Holy Spirit*, 226.

[930]Wood, *Meaning of Pentecost*, 90; Wood, "Third Wave of the Spirit," 125. See the objections of Greathouse in *Wholeness in Christ*, 69-70, based on his research in *Historical Development*, 241-244. Wood conceded that on some occasions, such as Acts 2:37-38; Acts 10 the Spirit's baptism may come at conversion ["Exegetical-Theological Reflections," 55].

[931]Wood, *Meaning of Pentecost*, 90; 172; 267.

not reveal that he made such a claim.[932]

What the Scripture describes concerning all new converts at and immediately following the day of Pentecost is the expected norm and standard of all who are regenerated in every age of this Holy Ghost dispensation. It cannot be proved that Fletcher or Wesley believed that, on the day of Pentecost, all new converts were simultaneously justified and fully sanctified as Wood claims. This minimal view of the Spirit's initial work of sanctification in the heart is repeatedly apparent in Wood's attempt at historical revisionism. Both Wesley and Fletcher consistently maintained that the work of holiness is begun in regeneration. Wood fails to acknowledge that both regeneration and entire sanctification are made possible only upon the descent of the Holy Spirit during and after the day of Pentecost. Initial salvation in the work of regeneration was sometimes equated by Wesley as a restoration, even if but a partial restoration, of the image of God in the soul.[933]

Ray Dunning felt that while the disciples may have experienced a baptism with the Spirit that resulted in their full or entire sanctification, "There may have been those, notably the three thousand, whose initial experience of the gift of the Spirit led them only so far as regeneration." Then Dunning commented that if the Pentecostal experience is a paradigm, it is the three thousand and not the hundred and twenty who provide the pattern.[934]

However, Ervin rejected the view of Dunn that there was a transition period in salvation history between the resurrection and Pentecost, calling it "a dispensational limbo." He argued that if the disciples were born again on the resurrection day, but if the Church did not come into existence until Pentecost, into what then were the apostles born? He wants the experience of the apostles to be considered the normative pattern of Christian spirituality.[935]

F. F. Bruce observed that the same verb ἐμφυσάω (*emphysao*) is used in the Septuagint translation of Genesis 2:7 and Ezekiel 37:9. Bruce argued that this is no mere anticipation of Pentecost, but a real impartation of the Spirit for the purpose specified. "But it is not the bestowal of life that is in view now, but empowerment for ministry."[936] Whitacre described this event as the conception of the church, which was born at Pentecost.

Thus, Dunn concedes more than is necessary and Ervin argues for more than he can prove. The verb for "breathe" (ἐμφυσάω- *emphysao*) is aorist

[932]Fletcher, *Works*, 1:592-594.

[933]McPherson, Review of *Meaning of Pentecost*," 9-11.

[934]Dunning, "Wesleyan Perspective on Spirit Baptism," 226; 317.

[935]Ervin, *Conversion-Initiation*, 137-139.

[936]Bruce, *John*, 397; 392.

indicative. John is describing a real event which happened before Pentecost. However, all that can be concluded from this verb is that Jesus actually did breathe on them at that time. Whether they actually received the Spirit, whether that action was merely symbolic, whether they received an empowerment for ministry, or whether they received a measure of the Spirit illuminating them and enabling them to tarry, or whether the new covenant was actually inaugurated at that time will have to be decided on grounds other than the Greek tense and mood.

In the book of Revelation John regularly uses the indicative mood to describe symbolic events. The general teaching of Scripture is that although the Spirit has always been in the world, he was given at Pentecost in fulfillment of the promises concerning the new covenant. Thus, the new covenant began at Pentecost and the actions of Jesus in John 20:22 should not be interpreted otherwise. The point of Jesus' actions was to declare that he became the baptizer with the Holy Spirit, following his resurrection. However, he did not send the Spirit until the day of Pentecost.

Donald Stamps also argued that the impartation of the Holy Spirit by Jesus to his disciples on resurrection day was not the baptism in the Spirit experienced at Pentecost. Instead Stamps contended that it was the infusing of the disciples for the first time with the regenerating presence of the Holy Spirit and with new life from the risen Christ. Stamps saw this action as the fulfillment of John 14:17, "He lives with you and will be in you" and the beginning of the Church. [937] However, the account of John 20:19-25 covers the same appearance of Jesus as recorded in Luke 24:36-49. But there is nothing in Luke's account to indicate that the disciples were regenerated or that the Church was born on this resurrection evening. Instead, Luke records the words of Peter referring to Pentecost as the "beginning" of the Church in Acts 11:15.

Stanley Horton argued that the new covenant was inaugurated by the death of Christ and that the church was commissioned before the ascension of Jesus. "By this we can see that those Jesus left behind were already the new covenant body, the church." Horton argued further that the leadership replacement, while waiting for the promised baptism in the Holy Spirit, indicated that the church was already in existence. Therefore, he concluded that Spirit baptism is a distinct experience subsequent to conversion.[938]

Dunning, however, gives the Wesleyan perspective that "the primary thrust of Acts relates most centrally to the theological doctrine of ecclesiology"

---

[937]Stamps, *Full Life Study Bible*, 1627. Adam Clarke preached that the phrase "he dwelleth with you" described the collective indwelling of the Spirit within the Church of God, while he also individually indwells the souls of true believers ["The Promise And Mission Of The Holy Ghost," Outline 2, *Works*, 8:416].

[938]Horton, "Spirit Baptism,"56-57.

and that with the exception of Saul, there are not accounts of an individual as an individual receiving the Spirit. Even with Saul, his reception of the Spirit awaited the coming of the church in the person of Ananias. . . . Luke's broadest and primary intent was to demonstrate how, in the power and under the direction of the Holy Spirit, the church, which originated as a Jerusalem-based, Judaism-oriented sect of Jewish believers, became a chiefly Gentile, worldwide phenomenon reflecting a belief in universal salvation based on grace alone. . . . It is not Luke's primary intention to provide a normative or normal pattern of individual experience."[939] J. I. Packer wrote,

> There is no way to establish the disciples' Spirit-baptism at Pentecost as a normative experience for all later believers. Indeed, quite apart from the fact that as an experience we know very little about it, its dispensational uniqueness rules that out. Nine o-clock on Pentecost morning was the singular, unrepeatable moment when the promised Spirit first began his new covenant ministry of communicating communion with the glorified Christ. Since that moment all Christians have enjoyed this ministry from conversion on. Because the disciples became believers before Pentecost, their experience had to be "two-stage" in a way no later Christian's can ever be.[940]

Thus, the question of the apostles' experience at Pentecost should not be tied to the question of when the Church began. God has always had a people. We see the beginnings of the church within the first family. Adam was the first priest and he led his family in worship through sacrifices. As the world became apostate, God called Noah out. The basic meaning of the Greek word for church, ἐκκλησία (*ekklesia*), is called out. The ark is an illustration of the Church. We are called out of this world to be saved from coming judgment.

Abraham was called out and entered into a covenant agreement with God. Abraham is the father of all who believe (Rom 4:12, 16). By the time of Moses the family had grown into a nation. The nation of Israel was God's Church in the Old Testament.

In the Septuagint, the Greek translation of the Old Testament, *ekklesia* is used to refer to Israel in places such as: Joshua 8:35; Ezra 2:64; Joel 2:16. Acts 7:38 refers to the Israelites as the "church in the wilderness." By the New

---

[939]Dunning, "Wesleyan Perspective on Spirit Baptism,"193; 214-215.

[940]Packer, "Charismatic Renewal,"17. Packer made a similar statement in "Piety on Fire," 22-23. While the disciples were believers before Pentecost, they were not Christians.

Testament the Church was no longer national, but international. The mystery referred to by Paul was that God intended both Jew and Gentile to be one body (Eph 3:4-6). There are eighteen descriptions of Israel given in the Old Testament which, in the New Testament, are used in reference to the Christian Church. In addition there are sixteen passages in the Old Testament referring to Israel which are quoted in the New Testament as referring to Christians. Therefore, the conditional privilege of old Israel has been transferred to the Church.[941]

Dispensationalists teach that the Church did not exist until Pentecost and that it is a digression from God's original plan. However, God does not have two peoples. Both Jew and Gentile are to be incorporated into "one new man" (Eph 2:15). Some have inferred from the words of Jesus in Matthew 16:18, "I will build my church," that the Church was not a present reality when Jesus spoke. But in Matthew 18:17 Christ speaks of the Church as a present reality.

Christ reformed the old Church (Heb 9:10) and the new Church was built upon the foundation of the old (Eph 2:20). The new Church began at Pentecost with the sending of the Spirit. Thus, Wiley is accurate in stating, "Pentecost was the birthday of the Christian Church."[942] Now we believe not only in the Father, but in the Son (John 14:1) and when we believe we are baptized by the Spirit into the body of Christ (1 Cor 12:13). All who are saved are added to the Church (Acts 2:47). Faith in Christ is not optional; Jews are saved the same way Gentiles are saved. The only way to the Father is through Jesus Christ.

Thus, the New Testament Church began with the inauguration of the new covenant at Pentecost and was entered by the disciples who were regenerated at

---

[941]Provan, *The Church is Israel Now.*

[942]Wiley, *Christian Theology*, 2:329; 3:107. However, in *Christian Theology*, 3:185-186, Wiley said the church first took its visible form in the covenant with Abraham and that the Christian church is the continuation of the Abrahamic covenant. While Richard S. Taylor regards these two statements as constituting opposite positions [*Theological Formulation*, 128], I do not see them as contradictory. Pentecost was the birthday of the *Christian* Church, but not the birthday of the Church. Charles Carter said Pentecost should be regarded as the consecration, dedication, or inauguration of the Church of Christ [*Person and Ministry*, 156]. See also Dunning, *Grace, Faith, and Holiness*, 492. This view is in line with Wesley's statement that Pentecost marked "the beginning of the Christian Church" ["The General Spread of the Gospel," Sermon #63, §20]. Certainly, however, Pentecost does not represent the perfection of the Church — which is the position of those who teach the disciples were entire sanctified at Pentecost.

It has also been argued that the New Testament Church began when Christ called the twelve disciples. Roger Stronstad argued that Pentecost did *not* mark the birthday of the Church, that it has no soteriological import, but that it means the charismatic Spirit of Jesus passed on to his disciples empowering them for their mission [Turner, *Power from on High*, 62].

Pentecost. However, this New Testament Church is the continuation of Old Testament Israel, but with greater privilege and universal expansion.

In the fourth century Chrysostom raised the question, How it is that Jesus said, "If I do not go away, he will not come" (John 16:7), and yet he gives them the Spirit here in John 20:22? Chrysostom concluded that Jesus did not give them the Spirit, but prepared them to receive the Spirit. While the disciples did not receive the Spirit until Pentecost, they did receive the authority to declare the gospel of forgiveness.[943]

The standard Methodist interpretation did not connect the bestowal of the Spirit in John 20:22 with either regeneration or entire sanctification. Wesley understood John 20:22 as "an earnest of pentecost."[944] Here Wesley used the language of Bengel.[945] Fletcher believed that our Lord breathed on his disciples imparting "the Spirit of grace and supplication" to help them wait in faith and unceasing prayer "till they were endued with power from on high."[946] Clarke called this "a measure of the Holy Spirit."[947] Benson understood the Lord's command to receive as referring to what the disciples would receive at the following pentecost.[948] Thomas Coke wrote that Jesus bestowed a token on his disciples and this resulted in an illumination of the disciples' minds concerning what they would afterwards receive in greater measure.[949] Whedon did not understand John 20:22 to be the full bestowment of the Holy Spirit.[950] Daniel

---

943Elowsky, *John*, B:362.

944Wesley, *Notes*, 271.

945Steele, *Gospel of the Comforter*, 136. Steele also cited Alford who said, "To understand John 20:22 as the outpouring of the Spirit, the fulfilment of the promise of the Comforter, is against all consistency, and most against John Himself, see John 7:39 and 16:7." And Steele cited Meyer who saw this impartation as a special first fruit, whilst the full outpouring, the baptism of the Spirit, remained attached to His exaltation" [Steele, p. 137]. Steele himself held that the apostles at this point were servants rather than conscious of their sonship.

946Fletcher, *Works*, 1:590.

947Clarke, *Commentary*, 5:655.

948Benson, *Notes*, 4:664. In his sermon "On Receiving the Holy Ghost," Benson referred to John 3:8 where wind or air, by which we breathe and live, illustrates the work of the Holy Spirit. Benson said it may have been Christ's intention to illustrate the work of the Spirit when he breathed on his disciples and said, "Receive ye the Holy Ghost" [*Sermons*, 4:214].

949Coke, *Commentary*, 5:919.

950Whedon, *Commentary*, 2:412.

Steele concluded "that something real was imparted, but far less than the fulness of the Spirit."[951] Thus, they agree that the only actual fulfillment of the promise of the baptism in the Holy Spirit is at Acts 2. The fact is that Jesus did not receive the Spirit to pour on his disciples until *after* his ascension (Acts 2:33).

2. The view that John 20:22 is figurative.

Jesus said that he would send the Holy Spirit after he ascended back to heaven and so it is best to view his action as a promise fulfilled on the day of Pentecost. A. J. Smith argued that there was no point to be gained by citing John 20:22 as the point in time when the disciples were born again, since there is no record that they were spiritually changed by being breathed upon by our Lord. The only great spiritual change that came to the disciples was at Pentecost. Just as God breathed into man the breath of life in creation (Gen 2:7), this act should be understood as symbolic of the new creation (2 Cor 5:17).[952] This view was suggested as early as the sixth century by Theodore of Mopsuestia.[953]

Thus, Thomas Summers called John 20:22 a symbolic act. On the basis of Luke 24:49; John 21 and Acts 1-2, Summers declared "it is certain they did not possess it till the day of Pentecost."[954] Binney wrote, "This was probably a symbolical act, a sort of *earnest* of that full bestowment of the Holy Spirit which they were to receive at the pentecost [sic] after his ascension."[955] Charles Carter declared, "All of the promises concerning baptism in the Spirit find their fulfillment in the Pentecostal effusion, but never before." He believes that in John 20:22 Jesus was acting symbolically and in anticipation of Pentecost.[956] George Eldon Ladd suggested that this "inbreathing" was "an acted parable promissory and anticipatory to the actual coming of the Spirit at Pentecost." While there are parallels between the two events, there is no overpowering reason why one cannot

---

[951]Steele, *Gospel of the Comforter*,136.

[952]Smith, *Bible Holiness*, 38.

[953]Elowsky, *John 11-21*, 361-362. The views of Theodore were condemned by the Second Council of Constantinople in A. D. 553 because he was considered a forerunner of Nestorius. Nestorianism was the teaching that Christ existed as two persons: the divine son of God and the human Jesus. However, his interpretation, cited above, was not necessarily condemned.

[954]Summers, *Commentary*, 4:300.

[955]Binney and Steele, *People's Commentary*, 304. Yet see Steele's own view stated under the first option.

[956]Carter, "Baptism with the Holy Spirit," 65.

be promissory of the other.[957]

Köstenberger explained that the action of Jesus represents a symbolic promise of the soon-to-be-given gift of the Spirit. This section does not represent John's equivalent to Pentecost lest John be found to stand in actual conflict with Luke's Pentecost narrative in Acts 2. Furthermore, if the Spirit was actually given at John 20:22, John would be in conflict with his own disclaimers that the Spirit would be given only subsequent to the glorification of Jesus, which entails his return to the Father (John 7:39; 14:12, 16-18, 25-26; 16:12-15; 20:17). The behavior of the disciples after this present incident would be rather puzzling if they had already received the Spirit since they exhibited fear of the Jewish leaders, since Peter returned to his previous occupation, and since Peter denies having *agape* love for Christ. Just as God breathed his Spirit into Adam at creation, here the disciples are commissioned as the new messianic community in anticipation of the Spirit subsequent to his ascension.[958]

3. There is one bestowal and John 20:22 is the Johannine Pentecost.

Ervin asked if the apostolic community experienced the new creation/regeneration twice, once on resurrection day (John 20:22) and again at Pentecost. Did John know of two bestowals of the Spirit, although he recorded only one? Or is John 20:22 the Johannine Pentecost?[959] Bloesch held that John 20:22 was a theological reconstruction of the historical event of Acts 1-2. He held that both Luke and John were describing the same event.[960] This is also the view of Robert Lyon. While some commentators see Luke's account and John's account as two divergent traditions of the same event which are impossible to harmonize, Lyon does not believe it is impossible to harmonize the two accounts. His solution is to incorporate redaction criticism. For Lyon, John 20:1-23 is "the resurrection package"and John 21 may well have been added at some later stage of the development of the text.[961]

This is the most radical interpretation and it raises unnecessary questions about the integrity of the text itself. However, Lyon was driven to this conclusion after rejecting the second option. He argued that John must not be interpreted through the lense of Luke. If this conclusion is valid, it solves the unanswered

---

[957]Ladd, *Theology*, 289. Dunning embraced this interpretation in *Grace, Faith, and Holiness*, 418.

[958]Köstenberger, *John*, 574-575.

[959]Ervin, *Conversation-Initiation*, 133.

[960]Bloesch, *Holy Spirit*, 305-306.

[961]Lyon, "John 20:22," 81-83.

questions left by the first option concerning two bestowals of the Spirit. Yet ultimately it is an attempt to harmonize the two accounts from Luke and John at the expense of John's account. It is better to let the two accounts stand as we have them and not try to harmonize them into one event.

However, the event described in John 20:22 is not the actual bestowal of the Spirit. It is symbolic and yet perhaps more than symbolic. How much difference in meaning is there between an earnest and a figurative action? Both the earnest and the figure anticipate the full gift. John 20:22 anticipates the actual bestowal of the Spirit in Acts 2. Therefore, any work of the Spirit prior to Pentecost cannot be used legitimately to define either regeneration or entire sanctification. And there were only ten disciples involved in the actions of John 20:22. This does not account for the rest of the one hundred and twenty. According to Acts 1:8 no one had yet received the Spirit until Pentecost.

4. Pentecost is not a model because there is no seven-day waiting period. The early disciples had to wait until the Spirit was poured out, but it is not scriptural for us to "tarry."

5. The concept of heart purity or cleansing is not prominent in the Acts passages concerning the gift of the Holy Spirit. The emphasis is on power. It was no accident that when the holiness movement adopted the Pentecostal model to explain Christian perfection, the emphasis switched from purity to an emphasis on power.

6. Jesus taught that we enter the kingdom of God through the new birth. Both John the Baptist and Jesus said that the kingdom of God was near. According to the words of Jesus, John was not in the kingdom. Jesus said, "He that is least in the kingdom of heaven is greater than [John]" (Matt 11:11). Christian regeneration affords us greater privilege than John the Baptist. Wesley also commented that in John "the old dispensation expired, and the new began."[962]

Then Jesus told his disciples that "some who are standing here will not taste death before they see the Son of Man coming in his kingdom" (Matt 16:28). Apparently the disciples preached the good news of the coming kingdom, but were not personally in the kingdom. The fact that Jesus told Nicodemus he needed to be born again (John 3:3-5) was no indication that Nicodemus was born again at that time. Bloesch concluded that the new birth did not take place until the Son

---

[962]Wesley, *Notes*, 40. At Luke 7:28 Wesley explained that the least teacher he sent forth was a greater teacher than John the Baptist. Richard S. Taylor regards these two explanations as different [*Theological Formulation*, 120]. Yet we have a greater knowledge and thus a greater aptitude to teach because we are under the new covenant, have entered the kingdom, and have been regenerated.

of Man is lifted up (John 3:14-15).[963] Apparently Nicodemus did not publicly identify with Christ until after his death (John 19:38-39).

Adam Clarke referred to the Jewish custom of baptizing proselytes in his comments on John 3:12. According to Clarke they were considered "as being born of baptism." This, he says was "practiced every day in the initiation of proselytes." Clarke then showed how Jesus was endeavoring to make Nicodemus "understand such heavenly things as the initiation of my disciples by the baptism of the Holy Ghost and fire from heaven."[964] Thus, it need not be inferred that the new birth was a common experience prior to Pentecost or that Christ was rebuking Nicodemus because he should have been familiar with regeneration.

Admission into the kingdom of the Messiah was not described as a new birth in the Old Testament. It cannot be proven that as early as the time of Christ the Jewish rabbis called a baptized person "born again." Therefore, Benson concluded that Nicodemus was not rebuked because he should have connected the new birth with the baptism of proselytes. Instead Nicodemus should have known the Old Testament doctrine respecting the necessity of a change of heart being experienced by all who would be the true people and spiritual worshipers of God. And he should have known about the effusion of the Spirit which the prophets had so clearly foretold would take place under the Messiah.[965]

Daniel prophesied that the kingdom of God would come after the fourth kingdom of man. It could not come until the days of the Roman empire. Amos looked forward to the kingdom as the time when David's fallen tent would be restored (9:11). This prophecy is quoted by James in Acts 15:16 as having been fulfilled. Peter explained in his Pentecostal sermon that while David was dead, the Messiah was seated on the throne of David. We know that the kingdom of Christ has been established because he poured out the Holy Spirit (Acts 2:33). Now if the kingdom came at Pentecost and if we enter the kingdom through regeneration, then the disciples were born again in Acts 2. John Fletcher concluded that all true believers in Christ, all real Christians, belong to the kingdom of God and that John the Baptist came to set up that kingdom. "Therefore we cannot measure the privileges of real Christians by those formerly given to the Jews."[966] Because of the transitional nature of Pentecost it does not make a good model to explain either regeneration or entire sanctification. Wayne McCown asked, "Is the reception of the Holy Spirit a concomitant of the initial experience of Christian grace, or is it representative of a subsequent experience and work?" He concluded, "That

---

[963]Bloesch, *Holy Spirit*, 304.

[964]Clarke, *Commentary*, 5:532.

[965]Summers, *John*, 43; Benson, *Notes*, 4:536.

[966]Fletcher, *Works*, 1:589-590.

question cannot be answered with certainty either, on the basis of the data in Acts." He did conclude, however, that the book of Acts represents no normative sequence for Christian experience.[967] "To compare true Christians who are in Christ to the disciples before Pentecost is as misleading as it would be to place a Christian today between Good Friday and Easter, blessed by the death of Christ but not by his resurrection."[968]

Acts 4

In the six accounts of the giving of the Holy Spirit, the account in Acts 4:31 is of a fresh filling, but not a fresh baptism. Adam Clarke explained,

> Though these disciples had received the Holy Spirit on the day of pentecost [sic], yet they were capable of larger communications; and what they had then received did not preclude the necessity of frequent supplies, on emergent occasions. Indeed, one communication of this Spirit always makes way and disposes for another. Neither apostle nor private Christian can subsist in the Divine life without frequent influences from on high. Had these disciples depended on their pentecostal grace, they might have sunk now under the terror and menaces of their combined and powerful foes. God gives grace for the *time being*, but no stock for *futurity*, because he will keep all his followers *continually dependent* on himself.[969]

However, W. B. Godbey believed this second Pentecost was to sanctify the converts of the first Pentecost.[970] This demonstrates a growing rigidity among the holiness movement that always equated the giving of the Spirit with entire sanctification. Mildred Wynkoop objected to the isolation of holiness preaching from gospel preaching and to study holiness as a doctrine separate from Christian theology as a whole. She concluded,

> When the continuity of grace between conversion and sanctification was lost, it became necessary to make clear

---

[967]McCown, "Spirit in the Book of Acts," 113-114; 112.

[968]Prior, *Way of Holiness*, 118.

[969]Clarke, *Commentary*, 5:713. Witherington, *Acts*, 204, calls it "a fresh filling."

[970]Godbey, *Commentary*, 5:109.

distinctions between them so that one could refer to emotional evidences to be sure of standing.[971]

Acts 8

Ben Witherington noted that the issue of sequence is not important to Luke. Luke records the diverse ways in which the Spirit came in Acts.[972] The usual formula is Acts 2:38, but in the remaining cases there is some variation from the standard order of Acts 2:38. These cases are not recorded as a pattern for us, but as exceptions to the pattern. The historical record of whatever happened at one location and at one time does not take precedence over the general teaching of Scripture. There is nothing in Acts 8 which commands us to follow this same formula. Stott concluded, "I cannot myself see how the abnormality in the Samaritan reception of the Spirit could be taken as a precedent for today."[973] However, Acts 8 is the most hotly contested passage in the interpretation of Luke/Acts.

It was predicted in Acts 1:8 that after the disciples received the Holy Spirit they would take the gospel to Samaria. In Acts 8:5-25 Philip preached Christ in Samaria. We are also told that the Samaritans believed and were baptized in the name of the Lord Jesus, but the Holy Spirit had not yet fallen upon any of them.

Does Luke intend to convey to us that they were born again and needed to be entirely sanctified? G. A. McLaughlin wrote that the Samaritans were not sinners, but believers. "Sinners are not eligible to receive the gift of the Holy Ghost. This passage alone ought to forever silence those who say we 'get all there is at conversion.' A careful study of the New Testament will show that there was always in that day a second work of confirmation that the church insisted upon after a company of people had been converted."[974] W. B. Godbey believed that Peter and John were sent to preach the second work of grace that they all might receive the Holy Ghost.[975] According to Grider, the revival at Samaria is "perhaps the Gibraltar of two-works-of-grace teaching."[976] However Charles Carter was

---

[971]Wynkoop, "Theological Roots," 80.

[972]Witherington, *Acts*, 154.

[973]Stott, *Baptism and Fullness*, 34; see also Stott, *Message of Acts*, 151-159.

[974]McLaughlin, *Acts*, 87.

[975]Godbey, *Commentary*, 5:179.

[976]Grider, *Entire Sanctification*, 45.

uncertain whether the Samaritans were sanctified on this occasion or another.[977] According to Ralph Earle, Luke's understanding of the gift of the Holy Spirit as an experience subsequent to conversion is certainly reflected here.[978] This view reflects a low and unscriptural standard of regeneration.

James Dunn contended that the verb form for "believe" is unique to the book of Acts and that it signifies intellectual assent rather than commitment because they did not believe into or upon the Lord, but simply that they believed Philip. The next verse tells us that Simon also believed, but only a few verses later Peter's rebuke demonstrates the fact that Simon had not really been born again.[979] Bloesch agreed with Dunn that the Samaritans lacked effectual faith or full conversion. Instead their faith was based on their fascination with the miracles and signs that accompanied Philip's ministry.[980] However, Marshall argued that it is the rest of the account which reveals Simon's faith or lack of faith. While Dunn argued that πιστεύω (*pisteuo*) the verb for faith, when used with the dative case indicates merely intellectual ascent, Marshall pointed to Acts 16:34 and 18:8 where this construction indicates genuine faith. He concluded, "On the whole, there is no clear evidence that the people were merely superficial in their belief."[981]

However, Luke related this incident because it was highly unusual. Dunn concluded that no explanation is given as to why the Spirit had been sovereignly withheld. He continues:

> The mistake of many commentators is to assume that because the conditions of 2:38 had apparently been fulfilled, therefore they were Christians and/or the Spirit had been given. The NT way is rather to say: Because the Spirit has not been given, therefore the conditions have not been met. This is why Luke puts so much emphasis on the Samaritans' reception of the Spirit (vv 15-20), for it is God's giving of the Spirit which makes a man a Christian, and, in the last analysis, nothing else.[982]

---

[977]Carter, *Wesleyan Biblical Commentary*, 4:535.

[978]Earle, *Beacon Bible Commentary*, 7:353.

[979]Dunn, *Baptism in the Holy Spirit*, 65.

[980]Bloesch, *Holy Spirit*, 310.

[981]Marshall, *Acts*, 5:156. R. C. H. Lenski wrote that *pisteuo* with the dative means to believe the person and what he says. Thus, the Samaritans accepted the gospel which Philip preached [*Acts*, 321].

[982]Dunn, *Baptism in the Holy Spirit*, 68.

Dunn is simply saying that we form our doctrine from the clear doctrinal passages, not from the apparent exceptions to the rule. Yet Ervin attempted to refute Dunn's conclusions in *Conversion-Initiation and the Baptism in the Holy Spirit* and more recently in *Spirit Baptism: A Biblical Investigation.* Although Ervin is charismatic, some holiness colleges also use his research to strengthen their own position that this is a second blessing. But Ervin's position is that Spirit baptism in the New Testament relates not to conversion or sanctification but to charismatic empowerment.[983] This is a second possible answer, that the Samaritans *were* converted, but has not yet received charismatic gifts. However, R. J. Knowling argued that it is difficult to believe that Luke meant to limit the expression "receive"to anything less than a bestowal of that divine indwelling of the Spirit which makes the Christian the temple of God. Paul made it plain in 1 Corinthians 12:30 that the advent of the Holy Spirit was not necessarily attested by any particular manifestations, nor were these manifestations essential accompaniments of it.[984]

Ironically, there is a consensus among Methodist commentators that the Samaritans *had* been regenerated by the Spirit. Their interpretation is here governed by the teaching of Paul in such passages as Romans 8:9. If they believed and were baptized into the name of the Lord Jesus, they belong to Christ and thus had received the Spirit. Here the Methodist commentators are in line with Calvin's interpretation that what is given is not the regenerating Spirit, but extraordinary graces of the Spirit.[985]

But the classic Methodist interpretation does not hold Acts 8:15 up as a second work of grace nor as a charismatic experience which all believers are to seek. Clarke said the purpose for which the Holy Spirit was thus given was "certainly not for the sanctification of the souls of the people: this they had on believing in Christ Jesus; and this the apostles never dispensed. It was the *miraculous* gifts of the Spirit which were thus communicated."[986]

Adam Clarke's point is that the Samaritans already had the Holy Spirit, whom they received when they believed on Jesus Christ. However, one of the marks of an apostle was his ability to perform miracles. The apostles wrote the New Testament and had authority to establish congregations. This authority was confirmed through their ability to do miracles. In this case, when Peter and John came to Samaria, their authority was confirmed through this manifestation of the Spirit. Notice that when Simon saw this confirmation of apostolic authority, he

---

[983]Ervin, *Spirit-Baptism*, 6.

[984]Knowling, *Expositor's Greek Testament*, 2:216.

[985]Calvin, *Acts 1-13*, 236.

[986]Clarke, *Commentary*, 5:741.

offered to buy it. But this ability comes from God and cannot be purchased. Clarke says the Samaritans had received the Spirit, but had not witnessed the miraculous power of the Spirit through apostles. This much is obvious, Clarke and the early Methodists clearly believed that all true believers received the Holy Spirit.

Is it possible that those who believe on Jesus Christ can receive the Spirit at a later time? Clarke did not even consider this as a possibility because this passage must be reconciled with all of the plain passages which teach otherwise. Therefore, he believed that this is confirmation of apostolic authority. Joseph Benson, another early Methodist commentator, took much the same position. He says that the church leaders at Samaria had not yet received gifts of the Spirit which would be needed in their leadership of the church. Again, the emphasis here is upon the apostles' authority to establish the local congregation. Chrysostom held the same view, that the Samaritans had received the Spirit of remission of sins, but not the Spirit of the signs.[987]

Wesley suggested that the Samaritans had not yet received the Spirit in his miraculous gifts and his sanctifying graces.[988] Benson explained that while not all in any church receive these gifts, yet it was necessary that some receive these gifts for the confirmation of the gospel and to honor the apostolic office.[989] Thomas Coke wrote,

> From what follows it is plain, that the Holy Spirit was here conferred in his supernatural and miraculous influences; for Simon the magician saw some of the wondrous effects of that divine gift immediately, by the new converts speaking languages which they had never learned, or prophesying, or working miracles; and it was this which made him so earnestly covet that apostolic power. . . .
>
> As the Samaritans were now Jews by religion, and many of them even descended from Jewish parents, and as our Lord himself had during his own personal ministry treated them as Jews, there was no occasion for the pouring down of the Holy Spirit, in any

---

[987]Martin, *ACCS*, 5:93.

[988]Wesley, *Notes*, 297. According to Laurence Wood, in an unpublished manuscript Fletcher quoted Wesley as teaching that the Samaritans received the Spirit as their full sanctification [*Meaning of Pentecost*, p. 341]. A careful reading of the source, reprinted in *The Asbury Theological Journal* 53:1 (Spring 1998): 45, will not bear this out. In fact, Fletcher quotes the same comments from Wesley's *Notes*, inserts the word "full" before "sanctifying graces" and then strikes it out.

[989]Benson, *Notes*, 4:733-734.

of his miraculous gifts, upon them before baptism, to prepare the way for their being received into the Christian church: as there manifestly was afterwards in the case of the first-fruits from among the Gentiles: and, on the other hand, supposing the Samaritans had not been favored with any spiritual gifts and miraculous powers; that is, neither before baptism nor after it; they would have come behind other churches, and might thereupon have been ready to question, whether they who had been so peculiarly odious to the Jews, were now accepted of God equally, and to like privileges with the Jews, from among whom came the Saviour and salvation to mankind. The two apostles, therefore, went down, and conferred upon them the extraordinary gifts of the Holy Ghost.[990]

Thomas Summers believed that the Samaritan believers had received the Spirit in his ordinary converting power, but not in the impartation of miraculous gifts as on the day of Pentecost.[991] Whedon explained that the Samaritans had been doubtless regenerated by the Spirit, but had not received his miraculous, extraordinary, charismatic manifestation.[992]

Edward Hare wrote that the Holy Ghost had not fallen in extraordinary and miraculous operations. While the Spirit of adoption brings its own evidence, it is an evidence only to the individual. What Simon saw was not the Spirit of adoption, but miraculous power conveyed.[993]

And so the classic Methodist interpretation is a variation on the charismatic answer, that the Samaritans were genuine Christians but had not yet received the gifts of the Spirit. But the Methodist answer does not promote the agenda of the modern charismatic movement, but rather apostolic authority.[994] Another variation of this position emphasizes that the Spirit was given to break down racial prejudice and cultural barriers.

Roy Aldrich suggested that the ministration of the Spirit by the official

---

[990]Coke, *Commentary*, 5:999.

[991]Summers, *Commentary*, 5:141.

[992]Whedon, *Commentary* 3:102.

[993]Hare, *Letter to Melville Horne*, 29-30.

[994]Wesley's view of the apostolic office was functional, not charismatic. Their argument for an episcopal form of church government was based on the continuation of apostolic authority. Thus, when Francis Asbury wrote, "The signs of an apostle have been seen in me" [*Journal*, 2:470], he was not referring to signs and wonders but to his authority as a bishop.

leaders from Jerusalem was necessary because of the traditional conflict between the Jews and the Samaritans, referenced in John 4:20-22.[995] William J. Larkin, Jr. concluded that the Samaritan experience must be viewed as extraordinary, not normative. He explained that if God had not withheld his Spirit until the Jerusalem apostles came, converts on both sides of the cultural barrier might have found Christ without finding each other.[996]

This is the position of Longenecker who argued that the time lapse between their profession of faith through water baptism and their baptism with the Spirit should not be used by Catholic theologians to justify a separation between baptism and confirmation. Nor should it be used by charismatics as justification for their doctrine of the baptism of the Spirit as a second work of grace. Instead, it should be understood that because of the Jewish/Samaritan prejudices God first sent Philip, with his Greek culture, to preach Christ since he would more easily be accepted than a Jew. Then God sent Peter and John, two leading apostles from the mother church in Jerusalem to impart the Holy Spirit. Had the Samaritans received the Spirit independent of the Jerusalem church, the rift would have been perpetuated.[997]

Wayne Grudem concluded that God, in his providence, sovereignly waited to give the new covenant empowering of the Holy Spirit directly through the hands of the apostles so that the Samaritans would be recognized as full members of the church. This was important because of the historic animosity between Jews and Samaritans (John 4:9) and was the next major step after the gospel had been preached in Jerusalem and Judea (Acts 1:8). However, it does not provide a pattern for us to repeat today, but was simply a transition between the old covenant and the new covenant.[998]

David J. Williams also observed that there is no hint of any deficiency in the faith of the Samaritans. Certainly Philip did not recognize any deficiency or he would have not baptized them. "It is hard to believe, then, that the Spirit's work of regeneration had not been done in their lives." But the apostles prayed that they might receive the Holy Spirit in his outward manifestations so that there could be no doubt that the Samaritans were fully incorporated into the Christian

---

[995]Aldrich, *Transition Problem*, 9. This was also the argument of Clark Pinnock who concluded that the experience at Samaria must not be made into a doctrinal principle since the pattern was reversed at the house of Cornelius later when the Spirit fell first and recognition was given on that basis [Pinnock, "Theological Evaluation and Critique,"134].

[996]Larkin, *Acts*, 5:128.

[997]Longenecker, *Acts*, 9:284-285; 359.

[998]Grudem, *Systematic Theology*, 774.

community.[999]

And yet the second position, in all three variations, assumes that the Samaritans *did* have the Holy Spirit. Therefore, those who hold this interpretation are forced to explain the statement in Acts 8:16 "the Holy Spirit had not yet fallen on any of them" as meaning something other than the new birth. And some who hold the first position do not really believe that the Holy Spirit comes in the new birth. But if Acts 2:38 governs our interpretation of Acts 8, those who truly repent are forgiven of their sins. And water baptism is the outward sign of the gift or baptism of the Holy Spirit.

All we are told is that the Samaritans did *not* have the Spirit. Therefore, it is best to assume that they were not yet saved. While the argument about whether the verb for "believe" indicated genuine faith is too technical, Robert Lyon observed,

> Everything that is said about the Samaritans is also said of Simon Magus who certainly had problems. If they were Christians, so was he at this point. Further, the reference in verse 16 to the fact that the Holy Spirit had not yet fallen up them sounds as though this is abnormal and a surprise. Something was not quite right. Finally, the repeated reference in the narrative to the miraculous (vv. 6, 7, 13) might suggest an emotion-laden atmosphere which hindered the clear reception of the word. There is precedent for this in the ministry of Jesus, for in John 2:23-24, we read that many believe on His name when they saw the signs He was doing; but Jesus did not in turn entrust Himself to them. I suggest, then, that the sending of Peter and John was to provide some sort of corrective. One thing, however, is quite certain, viz., that when Peter and John laid their hands upon them and they "received" the Holy Spirit, it was their first experience of the Spirit and cannot be counted as a second experience. In the schema of the book (see 1:8) it is the incorporation of the Samaritans into the body. It was, so to speak, the culmination of their conversion.[1000]

Ken Schenck explained, "Almost all Wesleyan Bible scholars today would see the problem here as the fact that these people were still lacking the most important ingredient in conversion — namely, they lacked the Holy Spirit. Peter

---

[999]Williams, *Acts*, 5:156-157. This is also the conclusion of Lampe [*Seal of the Spirit*, 70] and Marshall, *Acts*, 5:157.

[1000]Lyon, "Baptism and Spirit-Baptism,"19.

sets out the template for conversion in Acts 2:38."[1001]

Acts 9

The conversion of Paul is recorded in Acts 9. As Acts 9 opens, Paul was breathing out murderous threats against the Lord's disciples. Paul retells this story in Acts 22 and again in Acts 26. He tells us he was zealous for God. He said he was of the strictest sect, the Pharisees and had lived this lifestyle since he was a child. Therefore, he thought he ought to do everything possible to oppose the name of Jesus of Nazareth. He even voted that Christians be put to death.

Here is the portrait of a religious bigot. His religious prejudice has blinded him to truth. He is zealous for God, but he is spiritually dead in the sense that he has no personal relationship with God. Most wars have been fought over religion, in which both sides were zealous but did not know the God of love.

But suddenly on the road to Damascus, Paul was awakened. A light from heaven flashed around him and he heard a voice saying, "Saul, Saul, why do you persecute me?" Saul replied, "Who are you, Lord?" Paul then is led into Damascus blind. He is in the pangs of the new birth for three days,[1002] seeking God and eating nothing. Then his eyes are opened, he receives the Spirit, and was baptized as a profession of his faith. In Acts 22 his baptism was connected with the washing of his sins away. A great deal is often made that Ananias addressed Paul as "brother." Dunn believes Ananias used this term because Paul was in the process of becoming a Christian.[1003] God had just revealed to Ananias that Saul is a chosen instrument who will bear his name. Thus, Ananias and Saul are colleagues.

Both Bede and Chrysostom compared Paul's three days to the three days before the resurrection of Christ. Bede even suggested that because Paul did not

---

[1001]Online: Schenck, "Church and the Holy Spirit," 2.

[1002]Concerning the three days, Wesley commented, "An important season! So long he seems to have been in the pangs of the new birth" [*Notes*, 299; see also Wesley, *Journal*, 22 April 1738; *Works*, 9:93]. See also Fletcher, *Works*, 1:579. However, holiness evangelist Joseph H. Smith preached that Paul experienced Christian perfection [*Pauline Perfection*, 25-26]. While Wesley's notes on the New Testament tended to follow Bengel's *Gnomon*, Wesley takes a different position than Bengel here. This fact is noted by Laurence Wood, who then sided against Wesley's interpretation [*Pentecostal Grace*, 199]. A proper understanding of the three days illustrates the doctrine of the awakened sinner.

[1003]On the significance of Acts 9:17, see Dunn, *Baptism in the Holy Spirit*, 74. Dunn also said that Paul used *adelphos* (brother) in the sense of a "colleague" [*Romans 1-8*, 38A:31].

believe in Christ's resurrection, he was taught by his own experience.[1004] Wesley did not believe his conversion was a sudden conversion on the Damascus road, but described Paul's experience of being "filled with the Holy Ghost" as part of Paul's *conversion.*[1005] It does seem clear from Paul's testimony found in Acts 22:16 that he was not born again until Ananias prayed with him. Adam Clarke stated that Paul was not a Christian before being filled with the Spirit.[1006] Daniel Steele said Paul's prayers in Damascus "were doubtless entreaties for forgiveness." Steele felt Paul was entirely sanctified during the three years he was in Arabia (Gal 1:17-18).[1007] Lyon argued that the language of Acts 22:16, which recounts this event, is conversion language: baptism, forgiveness of sins, calling on the name of the Lord.[1008] Bloesch concluded that Paul had been converted from being an anti-Christian to a pre-Christian, between his Damascus road experience and his baptism, and then to a born-again Christian.[1009]

However, Grider informs us that "the interpretation of holiness scholars is that Paul was converted at the earlier time and that therefore being filled with the Spirit at the house of Ananias was subsequent to his justification."[1010] Although Paul did call Jesus "Lord"(κύριος - *kurios*), the term probably meant no more than "sir."[1011] According to Matthew 7:21-23 not all who use lordship language are in the kingdom or known by Christ (see also Luke 6:46). To ask "Who are you, Lord?" is hardly a confession of faith.

Richard S. Taylor sees those three days as "a real death to self," the time when Paul came to be crucified with Christ. This is a condition to be met before the baptism of the Holy Spirit or entire sanctification is experienced, according to Taylor.[1012] However, a careful reading of the Scripture, in this case Acts 22:16,

---

[1004]Martin, *ACCS*, 5:105.

[1005]Wesley, *Works*, 9:93.

[1006]Clarke, *Commentary*, 5:752.

[1007]Steele, *Half-Hours with St. Paul*, 14; *Steele's Answers*, 178.

[1008]Lyon, "Baptism and Spirit-Baptism," 19.

[1009]Bloesch, *Holy Spirit,* 312.

[1010]Grider, *Entire Sanctification*, 46.

[1011]Summers, *Acts*, 153. *Kurios* is translated "sir" in John 4:11; 12:21; 20:15. See also Longenecker, *Acts*, 9:371; Dunn, *Baptism in the Holy Spirit*, 73-74. Although Ervin argues that Paul was converted on the Damascus Road and filled with the Spirit three days later, he concedes that *kurios*, in the vocative case may mean simply "sir" [Ervin, *Conversion-Initiation*, 42].

[1012]Taylor, *Theological Formulation*, 172.

sheds a lot of light on the holiness commentators. Huntington wrote,

> The notion that he was justified on the way to Damascus, and sanctified the day upon which Ananias called upon him, is a misconception of the whole account. He never intimates this when he tells the story himself, nor does Luke when he relates it for him. It was at Damascus that he prayed, was baptized, and received the Holy Ghost. It was there that the scales fell from his eyes, and it was at that time and place that Paul locates his conversion from Judaism to Christ and Christianity.[1013]

Michael Green wrote, "It would be very precarious to found a doctrine of two-stage initiation on the three day delay in Paul's conversion experience. . . . [Luke] sees the whole three day experience as one."[1014] We do not formulate doctrine on the basis of experience, but we interpret experience on the basis of doctrinal teaching. According to Acts 2:38 those who repent and are forgiven also receive the Holy Spirit. Donald Guthrie recognized, "The key to the whole experience of the conversion of Saul of Tarsus is his infilling with the Holy Spirit."[1015]

Acts 10

The one passage of scripture which most defined servant theology for Wesley is the case of Cornelius.[1016] In Acts 10 we are told that Cornelius was a God-fearer who had not chosen to become a Jewish proselyte through circumcision. He feared God. He and his family were devout. He was a God seeker.[1017] He gave generously and prayed regularly. He was a servant of God, but not yet a son of God. Irenaeus observed that while he feared God, he was lacking in his knowledge of the Son.[1018]

It is easy to misjudge his state of grace because we are impressed with his good works. But we are not saved by works. His devotion to God was commendable, but not meritorious. Daniel Steele said he was living up to his best

---

[1013]Huntington, *Sin and Holiness*, 236.

[1014]Green, *I Believe in the Holy Spirit*, 134.

[1015]Guthrie, *New Testament Theology*, 543.

[1016]Olson, "Roots of John Wesley,"129.

[1017]Richardson, *Eternity in Their Hearts*, 160.

[1018]Martin, *ACCS*, 5:135.

light as a pagan and was an acceptable candidate for Christian salvation.[1019]

Holiness commentators frequently point to verses like 10:35 to demonstrate that Cornelius must have been a Christian. Bruce reminds us, however, that salvation is not of works, but of grace. (15:11) "Salvation did not enter his house until Peter came there with the gospel."[1020] Wesley explained that Cornelius in the Christian sense was an unbeliever because he did not have faith in Christ.[1021] Wesley went on to say that Cornelius had the faith of a servant and was accepted through Christ, "though he knows him not."[1022]

The Jews of Palestine would have still regarded Cornelius as a pagan. Peter struggled to accept Cornelius as an equal. God told Peter not to call anything common which God had cleansed. Holiness commentators frequently jump at the word "cleansed" in 11:9 and 15:9 as proof of a second crisis experience. They fail to remember that regeneration, too, is a cleansing act of the Holy Spirit (1 Cor 6:11; Titus 3:5; 1 Peter 1:22-23). According to Alex Deasley, when God told Peter that the Gentiles were cleansed he was saying that "the ritual barrier between Jews and Gentiles is annulled." Deasley concluded,

> The meaning to be attached to cleansing in 15:9 must be determined by the context, just as in all other examples of the term in Luke-Acts. It has been shown above that the surrounding context is concerned with the proclamation of repentance, faith, salvation and new life (Acts 15:1, 3, 7, 11, etc.).[1023]

An examination of Peter's message reveals that the subject was forgiveness, not a second blessing. When Peter arrives at his home, Peter preaches a gospel message. In 10:43 Peter preaches the forgiveness of sins. The

---

[1019]Steele, *Answers*, 56. Yet Charles Ewing Brown declared, "We have no doubt that he was like all others on the record — a saved man before he was baptized with the Holy Spirit. The evidence would completely convince any believer not prejudiced by a dogmatic bias" [Brown, *Meaning of Sanctification*, 109].

[1020]Bruce, *Acts*, 222.

[1021]Wesley, *Notes*, 302. At Acts 11:47 Wesley considered *receiving* the Spirit as synonymous with the *baptism* with the Spirit. This baptism was initiation into the Christian faith and was conditioned upon repentance [*Notes*, 305].

[1022]Wesley, *Notes*, 304. See also Wesley, *Works*, 8:283, "Minutes of Some Late Conversations."

[1023]Deasley, "Entire Sanctification," 44. This is also how John Wesley interpreted Acts 15:9 ["On Sin in Believers," Sermon #13, 2.4; "The Marks of the New Birth," Sermon #18, 1.4]. See also Pope, *Higher Catechism*, 254.

Holy Spirit was poured out. Cornelius was baptized in the name of Jesus Christ.

When Peter explained his actions in the following chapter, he described their baptism of the Spirit as the same gift they had received at Pentecost (11:16). Then the apostles glorified God because he had granted the Gentiles "repentance unto life" (11:18). They, too, had the opportunity to repent of their sins and obtain eternal life. Thus "life" means salvation. When they repented, they received the Holy Spirit just like Acts 2:38 promised. Then Peter baptized them as a public testimony of their faith in Christ.

In Acts 15:9 Peter reports that the heart of Cornelius was purified by faith. According to Titus 3:5, salvation is the washing of regeneration and the renewal of the Holy Spirit. Robert Wall concluded, "Purity of heart in Acts results from divine forgiveness."[1024] Mudge wrote that "this is simply an essential accompaniment of their conversion, nothing more. God purifies the heart of every man when he receives him into his family; to give a man a new heart is to give him a clean heart. Nowhere is it said that God perfectly purified the heart of Cornelius, or cleansed it from all sin. That is an entirely different thing."[1025] Huntington wrote,

> Cornelius was a religious man before the way of salvation was made known to him; not so much so, however, as was John Wesley before his conversion, and no more so than thousands of unconverted men at the present day. To make this the case of a justified believer, seeking and obtaining the destruction of his "inbred sin," is to read into it what is quite foreign to the history.[1026]

Acts 15:8-9 must be interpreted in line with Acts 11:15-18. Since "repentance unto life" is a clear description of regeneration, "purifying their hearts by faith" must be initial, and not entire sanctification. Awakened, God-fearers do not jump to Christian maturity.

Again in Acts 15:19 Peter concludes that Cornelius has turned to God. The verb "turned" is ἐπιστρέφω (*epistrepho*), the word for "conversion." And Acts 5:8 makes it clear that this was the same experience of the apostles at Pentecost. It is no wonder that Turner wrote, "It is difficult to affirm with full confidence that Cornelius and the disciples of John at Ephesus were Christians

---

[1024]Wall, "Purity and Power," 81.

[1025]Mudge, *Growth in Holiness*, 247.

[1026]Huntington, *Sin and Holiness*, 237.

before being baptized in the Spirit."[1027]

However, Godbey contended that Peter had not been sent to convert Cornelius because he was a Gentile disciple of Christ "vigorously pressing on to entire sanctification."[1028] In *The Evangelical Commentary,* Ralph Earle stated "to hold that Cornelius was a Christian before he met Peter is very precarious exegesis."[1029] However in the *Beacon Bible Commentary*, Earle stated that the experience of Cornelius is "commonly known as entire sanctification."[1030]

Acts 19

In Acts 18:24-26 Apollos knows only the baptism of John. Thus he is a Jewish follower of Jesus, but not yet a Christian since he does not know the baptism of the Spirit. Although he is fervent in his spirit, he does not have God's Spirit.[1031] Benson thought that Apollos had heard John the Baptist preach some twenty years prior to this point in time. It is possible that Apollos returned to Alexandria in Egypt after that.[1032] Aquila and Priscilla brought him up to date about the life of Christ, who baptized his disciples with the Holy Ghost and with fire, as John had foretold.[1033] Summers wrote that Apollos recognized Jesus as the Messiah, "but his views concerning him were vague, like those of the apostles before they were endued with power from on high on the day of Pentecost."[1034] According to Fletcher, Apollos was in the dispensation of the Son. This describes those who know about Christ and believe that he is the Messiah, but have never personally been born again.[1035]

[1027]Turner, *Vision Which Transforms*,153.

[1028]Godbey, *Commentary*, 5:199.

[1029]Carter and Earle, *Acts*, 154.

[1030]Earle, *Acts*, 7:380. Deasley wrote, "The only difficulty with this exegesis is that there is not a syllable in Acts 10:44 or 11:15 to suggest or support it" ["Entire Sanctification," 30].

[1031]Witherington, *Acts*, 564-566. Dunn says his case is parallel to the Ephesians except that he already possessed the Spirit [*Baptism in the Holy Spirit*, 88]. However, Romans 12:11 uses the same phrase to describe a fervent spirit. See Larkin, *Acts*, 5:270-271.

[1032]Coke, *Commentary*, 5:1099; 1103..

[1033]Benson, *Notes*, 4:803.

[1034]Summers, *Acts*, 297.

[1035]Fletcher, *Works*, 3:180.

The case of Apollos seems to introduce the circumstances Paul discovered in Ephesus. In Acts 19 the disciples at Ephesus had not received Christian baptism either. Oscar Cullmann demonstrated that for the Christian, forgiveness for the old life cannot be separated from the new life of the Spirit.[1036] Bloesch wrote, "It is obvious to me that the Ephesians when they first met Paul were not yet Christians, for they had received only the Johannine baptism of repentance."[1037] Witherington argued that for Luke, if one is without the Spirit, then one is not a Christian. Thus he argued that the Ephesians were not Christians.[1038]

The baptism of John was a baptism of expectation and preparation rather than one of fulfillment, according to Bruce.[1039] The major difference between John's baptism and Christ's baptism was that the Holy Spirit was imparted through Christ's baptism. John's water baptism was only a shadow and a symbol of Christ's Spirit baptism.[1040] Thus the superiority of Christian baptism demonstrates that the least in the kingdom of heaven is greater than John (Luke 7:28).

In his *Compendium of Christian Theology,* William Burt Pope spoke out strongly against taking Acts 19 as proof of a second blessing.[1041] In his sermon "The Pentecostal Test" Pope warned that were some who undervalued the sanctifying power of the Holy Ghost when the believer is first united to Christ by a living faith. But Pope declared it was wrong to speak of the regenerate life as separated from a higher kind of life. Scripture does not make a distinction between a state of regeneration and a state of higher religious life. The same Holy Ghost whom we receive in the new birth is given for our entire consecration; and from the very beginning there is no limit to His consecrating energy and grace. One and the same Spirit is given for all future grown in holiness unto perfection. The higher life is only an increase in degree. The Spirit of sealing was given to everyone when he believed. Pope preached that the Spirit is the Spirit of promise in two senses: He is promised to every believer and in every believer He is the promise of the highest attainment.

[1036]Cullmann, *Baptism in the New Testament*, 12.

[1037]Bloesch, *Holy Spirit*, 311.

[1038]Witherington, *Acts*, 570; see also Larkin, *Acts*, 273 who said they are "at best nominal Christians and at worst simply disciples of John." Yet Laurence Wood argues that they were Christians and that every Christian is incomplete until he receives the Spirit as a second work of grace [*Pentecostal Grace*, 83].

[1039]Bruce, *Acts*, p. 364.

[1040]Dunn, *Baptism in the Holy Spirit*, 19.

[1041]Pope, *Compendium*, 3:44; 64.

Pope concluded that in the present day none can be found precisely in the same condition as were the twelve men at Ephesus. He called them "relics, probably some of the last relicts, of John the Baptist's ministry, whose survival at so late a date is a curious problem with which we have nothing now to do."

There were three lesser Pentecosts after the great one: when Peter threw open the gates to the Gentiles, when Samaria was added to the fold, and now at Ephesus. Pope continued to explain that the signs which accompanied their reception into Christianity should be understood as tokens of honor for John the Baptist and his ministry. "After this there are no more renewals of the Pentecostal tokens in the history of the Acts: the extraordinary signs of the Spirit melt into the ordinary." While Pope put no emphasis on pentecostal signs and wonders, he said the pentecostal test remains valid and is always authoritative. He noted that the apostle makes the conscious reception of the Holy Ghost a test. "Did ye when ye believed receive the Holy Ghost?"

John the Baptist had spoken of a baptism of the Holy Ghost which the Messiah would impart. The Ephesians had nothing beyond this incomplete faith. If they were present they might assert that they held all that is necessary. They accept the teaching of Jesus as the best directory of true religion. They receive the doctrine of illumination, that of the influence of the Holy Ghost resting on the human mind. They hold a correct creed regarding the relationship of the Holy Spirit to the Godhead. But in the light of the day of Pentecost, such a faith cannot sustain the test, though there are great numbers even today who are little better than these imperfect disciples.

Pope then called the twelve Ephesians "half-disciples," who may be regarded as the type of a large class of Christians who have received the Holy Ghost in his preparatory influences, but not yet in the fulness of his sealing and regenerating and comforting grace. Paul had a similar experience in the case of Apollos. Pope felt certain that the experience of these imperfect disciples was recorded in Acts to serve as an illustration of a certain kind of imperfect Christianity. Like these twelve they know only the baptism of repentance. Their sins have been revealed to them but not their Savior. They are coming to the Lord, but have not fully come. They remain long between nature and grace, having a measure of life which is not the life of regeneration, a penitent life, which is not comforted by the conscious reception of the Holy Ghost. But Paul hastened to fulfill his mission when he saw their sincerity. The catechising is soon over. The perfect baptism of Christianity is at once received and a faint remembrance of Pentecost honors the reception of these disciples of John into the Christian fold.[1042]

[1042]Pope, "The Pentecostal Test," Sermon #14 in *Sermons*, 251-264. The previous five paragraphs were drawn from this sermon. See also Sangster, *Path to Perfection*, 83; 194-195.

This is the only instance of re-baptism in scripture. Perhaps they were instructed by Apollos who himself knew only the baptism of John (Acts 18:25). John the Baptist had spoken of the coming baptism with the Holy Spirit, but they did not know that this expected baptism was an accomplished fact.[1043] The Ephesians were asked, "Did you receive the Holy Spirit when you believed?" The action by an aorist participle may be before, after, or simultaneous with the main verb. Most commentators recognize this as a coincident aorist which is translated "when."[1044] Even if it is argued that receiving is antecedent to believing, this does not prove that both believing and receiving are not two components of one experience. Thus Brown did not grasp either biblical teaching or Wesleyan theology when he wrote, "Wesleyan preachers have long used Paul's question: 'Have ye received the Holy Ghost since ye believed?' as evidence that the Holy Spirit is received after the experience of believing for regeneration."[1045]

Paul's question put doctrine ahead of experience. According to Paul, all true believers have the Holy Spirit (Rom 8:9) and the fact that they did not receive the Spirit indicated that their faith was incomplete. Paul recalls the incident in Ephesians 1:13 saying they were "sealed."

Ordinarily the Holy Spirit is given when complete faith is put in Jesus Christ. This account is not given as a pattern, but given as an exception to the pattern. Marshall writes,

> These men can hardly have been Christians since they had not received the gift of the Spirit; it is safe to say that the New Testament does not recognize the possibility of being a Christian apart from possession of the Spirit (Jn. 3:5; Acts 11:17; Rom. 8:9; 1 Cor. 12:3; Gal. 3:2; 1 Thes. 1:5f; Tit. 3:5; Heb. 6:4; 1 Pet. 1:2; 1 Jn. 3:24; 4:13).[1046]

Mudge said,

> The implication plainly is that all who were full-fledged Christian believers, properly instructed and baptized, as believers are now, did receive the Holy Ghost when they became believers. The only way in which any capital can be made out of this incident, by those who seek in it proof that receiving the Holy

---

[1043]Bruce, *Acts*, 363.

[1044]Dunn, *Baptism in the Holy Spirit*, 87.

[1045]Brown, *The Meaning of Sanctification*, 195.

[1046]Marshall, *Acts*,305.

> Ghost means experiencing entire sanctification, is by ignoring the great difference between John's baptism and Christian baptism and assuming that, under the former preparatory and rudimentary teaching, Christian disciples, with the full privileges of the dispensation of the Holy Ghost, could be and were made.[1047]

While the Ephesians are called "disciples," Dunn observed that this is the only time in Acts that "disciples" is not preceded by the definite article. His conclusion is that Luke does this intentionally to indicate they were not part of "*the* disciples" which made up the Ephesian church.[1048] They were disciples of John, until their baptism in the name of the Lord Jesus.

However, Godbey claimed that Apollos had been preaching to the Ephesians a second work of grace "though he had not yet received it, and was consequently incompetent to lead others into it."[1049] By and large the holiness movement came to reject the scholarship of early Methodism and accept the view that the Ephesian disciples were entirely sanctified in Acts 19. It is ironic that in *A Contemporary Wesleyan Theology* nearly three pages are devoted to proving an exegesis of Acts 19 that is contrary to early Methodism.[1050] McGonigle concluded:

> Neither did the early Wesleyans clearly accept, as would generally be accepted by Wesleyan scholars today, that those instances in Acts as receiving the baptism of the Spirit were already justified believers. This is surely demonstrable with the disciples at Pentecost, the Samaritans in Acts 8, the Ephesians in Acts 19, and when all the evidence is weighed, it can also be advanced for Cornelius and his household.[1051]

[1047]Mudge, *Growth in Holiness*, 246.

[1048]Dunn, *Baptism in the Holy Spirit*, 84.

[1049]Godbey, *Commentary*, 5:268.

[1050]Dayton, "Entire Sanctification,"1:550-552. Laurence Wood also misrepresents Wesley at this point [*Meaning of Pentecost*, 340-341]. According to Wood, Fletcher taught that Acts 19:2 meant the Ephesian disciples were fully sanctified. A careful reading of Fletcher will not bear this out. Wood cites a previously unpublished writing of Fletcher, reprinted in the *Asbury Theological Journal* (Spring 1998):54.

[1051]McGonigle, "Pneumatological Nomenclature," 70. McGonigle saw this as an error on the part of the early Methodists which allowed modern Pentecostalism to

The Baptism with the Holy Spirit

Ralph Earle said he found it "difficult to understand the almost universal neglect in the Christian Church of the baptism of the Holy Spirit."[1052] However, the Bible never commands the believer to receive the baptism of the Holy Spirit. It is amazing how much is made of the baptism of the Spirit in light of how little is said concerning it in Scripture.

The biblical teaching concerning Spirit baptism is located in four passages or clusters of parallel passages. As we examine every passage in Scripture which refers to Spirit baptism, we will discover that this artificial distinction between Christ's baptism and the Spirit's baptism does not exist.

1. A parallel passage in the four gospels is a promise by John the Baptist that Christ will baptize with the Holy Spirit. In Matt 3:11 and Luke 3:16 the statement is that "he will baptize you εν the fire of the Holy Spirit." Εν can be translated in, with, or by. In Mark 1:8 no preposition is used, but "Holy Spirit" is in the locative case. The locative case refers to position. Christ baptizes us into the sphere of the Holy Spirit. While the declaration made in John 1:33 may not be exactly at the same time as the statement was made in the three synoptic gospels, John also uses the preposition εν.

2. Two parallel passages in Acts record the promise of Christ that his disciples will be baptized εν the Holy Spirit (Acts 1:5; 11:16).

3. Romans 6:3-4 describes being baptized into (εις) Christ Jesus and raised to a new life. The preposition εις was derived from εν and gradually took over its functions until εν dropped from usage in modern Greek. This passage does not specifically mention the Holy Spirit and commentators are divided as to whether this is a reference to water or Spirit baptism. Although many people see the word "baptize" and immediately associate it with water, it is questionable whether Paul is speaking of the ritual of water baptism here.[1053] When we are baptized into

---

usurp and use "the baptism with the Holy Ghost" for its own purposes. My own conclusion is that the holiness movement erred in misapplying "the baptism with the Holy Ghost" to entire sanctification and thus paved the way for the further error of modern Pentecostalism.

[1052]Earle, *Mark*, 30. H. C. Morrison declared that there is no doctrine more clearly taught in Scripture than the doctrine of the Baptism with the Holy Ghost. According to Morrison, if Christianity were to take this doctrine out of its theology it would be left with nothing but an empty shell [Jerry Wood, *Pentecostal Holiness*, 127].

[1053]Reasoner, *Romans*, 221-228.

Christ Jesus, we are uniting with him in his death and resurrection. Through this baptism we die to the old life of sin and are raised from the dead that we may live a new life. A similar statement is found in Galatians 3:27, "for as many as were baptized into (εις) Christ, have put on Christ."

Dunn says "baptism into Christ Jesus" is a metaphor. "It is drawn from baptism, but does not itself describe baptism, or contain within itself the thought of the water-rite, any more than did the synonymous metaphors of putting on Christ (Gal. 3:27) and being drenched with the Spirit (1 Cor 12:13)."[1054]

4. 1 Corinthians 12:13 declares that we were all baptized into one body by, in, or with (εν) one Spirit. According to a misguided exegesis, this passage describes the initiation of the forgiven sinner into the Church. This initial baptism is by the Spirit; Christ will then baptize the believer with the Holy Spirit as a later event. In other words while the Spirit has baptized every believer into Christ at conversion, it is claimed that Christ has not yet baptized every believer into the Spirit.[1055] The text does not allow for this interpretation for the following two reasons:

1) Because this initial baptism is εν the Holy Spirit. This same preposition has been the usual preposition used in the passages (listed under #1 and #2) which supposedly teach a subsequent baptism. No valid distinction can be made between a baptism *by* the Spirit and a baptism *with* the Spirit. The Greek preposition εν can have either meaning. Nowhere else in the New Testament does the Spirit do the baptizing, therefore εν should probably not be translated "by."[1056] The Spirit is not the agent, but the element into which we are baptized. It is likely that here,

---

[1054]Dunn, *Baptism in the Holy Spirit*, 140. See also Dunn, *Romans 1-8*, 38A:328.

[1055]Representing the Pentecostal view, Horton argued for such a distinction between the baptism *by* the Spirit into the body of Christ and the baptism *in* the Spirit ["Spirit Baptism," 129-130].

[1056]If Paul had wanted to specify that the Corinthians had all been baptized *by* the agency of the Holy Spirit he could have used ὑπό (*hypo*) with the genitive case, not ἐν (*en*) with the dative case [Grudem, *Systematic Theology*, 768]. In Greek syntax, the issue is whether we are dealing with a dative of agency or a dative of means. Stephen S. Kim concluded that the dative of agency was rare or non-existent in the New Testament ["Doctrine of Spirit Baptism,'"41-48].

M. J. Harris argued that there was no certain instance of the preposition *en* used with *baptizo* to carry the meaning that this baptism is accomplished by the agency of the Holy Spirit. Instead *en* carries the meaning of baptism in the realm or sphere of the Spirit. "It is always Jesus who is the baptizer, never the Spirit"[Harris, "Appendix," 3:1210]. See also Schreiner, *Paul, Apostle of God's Glory*, 373.

as well, the Spirit is not the agent by which we are baptized, but, as Gordon Fee translates the phrase, "we are all immersed in the one Spirit, so as to become one body."[1057]

2) Because this same verse gives further explanation that at the same time as this initial baptism we were all given one Spirit to drink. The distinction that we enter the body of Christ initially and that we receive the baptism with the Holy Spirit later contradicts the teaching of this verse. Both the verb "baptize" and the verb "give to drink" are exactly the same form (aorist indicative passive). This indicates that both actions occurred at the same time.

Fee writes that the clause "and were all given one Spirit to drink" does not describe a second experience of the same kind. Instead it is used metaphorically for baptism and both clauses should be interpreted as a form of parallelism making essentially the same point.[1058] Actually this second verb, ποτιζω (*potizo* - I give to drink), metaphorically carries the same meaning as to be filled. We drink of the Spirit and are filled with the Spirit at the same moment we are baptized with the Holy Spirit into the body of Christ. The command to be filled with the Spirit in Ephesians 5:18 is present passive imperative — keep filled or maintain the fullness of (εν) the Spirit.

According to Hebrews 9:10 there were various baptisms until the time of the new order:

- the washing or baptism of utensils, such as cups, pitchers, kettles, or couches (Mark 7:4)[1059]
- the baptism of Moses (1 Cor 10:2)
- John's baptism (Acts 19:3-4)

Yet no one could be baptized with the Spirit until Jesus gave the Spirit.

[1057]Fee, *First Corinthians*, 606. Although Pentecostal, Fee argued that Paul is referring to their common experience of conversion [p. 605].

[1058]Fee, *First Corinthians*, 604.

[1059]Κλίνη (*kline*) is translated "tables" in the KJV, but refers to a bed or a couch on which people reclined at meals. It occurs also in Mark 7:30. It is unlikely that such a piece of furniture was cleaned through immersion. According to G. W. Hughey, the first edition of the Liddell and Scott *Lexicon* included "to wet" and "to pour upon" as definitions of *baptidzo*. Yet subsequent editions of the lexicon omitted these definitions. Hughey claimed the American editor of the lexicon omitted these definitions because the publishers could not otherwise sell it to the immersionists of England and America [Hughey, *Scriptural Mode of Christian Baptism*, 60-62]. According to William Lane the washing, mentioned in v 3, was accomplished by pouring water on the hands and excludes all suggestion of immersing the hands [Lane, *Mark*, 246].

In the four Gospels, the baptism with the Spirit is always described as a future work of God. It is still future even in Acts 1:5. However, it is considered by some that has already occurred in the life of believers in Acts 11:16 and in Paul's writings. Richard Watson pointed out that

> whenever our Lord speaks of the gift of the Holy Spirit, in that fulness of influence which was to be administered to all that believed on him, he speaks of it as a *future* gift, "which they that believed on him should receive;" and the direction to the disciples was, that they should "tarry at Jerusalem until they were endued with power from on high." The declaration in the text was. first fulfilled at the day of pentecost; but not only then: it is fulfilled whenever the Holy Spirit is vouchsafed to believers; for when St. Peter gives an account of the result of his mission to Cornelius, he says, "And as I began to speak, the Holy Ghost fell on them, as on us at the beginning: then remembered I the word of the Lord; how that he said, John indeed baptized with water; but ye shall be baptized with the Holy Ghost," Acts 11:15, 16.[1060]

Matthew 3:11 and Mark 1:8 promised that Christ *will* baptize with the Holy Spirit. The disciples were to stay in Jerusalem *until* they were clothed with power from on high (Luke 24:49). According to John 7:39 the Spirit was not given *until* Jesus was glorified. If the power of the Spirit was to be Christlike power, it was necessary to see that power manifested first in the whole life of Christ. It had to be seen in humiliation and triumph, on the Cross and in the Resurrection. There had to be a total reorientation of the concept of power.[1061] Furthermore, the Spirit's coming was dependent on Jesus returning and sending the Spirit (John 16:7).

This baptism with the Spirit now comes when we believe in the name of Jesus Christ. No one could believe upon his name until he had come. He taught his disciples, "You believe in God, believe also in me" (John 14:1). In Acts 19:2 Paul asked, "Did you receive the Holy Spirit when you believed?" This baptism is regenerating. It is the Spirit who gives life (John 6:63; 7:38-39; Rom 6:3-4; Col 2:12). This baptism is purifying according to 1 Corinthians 6:11; Titus 3:5; 1 Peter 1:22-23. This baptism is empowering, enabling us to have victory over sin (Ezek 36:25-29; Acts 1:8; John 3:5-8; 1 Peter 1:23). It is entrance into the body of Christ, the Church according to 1 Corinthians 12:13; Galatians 3:27. It is entrance into the kingdom of God (John 3:5; Luke 7:28; Rom 14:17).

[1060]Watson, *Exposition*, 41.

[1061]E. Stanley Jones, *Way to Power and Poise*, 42, 47, 55.

After surveying these passages in Acts, it is the opinion of Robert Lyon that "the baptism in the Spirit, far from being a second experience and an experience subsequent to receiving the Spirit or being born of the Spirit, stands scripturally at the heart of conversion."[1062]

Just as Jesus was baptized in water and then the Holy Spirit descended upon him, so Acts 2:38 gives this pattern for us. There can be exceptions in a person's salvation experience, and some exceptions were recorded in Acts, but there is a correlation between water baptism and Spirit baptism. The baptism of the Spirit does inwardly what water baptism symbolizes outwardly. Robert Lyon stated that baptism terminology without exception always has reference to a believer's entrance into the body of Christ.[1063] This is what Paul teaches in 1 Corinthians 12:13, "For we were all baptized by one Spirit into one body—whether Jews or Greeks, slave or free—and we were all given the one Spirit to drink." In Galatians 3:27 Paul wrote, "for all of you who were united with Christ in baptism have been clothed with Christ." In both references their baptism was a past event which occurred when they entered the body of Christ.

Richard S. Taylor described the Spirit's baptism in 1 Corinthians 12:13 as "an event which occurs in regeneration." Then he argued that there is a distinction between the Spirit baptizing men into Christ and Christ baptizing men with the Holy Ghost.[1064] Other holiness and pentecostal teachers will say that the Spirit has baptized every believer into Christ, but they will not admit that Christ has baptized every believer with the Spirit. Actually the Bible never speaks of the baptism *of* the Spirit. It is the baptism "of" or "from" Christ. Christ baptizes "with" the Spirit "into" the body of Christ. The emphasis should be on the work of Christ.

According to Ephesians 4:5 there is only one baptism. Therefore, every believer is baptized once, not twice.[1065] Theologically, it boarders on modalism

---

[1062]Lyon, "Baptism and Spirit Baptism," 21. Yet Laurence Wood claims there are twelve places in the New Testament where "receiving the Spirit" is used as descriptive of Pentecostal fulness, which he equates with Christian perfection [*Pentecostal Grace*, 15-17]. He claimed that the reception of the Spirit and the new birth were not necessarily at the same time [p. 92].

[1063]Lyon, "Baptism and Spirit Baptism," 17. Whether the passages in Romans, Colossians, and Galatians refer to Spirit or water baptism, the point is that in each instance the description is linked to entrance and that the experience is inclusive of all believers.

[1064]Taylor, *God. Man, and Salvation*, 494.

[1065]The verb βαπτίζω (*baptizo*) in 1 Cor 12:13 is in the aorist tense, indicating unrepeated, once-for-all action, while the filling of the Spirit in Eph 5:18 is in the present tense, denoting progressive, continuous action. However, Howard Ervin

to divide up the Trinity and teach that the Holy Spirit baptizes every believer into Christ at the new birth, but that Christ has not baptized every believer with the Spirit at that time. Hoekema questioned how one can make a distinction between a baptism by the Spirit and a baptism by Christ. "If something is done by Christ, is it not done through the Spirit? And if something is done by the Spirit, is it not also done by Christ?"[1066] If there is a baptism by the Son and a baptism by the Spirit, why not also a baptism by the Father?[1067] This amounts to tritheism, not orthodox Trinitarian theology. We cannot say that Jesus saves and the Holy Spirit sanctifies. "This is one of the practical problems arising when 'baptism with the Holy Spirit' language is used as a metaphor for entire sanctification."[1068]

In the fourth century, Cyril of Jerusalem wrote on the Holy Spirit in his catechismal lectures, connecting water baptism and Spirit baptism. According to Cyril the Holy Spirit came down to clothe the Apostles with power and to baptism them, "for as he who plunges into the waters and is baptized is encompassed on all sides by the waters, so were they also baptized completely by the Holy Ghost. The water however flows round the outside only, but the Spirit baptizes also the soul within, and that completely."[1069]

Having looked at every scriptural passage referring to Spirit baptism, we must conclude that Christ is always the baptizer. He baptizes *with* the Spirit *into* the body of Christ or *into* the realm of the Spirit and the Church (the body of Christ). By making the baptism with the Holy Spirit an experience subsequent to entrance into the kingdom of God, the modern holiness movement has obscured the significance of water baptism. Water baptism and Spirit baptism are two halves of one act or the one baptism. That one act or baptism is entrance into the kingdom of God. Baptism consists of an inward effusion of the Holy Spirit, outwardly typified by the application of water as its emblem. Water baptism,

---

argued, "If, therefore, baptism in the Spirit is a once-and-for-all experience, and it is, then filling with the Spirit is a once-and-for-all experience also" [*Conversion-Initiation*, 35].

[1066]Hoekema, "The Reformed Perspective," 142.

[1067]William Durham, early theologian of Pentecostalism, taught that "in the first experience they received Christ and were made holy by Him. In the second, they received the Holy Spirit and were sealed unto the day of redemption" [*Articles by Durham*, 8; see also 38-39].

[1068]Leclerc, *Discovering Christian Holiness*, 188.

[1069]Cyril, *NPNF*, Second Series, 7:127; Lecture 17.14. See also his lecture on baptism were he declares that baptism is not merely the grace of remission of sins, but that it purges our sins, and ministers to us the gift of the Holy Ghost [7:148; Lecture 20.6].

properly understood, is an outward sign of this inward grace. This is one event, not two; it is an act of initiation which occurs at the time of regeneration.[1070]

Two of the gospel writers referred to the baptism of the Holy Spirit by adding the words "and fire" (Matt 3:11; Luke 3:16). Holiness commentators often argue that the fire spoken of is a purifying agent and therefore the baptism of the Spirit must be the second blessing which purifies the heart. In arriving at this conclusion they overlook passages which also describe regeneration as a cleansing work, such as 1 Corinthians 6:11; Titus 3:5; 1 Peter 1:22-23. The fire of the Holy Spirit should be understood as parallel to the "washing of regeneration" for the believer, but as the unquenchable fire of God's judgment upon the unbeliever. While Luke 3:17 describes Christ separating the wheat from the chaff, this is no reference to Christian purity.

Methodism never used the phrase "the baptism with the Spirit" to mark the moment one is entirely sanctified, even though their teaching is sometimes misrepresented by holiness advocates. The more honest writers from within the holiness movement acknowledge that their emphasis is not that of Wesley, but they sometimes claim to have "improved" on his teaching.[1071]

Whedon incorporated both the outward sign and the inward grace in his statement, "One affusion by the Spirit, symbolized by water, declaring to the world our living *one faith* in the *one Lord*."[1072]

The early Methodist theologians consistently argued for water baptism administered by affusion because of the close connection between the pouring out of the Spirit and the symbolic pouring of water.[1073] John Wesley commented,

> Either men have received the Holy Ghost or not. If they have not,

---

[1070]Oden, *Life in the Spirit*, 181-182. This is also the presupposition of D. D. Whedon in his essay "The Double Baptism" in which he stated that baptism by water is the visible type and symbolic of the baptism by the Holy Spirit [*Essays*, 216-248; also contained in Clark, *Methodism Episcopal Pulpit*, 410-436]. Jacob Ditzler also argued for effusion as the proper mode of water baptism based on its connection to Spirit baptism [*Baptism*, 23-25; 37-38; 145].

[1071]Grider wrote that the holiness writers "amended" Wesley [*Entire Sanctification*, 9].
Richard S. Taylor said the message of the holiness movement was basically the old Methodist doctrine "in slightly new dress" ["Why the Holiness Movement Died," 37]. These are both statements of denial. Diane Leclerc wrote that Grider believed the nineteenth century had improved on Wesley [*Discovering Christian Holiness*, 129].

[1072]Whedon, *Commentary*, 4:284.

[1073]Raymond, *Systematic Theology*, 3:320-338; Reasoner, "Paradigm Shift Concerning Pentecost," 132-134.

repent, saith God, and be baptized, and ye shall receive the gift of the Holy Ghost. If they have, if they are already baptized with the Holy Ghost, then who can forbid water?[1074]

Adam Clarke pointed out that Jewish proselytes were baptized in water, but Jesus told Nicodemus, "Unless a man is born of water and the Spirit, he cannot enter the kingdom of God" (John 3:5). Christians are not only baptized with water, but with the Spirit.[1075] Cullmann warned against separating water and Spirit baptism. Forgiveness of sins must always be connected with the gift of the Holy Spirit.[1076]

Stephen M. Merrill, made a Methodist bishop in 1872, explained that under Judaism there were many washings, but Christ merged them all into one baptism, "which He ordained as the symbol of the Holy Spirit, and made it the sign of regeneration—the emblematic washing of regeneration and renewing of the Holy Ghost."[1077] In fact, the association of water baptism with Spirit baptism was so strong in the early church that Pentecost Sunday became a major occasion for baptisms. Pentecost Sunday became known as "Whitsunday" because the baptismal candidates dressed in white robes.[1078]

John R. Church contended that the birth of the Spirit and the baptism with the Spirit were two separate experiences. He lamented, "There are many people in the Methodist church today, who have no clear cut conception as to why they have been baptized by affusion."[1079] Yet his own theology actually weakened his argument for affusion since he did not connect the outward sign with the inward grace.

The equation of entire sanctification with the baptism of the Holy Spirit appears nowhere in the collected works of Richard Watson, nor the systematic theologies of Miley and Pope. In the three volume theology of H. Orton Wiley it

---

[1074]Wesley, *Notes*, 305.

[1075]Clarke, *Commentary*, 5:531.

[1076]Cullmann, *Baptism in the New Testament*, 12-13.

[1077]Merrill, *Christian Baptism*, 285-289.

[1078]Nixon, "Pentecost,"763.

[1079]Church, *Why Baptize By Sprinkling*, 6. In *The One Baptism That Jesus Offers*, 51 Church declared that the one baptism of Eph 4:5 was the baptism with the Holy Spirit. Yet he also contended for sprinkling without ever making the connection that the affusion of the Spirit occurred at the point of the new birth.

is given only a single page.[1080] Wiley defined the baptism with the Spirit as "the induction of newborn individuals into the full privileges of the New Covenant," but then affirmed that "entire sanctification is effected by the baptism with the Spirit."[1081]

Yet in what was reprinted as a "great holiness classic," Albert Gray asserted that

> the experiences recorded in Acts uniformly describe the receiving of the Holy Spirit baptism as subsequent to conversion. In no instance does it appear that sinners were converted and baptized with the Spirit at the same time.[1082]

Godbey noticed that Cornelius was baptized with the Spirit, which he thought was a second blessing, and was then baptized in water. He missed the whole point by declaring,

> When you receive the baptism of the Holy Ghost no one can question your right to water-baptism, eucharist and every other privilege of the gospel church. You are then eligible to any and every office in the church, pursuant to the administration of the Holy Ghost.[1083]

Does this mean only those entirely sanctified are eligible to be members of or hold office in the church? Are they the only ones eligible to receive the sacraments? In time this kind of thinking leads to holiness denominations requiring a profession of entire sanctification to be received for membership.[1084] It leads to

---

[1080]Deasley, "Entire Sanctification," 28. The reference in Wiley is *Christian Theology*, 2:444. According to Quanstrom, Wiley did not base his doctrine of entire sanctification on Acts 2 although he accepted that premise [*Century of Holiness Theology*, 80].

[1081]Wiley, *Christian Theology*, 3:323-324. Kaiser objected that if "baptism with the Holy Spirit" is so flexible that it can legitimately be applied to conversion, subsequent infillings, and entire sanctification, then it ends up meaning nothing at all. "How can we show the exegetical intention of the author simultaneously to mean all these things at once?" [Kaiser, "Baptism in the Holy Spirit," 232].

[1082]Taylor, *Leading Wesleyan Thinkers*, 363.

[1083]Godbey, *Commentary*, 5:205.

[1084]This was the rule in the Holiness Church of California, which merged with the Pilgrim Holiness Church in 1946 [Timothy Smith, *Called Unto Holiness*, 34; Charles Edwin Jones, *Perfectionist Persuasion*, 58; Dieter, *Holiness Revival*, 228-230].

such declarations as, "if you are saved, you are my half brother and if you are sanctified, you are my full brother."

Tongues in 1 Corinthians 12-14

The same word γλῶσσα (*glossa*), which is used in Acts 2 to describe real languages, is used twenty-one times in 1 Corinthians 12-14. The burden of proof for charismatics is to show that Paul is not here talking about real languages. Boyce Blackwelder denied there was any scriptural evidence that anyone under the influence of the Holy Spirit ever spoke in an "unknown tongue." Since *glossa* means language, regardless of the language spoken it would be known to some people.[1085] Steadman argued that this gift was the ability to speak foreign languages. He asked, "Who can interpret mere ecstatic ejaculations?"[1086]

Paul states the purpose of the gift of languages is evangelistic. It is not to confirm the baptism with the Holy Spirit for those who have believed on Christ, but it is for unbelievers (14:22). It is not a prayer language. Paul used a third class conditional statement in 1 Corinthians 13:1. He is giving a hypothetical example. He overstates his argument with an exaggeration to make a point. Nowhere else in Scripture is an angelic language mentioned and this verse does not establish that men can or do speak in angelic languages. The groans of the Spirit are actually unexpressed groanings which are too deep for words.[1087] According to the Greek syntax Paul was not presently speaking in an angelic language, but even if he was to do so it would profit him nothing if he did not have divine love. Therefore, Paul is not advocating an unknown prayer language, but he is making the point that such a practice would be of no benefit if the prayer did not understand what he was praying. The context is not private devotions, but public worship.

Writing toward the end of the second century, Irenaeus described the use of spiritual gifts. "In like manner we do also hear many brethren in the church, who possess prophetic gifts, and who through the Spirit speak all kinds of languages and bring to light for the general benefit the hidden things of men, and declare the mysteries of God."[1088] The obvious use of the gift of languages was communication and edification.

[1085]Blackwelder, "The Glossolalia at Pentecost," 6.

[1086]Steadman, "Gift of Tongues," 693-694.

[1087]See Reasoner, *Romans*, 347-348 regarding Rom 8:26.

[1088]Irenaeus, *ANF*, 1:531. Almost all of the early Church Fathers, including Origen, Chrysostom, Theodoret, Gregory of Nyssa, and Gregory of Nazianzus understood the gift of tongues, as recorded in Acts to consist of bona fide languages or dialects given for the purpose of evangelization [Carter, "Gift of Tongues," 49].

Wesley explained God's purpose in bestowing the gift of tongues: "On the other hand, he may see good to give many other gifts, where it is not his will to bestow this. Particularly where it would be of no use; as in a Church where all are of one mind, and all speak the same language."[1089]

Gary Maxey has noted that there are few references in Scripture to speaking in tongues. The concept of "initial evidence," as distinct from the gift of tongues as a spiritual gift, is not supported in Scripture. Acts 2 is the *only* chapter in the Bible that gives a description of speaking in tongues. Since the same Greek words are used in Mark 16, Acts 2, 10, 19, and 1 Corinthians 12, we should assume that each context is describing the same thing. In each case no interpreter was needed. The biblical pattern of speaking in tongues *never* requires the gift of interpretation to accompany it because the purpose of the true gift of tongues is to communicate truth.

However, no other chapter in the New Testament is more superficially read and carelessly interpreted than 1 Corinthians 14. This chapter is addressing a different question and describing something different than the gift of tongues in Acts 2. The situation here is that people would speak in their own native language during public worship. Yet these exuberant Christians were incomprehensible to the other worshipers. While 1 Corinthians 14 also describes real languages, and not ecstatic utterances,[1090] in this case the languages spoken are unknown to the hearer. Thus, the understanding[1091] of the speaker is unfruitful because it does not bear the expected fruit of communicating truth to others. The utterance is fruitless

---

[1089]Wesley, *Letter* to Dr. Conyers Middleton, 4 January 1749, Section 6, ¶ 8.

[1090]In 1 Corinthians 14 the *New English Bible* uses the phrases "ecstatic utterance," "language of ecstasy," "tongues of ecstasy," "ecstatic speech," and "ecstatic language" eleven times. The Greek word γλῶσσα (*glossa*) occurs fifteen times and is the same word used in Acts 2 for languages. Thus these translations in the NEB are without warrant. Carter argued that the tongues in 1 Corinthians 12-14 were also bona fide languages, but many at the church at Corinth had worshiped at the pagan shrines. Therefore, they carried the pagan practice of ecstatic utterances into the church and Paul had to deal with the counterfeit in his Corinthian correspondence ["Gift of Tongues," 56-57; see also Grudem, *Systematic Theology*, 1073-1074]. Harvey Blaney believed the Corinthian believers were lapsing into a pagan ritual, carried away in the ecstasy, unaware of what they were doing. This "unknown" tongue was not a true gift of the Spirit. Paul believed in the true gifts of the Spirit, but not in an unknown tongue. "He recognized that speaking in unknown tongues was practiced in the Corinthian church, but he did not encourage it or accept it was a work of the Spirit [Blaney, "Speaking in Unknown Tongues," 52-60]. See also Wood, "Third Wave,"112-113.

[1091]The Greek word used, νοῦς (*nous*), means the mind, understanding, or thought.

because the hearers fail to grasp the message. So there is a need for the gift of interpretation.

The charismatic interpretation of 1 Corinthians 14:14 is that the spirit of a person prays in an unknown heavenly language that bypasses the understanding of his mind. This assumes that mankind is a trichotomy, but the Bible tends to use *mind*, *heart*, *soul*, *life*, and *spirit* interchangeably.

The charismatic interpretation of 1 Corinthians 14:2 is that *mysteries* are ecstatic speech. However, the biblical definition of *mystery* is the open secret of the Gospel, including both Jew and gentile, which was hidden in ages past but now revealed. Thus, when the tongues speaker speaks mysteries he is proclaiming the Gospel in other languages. He is also edified because he understands his own words, but there can be no edification for those who do not understand his language. Since the purpose is to bear fruit, his message much be translated.

Neither the gift of languages in Acts 2 or the gift of interpretation of languages in 1 Corinthians 14 has anything to do with ecstatic utterances, in which the speaker does not understand the meaning of the sounds he is making. Ecstatic speech is a pagan practice which is addressed twice in Scripture. Isaiah 8:19 contrasts the mumbling and prattle of mediums[1092] with the clear proclamation of God's Word by God's prophets. Charles Isbell argued that when ecstasy appears in the Hebrew Bible it is to be understood as strange *actions* rather than strange *utterances*.[1093]

The second passage is Matthew 6:7 where Jesus tells his disciples that their praying should not be like that of the pagans who babble. This word "babble" is βατταλογέω (*battalogeo*). While *logeo* means to speak or say, the prefix has no meaning. Therefore, Jesus describes pagan praying as saying or repeating "batta"as a meaningless mantra. Nor can true prayer be ecstatic if prayer involves two-way communication.[1094]

[1092]The Hebrew word for "medium" is אוב(*ob*)means one who mumbles or prattles. Their speaking is described as whispering, cooing and chirping like a bird (צפף - *sapap*) and murmuring.

[1093]Isbell, "Ecstatic Utterance, 63; 75.

[1094]The prefix "batta" is an onomatopoeia, which means it is a word which imitates a sound. A mantra is a sound symbol of one or more syllables used to induce a mystical state. It must be passed on by the living voice of a guru and cannot be learned any other way. One need not understand the meaning of the mantra; the virtue is in repetition of the sound. According to Hindu teaching it embodies a spirit or deity and the repetition of the mantra calls this spirit to the person repeating it. Thus, the mantra both invites a particular spirit to enter the one using it and also creates a passive state in the meditator which facilitates this fusion of beings [Maharaj, *Escape into the Light*, 204].

The previous four paragraphs have been drawn from unpublished class syllabus

Ethical Holiness

While the holiness of the Old Testament was ceremonial and the emphasis of today is often emotionalism, the holiness of the New Testament is an ethical holiness demonstrated by conformity to the law of God. Some theologies claim to accept the full authority of scripture and then deny that anyone can live up to the New Testament standard of holiness. Other theologies redefine sin and holiness until the doctrine they teach is very different from the New Testament. Early Methodism had a good grasp of the doctrine and the lifestyle of the New Testament. While the later holiness movement claimed to maintain the same doctrine, we have noticed how radically different they interpreted many key passages.

A careful study of the New Testament will reveal the following propositions are scriptural. A careful study of early Wesleyan literature will demonstrate the same positions are Wesleyan. A careful study of holiness literature will reveal a confusion and ambiguity on these issues:

1. *All Christians have the Holy Spirit.* "The New Testament is very explicit that the converted man possesses the Holy Spirit." As the divine Agent, the Spirit indwells the believer, becoming the source of regeneration.[1095] The issue is not birth versus baptism, or received versus filled. You have either received him or you have not. Commenting on Acts 1:5, "Ye shall be baptized with the Holy Ghost," Wesley said, "And so are all true believers to the end of the world."[1096] The believer is never commanded to receive or be baptized in the Holy Spirit, but he is commanded in Ephesians 5:18 to keep constantly filled with the Spirit.

2. *All Christians are sanctified.* They are separated from willful sin and are holy. Most references in Scripture to "sanctification" fall under the category of initial sanctification, not entire sanctification.

3. *All Christians have been cleansed from the guilt and power of sin in their life.* They still have inherited depravity, but they have been washed from acquired depravity. Most holiness writers pass over this fact.[1097] God used the graphic

---

notes of Gary Maxey ["Gifts, Signs, and Miracles," 24-58]. See also Geisler, *Systematic Theology*, 4:670.

[1095]Hall and Peisker, "The Work of the Holy Spirit in Salvation," 187-188; see also Ries, "The Holy Spirit and the Converted Man," 202-203.

[1096]Wesley, *Notes*, 275.

[1097]An exception is Doty, *Lessons in Holiness*, 26-31.

analogy of circumcision to teach us that our hearts are impure and that he wants to do spiritual surgery on us. The context of Colossians 2:11 implies that when we were living in sin we were uncircumcised, but at the moment of regeneration Christ circumcised us. We are the circumcision (Phil 3:2-3). This work of the Spirit is part of the new covenant (Jer 31:31-34).[1098]

4. *All Christians are in the universal Church.* We are added to the Church when we are born again (Acts 2:47).

5. *All who are Christians will go to Heaven.* The "holiness or hell" theory has led holiness professors to believe that a man could be "saved" and yet go to hell because he was not "sanctified." R. S. Foster, elected bishop of the Methodist Episcopal Church in 1872 cautioned,

> Do not depreciate the blessing of justification. Great wrong has been unwittingly done by unadvised teachings and expressions on the part of those who profess a higher state of grace, with regard to ordinary Christian experience. This is, and always must be, fruitful of several injurious results.
> Justification is sometimes represented as an unsafe state—as but little better, if any, than impenitency; and Christians not actually in the enjoyment of, or earnestly seeking after, a higher state of grace are considered but little more secure than the men of the world. This is most unwise.[1099]

Miley cautioned, "The doctrine of sanctification must not be so interpreted as to be made a doctrine of despair to all Christian who have not consciously attained to such an experience, particularly in the definite manner of the second-blessing theory. No such interpretation can be true, because it must deny the salvation of the truly regenerate. The truly regenerate are saved, and in

---

[1098]Under the old covenant it was the male alone who bore the mark of the covenant. Yet in the last days God gives his Spirit to both male and female (Acts 2:17-18).

[1099]Foster, *Christian Purity*,308. See also Peck, *Central Idea of Christianity*, 35-36. Peck recognizes the problem theologically for God to pardon a sinner and yet condemn him at the same time. Yet he seems to suggest an unconscious cleaning for many which makes them ready for heaven. Mudge said "this kind of bald assumption is precisely of a piece with the kindred and equally baseless assumption of the Calvinist, that no truly converted person can possibly fall away and be lost" [Mudge, *Growth in Holiness*, 116].

the maintenance of a truly regenerate life must be finally saved."[1100]

While I do not believe the historical account of the early church in Acts proves the doctrine of a second blessing, the issue is over hermeneutics not doctrine. I do believe the doctrinal books in the New Testament encourage the believer to go on unto perfection. The encouragement comes under four categories: promises, prayers, commands, and examples. God would not command what is impossible and he would not promise what is unattainable.[1101] Daniel Steele declared, "In every 'ought' there is an implied 'can.'"[1102]

C. S. Lewis contended, "The command 'Be ye perfect' is not idealistic gas. Nor is it a command to do the impossible."[1103] Miner Raymond introduced his discussion of entire sanctification with this compilation:

> He gave some, apostles; and some, prophets; and some, evangelists; and some, pastors and teachers; for the perfecting of the saints, till we all come in the unity of the faith and of the knowledge of God unto a perfect man; unto the stature of the fullness of Christ. The kingdom of heaven is like unto leaven which a woman took and hid in three measures of meal till the whole was leavened. First the blade, then the ear, then the full corn in the ear. We are glad when we are weak and ye are strong, and this we also wish, even your perfection. Leaving the principles of the doctrine of Christ let us go on unto perfection, not laying again the foundation of repentance from dead works and of faith toward God. And the very God of peace sanctify you wholly; and I pray God your whole spirit and soul and body be preserved blameless unto the coming of our Lord Jesus Christ. Faithful is he that calleth you, who also will do it. For this cause I bow my knees unto the Father of our Lord Jesus Christ, of whom the whole family in heaven and earth is named, that he would grant you according to the riches of his glory to be strengthened with might by his spirit in the inner man; that Christ may dwell in your hearts by faith; that ye, being rooted and

---

[1100]Miley, *Systematic Theology*, 2:379.

[1101]This is the premise of Gibson, *Sincerity of God*. Gibson calls this concept "the promise hermeneutic." In contrast, A. W. Pink taught that men have the responsibility to repent of their sins and come to Christ even though they are not elect and are unable to come to Christ [*John*, 2:49-50; *Man's Total Depravity*, 282; 299; 304; 309].

[1102]Steele, *Jesus Exultant*, 204.

[1103]Lewis, *Mere Christianity*, 160.

> grounded in love, may be able to comprehend with all saints what is the breadth and length, and depth and height, and to know the love of Christ which passeth knowledge; that ye might be filled with all the fullness of God. Now unto him that is able to do exceeding abundantly above all that we ask or think according to the power that worketh in us, unto him be glory, in the Church by Christ Jesus, throughout all ages, world without end. Amen.[1104]

The holiness described in the New Testament is not only an experience to seek, but a life to be lived. The emphasis of scripture is not on an emotional filling, but an ethical lifestyle. R. S. Foster wrote,

> God fills the soul with his love to overflowing. It thrills with gladness. It expels impurity. While it reigns there is no place for evil thoughts, evil desire, evil feelings. Heaven has already come. Can it be permanent at its highest pitch? We think we are safe in saying not, as an emotion. The thrill of love and joy must be intermittent in a life like ours on the earth. Other feelings must come and for the time obscure and replace these. But as a principle governing the life we are bold to say love may and should abide moment by moment and without alloy. That is all God wants; that is moral perfection; that is spiritual holiness; that opens heaven.[1105]

We get into confusion whenever we seek an experience instead of seeking to know God. There is all too often a uniformity of expression in praying, testifying, and preaching. Shallow preaching and an emphasis on experience has resulted in a shift from the objective authority of God's Word to the subjective authority of emotionalism. Holiness people tend to believe that they have arrived when they receive the second blessing. While they strongly oppose the teaching of "once saved, always saved," they tend to believe that the perfected with persevere. Rob Staples described the rationalization of holiness professors who see holiness as their permanent state, "Since I am sanctified, pure in heart, free from sin, none

---

[1104]Raymond, *Systematic Theology*, 2:372-373. Ironically, Raymond felt it was impossible to define that in which Christian perfection consists, though he believed it to be a state of grace which may be sought, obtained, and enjoyed. The difficulty of definition, however, was not a bar to the actual experience [2:383-384].

[1105]Foster, *Philosophy of Christian Experience*, 161-162.

of my actions or attitudes can be considered sinful."[1106] The emphasis should not be on receiving a certain experience, but upon living a consistent, Christlike life. Thomas Cook wrote, "We teach, therefore, not a state of purity, but a maintained condition of purity, a moment-by-moment salvation consequent upon a moment-by-moment obedience and trust."[1107] Too often when a sanctified professor is confronted with evidence of a deeper need in his life he rationalizes that these things cannot be sin because he is sanctified. Their certainty is usually based on an emotional experience. Edward Sugden wrote,

> The fact is, a man is at any moment fully sanctified, if he has full faith in Christ, and so realizes the presence of Christ in his heart by His Spirit; and this will continue, as long as his faith remains fixed on his Savior. Such happy periods will at first be often interrupted by the failure of his faith; but as he perseveres, they will become more and more habitual, until they are practically continuous; though there will always remain until death the possibility of occasional lapses from the height which he has reached. So that it is not wise to speak of "a sanctified state," but rather of a present experience of sanctification. This is the peril of the view of sanctification as "a second blessing"; it is a blessing repeated not once or twice, but scores of times in the course of the Christian life.[1108]

We have seen a difference in the work of the Spirit under the old covenant and under the new. He was with them, but he indwells us. It is our privilege today to be regenerated and entirely sanctified by the Holy Spirit. Since both are the work of the Spirit, a reference in the Bible to the Spirit's work cannot be assumed to refer always to a second blessing. The context must not be ignored. While we lift up the promise of entire sanctification, we must not minimize the transformation of the new birth. Pentecost is not a good model for entire sanctification because it was a transition from the old to the new. While some feel this is an attack on the doctrine of entire sanctification, I see it as a hermeneutical issue. In nearly every instance the standard holiness interpretation of a passage differed from the outlook of early Methodist commentators. The New Testament contains many references to a deeper work of God's grace. We should seek it because it is promised and commanded, not simply because it was someone else's

---

[1106]Staples, "Doctrine of the Holy Spirit," 107; see also Staples, "Wesleyan Perspectives," 226; Staples, "Sanctification: A Dangerous Doctrine?"36.

[1107]Cook, *New Testament Holiness*, 43.

[1108]Sugden, *Works*, 2:172.

experience. The emphasis of the holiness movement has become too experience oriented. We will always get confused when we seek someone else's experience, especially if some of the experiences in Acts were abnormal, not normal. Our theology must be based on the didactic and not the *narrative* portions of Scripture. The Gospels were largely prophetic, Acts was historical, and the Epistles are doctrinal. Even if all Scripture is profitable for doctrine we must not interpret narrative passages in a way which contradicts the major doctrinal sections.

Facing the Future with Full Assurance

The full assurance of understanding (Col 2:2) deals with an assurance regarding the fundamental doctrines which were given once for all to the saints (Jude 3). Thus, it looks back. The full assurance of faith (Heb 10:22) deals with our present relationship with God. According to Yates, "the full assurance of faith relates to present pardon; the full measure of hope, to future glory."[1109] The full assurance of hope (Heb 6:11) should also be understood as an objective confidence based on the promises in God's Word regarding the success of Christ's kingdom.

The full assurance of faith is promised in Hebrews 10:22. Wesley held that it was the common privilege of believers to have a consciousness of being in the favor of God, but he did not call this the full assurance of faith since it was frequently interrupted by the return of doubt and fear.[1110] The same year of his conversion, Wesley told his brother that he had some assurance of salvation, but not full assurance.[1111] Wesley had been taught by the Moravians that the experience of justification is followed after a short delay by the full assurance of faith, which shuts out all doubt and fear.[1112] Wesley broke with the Moravians, in part, because he misunderstood them as teaching there are no degrees of faith. He later retracted his accusation, but continued to hold the position that there are

---

[1109] Yates, *Doctrine of Assurance*, 128-132.

[1110] Wesley, *Letter* to Dr. Thomas Rutherforth, 28 March 1768.

[1111] Wesley, *Letter* to Samuel Wesley, 30 October 1738.

[1112] See the testimony of full assurance by Arvid Gradin in Wesley's *Journal*, 11-14 August 1738. Wesley referenced this same testimony in his *Plain Account of Christian Perfection*, ¶ 8, although as a disciple of Zinzendorf, Gradin would not have believed in Christian perfection as something beyond the new birth. Luke Tyerman wrote that this description of assurance is what the Methodists meant by entire sanctification. Tyerman suggested that Wesley had confused the witness of the Spirit with sanctification at that time in 1738 when he was influenced by Moravian teaching [Tyerman, *Life and Times of Wesley*, 1:202-203].

degrees of faith.[1113] He concluded,

> There are *degrees of faith*, and that a man may have *some degree* of it before all things in him are become new; before he has the full assurance of faith, the abiding witness of the Spirit, or the clear perception that Christ dwelleth in him.[1114]

He explained that the difference between a clear assurance of justifying faith and full assurance amounts to the difference between the light of the morning and that of the mid-day sun.[1115] He also defended himself against the misunderstanding that he did not distinguish between the common measure of faith and the full assurance of faith. He declared there may be faith without full assurance.[1116]

In his sermon "The Marks of the New Birth,"[1117] Wesley referenced the full assurance of faith and the full assurance of hope. While he taught that a living faith and a living hope were marks of the new birth, he did not define the full assurance of faith and of hope as explicitly as he does elsewhere. Instead he seems to equate them with the witness of the Spirit that we are children of God.

Richard Watson concluded that every Christian ought to aim at a full persuasion that we are the children of God and therefore heirs of his glory. Such assurance is attainable. "This, however, does not exclude occasional doubt and weakness of faith, from the earlier stages of his experience."[1118]

In 1883 Daniel Steele preached that the direct witness of the Spirit is usually intermittent in the early stages of Christian experience. In advanced

---

[1113]Wesley, *Journal*, 31 December 1739; 3 September 1741, ¶ 5. This is corrected in his preface to his second journal [*BE Works*, 19:217; 18:220]. See also "An Extract from a Short View of the Difference Between the Moravian Brethren (so called), and the Rev. John and Charles Wesley," *Works*, 10:201-204.

[1114]Wesley, *Journal*, 31 Dec 1739. See also Hunt, *Letters on Sanctification*, 51; 79.

[1115]Wesley, *Letter* to Thomas Church, 2 February 1745, 2.8.

[1116]Wesley, *Letter* to Richard Tompson, 5 February 1756.

[1117]Wesley, Sermon #18,2.2. Contrary to Wood, this sermon is not principally about entire sanctification. The regenerate have not fulfilled the command to be perfect, but are urged to go on unto perfection [*Meaning of Pentecost*, 228; 244].

[1118]Watson, *Dictionary*, p. 101. In this section Watson defined the full assurance of understanding, faith, and hope. The reference cited above was dealing with the full assurance of hope, based on the fact that we are heirs of his glory. However, Watson is also speaking of the full assurance of faith.

experience the witness to adoption is not intermittent but abiding. Steele urged all Christians to seek full assurance. He also acknowledged the full assurance of hope, but does not offer it as the privilege of all God's children.[1119]

There are stages of faith by which we move toward this goal. The full assurance of faith is divine assurance of present salvation which excludes all doubt and fear.[1120] It is associated with the perfect love which casts out all fear (1 John 4:18). John Hunt wrote that the first Methodists made a just distinction between the Spirit's witness in a justified believer and in an entirely sanctified believer. The one is light; the other is the clearest light. One is morning; the other is the perfect day. When the Spirit is given more fully to assure us of our acceptance with God, then we have the unclouded witness of the Spirit.[1121] Hunt then quoted from Charles Wesley

Come, then, my God, mark our thine heir,
Of heaven a larger earnest give!
With clearer light thy witness bear;
More sensibly within me live:
Let all my powers thine entrance feel,
And deeper stamp thyself the seal![1122]

In Romans 14, Paul says the one who is weak in faith struggles with these secondary issues. Entire sanctification is spiritual maturity and one of the marks of maturity is the ability to discern between what is essential and what is nonessential. Often we think the strictest person is the most spiritual. The more rules we have the more holy we are. Here Paul says that sometimes this indicates weakness. Nonessentials do not define the kingdom (v 17). In this chapter Paul refers to full persuasion in vv 5, 14.[1123] This is a mark of entire sanctification to have a full assurance of understanding, faith, and hope.

Perkins wrote that this full development and full assurance comes to

---

[1119]Steele, "The Full Assurance of Faith," in *Half-Hours with St. Paul*, 307-323.

[1120]Wesley, "On the Discoveries of Faith," Sermon #110, ¶ 15; *Letter* to Elizabeth Ritchie, 6 October 1778.

[1121]Hunt, *Letters on Sanctification*, 79. However, Hunt did not feel that a direct witness to entire sanctification was as absolutely necessary as a direct witness to justification [p. 45].

[1122]Wesley, *BE Works*, 7:533, Hymn #363.

[1123]In v 5 the word is πληροφορέω (*plerophoreo*); in v 14 πείθω (*peitho*) is in the perfect tense, meaning he knows and stands persuaded. Thus, the NIV renders it "fully convinced."

different people in a variety of religious experiences and in some measure according to their temperaments.[1124] According to Pope the full assurance or *plerophory* of faith, of hope, and of understanding are three various forms of the same thing — the sure conviction of the reality of the object personally trusted in, hoped for, and apprehended in knowledge.[1125]

According to Hebrews 6:11, we are to show diligence toward the full assurance (πληροφορία - *plerophoria*) of hope.[1126] This speaks of the full development of hope. We are to take hold of the hope offered to us (Heb 6:18). Hope is faith, but it is faith which is future oriented. It is not yet realized (Rom 8:24).

Wesley associated the full assurance of hope with perfect love.[1127] It is not only the hope of heaven, but the hope of progress in God's blessing. Thus, perfect love always hopes (1 Cor 13:7). Wesley described it as "such a confidence of receiving all the promises of God, as excludes the possibility of doubting; with that Holy Spirit, by universal holiness, stamping the whole image of God on our

---

[1124]Perkins, *Evangelical Perfection*, 58.

[1125]Pope, *Prayers of St. Paul*, 214; see also Joseph H. Smith, *Pauline Perfection*, 30. The word translated "full assurance,"πληροφορία (*plerophoria* or *plerophory*), occurs in Col 2:2; 4:12; 1 Thess 1:5; Heb 6:11; 10:22.

[1126]See Wesley's *Notes*, 575 for a distinction between the full assurance of faith and of hope. Wesley associated the full assurance of hope with future glory. He defined it as the "divine testimony that we shall endure to the end; or more directly that we shall enjoy God in glory"[*Works*, 13:60-61]. Wesley also connected the full assurance of hope with Rom 8:38-39 [*Works*, 10:291]. Yet Wesley also cautioned that while the full assurance of hope excludes all doubt of our final salvation, "it does not, and cannot, continue any longer than we walk closely with God" [*Letter* to a Young Disciple, 20 May 1771; *Works*, 11:421-424]. "And this confidence is totally different from an opinion that 'no saint shall fall from grace.' It has no relation to it" [*Letter* to Hester Ann Roe, 10 April 1781]. See also "Sermon on the Mount, I," Sermon #21, 2.4, where he described the full assurance of faith as swallowing up doubt, as well as all tormenting fear, God now giving them a sure hope. Wesley then made a disclaimer that this does not necessarily imply that it is impossible for those with this sure hope to fall away.

Thomas Summers explained that the full assurance of hope is restricted to the present state and has nothing to do with an assurance that grace cannot be lost [*Systematic Theology*, 2:209-210].

[1127]"On the Discoveries of Faith," Sermon #117, § 17. Yet he wrote, "This is by no means essential to or inseparable from perfect love. It is sometimes given to those that are not perfected in love, as it was to Mr. Grimshaw. And it is not given (at least not for some time) to many that are perfected in love" [*Letter* to Elizabeth Ritchie, 6 October 1778]; "pure love, on which the full assurance of hope generally attends" [*Letter* to Hester Ann Roe, 10 April 1781]. See also Hunt, *Letters on Sanctification*, 88.

hearts."[1128] It is a divine confidence in all the promises of God which excludes the possibility of doubting, especially with regard to our final salvation, so long as we walk closely with God. Wesley said those with the full assurance of hope have no more doubt of reigning with Christ in glory, than if they already saw him coming in the clouds of heaven. "But this does not prevent their continually increasing in the knowledge and love of God."[1129]

It seems, however, that Wesley did not fully develop his doctrine of a full assurance of hope. He seemed to concede that William Grimshaw had such an assurance and, not wanting to deny that God could give him such assurance, left it at that. And yet how can I have full assurance of a future contingent event?[1130] Watson said, "Assurance of final salvation must stand or fall with the doctrine of personal unconditional election."[1131] Clarke cautioned that this full assurance of hope cannot imply that a man will absolutely persevere to the end since the Scripture does not teach unconditional perseverance.[1132] Pope argued that it would not be the assurance of hope if it were the assurance of an eternal and inalienable salvation. When faith turns to the future it is hope — hope that is full of assurance and without fear, but only hope and not the end of probation.[1133]

The full assurance of hope might apply to assurance received from God by an intercessor that the one for whom he is praying will be saved. I would also suggest that the full assurance of hope should also be understood as an objective confidence based on the promises in God's Word regarding the success of Christ's kingdom. Wesley preached about the work of the Spirit in apostolic days and then said, "But shall we not see greater things than these? Ye, greater than have been yet from the beginning of the world? Can Satan cause the truth of God to fail? Or his promises to be of none effect? If not, the time will come when Christianity

---

[1128]Wesley, *Works*, 11:424.

[1129]Wesley, "On the Discoveries of Faith," Sermon #117, ¶ 17; see also "A Second Letter to the Author of *The Enthusiasm of Methodists*," § 20, *BE Works*, 11:398-399.

[1130]In private correspondence with the author, Ken Collins called this doctrine "a strange animal" which was based on divine foreknowledge, allowing the believer to catch a glimpse of eternity. Wesley was well aware of the possible antinomian implications [27 December 2008, see also Collins, *Theology of John Wesley*, 140-142].

[1131]Watson, *Dictionary*, 101. See also Watson, *Institutes*, 2:270-271; *Dictionary*, 25.

[1132]Clarke, *Commentary*, 6:727. Yet the Calvinistic doctrine of assurance is expanded to include the assurance of election and therefore of perseverance [Beeke, *Quest for Full Assurance*, 6; 39].

[1133]Pope, *Prayers of St. Paul*, 215.

will prevail over all, and cover the earth."[1134]

J. Edwin Orr documented a great move of God in every generation since 1725, the first great awakening of which George Whitefield was part, to the present. "One generation shall praise your works to another, and shall declare your mighty acts" (Psalm 145:4).[1135] John Fletcher wrote, "We can patiently and confidently expect those times of refreshing which shall assuredly come from the presence of the Lord looking forward to that promised restitution of all things."[1136] Charles Wesley also expected God's help:

Lord, if at Thy command
The word of life we sow,
Watered by Thy almighty hand,
The seed shall surely grow:
The virtue of Thy grace
a large increase shall give
And multiply the faithful race
Who to Thy glory live.

Now, then, the ceaseless shower
Of gospel blessings send,
And let the soul-converting power
thy ministers attend.
On multitudes confer
the heart-renewing love,
And by the joy of grace prepare
For fuller joys above.[1137]

John Wesley commented in 1779,

> The remark of Luther "that a revival of religion seldom continues above thirty years" has been verified many times in several countries. But it will not always hold. The present revival of religion in England has already continued fifty years. And, blessed be God, it is at least as likely to continue as it was twenty or thirty years ago. Indeed, it is far more likely; as it not only

---

[1134]Wesley, "Scriptural Christianity," Sermon #4, 3.1.

[1135]French, "The Next Great Awakening," 2.

[1136]Fletcher, *Works*, 2:165.

[1137]*A Collection of Hymns* (1876), hymn #734, based on Acts 11:21.

spreads wider but sinks deeper than ever, more and more persons being able to testify that the blood of Christ cleanses from all sin. We have therefore reason to hope that this revival of religion will continue, and continually increase, till the time when all Israel shall be saved and the fullness of the Gentiles shall come.[1138]

Negative holiness is false holiness. 1 Corinthians 13:7 says that love always hopes. So long as we persevere we can live in such a confidence that we shall see him that excludes all doubt and fear. Heaven is our hope; the full assurance of this hope is the highest state of sanctification. "This is the highest and happiest state we can attain on earth, and the best guardian against all apostasy and relapse."[1139] Therefore, Clarke describes the person who has the full assurance of hope as "he who knows and feels that his sins are forgiven *and* that his heart is purified from all unrighteousness, that the whole body of sin and death is destroyed, and that he is fully made a partaker of the Divine nature."[1140]

Bishop Edmund Janes declared in 1851, "A holy Church would soon make a holy world."[1141] We must declare the doctrine of holiness with confidence and live the holy life with consistency. Such a message is Scriptural and such a desire is created by the Spirit. The history of the true Church across twenty centuries has been the pursuit of perfection and we must continue that pursuit in the third millennium.

[1138]Wesley, *Letter* to Elizabeth Ritchie, 12 February 1779; see also "The General Spread of the Gospel," Sermon #63, § 16; "On Laying the Foundation of the New Chapel," Sermon #112, 2.6-7; *Farther Appeal to Men of Reason and Religion, Part III*, 1.6-8; 1745.

[1139]Sutcliffe, *Commentary*, 2:914; 912.

[1140]Clarke, *Commentary*, 6:727. However, the statement by Clarke that "without holiness, complete, entire holiness, no man can see God; so, without this, none can scripturally or rationally *hope* for eternal glory" is open to misinterpretation. The later holiness movement taught "holiness or hell," but this complete holiness will be imputed to all who are justified.

[1141]Foster, *Christian Purity*, 13.

II. HISTORICAL THEOLOGY

CHAPTER 5
DEVELOPMENT OF THE DOCTRINE OF HOLINESS BEFORE METHODISM

Harold William Perkins concluded that the doctrine of perfection must be divine because the desire for a state of perfect attainment is extremely widespread. It may even be traced outside Christianity. Evangelical perfection, however, believes that divine perfection has been communicated to man through Christ. Yet even within the Christian Church the desire appears to be confined to a small minority, but it normally emerges at a certain stage of human development.

However, the attainment of perfection is an inalienable part of the Gospel revealed in Christ. Perkins defined Christian perfection as "a spiritual state, mediated by the Holy Spirit, in which the believer in Christ has a full assurance of his redemption through the blood of Christ, and enjoys unbroken communion with the love of God."[1142]

It should be obvious from the previous survey of the New Testament, that the new birth is the beginning of Christian holiness, but not the end of Christian growth. The leadership of the early Church felt a keen sense of urgency to see that believers go on unto Christian perfection. But how does that happen? Adolf Köberle observed that there are three ladders on which men continually seek to climb up to God: moralism, which emphasizes the will; mysticism, which emphasizes the emotions; and speculation, which emphasizes the intellect. The Apostle Paul came in contact with all three in his ministry: Pharisaic moralism, the mysticism of the Asian cults, and Greek wisdom.[1143] But he wrote, "Having begun by the Spirit, are you now being perfected by the flesh?" (Gal 3:3).

Wynkoop also described three major heresies using different language.[1144] If knowledge is virtue, philosophy is salvation. This is the error of gnosticism. If matter is evil, then self-discipline, even emasculation, leads to perfection. This is the error of asceticism. If the personal experience of Christ is the heart of New Testament religion, the ecstatic, Spirit-prompted mystical and emotional

[1142]Perkins, *Evangelical Perfection*, 6-7; 15; 251-254.

[1143]Köberle, *Quest for Holiness*, 2.

[1144]Wynkoop, *Theology of Love*, 276.

experience is holiness. This is mysticism. Regardless of the language used, all three errors are still present within the Church.

W. E. Sangster offered three groupings in Protestant thought regarding the way to holiness: imputed, imparted, and improving. "A balanced view of Protestant sanctity will make an effort to harmonize all three." He also characterized the classic Catholic approach as three parts of one process: purgative, illuminative, and unitive. Sangster concluded their language was different and there was some difference in method from Protestantism, but "the cardinal features of sanctity are alike wherever we meet it, and the major elements of method are alike as well. . . . Holiness is not a monopoly of the cloisters, or of one branch of Christendom. The energies of the Holy Spirit are available to everyone who will see Him."[1145] In his survey of Christian perfection historically, Merrill Gaddis described five approaches:

- the enthusiastic approach is spectacular and emotionally based
- the ascetic approach emphasizes the mortification of the body and its desires
- the humanistic emphasis, such as found in Pelaganism, dignifies human nature through its emphasis on free will
- the mystical approach teaches discipline and self-enforced passivity
- the eclectic approach draws elements from all of the above

Gaddis observed that the New Testament writings were appealed to as the basic authority for every type of perfection movement in America.[1146]

R. H. Coats wrote about the esoteric holiness of gnosticism, the prophetic holiness of Montanism, the ascetic holiness of monasticism, the natural holiness of Pelagianism, the sacramental holiness of Catholicism, the subjective holiness of mysticism, the lay holiness of the Catholic orders, and the fiduciary holiness of Protestantism. Calvin taught an intensive holiness of the elect, based on the decree of God, the Scottish Presbyterians and English Puritans taught an austere holiness, the pietists taught an experimental holiness, and Methodism taught a perfect holiness.[1147]

I want to trace through the history of the Church some seventeen responses that have been given to this question. William Burt Pope said that some kind of Christian perfection has been held in every age. He said testimonies might

---

[1145]Sangster, *Pure in Heart*,184-196; 250. The Eastern Church made a distinction between the beginners, proficients, and the perfect. The perfect had a true experimental knowledge of God [Collins, *Exploring Christian Spirituality*, 118].

[1146]Gaddis, *Christian Perfection in America*, 4-17.

[1147]Coats, "Holiness,"6:745-750.

be gathered from writers of every period. There was a true golden chain, "proving that the Spirit of finished holiness has never left Himself without witness."[1148] R. Newton Flew asserted that from the earliest days of the Christian Church there were certain communities which believed that such an ideal life could be lived in this world.[1149] "Some phase of the idea and ideal of perfection has a place in the Christian thought of every generation."[1150]

Since these seventeen approaches to Christian holiness span four chapters, it may be helpful to list them here as a preview of what is to follow:

- Persecution, Suffering and Martyrdom
- The Philosophy of Gnosticism
- The Asceticism of Monasticism
- The Corporate Grace of Sacramentarianism
- The Rationalism of Scholasticism
- The Mystical Experience
- Imputed Righteousness and the Reformation
- Eschatological Perfection
- Imparted Righteousness and the Pietists
- The Puritans and Ecclesiastical Separation
- The Wesleyan Synthesis
- The American Holiness Movement and the Second Blessing
- The Keswick View of Consecration
- Dispensationalism and the Spirit-Filled Life
- Pentecostalism and the Power of the Spirit
- Legalism: Sanctification by Works
- A Psychological/Philosophical Theology of Sanctification

The whole Church everywhere has always taught holiness.[1151] Yet in different period of time and among different movements often a part has been taught as the whole. God has always had a people and his people have always been holy, but at different periods in Church history there have been different emphases on the holy life. While some differences are substantive, others are

---

[1148]Pope, *Compendium*, 3:61.

[1149]Flew, *Idea of Perfection*, 4.

[1150]Frederic Platt, "Perfection," 9:738. This statement is hard to reconcile with Platt's statement that the doctrine of perfection "is a bypath in Christian theological systems" [Flew, *Idea of Perfection*, xii].

[1151]This statement is an adaptation of the consensus theology of Vincent of Lérins in the fifth century, "Quod ubique, quod semper, quod ab omnibus creditum est" (That faith which has been believed everywhere, always, by all).

more a matter of accent and we can learn something from each emphasis. Ephesians 3:10 speaks of the manifold wisdom of God. This word "manifold" has been translated as "many-sided" or "variegated." Just as a diamond refracts light from many angles, so the Church has emphasized Christian holiness from many vantage points. However, some books I have evaluated strike me as an attempt by the author to systematize his own experience. There is always the danger in moving from a particular experience to a general conclusion.

Barry Callen raised the question, "how are disciples of Jesus to be God's holy people?" He replied that the answers have varied across the centuries. However, "the goal of 'going on to perfection' is a persistent stream of persistent concern in all holiness traditions of Christianity."[1152]

There are three attitudes toward early Church history. The first, represented by Leo Cox stated that before the Church was very old there was a departure from the ideal of Christian perfection. "From a very early date there was a defection from the original radiance of the classic spirituality of the Early Church."[1153] Wesley wrote,

> It is true, there were a few in every age of these burning and shining lights. But they shone in a dark place, in a benighted world, a world full of darkness and cruel habitations. As the mystery of iniquity began to work even in the days of the Apostles, so, not long after they were removed from the earth, it brought forth a plentiful harvest. It overspread the face of the earth; so that well-nigh all flesh corrupted their ways before the Lord. And from that time to this, it might truly be said, "The whole world lieth in the wicked one;" meaning thereby not only the Mahometan and Pagan, but also the Christian, world.[1154]

However, Wesley had an optimistic view of historical progress and "he did not cease to look upon the early centuries as an exemplary period in the life of the Christian community."[1155] And Wesley would not have published *The Christian Library*, fifty volumes of antiquity, if he had felt it was all corrupt.

[1152]Callen, "The Context: Past and Present,"11-12.

[1153]Cox, *Perfection*, 12-13; see also Lowrey, *Possibilities of Grace*, 14-32.

[1154]Wesley, *Works*, 14:299; see also "Scripture Christianity," Sermon #4, 2.9; "The Mystery of Iniquity," Sermon #61; §21-26; "Of Former Times," Sermon #102, § 18. However, it should be noted that in these references Wesley was commenting on the general state of the Church, not specifically the life and doctrine of Christian perfection.

[1155]Campbell, *Christian Antiquity*, 52.

The opposite historical philosophy held that the Church had never utterly fallen. The Church was at its best for the first four to five hundred years. John Jewel extended this period to six centuries. In fact, the Holy Spirit continued to oversee the progress of the early Church at least through the ecumenical councils so that the Church would begin on a firm footing. The consensus of the early Church could even be considered authoritative so far as it did not contradict biblical teaching. This approach was advocated by Vincent of Lérins, who died before A. D. 450, and more recently adopted by Thomas Oden.

Samuel Wesley urged his son to study Christian antiquity and in his early years John tried too hard to duplicate the ancient Church. As an Anglican, Wesley was influenced by the Caroline divines and non-jurors. By the time of his return from America, John had come to realize that he had put too much faith in the writings of the early Church. Thus, he arrived at a third or moderate position in which he determined to rely on the authority of Scripture and to view antiquity as a "subordinate rule" rather than a "co-ordinate" one.[1156] Yet Wesley was also indebted to the theology of the early and Eastern church for his emphasis on the doctrine of open-ended perfection in this life.[1157]

It should be understood that the Apostolic Fathers did not attempt to write exhaustive theologies of the Christian faith. Instead they responded to "specific problems and situations," just as the biblical writers had done.[1158] We must also remember that the early church was more fluid in its discussion of sanctification and justification. "It did not always use terms consistently. It did not have a well-established order of salvation."[1159]

According to Gaddis, the Anti-Nicene Fathers do not represent a perfection "movement." Their language is largely Pauline and their emphasis in on ethical aspects of the Church.[1160] Perkins concluded that, while the early Fathers provided noteworthy expressions of individual and ecclesiastical perfection, their statements are not systematic and they do not attempt to pursue the conclusions deduced from them.[1161]

Yet Chris Bounds concluded that, in general, the Apostolic Fathers taught that Christian perfection is a perfection of love summarized in the two great

---

[1156]Campbell, *Christian Antiquity* , 12-40.

[1157]Outler, "Early Fathers of the Church," 103.

[1158]Bassett, *Historical Development*, 26.

[1159]Elowsky, *We Believe in the Holy Spirit*, 171.

[1160]Gaddis, *Christian Perfection in America*, 49.

[1161]Perkins, *Evangelical Perfection*, 128.

commandments, the love of God and the love of neighbor. And they taught that Christian perfection entails freedom from sin — free from deliberate sin and complete obedience to the commandments of God. They taught the possibility of Christian perfection is this present life. Christian perfection is the work of God, made possible through the redemptive life of Christ and the sanctifying presence of the Holy Spirit. By the end of the second century, the "image of God" is synonymous with Christian perfection.[1162]

Bounds said that the earliest Church Fathers, addressing particular pastoral problems, gave only a glimpse of their views. However, he argued for a basic consensus among them. Yet Bounds acknowledged that some Fathers distinguished between Christians who were perfect in this life and Christians who were not. Other Fathers taught that all baptized Christians participate to varying degrees in perfection. Some Fathers taught complete freedom from sin as the essential aspect of perfection, while others taught that freedom from sin came gradually in the process of perfection. Some Fathers taught that being remade in the image and likeness of God meant having the law of God written upon our hearts and sacrificial service to humanity. Others taught it produced incorruptibility, sinlessness, or freedom from passions. Perfect love is displayed is submission to the authority of the elders, obeying the Lord's commands, or in the voluntary act of martyrdom.[1163]

Clement of Rome was a disciple of Paul and Peter. He wrote around A. D. 90-100, "Those who have been perfected in love, through the grace of God, attain to the place of the godly in the fellowship of those who in all ages have served the glory of God in perfectness."[1164] For Clement there is no perfection apart from the atonement. The perfection to which the elect are brought is a perfect love. One can only experience this perfection of love by the grace of God. While Clement is not specific, he does infer that this perfecting in love can and does take place in this present life.[1165]

> He that has the love that is in CHRIST, let him keep the commandments of CHRIST. Who can declare the bond of the love of GOD? Who is sufficient worthily to express the magnificence of its beauty? The height to which love exalts us

---

[1162]Bounds, "Christian Perfection in the Apostolic Fathers," 22-24; 26.

[1163]Bounds, *Christian Perfection in the Ante-Nicene Fathers*, 144; 149-151; 170-181.

[1164]Quoted by Pope, *Compendium*, 3:62.

[1165]Bounds, *Christian Perfection in Fathers*, pp. 37-40; see also Bounds, "Christian Perfection in the Apostolic Fathers,"19-10.

> cannot be spoken. Love unites us to Cod. Love covereth a multitude of sins. Love is long-sufferings, yea, bears all things. There is nothing mean in love, there is nothing haughty. Love has no schism, is not seditious. Love does all things in unity. By love were all the elect of GOD made perfect. without love nothing is acceptable to God. Through love has JESUS CHRIST our Lord received us: through his love to us has he given his blood for us, his flesh for our flesh by the will of GOD, and his soul for our souls.
>
> Ye see, beloved, how great and wonderful a thing love is, and that no words can declare its perfection. Who then is sufficient to be found therein? Who but they whom GOD vouchsafes to teach it. Let us therefore beseech him that we may be worthy thereof, that we may live in love, unblamable, without respect of persons. All the generations from Adam unto this day are passed away: but those who were made perfect in love, are in the region of the just, and shall appear in glory at the visitation of the kingdom of CHRIST. Happy then are we, beloved, if we fulfill the commandments of GOD in the unity of love, that so, through love our sins may be forgiven us. For "blessed are they whose iniquities are forgiven, and whose sins are covered." And this blessing comes on those who are elected by GOD, through JESUS CHRIST our Lord. To whom be glory for ever and ever. Amen.[1166]

Yet Clement is the first Christian writer to assume that sin is a permanent reality within the Church.[1167]

In the second century *The Shepherd of Hermas*, written before A. D. 150, also called for perfection of life without providing a clear doctrine of sanctification. This writing does not directly mention the perfection of an individual, but does discuss perfection in relationship to a person's faith and fasting. Yet Bounds explained that these references describe a whole way of life, "a life characterized by a mind wholly directed toward the Lord and by freedom from sin."[1168] This book addressed the question of post-baptismal sins. Bassett

---

[1166]Wesley, *Christian Library*, Vol. 1; *Epistle to the Corinthians* § 49-50.

[1167]Flew, *Idea of Perfection*, 132-133. Flew said the author of Clement's Second Epistle to the Corinthians himself is still struggling with sin and has not experienced the might of God's grace. Yet Eusebius raised questions regarding the authorship of this letter [*Ecclesiastical History*, 3.16].

[1168]Bounds, *Christian Perfection in Fathers*, 62.

said that this book "maintains the norm of sinlessness," while still allowing for the possibility of repentance when a baptized believer sins. Yet it does not contain a clear doctrine of sanctification nor a clear exposition of its relationship to the perfection and purity for which the writer continually calls.[1169]

In the face of backslidding within the Church, Hermas explained to those who had been baptized but had not been endued with the Holy Spirit had no advantage.[1170] Flew wrote, "The Shepherd of Hermas makes a new attempt to reconcile the ideal of sinlessness with the reality of sin in the Church. The aim of the book is that he who has sinned may sin no more." While Hermas had no doubt that sinlessness was possible, the idea of works of supererogation had entered into the Church.[1171] This refers to the teaching that merit could be obtained by going beyond the moral requirements of the Gospel and that sanctification was by works. This would find further development in the monastic emphasis on poverty, chastity, and obedience.

Around A. D. 135 Polycarp wrote,

> These things, my brethren, I write not unto you of myself, concerning righteousness; but because ye exhorted me thereto. For neither can I, nor any other such as I am, come up to the wisdom of the blessed and glorious Paul, who being present with you, taught you the word of truth perfectly, and being absent, wrote letters unto you; by which ye may be edified in the faith that is given you, which is the mother of us all which is followed by hope and led by love both of God, and Christ, and our neighbor. For if a man be in these, he has fulfilled the law of righteousness: for he who has love is far from all sin.[1172]

Polycarp, a disciple of John, discipled Irenaeus (A. D. 175-195). Bassett wrote, "One seeks in vain for particular passages of any great length in which Irenaeus expounds his understandings of sanctification and perfection."[1173] Yet

---

[1169]Bassett, *Historical Development*, 32; 34.

[1170]Bassett, *Holiness Teaching*, 57; *Pastor of Hermas*, 3.9.13, *ANF*, 2:48.

[1171]Flew, *Idea of Perfection*, 133-134.

[1172]Wesley, *Christian Library*, Vol 1; *Epistle to the Philippians*; § 3.

[1173]Bassett, *Holiness Teaching*, 66. Most of the material gathered by Bassett in *Holiness Teaching* is of a general nature; some does not even address the subject of Christian perfection. Bassett concedes that "one seeks in vain for particular passages of any great length in which Irenaeus expounds his understandings of sanctification and perfection." Bassett asked, "Did Irenaeus speak of or imply a 'second definite work of

Bounds asserted that in *Against Heresies* Irenaeus "offers the most extensively developed doctrine of perfection as yet in the Ante-Nicene period."[1174] In *Against Heresies* Irenaeus opposed the teaching of gnosticism. Against the gnostic teaching of redemption *from* the world, Irenaeus taught the redemption *of* the world. Gnosticism stressed knowledge, the understanding and grasp of certain propositional ideas about humanity's origin and nature. This knowledge resided in the man Jesus and was secretly revealed to certain individuals chosen by the spiritual Christ who emanated from the Supreme Mind. Irenaeus taught that the possibility of perfection was open to all, not just a select few. Irenaeus also emphasized the necessity of the Incarnation, teaching that if there is no real Incarnation there is no salvation. Based on the teaching of Paul in 1 Corinthians 15:45, Irenaeus emphasized the role of the first and last Adam. He emphasized that Jesus became like us in order that we might become like him. Without the Incarnation man could not attain his purpose and live in fellowship with God.

> For the glory of God is a living man; and the life of man consists in beholding God. For if the manifestation of God which is made by means of the creation, affords life to all living in the earth, much more does that revelation of the Father which comes through the Word, give life to those who see God.[1175]

Thus, the victory of Christ is reproduced or recapitulated within us, enabling us to achieve God's purpose for us. All things are to be summed up in Christ, the last Adam (1 Cor 15:45) and the second man (1 Cor 15:47; see also Rom 5:12-21). What was lost because of Adam's disobedience is restored in Christ's obedience.

> These things, therefore, He recapitulated in Himself: by uniting man to the Spirit, and causing the Spirit to dwell in man, He is

---

grace, subsequent to regeneration'? Did he talk of entire sanctification? The answer to both questions is yes and no." Bassett has already conceded that Irenaeus wrote nothing specifically on the question, yet Bassett wanted to read into the writings of Irenaeus his own bias that he "seems to be referring to a 'secondness' of sanctification in the context of baptism." But the symbolism of water baptism is initiation, not something subsequent. Bassett does not reprint a single classic text which either advocates a second crisis experience or equates the baptism with the Holy Spirit with Christian perfection [see Reasoner, "Holiness Propaganda," 2-3].

[1174]Bounds, *Christian Perfection in Fathers*, 65. See also Bounds, "Irenaeus," 161-176.

[1175]Irenaeus, *Against Heresies*, 4.20.7; *ANF*, 1:490.

> Himself made the head of the Spirit, and gives the Spirit to be the head of man: for through Him (the Spirit) we see, and hear, and speak. He has therefore, in His work of recapitulation, summed up all things, both waging war against our enemy, and crushing him who had at the beginning led us away captives in Adam, and trampled upon his head. . . . For indeed the enemy would not have been fairly vanquished, unless it had been a man [born] of a woman who conquered him. For it was by means of a woman that he got the advantage over man at first, setting himself up as man's opponent. And therefore does the Lord profess Himself to be the Son of man, comprising in Himself that original man out of whom the woman was fashioned, in order that, as our species went down to death through a vanquished man, so we may ascend to life again through a victorious one; and as through a man death received the palm [of victory] against us, so again by a man we may receive the palm against death.
>
> Now the Lord would not have recapitulated in Himself that ancient and primary enmity against the serpent, fulfilling the promise of the Creator, and performing His command, if He had come from another Father. But as He is one and the same, who formed us at the beginning, and sent His Son at the end, the Lord did perform His command, being made of a woman, by both destroying our adversary, and perfecting man after the image and likeness of God.[1176]

Irenaeus taught that our goal was to be perfected in Christ, having received the Spirit, living in communion with God. The Holy Spirit is received at conversion and baptism. Christians are spiritual because they have put aside the lusts of the flesh and have received the Holy Spirit. Yet Irenaeus also wrote that

> God is mighty to make that perfect which the willing spirit desires. . . . the Apostle calls them perfect who present body, soul, and spirit without blame before God: who not only have the Holy Spirit abiding in them, but also preserve faultless their souls and bodies, keeping their fidelity to God, and fulfilling their

---

[1176]Irenaeus, *Against Heresies*, 5.20.2-5.21.2; *ANF*, 1:548-549. According to Flew, Irenaeus based this concept on Eph 1:10; Col 1:19. In Eph 1:10 Paul used ἀνακεφαλαιόω (*anakephalaioo*), a compound word made up of *ana* (up) and *kephale* (head). Flew asserted that the doctrine of perfection is inherent in this word [*Idea of Perfection*, 127].

duties to their neighbor.[1177]

Irenaeus wrote that Christ sanctified each stage of human life:

> For He came to save all through means of Himself — all, I say, who though Him are born again to God — infants, and children, and boys, and youth, and old men. He therefore passed through every age, becoming an infant for infants, thus sanctifying infants; a child for children, thus sanctifying those who are of this age, being at the same time made to them an example of piety, righteousness, and submission; a youth for youths, becoming an example to youths, and thus sanctifying them for the Lord. So likewise He was an old man for old men, that He might be a perfect Master for all, not merely as respects the setting forth of the truth, but also as regards age, sanctifying at the same time the aged also, and becoming an example to them likewise. Then, at last, He came on death itself, that He might be "the firstborn from the dead, that in all things He might have the pre-eminence," the Prince of life, existing before all, and going before all.[1178]

1. Persecution, Suffering, and Martyrdom

By the end of the first century compromise and backsliding had entered the Church. Writers in this period recognized the possibility of perfection but tended to emphasize perfection through suffering and martyrdom, which was the perfect imitation of Christ.[1179] In the eighteenth century, the imitation of Christ was an ideal of Christianity advocated by a range of theological positions in Britain: Anglicans and dissenters, Methodists and evangelicals, as well as mystics.

Asbury Lowrey wrote, "The fathers had a morbid martyr spirit and reckless zeal that courted suffering and death. They were more anxious to die *for* Christ as martyrs, than to die *in* Christ to all sin."[1180] This shift is first detected in the writings of Ignatius of Antioch, who was himself martyred either in A. D. 98 or 117. In almost all of his letters, Ignatius mentioned that he had not yet been

[1177]Quoted by Pope, *Compendium*, 3:62.

[1178]Irenaeus, *Against Heresies*, 2.22.4; *ANF*, 1:391.

[1179]Forsyth concluded that the monks lost the way of life by thinking more of imitating Christ than of trusting Christ [*Christian Perfection*, 97].

[1180]Lowrey, *Possibilities of Grace*, 18.

made perfect or attained martyrdom. Turner wrote,

> In his Epistles may be seen a Christian expression of the idea of perfection by way of suffering, which perhaps first received classic expression in Job and won increasing influence when the Jewish people were the victims of persecution. This is a departure from what is central in New Testament teaching, but it is not without precedent in the canonical writings. It marks perhaps the first explicit indication of a shift from the New Testament ideal of perfection in love to the medieval ideal of perfection through renunciation.[1181]

Yet in his letters he tied Christian perfection to faith and love. Ignatius wrote,

> For nothing is better than peace, whereby all war is destroyed, both of things in heaven and things on earth. Nothing of this is hid from you, if ye have perfect faith in JESUS CHRIST, and love, which are the beginning and the end of life: faith is the beginning, love the end: and both being joined in one, are of God. All other things pertaining to perfect holiness follow. For no man that hath faith sins; and none that has love hateth any man. The tree is made manifest by its fruits. So Christians shall be known by their deeds. For it is not the work of an outward profession; but in the power of faith, if a man endure unto the end.[1182]

Ignatius wrote of a perfect faith, a perfect mind and intention, and of the perfect work of holiness.[1183] "For in as much as ye are perfect yourselves, you ought to think those things that are perfect. And when you are desirous to do well, God is ready to enable you thereunto."[1184] He advocated perfection in love as the Christian norm, but said nothing of how one enters such an experience nor how the doctrine relates to justification or sanctification. His emphasis is on the work of the Holy Spirit in the Church and not in the individual believer.[1185]

Clement of Alexandria (A. D. 153-217) produced the first attempt to

---

[1181]Turner, *Vision Which Transforms*, 164-165.

[1182]Wesley, *Christian Library*, Volume 1; *Epistle to the Ephesians* § 13-14.

[1183]Pope, *Compendium*, 3:62.

[1184]Wesley, *Christian Library*, Volume 1; *Epistle to the Smyrnaeans* § 6.

[1185]Bassett, *Historical Development*, 28-30.

represent a rational ideal of the Christian life. He also spoke of the Greek and barbarian philosophies of perfection, but said that one might dispense with philosophy and may take the short cut to perfection, that of salvation by faith.[1186]

Clement was definite regarding the possibility of perfection in this life, which exempts us from purgatory in the next life. Following Plato, Clement believed purgatory remained for those who did not reach purification in this life.[1187]

He also wrote, "For it is utterly impossible for any one to become perfect as God is. Now the Father wishes us to be perfect by living blamelessly, according to the obedience of the Gospel."[1188] Yet Clement also connected martyrdom and perfection because martyrdom is the ultimate testimony of love for God. "We call martyrdom perfection, not because the man comes to the end of his life as others, but because he had exhibited the perfect work of love." Since Christ calls a person in life to leave behind all possessions, all human relationships which would hinder in following the Lord, and all passions, by laying down his life the martyr testifies that he is dead to the world and fully alive in Christ. However, Clement was careful to caution people from eagerly seeking martyrdom. To do so is "rash," "foolhardy," and a "sin against God."[1189]

Passages like 1 Peter 5:10, as well as the entire book of 1 Peter, teach the significance of suffering and affliction. According to Hebrews 12:10 God disciplines us that we may share in his holiness and that discipline may involve suffering, adversity, persecution, and even pain. However the emphasis is not upon suffering, but upon grace. Suffering demonstrates our need for growth in grace. Although Peter's emphasis in this first letter is that Christians will suffer (see 1:6) and that trials should not take us by surprise (4:12), persecution and stress, trials and afflictions do not sanctify — they reveal to what degree we are sanctified. However, Wesley observed,

> We have now abundant proof that very many are made better by sickness; unless one would rather say in sickness. This is one of the grand means which God employs for that purpose. In sickness, many are convinced of sin, many converted to God, and still more confirmed in the ways of God and brought onward to perfection.[1190]

[1186]Clement, *Stromata*, 7.2; *ANF*, 2:526.

[1187]Perkins, *Evangelical Perfection*, 148.

[1188]Clement, *Stromata*, 7.14; *ANF*, 2:549.

[1189]Bounds, *Christian Perfection in Fathers*, 106-107.

[1190]Wesley, *Letter* to Mary Bishop, 15 March 1777.

Yet Wesley also observed that the Apostle John suffered the least, but loved Christ the most.[1191] Commenting on Hebrews 2:10, Fletcher observed

> Our Lord "was made a perfect *Savior* through sufferings" and we may be made perfect Christians in the same manner. We may be called to suffer, till all that which we have brought out of spiritual Egypt is consumed in a howling wilderness, in a dismal Gethsemane, or on a shameful Calvary. Should this lot be reserved for us, let us not imitate our Lord's imperfect disciples, who "forsook him and fled;" but let us stand the fiery trial, till all our fetters are melted, and our dross is purged away.[1192]

Of course, the ultimate form of suffering is martyrdom. But dying for the cause of Christ does not guarantee sainthood. It may be easier to die for Christ than to live for Christ in some circumstances. 1 Corinthians 13:3 warns, "If I surrender my body to the flames, but have not love, I gain nothing." Therefore, we do not seek persecution or suffering; we seek more grace. Yet Ignatius testified to that grace and died a martyr.

> Then Trajan pronounced this sentence against him; For as much as Ignatius has confessed that he carries within himself Him that was crucified, we command that he be carried bound to the great Rome, there to be thrown to the beasts, for the entertainment of the people. When the holy martyr heard this, he cried out with joy, "I thank thee, O Lord, that you have vouchsafed to honor me with a perfect love towards thee."[1193]

Tears are related to suffering . In a later period Symeon the New Theologian (949-1022) believed in the perfectability of man, but received the theology of tears from his teacher, Symeon the Studite. Symeon the New Theologian experienced tears at the time of his conversion and again when overwhelmed with the divine presence. He felt this gift of tears was necessary and should be sought by all Christians.[1194] Unless there is true repentance and tears, there is no holiness nor perfection. Spiritual gifts, such as tears, are essential for

---

[1191]Wesley, *Letter* to Mary Stokes, 16 June 1772; *Letter* to John Valton, 18 June 1782; Preface to the Life of Madame Guyon, ¶ 7, cited on p. 351 of this book.

[1192]Fletcher, *Works*, 2:644.

[1193]Wesley, *Christian Library*, Vol. 1; *The Martyrdom of St. Ignatius*, § 6-7.

[1194]deCatanzaro, *Catechetical Discourse* 29, 209-234.

true holiness. The Spirit of God will reward the faithful believer with the chrism of tears through which he is quickly lifted up to perfect purification and holiness.[1195]

T. G. Hegre, founder of the Bethany Fellowship community, taught four stages in salvation: awakening, conversion, baptism with the Holy Spirit, and the fellowship of sufferings. Hegre distinguished between the baptism by the Spirit into the body of Christ, the baptism by Christ with the Holy Spirit, and then urged us to "go on into the still-deeper step of the fellowship of the sufferings of Christ."[1196] While I am wary of too many steps or levels, suffering does seem to be an unavoidable part of living the holy life.

2. The Philosophy of Gnosticism

Gnosticism comes from the Greek word γνῶσις (*gnosis*) meaning knowledge, insight, or science. However, 1 Corinthians 13:2 warns that even if I can fathom all mysteries and all knowledge, but have not love I am nothing. Paul purposed that he would preach Christ crucified and not human philosophy. Yet he declared in 1 Corinthians 2:6 that his message was wisdom to those who were perfect. However, it was not gnostic wisdom. Wesley explained the difference:

> The doctrine of the Gnostics was not that a child of God *does not commit sin*, i.e. act the things forbidden in Scripture, but that they are *not sin* in him, that he is a child of God still; so they contended not for *sinless* but *sinful* perfection: just as different from what I contend for as heaven is from hell.[1197]

Gnosticism held that mankind was *hylikoi*, materialistic, without God and without hope. Those who knew the Gospel were the *psychichoi*. They possessed a soul and were capable of salvation, but not of entering into the Pleroma or fullness. The secrets of the kingdom were revealed to the *pneumatikoi*. Thus, redemption came through the *gnosis*. However in practice this led to antinomianism.[1198]

[1195]deCatanzaro, *Catechetical Discourse* 4, 360-402.

[1196]Hegre, *Message of the Cross* 23 (March-April 1970): 5.

[1197]Wesley, *Letter* to William Dodd, 12 March 1756.

[1198]These categories seem to be perpetuated by dispensational theology. See pp. 658-667. Ironically, it is possible to substitute man's rules for God's commands and be both legalistic *and* lawless (Matt 15:3, 6).

The basic error of gnosticism was a dualism of matter which was evil and spirit which was good. Enlightenment or knowledge was exalted above evangelical faith as pagan philosophy was assimilated into Christianity. Pagan gnosticism taught that redemption was a form of spiritual illumination which enabled the spiritual person to escape from the power of the material world into the realm of pure spirit. Salvation was in knowing how to move from the totally material to the stage of pure spirit. Except for the first and last stages, there was a spirit, a force, or god at each stage who would help the willing person grasp that stage and move on to the next.[1199]

In the second century Clement of Alexandria synthesized his knowledge of Scripture with the Greek philosophy of neoplatonism. Basic to neoplatonism is the emphasis on the mind or ideas as superior to the material world. "The monks tried to combine apostolic life with the philosophy which finds its highest expression in the renunciation of the material for the sake of the spiritual, in making the soul less of a partner with the body and more of a master."[1200] According to Clement, the Gnostic studied to acquire mastery over his passions.

Clement had been a philosopher prior to his conversion to Christianity. Unfortunately, he described the perfect Christian or "true Gnostic" in Stoic terms. He stressed the importance of keeping all emotion in check through reason and even described Jesus Christ as dispassionate.[1201]

Clement defined the *philosophein* as a striving for the perfect life.[1202] Thus, philosophy is the preparatory discipline for the perfection which is by Christ. The perfect man was a Christian Gnostic, having both faith and knowledge. While gnosticism teaches salvation through knowledge, Clement in his seventh book of the *Stromateis* (or *Miscellanies*), written about A. D. 200, contrasted the true Christian gnostic with the false teachings produced by Gnostic sects. He described a true gnostic as a perfect Christian, a "complete model of moral conduct," who have the knowledge of God in the heart through faith, not through the acquisition of wisdom. In contrast to the gnostics who regarded only themselves as perfect, Clement declared that all Christians are perfect from the moment of their entrance into the new life. And in contrast to gnosticism, Clement held that perfection was possible for all Christians. But they must continue that perfecting process throughout their lives.

[1199]Bassett, *Holiness Teaching*, 46-47.

[1200]Williams, *Early Church Fathers*, 187.

[1201]"Patripassionism," the belief that the Father suffers was condemned by the early Church as heretical. This resulted in the opposite error, impassibility, that God did not have any emotions.

[1202]Clement, *Stromata*, 6.17; *ANF*, 2:516.

Clement recognized that all believers were perfect in the sight of God, but urged these believers to go on unto perfection. Clement taught that those who were regenerated had attained perfection because the baptized individual has received the Holy Spirit and because that person, even in the lowest stage of Christian life, possesses love and likeness to God, even if only in an immature or embryonic form.[1203]

While we cannot be perfect in all virtues simultaneously, we can still excel in every virtue. We each have unique strengths and weaknesses, which provide us with varying capacities for acquiring these virtues. But we can become perfect with respect to our particular proficiencies, which results in a relative state of perfection.[1204]

Thus Clement understood perfection in dynamic terms. Absolute perfection was a reality only for Christ, yet perfection in love is a present possibility. Christian perfection is being made like Christ up to the measure of our capacity. In *Stromata* Clement described the steps to a higher degree of perfection: "Knowledge is added to faith and love to knowledge; and to love, the heavenly inheritance. This occurs whenever anyone clings to the Lord by faith and knowledge and love and ascends with Him to the very presence of God, the Keeper of our faith and love."[1205] Clement also emphasized a complete disinterestedness to the passions of the soul. The goal was not moderation, but *apatheia*, a complete eradication of desire.[1206] In fact, *apatheia* was a metaphor for Christian holiness.[1207]

While in one sense Clement was a gnostic, yet in another sense he opposed the fanaticism within gnosticism. "I cannot but sometimes wonder that some men dare to call themselves perfect and Gnostics, thinking of themselves more highly than the Apostle did."[1208]

[1203]Bounds, *Christian Perfection in Fathers*, 98-99; Flew, *Idea of Perfection*, 141. This is also the teaching of Notatian (A. D. 210-280) [Bounds, 136].

[1204]See the summary of Clement's teaching by Lowery on *Salvaging Wesley's Agenda*, 147-149.

[1205]Bassett, *Holiness Teaching*, 80. Earlier in Book 4 Clement wrote about Christian perfection as exemplified in martyrdom. Yet in *Stromateis*, 7.2.11.99 Clement wrote of "the short-cut to perfection, that of salvation through faith."

[1206]Clement, *Stromata*, 6.9; 7.11, 13, 14; *ANF*, 2:496; 541, 547. This *apatheia* could have only been learned from the Stoics [LaRondelle, *Perfection and Perfectionism*, 297]. For another opinion, see Dunning, *Grace, Faith, and Holiness,* 458.

[1207]Anderson, *Clement of Alexandria*, 168.

[1208]Clement, *The Instructor* [*Paedagogus*], ch. 6; *ANF*, 2:222.

Gnosticism claimed to be redeemed from the bondage of matter and the flesh. For them the spirit is good, but matter is evil. Therefore, sin is accepted as a necessary consequence of the body. Richard Watson objected that "we nowhere find the circumstance of the soul's union with the body represented as a necessary obstacle to its entire sanctification."[1209] Pope wrote that such writers as Clement and Irenaeus "were content to write as if sin was a necessary concomitant of the body."[1210]

According to Clement, gnostics who follow the apostles ought to be sinless.[1211] Pope suggested that Clement should have emphasized that believers may be sanctified *in* the flesh as well as *from* the flesh.[1212] Clement also wrote, "'But they who have been perfected in love, through the grace of God, hold the place of the godly, who shall be manifested at the visitation of the kingdom of Christ.' Love permits not to sin; but if it fall into any such case, by reason of the interference of the adversary, in imitation of David, it will sing: "I will confess unto the Lord, and it will please Him above a young bullock that has horns and hoofs. Let the poor see it, and be glad." For he says, "Sacrifice to God a sacrifice of praise, and pay to the Lord thy vows; and call upon me in the day of trouble, and I will deliver thee, and thou shalt glorify me." "For the sacrifice of God is a broken spirit."[1213]

Clement taught that those chosen by God are those who are perfected in love and once the knowledge of God is attained, virtue becomes habit and is incapable of being lost. Yet John Wesley was inspired by Clement's description of a perfect Christian and in 1742 Wesley also wrote a sketch, called "The Character of a Methodist." Outler said that Wesley took the description of a "true Gnostic," found in the Seventh Book of *Stromateis* by Clement, and updated it for

---

[1209]Watson, *Theological Institutes*, 2:451.

[1210]Pope, *Compendium*, 3:63.

[1211]Clement, *Stromata*, 4.9; *ANF*, 2:422.

[1212]Pope, *Compendium*, 3:62-63. Anders Nygren was critical of Clement in *Agape and Eros* regarding him as a perverter of the faith, while attempting to defend it. However, Claude Thompson wrote that "one begins to suspect that Nygren is actually imposing upon Clement his own theological presuppositions" ["Witness of American Methodism,"101]. But Clement held to a Docetic view of Christ, that he only appeared human [*Stromateis*, 6.9] and viewed sin as ignorance or weakness [*Stromateis*, 7.16]. Therefore, his view of faith is primarily a matter of intellectual assent. This was also the conclusion of Claude Thompson who also wrote that Clement's perfect life bears the marks of Greek contemplation rather than of reconciliation ["Witness of American Methodism," 104-105].

[1213]Clement, *Stromata*, 4.18; *ANF*, 2:430.

the eighteenth century.[1214] However, Wesley did not follow Clement's order nor use his precise words. He did not retain Clement's emphasis on the Christian's passionlessness nor on the contemplation of the divine.[1215] Outler wrote that it was almost as if Wesley read "love" were Clement had written "knowledge," "then had turned the Eastern notion of a vertical scale of perfection into a genetic scale of development within historical existence."[1216] Instead, he attempted to write "in a more scriptural manner." And in this same letter to *Lloyd's Evening Post*, Wesley replied to William Dodd by declaring "I am not perfect. . . . I tell you flat *I have not attained* the character I draw.[1217] Yet, "the fact that Wesley *thought of* his treatise on 'The Character of a Methodist' as being derived from Clement of Alexandria reveals that Wesley saw a continuity between the Methodism of his age and early Christianity."[1218] However, Wesley's admiration for Clement cooled in later years. He wrote that then he saw a Stoic and a Christian were different characters and he did not admire the description of Clement of Alexandria as he previously had.[1219]

It was said of Tertullian that "above all his life was the pursuit of holiness in the presence of the living God." He saw sanctification as "the path by which a man might attain a more perfect knowledge of God." For Tertullian the work of sanctification was "essentially one of restoration which led eventually to a renewal of life as it was before the Fall." Yet he held to a dualism which saw the flesh as the enemy of the soul.

Watson wrote that the doctrine of the necessary indwelling of sin in the soul till death assumes that the seat of sin is in the flesh. Thus it adopts pagan philosophy which attributes all evil to matter. Yet the doctrine of the Bible teaches that the seal of sin is in the soul. There is no need to wait for the separation of the soul from the body in order to be saved from evils of the spirit.[1220]

However, Tertullian felt that perfection was fragile and needed to be maintained through asceticism. Thus, he equated holiness with denying the flesh.

[1214]Wesley, *BE Works*, 1:75.

[1215]Campbell, *Christian Antiquity*, p. 42. Anderson analyzed the influence of Clement upon Wesley in *Clement of Alexandria*, 205-286.

[1216]Outler, *John Wesley*, 31.

[1217]Wesley, *Journal*, 5 March, 1767.

[1218]Campbell, *Christian Antiquity*, 4.

[1219]Wesley, *Letter* to Miss J. C. March, 30 November 1774.

[1220]Watson, *Theological Institutes*, 2:454.

He emphasized fasting and chastity or sexual continence.[1221] Perkins observed that Tertullian never dreamed of the Church redeeming the world. For Tertullian, the Christian must aim at perfection through complete renunciation of the world.[1222]

Origen, a disciple of Clement of Alexandria, carried gnosticism further. Origen taught that man's present state is the result of his original sin in a pre-existent state. Origen believed in the soul's pre-existence through the teaching of Pythagorean and Platonic philosophy. He also felt that all punishment was remedial, making no distinction between the fires of hell and purgatory. Thus, Origen held out hope even for the conversion of the devil and his angels.[1223]

He taught that faith saves, but knowledge perfects. Faith was a useful thing for the multitude, but to ascend to truth beyond "mere faith" Origen advocates the ladder of knowledge. Faith is not personal trust, but mental assent to truth. This ladder is climbed gradually. No sudden break with sin occurs. Conversion is only a change of the will. Origen taught that the Christian is not a servant of sin; he sins but he is not a sinner. Yet the spiritual man can rise above his body and enter the battle against demons. He may be wholly united with God or deified in this life. Salvation was the adaptation of the Gospel to philosophical language. Origen held that the true gnostic, the perfect man, had reached the stage where Jesus the crucified has no longer any meaning for him.[1224]

For those who desired to go on unto perfection, his first advice was "know thyself." Thus, while Origen defended the possibility of moral perfection, it was essentially a humanistic perfection in which man takes the initiative. Yet perfect purity, which was celibacy and chastity, was the gift of God. The perfect Christian has turned his back on the outward and visible world, as well as his own emotions. Origen considered the body the fetter of the soul which hindered it from gaining the knowledge of God. Taking literally the words of Jesus in Matthew 19:12, Origen had himself castrated.[1225] According to Flew, "Origen is the precursor of Monasticism."[1226] Origen opened the door to monasticism with his emphasis on asceticism.

[1221]Bray, *Holiness and the Will of God*, 31; 63; 36-37. Ironically, before the Fall, God told mankind to be fruitful and multiply, not to abstain from sex within marriage.

[1222]Perkins, *Evangelical Perfection*, 131.

[1223]This doctrine was condemned by Augustine in the *City of God*, 21.17.

[1224]Harnack, *Monasticism*, 367.

[1225]Eusebius, *Ecclesiastical History*, 6.8.

[1226]Flew, *Idea of Perfection*, 151-156.

Tatian was the leader of the Encratites, a second century Christian sect named for their doctrine of continence or abstinence from sexual activity. The Greek word was *enkrateia*. Tatian wrote *Concerning Perfection According to the Redeemer*, in which he advocated abstinence from marriage, from wine and flesh, and from earthly possession, as the only true following of Christ.[1227]

In the early Church, the martyr was regarded as the best personification of holiness. However, after Constantine legalized Christianity the state no longer executed Christians. Thus the new martyrdom was the rise of asceticism. If a person could not longer be literally crucified with Christ, at least he could practice self-mortification.

"Asceticism" comes from the Greek word ἄσκησις (*askesis*) which refers to the physical training of athletes and the self discipline, even self denial, of the Stoics and Cynics. Within monasticism, asceticism meant training the thoughts, controlling the tongue, and disciplining the body through chastity and temperance. Ascetic spirituality appeals to the *kenosis* or Christ emptying himself of his glory in Philippians 2:7 and teaches that we must empty ourselves as well. In holiness theology this may be described in terms as death to self or consecration.

Simeon the Stylite began as a solitary in a cell near Antioch. After three years he took his stand on a nearby height, chained to a large stone. Gaining confidence, he stood unchained for four years without lying or sitting down, enduring summer heat and winter snow. Yet the devotion of the crowds distracted him, so he stood on a column which over time he made higher and higher until it reached sixty feet. This pillar was also called a "style," thus the name "stylite." There he lived for over thirty years without ever coming down. His disciples brought his necessary food up on a ladder.[1228] Some of his disciples even fought sleep. Bernard of Clairvaux regarded all time given to sleep as wasted. Whips and iron girdles were used to subdue the flesh. Francis of Assisi sprinkled ashes on his food if it tasted too good.[1229] He also referred to his body as "Brother Ass."

More recently a biography of Pope Paul II confirmed that the pope regularly whipped himself as an act of penance. The author explained that self-flagellation was "an instrument of Christian perfection emulating the sufferings

---

[1227]While this work is not extant, fragments have been collected in *ANF*, 2:82-83. The Encratites even substituted milk for wine in the Eucharist.

[1228]Yet Bradley Nassif asserted that his preaching converted Bedouin Arab tribes to Christ. Despite their extreme personal discipline, Nassif claimed these "athletes of God" were driven by love for God ["Poverty of Love,"34-37].

[1229]See the discussion by Sangster, *Pure in Heart*, 176-177.

of Jesus Christ."[1230]

Yet Richard S. Taylor explained that disciplined living is not necessarily holy living. Discipline is not a substitute for holiness nor is discipline the way to holiness. Suffering does not necessarily sanctify. However, the holy still need discipline.[1231]

For modern expressions of spiritual discipline, though not necessarily ascetic, see Richard Foster, *Celebration of Discipline* (1978) and Dallas Willard, *The Spirit of the Disciplines* (1988). Willard believes that justification is by grace alone, through faith alone, in Christ alone. But sanctification involves the mortification of the old self and vivification of the new self. This is not only God's gift, but requires our effort. Willard advocates solitude and silence, fasting and meditation, chastity, secrecy about our good works, study of God's Word, worship and celebration, consciousness of God's presence everywhere, prayer and confession of our sins to God and each other.[1232]

3. The Asceticism of Monasticism

The hermit Antony is considered the father of monasticism. Harnack called this movement "the greatest organized quest for perfection in history."[1233] Since perfection was defined as the renunciation of the world, including property, marriage, personal will, and honor, the true monk was considered to be the true and most perfect Christian.[1234]

On his way to church Antony was distressed by the thought of his own unworthiness. The sermon was from the words of Jesus to the young ruler, "If you would be perfect" (Matt 19:21).[1235] And so about A. D. 270 Antony sold all he had and purchased his freedom from the chains of the world.

Yet according to 1 Corinthians 13:3, "If I give all I posses to the poor, but have not love, I gain nothing." "Such regulations indeed have an appearance of wisdom, with their self-imposed worship, their false humility and their harsh treatment of the body, but they lack any value in restraining the flesh" (Col 2:23

[1230]Oder, *Why He Is a Saint*. This practice reveals a misunderstanding of the substitutionary nature of Christ's passion.

[1231]Taylor, *Disciplined Life*, 48-62.

[1232]see Plantinga, "Dr. Willard's Diagnosis,"49-51.

[1233]Harnack, *History of Dogma*, 5:10. See also Flew, *Idea of Perfection*, 158.

[1234]Harnack, *Monasticism*, 10-11.

[1235]According to Platt, this perfection constitutes a perfect conversion at the beginning of Christian discipleship and is not Christian perfection ["Perfection,"9:728].

[NIV]; see also 1 Tim 4:3-4).[1236] We must remember that Christian perfection is received, not achieved.

> A long and dreary chronicle of horrors could be cited to illustrate the ways in which men have sought sanctification apart from the law. Self-torture, flagellations, fastings, hairshirts, and a great variety of devices have been used in order to give the seeker sanctification. The result has been neither peace nor holiness. Men have rolled themselves into thorn bushes, treated their bodies as a satanic enemy, and still found evil resting in the essence of their thoughts. Weak bodies have not made for strong souls.[1237]

Monasticism emphasized holiness through withdrawal from the world. This withdrawal was a protest against the encroachment of the world upon the Church and an attempt to build model colonies of the kingdom of heaven. The emphasis is upon detachment from the world by withdrawing into the desert of solitude.

While Jesus bade all his followers to be perfect, and in the New Testament the *holy* and *perfect* were sanctified or mature Christians in the ordinary walks of life, monasticism confined the *religious* to a professional class who made the cultivation of holiness a distinct calling by fleeing from the world.[1238]

Vows and religious orders came to be viewed as a shortcut to holiness. Holiness was defined as poverty, chastity, and submission to authority. Ambrose tended to emphasize celibacy, Aquinas emphasized obedience, while the Franciscans emphasized poverty or detachment to material possessions.[1239] Regardless of the differences of emphasis, the common point was that this search for perfection must be made within the pale of the Roman church. The Jesuit, Jean-Pierre deCaussade concluded, "holiness may be reduced to one point only:

[1236]The English Standard Version actually uses the word "asceticism" in Col 2:18.

[1237]Rushdoony, *Institutes of Biblical Law*, 550. While Rushdoony argued that this approach to sanctification was based on pagan philosophy, Calvinism is also tainted with this same dualistic philosophy when it declares that we cannot be holy so long as we live in this physical body.

[1238]Coats, "Holiness,"6:746.

[1239]Later we will notice various emphases within the Protestant tradition, as well.

fidelity to the Order of God."[1240] While resignation to the "order of God" meant that we should accept any cross sent by Providence, this submission was also extended to a regular system of spiritual formation and obedience to spiritual directors.

Within a hundred years of Antony this movement would be organized and monks would live in monasteries. Monks withdrew from the world in order to discipline the flesh. Holiness was the practice of the spiritual disciplines. Yet Thomas Merton wrote that a man "can spend forty or fifty or sixty years in the monastery and still have a bad temper."[1241]

Their solitary devotion did not mean their spirituality was individualistic. It was understood that they held to the faith of the Church. Those who continued to live in this world system concluded they could not be holy and would have to be purified in purgatory. This created two classes of Christians —the holy and the unholy. The unholy developed a lax attitude believing holiness could not be attained in this life. The *Didache*, a church manual from the last half of the second century taught, "For if you can bear the whole yoke of the Lord, you will be perfect, but if you cannot, do what you can."[1242] Bounds concluded that the *Didache* presents perfection as a state which involves human effort, but is accompanied and sustained by God's intervention.[1243]

Two hundred years later Chrysostom counseled that forsaking all should not be attempted all at once, but it is a ladder that leads up to heaven and must be ascended little by little.

[1240]deCaussade, *Self-Abandonment*, 6. This devotional classic is based on the teaching of Francis de Sales and John of the Cross.

[1241]Merton, *Elected Silence*, 334; first published in 1948 as *The Seven Storey Mountain*. Merton's theme is the revelation of the false self and the discovery of the true self in God.

[1242]*Didache*, 6.2. Bounds explained, "This statement appears to point to the role of human effort in striving for perfection. If one is unable to become perfect, the he must do his best to walk in the way of life" *[Christian Perfection in Fathers*, 51]. Pope cautioned against the undue emphasis on human effort and asceticism [*Compendium*, 3:65-66].

Wesley observed that everyone who is redeemed has a choice of walking in the higher or the lower path. Those who do not accept the invitation of the Holy Spirit to walk the more excellent way decline into the lower order of Christians. He did not believe that those who do not walk the higher road are in the high road to Hell. While they will find mercy at the close of life, they will forfeit a greater reward [Wesley, "The More Excellent Way," Sermon #89, § 6-8]. The point is, however, that for Wesley the high road was not monasticism, but Christian perfection.

[1243]Bounds, "Doctrine of Christian Perfection," 14-16.

> And thou then, art thou unable to practice virginity? Be chaste in marriage. Art thou unable to strip thyself of thy possessions? Give of thy substance. Canst thou not bear that burden? Share thy goods with Christ. Art thou unwilling to yield Him up all? Give Him but the half, but the third part.[1244]

Ambrose (c.339-397) marked a transition from Eastern monasticism to Augustine. The ethical teaching of Ambrose was based on Stoic philosophy. While not disparaging marriage, Ambrose stressed virginity more than most other monastic writers. Although he did not directly identify perfection with either poverty or virginity, he did consider perfection attainable for the few in this life.[1245] However, R. C. H. Lenski wrote that it is incorrect to interpret Matthew 5:3-12 as "counsels for the perfect" which are unattainable on the part of lesser Christians. "Christ has no double standard. His greatest saints are found among the common believers who by grace have become pure in heart."[1246]

Basil of Caesarea argued that the solitary life can come into conflict with the law of love. Love is not self seeking (1 Cor 13:5). Instead Paul taught that everyone should see the good of others, not merely their own good (1 Cor 10:24). Basil believed that the heart could be purified from sin in this life and that the commandments of love could be kept.[1247] Basil also argued against the comparative fruitlessness of the solitary life in contrast with the Christian influence of the common life. And Basil argued that spiritual gifts were given individually for the common good (1 Cor 12:7).[1248]

However, John Cassian advocated the superior monastic life of renunciation of the world and the contemplation of God. Gregory the Great taught that while sanctification was a gift given at baptism, perfection is a goal to be striven for through monasticism. In fact, the monks were called "the perfect." For the next nine hundred years, from the time of Gregory, the monk became the ideal Christian and perfection came to be tied to that ideal.

Through Thomas Aquinas the Roman Church adopted the view that the solitary life was superior. In the Eastern Church, Chrysostom and Jerome followed the teaching of Basil. While Wesley admired Chrysostom and Basil, his

---

1244 *NPNF*, First Series, 10:389; 286.

1245 Flew, *Idea of Perfection*, 192.

1246 Lenski, *Matthew*, 253.

1247 Greathouse, *From the Apostles to Wesley*, 53.

1248 Flew, *Idea of Perfection*, 164-165. Basil had also advocated monasticism, which could help the Christian avoid sin, but he left that life to become the bishop of Capadocia at the request of his bishop.

two heroes were Macarius the Egyptian and Ephraem Syrus.[1249] Outler explained that in the descriptions of these two writers Wesley discovered "the normative pattern of catholic Christianity."[1250] In his diary for July 30, 1736 Wesley wrote that he read Macarius and sang.[1251]

Wesley was attracted to Macarius because of his emphasis on holiness and perfection which Wesley believed characterized the Church as a whole when it was pure.[1252] More recently some textual critics have concluded that Macarius was influenced by and copied from Gregory of Nyssa.[1253] But Reinhart Staats has argued that Gregory is the one who copied from Macarius.[1254] The similarities which exist between Macarius, Gregory, Ephraem Syrus and other Eastern writers at least demonstrate that a theology of perfection was developed in the Eastern church prior to Augustine and that represented "the high point of Eastern ascetical teaching."

According to Snyder, Wesley was drawn to seven particular themes in the writings of Gregory and Macarius: Salvation is fundamentally seen in terms of the restoration of the image of God; Human beings have free will, perfection is participation in the divine Spirit, love is the supreme virtue in perfection, Christians must strive to attain perfection, Christ is the Christian's model, and Christ's work is universal.[1255]

The fact that Wesley used the term "Christian perfection" more frequently than "sanctification" or "holiness" reflects his indebtedness to Eastern thought.

[1249]Whaling, *John and Charles Wesley*, 12. According to K. Steve McCormick it was primarily through Chrysostom that Wesley adopted his assessment of the Christ life as "faith filled with the energy of love" ["Wesley's Use of John Chrysostom].

[1250]Outler, *John Wesley*, 9.

[1251]Wesley, *BE Works*, 18:405-406.

[1252]See Wesley's statement about the religion of the primitive church as expressed in the writings of Clement of Rome, Ignatius, Polycarp, Tertullian, Origen, Clement of Alexandria and Cyprian. "And even in the fourth century it was found in the works of Chrysostom, Basil, Ephrem Syrus, and Macarius. It would be easy to produce a cloud of witnesses testifying the same thing" ["On Laying the Foundation of the New Chapel," Sermon #112, 2.3].

[1253]See Outler's comments in Wesley, *BE Works*, 2:159.

[1254]Snyder, "Macarius the Egyptian," 55. Kallistos (Timothy) Ware stated there was general agreement that the author of the Macarian writings has no connection with the Coptic Desert Father, Macarius the Egyptian. Instead the author depended on Gregory of Nyssa and is believed to be a Syrian monk of the fourth century [*Pseudo-Macarius*, xi; 11].

[1255]Snyder, "Macarius the Egyptian," 56-57.

The significance of this Eastern influence, as opposed to Western thought, was their emphasis upon perfection as a process rather than a state.[1256] To the Latin (Western) Church, *perfection* was that which is complete in and of itself. However, the Greek or Eastern approach emphasized that *perfection* meant becoming that which God intended us to be. Thus the emphasis is on divine enablement rather than human discipline.

Gregory of Nyssa defined human perfection as perpetual progress "from glory to glory" or "constant growth in the good."[1257] In "The Scriptural Way of Salvation" Wesley quoted a warning from Macarius to those who imagined they were entirely free from sin.

> The unskilful (or unexperienced), when grace operates, presently imagine they have no more sin. Whereas they that have discretion cannot deny that even we who have the grace of God may be molested again. . . . For we have often had instances of some among the brethren who have experienced such grace as to affirm that they had no sin in them. And yet after all, when they thought themselves entirely freed from it, the corruption that lurked within was stirred up anew, and they were wellnigh burnt up.[1258]

Wesley printed twenty-two homilies by Macarius in the first volume of his *Christian Library*.[1259] These homilies are primarily concerned with the Christian's pursuit of perfection. In his eighth homily he referred to twelve steps to perfection. After attaining this height, the perfect Christian then steps down to the eleventh step so that he can still preach and minister to his brethren.[1260]

Pope concluded that there was an undue stress on human effort.

[1256]Outler, *John Wesley*, p. 10; see also Outler in Wesley, *BE Works*, 1:74-76.

[1257]Quoted by Bassett, *Historical Development*, 81.

[1258]Wesley, Sermon # 43, 1.7.

[1259]In the first edition this comprises pages 81-155; in the second edition pages 69-131. It should be noted that in the first volume Wesley included writings from Clement, Ignatius, and Polycarp, as well as reports on the martyrdom of Ignatius and Polycarp. This is all Wesley reprinted of the early Church fathers. The first volume then jumped to the fourth century and incorporates Macarius and then jumps to the seventeenth century, concluding with German pietist Johann Arndt. Wesley wrote, "John Arndt's nervous account of true Christianity [is] worthy of the earliest ages." The next three volumes contain what is commonly referred to as *Foxe's Book of Martyrs*.

[1260]Flew, *Idea of Perfection*, 185-186.

Asceticism felt that "something must remain for human vigilance to watch and keep down, without which humility would not be perfect. . . . The Ascetic theory has always rested in the contest between the human spirit and the flesh: too often forgetting that the Divine Spirit is not merely the umpire and witness but the Almighty Agent also in the destruction of sin. . . . There is but a step between such views as these and the Scriptural truth that the Divine strength not only aids but is perfected in our weakness. That step, however, was never taken by the Ascetic theory."[1261]

For Macarius there was hardly any other way of following Christ except through monasticism.[1262] In his homilies he described degrees of perfection and taught that a person grows and comes to a perfect man only gradually. "It is only gradually that a man grows and comes to *a perfect man, to the measure of the stature*, not as some say, 'Off with one coat and on with another.'"[1263] Wesley did not include this quote in *The Christian Library*. He does, however, include in Homily 15,

> For a man does not immediately arrive at perfection. First, he enters the lists and fights with SATAN, and after a long course and fight he carries off the trophies of victory, and becomes a Christian. For if merely by hearing a man is made perfect without any further trouble; then even those that frequent the theatre, and whoremongers, shall all go into the kingdom. But this cannot be: the *way is strait and narrow*: we must go through this rugged way, and hold out with patience, and be afflicted, and so enter into life.[1264]

Macarius also preached

> Christians are clothed with the Spirit, and are at rest. And though war arises from without, they are inwardly fortified with the power of the Lord, and are no more concerned for SATAN. Just so, when he tempted our Lord in the wilderness for forty days, what real hurt was it, that he could outwardly approach his body? for within was God. In like manner Christians, though

---

[1261]Pope, *Compendium*, 3:66-69. Pope referenced 2 Cor 12:9 where our weakness or impotence is perfected [τελέω - *teleo*] through God's power.

[1262]Flew, *Idea of Perfection*, 181.

[1263]Quoted by Flew, *Idea of Perfection*, 183.

[1264]Wesley, *Christian Library*, 2nd ed, 1:114.

> outwardly they are tempted; yet inwardly are they. filled with the Divine nature, and so nothing injured. These degrees, if any man attain to, he is come to the perfect love of CHRIST, and to the fullness of the Godhead. But he that is not so, still inwardly retains the war. He is one hour refreshed in prayer, and another in a state of affliction: for so is the will of the Lord; because he is as yet but an infant, he trains him up to the battle: and there spring up in him both light and darkness, and rest and affliction: and that, whatever gifts he has, for many of the brethren have had the gifts of healing, and revelation and prophecy; however, not having attained to perfect charity, the war came upon them, and they fell. Indeed, if any one comes to perfect love, he is for ever after bound and captivated by grace. But if any one make but small advances towards this, he is still in bondage to fear, and to war, and to falling.[1265]

In another homily Macarius wrote, "the mischief is strained out and refined off bit by bit, and not all at once."[1266] Macarius also declared, "A perfect Christian man, one completely free, I have not yet seen . . . Sin is still present within."[1267] Flew concluded that he was at war with the primitive doctrine that after baptism a Christian does not sin.[1268] However, Macarius asked, "Is the natural concupiscence rooted out by the coming of the Holy Spirit? Sin is rooted out, and man receives the original formation of Adam in his purity. Through the power of the Spirit, he comes up to the first Adam; yea, is made greater than him."[1269]

Yet Macarius also wrote of sanctification of the Spirit, entire redemption from sin, and the baptism of fire and of the Holy Ghost. For Macarius spiritual perfection is accomplished through the baptism into the Holy Spirit which burns up demons and consumes evil so that those who have received it "have no

---

[1265]Wesley, *Christian Library*, Volume 1; Homily 14.5.

[1266]Ware, *Pseudo-Macarius*, Homily 15.7. Wesley omitted this statement in his *Christian Library.*

[1267]Ware, *Pseudo-Macarius*, Homily 8.5. Wesley also omitted this statement in his *Christian Library*. Platt concluded that for Macarius, "Christian perfection never becomes more than aspiration and approximation in religious experience" ["Perfection," 9:734].

[1268]Flew, *Idea of Perfection*, 181.

[1269]Wesley, *Christian Library*, Volume 1; Homily 14.2.

experience of evil."[1270] Campbell noted that Wesley himself did not make this connection but allowed it to stand when he edited Macarius.[1271]

In medieval times the Waldensians preached a message of apostolic poverty. Waldo, a rich merchant of Lyons gave away his property in 1176 and attracted followers known as the Poor Men of Lyons. They were followed by heretical groups of the thirteenth and fourteenth centuries, such as the Beghards, who were self-proclaimed "holy beggars." They often entered towns crying, "Bread for God's sake." In fact, our words "beg" and "beggar" are derived from "Beghard."[1272]

In the summer of 2004 several communities, some of which had begun as early as the 1970s, met in Durham, NC. They did not advocate a return to old monastic rules, but to joyful discipline within small groups. According to Elaine Heath, the new monastic movement is nothing less than a new holiness movement.[1273] Yet the new monasticism embraces a Benedictine view of conversion as *conversation morum*, that conversion happens not once but upon ever return to their common prayer.[1274] While salvation is an ongoing process, I am concerned that initial salvation, as a radical encounter with Christ that turns us away from sin, may be obscured in place of a progressive conversion.

4. The Corporate Grace of Sacramentarianism

Sacramental theology describes the life of the Church. In A. D. 251 Cyprian declared, "He can no longer have God for his Father, who has not the Church for his mother."[1275] Irenaeus also believed the perfecting work of the Holy Spirit was confined to the Church and that perfecting work takes place

---

[1270]Ware, *Pseudo-Macarius*, Homily 43.3; Wesley, *Christian Library*, first ed, 1:140. See also King, "Eastern Patristic Spirit-Christology,"114.

[1271]Campbell, *Christian Antiquity*, 66; 148. However, the second edition of the *Christian Library* does not contain these references [1:112-114]. Fletcher quoted from the writings of Macarius in his essay on the new birth and concluded Macarius preached "the baptism and dispensation of the Holy Spirit" [Fletcher, "Doctrine of the New Birth," 42].

[1272]Beghards were male and Beguines were female. See Stark, *Glory of God*, 58-59.

[1273]Heath, *Naked Faith*, 110. See also Moll, "New Monasticism,"38-46.

[1274]Wilson-Hartgrove, "Joining the Eternal Song," 44.

[1275]Cyprian, "On the Unity of the Church," ¶ 6 [*ANF*, 5:423]. He also said, "Whoever he may be, and whatever he may be, he who is not in the Church of Christ is not a Christian" [*Epistle*, 51.24; *ANF*, 5:333].

within the Church.[1276] He opposed the gnostic view that personalized perfection. Eventually it was held that people were holy simply because they belonged to the Church. However, the ideal of a holy Church and reality of a mixed multitude leads to the conclusion that all are not actually within the Church or the conclusion that there is a high way and a low way.

Sacramentarianism emphasizes the rituals of the church as the means of receiving saving and sanctifying grace. Baptism was understood as imparting justifying grace. Communion imparted sanctifying grace. However, since justification was regarded as imparted righteousness, righteousness and holiness were synonymous and not "two works of grace."

Joel C. Elowsky wrote that a core component of the ancient liturgical life was the sanctifying work of the Spirit in baptism and Eucharist. Thus, the sacraments impart holiness. "It is not so much that sanctification has made one into a morally better or superior person, although this is indeed what sanctification does, but it accomplishes this by returning us to what God always intended us to be — a bride without any spot or blemish for his Son." Again, the emphasis is not such much on personal sanctification, as on corporate identification.[1277]

Robert Wilberforce taught that Christ was the "pattern man" to whom each human being must approximate through sacramental grace.[1278] According to Dunn, sacramentalists regard "water baptism as the focus of conversion-initiation, so that forgiveness, the gift of the Spirit, membership of Christ, etc, become a function of the rite, and can be said to be mediated or conveyed through it."[1279]

Thus the Donatists, a group of North African believers in the fourth and fifth centuries, believed that it was necessary to have a holy priesthood. They felt the Holy Spirit would not come if an unholy priest administered baptism. Only holy hands could administer grace through the Lord's Supper. The means of grace through the sacraments was thwarted if celebrated by an unholy priest. Thus the Church could be holy only if its priests were holy.

However, Augustine taught that the validity of the sacraments does not

---

[1276]Bassett, *Historical Development*, 46-47. This emphasis on the perfection of the Church was also found in the writings of Novatian and in the *Didache* [Bounds, *Christian Perfection in Fathers*, 52; 136].

[1277]Elowsky, *We Believe in the Holy Spirit*, 172; 182-190.

[1278]Wilberforce, *Doctrine of the Incarnation*, chapters 1-4. Robert was the son of William Wilberforce.

[1279]Dunn, *Baptism in the Holy Spirit*, 3.

depend on the moral or doctrinal purity of the priesthood.[1280] The Spirit is free to blow wherever he wills. Thus holiness is a gift of grace to the Church and does not depend upon the moral character of priest nor member. The sacraments are vehicles of holiness regardless of the moral character of the priests who administer them or the congregation who receives them. Holiness, then is objective and corporate. Where the Church is, there will be spiritual perfection.

By the middle of the fourth century it was possible to speak of being holy in distinction from being pure or perfect. One was holy because he belongs to Christ and the Church. The holiness of Christ covered any lack of holiness. Perfection came to refer to the renunciation of possessions and desires.

In the Middle Ages Aquinas define a sacrament as "the sign of a holy thing insofar as it makes men holy."[1281] Aquinas went on to share three ways the sacraments sanctify. First, they are signs of the Word incarnate, who is the cause of sanctification. Second, since man is made up of soul and body as the sensible element touches the body, faith in the words reaches the soul. Third, Aquinas refers to Augustine's definition that the sacraments are visible words which express concepts with greater precision. Therefore, we use sacramental formulas to signify spiritual blessings.[1282]

The Oxford Movement within the Anglican Church, also known as Tractarians because of the series of *Tracts for the Times* issued from Oxford between 1833-1841, emphasized symbols in worship. They were reacting to the Enlightenment emphasis on reason and adopted a Romantic philosophy which emphasized intuition. The sacraments were the heart of their quest for holiness. Baptism was the taproot of all grace.

E. B. Pusey had written three tracts vindicating baptismal regeneration. He also asserted the real presence of Christ in the bread and wine of the Lord's Supper. For Tractarians, the Lord's Supper was the chief way in which believers became united with Christ.[1283] The Tractarian movement was also attracted to the self-denial of asceticism and the tradition of the ancient church. They emphasized the corporate dimension of spirituality and denied personal assurance of

---

[1280]Wesley also taught that the Methodists should attend the Church of England services regardless of the spiritual state of the priest. "The validity of the ordinance doth not depend on the goodness of him that administers, but on the faithfulness of him that ordained it" ["Sermon on the Mount, XII," Sermon #32, 3.8; see also "On Attending the Church Service," Sermon #104, § 27-33; *Works*, 8:280-281; 322].

[1281]Aquinas, *Summa Theologica*, 3, q. 60, a. 2, c.

[1282]Aquinas, *Summa Theologica*, 3, q. 60, a. 6, c.

[1283]Bebbington, *Holiness in Nineteenth-Century England*, 13-15.

salvation.[1284]

While the sacraments are a means of grace, our faith must be in what they symbolize and not in the ritual itself. Participation in the sacraments does not automatically result in added grace. Dunning explained that initially "the ritual was perceived as the symbol through which the reality became actualized, but in the process of time the sacramentarian view set in, and the rituals were seen as operating automatically."[1285] Circumcision in the Old Testament and confirmation in the Roman church may symbolize holiness, but they do not necessarily produce it.[1286] Symbolic holiness does not necessarily equal righteousness. Furthermore, confirmation would correspond to the doctrine of assurance, not Christian perfection.[1287]

[1284]Bebbington, *Holiness in Nineteenth-Century England*, 21-27.

[1285]Dunning, *Grace, Faith, and Holiness*, 461.

[1286]The argument for two works of grace based on sacramental liturgy was first made by Brown in *Meaning of Sanctification*, 38-43; 112. Bassett also referred to baptismal procedures within the early Church and attempted to impose a nineteenth century holiness paradigm on these symbolic expressions [*Historical Development*, 35-50; 72; *Holiness Teachings*, 109]. While baptism is a rite of purification, it is also a rite of initiation. According to Irenaeus, Cyprian, and Tertullian baptism included renunciation of Satan, a confession of faith, immersion, anointing with oil, the laying on of hands, and the kiss of peace. While this anointing with oil symbolizes the baptism of the Spirit, according to a fourth century document called the *Apostolic Constitutions*, there is no basis for teaching two works of grace — baptism with water first, then a subsequent baptism of the Spirit. All components were part of *one* ritual. See the "Ceremonies of Baptism and Chrism" which is based on Cyril's Catechetical Lectures. The candidate for baptism is anointed with exorcised oil before baptism and with consecrated ointment after baptism [Gifford, "Introduction," *NPNF*, Second Series, 7: xxi-xxvi].

An anonymous monk of the Eastern Church explained that while the Apostles received Pentecostal grace after Paschal [passover/Easter] grace, at the time of the first Easter the Apostles obtained only an incomplete experience of Paschal grace. They shared in the Lord's Supper, but they did not share in the immolation [sacrifice] of Christ. Pentecost for them was the necessary condition of this full Paschal grace, just as the gift of the Spirit is for us the necessary condition of a full eucharistic life. While in church ritual, the Chrisma precedes the Eucharist, Baptismal grace, Pentecostal grace, Paschal grace are but aspects of one and the same divine grace [Collins, *Exploring Christian Spirituality*, 120].

[1287]In fact, Wesley quoted the rite of consecration of the oil used in consecration, called "chrism" [*Works*, 10:117]. While the chrism was itself fully sanctified, it's purpose was "for the adoption of sons by the Holy Spirit." In explaining Orthodox theology Alexander Schmemann wrote that the second sacrament of initiation, confirmation, "has always been an integral part of the baptismal liturgy. For

The Anglican church commonly refers to Pentecost Sunday as Whitsunday, because the baptismal candidates typically all wear white baptismal gowns when they are baptized on Pentecost Sunday. Douglas Crossman told me that in England the Anglican bishop touches each baptismal candidate on the head or cheek and says, "Receive the Spirit."

Sacramentalism and sacerdotalism go hand in hand. The sacerdotalist view is that the grace of God is controlled by a spiritual elite priesthood, who themselves may not be holy but are vested with authority. Sacerdotalists claim that sanctification comes before justification.

The Council of Trent described the infusion of divine grace, derived from the inexhaustible treasury of the merits of Christ and imparted by the sacraments. This sanctifying grace within the soul secures the remission of original sin, imparts a permanent habit of inherent righteousness, and the potential of further development — even perfection. This good work can be neutralized or destroyed by mortal sin, but guilt from venial sins can be removed by the Eucharist. Guilt from mortal sin is absolved by the sacrament of penance. The result of this process was known as justification rather than sanctification, since it made men just before God.[1288]

Thomas Merton, a Trappist monk, taught five components intertwine to constitute holiness: faith in God's grace, an inner conversion which creates a new man, self-surrender which establishes a mystical bond with God, an ever-deepening process of growth in grace; a dependence upon the Church and her sacraments.[1289] While Merton placed conversion prior to perfection, sanctification, from start to finish, took place within the context of the Church. Merton declared that "we receive the Holy Spirit through the Church and her sacraments."[1290]

Stanley Hauerwas, writing as an evangelical Catholic, argued that we are made perfect through our habits. "The monks have been right to think that nothing is more important for the shaping of communities of holiness than how our days are structured. . . . After all, the Eucharist is the only true sanctified

---

it is not so much another sacrament as the very fulfillment of Baptism, its 'confirmation' by the Holy Spirit. It can be distinguished from baptism only insofar as life can be distinguished from birth. . . . Confirmation is thus the personal Pentecost of man, his entrance into the new life in the Holy Spirit, which is the true life of the Church." Schmemann continued to explain that baptism and confirmation were immediately followed by a procession to the doors of the church, symbolizing their entrance into the kingdom [*For the Life of the World*, 54-56].

[1288]Berkhof, *Systematic Theology*, 529-530.

[1289]Reed, "Thomas Merton," 93.

[1290]Merton, *Life and Holiness*, 65.

body."[1291]

In seeking support for Pentecostalism, Ervin appeals to a "strange bedfellow" for Pentecostals. Ervin tried to connect Pentecostalism with sacramentalism by arguing that both believe in the reality of the divine presence and not just a propositional symbolism.[1292] Yet traditionally, pentecostal theology has been an adaptation of basic fundamental Christianity. And Pentecostal worship has been a revolt against sacramental liturgy. While Ervin tries to argue for an open world in which miracles may happen, the tendency in sacramentalism is to say that the miracle is in transubstantiation — which amounts to a theological proposition. Methodism, as distinct from both alternatives, holds to the real presence of Christ in the Lord's Supper *and* that the baptism of the Spirit is conversion-initiation. And yet that Spirit baptism was real and not merely a logical deduction. It really delivered from sin and produced a new life.

In his study of the sacraments, Rob Staples calls baptism the sacrament of initiation and the eucharist the sacrament of sanctification. Staples explained

> The Eucharist may be understood as that means of grace, instituted by Jesus Christ, to which we are invited for repentance, for self-examination, for renewal, for spiritual sustenance, for thanksgiving, for fellowship, for anticipation of the heavenly kingdom, and for celebration in our pilgrimage toward perfection in the image of Christ. All these are involved in our sanctification, and all these are available to us at the Lord's table.[1293]

Wesley himself defined the Lord's Supper as a means of conveying to men either preventing, justifying, or sanctifying grace, "according to their several necessities."[1294] And yet this emphasis does not imply that the sacraments are the sole means by which salvation is conveyed.

It was the Baptist theologian A. H. Strong who noted that "it was John Wesley who did most to establish the doctrine of regeneration. He asserted that the Holy Spirit acts through the truth, in distinction from the doctrine that the Holy Spirit works solely through the ministers and sacraments of the church."[1295]

[1291]Hauerwas, "The Sanctified Body,"36-37.

[1292]Ervin, *Conversion-Initiation*, 82-83.

[1293]Staples, *Outward Sign*, 202-203.

[1294]Wesley, *Journal*, 28 June 1740.

[1295]Strong, *Systematic Theology*, 816.

5. The Rationalism of Scholasticism

By Mediaeval times theology was the Queen of the Sciences, but philosophy was her handmaid. Human intellect was seen as the primary agent in man's quest for perfection. Spirituality was expressed through theological research and education. God's Word was authoritative in the areas of redemption and the Christian life, but Aristotle became the source of valid knowledge in the realm of the natural sciences.

Human reason was accepted as adequate to organize the wisdom of God into a system and the Roman church claimed to possess a revelation of truth which transcends logic. Perfection became inseparable from the institutional church. Thomas Aquinas also developed levels of perfection within the offices of the church. Bishops are in a higher state of perfection than those under them, such as parish priests and archdeacons, because their office gives them authority to confer grace and enlightenment to those in their charge. Bishops are the perfectors, while those in religious orders are the perfected.[1296] While all human beings may attain to perfection apart from vows and orders, the religious orders are a shortcut to perfection. Claude Thompson wrote, "To relegate these grades of perfection to offices within the Church is a sheer arbitrary imposition upon Christian morality of the views of Pseudo-Dionysius and his conception of the 'heavenly hierarchy.'"[1297]

Dionysius taught that the threefold grace of purification, enlightenment, and perfection flows through the three choirs of heavenly angels. Thus it is fitting that there should also be orders in the earthly ministry. There are three sacraments: baptism, the Eucharist, and unction; three orders: deacon, priest, bishop; and three orders denoting states of spiritual progress: those who have received baptism and are being prepared by the deacon, those who share the Eucharist from the priest, and finally those who are monks, having renounced the world and who have received from the bishop the final perfecting which fits them for divine unction.[1298]

Thomas Aquinas taught that life is a balance between the active and contemplative life. It is not possible to remain long in the highest state, the vision of the Divine Being. We should set before ourselves the Beatific Vision or knowledge of God. Aquinas believed that man's capacity to think about things divine was the highest level of human activity. Such human reason, when coupled with love, amounted to the highest perfection attainable in this life. Aquinas

---

[1296]Aquinas, *Summa Theologia*, 2.2.Question 184.7-8; see also Flew, *Idea of Perfection*, 237-238.

[1297]Thompson, "Witness of American Methodism," 132.

[1298]Perkins, *Evangelical Perfection*, 177.

began with the philosophy of Aristotle and his concept of the unmoved mover. Aristotle argued that motion must always continue without interruption, so there must be something eternal which imparts motion but is unmoved itself. Thus, the unmoved mover ceaselessly contemplates himself and man's highest function is our contemplation of the divine. God is a rational Being and he reaches out to his rational creation, drawing them through their exercise of divinely given reason. This emphasis on intellectualism led Aquinas to four theses:

- The contemplative is superior to the active life
- Christian perfection consists in love
- God must be loved for his own sake
- Full perfection is in the life beyond the grave

The greatest mistake of Aquinas was to adopt the ladder by which humanity reaches God. This ladder can be traced back to Dionysius. Aquinas conceived of perfection as a state to be reached through the organization of the church. The bishop is the dispenser of perfection to others.

In *Summa Theologia* Aquinas taught a threefold perfection. Absolute perfection is found in God alone. A second perfection will be realized in heaven, and described in 1 Corinthians 13:10, when the soul loves God as much as it possibly can. This perfect love is possible only on the basis of perfect knowledge. A third perfection may be had in this life by the removal from man's affections of all that is contrary to love and of whatever hinders the mind's affections from tending wholly to God. This perfection is the contemplative life activated by love. Mortal sin is eliminated in this condition, although venial sins are still present.[1299]

In *De Perfectione* or *The Perfection of the Spiritual Life* Aquinas counseled monasticism and the vows of poverty, chastity, and obedience in order to eliminate obstacles to Christian perfection. He regarded monasticism as the short cut to perfection. Aquinas defined perfection as the love of God and love of our neighbor. We so love God if all our actions are directed to God, if our understanding is subjected to him, and if all our affections are directed to the love of God. But to achieve perfection we are counseled to renounce earthly possession, renounce earthly ties including matrimony, and deny our own will. Those who belong to the religious order follow this counsel above all others by taking upon themselves the three vows of poverty, chastity, and obedience.[1300]

Immanuel Kant carried this intellectual influence of Aquinas forward with his emphasis on moral perfection, the very concept of which should give us the

---

[1299]Aquinas, *Summa Theologia*, 2.2. Question 184.2.

[1300]Flew, *Idea of Perfection*, 230-237.

power to achieve through emulation of the Son of God.[1301] Thus sanctification was not considered to be the supernatural work of the Spirit, but moral improvement based on man's natural powers. The ego became both God and the world.

The new Enlightenment ideal was based on the perfectibility of man and society. Robespierre and the Jacobins had faith in the perfectibility of humanity. Voltaire outlines four epochs of history, holding that his own was the apex. Yet this secular perfection produced the reign of terror and the General Will of society was replaced by a dictatorship under Napoleon Bonaparte. Enlightenment reason does not focus on the *telos*, the purpose or end of God's work in mankind. It divorces the head from the heart.

Yet John C. English asserted that "John Wesley was a man of the Enlightenment," by establishing a connection between the thought of John Wesley and John Locke.[1302] John Locke (1632-1704) was considered the founder of the Enlightenment, but he was one of the few philosophers of this period who believed in God. While John Locke influenced both John Wesley and Jonathan Edwards, the Calvinist theologian, yet Wesley was never completely satisfied with his empiricism.[1303] And Locke does not represent the extreme skeptical positions of later empiricists.[1304]

Although Wesley was Arminian, he was not a humanist. Carl Bangs pointed out that "Arminianism" can mean the theological position of Arminius himself, it can mean some kind of protest against Calvinism, or it can mean a rallying point for dissent under the banner of toleration.[1305]

Wesley's thought was influenced by Enlightenment philosophy with its emphasis on the reasonableness of Christianity.[1306] Yet the theology of Jonathan

---

[1301]Kant, *Religion Within the Limits of Reason Alone*, 3, 79, 110.

[1302]English, "John Wesley and the English Enlightenment," 400.

[1303]Wesley, *BE Works*, 2:589.

[1304]See Wesley's reference to Hume and Voltaire [*Journal*, 5 March, 1769; 5 May 1772; 3 August 1773]. Descartes is more representative of the current rationalism. Wesley published a digest of Locke's work, with his critical comments, in the *Arminian Magazine* 1782-1784 (volumes 5-7). However, Wesley felt no need to appeal to anything other than Scripture [see Thorsen, *Wesleyan Quadrilateral*, 179-182; 187-193].

[1305]Bangs, "Arminius and Reformed Theology," 249.

[1306]Kevin Lowery has attempted to link Wesley's thought to Enlightenment philosophy, devoting a couple of chapters to connections between Wesley and Locke [*Salvaging Wesley's Agenda*, xv; 65-121). Yet Long distances Wesley from the Enlightenment in *John Wesley's Moral Theology*.

Edwards escapes being labeled as Enlightenment, although he was also influenced by John Locke, because Calvinism holds that the human mind is so darkened by sin that the elect must first be regenerated, then they repent and believe as evidence of their regeneration. Yet Wesley's theology is not properly humanistic because it is prevenient grace, not human reason, which awakens the sinner and enables him to repent and believe.

Wesley was concerned about charges of "enthusiasm," which were actually accusations of being irrational or emotional. But Wesley did not contend for rationalism or deism. He did believe in a warm heart, along with a clear mind. He certainly advocated a supernatural work of regeneration and sanctification. It was actually Methodism which prevented England from the ravages of the French Revolution, which was the culmination of Enlightenment philosophy.[1307]

Evolution is a secularization of the Christian view of progress. According to Charles Darwin, "And as natural selection works solely by and for the good of each being, all corporeal and mental endowments will tend to progress towards perfection."[1308] Herbert Spencer also declared, "Progress, therefore, is not an accident, but a necessity. . . . so surely must the human faculties be moulded into complete fitness for the social state; so surely must the things we call evil and immorality disappear; so surely must man become perfect."[1309] Yet this progress toward perfection was to occur without a God of providence. Thus, instead of history from creation to kingdom, it is from barbarianism to civilization.

Karl Marx used soteriological language to describe revolution."Regeneration through total chaos was his goal, and the proletariat would serve as the priestly class in this ritual so that the whole society might be

---

[1307]This evaluation is sometimes called "The Halévy Thesis." Elie Halévy concluded that England escaped the kind of social turmoil experienced in the French Revolution largely because of the evangelical revival in the eighteenth century. The effectiveness of the early Methodists in meeting the needs of the urban poor and organizing many of them into responsible communities made a notable impact on English society. Wesley's compassion for the needy spread until the entire complexion of the working class in England was changed. The revival was also a dominant force in mobilizing a group of influential political figures to crusade for reform. Included in this group was William Wilberforce, who devoted his life to the abolition of the slave trade [Hatch, Noll, Woodbridge, *The Gospel in America*, 225]. See Bready, *England: Before and After Wesley*, 19-160. See also Warner, *Wesleyan Movement in the Industrial Revolution*.

[1308]Darwin, *Origin of Species*, 459. Darwin built upon the concept of Jean Baptiste Lamarck which saw God at work in the world. This was the time-honored idea of a tendency toward "perfection" [Gould, "Ideas About Life," 7; 32-34].

[1309]Spencer, *Social Statics*, 60.

freed from its alienation."[1310] Raymond Aron explained, "Only revolution, because it is an adventure, or a revolutionary regime, because its accepts the permanent use of violence, seems capable of attaining the goal of perfection. The myth of the revolution serves as a refuge for utopian intellectuals; it becomes the mysterious, unpredictable intercessor between the real and the ideal."[1311]

According to the rationalism of Albrecht Ritschl (1822-1889) we attain ethical perfection by fulfilling our vocation as members of the kingdom of God.[1312] Essentially, perfection is the Christian exercising dominion over the world. This ever increasing redemption of the lower self by the dominion of the higher self presupposes that the human intellect was not affected by the fall. However, Jeremiah 17:9 warns that the unregenerate mind is deceitful and wicked. We cannot reason our way into a relationship with God.

While we cannot be like our Maker in his essence, we strive to imitate him as much as possible. Since God's essence is evidenced primarily in his love, true perfection must combine knowledge with love. Love unites us with God and it is more excellent to love the divine than to know it. However, in the world to come perfection will also involve knowing God in his essence. This will be perfect intellect, which may be similar to that of the angels. However, until that perfection we are dependant upon divine revelation not rationalism.

6. The Mystical Experience

There is a mystic element in all religions. W. B. Pope described this emphasis as "such oneness with God as excludes or suppresses the consciousness of individuality and of a phenomenal universe on the way to Him; and, when that goal is reached, destroys all distinction between Him and His creature for ever."[1313] Thus, the finite is absorbed by the infinite. Mysticism is not necessarily Christian, but it is when it looks back to Christ. Mysticism begins and ends with

---

[1310]North, *Marx Religion of Revolution*, 85.

[1311]Aron, *Opium of the Intellectuals*, 65.

[1312]See the evaluation of Warfield, *Perfectionism*, 1:3-110. According to Warfield the perfectionism of Ritschl was not based on either mystical or Wesleyan influences. According to John Alfred Faulkner, in his chapter "Ritschl or Wesley?," the theology of Ritschl is too subjective. It is our moral development in which we each become whole in our own way [Faulkner, *Modernism and the Christian Faith*, 208-236].

[1313]Pope, *Compendium*, 3:77. Pope said there were two kinds of mysticism: the false type tending to pantheism and the true type filled with the Spirit of love [*Higher Catechism of Theology*, p. 268]. After his death Pope's children honored him with a tablet inscribed with the description "theologian, *mystic*, saint, a master in Israel" [*W. B. Pope*, 126]. See also his defense of mysticism in *Compendium*, 3:231.

the human soul.

Yet in an evangelical sense, Clarke declared, "Our souls can never be truly happy till our wills be entirely subjected to, and become one with, the will of God."[1314] Anyone who professes to have communion with God through Christ in prayer, a direct assurance from God regarding their salvation, and seeks to be led by his Spirit are usually labeled "mystic." Yet the Spirit will never lead contrary to the word he inspired. Our focus here is on extra-biblical mysticism.

Richard Watson observed that Scriptural Christianity, in its inward influence, has been labeled as mysticism. However, true mysticism is to be regarded as an error arising out of partial views of truth. It is a type of fanaticism which exhibits a disregard for divinely appointed ordinances. Mystics tend to mishandle the scriptures and profess to be inwardly taught of God. They also emphasize a disinterested love of God, free from all selfish considerations.[1315] Mysticism tends to express itself in symbols of pain, death, and eroticism.

"Mysticism despairs of the regular process of science; it believes that we may attain directly, without the aid of the senses or reason, and by an immediate intuition, to the real and absolute principle of all truth, God. It finds God either in nature . . . or in the soul."[1316] Because of its emphasis on intuition, Gaddis called mysticism the emphasis of the feminine.[1317]

Mysticism, also known as quietism or the contemplative approach, is a general name for the belief that God permeates the universe and is immanent in both man and creation. However, the evangelical doctrine of God's immanence is not identical with the mystical doctrine of human identity with God. Mysticism emphasizes the spark of divinity within mankind and the union of the soul with the divine.

Bloesch warned that mysticism tends to view sin as separation from a preexistent union with God, not so much as transgression of God's law. And salvation is seen as the return of the soul to its original, undivided unity with God.[1318] Yet the biblical teaching is that union with Christ is the starting point

---

[1314]Clarke, *Christian Theology*, 203.

[1315]Watson, *Dictionary*, 682-683.

[1316]McClintock and Strong, *Cyclopedia*, 6:794. The article on "mystics" concludes with the observation that there are two types of mysticism: quietism and pantheism [p. 804].

[1317]Gaddis, *Christian Perfection in America*, 55.

[1318]Bloesch, *Jesus Christ*, 190. Sangster distinguished between the active and the passive way to oneness with God. The passive way was quietism, which included the dark night of the soul [*Pure in Heart*, 194-195]. Cox said that when Wesley spoke harshly of the mystics he apparently was referring to quietism [*Perfection*, 115].

of the Christian life. Purification and illumination are part of what follows.

Dunning said that sanctification could be interpreted four ways: in terms of law, in terms of love, in terms of transformation of being, and ceremonially. The earliest expositions of the doctrine of sanctification were developed in terms of a transformation of being. Eastern theologians, such as Irenaeus and Athanasius tended to understand redemption in a substantive, and not a relational sense. While the change is real, it is not necessary to understand it as deification.[1319] Irenaeus carried this participation in God so far as to amount to deification.[1320]

In his *Christian Library* Wesley eliminated the word "deification" from his edition of the homilies of Macarius.[1321] This term can refer to the pantheistic identify between God and humanity or a participation, through grace, in the divine life. Some Eastern mystics viewed deification, not only spiritually, but as bodily transformation in this life. However, such transformation will come only in the next life. In the ancient Greek religion, mythological heros were never regarded as fully divine, but they constituted a link between the human and divine world.

The eastern theological tradition maintains that *theosis* is the union of the gift of divine energy and human freedom. Michael Christensen noted that theosis, which means deification or becoming god, can mean either union, in which humanity literally becomes divine or communion, in which humanity becomes *like* God.[1322] According to Culp, theosis can be defined three different ways: as pantheistic or ontological union in which the human becomes part of the divine, as a literal participation in God's activities and characteristics without a confusion of substance or loss of identity, or as a metaphor describing how we become like

---

According to Leclarc, Wesley rejected the mystic doctrine that the goal of Christian experience was unification with God and he also rejected their quietism [*Discovering Christian Holiness*, 242].

1319Dunning, *Grace, Faith, and Holiness*, 457-458.

1320McGiffert, *History of Christian Thought*, 1:141. This view was rejected by Flew, *Idea of the Holy*, 127-128.

1321Campbell, *Christian Antiquity*, x; 66. See also Collins, "Critical Appropriation of Tradition," 85; Collins, *John Wesley: Theological Journey*, 199; Bundy, "Visions of Sanctification,"114. James R. Payton attempts to link the Wesleys to the doctrine of theosis in "Keeping the End in View," 66-68. However, the only evidence he cites is to quote from two hymns by Charles Wesley in which he prays to be conformed into the image of Christ. This may be the language of theosis in Orthodox theology, but in Wesleyan theology it is the language of sanctification.

1322Christensen, "Theosis and Sanctification," 72-73. *Theosis* is synonymous with another term *theopoiesis*. *Theosis* literally means "becoming god." *Theopoiesis* means "making divine" or "making into a god."

God.[1323] According to Thomas Torrance, the Greek Fathers did not use *theosis* to mean "divinization," but to describe

> the utterly staggering act of God in which he gives himself to us and adopts us into the communion of his divine life and live through Jesus Christ, and in his one Spirit, yet in such a way that we are not made divine but are preserved in our humanity.[1324]

Randy Maddox said that the doctrine of sanctification "has significant parallels with the Eastern Orthodox theme of deification."[1325] Eastern Orthodoxy teaches a deification of man through God's perfecting grace, the spiritual disciplines, and being made partakers of the divine nature (2 Peter 1:4). "The Eastern fathers were impressed by the grace that deifies humans and makes them sharers of divine life. They believed that through the incarnation the mortal had been changed into immortal and from passible into impassible."[1326]

Yet it is important to consider the exegesis of Adam Clarke on 2 Peter 1:4. Clarke preached concerning 2 Peter 1:4 that this was "not *the* divine nature, as if the *nature of God* were meant; but *a* divine nature, a holy frame of soul, a holy heart, full of pure and righteous tempers, affections, and desires."[1327] Tuttle also pointed out that the Roman Catholic mystics, who had the greatest influence on Wesley, did not lean toward pantheism or the "progressive deification" of the soul.[1328]

The modern Faith movement teaches that we are little gods and can create simply by speaking matter into existence. Notice however, the faith teachers bypass all striving after holiness and simply become little gods by declaring

---

[1323]Culp, "Supernatural and Sanctification," 152. See Oden, *Life in the Spirit*, 208-209. According to Gomes the early fathers distinguished between communicable and incommunicable attributes. While they did hold that God does impart such communicable attributes as holiness and immortality to his creatures, he does not impart incommunicable attributes such as aseity or self-existence. Therefore, their doctrine of theosis did not lead to polytheism, as taught by Mormonism, in which we all can become gods [Gomes, "Value of Historical Theology," 5-6].

[1324]Torrance*, Meditation of Christ*, 61-67.

[1325]Maddox, *Responsible Grace*, 122.

[1326]Kärkkäinen, *Pneumatology*, 43; 69. "Impassible" means not able to experience emotions.

[1327]Clarke, "Corruption That Is In The World Through Lust," Sermon #30, *Works*, 6:382.

[1328]Tuttle, *Mysticism in the Wesleyan Tradition*, 26.

themselves to be so. While most of the evangelical community underestimates the power of regenerating grace, the faith teachers overstate it because of their metaphysical foundation. Thus they tend to fall into the first category. For example Kenneth Copeland insists, "You have the same creative faith and ability on the inside of you that God used when he created the heavens and the earth."[1329] However, if Jesus is born again and is now exalted to the right hand of God, then we who are also born again are equal with Jesus Christ.

Not only have they distorted regeneration, but they have emphasized the humanity of Christ at the expense of his deity. Jesus becomes a "pattern Son" instead of the unique Son of God. Jesus walked on earth as an anointed man, empowered by the Holy Spirit. Christians now have this same anointing. Therefore, according to Benny Hinn, we are now little gods on the earth. According to this teaching, all the fullness of God dwell in *us* (Col 2:9). This is not the power to live a holy life, but power to walk in the miraculous.[1330]

While not usually considered a mystical theologian, Clement of Alexandria regarded contemplation as a demonstration of the virtue and holiness of the Christian gnostic.[1331] Tuttle explained that while "contemplation is essential to mystical theology, nonetheless, it is a treacherous and equivocal word."[1332]

The mystic seeks God through meditation and intuitive methods, rather than through academic or rational disciplines. William James used four words to define mysticism: *ineffability* means the experience cannot be imparted or transferred; it contains a noetic quality of *illumination*; *transiency* means the experience cannot be sustained; and there is *passivity* on the part of the recipient.[1333]

Contemplative praying is found within the mystic tradition. There are so many variations that it is hard to give a blanket endorsement or condemnation.[1334] The problem is that since mysticism is not based on the ultimate authority of the

---

[1329]Copeland, "Inner Image of the Covenant,"side 2.

[1330]Reeves, *Other Side of the River*, 23, 27, 30, 121. On bodily perfection, see the teaching of Charles Parham, p. 678 in this book.

[1331]Anderson, *Clement of Alexandria*, 184.

[1332]Tuttle, *Mysticism in the Wesleyan Tradition*, 27.

[1333]James, *Varieties of Religious Experience*, 380-381. James was a conservative Hegelian. See p. 36.

[1334]In his description of contemplation, a monk of the Eastern Church said we must place ourselves in the presence of God and maintain ourselves in his presence for a certain time of inward silence. It is not difficult and even a few minutes is fruitful. However, the contemplative life is better still [Collins, *Exploring Christian Spirituality*, 118].

Word there is a tendency toward heresy. Not all mystics are heretics, but their openness to the New Age has caused some of them to incorporate meditation techniques from other religions such as Hinduism.

Biblical meditation involves filling our mind with the Word of God.[1335] Pagan meditation practices generally involve emptying our minds and opening ourselves. The problem is that sometimes we open ourselves to deception. For example, the Hindu practice of meditation involves saying a mantra over and over. A mantra is a sound syllable which has no meaning to person using it, but is used to induce a mystical or passive state of mind.[1336]

The contemplative method advocates climbing the ladder of love as a spiritual exercise. In the fourth century, Gregory of Nyssa wrote *The Life of Moses* in which he outlined the stages Moses passed through in his ascent to God. According to his interpretation of 2 Corinthians 3:18, Gregory taught this as a paradigm we must all follow. The first state, the way of light, was a detachment from the love of things and the purification of the soul. The second stage, illumination, was when Moses entered the cloud. All sights and sounds were dampened by the cloud until only an awareness of God's presence remained. The third stage, Moses became more perfected when he entered into darkness and saw God in Exodus 20:21. According to Gregory, this darkness expressed the fact that God is infinite and there is infinite growth in our knowledge of him.[1337]

In the tenth century Bernard of Clairvaux wrote in a letter on love that there were four levels of love. He wrote, "A first sort of recognition is the love of a slave who fears for his own skin. The second sort is that of a hireling who thinks only of himself. The third sort is that of a son who reveres his father. . . . Sometimes even a slave is able to do God's work, but it is not done willingly. The hireling is also able to do God's work, but not willingly. . . . The slave does not love God, and the hireling loves something more than he loves God."

Bernard taught in *On Loving God* that the first level is love of self for the sake of self. "This is carnal love, the love by which one loves himself above all for his own sake. One is only aware of oneself."

Second is the love of God for the sake of self. "Such a human being loves God, but for its own profit and not yet for God's sake. Third is the love of God for the sake of God. "The fulfillment of our desires pleases us less than to seek his will done in us and for us, as we beg every day in prayer, saying, 'Your will be done on earth as it is in heaven.'" The highest level of loving God is loving self for the sake of God. "For now we do not love ourselves, except for his sake, that

---

[1335]For example, Luther taught contemplation on the sufferings of Christ gives strength against temptation [Köberle, *Quest for Holiness*, 159-160}.

[1336]See ftnt #1093.

[1337]Williams, "Reveling in the Mystery," 48-49.

he may be the reward of those who love him and the eternal recompense of those who love him forever." Bernard believed one remained at the third level a long time and doubted whether anyone had arrived at the fourth stage.[1338]

Bernard offered this prayer for those in bondage to themselves, "Let me be moved by your Spirit, the Spirit of freedom, by which your children act; the Spirit that bears witness with my spirit that I, too, am one of your children."[1339] While Bernard's analysis corresponds to the Wesleyan paradigm,[1340] the contemplative method puts too much emphasis on human effort. Yet Bernard did emphasize that our love can be perfect in this life and this emphasis had been lacking since the time of Augustine. And unlike most monks who connected perfection with celibacy, Bernard used marriage as a metaphor of the devout life.[1341]

John of Fidanza, better known as Bonaventure, (1221-1274) taught the triple way of purgation, enlightenment, and perfection. Purgation disciplines the outer man. Illumination disciplines human reason, and perfection bring an experiential knowledge of God. There are three levels of activity: meditation, prayer, and contemplation which function at all three levels of purgation, enlightenment, and perfection. Finally there are three levels of perfection: freedom from improper attachment to worldly things, freedom from evil, and the level of beatitude, the conscious experiencing of God.[1342]

In the late fourteenth century Julian, a Catholic mystic, of Norwich, England prayed for three gifts: a recollection of Christ's passion, bodily sickness, and three wounds. Her *Revelations* is believed to be the first English-language book written by a woman. Julian declared in 1373, "I wanted to have every kind of pain, bodily and spiritual, which I should have if I died, every fear and temptation from devils, and every other kind of pain except the departure of the spirit."[1343]

On May 13, 1373 she received a revelation. Her theology was based her mystical experience. Julian spoke of "oning" or "oneing," which she used to convey God's desire for union with us. "He ones us to himself." According to

1338Flew, *Idea of Perfection*, 223.

1339Bassett, *Holiness Teachings*, 236-243; see also Evans, *Bernard of Clairvaux*, 192-197.

1340See Wesley's *Notes* on 1 John 4:18.

1341Bernard wrote 86 sermons on the first two verses of Solomon's Song of Songs in which he suggests that the union of the soul with God is analogous to the marital bliss of wife (soul) and husband (God).

1342de Vinck, *Works of Bonaventure*, 59-94.

1343Wilson-Hartgrove, "A Curious Saint,"51-53.

Julian, "Unmade kind is God." She taught a divine Motherhood, "As truly as God is our Father so truly is God our Mother." She also declared that sin is necessary.[1344]

An anonymous monk also wrote *The Cloud of Unknowing* at the end of the fourteenth century. He advocated a leap of love, writing that love, not understanding, breaks through the cloud separating God and man. Here the emphasis is on apophatic mysticism or the *via negativa*, in which God is described according to what he is not. This emphasis leads to extreme passivity and quietism. While this approach is regarded as a bridge to non-Christian mysticism, the mysticism of the Hebrew prophets was kataphatic or the *via affirmativa*.

With reference to the Holy Spirit, λαμβάνω (*lambano*) is used a total of ten times, always in the active voice.[1345] Thus, the Holy Spirit is not received passively, but he is taken, seized, or appropriated by faith.

William Johnston has observed that God spoke to Moses in a burning bush, not in silence and nothingness. Ezekiel saw visions of God, as did Isaiah, Jeremiah, Amos, and others. Jesus Christ is the image of the invisible God (Col 1:15, 19). The New Testament is full of visions, dreams, actions, experiences and encounters. Kataphatic mysticism is overwhelmingly present. Therefore, Christian mysticism must include more than an emphasis on nothingness, dark nights of the soul, detachment, emptiness, letting go, not knowing, or clouds of unknowing.[1346] In fact, Harvey Egan argues that the apophatic mystic's very act of writing about his or her apophasia is itself a kataphatic experience.[1347]

In the fourteenth century we find Master Eckhart, Henry Suso, Nicholas of Basle, and John Tauler, who called themselves "Friends of God." Eckhart was a Dominican mystic who advocated human perfectability. He taught a detachment and return of the soul to God, being formed again into God, and the birth of the Son in the soul. His view of a total love of God led to his position that we ought to love all things equally. His writings are hard to read, but he has often been accused of pantheism although he also seems to maintain the transcendence of the Creator. His concept that there should be no differentiation among the objects of love and his emphasis on the divine spark, leaves him open to this accusation.

Bernard of Clairvaux was more careful to define our union with God as one in spirit, but not one in essence. Eckhart was not as careful in his language. He also taught the interior act alone counts. The exterior act adds nothing to the

---

[1344]Colledge and Walsh, *Julian of Norwich*, 225; 70.

[1345]John 20:22; Acts 1:8; 2:38; 8:15, 17, 19; 10:47; 19:2; Rom 8:15; Gal 3:2.

[1346]Johnston, *Arise My Love*, 116-117.

[1347]"Christian Apophatic and Kataphatic Mysticisms," *Theological Studies* 39 (1978): 399-426.

goodness of the interior one. As Wesley noted, this emphasis destroys social holiness. A distorted perfectionism and self-absorption go hand in hand.

At this same time in England Walter Hilton wrote *The Ladder of Perfection*. Hilton distinguished between rigid discipline and an inward delight in loving God. He wrote of three stages of the contemplative life: knowing God, a burning love in devotion, and a burning love in contemplation. The distinction between the second and third stages is that the second stage was not as permanent. The third stage was perfection.

Turner compared Hilton's distinctions to Wesley's distinction between a servant and a son. While Hilton did not regard a complete and permanent deliverance from sin as possible in this life, he does distinguish, perhaps for the first time in English thought, between a Christian who is saved by faith and one who is perfected in love.[1348] Yet Hilton declared, "In the justification of a soul, our Lord Jesus manifests His greatest love to a soul, for He disposes of all sin and unites the soul to himself. Such is the greatest thing that He is able to do for the soul, and for this reason it is allotted to the Holy Spirit to do it."[1349]

Hilton, in his letters to Adam Horsley, distinguished between three types of Christian commitment: the active life, the life of ordinary Christians; the contemplative life, the life of monks and nuns; and the mixed life, the life Hilton advocated. Hilton wrote that we do not have to leave the world in order to be sanctified. In fact, while we are not *of* the world, it is beneficial for us to be *in* the world in order to be salt and light.[1350]

In the sixteenth century John of the Cross was a Spanish Carmelite mystic, considered by the Catholic community to be *the* mystical doctor. He emphasized the "dark night of the soul," when God withdraws his presence in the life of a believer. This is not a period of blindness and stupidity, but a state in which our own interests are sacrificed to a pure, disinterested love.[1351]

John actually envisioned two nights. One is "the night of the senses" in which we play a part in the purification of the senses. The second is "the night of the spirit" in which love takes control and wipes out the last vestiges of self-centeredness so that we can become one with God. All this is explained as the process of purification through "the refiner's fire."[1352]

John Wesley was initially attracted to mysticism during his years at Oxford due to the influence of William Law. He wrote that he "dragged on

---

[1348]Turner, *Vision Which Transforms*, 173-174.

[1349]Bassett, *Holiness Teaching*, 255.

[1350]Jeffrey, *Toward A Perfect Love*, xxi.

[1351]Flew, *Idea of Perfection*, 273.

[1352]Hinson, "Contemplative View,"178-180.

heavily, finding no comfort or help" from the mystic writers until the time he left England, 14 October, 1735. It was on the ship to America that he came in contact with the Moravian brethren who showed him a more excellent way.[1353]

According to Outler, Wesley was exposed to three types of mysticism: the antinomian mysticism of Molinos, Madame Guyon, and Francois de Sales, the voluntaristic mysticism of Kempis, Law, and Scupoli, and the quietistic mysticism of the Molinists. Outler concluded that the doctrine of perfection, as taught by Wesley, is strikingly different, both in substance and form from these types of mysticism.[1354]

While Warfield was no admirer of Wesley, on the first page of his treatise on perfectionism, he declared it was a mistake to lump Wesleyan perfectionism in with mystical perfection.[1355] Colin Williams explained that while medieval theology considered perfection as a possibility, it was described as a ladder of ascent, available only for those in the contemplative vocation. Wesley saw that perfection must be taken away from the ladder of merit, brought under the Reformation doctrine of salvation by grace through faith alone, and presented as a promise which is for all.[1356]

And so from that turning point when Wesley came to America to the end of his life he consistently criticized mysticism. In 1734, John wrote his father

> By holiness I mean, not fasting, or bodily austerity, or any other external means of improvement, but that inward temper to which all these are subservient, a renewal of soul in the image of God. I mean a complex habit of lowliness, meekness, purity, faith, hope, and love of God and man.[1357]

In a letter to his brother, Samuel, John wrote that the writings of the mystics had almost at one point in his life caused him to make "shipwreck of the faith." He objected that mysticism depreciates the means of grace, including church attendance; that it was too subjective, and that it usurped the priority of

---

[1353]Wesley, *Journal*, 24 May, 1738, ¶ 8. The first two editions of his journal also included the statement that he believed the mystics "to be one great antichrist."

[1354]Outler, *John Wesley*, 252; see Tuttle, *John Wesley: Life and Theology*, 337-345. Tuttle concluded that Wesley emphasized resignation to the will of God as basic to Christian perfection.

[1355]Warfield, *Studies in Perfectionism*, 1:3.

[1356]Williams, *John Wesley's Theology Today*, 174.

[1357]Wesley, *Letter*, 10 December 1734, ¶ 6.

the Word.[1358] According to Collins, Wesley had three major complaints against mysticism: their depreciation of the means of grace, their understanding of "the dark night of the soul," and their concept of union with God which some called perfection. Wesley preferred the language of communion to that of union and the language of the perfection of love to that of the melding of the soul into the dark abyss of God.[1359] Thus, Wesley emphasized an active, not a passive spirituality.

In 1739 John and Charles published *Hymns and Sacred Poems*. In the preface they accused mysticism of laying another foundation other than the righteousness of Christ. They wrote that while common writers suppose that we are justified by outward works, the mystics suppose we are justified for the sake of our inward righteousness.

> For neither our own inward nor outward righteousness is the ground of our justification. Holiness of heart, as well as holiness of life, is not the cause but the effect of it. The sole cause of our acceptance with God, (or, that for the sake of which on the account of which, we are accepted,) is the righteousness and the death of Christ, who fulfilled God's law, and died in our stead. And even the condition of it is not (as they suppose) our holiness either of heart or life; but our faith alone; faith contradistinguished from holiness, as well as from good works. Other foundation therefore can no man lay, without being an adversary to Christ and his gospel, than faith alone; faith, though necessarily producing both, yet not including either good works, or holiness.

[1358]Wesley, *Letter*, 23 Nov 1736. In this letter he mentioned John Tauler, Miguel de Molines, and *Theologia Germanica*, an anonymous German mystical book, first given to Wesley by William Law. In his letter to William Law, Wesley later rejected *Theologia Germanica* for failing to include any emphasis on Christ as our atonement [20 May 1738]. Ironically, Martin Luther was so impressed with *Theologia Germanica* that he prepared it for re-publication twice, adding his appreciation for its rare service to his life [Gaddis, *Christian Perfection in America*, 72].

See also Weeks, *Mysticism, Antinomianism and the Positive Gospel*. In this pamphlet Weeks critiqued the holiness movement as making void the written law by obedience to an imaginary law — mysticism. But mysticism frequently forgets the law and the testimony. Thus, believers do not obey God's law unless they feel led. Yet they justify their lawlessness on the basis that they get blessed emotionally. If they "feel the fire" they can be sure they are still among the elect.

[1359]Collins, "Critical Appropriation of Early German Pietism," 75-76. This concept of union is the doctrine of theosis or deification.

The also rejected the emphasis on solitude in order to purify the soul. "They advise, 'To the desert! to the desert! and God will build you up.'" Yet the Wesleys quoted Acts 2:42, that the early Christians continued in the apostles' teaching, fellowship, breaking bread, and communion. Therefore, they concluded the gospel of Christ was directly opposed to mysticism.

> Directly opposite to this is the gospel of Christ. Solitary religion is not to be found there. "Holy solitaries" is a phrase no more consistent with the gospel than holy adulterers. The gospel of Christ knows of no religion, but social; no holiness but social holiness.[1360]

Wesley preached, that Christianity is essentially a social religion, and that to turn it into a solitary one is to destroy it.[1361]

Our union with Christ is not a mystical, private union, but a social union; it is life in the body of Christ (1 Cor 12:27; Eph 4:13-16). Wesley ultimately rejected the emphasis of à Kempis because it led to "self-denigration aimed merely at total resignation which becomes a kind of detached fatalism. The holiness advanced by the 'quietists' (e. g. Madame Guyon) at first attracted Wesley, but then repelled him because of its antinomian and subjective tendencies. He saw clearly that holiness is more than consecration — it is a divine cleansing and

---

[1360]Wesley, *Works*, 14:319-321. In a letter to his niece, Sally, John wrote that both his brother Charles and John Fletcher had been adversely influenced by mystics. "The reading of those poisonous writers the Mystics confounded the intellects of both my brother and Mr. Fletcher and made them afraid of (what ought to have been their glory) the letting their light shine before men" [26 September 1788]. For a defense, see "On Evangelical Mysticism" [Fletcher, *Works*, 4:7-13].

For other references to mysticism, see Wesley's *Journal*, 16 July 1740; 11 November 1741; 5 June 1742; 15 May 1746; 10 April 1747; 5 February 1764; Letter to Count Zinzindorf and the Church at Herrnhut, 5-8 August, 1740, ¶ 14-15; Letter to Dr. John Robertson, 24 September 1753; Letter to William Law, 6 January 1756; Letter to Dorothy Furly, 18 June 1757; Letter to the *London Chronicle*, 17 September 1760; Letter to Ann Bolton, 25 March 1772; Letter to Penelope Newman, 23 October 1772; Letter to Ann Bolton, 25 October 1772; Letter to Mary Bishop, 19 September 1773. Wesley wrote to Mary Bishop on 30 November 1774 that Lopez advocated "au désert! au désert! Nay, but I say, 'To the Bible! To the Bible!"

[1361]Wesley, "Sermon on the Mount, IV," Sermon #24, ¶ 5. In the days of Oxford Methodism Wesley was advised, "Sir, you are to serve God and go to heaven. Remember you cannot serve Him alone; you must, therefore, find companions, or make them; the Bible knows nothing of solitary religion" [Telford, *Life of Wesley*, 147].

empowering."[1362]

Wesley also rejected the "dark night of the soul" teaching of mysticism, which asserts that God withdraws himself from the believer and forces him to fly by the instruments.[1363] "It is repugnant to the very nature of God; it is utterly beneath his majesty and wisdom 'to play at *bo-peep* with his creatures.'"[1364] Wesley first struggled to understand the dark night during his early attraction to mysticism, but abandoned the attempt because he could not feel assurance and at the same time embrace the "unknowing" of the night.[1365] Thus Wesley challenged the universality of the experience of the dark night of the soul, insisting that it was not essential to the Christian life.

He also differed with John of the Cross, Teresa of Avila,[1366] and William Law regarding the causes for this "dark night." While they saw it as part of God's design for Christian maturity, Wesley felt this experience was brought on by sin, ignorance, or disappointment arising from unrealistic expectations about the Christian life. For those in such a condition, Wesley counseled repentance of sin, study of the Scriptures, and a more realistic view of the Christian life. Wesley argued from John 8:12 that God never deserts any man unless he first deserts God. "Abstracting from bodily disorders on the one hand and violent

---

[1362]Knight, "Presidential Address," 11; see also Knight, *Holiness Pilgrimage*, 17. Consecration is the result of human dedication and can become legalistic. Sanctification is the work of the Spirit.

[1363]Wesley, "The Wilderness State," Sermon #46, 2.1, 12.

[1364]Wesley, "Heaviness through Manifold Temptations," Sermon #47, 3.7. Rick Warren wrote, "Sometimes God intentionally draws back, and we don't sense his closeness. A king named Hezekiah experienced this test" [*Purpose-Driven Life*, 43]. While Warren cited 2 Chron 32:31 as his proof-text, in context Hezekiah had become proud (v 25). While he repented (v 26), he then received envoys from Babylon (see also Isa 38-39) and it was at that point that God tested him to see whether he would trust in human treaties or in God. According to Selman, Hezekiah incurred God's wrath because of his pride and because he entertained the enemy. Although Hezekiah repented, his motives were still not entirely pure and God forsook him as an act of divine judgment. God already knew his heart, but Hezekiah needed to know himself and repent [*2 Chronicles*, 10b:515-516].

[1365]Tuttle, *Mysticism in the Wesleyan Tradition*, 106-107.

[1366]Teresa of Avila (1515-1582) portrayed the spiritual journey as inward progress through seven mansions, beginning with humility, which she linked with self-knowledge, and ending with spiritual marriage, "where the most secret things pass between God and the soul" [*Interior Castle*]. Yet her passion was that her life conform to the sufferings of Jesus, so that she undertook severe mortification. Her motto was, "Lord, either let me suffer or let me die."

temptation on the other, every believer may be happy as well as holy, and 'walk in the light all the days of his life.'"[1367]

In his afterword to the second edition of *Rediscovering Holiness*, Packer devoted fourteen pages to an analysis of the case of Mother Teresa who felt abandoned by God for half a century although she was fully committed to God and had an experiential union with God for twenty years previous.[1368]

In this analysis Packer references the teachings of John of the Cross. He then compared this teaching with evangelical teaching, pointing out that evangelical theology is based on scriptural authority, an emphasis on the work of the Holy Spirit, on justification by faith, and on the work of the Spirit in regeneration. Thus, the evangelical emphasis is not on climbing from lower to higher levels of attainment nor the monastic life.

However, Packer said older evangelical literature taught that God sovereignly brings episodes of spiritual darkness on us from time to time. Packer explained these as wake-up calls or tests of fidelity. Packer, however, counseled that God's covenant is unbreakable and this knowledge helps Christians, even if they are in darkness.

Packer concluded that Mother Teresa's experience was not an experience of doubt or depression. Nor was it the "dark night of the soul," for Catholic tradition teaches that to be a temporary experience. Packer did not feel that the purpose of this permanent darkness was a call to repentance. He felt it was

---

[1367]Wesley, *Journal*, 31 January 1767. Yet it should be noted that seven months after Wesley's conversion he declared in his *Journal* that he was not then a Christian [4 Jan 1739]. John also wrote to Charles, "I do not love God. I never did. Therefore I never believed in the Christian sense of the word. Therefore I am only an honest heathen. . . . And yet I dare not preach otherwise than I do, either concerning faith, or love, or justification, or perfection. And yet I find rather an increase than a decrease of zeal for the whole work of God and every part of it. I am so swept along I know not how that I can't stand still. I want all the world to come to what I do not know myself" [27 June 1766; see Outler, *John Wesley*, 81-82]. This letter is discussed by Felleman, "'Servant of God,'" 72-86. However, I do not accept her conclusion that servants of God are justified.

Wynkoop said that all of this is not inconsistent with the kind of perfection of love Wesley tried to describe as the fulfilling of the whole law [*Theology of Love*, 86]. See also the explanation of Collins, "Twentieth-Century Interpretations," 25-26, "Wesley does not claim that the new birth cannot be followed by a measure of doubt, fear, or even depression."

Olson points out that theologically Wesley separated justification and the new birth. The servant is justified, but not born again. The child is justified *and* born again. Thus, Wesley judged himself to be pre-new birth, but post-justification ["Aldersgate II," 166].

[1368]Mother Teresa, *Come Be My Light.*

partially demonic attack. He discussed the suggestion that it was disciplinary, meant to enhance the quality of her discipleship. Ultimately, Packer concluded the purpose of this darkness was so that she could have a greater identification with the poor.

Packer then moved from this specific case to the general conclusion that God uses darkness experiences for instruction, correction, edification, and preparation for usefulness so that we can comfort those in any trouble. However, God does not usually explain the reason for such experiences. The persevering commitment of Mother Teresa, however, shows us how to respond.[1369] There is always a danger, however, in working from a specific case to a general conclusion. We cannot formulate theology from experience. Rather, we must interpret our experience based on biblical revelation. The normal Christian life is a life of assurance.

According to Elaine Heath, Mother Teresa did spend much of her adult life in a dark night of the soul and she embodied Phoebe Palmer's concept of naked faith.[1370] John MacMillan was more theologically correct in writing, "One of the hard lessons that must be learned by every seeker after the deeper life in Christ is that each new appropriation of heavenly grace and knowledge brings him often into a more subtile conflict."[1371]

Yet Wesley did not dismiss all mystics without recognizing some value. He included some mystics in his *Christian Library*, including Brother Lawrence, Gregory Lopez, Antoinette Bourignon, Don Juan D'Avila, Miguel de Molinos, Francis Fénelon, Marquis de Renty, Madame Guyon, and Thomas à Kempis.[1372] In the preface he expressed his desire to "extract the gold out of these baser mixtures. Who will separate the pure, genuine divinity out of this huge, mingled mass? I have made, as I was able, an attempt of this kind." He declared that he had endeavored to extract such a collection of English theology, which he believed was true and agreeable with the oracles of God.

> But, in order to this, I have been obliged, not only to omit the far greatest part of several eminent authors, but also to add what was needful, either to clear their sense, or to correct their

[1369]Packer, *Rediscovering Holiness*, 249-263.

[1370]Heath, *Naked Faith*, 112-113.

[1371]MacMillan, *Authority of the Believer*, 82.

[1372]In his preface to her *Solid Virtue*, Wesley wrote that some might be tempted to dismiss Bourignon for not giving adequate attention to Jesus Christ. "Be pleased then friendly reader, to pursue this book with a sincere resolution, by the divine grace, to put the directions of it in practice, so far as you find them conformable to the gospel of Jesus Christ" [*Christian Library*, 36:177; second edition, 21:299].

mistakes. And, in a design of this nature, I apprehend myself to be at full liberty so to do. I therefore take no author for better; for worse; (as indeed I dare not call any man Rabbi;) but endeavor to follow each so far as he follows Christ. And not (knowingly) one step farther.[1373]

In some cases he published a biography about the mystic instead of reprinting the writings of the mystic. Such was the case with Monsieur de Renty.[1374] Wesley's abridgement of de Renty's biography reduced it from 358 pages to 67.[1375] According to Martin Schmidt, John Wesley was impressed with the way deRenty was dominated by the thought of God. He lived in the conscious presence of God.

In everything he was led by the wish to be wholly dedicated to God. He saw through all external things to an ultimate spiritual

---

[1373]"Preface," ¶ 9-10, *Works*, 14:222-223.

[1374]See references to de Renty in "The Repentance of Believers," Sermon #14, 1.15; "On the Trinity," Sermon #55, ¶ 1, 17; "Of Evil Angels," Sermon #72, 2.15; "On Temptation," Sermon #82, 3.6; "On the Death of John Fletcher," Sermon #114, 3.12; "On the Discoveries of Faith," Sermon #117, ¶ 17 (not mentioned by name). Wesley called de Renty "one of the brightest patterns of heavenly wisdom" [*Journal*, 6 January 1738]. However, in Wesley's *Plain Account of Christian Perfection* he used de Renty to illustrate how a mistake in judgment may occasion a mistake in practice [*Works*, 11:394-395]. Here Wesley refers to his wearing an iron girdle.

An extract of the life of Monsieur de Renty was first published by Wesley in 1741 (London: Strahan). It was reissued in new editions (but with little change) four times during his life: Bristol: Farley, 1746; Bristol: Grabham & Pine, 1760; London: Hawes, 1778; London: New Chapel, 1788.

It was not included in the first edition of the *Christian Library* (1749-1756), but was added by Thomas Jackson to the second edition [1819-1826; Vol. 29:212-275] when he discovered he would have extra room. It was reprinted by Schmul Publishing Company in 2002.

In a letter to John Wesley 26 March, 1770, Toplady criticized him for raising "the ghost of Monsieur de Renty the French Papist, and many other Romish enthusiasts, by translating their lives into English for the edification of Protestant readers" [*Works*, 719-728]. However, Wesley edited 347 pages of a biography by Jean Baptiste de Saint-Jure to 67 pages, frequently condensing entire chapters into mere sentences. Tuttle explained that Wesley omits excessive mortification, any reference to the highly philosophical mystical path, and material leaning toward Rome [*Mysticism in the Wesleyan Tradition*, 93].

[1375]See Wesley's comments about the injudicious manner in which the biographer related de Renty's life in his *Journal*, 6 January 1738.

> point and there he perceived God. Wesley found in him perfection which attains to holiness as a higher nature. To read de Renty's life is to gain the impression that he never needed to submit himself to law, although he does make incidental reference to his inner struggles. He was one in whom sanctification and joy in salvation had attained a deep unity. His perfection was rooted in love toward God.[1376]

Nicolas Herman (1605-1691), better known as Brother Lawrence, entered the Carmelite monastery at Paris in 1649. He was given the task of managing the kitchen. Best known for his book, *The Practice of the Presence of God*, a conversation was recorded from 25 November, 1667.

> His very countenance was edifying; such a sweet and calm devotion appearing in it, as could not but affect the beholders; and it was observed, that in the greatest burry of business in the kitchen, he still preserved his recollection and heavenly-mindedness. He was never hasty nor loitering, but did each thing in its season, with an even uninterrupted composure and tranquility of spirit. " The time of business," said he, "does not, with me, differ from the time of prayer; and in the noise and hurry of my kitchen, while several persons are at the same time calling for different things, I possess GOD in as great tranquility as if I were upon my knees at the sacrament."[1377]

Wesley also exhorted Lady Maxwell to be "all a Christian; such a Christian as the Marquis de Renty, or Gregory Lopez, was."[1378] He declared that a person may truly be real Christians and yet hold wrong opinions, such as à Kempis, Gregory Lopez, and the Marquis de Renty.[1379] In his sermon "On God's Vineyard" Wesley recommended Francis de Sales and Juan de Castaniza as having written "strongly and scripturally on sanctification. But he went on to say that they were unacquainted with the nature of justification because the Council

---

[1376]Schmidt, *John Wesley: Theological Biography*, 1:216.

[1377]Wesley, ed, *The Christian Library*, first ed, 38:92; second ed, 23:66. Tuttle observed that in his *Christian Library* Wesley omitted Lawrence's statement that perfection necessarily implies long and tedious diligence [*Mysticism in the Wesleyan Tradition*, 157].

[1378]Wesley, *Letter* to Lady Maxwell, 22 September 1764.

[1379]Wesley, "On the Trinity," Sermon 55, ¶ 1.

of Trent had confused sanctification and justification.[1380]

Francis de Sales emphasized the ideal that perfection was possible for all men, not simply for monks. But the search for perfection must be made within the pale of the Roman church.[1381] Although the Reformation was needed in order to assert the possibility of attaining holiness in ordinary life, according to Flew, "The chasm between monk and layman was at least diminished."[1382] Contemplation is still possible for those who are engaged in the lawful occupations of a busy life through detachment.

According to de Sales, perfection of the soul is simple resignation. Human reason does not enter the holy place.[1383] Instead, the mind acquiesces and submits to the will of God. Thus the soul enjoys contemplation, the goal of which is ecstasy or the rapture of the mind in which we experience the peace of God. To feel God and to be free from vain attachments is a relative perfection. This emphasis connected with the Renaissance and earned de Sales the title of "the most perfect incarnation of Devout Humanism."[1384] Implied in this label is the belief that human perfection and happiness can be attained through contemplation. The Renaissance emphasis on individualism, self worth, and self determinism was integrated with resignation to providence as the means to attaining self fulfillment.

Castaniza was a Spanish theologian, of the order of Benedictines and chaplain of Philip II. His well-known book on Christian perfection, published in 1599, has more recently been attributed to a monk, Lorenzo Scupoli.

Miguel de Molinos published his *Spiritual Guide* in Italian in 1675. He distinguished between meditation, which is for beginners, and contemplation, which had two stages. Flew described this highest stage as an abandonment of meditation, even on the truths of the Christian religion. He rejected the use of images, figures, ideas, or conceptions; both physical and mental images. This "deification" occurs by the silence of not speaking, not desiring, and not thinking. The soul has lost itself in God's immeasurable sea.

There is also a holy indifference that surpasses Stoicism. And there is unbroken communion with God. The best kind of prayer is the prayer of

---

[1380]Sermon #107, 1.5.

[1381]Perkins, *Evangelical Perfection*, 184.

[1382]Flew, *Idea of Perfection*, 258.

[1383]Sangster said that reason wants to know *why*; the saint only wants to know *what* [*Pure in Heart*, 203-204]. Yet Sangster argued later in his book that the saints do not deny the validity of reason [p. 213].

[1384]Flew, *Idea of Perfection*, 261. Greathouse said he reflected both Neoplatonic mysticism and Renaissance humanism [*From the Apostles to Wesley*, 82].

silence.[1385] This complete passivity "as wax awaits a seal,"is known as quietism. Yet Wesley included an edited edition of his *Devotional Tracts* and *Spiritual Guide* in Volume 36 of the first edition of *The Christian Library* and in Volume 23 of the second edition.

Tuttle expressed surprise that Wesley included Molinos' *Spiritual Guide*, since he had some lingering problems with quietism among his societies. In contrast to Wesley, Molinos taught that one can achieve perfection through his own efforts. Yet Wesley reduced the original 180-page *Spiritual Guide* to 44 pages. "One could read descriptions of the original *Spiritual Guide* and Wesley's extract and never suspect that they were describing the same book." Tuttle concluded that Wesley cut the heart out of what Molinos was really saying. Yet he went to the trouble of sifting gold from Molinos because he had a unique contribution to make concerning pure love and humility.[1386]

Wesley began reading Thomas à Kempis in 1725, about the time he was ordained. "I began to see that true religion was seated in the heart and that God's law extended to all our thoughts as well as words and actions. I was, however, very angry at Kempis for being *too strict*, though I read him only in Dean Stanhope's translation. Yet I had frequently much sensible comfort in reading him, such as I was an utter stranger to before."[1387]

Wesley wrote his nephew about "the religion of the heart; the religion which Kempis, Pascal, Fénelon enjoyed: the life of God in the soul of man, the walking with God and having fellowship with the Father and the Son."[1388] The phrase "the life of God in the soul of man" was the title of a very popular eighteenth book by Scottish mystic Henry Scougal, first published in 1677. Susanna Wesley recommended it to her boys.[1389] John Wesley abridged and published it in 1742.

While *The Imitation of Christ* first appeared in print in 1471, Wesley produced his own translation in 1735 under the title *The Christian's Pattern.*[1390] It was revised extensively, a more literal translation of the Latin, yet more modern and "closer to the language of the man in the street."[1391] Wesley continued to reprint Kempis in four different forms and at least 120 editions. In his

---

[1385]Flew, *Idea of Perfection*, 262-263.

[1386]Tuttle, *Mysticism in the Wesleyan Tradition*, 136-137.

[1387]Wesley, *Journal*, 24 May, 1738, § 4.

[1388]Wesley, *Letter* to Samuel Wesley, 29 April 1790.

[1389]Clarke, *Memoirs of the Wesley Family*, 222.

[1390]Wesley, *Christian's Pattern*; Baker, *Heart of True Spirituality.*

[1391]Baker, *Heart of True Spirituality*, 2:17.

introduction Wesley wrote,

> Whatever relates to Christian perfection, may be reduced to one of these three heads;
> (1.) The essence of it:
> (2.) The ways and degrees by which it is attained: And,
> (3.) The means or instruments of it.
> The scope of this treatise is, that perfection which every Christian is bound to aspire to. Now, although the whole essence of this consists in love, which unites the soul to God; yet, because perfect love implies,
> (1.) Entire humility,
> (2.) Absolute self-renunciation,[1392]
> (3.) Unreserved resignation,
> (4.) Such a union of our will with the divine as makes the Christian one spirit with God; a great part of it describes these tempers, whereby he that loves God is made partaker of the divine nature.

Wesley had a great admiration for Kempis, but in a letter to his mother objected to the position of Kempis that God has decreed we should be miserable in the world. Wesley also objected to his contentions that "mirth is vain and useless."[1393] In *A Plain Account of Christian Perfection* Wesley referred to Kempis who had written,

> Simplicity and purity are the two wings by which a man is lifted up above all earthly things. Simplicity is in the intention, purity in the affection; simplicity tends to God, purity apprehends and tastes him.[1394]

[1392]Wesley felt that this word is preferable to "self-denial" for two reasons: it is a more general term, including both "self-denial" and "taking up the cross," and it is a more literal translation of our Savior's expression, "let him deny himself" (Matt 16:24). While the translation "deny himself" carries the baggage of asceticism, the word ἀπαρνέομαι (*arneomai*) means to disown and is used three times in the account of Peter's denial (Matt 26:34, 35, 75). While Wesley advocated a renunciation of self-will, he also stated that a proper love of self "is not a sin, but an indisputable duty" [*Notes*, 500]. See also John Hunt, *Letters on Sanctification*, Letter 21 on self-love.

[1393]Wesley, *Letter* to Susanna Wesley, 28 May 1725.

[1394]Wesley, *Christian's Pattern*, 37; Baker, *Heart of True Spirituality*, 2:26; Wesley, *Works*, 11:367, § 3.

Francis Fénelon was the chaplain in the court of Louis XIV. His devotional classic in French has been translated into English under the title of *Christian Perfection*. No one influenced Wesley with regard to pure love more than Fénelon.[1395] Fénelon taught that the state of pure love was a "passive state." While this opened him to charges of quietism, Flew claimed that he simply meant the opposite of hurry and distraction. To be in a perfect passive state of contemplation would mean that the human soul had become one with God. According to Fénelon such a state of continuous contemplation was impossible in this life. While Aristotle had first advocated passivity, Christian mystics have tended to emphasize the awakening by divine grace of the soul's energy.[1396]

In *Christian Perfection* he has much to say about mortification, yet he saw perfection as a work of God's grace. God wants a pure intention, a sincere detachment from ourselves. Stated in positive terms, the perfect life is the imitation of Jesus. Fénelon argued,

> If anyone imagines that this perfect love is impossible and visionary, and that it is a foolish subtlety which can become a source of illusion, I have only two words with which to answer him. Nothing is impossible to God. He himself calls himself the jealous God. He only keeps us in the pilgrimage of this life to lead us to perfection. To treat this love as a visionary and dangerous subtlety is to accuse of illusion the greatest saints of every age, who have admitted this love, and who have reached through it the highest degree of spiritual life.[1397]

Fénelon contended that the highest love is disinterested love and this state of pure love is possible. According to Flew he means by "disinterested" that our own interests are sacrificed in order to please God.[1398] Yet according to Tuttle he "insisted that the Christian's ascent toward union with God must be made by the stages of love where resignation becomes indifference, and self (even one's own salvation) becomes less and less important."[1399] Pope observed that this doctrine of disinterested love, "pressed to the extreme of the utter extinction of desire of heaven and fear of hell, overturns the very foundation of any theory of personal

---

[1395]Tuttle, *Mysticism in the Wesleyan Tradition*, 153.

[1396]Flew, *Idea of Perfection*, 270-272.

[1397]Fénelon, *Christian Perfection*, 41.

[1398]Flew, *Idea of Perfection*, 267.

[1399]Tuttle, *Mysticism in the Wesleyan Tradition*, 40.

evidence of salvation.[1400] There is a difference, however, between dying to self-centeredness and dying to self.

Quietism seems to teach that we attain a victorious life through the obliteration of our personality. I cannot lose myself, but I can be delivered from self-centeredness. Wynkoop explained, "The personality *is* the self. Remove the self and no personality remains."[1401] The New Testament is not pantheistic, urging that natural self love be eradicated. We are to love our neighbor *as ourselves.*

Wesley taught that love of self was not a sin, but an indisputable duty.[1402] The sin is selfishness, which is a distortion of love.[1403] According to Kevin Lowrey, when Wesley spoke of "disinterested love," he did not mean the absence of self-love altogether. Rather he meant that genuine love for others is not ultimately motivated by self-love. Thus, people are loved for their own sakes.[1404]

Fénelon held that this state may be interrupted by venial sins. Roman Catholics distinguish between *venial* and *mortal* sin. A sin may be willful, but considered *venial* if it is a small matter. "A sin can be venial in two ways: (1) when the evil done is not seriously wrong; (2) when the evil done is seriously wrong, but the sinner sincerely believes it is only slightly wrong or does not give full consent to it."

While Franciscans, Jesuits, and Molinists hold that perfection is attainable in this life, they rest the doctrine largely on this distinction between mortal and venial sins. Based on the theology of Augustine the Dominicans and Jansenists deny the possibility of perfection in this life.[1405] In contrast Wesley

---

[1400]Pope, *Compendium*, 3:123-124.

[1401]Wynkoop, *Foundations*, 113-114; see also Doty, *Lessons in Holiness*, 89; Sangster, *Pure in Heart*, 229; Yocum, *Conformed to Christ*, 76-78; Seamands, *Childish Things*, 112-119.

[1402]Wesley, *Notes*, 500.

[1403]Wynkoop, *Theology of Love*, 141; 203.

[1404]Lowrey, *Salvaging Wesley's Agenda*, 290.

[1405]Noll, *Father Smith Instructs Jackson*, 76. See also McClintock and Strong, *Cyclopedia*, 7:943. Augustine held that while a man might avoid all mortal sin, venial sins were absolutely unavoidable and the holiest men often fell into them [Peck, *Christian Perfection*, 98]. The Jesuits held to a legal perfection, while the Jansenists maintain that it is impossible for believers to fulfill the divine law because of the influence of Augustine upon their theology [Peck, *Christian Perfection*, 124-127; see also Platt, "Perfection," 734].

distinguished between willful sins and unintentional sins.[1406]

While Wesley included Fénelon in volume 38 of his *Christian Library*, yet he omitted Fénelon's description of the slow, painful process necessary to attain perfection.[1407] Wesley wrote to a young disciple,

> Although there may be some use in teaching very young children to "say their prayers daily;" yet I judge it to be utterly impossible to teach any to "practice prayer," till they are awakened. For, what is prayer, but the desire of the soul expressed in words to God, either inwardly or outwardly? How then will you teach them to express a desire who feel no desire at all? When, therefore, Madame Guion [Guyon] talks in that manner, it often makes me afraid, that both she and her teacher, Archbishop Fenelon, talked by rote of the things they knew not. Both of them had an amazing genius, but, I doubt, full little experience. It is exceeding certain, neither his nor her writings are likely to do us any solid service. We have all the gold that is in them, without the dross; which is often not only useless, but dangerous.[1408]

Yet Wesley was impressed with Fénelon's statement on simplicity. In his correspondence he cited it on at least four occasions. "Simplicity is that grace which frees the soul from all unnecessary reflections upon itself."[1409]

Madame Guyon was a French mystic who read Kempis and de Sales. A Franciscan monk urged her to look within instead of without for peace and to seek God in her heart. She taught that if you feel the presence of God while praying, you should remain quiet and "cherish this sensation while it continues." You must "sink into yourself" in order to find God "in your innermost center." She explained,

> When you have fully entered into yourself, you will sense within you the warm presence of God when the senses are recollected and withdrawn from the circumference to the center and the soul is sweetly and silently employed on the truths we have read, not

---

[1406]Wesley, *Works*, 10:394.

[1407]Tuttle, *Mysticism in the Wesleyan Tradition*, 156-157.

[1408]Wesley, 8 September, 1773; *Works*, 12:449-450. The letter was written to Philothea Briggs.

[1409]Wesley, *Letter* to Miss J. C. March, 6 July 1770; Mary Bishop, 30 November 1774; Ann Bolton, 27 September 1777. In another letter to Mary Bishop Wesley wrote "all unprofitable reflections" [12 January 1773].

in reasoning, but in feeding thereon.[1410]

Soon after the pope condemned the quietism of Molinos in 1687, Guyon was imprisoned. Released in 1689, Fénelon was among her circle of friends and had an affection for her which was "stronger than persecution or death." She was rearrested on charges of heresy in 1695 and was not released until 1701. Wesley said that she "imagined herself to be infallible" because she believe the strong impressions she felt were all from God. Wesley continued,

> The grand source of all her mistakes was this — the not being guided by the written word. She did not take the Scriptures for the rule of her actions; at most, they were but a secondary rule. Inward impressions, which she called inspirations, were her primary rule. The written word was not a lantern to her feet, a light in all her paths. No; she followed another light — the outward light of her confessors, and the inward light of her own spirit. It is true, she wrote many volumes upon the Scriptures. But she read them not to learn, but to teach; and therein was hurried on by the rapid stream of her overflowing imagination. Hence arose that capital mistake which runs through all her writings, that God never does, never can purify a soul but by inward and outward suffering. Utterly false! Never was there a more purified soul than the apostle John. And which of the apostles suffered less — yea, of all the primitive Christians? Therefore, all that she says on this head, of "darkness, desertion, and privation," and the like, is fundamentally wrong. This unscriptural notion led her into the unscriptural practice of bringing suffering upon herself — by bodily austerities; by giving away her estate to ungodly, unthankful relations; by not justifying herself, than which nothing could be unjust or uncharitable; and by that unaccountable whim (the source of numberless sufferings which did not end but with her life), the going to Geneva to convert the heretics to the Catholic faith. And yet with all this dross, how much pure gold is mixed! So did God wink at involuntary ignorance. What a depth of religion did she enjoy! Of the mind that was in Christ Jesus! What heights of righteousness, and peace, and joy in the Holy Ghost! How few such instances do we find of exalted love to God and our neighbor; of genuine humility; of invincible meekness and unbounded resignation! So that, upon the whole, I know not

[1410]Guyon, *Experiencing Union with God*, 16-17; 28.

whether we may not search many centuries to find another woman who was such a pattern of true holiness.[1411]

Daniel Steele concluded that "through all her writings runs the capital mistake that God never does, never can, purify a soul but by inward and outward suffering. This led her into the Romish practice of bringing suffering upon herself by bodily austerities. But with this dross much pure gold was mixed."[1412]

Madame Guyon wrote that love pure and holy, is a deathless fire and is ethereal fare [heavenly food]. Her theology influenced both the Quakers and Romanticism.[1413]

Later the Quakers would emphasize the inner light. The way of perfection to the Quaker is simply obedience to the Voice within. "The Methodist has no confidence in any witness within unless he can confirm it from the Word: the Quaker does not feel bound by any Scripture, unless it is in accord with the immediate revelation of the spirit to his own soul."[1414]

Quakers taught that God gives every man an inner principle which tells him of his duty toward God. God awakens within man a desire to live up to this principle. This inner light could be linked with John 1:9 or it could be a substitute for divine revelation of Scripture. While Quakers believe the Bible to be a revelation of God, they did not believe it to be the only revelation. Revelation is ongoing and to be received in silence.

The Quakers came under much criticism for their refusal to call the Bible the Word of God. George Fox preached that to properly understand a particular Scripture one must be in the same spirit that the writer was in when he wrote the Scripture. As a young Christian, Fox said that he often had openings from the Spirit and in reading the Scriptures afterward he found that they were in perfect agreement with what the Spirit had previously taught him. Fox eventually committed large portions of the Scripture to memory and was able to use it successfully against those with whom he debated. The Northwest Yearly Meeting of Friends have declared, "We believe the Spirit will not lead persons or groups

---

[1411]Wesley, *Works*, 14:276; 278, ¶ 7-9. According to Warfield, Guyon had nothing in common with Protestantism except the inwardness of her religion and her exaltation of Christ. Her concept of faith was Roman Catholic and in practice she was a quietist [*Perfectionism*, 2:376-380; 429-430].

[1412]*Steele's Answers*, 202-203.

[1413]James, *Pure Love of Madame Guyon*.

[1414]Perkins, *Evangelical Perfection*, 234. Perkins wrote that while all light comes from Christ, according to Quaker doctrine, there seems no real place for the Atonement in their system [p. 236].

contrary to the teachings of the Scriptures."[1415]

On the other hand Elias Hicks (1748-1830) emphasized following the light of God in the human heart to the point of abandoning Scripture. The guidance of the historic Christ was separated from the inward Christ, resulting in a conformity to the conclusions of the Enlightenment. Rejecting the Trinity and the Atonement, in 1827 Hicks withdrew from the Society of Friends and established his own Quaker sect. The doctrine of the "Light" carried Hicks to the very verge of the doctrine of election. The decisions of life are not determined by reason. The Light acts best when man himself is still and reason is in a state of inactivity. The Fall consists "in turning away from the inward spiritual guide, in trusting the outward senses and outward passions, and especially in following the desire 'to know good and evil' without the instruction of the Light within."[1416] Thus, there is no emphasis on racial corruption. All that is necessary is for the individual soul to be awakened, so that Christ may shine upon in. According to Otto Scott, the "Inner Light" sometimes led some of them to appear naked, with blackened faces, or swathed in sheets, to reinforce their protests before Magistrates.[1417]

While Protestants have so reacted to "works righteousness" that they had swung to the opposite antinomian extreme, the early Quakers protested this "cheap grace." Thus, George Fox rejected any doctrine of imputation. Barbour and Roberts wrote,

> Early Friends were clearly describing "experimentally" (we would say, existentially) what the later, more rationalistic Methodists would systematize in their doctrine of sanctification. Quakers did not imagine that they had been given instant sanctification at any time. But they had seen perfect obedience to the Light as ever a possibility, and they could announce this possibility as a doctrinal truth.[1418]

[1415]Online: "Faith Expressed as Doctrine," ¶ 4.

[1416]Jones, *Later Periods of Quakerism*, 447-452.

[1417]Scott, *Great Christian Revolution*, 246.

[1418]Barbour and Roberts, *Early Quaker Writings*, 248; 24. Perkins wrote that the impact of Methodism on Quakerism was a great blessing [*Evangelical Perfection*, 240]. While the Quakers began around 1640, Rufus M. Jones observed that after Methodism arose in the following century there was a marked tendency to mold and formulate Quaker thought in the direction of evangelical doctrine. Where the influence of Methodism upon Quakerism waned, Quakerism tended toward a more anti-evangelical and Enlightenment direction [*Later Periods of Quakerism*, xiii, 275].

While in Derby Jail, George Fox testified to holiness. "If your faith be true, it will give you victory over sin and the devil, purify your hearts and consciences (for the true faith is held in a pure conscience), and bring you to please God, and give you access to Him again."[1419] However, his jailers "could not endure to hear of purity, and of victory over sin and the devil. They said they could not believe any could be free from sin on this side of the grave."[1420] According to Asbury Lowrey, Fox taught that the mark of the prize of the high calling of all true Christians was "Perfection from sin, according to the Scriptures of truth, which testify it to the end of Christ's coming, and the nature of His kingdom for which His Spirit was given."[1421] Yet he taught that man could be restored to the innocence of Adam before the fall.[1422]

Robert Barclay argued that it is possible so far to keep to it as not to be found daily transgressors of the law of God.

> First, that we place not this possibility in man's own will and capacity, as he is a man, the son of fallen Adam, or as he is in his natural state, however wise or knowing, or however much endued with a notional and literal knowledge of Christ, thereby endeavouring a conformity to the letter of the law, as it is outward.
>
> Secondly, That we attribute it wholly to man as he is born again, renewed in his mind, raised by Christ, knowing Christ alive, reigning and ruling in him, and guiding and leading him by his Spirit, and revealing in him the law of the Spirit of life; which not only manifests and reproves sin but also gives power to come out of it.
>
> Thirdly, that by this we understand not such a perfection as may not daily admit of a growth, and consequently mean not, as if we were to be as pure, holy, and perfect as God in his divine attributes of wisdom, knowledge and purity; but *only a perfection proportionable and answerable to man's measure*, whereby we are kept from transgressing the law of God and enabled to answer what he requires of us, even as he that improved his two talents so as to make four of them perfected his work, and was so accepted of his Lord as to be called a "good

---

[1419] *Journal of George Fox*, 1:56.

[1420] *George Fox, An Autobiography*, 123.

[1421] Lowrey, *Possibilities of Grace,* 442.

[1422] Greathouse, *From the Apostles to Wesley*, 98-101.

and faithful servant," nothing less than he that made his five ten. Even as a little gold is perfect gold in its kind, as well as a great mass, and a child hath a perfect body as well as a man, though it daily grow more and more. Thus Christ is said (Luke 2:52) to have "increased in wisdom and stature, and in favour with God and man," though before that time he had *never sinned*, and was (no doubt) perfect, in a true and proper sense.
Fourthly, though a man may witness this for a season, and therefore all ought to press after it, yet we do not affirm but *those, that have attained it in a measure, may, by the wiles and temptations of the enemy, fall into iniquity, and lose it sometimes, if they be not watchful, and do not diligently attend to that of God in the heart.* And we doubt not but many good and holy men, who have arrived to everlasting life, have had divers ebbings and flowings of this kind, for though every sin weakens a man in his spiritual condition, yet it doth not so as to destroy him altogether, or render him incapable of rising again.
Lastly, though I affirm that after a man hath arrived to such a condition in which a man may not sin, he yet may sin; I will nevertheless not deny but there may be a state attainable in this life, in which to do righteousness may become so natural to the regenerate soul, that in the stability of this condition they can not sin. Others may perhaps speak more certainly of this state, as having arrived to it. For me, I shall speak modestly, as acknowledging myself not to have arrived at it; yet I dare not deny it, for that it seems so positively to be asserted by the apostle, in these words (1 John 3:9), "He that is born of God sinneth not, neither can he, because the seed of God remaineth in him."[1423]

[1423]Barclay, *Apology*, Eighth Proposition, § 2, 205-206. Wesley abridged Barclay under the title *Serious Considerations on Absolute Predestination: Extracted from a Late Author.* However, Wesley omitted the passages from Barclay where he asserted that the light in every man meant Christ was already present in every heart [McGonigle, *Sufficient Saving Grace*, 133-134]. There is some question regarding whether George Fox held to total depravity. He wrote that he was renewed into the image of God so that he measured up to the state in which Adam was before his fall. Then he was taken by the Spirit into a state more steadfast than Adam's innocence before he fell [*Journal of George Fox*,1:28; Flew, *Idea of Perfection*, 290].

After categorizing Quaker teaching on Christian perfection as a combination

Quaker theology taught that it is possible to attain immediate union with God, which amounted to perfection. This perfection should not be confused with any office, but was based on the true glory of humanity. Concerning the difference between Quaker teaching and Methodist teaching, Wesley wrote,

> Here there is a difference. The Scriptures are the touchstone whereby Christians examine all, real or supposed, revelations. In all cases they appeal "to the law and to the testimony," and try every spirit thereby.[1424]

Emanuel Swedenborg (1688-1722), was a Swedish scientist and mystic. He attempted to prove through scientific means that the universe had a spiritual structure. For twenty-seven years he claimed direct contact with angels and departed spirits, having visions both while awake and asleep. He eventually founded the Church of the New Jerusalem. Wesley recorded in his *Journal*,

> I sat down to read and seriously consider some of the writings of Baron Swedenborg. I began with huge prejudice in his favor, knowing him to be a pious man, one of a strong understanding,

---

of mysticism and Arminianism, Pope cited some extracts from Barclay's *Apology* which "show how high it is and how much nearer to the Methodist doctrine than any other" [*Higher Catechism* , 273]. Claude Thompson said that Barclay's seventh proposition comes nearest to the doctrine held by the Methodists ["Witness of American Methodism,"168; however I think he mean the eighth proposition]. Yet in his *Compendium* Pope categorized the Quakers as among the best representatives of modern mysticism. He felt that Barclay regarded the new birth as a developing process [3:75-76]. Rufus Jones maintained that Barclay introduced a quietist, passive mysticism to Quakerism and that Fox exemplified a more dynamic active mysticism ["Introduction,"xii].

[1424]Wesley, "Letter to a Person Lately Joined with the People Called Quakers,"*Works*, 10:178. William Law held many views in common with the Quakers, such as the "inward light," but wrote five letters to a young lady to persuade her not to leave the Church of England and join the Quakers. George Croft Cell catalogued the strong language Wesley used in warning against Quaker mysticism and concluded that these warnings are found in all his writings, sermons, Journals, Letters, Monographs, in every period of his ministry from 1736 to 1791 [*Rediscovery of John Wesley*, 117].

Platt concluded that the Quakers held a mediating position between antinomian indifference and ascetic discipline. He described them as evangelical and teaching a Christian type of mystical perfection ["Perfection," 9:735].

> of much learning, and one who thoroughly believed himself. But I could not hold out long. Any one of his visions puts his real character out of doubt. He is one of the most ingenious, lively, entertaining madmen that ever set pen to paper. But his waking dreams are so wild, so far remote both from Scripture and common sense, that one might as easily swallow the stories of Tom Thumb or Jack the Giant-killer.[1425]

In 1782 Wesley wrote, "True, his tales are often exceeding lively, and as entertaining as the tales of the fairies: But I dare not give up my Bible for them; and I must give up one or the other. If the preceding extracts are from God, then the Bible is only a fable: But if 'all Scriptures are given by inspiration of God,' then let these dreams sink into the pit from whence they came."[1426]

Wesley asserted that Swedenborg borrowed many of his ideas from Jacob Behmen (1575-1624).[1427] Late in life William Law became fascinated with the writings of Jacob Behmen and after his death a translation of Behmen's works was published in four volumes with Law's name on the title page. He utilized chemical and Latin phrases and couched his teaching in allegorical symbols. Watson concluded, "The essential obscurity of the subjects indeed he could not remedy. If they were understood by the author himself, he is probably the only one who ever made that attainment."[1428] In 1780 Wesley concluded,

> I allow he wrote many truths; but none that would have appeared at all extraordinary, had he thrown aside his hard words, and used plain and common language. . . . The whole of Behmenism, including both phrase and sense, is useless. It stuns and astonishes its admirers. It fills their heads, but it does not change

---

[1425]Wesley, *Journal*, 28 February 1770. Wesley felt that a fever he had really introduced him into the society of lunatics [*Journal*, 8 December 1771; see also *Journal*, 22 April 1779].

[1426]Wesley, "Thoughts on the Writings of Baron Swedenborg," *Works*, 13:425-448; see also Wesley, "Account of Baron Swedenborg," 46-49; Watson, *Dictionary*, 878-880. Watson concluded that no one except Mohammed claimed to have such extensive correspondence with the invisible world. See also Van Baalen, *Chaos of Cults*, 177-187 where the author identified Swedenborgianism as a type of gnosticism.

[1427]The German spelling was Böhme.

[1428]Watson, *Dictionary*, 145.

> their hearts. It makes no eminent Christians. For many years I have diligently inquired concerning the grand patrons of it. And I have found none of them who were burning and shining lights; none who adorned the doctrine of God our Savior.[1429]

In his *Journal* Wesley objected to the mystic writers on three grounds:

1. The chief of them do not appear to me to have any conception of Church communion. Again, they slight not only works of piety, the ordinances of God, but even works of mercy. And yet most of them, yea all that I have seen, hold justification by works. In general, they are "wise above what is written."

2. Most of them are of a dark, shy, reserved, unsociable temper. And that they are apt to despise all who differ from them as carnal, unenlightened men.

3. I object to their whole phraseology. It is both unscriptural and affectedly mysterious. I say, "affectedly." For this does not necessarily result from the nature of the things spoken of. St. John speaks as high and as deep things as Jacob Behmen. Why then does not Jacob speak as plain as him?[1430]

While the name of Behmen and Swedenborg may not be known in our day, the influence of mystics was passed on to a new generation through Thomas Upham (1799-1872). Led into experience of perfect love by Phoebe Palmer, Upham pioneered the integration of psychology to holy living. Upham believed that God was interested in man's harmony, happiness, and holiness. He taught that desires for security, knowledge, recognition, curiosity, and gregariousness were not exterminated but rather sanctified and disciplined. Yet he emphasized the necessity of suffering in the sanctifying process.

> Whether he suffers or does not suffer, the throne of peace is erected in the centre of his soul. Wretchedness and joy are alike. He welcomes sorrow, even the deepest sorrow of the heart, with

---

[1429]Wesley, "Thoughts Upon Jacob Behmen," *Works*, 9:511-514; Wesley, "Thoughts Upon Jacob Behmen," 268-274. Wesley concluded that Behmen was not a theosopher, but a "demonosopher" [*Works*, 9:518]. Thomas Bromley, a follower of Behmen, taught that marriage was unfit for perfect Christians [*Way to the Sabbath of Rest*, 53-55].

[1430]Wesley, *Journal*, 5 February 1764.

as warm a gush of gratitude, as he welcomes happiness, if the will of God is accomplished.[1431]

The professor of moral philosophy for 43 years at Bowdoin College in Maine, Upham's most well known title was *Principles of the Interior Life.* He contended that the human will, as well as human desires and powers, actually died at the moment of sanctification. Palmer disagreed with him in a series of letters, claimed that God did not destroy human nature but rather purified it.[1432] Palmer also expressed concern that he was moving beyond the clear teachings of the Scripture concerning the possibilities of "divine union."[1433] Upham connected the holiness teaching of his day with the experience of Catholic mystics such as Fénelon, Guyon, and Molinos, producing a psychological analysis of the sanctified life.[1434] Dieter concluded that Upham "really assimilated Quietism to Wesleyanism."[1435]

Upham advocated an inward quietness or stillness and self-annihilation which resulted in nothingness or the loss of the will. "We have no pleasure of our own; we have no desires of our own; we have no will of our own." Therefore, temptation loses all it appeal.[1436]

[1431]Upham, *Principles of the Interior Life*, 109. However, Wesley observed that even "Our Lord Himself desired ease in pain" [*Works*, 11:379].

[1432]Smith, *Revivalism and Social Reform*, 144; White, "Holy Spirit Can and Cannot Do," 108.

[1433]Wheatley, *Life and Letters of Phoebe Palmer*, 518-523. However, the thesis of Heath is that Palmer's theology was developed in light of her mystical experiences ["*Via Negativa*," 87-111]. According to Heath, Palmer should be understood as a mystic. However, Palmer's concern was with Upham's antinomian forms of mysticism which emphasized a third work of grace and the death of the will [Heath, *Naked Faith*, 36-37].

[1434]In particular see Uphan, *Principles of the Interior*; see also Warfield, *Studies in Perfectionism*, 2:337-459.

[1435]Dieter, *Holiness Revival of the Nineteenth Century*, 48.

[1436]*Principles of the Interior*, 364-365. This led some of Palmer's disciples to conclude that every desire in the heart of the perfected Christian comes from God. Sin is impossible since the believer is united with God. Therefore ordinary spiritual discipline is not necessary and anything which attracts the believer is right. Therefore, the believer is free to do anything. If that believer feels like breaking one of the ten commandments, God is leading him into "sin" for His own greater glory. Of course,

Upham also taught a third stage of spiritual experience beyond justification and sanctification, which he called divine union. "The divine mind brings the human mind into a state that is free not only of desires and passions but of unnecessary and wandering thoughts."[1437] He frequently implied that the human will could be so absorbed into the divine mind that we could become oblivious to natural desire.

More recently Evelyn Underhill has argued for Christian mysticism. Initially an atheist, in her spiritual quest, Evelyn visited both English and Roman churches. After visiting at the convent of Perpetual Adoration, Evelyn was converted "quite suddenly once and for all by an overpowering vision, which had really no specific Christian element but yet convinced me that the Catholic religion was true. It was so tightly bound up with Roman Catholicism that I had no doubt . . . that the Church was my ultimate home."[1438]

Her book, *Mysticism: A Study in Nature and Development of Spiritual Consciousness* (1911) provided a general introduction to the subject. A certain type of mind has always reached out to the Absolute through religion, in pain, and in the appreciation of beauty. *Mysticism* is considered a classic and was used to introduce Protestants to Catholic mystics. The second part of her book contained a detailed study of the nature and development of man's spiritual consciousness. This part was called "The Mystic Way" and it contained records of mystical experience. Instead of the usual trajectory of purgation, illumination, and union Underhill mapped five sections: the awakening of self, the purgation of self, Illumination, the Dark Night, and the Unitive Life.

The modern contemplative spirituality/Emergent Church movement attempts to blend Universalism as well as New Age belief and practice with the Christian faith. Robert Tuttle, after warning against gnostic dualism, new age pantheism, and occult tendencies with "pop" mysticism, pointed out that the great Christian mystics emphasized that God is present and at work.[1439]

Joseph H. Smith concluded that mysticism was too vague and indistinct, that it savors too much of merit of works, and that it tends to abstraction from the world. In contrast the perfection taught by Scripture is clear, is by faith alone,

---

Palmer rejected such conclusions [White, "Holy Spirit Can and Cannot Do," 112].

[1437]Salter, *Spirit and Intellect*,105; see also Salter, "Mysticism in American Wesleyanism," 101.

[1438]Cropper, *Life of Evelyn Underhill*, 29.

[1439]Tuttle, *Mysticism in the Wesleyan Tradition*, 167-183.

and does not take us out of the world but send us forth into the world.[1440]

7. Imputed righteousness and the Reformation

The Protestant Reformers asserted that mankind was so sinful that we can never be delivered from sin in this life. Any holiness, then, is positional or imputed. Thus, the doctrine of imputed righteousness was a reaction against sacramentalism. Having rejected salvation by works and the doctrine of purgatory, Lutherans asked how is it possible for the imperfect to enter heaven. The obedience of Christ is imputed or reckoned to our account so that a person who is morally impure is accounted as holy.

It is sometimes asserted that the active and passive righteousness of Christ is imputed to believers. The active obedience of Christ refers to his sinless life, while the passive obedience of Christ refers to his atoning death. An emphasis on the imputation of both active and passive righteousness of Christ leads to antinomianism. Daniel Steele wrote,

> Theologians who state the doctrine of the atonement with proper safeguards, are careful to limit its vicarious efficacy to the *passive* obedience of the Son of God, His sufferings and death. His *active* obedience constitutes no part of His substitutional work. The germ of Antinomianism is found in the inclusion of the latter in the atonement.[1441]

Sutcliffe concluded that if the active and passive righteousness of Christ is imputed to us, we do no need the sanctifying grace of the Holy Spirit to make us righteous.[1442] Fletcher explained that we are made righteous, not by speculative imputation of the works of Christ, but by being made partakers of the divine nature, begotten of God, and clothed with righteousness and true holiness.[1443] Watson concluded that imputation is never used in scripture "in the sense of accounting the actions of one person to have been performed by another." Instead, the imputation of righteousness is the non-imputation, or pardon, of

---

[1440]Smith, *Pauline Perfection*, 11.

[1441]Steele, *Antinomianism Revived*, 21.

[1442]Sutcliffe, *Commentary*, 2:452-453.

[1443]Fletcher, *Works*, 1:308.

sin.[1444]

Our standing in Christ may be very different from our actual state. Flew observed that among German theologians the term *Perfektionismus* (*perfectionism*) was almost always a term of reproach.[1445] For Luther the emphasis was not on being made holy, but on being accounted holy.[1446]

Aurelius Augustine

Augustine, in his *Exposition of certain Propositions in the Epistle to the Romans* and in his book addressed to Simplicianus, Bishop of Milan, made two assertions: that Romans 7 must be understood as relating to a man under the law and that this chapter must not be understood as relating to a man under grace. Summers declared "the most enlightened commentators, ancient and modern are agreed that the apostle here is not speaking of himself for that would be contrary to the whole scope of his discourse."[1447]

Chris Bounds observed that as Augustine grew older his interpretation of Romans 7 changed. Initially, Augustine interpreted the subject of Romans 7 as one "under the law, prior to grace." Some twenty years later Augustine held that

---

1444Watson, *Theological Institutes*, 2:224; 241.

1445Flew, *Idea of Perfection*, 244.

1446Recently Finnish scholars at the University of Helsinki have argued that Luther's views on salvation are much closer to the Easter Orthodox doctrine of theosis. For them Luther's doctrine of justification is participation in Christ, not just legal imputation [Braaten and Jensen, *Union with Christ*]. This theory has not gained broad acceptance.

1447Summers, *Treatise on Sanctification*, 94. Summers cited Samuel Thomas Bloomfield as his authority. Bloomfield had written,

> Augustin, and most of the early *modern* Commentators (especially of the Calvinistic school) maintain that the Apostle here speaks of *himself*, and of *regenerate* Christians. But the ancient Commentators, and the later modern ones are of the opinion that he speaks of the *unregenerate*, and consequently *per* μετασχηματισμὸν, as before [*Greek Testament*, 2:44].

Bloomfield said that consequently by means of a figure of speech Paul transferred himself to before his conversion. Bloomfield's observation is confirmed by Bray, *Romans*, 189-190.

Romans 7 was Paul's personal testimony of Christian experience, as well as every individual under grace.[1448]

Yet Augustine regarded Romans 7 as the Christian's struggle with concupiscence, not the act of sinning. It was not until Jerome that we have any record of a theologian who attempts to use Romans 7 to justify his own personal lapses into sin. Jerome wrote

> For we do not what we would but what we would not; the soul desires to do one thing, the flesh is compelled to do another. If any persons are called righteous in scripture...they are called righteous according to that righteousness mentioned in the passage I have quoted: "A just man falleth seven times and rises up again,"...Zachariah the father of John who is described as a righteous man sinned in disbelieving the message sent to him and was at once punished with dumbness. Even Job, who at the outset of his history is spoken of as perfect and upright and uncomplaining, is afterwards proved to be a sinner both by God's words and by his own confession. If Abraham, Isaac, and Jacob, the prophets also and the apostles were by no means free from sin and if the finest wheat had chaff mixed with it, what can be said of us of whom it is written: "What is the chaff to the wheat, saith the Lord?"[1449]

Jerome by his own admission was a man prone to sin. In a discussion with Ctesiphon which involved Romans 7 he confessed "Yet, to lay bare my own weakness, I know that I wish to do many things which I ought to do and yet cannot. For while my spirit is strong and leads me to life my flesh is weak and draws me to death."[1450]

The debate with Pelagius around A. D. 419, however, drove Augustine to an extreme pessimism. Augustine over-reacted to the Pelagian heresy, which taught the perfectibility of human nature through the exercise of human will, and retracted his original position. He reinterpreted Romans 7 to be the highest state of Christian experience. In his debate with Pelagius, Augustine retracted the

---

[1448]Bounds, "Augustine's Interpretation of Romans 7:14-25," 20-35.

[1449]Jerome, *Letter* to Rusticas (A. D. 406) 122:3. *NPNF*, Second Series, 6:228-229.

[1450]Jerome, *Letter* to Ctesiphon (A. D. 415) 133:9. *NPNF*, Second Series, 6:278.

second position, but never denied the first. In other words, he applied the chapter to both categories. However, when Augustine allowed that this chapter might apply to the regenerate, he interpreted it as describing concupiscence or sexual lust and not the actual commitment of sin by the regenerate.

By reducing original sin to sexual desire, Augustine perpetuated the Greek concept that the human body is sinful. Augustine was fascinated with the inability of men to control their libidos.[1451] Augustine never managed to go beyond his early neo-Platonistic philosophy. For Augustine, all sexual activity, even marital sex, is tainted with sin.

For nine years Augustine was a disciple of Manichaean philosophy. Mani was a Persian who lived in the third century. He developed a dualism from ancient Babylonian mythology which resulted in a separation from the evil in the world. While this asceticism was possible for only a few, it was marked by three signs: the mouth was sealed against unclean food and speech; the hand was kept from unclean occupation; and the breast was to be guarded from impure thought, including desire for sexual intercourse, even in marriage.

Harnack said that Augustine became a Manichaean because of his sense of sin and because "he did not get past the idea that Catholic doctrine held God to be the originator of sin."[1452] He never threw off the influence of that teaching.

Greathouse wrote that Augustine's pessimistic doctrine of original sin, with its notion of ineradicable concupiscence has been the single greatest foe of the doctrine of Christian perfection. "The church has found it almost impossible to rid itself of the feeling that carnality is virtually synonymous with sexual desire. The New Testament knows no such identification of human nature with sin. . . . The essence of original sin is not lust, but 'pride, whereby we rob God of his inalienable right, and idolatrously usurp his glory.'"[1453]

Sigmund Freud traced everything back to a basic sex drive and created a form of biological determinism based on the survival of the fittest. For Freud guilt was a primitive relic lingering from the primal horde. Augustine also traced

---

[1451]Jacobs, *Original Sin*. According to Jacobs, Augustine's define of universal depravity is "curiously liberating." If we are all sinners, there can be no false optimism that we can live holy. Thus, we are all dependant upon divine grace.

[1452]Harnack, *Monasticism*, 110; 253.

[1453]Greathouse, *From the Apostles to Wesley,* 9; 64; 69-70; 110. Greathouse cited Wesley, "Original Sin," Sermon #44, 2.7. See also Dunning, *Grace, Faith and Holiness*, 389-390; Taylor, *Theological Formulation*, 3:94; Wynkoop, *Theology of Love*, 49; 251.

everything back to human sexuality and sought unsuccessfully to repress it. The result was a determinism based on the inevitability of sin. Freud sought the freedom to express human sexuality, but sought unsuccessfully to repress the guilt associated with sinful behavior. The Apostle Paul traces the problem of mankind to the Fall and our sinful nature and does not reduce our sinful nature to sexuality. Christian perfection is not the eradication of desire, but the discipline of every human desire and submission of God's standard of holiness as stated in his law.

Sexual desire must be disciplined and channeled into the confines of marriage. While we are tempted through our sexual desires and that vulnerability can easily lead to sins of immorality, sexual desire, in and of itself, is not sin.[1454] By viewing all sexual desire as sin, Augustine made popular the view that this struggle, described in Romans 7, would continue until death, even in the regenerate. "No one in this life can be so privileged that there should not be in his members a law fighting against the law of his mind."[1455] Augustine exempted no one except Jesus and his mother, indicting even the apostles.[1456] Augustine is famous for the phrase concerning the human state *non posse non peccare* (not able not to sin).

In a letter to Boniface, written in A. D. 418, Augustine warned that he should not believe he was free from sin as long as he was in this life. To support his statement, Augustine quoted from the Septuagint translation of Job 7:1, "Is not the life of man upon earth a life of temptation?" Yet liability to temptation does not necessitate bondage to sin.[1457]

While Augustine felt that God permits the continuance of sin for the discipline of the soul, Pope objected that this plea sounds very much like continuing in sin that grace may abound."[1458] Yet while the struggle still remains,

---

[1454]"Augustine, and some of 'the fathers,' regarded sin as inseparably connected with carnal desires, seemingly not excepting those which are natural and necessary to human propagation" [Lowrey, *Possibilities of Grace*, 142]. See the discussion by Leclerc, *Discovering Christian Holiness*, 212-213.

[1455]Augustine, *Retractions*, 1.19; quoted by Flew, *Idea of Perfection*, 208.

[1456]Augustine, *On Nature and Grace*, § 41-42; *NPNF*, 5:135. See the retraction at ftnt #850.

[1457]Augustine, *Letter* 189. *NPNF*, First Series, 1:554.

[1458]Pope, *Compendium*, 3:73. Pope was referring to Rom 6:1.

there is a relative perfection possible in this life.[1459] Augustine adopted Cyprian's statement, "There is one perfection in this world, another after this is completed." Flew concluded that his whole theology is essentially perfectionist because his thesis is the *summum bonum* or the final blessedness of man.[1460]

Augustine held that the goal of life was to know God in conscious communion. So long as man is on the earth, that love is capable of increase. Thus, in a letter to Jerome, Augustine concluded that perfection is never perfectly attained here below.[1461] Perkins observed that no man ever made a more strenuous effort to attain the state of perfection than Augustine, but that he did not distinguish between evangelical perfection and the beatific vision. This prevented him from perceiving that Christ has brought a salvation which is appropriate and sufficient for this life, and in the flesh, whatever further salvation beyond the world and apart from the flesh may be implicit in it. Thus Augustine transferred the Christian ideal to the next life.[1462]

From Augustine to Aquinas, the Western writers across the next eight centuries tended to echo the conclusions of Augustine.[1463] Thus, the premise is often accepted that to be human is to be sinful. Millard Erickson asked if Jesus could be fully human if he never sinned. Is the humanity of Jesus the same as ours if free from the sin nature? He said that for some, to be human by definition is to sin.[1464]

Bassett concluded that Augustine contributed to the doctrine of entire sanctification by insisting that God's perfect love is present in us by the Spirit. But Augustine militated against the doctrine by confusing it with justification and making it imputed, by identifying humanity with sinfulness, and by associating

---

[1459]See the summary by Flew, *Idea of Perfection*, pp. 208-209; Gregory, *Perfect in Christ Jesus*, 36-38. Yet see George Peck, *Christian Perfection*, 106.

[1460]Flew, *Idea of Perfection*, 193.

[1461]Augustine, *Letters*, 167.4.15; written about A. D. 415; *NPNF*, 1:537.

[1462]Perkins, *Evangelical Perfection*, 162-166. The beatific vision refers to a perfect knowledge of God as we behold him in heaven. Yet according to 1 John 3:2-3 those who anticipate this hope purify [*hagnizo*] themselves as God is pure [*hagnos* - the noun form of the verb just used]. Yet Augustine denies that we can be pure and holy in this life.

[1463]Flew, *Idea of Perfection*, 217.

[1464]Erickson, *Christian Theology*, 2:719-720.

sanctification so closely with good works.[1465] After his debate with Pelagius, Augustine wrote this retraction around A. D. 427 which did not carry the influence of some of his more negative statements:

> We do not think that the Apostles on this earth were exempt from the struggle of the flesh against the Spirit. But we believe that these promises can be fulfilled here just so far as they were fulfilled according to our belief in the Apostles, that is to say in the measure of human perfection in which perfection is possible in this life.[1466]

Pope's conclusion was that Augustine was not an opponent of the doctrine of entire sanctification, but that he was bounded by a false interpretation of certain sayings of Scripture and by an excessive dread of Pelagianism.[1467] According to Flew, Augustine taught a relative perfection in this life. Augustine seems to be of two minds. Within his writings he can be found to say that no one is perfect in this life. Elsewhere he declared there is a perfection is this life.[1468] Augustinian theology, as advanced by Calvin, however, tended to emphasize Christian imperfection.

Martin Luther

In the sixteenth century Luther taught that we are justified through the righteousness of Christ imputed to believers. He called this an alien righteousness. "Our faith depends solely on Christ. He alone is righteous, and I am not."[1469] Luther taught that man was at the same time just and yet sinful (*simul justus et peccator*). Luther wrote,

> A Christian is at the same time a sinner and a saint; he is at once bad and good. For in our own person we are in sin, and in our

---

[1465]Bassett, *Historical Development*, 107.

[1466]Augustine, *Retractions*, 1.19; quoted by Flew, *Idea of Perfection*, 208; Greathouse, *From the Apostles to Wesley*, 68.

[1467]Pope, *Compendium*, 3:70-73.

[1468]Flew, *Idea of Perfection*, 208-209.

[1469]"Lectures on Titus," in *Luther's Works*, 29:41.

own name we are sinners. But Christ brings us another name in which there is forgiveness of sin, so that for His sake our sin is forgiven and done away. Both then are true. There are sins ... and yet there are not sins. The reason is that for Christ's sake, God will not see them. They exist for my eyes; I see them, and feel them, too. But Christ is there who bids me preach that I am to repent...and then believe in the forgiveness of sin in His name... . Where such faith is, therefore, God no longer sees sin.[1470]

Luther explained,

Original sin, after regeneration, is like a wound that begins to heal; though it be a wound, yet it is in course of healing, through it still runs and is sore. So original sin remains in Christians until they die, yet itself is mortified and continually dying. Its head is crushed in pieces, so that it cannot condemn us.[1471]

Thus Luther declared that

the saints are always aware of their sin and seek righteousness from God in accordance with his mercy. And for this very reason, they are regarded as righteous by God. Thus in their own eyes (and in reality!) they are sinners; but in the eyes of God they are righteous, because he reckons them as such on account of their confession of their sin. In reality they are sinners; but

---

[1470]Quoted by Warfield, *Perfectionism*, 1:116. Emil Brunner followed the same doctrine as Luther's [Brunner, *Divine Imperative*, 30; 199]. Yet both Brunner and Barth rejected Luther's emphasis upon a transformed life. The neo-orthodox position of Brunner and Barth sees redemption entirely as a forensic act of God which ignores man both in the process and the result [Cox, *Perfection*, 84]. The emerging church shares a conversion narrative, "not a story of salvation in the strict sense, but of having been delivered from a small life into a big life" [Crouch, "Emergent Mystique," 38]. There is an implicit universalism in Barth and the emerging church which de-emphasizes salvation. Here the emphasis Crouch describes is a kingdom-consciousness. While this corporate mentality is legitimate, one cannot enter the kingdom except through personal salvation.

[1471]Luther, *Table Talk*, § 223; 157-158.

> they are righteous by the imputation of a merciful God. They are unknowingly righteous, and knowingly sinners. They are sinners in fact, but righteous in hope.[1472]

Luther taught "that sin and the sinful passions remain in us till the body is turned into ashes, and a new glorified body is raised up which is free from passion and sin."[1473] And Luther taught that no one on earth loved God and his neighbor as the law requires. Perfection of love will be a reality in the future life.[1474] Luther taught, "The sins of a Christian are for his good; and if he had no sin, he would not be so well of, neither would prayer flow so well."[1475] Therefore, he advised that we sin boldly. In a letter from Luther to Melanchthon, Luther advocated the breaking of vows of celibacy which held men and women in monastic orders. While I have no problem with his specific advice concerning unscriptural vows, Luther's letter closed with this more general advice, which is antinomian and usually has been translated, "sin boldly."

> Be a sinner, and let your sins be strong, but let your trust in Christ be stronger, and rejoice in Christ who is the victor over sin, death, and the world. We will commit sins while we are here, for this life is not a place where justice resides. We, however, says Peter (2 Peter 3:13) are looking forward to a new heaven and a new earth where justice will reign. It suffices that through God's glory we have recognized the Lamb who takes away the sin of the world. No sin can separate us from Him, even if we were to kill or commit adultery thousands of times each day. Do you think such an exalted Lamb paid merely a small price with a meager sacrifice for our sins? Pray hard for you are quite a

---

[1472]Cited by McGrath, *Reformation Thought*, 107.

[1473]Luther, *Romans*, 84; see also his 1535 commentary on Gal 3:25, "Therefore the defect is not in Christ; it is in us, because we have not yet shed the flesh, to which sin clings as long as we live"[*Luther's Works*, 26:349].

[1474]Bassett, *Historical Development*, 163. Here Bassett cited from Luther's exposition of 1 John 4:18.

[1475]Bogatzky, *Golden Treasury*, 328.

sinner.[1476]

Wesley concluded,

> Many who have spoken and written admirably well concerning justification had no clear conception, nay, were totally ignorant, of the doctrine of sanctification. Who has wrote more ably than Martin Luther on justification by faith alone? And who was more ignorant of the doctrine of sanctification, or more confused in his conceptions of it? In order to be thoroughly convinced of this, of his total ignorance with regard to sanctification, there needs no more than to read over, without prejudice, his celebrated comment on the Epistle to the Galatians.[1477]

> In his preface to his 1535 lectures on Galatians, Luther declared,

> "Although I am a sinner according to the Law, judged by the righteousness of the Law, nevertheless I do not despair. I do not die, because Christ lives who is my righteousness and my eternal and heavenly life. In that righteousness and life I have no sin, conscience, and death. I am indeed a sinner according to the present life and its righteousness, as a son of Adam where the Law accuses me, death reigns and devours me. But above this life I have another righteousness, another life, which is Christ, the Son of God, who does not know sin and death but is righteousness and eternal life. For His sake this body of mine will be raised from the dead and delivered from the slavery of the Law and sin, and will be sanctified together with the spirit."
> Thus as long as we live here, both remain. The flesh is accused, exercised, saddened, and crushed by the active righteousness of the Law. But the spirit rules, rejoices, and is saved by passive righteousness, because it knows that it has a Lord sitting in heaven at the right hand of the Father, who has abolished the Law, sin, and death, and has trodden all evils underfoot, has led

---

[1476]Luther, *Saemmtliche Schriften*, Letter #99, 1 August 1521, Vol. 15, cols. 2585-2590.

[1477]Wesley, "On God's Vineyard," Sermon #107, 1.5; see also Wesley, *Journal*, 15 June 1741.

them captive and triumphed over them in Himself (Col. 2:15).[1478]

In his commentary on Galatians Luther declared that the believer "should not presume that 'by-and-by' he will be changed thoroughly into a new man. He will keep some of his old vices cleaving to him, however good and perfect a Christian he is. . . . The Christian man hath a body, in whose members sin dwelleth and warreth. This sin is the root and the tree, rooted in the baptized flesh of every Christian and holds it captive. It forces him to do wrong."[1479]

Köberle expressed the Lutheran interpretation that Galatians 5:17 taught a dualism in which the believer is always dead and alive at the same time.[1480] Luther himself said in his comments on Galatians 5:17-18 that it was wicked to make excuses for Paul, who himself said that he was sinful. Paul describes the conflict going on between the flesh and the Spirit in his own body. No one should be surprised or frightened when he feels this conflict of the flesh against the Spirit in his body. By the Spirit he should fight back and say, "I am a sinner, and I am aware of my sin; for I have not yet put off my flesh, to which sin will cling as long as it lives." When his flesh impels him to sin, he is aroused and incited to seek forgiveness of sins through Christ and to embrace the righteousness of faith, which would otherwise not have been regarded as so important or yearned for with such intensity. And so it is very beneficial if we sometimes become aware of the evil of our nature and our flesh. Even though he has sin and commits sin, he remains godly. In the godly, therefore, the Law does not dare accuse as sin that which truly is a sin against the Law.[1481] According to Luther, the Law is a snare of the harshest slavery, which Paul calls a "yoke" in Galatians 5:1. It is impossible for Christ and the Law to dwell in the heart at the same time.[1482] While Augustine over-reacted against Pelagius, Luther over-reacted against legalism.

Wesley objected to Luther's concept of the law as an evil power, along with sin, death, and the devil, which Christ conquered. Luther defined a Christian as one "to whom God imputeth not his sin," not as one who has no sin.[1483] In his

---

[1478]*Luther's Works*, 26:9.

[1479]Luther, *Galatians*, 164-165; 304.

[1480]Köberle, *Quest for Holiness*, 154.

[1481]Summary from *Luther's Works*, 27:70-77, from 1535 edition of Luther's Lectures on Galatians.

[1482]*Luther's Works*, 27:7; 17.

[1483]Luther, *Galatians*, 114.

Journal he declared he was "utterly ashamed" of Luther's *Commentary on Galatians*. "Here (I apprehend) is the real spring of the grand error of the Moravians. They follow Luther, for better, for worse. Hence their 'No works, no law, no commandments.'"[1484]

Yet Luther also wrote, "We say that justification is effective without works, not that faith is without works. For that faith which lacks fruit is not an efficacious but a feigned faith. It is one thing that faith justifies without works; it is another thing that faith exists without works."[1485]

In his struggle against antinomianism, Wesley rejected the idea that Christ fulfilled the law by proxy. "Wesley wanted to guard against any idea that Christ kept the law for us in any sense that would excuse the believer from obedience."[1486] The atonement satisfied the penalty, and not the demands of the law. Sanctification is the fulfillment of the moral law.[1487]

For Lutherans sanctification is the process of becoming what we are declared to be at justification. Köberle expressed Lutheran theology thus: "Because sin prevents us from ever attaining the perfect image of Christ, faith never comes to its full perfection either in knowledge or in the fulfillment of the divine purposes or commands."[1488] Luther took holiness out of the monastery and away from mysticism, but stopped short of emphasizing the transformation that necessarily flows from our faith relationship to Christ. Instead he accepted the

---

[1484]Wesley, *Journal*, 15 June 1741. See also Lindström, *Wesley and Sanctification*, 13; 75-76. The Moravians taught the only commandment in the New Testament is the command to believe.

[1485]*Luther's Works*, 34:175-176.

[1486]Cox, *Perfection*, 38.

[1487]Lindström, *Wesley and Sanctification*, p. 75. Warfield declared, "All perfectionist doctrines run into antinomianism" [*Perfectionism*, 1:94]. In his critique of perfectionism, Charles Hodge noted that it sometimes lapses into antinomianism, but Hodge exempted the Methodists from this observation [*Systematic Theology*, 3:258].

[1488]Köberle, *Quest for Holiness*, 163. While Köberle argued for a progressive sanctification, he said that the teaching of Romans 7 dismissed the delusion of a complete conquest of the old nature [p. 239]. Köberle declared that prayer and asceticism were the two powerful weapons of faith for the preservation of the life of the new man and for the mortification of the old [p. 194].

necessity of sin in this life.[1489] Yet because we groan on account of it, it becomes venial and is not imputed lest God should damn us for it.[1490]

> Luther's concept of *simul justus et peccator* is fundamental for a Lutheran understanding not only of justification but also of sanctification. Before God the person is totally justified and the same person is in himself and sees himself as a sinner. What is important in this understanding is the Latin word *simul,* at the same time, and not in a sequential sense as if one followed the other in point of time.
> But let it be immediately said that the Christian is never completely Christian. As sinner—and he never escapes his sin—he is subject to the civil and accusatory functions of the law, since the old man does not believe, has never believed, and will never believe. He is finally destroyed only in death. The unregenerate part, the Old Adam, is an enemy of God and must be threatened by the law to conform to outward standards. He must be reminded that he has offended God continually. Such outward conformity to the law by unbelievers or by the unbelieving part of Christians has nothing to do with sanctification. Fear of penalty or the fear of God's wrath can never be a motivation for performing works which are pleasing to God as signs of faith and flowing from the Holy Spirit. Works performed in the civil sphere are called good works because they contribute to the well-being and outward serenity of society.[1491]

Yet in his treatise *On Monastic Vows* (1521), Luther declared "the state of perfection is to be filled with faith and to be a despiser of death, life, glory and the whole world, and in fervent love to be the servant of all." Luther argues that this state is better attained in the *obedient* life of laity than in monastic

---

[1489]See discussions by Williams, *John Wesley's Theology Today*, 178; Flew, *Idea of Perfection*, 246.

[1490]Rupp, *Righteousness of God*, 178.

[1491]Scaer, "Sanctification in Lutheran Theology," 187; 185. Regarding *simul justus et peccator*, see pp. 367, 382, 402 of this book.

observances, since works have nothing to do with personal holiness.[1492]

Melanchthon went beyond Luther is recognizing both that the law requires perfection and that in Christ we have power to fulfil the law.[1493] Melanchthon saw sanctification as the fulfillment of the law. However, this fulfillment, as well as sanctification, will always be imperfect. The Augsburg Confession (1530) separated the language of Christian perfections from the idea of justification, especially the language of vows and counsels.

> For they also who attribute justification to their vows, attribute to their own works what properly belongs to the glory of Christ. . . . Christian perfection is this, to fear God sincerely, and again, to conceive great faith, and to trust on account of Christ that we have a God who is appeased; to ask and certainly to look for help from God in all our doings, according to our calling; and outwardly to do good works diligently, and to be subject to our calling. In these things doth true perfection and the true worship of God consist; it doth not consist in singleness of life, in beggery, or in vile apparel.[1494]

Ritschl attempted to develop a Lutheran doctrine of perfection, but admitted that he had only meager references in Lutheran theology. Furthermore, he failed to convince his critics of any Lutheran doctrine of perfection. Ritschl taught that Luther diverged from Paul by teaching that sin was unconquerable in this life. On the other hand, Ritschl concluded that Paul assumes that Christians need not sin.[1495] Harnack concluded that the Lutheran church "neglected far too much the moral problem, the *Be ye holy for I am holy*."[1496]

[1492]Luther, *Werke*, 8:584. Italics mine, to highlight that Luther had some expectation of righteous actions.

[1493]Flew, *Idea of Perfection*, 247. Yet Melanchthon concluded that Paul himself declared openly that he serves the law of sin [George Peck, *Christian Perfection*, 115-116].

[1494]Augsburg Confession, 2.6 in Schaff, *Creeds of Christendom*, 3:56-57.

[1495]Flew *Idea of Perfection*, 254-257; Warfield reacted to this view of Paul by Ritschl in *Perfectionism*, 1:133-136; 92, defending his own "miserable-sinner" Christianity from the hands of such rationalists.

[1496]Harnack, *History of Dogma*, 7:266-267.

Both Lutheran and Reformed churches agree on the continued sinfulness of the Christian. The Heidelberg Catechism (1563) declared that we increase our guilt daily and that the best works of Christians in this life are defiled with sin. A more modern Reformed catechism declares that all flesh is subject to sin. Even when men do good, they sin in the best things they do. A modern Lutheran liturgy declares, "We transgress Thy divine commandments unceasingly in thoughts, words and deeds."[1497]

John Calvin

Karl Barth wrote that Luther oriented his whole theology around the reality of the justification of the sinner, while Calvin oriented his whole theology around the sanctification of the same sinner.[1498]

While Luther insisted sanctification is "an alien holiness," Calvin saw the holiness of God as the source of our holiness. Yet the holiness that this moral transformation beings is not complete in this life.[1499] Thus for all three theologians, Luther, Calvin, and Barth, the man who is apprehended in the reconciling, justifying, sanctifying work of God in Christ, is still a sinner. "Barth finds it perfectly natural to continue to speak of the Christian as a sinner in the present tense."[1500] Barth described himself as a man who "has sinned, is sinning, and will sin."[1501] For Barth, holiness is not a possession or a state of being, it is a change in orientation. It is a calling and an encounter with God which results in covenant, but not necessarily moral improvement. The Church is still composed of sinners, even if they are disturbed sinners.[1502]

No passage of Scripture has been more frequently resorted to, for the purpose of furnishing proofs of the necessary continuance of indwelling sin, than

---

[1497]Warfield, *Perfectionism*, 1:118-121.

[1498]Barth, *Church Dogmatics*, 1/2:208.

[1499]Bassett, *Historical Development*, 176-177.

[1500]Spross, "Sanctification in Karl Barth," 71. Thus, Barth would give no credence to the view that sanctification can be entire [p. 72].

[1501]Barth, *Christian Life*, 12-13.

[1502]Barth, *Church Dogmatics*, 4/2:526-616. See Samuel Powell's discussion of Barth and sanctification in *Embodied Holiness*, 169-172; 184.

the statements made by Paul in Romans 7:14-25.[1503] John Calvin was influenced by Romans 7:25, which he interpreted to describe one who had been enlightened by the Spirit. Calvin concluded that believers never reach the goal of perfection in this life, but that God works an honest desire for it in our hearts. "As long as the faithful dwell in the flesh, they never arrive at the end of righteousness."[1504] Thus Calvin wrote, "We shall not find a single saint who, clothed with a mortal body, ever attained to such perfection as to love the Lord with all his heart, and soul, and mind, and strength."[1505]

Calvin taught that Christians are positionally sanctified at the time of conversion since "Christ justifies no one whom he does not at the same time sanctify."[1506] Yet although the process begins in this life, believers remain sinners until the time of their death.[1507] Thus, the emphasis is on positional sanctification, not progressive sanctification. We will always be dissatisfied with our sanctification. We have no holiness apart from Jesus Christ. Believers borrow their holiness from him by faith. He is our holiness.

Calvin believed "there is always sin in the saints, until they are freed from their mortal frame, because depraved concupiscence resides in their flesh." He held that "all human desires are evil." Thus he concluded, "Therefore, so long as we dwell in the prison of the body, we must constantly struggle with the vices of

---

[1503]Treffry, *Treatise on Christian Perfection*, 72.

[1504]*Calvin's Commentaries: Romans and Thessalonians*, 155. Calvin continued to say that he felt this passage was significant for condemning "that most pernicious dogma of the Purists (Cathari) which some turbulent spirits are attempting to revive at the present time." Gerrit J. tenZythoff explained that Calvin was reacting to Anabaptist perfectionism ["The Non-Perfectionism of John Calvin,"196-201]. In his *Treatise Against the Anabaptists* Calvin reacted to their doctrine of the ban. He referred to the Cathari, who held the fantasy, as do these poor dreamers today, looking for a church in which one could find no fault. Therefore, they separated themselves from all of Christianity in order not to be in any way soiled by the imperfections of others [*Treatises Against the Anabaptists and Against the Libertines*, 70-71]. Therefore, Calvin was not reacting against the personal pursuit of holiness, but against perfectionism as found in ecclesiastical primitivism.

[1505]Calvin, *Institutes*, 2.7.5.

[1506]Calvin, *Institutes*, 3.16.1.

[1507]Calvin, *Institutes*, 3.2.2.

our corrupt nature, and so with our natural disposition."[1508]

Yet Calvin exhorted, "In this earthly prison of the body, no man is supplied with strength sufficient to hasten in his course with due alacrity, while the greater number are so oppressed with weakness, that hesitating, and halting, and even crawling on the ground, they make little progress, let every one of us go as far as his humble ability enables him, and prosecute the journey once begun."[1509]

Calvin also declared, "For concupiscence never wholly dies or is extinguished in men, until, freed by death from the body of death, they have altogether laid aside their own nature. . . . For as long as we live shut up in this prison of the body, the remains of sin dwell in us."[1510]

This teaching is based on a dualistic view that anything physical is sinful, therefore the body is sinful and we will be sinful until we leave the body.[1511] Sin is practically inevitable because being finite is too closely identified with being sinful. The inclination to sin therefore is regarded as truly sin.

Neoplatonism viewed the body as the prison house of the soul. Pagan mystics prayed to be delivered from the flesh rather than from sin. While the biblical doctrine of the resurrection of the body prevented Christians from going that far, often they were inconsistent. In his *Genevan Confession of Faith*, Calvin declared that although we are regenerate,

> until we slough off this mortal body, there remains always in us much imperfection and infirmity, so that we always remain poor

---

[1508]Calvin, *Institutes*, 3.3.10; 12; 20. Roman Catholic theology holds that concupiscence is not sin unless actualized. For Augustine concupiscence was actually sin. Luther and the Reformers followed Augustine [Online: "Theology of Luther"]. Calvin deemed concupiscence itself to be sin and maintained that sin always exists in the saints until they are divested of the mortal body [*Institutes*, 3.3.10].

[1509]Calvin, *Institutes*, 3.6.5.

[1510]Calvin, *Institutes*, 4.15.11.

[1511]Bassett argued that Calvin did hold to a platonic view of the body. According to Bassett, Calvin did not actually view the body as evil; it is not the source but the occasion of sin [*Historical Development*, 171]. However, Greathouse accused Calvin of having a Platonic view of the body. Calvin quoted Plato immediately after his reference to dwelling in the prison of the body resulting in a constant struggle with the vices of our corrupt nature in *Institutes*, 3.3.20 [Greathouse, *From the Apostles to Wesley*, 94-95].

and wretched sinners before the face of God. And, however much we ought day by day to increase and grow in God's righteousness, there will never be plenitude or perfection while we live here.[1512]

Wesley objected that "sinful body" is never found in Scripture. "And as it is totally unscriptural, so it is palpably absurd. For no *body*, or matter of any kind, can be *sinful*: spirits alone are capable of sin. Pray, in what part of the body should sin lodge? It cannot lodge in the skin, it cannot be in the bones any more than in the hair or nails. Only the soul can be the seat of sin."[1513]

Yet in his *Institutes* Calvin declared that "we shall never reach the goal until we have laid aside the body of sin, and been completely united to the Lord. If any one chooses to give the name of perfection to the Saints, I shall not obstinately quarrel with him, provided he defines this perfection in the words of Augustine, 'When we speak of the perfect virtue of the saints, part of this perfection consists in the recognition of our imperfection both in truth and in humility.'"[1514]

According to Calvin, while there is no freedom from sin, the saints are free from guilt.[1515] Calvin explained, "Whatever is imperfect in them is covered by the perfection of Christ, and all their blemishes and pollutions are wiped away by his purity, so as never to come under the cognisance of the divine tribunal."[1516]

Calvinistic Exegesis

In 1665 William Gurnall wrote *The Christian in Complete Armour*. This exposition of Ephesians 6:11-20 runs over 1100 pages. From start to finish the way of sanctification is essentially the inner struggle of a man who is engaged in

---

[1512]*The Genevan Confession* (1536), ¶ 9. Peliken and Hotchkiss, *Creeds and Confessions*, 2:315.

[1513]Wesley, "On Perfection," Sermon #76, 2.9.

[1514]Calvin, *Institutes* 3.17.15. Calvin quoted Augustine, *A Treatise Against Two Letters of the Pelagians*, Book 3, ch. 19, *NPNF*, First Series, 5:411. Augustine argues for imperfection in chapters 14-22.

[1515]Calvin, *Institutes*, 3.3.11.

[1516]Calvin, *Institutes*, 3.17.8.

a bitter life and death struggle with the devil until his dying breath.[1517]

In 1668 John Owen wrote *The Nature, Power, Deceit, and Prevalency of the Remainders of Indwelling Sin in Believers*. He began the book by assuming that Paul described himself, and the condition of all who are regenerate in Romans 7. Two laws operate within the regenerate, the law of the Spirit of life *and* the law of sin. Although the law of sin has its rule broken and its strength weakened, yet it is still a law of great force and power. Anyone who contends against it shall know and find that it is present with them, that it is powerful in them. While this law remains *in* the believer, it is not *to* them, as it is to unbelievers.

Owen wrote that if grace is maintained in the believer, the will to do good prevails against the power of indwelling sin. But the believers *worst* condition, unwilling sin, is better than the sinners *best* condition, which is willing sin. Yet the law of sin dwells in the heart of the believer, where it maintains a rebellion against God all our days. Sometimes it has more strength, sometimes less, but it is always in rebellion as long as we live and may bring us into captivity, causing us to sin against our will. Since we carry this enmity against God in us all our days, we must be on guard constantly.

Owen admitted that a believer might be led captive for a season by some particular sin. It may have power over him as it seems to have done with many Old Testament saints, but after awhile the desire to be freed from the law of sin will produce a sigh and cry for deliverance. While God may even take the life of an unbeliever, to stop the progress of his sin, God does not judicially cut off and take away the life of any who are his.[1518]

While Calvin taught that the believer is wholly passive with regard to his effectual calling and regeneration, he is active in sanctification. This involves self denial and a total resignation of the whole man to the sovereign will of God.[1519] The believer's life is thus entirely engaged in mortification and vivification.[1520]

Owen also advocated mortification. According to Packer this is more than suppression or counteraction of the sinful impulse, "it is nothing less than a

---

[1517]Gurnall, *Christian in Complete Armour*.

[1518]*Works of John Owen*, 6:157-322. Henry Brockett observed that while Owen taught the "two natures" doctrine, he was quite clear that the seat of sin was not the physical body but the heart [*Scriptural Freedom from Sin*, 44-45].

[1519]Calvin, *Institutes*, 3.7.1-10.

[1520]Calvin, *Institutes*, 3.3.3.

gradual eradication of it."[1521] Owen taught, "The whole work is by degrees to be carried on towards perfection all our days."[1522]

Yet he also warned the fight with sin is a lifelong battle. Owen taught that sin is put to death through the work of the Spirit. The Spirit kills sin by causing our hearts to abound in grace and the fruits of the Spirit, by enabling us to walk after the Spirit, and by weakening and destroying by degrees the root of sin. No self endeavor, such as praying, fasting, watching, or meditation can accomplish mortification. When these human efforts wax cold and the sense of sin wears off, then mortification goes out the door and sin returns to its former dominion.

> Sometimes a soul thinks or hopes that it may through grace be utterly free from this troublesome inmate. Upon some secret enjoyment of God, some full supply of grace, some return from wandering, some deep affliction, some thorough humiliation, the poor soul begins to hope that is shall now be freed from the law of sin. But after a while . . . sin acts again, makes good its old station.[1523]

Martyn Lloyd-Jones taught that "sin still has power over the body even in the man who is 'in Christ.'" He equated "the body of sin" in Romans 6:6 with "the flesh" and saw no deliverance until the physical death of the body. Pope, however, wrote, "The notion that we are not finally separated from the evil adhering to our nature until we are separated from the flesh is a subtile relic of Gnosticism."[1524]

While "the old man" has died, according to Lloyd-Jones, we believe this has happened on the authority of Scripture even though "I may feel that I am a sinner, that sin is in me." Every time we fall into sin we must realize "that whether you have sinned or not, you are in Christ; that sin does not affect you yourself as a person, and that it cannot bring you again into its realm and reign; that sin only remains in your mortal body. . . . Why then do I sin? Because sin is in my members, because 'this body of sin' remains. . . . When a Christian sins he does not sin as a slave, but he sins as a free man who is choosing to do that which

---

[1521]Packer, *Quest for Godliness*, 200.

[1522]Owen, *Works*, 6:8.

[1523]Owen, *Works*, 4:204.

[1524]Pope, *Compendium*, 3:49.

is wrong." Yet we are never to doubt that "the old man" died, because it was not us, but only our body which sinned.[1525]

Thus the Christian sins inevitably, but never necessarily. R. C. Sproul declared, "We still sin, and we still sin wilfully but a Christian can never say that he had to sin. . . . Given the strength of the power of sin that still resides within us, along with the astronomical number of opportunities that we have to sin, it is inevitable that sooner or later, and most often it is sooner, we do succumb to sin."[1526] John Piper also stated that sin is inevitable, "But sooner or later, whether it's that sin or another, you are going to fall."[1527]

Yet Jude declared that God is able to keep us from falling (Jude 24). While it is always possible to sin it is also possible, by the grace of God, to not sin. Thus, sin is not inevitable. Either God or sin is sovereign. If God is sovereign, he has the power to deliver us from sin.

Charles R. Swindoll wrote, "We have been programmed to think, *I know I am going to sin, to fail . . . to fall short today. Since this is true I need to be ready to find cleansing.* You have not been programmed to yield yourself unto God as those who have power over sin. . . . Yes, I know there will be times when we may momentarily fail, but they will be the exceptions rather than the rule of our day. We are under new management."

However, twenty-some pages later Swindoll wrote, "I wish I could guarantee all of us full freedom from sin 365 days a year, but that is not possible — not so long as we are earthbound. Perpetual sinlessness (theologians call it 'sinless perfection') will not be ours to enjoy until we are given glorified bodies and we are at home in heaven. But the good news is that we don't have to sin on a constant, day-after-day basis. Grace has freed us to obey Christ."[1528]

Richard Haldane wrote that the believer dies to the guilt of sin, but not to the influence or power of sin. He argued that Romans 7 proves no believer is dead to the power of sin. Concerning the statement in Romans 6:2 that we are dead to sin, Haldane wrote, "The expression, then, dead to sin, does not in any degree relate to their *character* or *conduct*, but exclusively to their *state* before God."[1529] Thus sanctification is imputed and positional; it is demonstrated by the fact that

---

[1525]Lloyd-Jones, *New Man*, 61-80; 84; 92; 128; 153.

[1526]Sproul, *Gospel of God*, 112-113.

[1527]Piper, "Gutsy Guilt," 74.

[1528]Swindoll, *Grace Awakening*, 113-114; 137.

[1529]Haldane, *Romans*, 239-241.

believers no longer *want* to sin. Yet Abraham Kuyper declared that the body was so corrupted that there was no freedom from sin apart from freedom from the body.[1530]

In *The Holiness of God* Sproul emphasized transcendence, trauma, and struggle, concluding with Luther's phrase *simul justus et peccator*. Sproul emphasized imputed righteousness:

> That a saint is still a sinner is obvious. How then can he be just? The saint is just because he has been justified. In and of himself he is not just. He is made just in the sight of God by the righteousness of Christ. That is what justification by faith is about. When we put our personal trust for our salvation in Christ and in Him alone, then God transfers to our account all of the righteousness of Jesus. His justness becomes our when we believe in Him. It is a legal transaction. The transfer of righteousness is like an accounting transaction where no real property is exchanged. That is, God puts Jesus' righteousness in my account while I am still a sinner.[1531]

While Sproul admits this sound something like a fraud, like God is playing legal games, he declares that this is the gospel. "God sees us as righteous because we have been covered and clothed by the righteousness of Jesus."[1532] Sproul made no reference to sharing in God's holiness (Heb 12:10) or being made partakers of the divine nature (2 Peter 1:4).

Participation in the divine nature produces victory over sin. God's seed remains in us enabling us not to sin (1 John 3:9; 1 Peter 1:23). This is Peter's primary emphasis because of the clause which follows. The result of partaking of the divine nature is that we escape the corruption in the world caused by corrupt desires. When do we escape this corruption? Some theologies say only at death, but the aorist participle in 2 Peter 1:4 puts that escape in the past. According to 2:20 we escape the corruption of this world by knowing our Lord and Savior Jesus Christ. Therefore, the new birth enables us to live a victorious life, in contrast to the defeated life described in Romans 7.

Sproul began *Pleasing God* with a reference to the two-stage healing in

---

[1530]Kuyper, *Work of the Holy Spirit*, 450.

[1531]Sproul, *Holiness of God*, 212.

[1532]Sproul, *Holiness of God*, 213.

Mark 8. Sproul interpreted the blindness to illustrate our fallen state. After the first touch, the clouded vision indicated regeneration; yet the healed man still sinned. The second touch represented glorification. While Sproul conceded there may be progress in this life, sanctification is a lifelong progress. He regarded perfectionism, a second work of grace, or the second blessing as "a poisonous doctrine" and "a pious fraud."[1533]

B. B. Warfield described this Augustinian emphasis as "miserable-sinner Christianity." He wrote, "Though blessed with every spiritual blessing in the heavenlies in Christ, we are still in ourselves just "miserable sinners": "miserable sinners" saved by grace to be sure, but "miserable sinners" still, deserving in ourselves nothing but everlasting wrath. Warfield concluded that "Paul knows nothing of a sinless man in this life."[1534] Although writing on *God's Way of Holiness*, Horatius Bonar did not see how anyone could have thought that Romans 7 refers to the unregenerate condition or to a transition state while groping his way to rest.[1535]

As Everett Cattell noted, Warfield does not critique the theology of Wesley, but simply assumes him to be in error. Warfield defined sin as any lack of conformity to the law of God and held that the call to holiness was a call to absolute holiness which could only be attained in heaven. Cattell acknowledged that when the Wesleyan argues for relative perfection as attainable now, he is not oblivious to the absolute claims of God. While there is cleansing for the area of conscious motive, that is not the whole of life nor the whole of God's demand.

Calvinists may feel that Wesleyans have an inadequate view of sin and accuse them of teaching a sinless perfection. But Wesleyans may feel that there is a greater victory than Calvinists teach and accuse them of condoning sin. Cattell concluded, "It is no more fair to charge the responsible Calvinist leaders with antinomianism than it is for them to charge Arminians with sinless perfection."[1536]

Edwin H. Palmer declared that the spiritual life of the regenerate

> is often a sickly one. For it is a fact that the Christian still sins.

[1533]Sproul, *Pleasing God*, 23-24. Pope also referenced this second touch and compared it to the disciples in Acts 19 in which the twelve at Ephesus moved from the preparatory influences of the Spirit to regenerating grace (see p. 261).

[1534]Warfield, *Perfectionism*, 1:113-114; 301.

[1535]Bonar, *God's Way of Holiness.*

[1536]Cattell, "Keswick and Wesleyan," 266-267; 270.

> Sometimes he sins so much that it almost looks as if the new life had left him entirely, and he were dead again. But we know that he is not dead. His infirmities will not be unto death, nor are they incurable. On the contrary, these infirmities will gradually disappear. In the meantime, however, there is no doubt that he is really sick.

Palmer continued to explain that victory over sin occurs gradually through God's sanctifying work in us through the Spirit and through our action. Thus, sanctification is both a grace and a duty which is never completed in this life. "But there will be a marked and definite progress toward complete sanctification."[1537]

The Westminster Confession of Faith, Chapter XIII "Of Sanctification" declared that sanctification was imperfect in this life.

> This sanctification is throughout in the whole man, yet imperfect in this life, there abiding still some remnants of corruption in every part; whence arises a continual and irreconcilable war, the flesh lusting against the spirit, and the Spirit against the flesh. In which war, although the remaining corruption, for a time may much prevail; yet, though the continual supply of strength from the sanctifying Spirit of Christ, the regenerate part does overcome and so the saints grow in grace, perfecting holiness in the fear of God.[1538]

R. J. Rushdoony declared that this statement on sanctification was excellent as far as it goes, but it fails to specify precisely what the *way* of sanctification is." According to Rushdoony, "Man's *justification* is by the *grace* of God in Jesus Christ; man's *sanctification* is by means of the *law* of God."[1539]

[1537]Palmer, *Person and Ministry of the Holy Spirit*, 87-99.

[1538]Clark, *Sanctification*, 100. John Wesley deleted out of the Westminster Shorter Catechism material that delayed perfection until after death in his abridgement for the *Christian Library,* 25:187-222 (2nd ed. 14:321-51) [MacDonald, *Wesley's Revision of the Shorter Catechism*].

[1539]Rushdoony, *Institutes of Biblical Law*, 549-556; 4. "The true holiness of man is man's separation unto God in faith and in obedience to God's law. The law is thus the specified way of holiness" [p. 36]. "Sanctification depends on our law-keeping in mind, word, and deed" [p. 307]. See also Rushdoony, *Law and Society*, 227 where

It would be better to say that sanctification is by means of the blood that cleanses and the Spirit that purifies. The law cannot sanctify, but it does define how the sanctified are to live. In spite of Rushdoony's opposition to antinomianism and his understanding that in sanctification we are renewed and remade after the image of God, transferred by Christ's justification into the new humanity, and led by God's Spirit into the holiness of that new race of Jesus Christ, in this life we are never wholly sanctified but die more and more to sin by the renewing of the Spirit.[1540]

By the nineteenth century Calvinists emphasized conversion, although as the century wore on there was often less precision about the experience. Conversion was sustained by the power of the cross and was fed by reading the Bible. Conversion resulted in vigorous activity. In contrast with the high-church Anglicans, they emphasized the atonement over the Incarnation, the Word over symbol, and the sermon over the sacraments.[1541]

In 1879 Anglican Bishop John Charles Ryle provided a twelve-point description of a holy person as a rebuttal to the Keswick position.

- He said holiness is the habit of being of one mind with God. We agree with his judgment, hate what he hates, love what he loves, and measure everything by the standard of his Word.[1542]
- A holy man will endeavor to shun every known sin and keep every known commandment.

---

sanctification is defined as "the destruction of the power of sin and death over man and the world by means of the effectual calling of the regenerated man, who, as a new creation, exercises righteousness, holiness, knowledge, and dominion over all things and brings all things into submission to God through Christ; the way of sanctification is the law of God." Notice that Rushdoony saw the effectual calling as the means of sanctification and that Daniel Steele declared election is unto sanctification [see p. 102 of this book]. Both appeal to 1 Peter 1:2. The difference between the Calvinist and the Arminian is whether or not this calling is coercion and this election is unconditional.

[1540]Rushdoony, *Systematic Theology*, 1:537. It is in this passage that Rushdoony appeals to 1 Peter 1:2.

[1541]Bebbington, *Holiness*, 37-41.

[1542]John Brown wrote, "Holiness does not consist in mystic speculations, enthusiastic fervours, or uncommanded austerities; it consists in thinking as God thinks, and willing as God wills" [*1 Peter*, 1:106]. However, it is one thing to agree with God's law and another thing to keep it. This is the condition of the unregenerate man in Romans 7:16.

- A holy man will strive to be like our Lord Jesus Christ.
- A holy man will follow after the fruits of the Spirit.
- A holy man will labor to mortify the desires of the flesh.
- A holy man will follow after charity and brotherly kindness. He will endeavor to follow the golden rule.
- A holy man will follow after the spirit of mercy and benevolence toward others.
- A holy man will follow after purity of heart. He knows his own heart is like tinder and will diligently keep clear of the sparks of temptation.
- A holy man will follow after the fear of God.
- A holy man will follow after humility.
- A holy man will follow after faithfulness in all the duties and relations in life.
- A holy man will follow after spiritual-mindedness. He will endeavor to set his affections entirely on things above and to hold things on earth with a very loose hand.[1543]

J. I. Packer considers this to be a classic account of holiness from a Reformed Augustinian standpoint.[1544] While there is certainly nothing objectionable about these aspirations, the question which arises is how much progress and how much consistency is expected? Ryle held that sanctification is always a progressive work. In his elaboration on Romans 7, Ryle considered the struggle itself as an evidence of sanctification, rather than an evidence of its lack.[1545]

Packer himself subscribes to Warfield's "miserable sinner" Christianity and believes that the "wretched man" of Romans 7 describes a "dynamic, spiritually healthy man." Over and over again this wretched man dares to hope that he has overcome the downdrag of sin and over and over God humbles him by letting him discover that is not yet so. Thus, Packer describes the life of holiness as ongoing repentance.[1546] Packer declared, "I know that I have never framed a prayer, preached a sermon, written a book, shown love to my wife, cared for my children, supported my friends, in short, done anything at all, which I did not in

---

[1543]Ryle, *Holiness*, 34-37.

[1544]Packer, *Keeping in Step with the Spirit*, 273. Ryle's book was written as a rebuttal to the Keswick position which will be discussed on p. 651.

[1545]Ryle, *Holiness*, 39; 21. Yet Wesley's emphasis was that life did not have to remain a perpetual struggle [Maddox, "Reconnecting the Means to the End," 44].

[1546]Packer, *Rediscovering Holiness*, 221-222; 132.

retrospect realize that it could and should have been done better; nor have I ever lived a day without leaving undone some things that I ought to have done."[1547]

Calvin taught that the remains of sin survive in the children of God "to humble them under a consciousness of their infirmity."[1548] While it is supposed that indwelling sin is useful in keeping true believers humble, Clarke explained that pride is the essence of sin. Yet it is absurd to think that pride can humble us. It is not sin that humbles us; it is the grace of God. While it is claimed that the greater sense we have of our own sinfulness the more we will appreciate a Savior, yet the same grace which awakens us to sin can also deliver from sin.[1549]

In his evaluation of holiness doctrine, R. H. Coats wrote,

> Where the Divine "seed" of the Holy Spirit abides in the child of God, the kinship to Satan is necessarily annulled, and the Christian need not, must not, does not, and cannot sin, since it is impossible that Christ and sin should dwell together in the same breast. Whether John is here speaking of an actual attained experience or is merely affirming the moral implication of an ideal faith is a matter of dispute.[1550]

Coats cited the Methodist commentator, George G. Findlay as representative of those who hold that John is describing an actual attained experience.[1551] Coats then cited Forsyth as representative of those who hold John is describing the moral implications of an ideal faith. Olin Curtis listed the ten most important books on Christian perfection, with Forsyth's *Christian Perfection* being one of the ten he cited.[1552]

Scottish theologian P. T. Forsyth stated essentially a Lutheran view that the only holiness possible is that of faith, continually appropriating Christ as the believer's righteousness. Forsyth argued for sinful perfection, insisting that

---

[1547]Packer, *Rediscovering Holiness*, 127.

[1548]Calvin, *Institutes*, 3.3.11. For Fletcher's reaction to the notion that sin humbles the soul, see *Works*, 2:503; 586-593. If sin produced humility, the devil would be the most humble of all creatures.

[1549]Clarke, *Christian Theology*, 186-187.

[1550]Coats, "Holiness," 6:745. Coats was referencing 1 John 3:9.

[1551]Findlay, *Studies in John's Epistles*, 127; 269-285.

[1552]Curtis, *Christian Faith*, 526.

perfection is not sanctity but faith. He argued that visitations of sin have a ministry in the redeemed life. They are a barrier against spiritual pride and a motive for faith. "To cease to feel defect is to cease to trust."[1553]

Yet Forsyth declared that we not only can, but we must enter into the perfection of God in Christ. Forsyth then distinguished between three notions of perfection. He defined the pietist idea as a state of sinlessness based on withdrawal from life and with a tendency to ecstasy. The popish idea of perfection also flees from the world in the form of the monk and the nun. They alone are called to perfection, while the majority live a more ordinary life with less demands. This Stoic paganism is based on Plato and Aristotle, not Paul

Forsyth advocated a third way. He defined it as the Protestant idea of perfection, a gift of God to us and based on faith and not our conduct. Forsyth began at 1 John 3:9, but argued that believers continue to sin. Thus, once a sinner always a sinner. The more Christian we become the more conscious we are of sin. To declare "I have now no sin" is to give up our faith in Christ and to become legalistic. There is no higher relationship possible than that of faith. The man who trusts in his works tries to attain a higher relationship than that of faith and therefore falls out of faith.

Therefore, "faith is not the faith of the sinless but of the redeemed, not of the holy but of the sanctified. . . . It is a fatal mistake to think of holiness as a possession which we have distinct from our faith."[1554] Forsyth labeled this as a Catholic idea. He also warned that a faith which is based wholly on experience is too subjective. "To claim sinlessness as the perfect state superseding faith is to fall from faith, not to rise from it."[1555]

Forsyth warned that sinlessness tends to an ascetic way of life. On the other hand, faith is positive and social. Love, not sinlessness, is the maturity of faith. Our perfection is to trust him. His great object with us is not our sinlessness, but our communion. Our holiness is a matter of worship. Any sinlessness of our is the adoration of his holiness. The height of sinlessness means the deepest sense of sin.

Forsyth argued that sin must abide, even while it is being conquered, as an occasion for faith. It has pleased God to leave us *in* our sin that we may be driven to seek more than his help, namely himself. We are pressed by our cleaving sin to press into a close and permanent communion with God.

[1553]Forsyth, *Christian Perfection*, 12.

[1554]Forsyth, *Christian Perfection*, 7.

[1555]Forsyth, *Christian Perfection*, 9.

According to Forsyth the solution to 1 John 3:9 is that John taught two kinds of sin in 1 John 5:16-17. There is a sin unto death, when a man falls completely out of communion with God. But Forsyth does not even see that this is a final apostasy. But the man is dead while remaining in this condition. The sin not unto death refers to lapses when he falls into sin but not into godlessness. He is not cut off from the divine life. Thus, whosoever is born of God may sin, but his sin will not result in spiritual death. Forsyth explains that John has forgotten for the moment the actuality of man. He is possessed with the sense of the omnipotence of Christ.[1556] His words were not written because he had attained sinlessness. They came from his faith in the power of Christ.

Forsyth stressed the difference between the sinner's sin and the saint's sin. The world is not troubled by sin, but the Christian man fears and hates sin. Yet he may lapse into sin. The difference is the final outcome. "Beethoven was not troubled when a performer struck a wrong note, but he was angry when he failed with the spirit and idea of the piece."[1557]

Forsyth said that sin is essentially an act of the will and we cannot say the condition described in Romans 7 is that the regenerate man is not really sinning, but simply his flesh sins against his will. Forsyth then declares that the will may chose certain good or evil acts which are not central to the personality. Thus the sinful principle does not really own us. Sin may capture certain volitions, but not the whole personality. Sin is not necessarily the prevailing habit of the soul. Sin may be at the circumference and the center of our being. Sin may be an incident and not the principle of our lives. This seems to argue against the point he has just made, that sin involves the whole of our personality.

But while perfection is not sinlessness, Forsyth conceded there is a perfection taught in the New Testament. He declared that it is wholeness. It contains a permanent element of repentance. We sin, but sin does not reign in us. It is not our life principle. We sin, but not unto death. We may still sin, but we are not sinners. The saints in the New Testament, according to Forsyth, are not the saintly, but the believing. Perfection is not sanctity but faith. "It is that surrender of the *will* which is involved in the act of personal faith in the living, saving Person of Jesus Christ. That is Christian perfection."[1558] However, the perfectness of their trust is the only perfect aspect of their being. They have not reached the point where faith has its perfect work in love, according to Forsyth.

[1556]Forsyth, *Christian Perfection*, 26.

[1557]Forsyth, *Christian Perfection*, 36.

[1558]Forsyth, *Christian Perfection*, 84.

Forsyth declared that Christian perfection is the faith which justifies. Sanctification is not a perfection added to justification. Therefore, he counseled, "You may perfectly trust your perfect Lord, and charge Him with the responsibility both for your sin and your sanctification."[1559] Thus, we are always being perfected. There will be lapses, yet we are growing and God will judge our life as a whole, not in pieces.

Forsyth defined Christian perfection as faith, humility, patience, thankfulness, prayer, duty, and love. He did not believe it was possible for any Christian at any one time to fulfill all these features. He declared that a man is perfect when he comes to belong to Christ, but he has as his goal a perfection in which perfection itself is perfected.[1560]

The emphasis on imputed righteousness, whether Lutheran or Calvinistic, is based the declaration that we are complete in him (Col 2:10), that by one offering he has perfected forever them that are sanctified (Heb 10:14), and that he is made unto us sanctification (1 Cor 1:30). Yet Pope remarked that these passages are very partially applied. Sin itself cannot be done away by imputation of righteousness or non-imputation of guilt. Calvinists deny that sin is done away; it is never abolished as a principle and power in the present age. Therefore, the emphasis is on a positional holiness. In some cases this leads to antinomianism.

Mildred Wynkoop warned against an exaggerated concept of substitution in which Christ pays the penalty for all our sins — past, present, and future; when his active life of obedience is also transferred to our account and covers our own filthy rags; where both justification and Christian character are considered included in the finished work of Christ on Calvary which is applied to us; so that our personal righteousness and full sanctification are drawn unconditionally from Christ without regard to the actual life we live or the sins we commit.[1561]

In other cases it is taught that since Christ is our substitute, his perfection already belongs to his people. But Pope also conceded that in some cases this doctrine stimulated the pursuit of personal perfection, exciting an unbounded

---

[1559]Forsyth, *Christian Perfection*, 93.

[1560]Forsyth, *Christian Perfection*, 111. This statement comes the closest to a recognition that there is something beyond initial justification by faith.

[1561]Wynkoop, *Foundations*, 110-111. Reformed Arminians hold that "all the believer's sins — past, present, and future, are forgiven" [Brown, *Modified Arminian Theology*, 336]. However, the Remonstrants rejected this doctrine with their whole heart and soul [Watson, *Dictionary*, 899].

horror of sin and a thirst for holiness.[1562] Wayne Grudem has stated that "we must affirm two things to be true. We will never be able to say 'I am completely free from sin, because our sanctification will never be completed." Yet Grudem also held that the Christian should never say "This sin has defeated me. I give up."[1563]

In his comments on 1 John 3:9, John MacArthur wrote on "Why Christians Won't Habitually Sin." He explained that genuine Christians cannot practice sin because sin is incompatible with the law of God, which they love. Habitual sin is lawlessness. Sin is incompatible with the work of Christ who died to make the believer holy and break the dominion of sin in the believer's life. Christ came to destroy the work of the arch-sinner, Satan. Sin in incompatible with the ministry of the Holy Spirit who has imparted a new nature to the believer. Yet MacArthur interprets the one defeated and bound by sin in Romans 7 as describing all Christians, "even the most spiritual and mature."[1564]

Gordon Clark defined sanctification as "the life-long battle against sin." He declared that "theology is the road to holiness." He also advocated the administration of the sacraments[1565] and other means of grace for the perfecting of the saints. About half of his book on *Sanctification* develops and defends the sacraments.

Louis Berkhof wrote that "sanctification is usually a lengthy process and never reaches perfection in this life. . . . the Bible teaches that in the present life no one can claim freedom from sin. . . . Sanctification does not engender a holy disposition, and does not gradually purify man. It does not put him in possession of any personal holiness, does not make him a saint, but leaves him a sinner."[1566]

Herman Bavinck taught that the believer can and will *become* holy

---

[1562]Pope, *Compendium*, 3:83-84. For example, see the prayer of Robert Murray M'Cheyne on p. 201.

[1563]Grudem, *Systematic Theology*, 747-748.

[1564]*MacArthur Bible Commentary*, 1951; 1528. In his response to those who say "whosoever is born of God doth not commit sin *habitually*," Wesley asked, "Whence is that? I read it not. It is not written in the Book. God plainly saith, he 'doth not commit sin'. And thou addest, 'habitually'! Who are thou that *mendest* the oracles of God? That 'addest to the words of this Book'? Beware, I beseech thee, lest God 'add to thee all the plagues that are written therein'!" ["The Marks of the New Birth," Sermon #18, 1.5].

[1565]Clark, *Sanctification*, 2; 6; 74.

[1566]Berkhof, *Systematic Theology*, 534-537.

because in Christ they *are* holy. Yet within the believer there is a struggle between the flesh and the spirit, between the old and the new man. "These two forces are not spatially separated, as though one part of the man — the reason, for example — were regenerated, and another part of him — the heart, for example — were not. Rather, these two forces spread themselves out over the whole man and over all his powers and abilities, so that either one of them can be called a man — the one the old, and the other the new. . . . The seriousness of this struggle already intimates that it will be a long time before the new man achieves the victory."

Wesley also said that generally it is a long time, "even many years, before sin is destroyed." But Wesley also argued that God could cut short his usual work.[1567] Yet Wesley saw the new birth as a victory over sin and he was speaking about the work of Christian perfection. However, Bavinck fails to see the connection between holiness and Christian perfection. Berkhof also declared, "sanctification is usually a lengthy process and never reaches perfection in this life."[1568] Representing the Calvinistic view, Anthony Hoekema declared, "I do not believe that the Bible allows for the possibility of living without sin, even with 'willful sin,' in this life and therefore I do not accept Wesleyan teaching about entire sanctification."[1569] Yet Wesley held that even babes in Christ, not yet entirely sanctified, have victory over willful sin.[1570]

While Bavinck concluded that perfection is not attainable in this life, yet he wrote that the admonishments and appeals in Scripture to perfection are useful and serious. Bavinck argued that a man may have to pay a sum of money and yet not be able to pay it, but the obligation still remains. "One can hold to the perfectibility of the saints only if one does not take seriously the sinful nature of man, if one does not regard his sinful thoughts and inclinations as sin, and if one does violence to the absolute holiness of the law." Yet "no sin or infirmity which still remains in us *against our will* can hinder us from being received of God in grace."[1571]

[1567]Wesley, *Works*, 11:423.

[1568]Berkhof, *Systematic Theology*, 534.

[1569]Hoekema, "The Reformed Perspective," 49.

[1570]"But even babes in Christ are so far perfect as not to commit sin" [Wesley, *Works*, 11:375].

[1571]Bavinck, *Our Reasonable Faith*, 469-513. Bavinck's description of the two natures is an attempt to disassociate his position from the more antinomian position of

Jerry Bridges explained that holiness is to be the lifelong pursuit of the Christian. It is through continual discipline that we break negative habits and form positive ones. Yet he says Romans 7 mirrors our struggle with sin. While we want instant victory, God wants us to learn to persevere in the discipline of holiness. Thus, we must persevere in spite of failure. The emphasis of Bridges is on obedience, not victory.[1572] Jonathan Edwards emphasized the believer's responsibility for growth in this life in his pursuit of holiness. The rules he resolved to maintain is impressive. Yet he confessed, "When I look into my heart and take a view of my wickedness, it looks like an abyss infinitely deeper than hell."[1573]

The problem with this emphasis is that imputed righteousness has been separated from imparted righteousness. God does not require the righteousness of Christ from any man. He required that only of Christ. It is true that we have no righteousness of our own, but God requires the sinner to believe in Christ. When we truly believe, our faith is reckoned as righteousness. Christ is not righteous in our stead but provides the basis by which we may become righteous through the power of the Holy Spirit. Wynkoop explained, "Holiness of character is never said in Scripture to be transferred from one person to another — nor is this possible. Christ's death is a substitute for our punishment but not for our holiness."[1574]

Romans 4 teaches that Abraham believed God and it was credited to him as righteousness. However, we not only have peace with God through justification by faith (Rom 5:1), he also pours out the Holy Spirit into the heart of the justified (Rom 5:5). The love of God was poured into our hearts through the Holy Spirit given to us[1575] when we were justified.[1576] Justification and the gift of the Holy Spirit both occur at the same time — *having been justified* and *having been given* both occurred at the moment of saving faith.

Therefore, God does not impute grace without imparting grace. For God to impute to us what he does not impart to us is legal fiction. He declares us to be without guilt and imparts his righteousness. To justify means to make just.

---

dispensationalism, which is discussed on pp. 645-654 of this book.

[1572]Bridges, *Pursuit of Holiness*, 103-105; 17; 77-81.

[1573]*Works of Jonathan Edwards*, 1:xlviii.

[1574]Wynkoop, *Foundations*, 110.

[1575]aorist passive participle

[1576]aorist passive participle

The same word δίκαιος (*dikaios*) is translated in Romans as "just" four times and "righteous" three times in the King James Version.[1577] A. W. Tozer wrote that God shares his holiness with his children "by imputation and by impartation, and because He has made it available to them through the blood of the Lamb, He requires it of them."[1578]

Calvinists generally hold that human goodness is exclusively imputed, but never actually imparted. The emphasis is that God only looks through Christ at the redeemed as if they were good, but that they cannot even by God's grace become actually good. While it is true that the biblical concept of atonement included the idea of a covering for sin, the Bible comes down on the side of genuine goodness. By God's regenerating grace we can have more than a provisional, pretended goodness. Redemptive grace includes giving people a measure of moral rightness, in addition to their standing before God. This redemptive grace goes beyond justification and includes regeneration and sanctification.[1579]

Wesley wrote, "Do not dispute for that particular phrase 'the imputed righteousness of Christ.' It is not scriptural."[1580] The Bible does not teach that the obedience of Christ is credited to my account. Instead Paul teaches that by faith in Christ as my substitute my sin is not charged to my account. In justification my sin is not imputed to me; in regeneration righteousness is imparted to me through the Holy Spirit (Rom 5-6).

We are not justified in our sin, we are set free from sin. God implants righteousness in every one to whom he has imputed it. Wynkoop said that this separation of legal standing from the actual possibility of perfection is a form of dualism.[1581] We must maintain a balance between separation from sin which leads to a feeling that we are never good enough and an emphasis on the father's love which seems to imply that we can come as we are and remain as we are.

Yet Wesley affirmed the doctrine of imputed righteousness, that faith is initially imputed for righteousness. He denied that the righteousness of Christ is imputed in lieu of any subsequent obedience. He explained the problem when

---

[1577]See Reasoner, *Romans*, 48-49.

[1578]Tozer, *Knowledge of the Holy*, 113.

[1579]The previous paragraph is a summary of Murphree, *Divine Paradoxes*, 83.

[1580]Wesley, *Works*, 10:318; 340; 430; see also Sermon #40, "The Lord Our Righteousness, 2.1-20.

[1581]Wynkoop, *Theology of Love*, 279.

imputed righteousness is not balanced with imparted righteousness.

> 'But when is it imputed?' When they believe. In that very hour the righteousness of Christ is theirs. It is imputed to every one that believes, as soon as he believes: faith and the righteousness of Christ are inseparable. . . .
> I believe God *implants* righteousness in every one to whom he has *imputed* it. I believe 'Jesus Christ is made of God unto us sanctification' as well as righteousness; or that God sanctifies, as well as justifies, all them that believe in him. They to whom the righteousness of Christ is imputed are made righteous by the spirit of Christ, are renewed in the image of God 'after the likeness wherein they were created, in righteousness and true holiness'.
> In the meantime what we are afraid of is this: lest any should use the phrase, 'the righteousness of Christ', or, 'the righteousness of Christ is "imputed to me",' as a cover for his unrighteousness. We have known this done a thousand times. A man has been reproved, suppose for drunkenness. 'Oh, said he, I pretend to no righteousness of *my own*: Christ is *my righteousness*.' Another has been told, that 'the extortioner, the unjust, shall not inherit the kingdom of God.' He replies with all assurance, 'I am unjust in myself, but I have a spotless righteousness in Christ.' And thus, though a man be as far from the practice as from the tempers of a Christian, though he neither has the mind which was in Christ nor in any respect walks as he walked, yet he has armor of proof against all conviction, in what he calls the 'righteousness of Christ.'[1582]

Yet Wesley stated that Methodism came to the very edge of Calvinism in ascribing all good to the free grace of God, in denying all natural free-will and all power antecedent to grace, and in excluding all merit from man, even for what he has or does by the grace of God.[1583] Yet Wesley would reject the conclusion of Kevin DeYoung, who said that when he looks at Galatians and Romans he feels, "If people hear us talking about justification and don't almost think that we are

---

[1582]Wesley, "The Lord our Righteousness," Sermon #20, 2.1, 12, 19.

[1583]Wesley, *Works*, 8:285.

giving them a license to sin, we aren't preaching grace strong enough."[1584] Wesley declared,"The imagination that faith *supercedes* holiness is the marrow of antinomianism."[1585]

8. Eschatological Perfection

Purgatory

While Jesus promised the thief on the cross, "Today you will be with me in paradise (Luke 23:43)," by the fifth or sixth century purgatory was substituted for paradise. Perfection was held to be the privilege of the few who took the high road of monasticism.[1586] For the imperfect, holiness is possible only after death in purgatory. The Roman church taught that the rest, who were in the Church, were too good for hell, but not ready for heaven. "All who die in God's grace and friendship, but still imperfectly purified, are indeed assured of their eternal salvation; but after death they undergo purification, so as to achieve the holiness necessary to enter the joy of heaven."[1587]

The concept of an intermediate state developed from the Jewish tradition of Sheol, from the account of Lazarus (Luke 16:19-31), and from the passages of Christ's descent into hades. Based on Matthew 5:20, Tertullian and Cyprian taught that a special satisfaction and penance was required for sins committed after baptism. While Christian martyrs and confessors passed immediately after death into heaven, the majority of Christian believers were imperfect and entered a preparatory state call Paradise or Abraham's Bosom for an indefinite period. There they were gradually purged until they were ripe for heaven.

The doctrine of purgatory was first taught from a dream of Perpetua, a North African martyr, around A. D. 202. It was based on 2 Maccabees 12:43-45,

---

[1584]Wax, "The Justification Debate," 36.

[1585]Wesley, "On the Wedding Garment," Sermon # 127, § 18.

[1586]Turner, *Vision Which Transforms*, 170. Turner cited Cassian as perhaps the best example of this tendency. Yet Cassian knew that practices which aid purity are not ends in themselves. According to Columba Stewart, Cassian knew that "not even total destitution can assure perfection unless there is also the love that 'consists of purity of heart alone'" [*Cassian the Monk*, 43].

[1587]*Catechism of the Catholic Church*, 1.2.3.3. §1030. However, Grider insisted that the Roman Catholic Church teaches purgatory cleanses venial and mortal sins, not original sin [*Wesleyan-Holiness Theology*, 457].

which is an apocryphal book and thus not part of the canon of Scripture, on Matthew 12:32, which only warns that blasphemy against the Holy Spirit will *not* be forgiven in this age or in the age to come, and on 1 Corinthians 3:13 which was interpreted as referring to purgatorial fire. Thus Roman Catholic theologian Michael Schmaus admitted that the doctrine of purgatory was not based on Scripture but rather on the church's practice of prayer and penance.[1588] The Eastern Orthodox Church rejects the notion of purgatory as a place distinct from heaven and hell. At the same time it concedes that there is an intermediate period of temporal pain in which penance for sins is carried out by those destined for heaven.

Purgatory means to purify[1589] and it was thought that in purgatory the temporal consequences of sin and a painful struggle after holiness took place. Origen spoke figuratively of purgatorial fire which burned away the remaining stains of the soul. Augustine and Gregory the Great, in the seventh century, are usually considered the inventors of purgatory, since they transferred the concept to the middle state.[1590] The dogma was not confirmed until the Council of Trent (1545-1563). However, there is no biblical evidence for such a place as purgatory after this life.

Perkins wrote, "The belief in an uninterrupted endeavor after a higher degree of Perfection, which death itself cannot interrupt, degenerated into a belief in Purgatory." Some concept of purgatory is bound up with the doctrine of perfection.

> Purgatory, which lies direct in the way to Heaven, is for those who have been baptized, and so washed from original sin, whose mortal sins have been forgiven in this life, but who have not yet attained perfection: it is even for those who may have been in the state of perfection, but have not yet attain. The fire of Purgatory is the same as the fire of Hell, and only differs in its effects.[1591]

John Fletcher argued the scriptural doctrine of purgatory was that the

[1588]Schmaus, *Justification and the Last Things.*

[1589]The Latin *purgatorium* is from *purgo*, I cleanse.

[1590]Schaff, *History of the Christian Church*, 2:600-606.

[1591]Perkins, *Evangelical Perfection*, 171; 198-199.

blood of Christ cleanses us from all sin.[1592] Richard Watson argued "that the entire sanctification of the soul, and its complete renewal in holiness, must take place in this world."[1593] Wiley pointed out the failure to recognize the present power of the atoning blood of Christ for full and complete cleansing and substitute a mechanical process of cleansing after death.[1594]

John S. Banks wrote, "Purgatory is a device for perfecting the good and fitting them for the vision of God. But why at death or after death rather than before? What prerogative is there in time, or what power will be at work then that is not at work now?"[1595]

Millennial Perfection

Joachim of Fiore (1130-1202) saw history in three stages. The first stage was the age of the Father. The second era was the age of the Son. The third period was the age of the Holy Spirit. However, for Joachim the Spirit was the "activating intellect" in every man and as man used his intellect he became God. Thus, the Holy Spirit was identified with the spirit of man, so that the new era was to be the age of man and man could create a paradise on earth through the power of natural reason.

Therefore, Joachim taught that those who would be perfect must wait for a third age in which spiritual men would lead a pure Church in an environment of peace, freedom, and contemplation. According to the apocalyptic visions of Joachim Christ was to return and inaugurate his millennial reign on earth in 1260. This new age would strengthen, not replace the Church of Rome. During this third age spiritual men would know the truth and would receive directly from the Holy Spirit all the charismatic gifts necessary for perfection.

Most medieval millennialists believed in a coming age when the world would be inhabited by a perfected humanity. However, millennial expectation in medieval times usually saw the kingdom coming with upheavals and met with resistance. The Taborites, took their name from Mount Tabor, where they believed Christ foretold his second coming. They expected the Lord's return in February 1420. When this date proved false, they became a revolutionary millennial movement. They formed armies to fight God's battle. They formed

---

[1592]Fletcher, *Works*, 2:488-489.

[1593]Watson, *Theological Institutes*, 2:450-451.

[1594]Wiley, *Christian Theology*, 2:452.

[1595]Banks, *Christian Doctrine*, 259.

themselves into communal groups and sold their possessions. They attempted to hasten the end by launching armed attacks upon their opponents, until they were crushed in 1434.

Initially, radicals saw hope in Martin Luther as a prophet of transition. However, Luther did not teach a radical transformation of society. While he believed he was living at the end of time, he rejected millennialism. Therefore, the militant premillennial leaders, such as Thomas Muntzer, turned away from Luther in disappointment. Thomas Muntzer, the spiritual leader of the German peasants who revolted in 1524-1526, announced the Millennium was about to begin. Unlike Martin Luther who believed that the Kingdom of Heaven was not earthly and that Rome would be overthrown by the preaching of the gospel, Muntzer taught a holy war of extermination had to take place before Christ would return and the Millennium begin. Muntzer became obsessed with the Book of Revelation. Convinced that God was on their side, in 1524 Muntzer led the Peasants' War, which claimed over a hundred thousand lives.

Ten years later Melchoir Hofmann and his successor, Jan Matthys, declared that the New Jerusalem was coming to Munster. Matthys preached violence to cleanse the earth from the ungodly and prepare for the return of Christ on Easter 1534. Matthys died, after he was convinced his small band could vanquish the enemies besieging the town. John Bockelson (also known as John of Leiden) took over and became even more fanatical, proclaiming himself as the "Messiah of the Last Days." This "kingdom" also came to a violent end.[1596]

In more recent times dispensationalism has tended to relegate the entire Sermon on the Mount to a future kingdom age, including the possibility of being "pure in heart." But Purkiser argued that all the other qualities names in the beatitudes are aspects of life here and how: the poor in spirit, those who mourn, those who hunger and thirst after righteousness, the persecuted. "It would be totally arbitrary to deny the possibility of heart purity in light of Christ's present tense: 'Blessed *are* the pure in heart.'"[1597]

[1596]Reasoner, *Hope of the Gospel*, 202-204; 225-226. While I concluded that Joachim held a type of postmillennialism, see Burgess, "Medieval Models of Perfectionism,"155-163. Burgess described Joachim as premillennial. See also Cohn, *Pursuit of the Millennium*.

[1597]*Biblical Foundation*, 1:81. See also section #14 on dispensationalism. There is no direct connection between the dispensational doctrine of sanctification and eschatology. See the discussion of the "Augustinian-Dispensational" view of sanctification on p. 652.

The Article of Death

Calvinism has sometimes emphasized entire sanctification in the article of death or that death releases the justified from the effects of the Fall, allowing us to become what we are positionally in Christ. Until then, a believer daily grows in grace, coming nearer and nearer to perfection. We ought to be continually pressing after this and to exhort all others so to do. Louis Berkhof wrote that the sanctification of the believer must be completed either at the very moment of death, or immediately after death, so far as the soul is concerned, and at the resurrection, so far as it pertains to the body.[1598]

Yet death is our enemy (1 Cor 15:26), not our friend. We can serve God in holiness and righteousness "all our days" (Luke 1:75). Sin is not sovereign. It would be a denial of the sovereignty of God to assert that the Spirit is impotent to save us wholly from our sins while soul and body are united. Thus Wesley and the early Methodists taught that we should expect to be saved from all sin before the article of death. They granted that many of those who have died in the faith,

> yea, the greater part of those we have known, were not sanctified throughout, not made perfect in love, till a little before death, that the term "sanctified" is continually applied by St. Paul to all that were justified, were true believers, that by this term alone, he rarely, if ever, means saved from all sin, that, consequently, it is not proper to use it in this sense, without adding the word "wholly, entirely," or the like, that the inspired writers almost continually speak of or to those who were justified; but very rarely, either of or to those who were wholly sanctified, and that, consequently, it behooves us to speak in public almost continually of the state of justification; but, more rarely, in full and explicit terms, concerning entire sanctification.

But having made these concessions, Methodism stated the point wherein we divide is this: "Whether we should expect to be saved from all sin before the article of death." They declared that there is clear scripture promise of this; that God will save us from *all* sin.[1599]

[1598]Berkhof, *Systematic Theology*, 534.

[1599]Wesley, *BE Works*, 10:195-197; see also *Works*, 11:388-390; Peck, *Christian Perfection*, 321-340. Wynkoop observed that the question of timing is not directly handled in the New Testament, except by implication. When one ought to come

Clarke declared, "God sets no bounds to the communications of his grace and Spirit to them that are faithful."[1600] Watson concluded that the destruction of the body of sin cannot refer to the hour of death nor placed subsequent to this present life. The attainment of perfect freedom from sin is one to which believers are called during the present life.[1601]

John Fletcher argued that since this full circumcision of the heart, which purifies the soul, is based on saving faith, which can be so sharp and searching as to be compared to a baptism of fire, it seems absurd to suppose that God's infinite wisdom has tied this powerful operation to the article of death when people are frequently so weak or delirious that they are unable to even think or receive nourishment.[1602] Thus, David Cubie described Christian perfection, as taught by Wesley and Fletcher, as "realized eschatology." Cubie explained, "They yet affirmed that, because it was God's work, it could and would be fulfilled in the believer provided he met the condition of faith. Though perfection usually occurred many years after the new birth, God can 'cut short his work.'"[1603]

9. Imparted Righteousness and the Pietists

Arndt, Spener, and Francke

Pietism, as well as later Moravianism and Methodism, emphasized the new birth and a personal relationship with God, personal piety, holiness, and discipline, religious idealism, and the centrality of the Scripture. In contrast to the established Church, they also regarded the early Church as normative and attempted to restore aspects of primitive Christianity.[1604]

---

into entire sanctification is a question neither raised nor answered [*Theology of Love*, 335-336]. For Wesley the only consistent answer was "now" [Wesley, "On Patience," Sermon #83, § 13; *Works*, 11:382; 393]. As Fletcher explained, if it is not expected every moment, it is never" [*Works*, 1:57].

[1600]Clarke, *Christian Theology*, 197.

[1601]Watson, *Theological Institutes*, 2:455.

[1602]Fletcher, *Works*, 2:566. See also Ralston, *Elements of Divinity*, 466-470; see Wakefield, *Christian Theology*, 2:450-452

[1603]Cubie, "Perfection in Wesley and Fletcher," 26.

[1604]Stoeffler, *Rise of Evangelical Pietism*, 13-23. See also Howard Snyder, "Pietism, Moravianism, and Methodism."

Kasper Schwenkfeld (1489-1561) reacted to Luther and became the forerunner of pietism by teaching that God actually makes us righteous. Pietism developed within the German Lutheran Church in the eighteenth century. Flew said its impulse came from the desire for personal holiness and the dissatisfaction with the hardness and objectivity of the prevailing Lutheranism — the state church. Yet is it narrowly individualistic.[1605] It laid great stress on the new birth, separation from the world, right living, and the inward witness of the Spirit. However, pietism is not necessarily the equivalent of perfectionism.[1606] The emphasis of pietism in the seventeenth century shifted from justification to regeneration. John Wesley was influenced by this emphasis on the new birth in pietistic theology.[1607]

While there is a streak of mysticism in all pietism, pietism tended to retain Lutheran theology. While there was some overlap between pietism and the Anabaptist movement, pietism is more closely related to the Moravian movement of Zinzendorf.

Johann Arndt (1555-1621) held that the Bible describes holiness, not learning, as the ideal desired by God for mankind. Arndt accepted Luther's theology of *simul justus et peccator*, that the believer is at one and the same time justified and a sinner. However, Arndt was also concerned about holy living and believed that holiness was not only imputed, but imparted. The way to "true Christianity" was to appropriate aspects of medieval Catholic spirituality.

First there was purgation through repentance. Arndt believed Christian experience should be grounded in repentance. This repentance creates a sensitivity within the believer toward sin and causes the believer to trust and obey. This relationship is absolutely dependant upon and maintained by the community of faith — the Church. Arndt taught that baptism bestows a perfect cleansing from original sin. Therefore being made perfect in baptism, we seek to lead a holy life. And the source of this holy life is the presence of Christ within us through regeneration.

As our gifts increase and our love grows, we receive illumination. Finally there is the full union of love, when we find the kingdom of God within ourselves. Thus, union with Christ is mystical and yet ethical. While we are never perfect in this life, never entirely sanctified, Arndt believed that our love may be perfected

---

[1605]Flew, *Idea of Perfection*, 275; 279.

[1606]Gaddis, *Christian Perfection in America*, 85.

[1607]Schmidt, *John Wesley: Theological Biography*, 1:246. See also Collins, *Theology of John Wesley*, 208-215.

in this life.[1608] Wesley included Arndt's *True Christianity* in the first volume of his *Christian Library.*[1609]

Arndt was followed by Philipp Jakob Spener (1635-1705). Spener began his ministry at Berlin with sixty-two sermons on the new birth.[1610] Spener reprinted Arndt in 1675 and added his own lengthy preface. This preface was eventually published separately as *Pia Desideria*.[1611] Regeneration was for Spener what justification had been for Luther.

Spener taught a regeneration that occurs in baptism and a regeneration which begins in baptism, but which continues only as we conform to the will of God. For Spener the process of sanctification began at baptism and this process of sanctification is manifesting and cultivating regeneration. In his emphasis on community, Spener formed small devotional groups or conventicles, called *collegia pietatis* (schools of piety). The label "pietism" was derived from this. Gaddis observed that Wesley's bands were comparable to the *collegia pietatis* of Spener.[1612]

August Hermann Francke (1663-1727) was a student of Arndt's. Wesley referred to the name of Francke as "precious ointment. O may I follow him, as he did Christ!"[1613] Francke also taught perfection in Christ. But that perfection is also improvable and we can never be fully perfect in this life. Francke advised the preacher:

[1608]Bassett, *Historical Development*, 187-192.

[1609]*Christian Library*, 1:157-2:206 [2nd ed. 1:133-427]. Arndt wrote of the *plerophory* or full assurance of faith in his *True Christianity.* On the significance of Arndt to Wesley, see Collins, *John Wesley: Spiritual Journey*, 64-66.

[1610]Brown, *Understanding Pietism*, 66-67.

[1611]"Pious Wishes" or "The Piety We Desire." Spener's agenda was a return to the Scriptures, involvement of laity, an emphasis on godliness, and end to theological controversies, the ministry must be reserved for true Christians, students training for ministry should be versed in the practices of godliness, not simply theory.

[1612]Gaddis, *Christian Perfection in America*, 133. According to Richard Foster, the three historical expressions of the *ecclesiola in ecclesia* worthy of particularly study are Spener's *collegia pietatis*, Wesley's society, and Hans Nielsen Hauge's nineteenth century "inner mission" in Norway [Foster, "Spiritual Formation Agenda," 31-32].

[1613]Wesley, *Journal*, 26 July 1738. Francke held to hopes of world-wide social regeneration.

> Nor is it enough to explain that first and mighty Change which is at once made in a Sinner at his conversion, when he comes to love that God which before he hated, and to hate the Evil which he before loved, when from being an Unbeliever he becomes a Believer, or when his false and dead Faith is changed into a true and saving one: But that further progressive Change should also be much recommended, in which the Christian must be improving to the very End of his Life.[1614]

Unlike the mystics Eckhart and Tauler, Gerhard Tersteegen (1697-1769) did not hold that God is inherently present in the depths of every soul, only waiting to be discovered and obeyed through a program of asceticism. Unlike Zinzendorf, Tersteegen did not conflate justification and sanctification. Instead, he emphasized the need for steady, daily growth in the praxis of saving grace that follows justification. While righteousness is first imputed to the believer, it then is to become progressively imparted through the indwelling Spirit of God. Through his poetry and prose he spoke of the believer's progressive transformation into the image of God.[1615]

In the sixteenth century the Anabaptists were the more radical Protestant reformers. They went beyond Luther's imputed righteousness and insisted upon holiness of heart and life. They did not dwell on what one must do to be saved, but emphasized how a Christian should live. Among these radical reformers, Peter Riedemann (1506-1556) was a leader of the Hutterite Brethren. He taught that Christ came to free us from sin in order that we might be servants of righteousness. As soon as one believes God's Word with his whole heart, God seals the covenant in them with the gift of his Spirit. The Christian Church is pure and holy as Christ himself is holy.

Richard Hughes termed the Anabaptists "ethical primitivists." They sought to recover the ethical and moral purity of the apostolic community. They felt that this was not possible as long as the church and state were connected. Thus, they separated from the state church. The term "Anabaptist" means to baptize again. Although George Blaurock had been baptized into the state church as an infant, on January 21, 1525 he was baptized again upon his confession of faith.

[1614]"Letter to a Friend concerning the Most Useful Way of Preaching," in Jennings, *Two Discourses*, 77. See also Bassett, *Holiness Teaching*, 283-323; Brown, *Understanding Pietism*. Gerhard Tersteegen (1697-1769), *Recluse in Demand*.

[1615]O'Malley, "Pietistic Influence," 60-65.

Menno Simons accused the state church of being a "worldly church" and an "adulterous bride." He insisted upon church discipline. In order to enforce this discipline, candidates for baptism had to promise to submit to exclusion or the ban, if they became entangled again with the world. Thus, the ban, or excommunication, or separation was fundamental to restoring the purity of the Church.[1616]

Not only do Anabaptists insist on baptism by immersion, but they are pacifists and emphasize separation from the world — even to the point of not voting. While their emphasis is a variation of the monastic model of holiness, instead of withdrawing into solitude they withdraw from the world to live in community. They insist that their discipline is not to make them holy, but rather to give witness to the holiness that God has given them. However, sometimes their discipline becomes confused as a means of salvation rather than its consequence.[1617]

Around 1580 an Anabaptist sect received the name Adamites because it required candidates for admission to appear naked before the congregation to show that physical desire had no power over them. Similar groups also went unclothed to imitate original perfection and purity, as well as their separation from the fallen world around them. The essential characteristic of all these groups was their emphasis on primitivism.[1618]

Fredrich Schleiermacher (1768-1834) first rejected his pietistic background, then finally regarded himself as a pietist of a higher order. Often described as the father of modern theology, he realized that religion could not be appropriated by purely intellectual means. He emphasized that religion was intuitive and defended religion on an experiential basis. Thus, he emphasized the mystical and subjective. Revelation springs from the God-consciousness within. He understood sanctification as the progressive dominion of the God consciousness within us over a defective world consciousness.[1619] Mankind has always possessed this capability.

He was critical of those who relegate the unclouded blessing of Christ to the next life. Yet he held an inadequate doctrine of sin and of Christ's atonement, feeling that sin would gradually be overcome as our consciousness of the Infinite increases. He felt that the individual is nothing if severed from the community and

---

[1616]Hughes, "Christian Primitivism as Perfection," 215-217.

[1617]Bassett, *Holiness Teaching*, 269-279.

[1618]Rushdoony, *Noble Savages*, 17.

[1619]Schleiermacher, *Christian Faith*, 238-244.

that corporately both sin and salvation would be overcome.[1620]

In his dissertation entitled *Christian Perfection in America*, Merrill Gaddis documented the fact that Quaker and German Pietistic perfectionism preceded Methodism to America. In particular he cited the Mennonites, Dunkards, Moravians, as well as followers of John Kelpius[1621] and Matthais Bauman.[1622]

In 1875 the holiness evangelism of Robert Pearsall Smith reached Germany where his message was embraced by the old Pietist areas. The German holiness movement remained within the established church but formed small-group fellowships within the church. This movement was severely divided by the Pentecostal movement in the early decades of the twentieth century. The church within the church concept broke down and produced distinct Pentecostal denominations.[1623]

Zinzendorf and the Moravians

[1620]Powell incorporates this theme in *Embodied Holiness*, 172-175; 179-183.

[1621]Kelpius was a mystic philosopher, associated with the German Pietist movement, who emigrated to America with others in 1694. They lived communally, but their spirituality also included solitary meditation. This group of celibates waited in the American forest for the end of the world. Like the earlier desert monks in Africa, their goal was to escape the world's temptations and enter into communion with the Divine Spirit. Thus, Kelpius lived in his cavern by the banks of the Wissahickon River in Pennsylvania. Eventually his followers became part of the Seventh Day Baptist movement. In his 1872 poem, "Pennsylvania Pilgrim," John Greenleaf Whittier said that Kelpius was the "maddest of good men" who "aired his perfection in a world of sin" [Bach, *Voices of the Turtledoves*].

[1622]Among the German Pietists, a day laborer named Matthias Baumann experienced religious visions over a five-day period. Baumann believed God commissioned him to preach repentance before the impending final judgment. He stopped attending the Reformed Church and worshiped with local Mennonites. After arrests in 1702 and 1706, Baumann emigrated to Pennsylvania in 1719 and founded a small group, the Neugeboren (the Newborn). Some years later Baumann reportedly visited Georg Conrad Beissel, the founder of the Ephrata Cloister, who had also emigrated to Pennsylvania. While Baumann preaching sinless perfection, Beissel told him to smell his own excrement and see if that pertained to perfection.

[1623]Dieter, "Holiness Revival in Nineteenth-Century Europe," 20-23. See Warfield, *Studies in Perfectionism*, 1:345-347. See also the Berlin Declaration on pp. 685-689 of this book.

The pietist Nicholas Ludwig, count of Zinzendorf taught that we are as holy as we will ever be when we are regenerated. Zinzendorf was the leader of the Unitas Fratrum, a religious society which began in Bohemia in 1457 under John Huss. Zinzendorf, himself, was a godson of Philipp Jakob Spener and a student of August Hermann Francke.

Wesley argued against the views of Zinzendorf that the epistles of the New Testament contain promises, prayers, and commands that believers go on unto perfection. In combating the view that regeneration and entire sanctification occur simultaneously, Wesley reasoned

> 1. There is such a thing as perfection; for it is again and again mentioned in Scripture. 2. It is not so early as justification; for justified persons are to "go on to perfection."
> 3. It is not so late as death; for St. Paul spake of living men that were perfect.[1624]

Wesley and Zinzendorf debated this issue on September 3, 1741. Zinzendorf asserted,

> The best of men are most miserable sinners, even unto death. . . . I acknowledge no inherent perfection in this life. This is the error of errors. I pursue it through the world with fire and sword. I trample upon it: I devote it to utter destruction. Whoever follows inherent perfection, denies Christ. . . . . Our whole Christian Perfection is imputed, not inherent. We are perfect in Christ; In ourselves we are never perfect. . . . But he is holy in Christ, not in himself. . . . He hath no holiness at all in himself. . . . He is not more holy if he loves more, or less holy, if he loves less. . . . In the moment he is justified, he is sanctified wholly. From that time he is neither more nor less holy, even unto death. . . . Our whole justification, and sanctification, are in the same instant, and he receives neither more nor less. . . . We reject all self-denial. We trample on it. We do, as believers, whatsoever we will, and nothing more. We laugh at all mortification. No purification precedes perfect love.

[1624]Wesley, *Works*, 11:441-442.

Wesley argued that every believer increased in love and therefore equally increased in holiness. He asserted that a father in Christ is holier than a new-born babe and that we should grow in grace. Wesley also argued that the apostles were justified before the death of Christ, but that they were more holy after the day of Pentecost than before Christ's death.[1625]

The Influence of Zinzendorf within Methodism

In 1848 Merritt Caldwell, professor at Maine Wesleyan Seminary, opposed the holiness teaching by claiming that regeneration restored our ability to exercise control over unholy inclinations. He was not in opposition to Wesleyan doctrine.[1626] However, this concept was picked up by W. C. Hosmer, who concluded that all necessary to salvation is given in regeneration. If sanctification is necessary to salvation, then it is given in regeneration and there

---

[1625]Wesley, *BE Works*, 19:211-215. According to W. Stephen Gunter, Wesley utilized this dialogue as the basis for his essay "A Dialogue Between an Antinomian and His Friend" in *Works*, 10:270-276. Zinzendorf's words are the basis for the antinomian part of the dialogue [*Limits of "Love Divine*," 105].

Leslie Wilcox mistakenly cited this debate as an instance where Wesley connected Pentecost and entire sanctification [*Be Ye Holy*, 280-281]. However, Wesley did not specify what the standing of the disciples was either before or after Pentecost, but simply used them to illustrate the fact that there can be improvement. Rob Staples observed that the question of when the baptism of the Holy Spirit occurs was not the subject under their discussion ["Current Debate," 4]. However, Laurence Wood resurrected this fallacious argument in his failed attempt to answer Kenneth Collins ["Need for a Contextual Interpretation," 260].

Reinhold Niebuhr recognized this conversation between Zinzendorf and Wesley as "a miniature of the whole controversy between the Renaissance and Reformation." In this debate Wesley held that "deliverance must be from sin and not from finiteness." Wesley also rejected the mystical influence that this deliverance would be in purely contemplative terms. Nor can Wesley accept the Moravian antinomianism that there is only one commandment in the New Testament, the command to believe. Niebuhr described Wesley rightly as clearly understanding "the moral imperatives of the gospel." Ultimately, however, Niebuhr is wrong in labeling Wesley's doctrine of sin as Pelagian and also misstated Wesley's doctrine of perfection [*Nature and Destiny of Man*, 2:173-175].

[1626]Caldwell, *Philosophy of Christian Perfection*.

is essentially no difference between the two.[1627]

In 1851 Thomas O. Summers argued theoretically that if a sinner recognized all the depravity of his nature and had the faith he could be perfectly sanctified at the moment of his justification. But Summers questioned the probability of such complete self-knowledge. Thus he concluded that indwelling sin in the heart of the regenerate is entirely destroyed by gradual mortification or by an instant and powerful exercise of faith.[1628]

In 1866 Samuel Franklin argued that regeneration is a sinless state since God would not create sin in the new creation. Franklin denied any blessing beyond regeneration in this life and rejected entire sanctification. If man was originally created perfect, then his regeneration is also perfect. While Franklin advocated growth in grace, he declared that "growth cannot mean an increase of purity above the new birth."[1629]

[1627]Hosmer, "Philosophy of Christian Perfection," 484-491. As a result, in 1848-1849 George Peck expanded his book *Scripture Doctrine of Christian Perfection*, first published in 1842, to address this attempt to modify Wesleyan theory [Reprint, Salem, OH: Schmul, 1990-1991, 363-364]. Peck associated the modification with Zinzendorf. Peck was the first American Methodist to publish an extended theological treatise on Christian perfection. According to Daniel Steele, around 1836 the New York Conference which had tried Dr. Francis Hodgson for Zinzendorfism also requested that George Peck write a refutation of this error. Thus originated his *Christian Perfection* [Steele, *Defense of Christian Perfection*, 70].

According to Peck's autobiography he thoroughly revised his book *Christian Perfection* in 1848. According to McClintock and Strong, *Cyclopedia*, 7:862 it was revised in 1848. According to Peters, *Christian Perfection*, 123, he issued a new edition in 1849. The book went through ten editions, but perhaps only one revision.

If Peters is correct that Peck expanded his book in response to Hosmer and Hosmer's article appeared in 1849, then the 1849 date for Peck's revision makes more sense. Perhaps, however, Peck was responding to this growing position and not specifically Hosmer. Peck does not reference Hosmer by name in his expanded Lecture 16 in *Christian Perfection*. As editor of the *MQR* from 1840-1848, Peck was also thrust in the middle of the controversy. Ironically, Peck's daughter, Mary Helen, was married to J. T. Crane who would publish his own work in 1874 which took the opposite position from Peck. Mary and J. T's son was Stephen Crane, author of *Red Badge of Courage* (1895).

[1628]Summers, *Treatise on Sanctification*, 117.

[1629]Franklin, *Critical Review of Wesleyan Perfection*, 19-213; 569. Franklin's approach was exegetical and he did not deal with such issues as Wesley's abridgement of the 9th Anglican Article of Religion.

However, in 1869 R. S. Foster wrote that regeneration is not perfect holiness. While all the elements of holiness are imparted and all the graces implanted in regeneration, all the rudiments of inbred sin are not destroyed. Regeneration is sanctification so far as it extends, but it is not as extensive as entire sanctification. "It is a degree, but not the whole of that work." The phrases "inbred sin," "remains of the carnal mind," "roots of bitterness," and "seeds of evil" describe the sin that remains after regeneration.[1630]

In 1874 Jonathan Townley Crane also argued that original sin does not remain in the regenerate. He argued against the "residue theory" and the progressive work of sanctification. Continuous victory over sin is the birthright of the Christian.[1631] D. D. Whedon wrote,

> Had we been privileged to peruse Dr. Crane's brochure, *Holiness the Birthright of All God's Children*, before publication, we should doubtless have endeavored to convince him that there is no such difference in his views as to require him to place them in so frank an antagonism to Mr. Wesley's. Mr. Wesley holds that regeneration is at first so incomplete that *traces of depravity remain in the soul*, as evidenced by the "sins willfully committed" (according to our Twelfth Article) "after justification." Dr. Crane admits that "after justification" there are "weak faith," "temptation," and "sin," but denies that their base is a "residue" of our natural pravity within us. This may seem to some a shadowy difference, bit it really leads him to a brave contest with Mr. Wesley's sermon on *Sin in Believers*, which has been accepted as standard by our Methodism the world around. We think it must still remain standard.

Whedon continued by asserting that Wesley and Crane agreed that at justification there is conferred a degree of power over sin and temptation. But there is a difference between initial sanctification and final sanctification, which is completed at the resurrection. In the mean time there is enough power to enable one to maintain the avoidance of such sin as diminishes the light of God's smile upon us. "Let us not be impatient because God is so slow as to leave an imperfect 'residue' within us." The sin of the unregenerate is the hostile act of an enemy;

[1630]Foster, *Christian Purity*, 109; 119.

[1631]Crane, *Birthright of All God's Children*, 64-118.

the sin of the regenerate is the offense of a child. Whedon concluded that Crane had reacted to the vast amount of both false showiness and extravagance under the guise of sanctification which the holiness movement has provided and that he unnecessarily went outside the Methodist system of doctrine to provide a countercheck.[1632]

In a 1878 article for the *Methodist Quarterly Review* Crane strove for points of theological agreement, noting that all schools of theology agree that complete sanctification is an integral part of redemption. All agree that perfection is not absolute. And all agree that in this life we are subject to temptation and sources of danger within us. Yet Methodists believe this complete sanctification may be completed in this life, while Calvinists believe it cannot be completed until death. Roman Catholics believe that baptism cleanses from original sin and whatever remains is dealt with in purgatory.

After making concessions, Crane said there were two questions which needed an answer: What scriptural ground is there for the belief that there is deliverance from moral depravity in this life? and To what extent can we be kept by the power of God from the commission of sin? Crane accepted the doctrine of depravity, defining us as "utterly indisposed, disabled, and made opposite to all good, and wholly inclined to all evil." Yet he argued against the ambiguity of the

---

[1632]Whedon, "Quarterly Book Table," 490-493. Whedon concluded that Crane overrated justification and underrated sanctification. This review was incorporated into Whedon, *Statements*, 331-338. Whedon argued that total depravity extended to the entire personality, but no so intensive as to make a man as bad as he could be. Thus, regeneration also extends to the total person, but not so intensive as to eliminate the possibility of sin [*Statements*, 331].

Yet Asbury Lowrey complained about Whedon's endorsement of Crane's book and Whedon responded ["Quarterly Book-Table,"662-681]. As editor of the *Methodist Quarterly Review*, Whedon described the new periodical, *The Christian Standard and Home Journal*, the successor to the late *Methodist Home Journal*, with Dr. Lowrey as editor, as having for its speciality the Wesleyan doctrine of holiness. "The editor quickly showed a sense of his high office by impeaching the sound Wesleyanism of our *Quarterly Review*. He seems to advocate a doctrine nearer to the type of George Bell than of John Wesley" [pp. 662].

Whedon continued his rebuttal of Lowrey by denying that he endorsed Crane's book. However, Whedon denied that Crane was Zinzendorfian. Whedon explained that Zinzendorf taught that sanctification was imputed at justification and that resulted in antinomianism. That was not Crane's teaching. Whedon went on to accuse Lowrey of "hyper-Wesleyanism" and then discussed the holiness abuse of figurative terms in Scripture. This rebuttal was edited into Whedon's statement on "Christian Perfection" in *Statement*, but all references to Lowrey were edited out.

term "original sin." Crane rejected attempts to explain away perfection or to postpone its completion to death. Instead he argued that it occurred at conversion. "Very many of us do not believe that Christian Perfection is a second, special blessing 'gained instantaneously by an act of faith' and 'not through any process of gradual growth, striving, or any advancement toward sinless perfection.'"

Crane rejected eradication and argued that instincts and passions do not need rooting out but discipline, restraint, and chastisement. He noted that Huntington and Franklin collided with Steele and McDonald as if they did not belong to the same church. "Very many of us do not believe that Christian Perfection is a second special blessing "gained instantaneously by an act of faith."

Crane also rejected Palmer's teaching. "Nor do we believe that the mere fact that a man thinks that he is conscious of having made a complete consecration of himself and all that he possesses justifies him in announcing that a second mighty work of renewal has not been wrought in him."

Crane noted that Jabez Bunting and others "dissented from the idea that the innate depravity of the human heart is removed by two distinct and instantaneous processes, one of which occurs at conversion, and the other at some subsequent period, when such a second work is made a definite aim, and sought by a specific act of faith."[1633]

In 1877 J. O. A. Clark wrote an essay on holiness in which he taught that complete cleansing from inbred sin and the being of sin and the sanctifying power of the Holy Ghost occurred at the initial moment of conversion. Perfection after the new birth could be summed up in a single word — "growth."[1634]

In 1881 Thomas Summers, editor of the Southern *Quarterly Review* asked, "who would have though that Osiandrianism and Zinzendorfianism would be revived in the close of the nineteenth century? Yet such is the case." He advocated a balance between the "rationalists" who denied innate depravity and the "fanatics" who distorted the doctrine of entire sanctification. Summers advocated a median line between Pelagianism and Augustianism.[1635]

[1633]Crane, "Christian Perfection and the Higher Life," 688-714. At the close of this article Whedon, the editor, placed a disclaimer stating that the author is responsible for any specialties of opinion in the article. However, within this article Crane commended Whedon's "snakes'head" railroad illustration as perfect. See p. 421 of this book.

[1634]Clark, "Holiness," 505-522.

[1635]Summers, "Osiandrianism and Zinzendorfianism," 88. Andreas Osiander (1498-1552) was a Lutheran pastor who attacked Melanchthon, arguing that in justification the new believer partakes in the divine nature. Thus he held justification

Although the teaching of Osiander and Zinzendorf are typically contrasted with the holiness message, in the same article Summers cited a correspondent who complained about teaching found in a holiness periodical, "The King's Highway," published in Spartanburg, SC. The correspondent wrote,

> It matters not what a man's general Christian experience may be, he always closes with these words: "I am all on the altar, and the altar being greater than the gift, it sanctifieth the gift, and I am wholly sanctified." They read in connection Heb. 13:10 and Exod 29:37, and feel assured that Christ is the Christian's altar, and that whatsoever toucheth it is wholly sanctified. They oppose all scriptural interpretation by their own experience. They say, "I know," and hence they are closed to all argument. They predicate the necessity of sanctification on the *universal carnality of all regenerate persons*, and therefore treat all regenerate persons as unsaved.

The correspondent declared this to be the baldest antinomianism because it considers justified people as sinners. Furthermore, the two passages cited from Scripture do not support the doctrine taught.

Summers then compared this holiness teaching with the Osiandrianism heresy which taught that justification and sanctification were one in the same act. Summers felt that Zinzendorfianism amounts to nearly the same result, although it comes through a different route. The result of the teaching of Osiander and Zinzendorf is that there is no progress in holiness after justification. The result of the holiness teaching, influenced by Phoebe Palmer, is that there is no holiness which accompanies justification. Thus, there can be no progress in holiness until a second blessing is received.

Regarding the empirical argument of the experience of instantaneous sanctification, Summers wrote that there is such a state, whether preceded by a longer or a shorter period, silent or more demonstrative processes. However, some people are naturally sanguine, enthusiastic, sensational, and may think the carnal mind is all destroyed because they are so happy that they do not feel its working in them. However, such may not be the case. The fallacy resulting from the use of metaphors carries them beyond the boundary line of truth and

---

and sanctification were one in the same act; that a real inner transformation was part of the justification process.

soberness.[1636] Yet Summers maintained a balance between excesses on both extremes. However, it was becoming more common for the excesses within the holiness movement to push Methodists toward the opposite extreme of Zinzendorf's teaching.

This view also surfaced with Jeremiah M. Boland's *The Problem of Methodism* in 1888. According to Peters, "No book, by a Southern author, and published by a Southern house, has been discussed so extensively. . . . Despite the inaccuracy of its principal thesis Boland's book received wide circulation and considerable acclaim."[1637]

Boland declared that the only controversy among the Churches regarding sanctification is in regard to the time, the place, and the means by which the work is done. "Methodism stands alone among all the Churches, in preaching *a present salvation from all sin, but faith in the blood of the Lamb, and the possibility of such a one 'abiding in Christ and sinning not.'*"[1638]

Yet Boland claimed, drawing from Crane, "The great mistake Mr. Wesley made was in adopting the 'residue theory of regeneration' and the 'second change theory of sanctification.'"[1639] The residue theory tends to minify regeneration and magnify sanctification.[1640]

According to Boland, "the old man,""the body of sin,""inbred sin," and "the carnal mind"all mean the same thing in Paul's psychology.[1641] Yet "the old

---

[1636]Summers, "Osiandrianism and Zinzendorfianism," 83-89.

[1637]Peters, *Christian Perfection*, 154; 156. Here Peters referenced Boland's claim that Wesley came to repudiate his earlier belief concerning sin in believers because he omitted over half of the ninth article in the Anglican Articles of Religion in preparing the Articles of Religion for the American Methodist Church. While the seventh Methodist article dealt with original sin, Wesley only omitted that portion which referred to original guilt. Furthermore, this article does not address the issue of sin remaining after regeneration. Peters concluded, "This was building a weighty assumption on a flimsy deduction" [*Christian Perfection*, 155; see also Rosser, *Reply to the "Problem of Methodism."* Rosser was the editor of the *Southern Methodist Review* and later became a bishop].

[1638]Boland, *Problem of Methodism*, 25-26.

[1639]Boland, *Problem of Methodism*, 27.

[1640]Boland, *Problem of Methodism*, 30.

[1641]Boland, *Problem of Methodism*, 89.

man" cannot be the same thing as the "body of sin" because Romans 6:6 says the one is crucified in order that the other might be destroyed. God does not fulfill a prerequisite in order that he might do the same thing again. According to Romans 6:6, our "old man" was crucified. Here an aorist passive indicative verb is used to indicate a past event. Then a purpose clause is used to speak of a future contingent event — "in order that" the body of sin might be destroyed. Here Paul uses ἵνα (*hina*) with the verb *katargeo* in the subjunctive mood. According to Kenneth Grider, "Paul is saying that our unregenerate self is crucified as surely as Christ on the Cross was crucified, and that God brings about this death to the former life in order that the state of original sin might also be destroyed."[1642]

But Boland denied that the carnal mind survives the work of regeneration[1643] and referred to Wesley's sermon "On Sin in Believers" as "that mysterious sermon."[1644] He decried the low estimate put on regeneration and held that the regenerate are entirely sanctified.[1645] "Regeneration is a complete work in its nature, and *includes* sanctification, or moral purity, while Christian perfection is a state of freedom from sin, and includes a maturity of the Christian graces. The one is instantaneous and complete, admitting of no degrees; the other is progressive — a growth, a going on, until the full stature of a perfect man in Christ is reached."[1646]

According to Boland the regenerate do not struggle with the sin nature, but with temptation. Yet Wesley declared that the whole body of ancient Christians who left any writings declare with one voice that an evil nature of sin remains even in believers until they are strong in the Lord.[1647]

Wesley's second mistake, according to Boland, was confounding sanctification with Christian perfection.[1648] While sanctification was complete in

---

[1642]Grider, "The Meaning of 'Old Man,'"15-16; 46.

[1643]Boland, *Problem of Methodism*, 83-96.

[1644]Boland, *Problem of Methodism*, 27-28; 61; 59. Boland claimed that Wesley wrote "Sin in Believers" under the influence of the ninth article of the Church of England, yet he finally rejected that dogma in the articles of faith he prepared for the American church [p. 72].

[1645]Boland, *Problem of Methodism*, 161.

[1646]Boland, *Problem of Methodism*, 28-29.

[1647]Wesley, "On Sin in Believers," Sermon #13, 1.2.

[1648]Boland, *Problem of Methodism*, 27.

regeneration, Christian perfection was not an instantaneous second change but a matter of growth in grace.

Summers explained that Wesley omitted the ambiguous portion of Anglical Article 9, which read "so that the flesh lusteth always contrary to the Spirit, and, therefore, in every person born into this world it deserves God's wrath and damnation. . . ." Summers observed that Wesley upheld the doctrine of original sin in Methodist Articles 2 and 20, yet he held that Christ made unconditional satisfaction for original guilt.[1649]

Concerning Wesley's abridgment of the ninth article, Tillett wrote that "some have taken the position that it indicates that in later life he abandoned the doctrine of indwelling sin in the regenerate as an article of his own faith; while others think that he continued to hold this doctrine to the last, but omitted the objectionable part of the Article only because it affirmed that this remaining sin involves moral guilt and is deserving of damnation."[1650]

While Tillett thought Wesley was inconsistent on his doctrine of sin in believers, this statement by Tillett actually undermined the view that Wesley abandoned the doctrine of original sin.

Boland's book became a hot topic in *The Quarterly Review of the Methodist Episcopal Church, South*, under the editorship of W. P. Harrison. The initial review of John E. Edwards was favorable.[1651] In January 1889 Josephus Anderson concluded that Boland "failed in his attempt to show that the doctrine of our church does not embrace the residue theory, as he calls it."[1652] In the April 1889 issue Joseph B. Cottrell arrived at the same solution as Boland.[1653] In October 1889 R. H. Mahon, writing on "The Nature of Sin and Holiness" does not name Boland but obviously referred to him as Zinzendorfian.[1654] In April 1894 S. H. Wainwright suggested that Boland did not read Wesley sufficiently.[1655]

[1649]Summers, *Systematic Theology*, 2:19-44.

[1650]Tillett, *Personal Salvation*, 526.

[1651]Edwards, "Problem of Methodism,"25-45.

[1652]Anderson, "Problem Examined,"373-393; 414-418.

[1653]Cottrell, "Problem of Methodism," 97-107.

[1654]Mahon, "Nature of Sin," 21-35.

[1655]Wainwright, "Dr. Boland on the Ninth Article," 36-40.

In the July 1894 issue H. R. Withers took issue with Boland and Hayes.[1656]

Boland himself replied with two articles for *The Methodist Review*, "Psychological View of Sin and Holiness" in July 1892[1657] and "'Problem' and Its Critics" in January 1893.[1658]

John James Tigert was editor of *The Southern Methodist Review* which was previously the *Quarterly Review of the Methodist Episcopal Church, South* until 1886 and after 1889 was renamed *The Methodist Review.* In 1894 Tigert declared that Methodism has a doctrine of perfect love. While Tigert did not personally profess it, he warned those who thought it necessary to root out the tares to be careful of the wheat.[1659]

George H. Hayes wrote *The Problem Solved* in which he argued against a second blessing on the basis that depravity is inseparable from humanity. This position was challenged by Benjamin F. Orr.[1660] While Hayes departed from the Zinzendorfianism of Boland, Hayes had no place for any second blessing.

Writing in 1893, William McDonald argued, "If Mr. Wesley abandoned his doctrine of "Sin in Believers," he succeeded in so far concealing the fact, that his most intimate associates and lifelong friends utterly failed to discover it, and his followers, for more than a hundred years, have never had a suspicion of any such change, until Drs. Crane and Boland made the wonderful discovery."[1661]

Writing in 1914 Watson Boone Duncan concluded, "The main feature of the book is it tendency to check the extremist who would either minimize or eliminate the work of regeneration."[1662]

John L. Brasher had been convinced by reading Boland in 1893 and preached "one work." However, in 1900 he was sanctified under the ministry of Samuel Logan Brengle and became an advocate for two works of grace.[1663]

In 1898 Isaiah Villars presented a paper before a district ministerial

---

1656Withers, "Problem of Methodism: Problem Solved," 338-360. See also O. E. Brown, "Comparative Study of Methodist Theology,"193-203.

1657pp. 342-354.

1658pp. 339-353.

1659Tigert, "Colossians," 274-277.

1660Orr, "'Problem Solved,'"Oct 1892: 91-106.

1661McDonald, *John Wesley and His Doctrine*, 109.

1662Duncan, *Studies in Methodist Literature*, 171.

1663Brasher, *Sanctified South*.

association of the Methodist Episcopal Church in Illinois. It met with their general approval and it was printed for general circulation. Villars declared that what the modern holiness movement taught was not the same as what Wesley taught. Villars believe that John Wesley's justification in 1737 was an Episcopalian justification, which carried with it no personal and conscious experience of pardon, regeneration, and witness of the Spirit. Villars called this a sacramental justification. Thus, Wesley's sanctification or experiential attainment of holiness of heart and perfect love in 1738 "was nothing more or less than our doctrine and experience of Justification by Faith."[1664]

DeWitt Clinton Huntington also claimed that regeneration and sanctification were essential the same. Huntington denied the theory of passive sin, claiming that all sin is voluntary in nature. He claimed that the doctrine of inbred sin was not Wesleyan. Calling inbred sin "guiltless sin," he claimed the deliverance from the misfortune of Adam's sin involves no change in moral character.[1665] Huntington believed that every believer is entirely sanctified at the moment of regeneration, but few, if any, abide without interruption in this state.[1666]

M. P. Zink objected to Huntington's position that all sin as a voluntary transgression of law, that Wesley taught the sinful sensibilities constitute original

---

[1664]Villars, *Theory of the Second Blessing*, 8. According to this interpretation, when candidates for admission into full membership in the conference were asked if they were going on to perfection, Villars said this question was asking if the preacher was actually converted. Villars pointed out that Wesley himself was an ordained clergyman *before* his 1738 conversion, as Methodism understands conversion [p.19].

[1665]Huntington, *Sin and Holiness*, 60; 81; 100. This book was based on an essay first given in 1869. Timothy Smith described this book as an elaborate reworking of Boland's thesis [*Called Unto Holiness*, 45].

[1666]Huntington, *Sin and Holiness*, 160; 202. Thus, Huntington believed entire, permanent sanctification is subsequent to the first moment of regeneration in time, but in nature one and the same [p. 278]. J. A. Wood recalled that during his early pastorates at Susquehanna and Binghamton, Huntington assisted him and was more clear in his experience of entire sanctification than was Wood. However, Wood acknowledged that Huntington's views respecting the Wesleyan doctrine of entire sanctification had changed. Wood felt this was due to a very trying ministry in the Genessee Conference. Wood concluded that if Dr. Huntington had held on to his early experience, he would never have written his book on *Sin and Holiness* [*Autobiography of Rev. J. A. Wood*, 48-49. Of course, this is merely speculation.

sin, and that entire sanctification is not the removal of the effects of ancestral sin.[1667]

In his book *Methodist Theologians vs. Methodist Theology* George W. Wilson devoted an entire chapter to refute Huntington. Wilson objected to Huntington's denial of inbred sin and concluded that Huntington held to righteousness effected by the free choice of the will — even though the freedom of the will was lost with Adam's original sin. Our will is only free as Christ makes it free.[1668]

Wilbur Fisk Tillett, influential theologian of the M. E. Church, South and dean of the theological faculty at Vanderbilt University, conceded that if Wesley's doctrine of "sin in believers" is true, there would be a place for the doctrine of a second work of grace. However, Tillett denied the regenerate believer retains the sinful nature. He declared every regenerate believer should live a sinless and holy life every day. According to Tillett, the most serious breach in the logic and harmony of Wesleyan Arminian theology is the unscriptural view of sin in the regenerate.[1669]

Tillett affirmed the doctrine of original sin and disassociated his views from Zinzendorf.[1670] He taught that all justified believers are sanctified, that "willful sin incompatible with the regenerate state," and that there is no middle ground between sin and salvation.[1671] Yet he said that a liability to sin remains after regeneration.[1672] While he argued for the possibility of Christian perfection, he did not call it salvation from all sin, which occurs in regeneration; it is completeness in Christ. Christian perfection is the ideal life of every child of God, not an instantaneous experience subsequent to regeneration.[1673] He advocated, "Let us preach that doctrine of progressive holiness which is marked by freedom from all known sin at every stage of the Christian life – that gradual work which,

---

1667Zink, *Review of Dr. Huntington*, 3.

1668Wilson, *Methodist Theologians*, 127-223.

1669Tillett, *Personal Salvation*, 520-521. At this point Tillett cited Miley for support, "We cannot think Mr Wesley's notable sermon on Sin in Believers entirely clear of this error" [Miley, *Systematic Theology*, 2:367].

1670Tillett, *Personal Salvation*, 84; 455.

1671Tillett, *Personal Salvation*, 255-270; 241-244.

1672Tillett, *Personal Salvation*, 378; 385.

1673Tillett, *Personal Salvation*, 514-519.

beginning at regeneration "may increase," to use Wesley's words, "more and more unto the perfect day."[1674] Tillett declared,

> Methodist theology has always maintained that it is not only possible, but the privilege and duty of every regenerate child of God to be entirely holy and free from all sin, and that this experience and state are included in God's gracious provisions for this present life, and not simply for realization at and after death. But, while Methodists are generally agreed as to this, they differ widely in opinion as to how this ideal Christian state is fully and finally attained; whether, recognizing its beginning in regeneration, it be by a work of grace wrought gradually or instantaneously after regeneration.[1675]

Tillett himself argued that Wesley was inconsistent for teaching two perfections: a thorough regeneration with no known sin and an incomplete regeneration with certain sins of the spirit which necessitate entire sanctification. Wesley preached a thorough regeneration with resulted in a victory over sin, but Christian perfection is a further work of grace which completes what was begun in regeneration. This is necessary because of the two-fold nature of sin.

In *The Hole in the Holiness Movement*, I cited John L. Peters' criticism that the views of D. D. Whedon were nearer the teaching of Zinzendorf than of Wesley.[1676] However, Whedon's definition and defense of Christian perfection in *Statements: Theological and Critical* cannot accurately be classified with Zinzendorf. Leslie Wilcox also concluded that Peters did not interpret Whedon properly.[1677] Whedon gave this summary of his view:

> Through a maturity of Christian experience and the fullness of the Spirit imparted, the spiritual powers of the faithful Christian may be so strengthened that he may, and often does, maintain, through grace, for a longer or shorter period, a permanent state of the undiminished fullness of his acceptance with God, and

---

[1674]Tillett, *Personal Salvation*, 532.

[1675]Tillett, *Personal Salvation*, 400.

[1676]Reasoner, *Hole in the Holiness Movement*, 98; see Peters, *Christian Perfection*, 151-152.

[1677]Wilcox, "Whedon's Position on the Doctrine of Holiness."

under no more actual condemnation than at the moment of his justification.[1678]

Maddox described this statement as a revision of Wesley's model in which perfect holiness was an ideal to be endlessly pursued, "being achieved, at best, sporadically and temporarily."[1679]

Whedon declared that the regenerate has power over sin, but is still able to yield to temptation. Whedon then gives five levels of power over sin, attempting to distinguish between initial and entire sanctification. Entire sanctification is "the power, through divine grace, more or less complete, and more or less permanent, so to resist temptation and avoid sin as to live in the fullness of divine favor." However, even the entirely sanctified are liable to apostasy. Thus, Whedon argued for the power of the Holy Spirit in repressing, not eradicating sin.[1680]

At Revelation 7:14 Whedon defined sanctification as the power to resist temptation, to repress our disordered affections, and bring all into obedience to the law of Christ.[1681] Whedon declared that sanctification is "perhaps, less the taking away anything from our inward nature than the bestowment of a repressive power over our inner sinward tendencies." Just as Paul found it necessary to *keep his body under*, so sanctification is a repression, not a removal. The cessation of our hereditary depravity occurs only in the sense of a complete repression, not a removal.

Whedon illustrated his point from the railroads of his day. The rails were mere flat iron bars spiked upon long timbers laid upon the cross-ties. Now and then the end of a rail loosened from the wood, lifted itself up, like the head of a serpent, and threw the train from the track. Yet the iron bar was an essential part of the railroad. In its proper place and doing its proper work, it was not only innocent, but necessary. Breaking loose from restraints, and getting out of its proper place, it became a source of danger and a cause of wreck and ruin. Safety

---

1678Whedon, *Essays*, 141-142. This book was a collection of Whedon's shorter writings. The section entitled "Doctrines of Methodism," from which this citation came, was published in *Bibliotheca Sacra* (April 1862): 241-274; reprinted by Langford, *Wesleyan Theology*, 102-103.

1679Maddox, "Reconnecting the Means to the End," 46.

1680Whedon, *Statements*, 330-350; Mudge said this "fivefold division is very cloudy"[*Growth in Holiness*, 153].

1681Whedon, *Commentary*, 5:388-389.

required some way of holding the iron rails securely in place, but not their abolition. This became known as Whedon's "snakes' head" theory through which he advocated the doctrine that sanctification was a force that kept our natural instincts and emotions "more or less completely" suppressed.[1682]

The view that full cleansing of the soul in entire sanctification was attributed rather than real, surfaced among some within the Church of God (Anderson) camp around 1899. Those who taught this were labeled "Anti-Cleansers," it was considered to be heresy and attributed to Zinzendorf.[1683]

In March 1907, William H. Durham, the Baptist pastor of the North Avenue Mission in Chicago spoke in tongues at Azusa Street, but by 1910 he denounced the "second blessing" doctrine of sanctification within pentecostalism. Durham did not find Wesley to teach what the holiness movement had represented him as teaching.

Durham concluded that the Acts account as well as his own experience did not square with the three works of grace paradigm. There were two crises, not three. He declared that after his baptism he could never preach another sermon on the second work of grace theory. He could preach holiness as never before, but not as a second work of grace.[1684] In opposition to the original pentecostal teaching of three works of grace, Durham argued for two works of grace: conversion and the baptism of the Holy Spirit with the initial evidence of speaking in tongues. He complained that justification was lowered if the converted man still had the old man, a serpent in his heart, or the Adamic nature in him. He argued that salvation was not a half-way work and those who were saved were not going to hell. "I began to write against the doctrine that it takes two works of grace to save and cleanse a man. I denied and still deny that God does not deal with the nature of sin at conversion. I deny that a man who is converted or born again is outwardly washed and cleansed but that his heart is left unclean with enmity against God in it."

Durham's message was that identification with Jesus Christ saves and sanctifies, no second work of grace is taught by Scripture of necessary. "We believed then, as now, that when God saves a man . . . . He cleanses him from all sin" However, he denied this was a separate experience apart from

---

[1682]Whedon, *Statements*, 335-341.

[1683]Smith, *Quest for Holiness and Unity*, 184-191; Strege, "Quilting a Church,"136-138. This was known as the "Anti-Cleansing Heresy."

[1684]Durham, "Open Letter To My Brother Ministers," 14.

justification.[1685]

Durham called his view the "finished work at Calvary," teaching that the work of Christ on the cross was sufficient for both salvation and sanctification. He argued that "the old man, or old nature, which was sinful and depraved and which was the very thing in us that was condemned, is crucified with Christ."[1686] Durham wrote, "When one really comes into Christ he is as much in Christ as he will ever be."[1687] He also declared, "No believer is justified without being entirely sanctified."[1688]

Over time "finished work" Pentecostals came to stress the gradual process of sanctification over a lifetime and this became the view of most American Pentecostals. However, Durham's teaching, before its modification to accept gradual sanctification, seemed to reflect the position of Zinzendorf.[1689] Stephen Lewis characterized him as "a single work perfectionist."[1690] More recently, David Peterson concluded,

> The popular view that sanctification is a process of moral renewal and change, following justification, is not the emphasis

---

[1685]Durham, "Finished Work of Calvary,"1.

[1686]Durham, "Finished Work of Christ," 2.

[1687]*Articles by Durham*, 2.

[1688]Quoted by Lewis, "William H. Durham," 26. While Lewis cites *Articles by Durham*, 28, I cannot find this direct quote. However, on p. 27 Durham declared that no man can be justified in an experience short of entire sanctification.

Durham sounds so much like Boland, that I think Durham must have been influenced by Boland. Both men stated their deep respect for Wesley, but felt they had improved on Wesley. Both men held to the completeness of regeneration, but added something subsequent to regeneration. Those who followed Boland within Methodism and those who followed Durham within Pentecostalism tended to drop their radical emphasis on regeneration while retaining their respective emphases on what followed regeneration.

[1689]This is the opinion of Clayton, "Significance of William H. Durham, 30-31; 34. Faupel thinks it is more Keswickian theology [*Everlasting Gospel*, 230; 264].

[1690]Lewis, "William H. Durham,"51-52. Simmons thinks that Durham got his "finished work" doctrine from E. W. Kenyon, who had taught it for over a decade prior to Durham [*E. W. Kenyon*, x; 292-293]. According to Bruce Barron, *Health and Wealth Gospel*, 35-63, Kenyon was Pentecostal. According to McConnell, *Different Gospel*, 16; 28; 185, he was not.

of the New Testament. Rather, sanctification is primarily another way of describing what it means to be converted or brought to God in Christ and kept in that relationship. It would be more accurate to say that renewal and change flow from the regeneration and sanctification that God has already accomplished in our lives.[1691]

10. The Puritans and Ecclesiastical Separation

In addition to the category of "ethical primitivism," Richard Hughes also identified a second form of primitivism, "ecclesiastical primitivism." This movement emphasized the restoration of forms and structures of the primitive church. There have been many primitive movements which attempted to restore apostolic Christianity. They differed, however, in their concept of apostolic Christianity. The best definition is found in Acts 2:42.

Novatian of Rome held that those who had apostatized during the Decian persecutions (A. D. 249-250) should not be welcomed back into the church. When Cornelius was elevated as pope in A. D. 251, Novatian was elected the "antipope" of the Puritan party in the church.[1692] This group formed under strict discipline and their separatist movement lasted many centuries. They were also called the Cathari, from the Greek word *katharoi* which meant "pure ones."

By medieval times they had spread and were known by different names, usually a location where they were strong. They were divined into two classes: believers and *perfecti*. The perfect had received the baptism of the Spirit by the imposition of hands, which removed original sin and restored immortality. They

---

[1691]Peterson, *Possessed by God*, 136.

[1692]The Donatists were Africans who separated from the Roman church in A. D. 312. In an open letter to Rev. William Dodd, Wesley said he did not know who they were but he suspected they were the real Christians of that age [*Works*, 11:453]. Wesley also expressed sympathy for the Novatians by expressing his agreement with the statement of John Gambold to his brother Charles. In this letter Gambold declared, "I am persuaded that a Montanist or a Novatian, who from the height of his purity should look down with contempt upon poor sinners, and exclude them from all mercy, would not be thought such as overthrower of the gospel as he who should learn from the Author of it to be a friend of publicans and sinners, and to sit down upon the level with them as soon as they begin to repent" [*Journal*, 14 May 1738]. Wesley shared a common concern with them for the purity of the church, however, without necessarily endorsing all their beliefs.

rejected marriage and sexual intercourse. Because of their contempt for the flesh, they despised human sexuality. Marriage was evil because it gave respectability to an evil act. To show their contempt for the holiness of marriage, in some cases the Cathari practiced homosexuality as a means of desecration and de-sacralizing the body. While some were evangelical dissenters, others were pantheistic or dualists.[1693] They were exterminated by the Inquisition of the fourteenth century.[1694]

Huldreich Zwingli condemned both singing and organs in the church since they were not commanded in apostolic churches. In 1550 Martin Bucer wrote *De Regno Christi*, in which he argued that England could become the kingdom of Christ if proper attention was given to the ancient church.

After the attempt of Mary Tudor to crush Protestantism in England, the Puritans were committed to embracing the apostolic faith. While the earliest Puritans were Presbyterians, by the 1580s some Puritan separatists had concluded that the model of primitive Christianity was congregationalism. Thus, John Robinson argued that the congregational form of government was "cast in the apostolical and primitive mold, and not one day nor hour younger, in the nature and form of it, than the first church of the New Testament."[1695]

The term "Puritans" was coined in the 1560s. As nonconformists they advocated a full Calvinistic reform within the Church of England based on the "pure" Word of God. They emphasized the need for a "continuing cycle of endeavour and self-evaluation within the context of faith in the effectual work of God," so that no one might be content with self-deception.[1696]

They emphasized personal holiness through union with Christ and social holiness. For the Puritans the work of holiness was the establishment of Christ's kingdom. According to Packer there was for them no disjunction between sacred and secular. All creation was sacred and all activities must be sanctified. Thus, they made everything "holiness to the Lord" by doing all to the glory of God.[1697] This Puritan work ethic, by which Max Weber described the Calvinists of the

---

[1693]Rushdoony, "The Cathars," Chalcedon Position Paper #63; reprinted in *Roots of Reconstruction*, 283-287.

[1694]See their description by Stark, *For the Glory of God*, 53-56. See also John Calvin's reaction to them on p. 376 of this book.

[1695]*Works of John Robinson*, 2:43.

[1696]Hawkes, "Logic of Assurance in English Puritan Theology," 252.

[1697]Packer, *Quest for Godliness*, 23-24; 29; 39; 271;330.

seventeenth century, emphasized worldly success as an indication that sanctification had begun. "Hence, in order to alleviate their fears, they strove with all their might and ingenuity for commercial achievement. The consequence was capitalism."[1698]

The fifth volume of Wesley's *Christian Library* continues with Puritan authors. Thirty-two Puritan authors were included in the project. In fact, the bulk of Wesley's sources were Puritan, but their predestination had been edited out.[1699]

Among these sources Wesley abridged was John Preston's work, *The New Covenant*. Wesley agreed with Preston that Christian perfection is by faith and not works. He also agreed there is a progressive element and that sanctification is the work of the Spirit. Robert Monk concluded,

> Although Wesley's perfection was a present possibility, it still must improve or increase in love, just as Preston demanded a constant increase in love. Preston's concept of perfection, on the other hand, certainly allowed some sense of "present perfection" in his concentration on purity of intention or dedication present now in a believer. Both authors sought a very similar, if not identical, end product — a pure, perfect, or sound heart in the believer.[1700]

However, the Puritans taught that this work could never be consummated in this life. For them entire sanctification comes only after death. John Cotton (1584-1652), a leader of the Puritan movement encouraged sanctification, but taught that in no way did a person's salvation hinge on a godly lifestyle. There was no necessary relationship between the outward life and the inner work of the Holy Spirit.[1701] Wesley felt it often came before death and he would not limit the work of the Spirit. After all, if God is sovereign, we are in error to limit what God can do.

In *Grace Abounding*, John Bunyan (1628-1688) denounced Richard Baxter and all who allowed for any possibility of "perfection in love" in this life. However, in Bunyan's *Holy War* he told how Diabolus petitioned Immanuel that

---

[1698]Bebbington, *Holiness*, 30-31.

[1699]Monk, *John Wesley: His Puritan Heritage*, pp. 38; 55-56; Wesley, *BE Works*, 1:26.

[1700]Monk, *John Wesley: His Puritan Heritage*, 116-117.

[1701]Cotton, "Hypocrites and Saints," 1:316.

he might have only a small part of the city of Mansoul. When this petition was rejected, Diabolus begged to have a little room within the walls. Immanuel answered that he should have no place at all to rest the sole of his foot. Wesley, who abridged *Holy War* for the *Christian Library* exclaimed,

> Had not the good old man forgot himself? Did not the force of truth so prevail over him here as utterly to overturn his own system? To assert perfection in the clearest manner? For if this is not salvation from sin I cannot tell what is.[1702]

Puritan Thomas Manton (1620-1677) described the divine nature which is promised in 2 Peter 1:4. Yet this does not imply a cleansing from the old nature.

> There may be such a sense of the goodness, wisdom, and power of God, as may produce a sudden passion, as suppose of fear or love; yet it may only affect us for the present, and not produce a thorough change of heart and life. There is an impression we cannot deny, and an impression suitable to those apprehensions that we have of God; but it is not a constant principle of holy spiritual operation. But the promises of the Gospel are to breed in us such a temper of heart as may be a second nature to us; an habit or constitution of soul that may incline as to live to God.
> A habit serveth for this use, that a man may act easily, pleasantly, and constantly. (1.) To act easily. There is an inclination and propensity to holiness. God created all things with an inclination to their proper operations; as fire to ascend, and water to descend. So true Christians have a tendency to holy actions; their hearts are bent to please God, and serve him, and they do whatever they do with a kind of naturalness, because of this bent and inclination. They act not only as enjoined, but as inclined.
> There is an inclination and propensity to holiness. God created

---

[1702]"On Perfection," Sermon #76, 3.11. Bunyan's *Holy War* is found in the *Christian Library*, 32:3-137; 2nd ed. 19:123-227.

all things with an inclination to their proper operations; as fire to ascend, and water to descend. So true Christians have a tendency to holy actions; their hearts are bent to please God, and serve him, and they do whatever they do with a kind of naturalness, because of this bent and inclination. They act not only as enjoined, but as inclined.

The law of God is in their hearts, and consequently they act not by constraint, but with a ready mind. (2.) To act pleasantly. They have not only a new bent, bias, and tendency, but it is a delight to them to do what is holy, as being in their element when they are thus employed. What is against nature is harsh, but what is with nature is sweet and pleasant. It is hard, a kind of force to bring them to do the contrary. There needeth some kind of violence to bring a good man to sin, as also a bad man to do good. (3.) It is a constant principle of holy operations, so that a man does not only obey God easily, but evenly, and without such frequent interruptions of the holy life. Many do that which is good, or forbear evil uneasily, because of the restraints of Providence, or dictates of conscience; and unevenly by fits and starts. But, Psalm 106:3, "Blessed is he that keepeth judgment, and does righteousness at all times." They are continually exercising all duties of Godliness, righteousness, and mercy; for the operations of nature are constant, however obstructed or diverted at certain times. This we are to look after, that the sanctifying grace we have received become a new nature; that the soul have a tendency and delight as to spiritual objects, and be constantly and easily carried to them, and that this be the whole frame and drift of our lives.[1703]

Walter Marshall, a Presbyterian divine, was a fellow of New College at Oxford. After his death his book, *The Gospel Mystery of Sanctification Opened in Sundry Practical Directions*, was published in 1692. The phrase "gospel mystery" indicates sanctification is a supernatural work of grace.[1704] Marshall

---

[1703]Wesley, *Christian Library*, 2nd ed, Vol. 7, Sermon #3, 1.1-2.

[1704]Packer, *Keep in Step with the Spirit*, p. 149. In his second edition *Rediscovering Holiness*, Packer expressed the hope that his book would facilitate in a reconnection with what Walter Marshall called the "gospel mystery of sanctification"[*Rediscovering Holiness*, 2nd ed, 9].

directed that holiness be sought in its due order, after union, justification and the gift of the Holy Ghost, and by faith. Marshall taught sanctification by faith, following the semi-mystical strain of some later Puritans. Although the Keswick tradition appeals to him as a precursor to their emphasis, there is really no continuity between his emphasis and theirs.[1705] Wiley said this book was written "as one of the earliest supplements to the legalism of the Reformation theology. While stated largely in Calvinist terminology, the emphasis upon an inward work of grace is wholesome and worthy of careful study. Theologically it forms an interesting transition to the teachings of the Wesleys in the eighteenth century."[1706]

John Goodwin, an Arminian Puritan, writing fifty years before Wesley, taught that the fullness of the Spirit gave the believer the full assurance of faith and their hearts would be made perfect in love.[1707] Fletcher called John Wesley "the John Goodwin of the age."[1708]

Various sects of Puritanism typically defended themselves by appealing to primitive Christianity. In 1639 Roger Williams formed the Baptist church in Rhode Island, believing that believers' baptism was clearly practiced in the apostolic church. In 1851 the Landmark Baptist movement began. They contended that the true church had preserved itself without interruption from the days of the apostles and could be identified by the "trail of blood" which had marked the martyrs of the true church in every age. Landmark Baptists claimed their own church began at Pentecost and any other religious body organized since Pentecost could not claim to be a church.

Just as sacramentalism had taught that perfection came to those who were united to the Roman Catholic church through communion, so these expressions of separation all taught perfection through membership in their sect. The emphasis was not so much on ethical primitivism or holy living nor on experiential primitivism or the apostolic gifts of the Spirit, but upon proper structure, form, and ritual.

In his book *In Pursuit of Purity*, David O. Beale traced the fundamentalist movement's pursuit of doctrinal purity through separation. There is no emphasis

---

[1705]Bebbington, *Holiness*, 73-74.

[1706]From the back flap dust jacket notes of Zondervan's 1954 reprint.

[1707]Goodwin, *A Being Filled With the Spirit*. Wesley reprinted Goodwin's *Treatise on Justification*.

[1708]Fletcher, *Works*, 1:29

on personal holiness.[1709] However, in another book by the same publisher, Bob Jones University, Fred Moritz taught the holiness is the result of justification by faith. As the Christian abides in Christ and surrenders to the control of the Spirit, he is progressively given victory over sin. When he tolerates sin in his life, the work of holiness is hindered but when the Spirit fills and controls then holiness is the result. Thus, Moritz advocated a personal separation from sin and from sinners, even when they are Christian brothers. However, the believer's sanctification will not be completed until heaven.[1710]

Under the leadership of Barton W. Stone, in 1804 the Christian movement in Kentucky was dedicated to ecclesiastical primitivism. They rejected all creeds and called upon all Christians in the sects to come out of Babylon and unite on the one apostolic foundation. When this was accomplished the millennium would begin. Influenced by Alexander Campbell in 1823, this Christian movement adopted baptism by immersion for the forgiveness of sins as the mark of the primitive faith.[1711] This restorationist movement split from the Presbyterian"old lights." These "new lights" taught a sinless perfection based on the limited time remaining for the world to be redeemed. The Cumberland Presbyterian Church in Kentucky embraced this new light theology and became a "holiness" church.[1712]

Beginning in 1989 a dialogue was initiated between Campbell's Restoration Movement and the Church of God (Anderson). The hope was that the Restoration Movement could teach the Church of God about baptism and the Church of God could expose the Christian Church to the holiness message.[1713]

[1709]Beale, *In Pursuit of Purity*.

[1710]Moritz, *"Be Ye Holy*," 28; 30-33; 35. The passages cited, 1 Thess 3:13; 5:23 actually state that the believer is to be in a condition of holiness when Christ returns, not that their sanctified is completed by the return of Christ or in heaven. See also Eph 5:27. I do not deny that we will grow more perfect throughout eternity, but I am wary of an emphasis which projects present grace into the next life.

[1711]Hughes, "Christian Primitivism as Perfection," 217-234.

[1712]Gaddis, *Christian Perfection in America*, 202.

[1713]Online: Strege, "Union Heaven Gave Us," 15-16; Callen and North, *Coming Together in Christ*.